By

PAUL W. MARSHALL

Associate Professor of Business Administration

WILLIAM J. ABERNATHY

Associate Professor of Business Administration

JEFFREY G. MILLER

Assistant Professor of Business Administration

RICHARD P. OLSEN

Assistant Professor of Business Administration

RICHARD S. ROSENBLOOM

David Sarnoff Professor of Business Administration

D. DARYL WYCKOFF

Associate Professor of Business Administration

All of the
Graduate School of Business Administration
Harvard University

Operations Managemen

Text and Cas

Operations Management
Text and Cases

 1975

Richard D. Irwin, Inc.   Homewood, Illinois   60430

Irwin-Dorsey Limited   Georgetown, Ontario   L7G 4B3

© RICHARD D. IRWIN, INC., 1975

67890 K 54321098

Case material of the Harvard Graduate School of
Business Administration is made possible by the
cooperation of business firms who may wish to remain
anonymous by having names, quantities, and other
identifying details disguised while basic relationships
are maintained. Cases are prepared as the basis for
class discussion rather than to illustrate either effective
or ineffective handling of administrative situations.

ISBN 0-256-01682-8
Library of Congress Catalog Card No. 74–27548
Printed in the United States of America

Preface

THIS BOOK was written with a specific audience in mind—the students of management who do not plan to become production managers or specialists. Many of these students will begin their management careers in finance, marketing, or in some part of the organization other than operations. However, some knowledge of production and operations management is vital to their success as managers. This book was designed to be used in its entirety as the basis for a course for these students. Such a course might have as its theme: What the general manager needs to know about production and operations management.

For such a course to be successful we believe the student must be given the opportunity to develop three skills:

1. Ability to describe and understand the operating process.
2. Ability to measure and analyze this process.
3. Ability to develop and evaluate plans for changing the operating process within the context of the entire organization and its strategy.

The first two skills are mainly analytical and the third is focused on the management issues of decision making and implementation. The text and cases in this book have been written with the express purpose of providing a medium for developing these skills.

The book is divided into three sections, each composed of several chapters of related text and a number of cases describing actual operating problems. The first section, "A Framework for Analysis," is designed to concentrate on developing the first two skills. The second, "Capacity Management," introduces some new analytical issues and reinforces those developed in the first section. However, these cases and associated text emphasize the need to take management action once the analysis is completed. The last section, "Integration and Overview," is designed to provide ample opportunity for the student to develop operating strategies and plan for their implementation.

Section I has three chapters, the first two of which are devoted to Process Analysis and Tradeoff Analysis. In Chapter 1 we present the idea of a process flow chart as a method of describing the operating system. We identify inputs and outputs of the process, and discuss the arrangements of tasks, flows, and storage within the process. We define four major characteristics of a process, namely, efficiency, effectiveness, capacity, and flexibility. A major goal of this chapter is to convince the student that operating problems can be addressed in a systematic framework which can be applied by anyone regardless of technical background.

In Chapter 2 we present a framework for looking at how a manager can attempt to balance the output characteristics of the operating process. We focus on three of the many characteristics that can describe the output of an operation, namely, cost, quality, and timeliness. There are situations where quality or delivery time can be improved if the manager is willing to also increase cost. Our goal in this chapter is to instill in students an awareness of the fact that some price or cost must be paid to obtain an improvement from the operating system and to give them a framework for analyzing this tradeoff situation.

The final chapter in Section I is entitled "Types of Processes." Its aim is to provide a method for categorizing different operating processes. We focus on job shops as one extreme and assembly lines as the other. The major emphasis is on highlighting the different management problems inherent in these diverse processes.

Section II is entitled "Capacity Management." There are many characteristics of the operating system around which we could focus material that allows the student to develop plans of action. We have chosen capacity because it is the characteristic we feel most often is considered by managers outside the operating function. The marketing function is concerned with the ability to meet future demand; this requires a capacity analysis. The finance function is concerned with capital budgeting and for the operating department a capital request is often the end result of capacity planning. Thus we believe that capacity management is an issue of broad interest to all managers and future managers.

This section is divided into three chapters paralleling the different time dimension of the capacity decision involved: (1) "Aggregate Planning, Scheduling, and Dispatching," (2) "Facilities Planning," (3) "Technology Planning."

The cases in the "Aggregate Planning" chapter focus on the six-month to one-year problem. In most of these cases physical capacity is fixed. Capacity can be changed, however, by varying the size of the workforce, or the length of the work day. Inventory levels can also be planned to smooth out the requirements for the capacity over time. In this type of capacity decision the major problem is to adapt short-run capacity by manipulating inventory level and workforce and to allocate this capacity to various product lines to meet a short-run sales forecast.

The second chapter in this section, "Facilities Planning," moves the time horizon of the capacity decision beyond one year. These cases allow the management to increase or decrease the amount of physical capacity. The issue of where to locate the additional capacity and what type of process technology to incorporate in the new capacity are added to the obvious problem of how much additional capacity to provide.

The final chapter of this section, "Technology Planning," focuses on the long-range capacity plan. The management issues in these cases are how to plan for new product technology, select new process technology, and implement this new technology into the existing organization.

In the last chapter of the book "Integration and Overview," the cases are very broad and provide considerable data on the company in addition to the operating function. The student is challenged to identify all the important problems, operating and nonoperating, and to develop a plan of action centering on the operating function, but giving major consideration to how this plan will affect the entire organization.

The material in this book was developed for a required course in Production and Operations Management at the Harvard Graduate School of Business Administration. The course was taught in the first year of the M.B.A. program to students with varying undergraduate training, including some who had taken no business courses in college. It is our belief that this material can be taught successfully to undergraduates as well as graduate students in a course for general management students.

We also think much of this material could be used in a management course for industrial engineers or future production managers. The sections on capacity planning and overview would be particularly useful in such a course. These cases present problems that concern general managers. If the specialist is to be useful in solving these problems he must understand how they influence the rest of the organization and try to develop a solution that will integrate all the parts of the organization into a meaningful plan of action. We believe practice in solving such problems would be valuable to all students of production and operations management.

Many topics familiar to readers of production and operations management textbooks are not included in this volume, for example, plant layout, methods, and time studies. Our test for material was a determination that it would be relevant and important to managers in an organization *in addition* to the operations and production managers.

The textual material in this book was written to support the analysis of the cases. It is our intention to provide a general framework for solving the operating problems found in the cases. We believe there is much good material available to explain analytical techniques like linear programming but that there is not much material that attempts to explain how to structure and analyze operating problems for *general managers*. It has been our intention to try to provide this latter type of material.

Finally, we have tried to make the material in this book relevant to managers in organizations that provide a service as their ultimate product. A large majority of the cases are about manufacturing companies. However, we have tried to include at least one case in each chapter on a service organization. In the textual material we have tried to show how many of the concepts apply to service as well as manufacturing organizations, and where this is not true we have tried to point it out.

April 1975

PAUL W. MARSHALL
WILLIAM J. ABERNATHY
JEFFREY G. MILLER
RICHARD P. OLSEN
RICHARD S. ROSENBLOOM
D. DARYL WYCKOFF

Acknowledgments

WE HAVE written a book that will help train general managers. Much of the work of a general manager is coordinating the efforts of others, and taking the good work of one person and combining it with the good work of others to reach some organizational goal. In this sense the development of this book was a general management activity for us. However, not only did we have to coordinate our own efforts, we also had the privilege of using ideas and material from our colleagues and associates. For this privilege we are most grateful.

As any teacher knows, the development of a teachable set of materials evolves over time. The material in this book has evolved from our efforts in teaching the required Production and Operations Management course at the Harvard Graduate School of Business Administration. Previously, this course was headed by Wickham Skinner and before him by William Holstein. Both of these men provided much for us to build upon. Professor Holstein wrote some of the cases in this volume, specifically Fabritek and Kool King, Inc. He also demonstrated in his classroom work that the necessary analytical techniques to support good case analysis can be successfully taught to general management students. His example has been important to many of us. Professor Skinner has written Chapter 7, the capstone to our book, and several excellent cases (Sunshine Builders, North American Rockwell Draper Division). His philosophy of management education has been a strong guide to all of us. Both of these men are now deans—Professor Holstein of the Business School at the State University of New York (Albany) and Professor Skinner of the M.B.A. program at Harvard. We trust they will continue to encourage the teaching of production and operations management. We know they have made this book possible through their inspiration and example.

During the past three years all of the authors have taught at least two years in the Production and Operations Management course. We have had other colleagues teach one of the three years and they have contributed greatly to our project. Many wrote cases and all of them discussed teaching ideas and aided us in developing the material for this book. Earl Sasser, Robert Hayes, and John Russell had taught the Production and Operations Management course in prior years. They have written cases and because of their excellent classroom skills have had a major influence on our teaching ideas. Tony Edwards, William Fulmer, Robert Leone, Alexander Morton, Roger Schmenner, and Steven Wheelwright have all taught Production and Operations Management for the first time using this material. Their suggestions and ideas have helped us to modify the material to make it more useful to a beginning instructor. Their willingness to try new ideas and give us useful critique has been invaluable.

Other people have written cases that we have used in this volume. Some of these cases are being published for the first time. Jim Jucker developed the material for National Cranberry Cooperative, and John Hammond for Productos de Concretos S. A. (D). Larry Bennigson wrote The Ferdanna Company; Lou Wells, P. T. Pertamina-Gulf Industrial Processing; and Curtis Jones, the Roblin-Seaway Industries case. Some of our other cases have been published before and have weathered the test of time. Franklin E. Folts wrote the first version of New Process Rubber Company (B); Robert E. McGarrah, Fawcett Optical Equipment Company; Hal Eyring, Art-Tone Cards; James R. Bright, Sarepta Paper Company; and Robert Ackerman, Zenith Radio. Besides authors and teachers there are many people who aided in the development of this book. Specifically, our secretaries have typed the manuscript and teaching notes and made useful editorial suggestions. The Intercollegiate Case Clearinghouse staff at Harvard has been most generous in their support of our efforts. To all of these people we are indebted.

Finally, we wish to express our thanks to the Harvard Graduate School of Business Administration and its dean, Lawrence Fouraker, for challenging us with the assignment to teach Production and Operations Management to M.B.A. students in a required course. We must also thank those students who have prepared and discussed these cases and made our teaching experience a rewarding one.

P. W. M.
W. J. A.
J. G. M.
R. P. O.
R. S. R.
D. D. W.

Contents

SECTION ONE

A Framework for Analysis

INTRODUCTION

As the title implies this section is intended to help you develop a frame-work for analyzing the operating system or process of an organization. It is important for you to realize what we hope you will learn from reading the textual material and analyzing the cases in this section. You should try to develop a personal approach for looking at operating problems; an "internal checklist" of what to do when you encounter certain situations as a manager. Such a learning process is not like memorizing the multipli-cation tables—the accomplishment of which allows you to "solve" all future multiplication problems you will encounter.

Most real management problems cannot be "solved" with a "correct solution." Some solutions may be better than others, but it is almost always impossible to prove that one solution is the "best." This is because of the complex nature of management problems and the conflicting interests that usually surround their resolution. For example, consider the simple prob-lem of how large an inventory to have on hand for some product in a company that makes many products. The sales department usually will want a large inventory to ensure quick delivery and good customer service. The operating department may want a large inventory to give them flexi-bility in scheduling their activities and to allow for a smooth work flow. This same department may want a small inventory of this product if it is costly to store or has a good chance of becoming obsolete. Finally, the finance department will usually want a small amount of inventory because of the cost of funds needed to finance or carry the inventory until it is sold. If you are the manager trying to decide the size of inventory you cannot have the "right answer" for all departments. In fact, you may not be able to find the right answer for any one department. Even more irritat-

1

ing is the fact that if you find the "right answer" for one product for one company, it will certainly not be the "right answer" for another product or another company.

If you agree with us that there are no "right answers" to most interesting management problems, then you should ask "What is it that a good manager should know?" We believe there are several basic skills a good manager should have and that these skills are learnable. First, a manager must be able to define the problem he or she is facing. This is a skill that is best developed through practice and each case in this section will give you such practice. In addition it is useful to know a vocabulary that is understood and accepted by other managers if you are to communicate your definition of the problem. The text of this section is intended to increase your vocabulary for operating problems.

A second skill that a good manager must learn is to develop a set of reasonable expectations for what will happen under a given set of circumstances. Once the problem is defined and alternative solutions proposed it is necessary to analyze what will happen. Such an analysis can become very technical, particularly if the problem involves the operating function. Good managers will test the results of these analyses against their expectation and ask for better explanations of areas where their expectations are not satisfied. Giving you the opportunity to develop such a set of expectations for operating problems is a primary goal of this section. For example, most of you would have some reasonable expectation of what a 50 percent reduction in price would do for the sales volume of some commodity. Do you have a similar set of expectations for what a 50 percent increase in volume will do to the scheduling of an operation or how such an increase might change the cost of a unit of output?

One final skill we believe is needed by a good manager is the ability to decide and act even when he or she knows the solution is imperfect. This is a skill that results only from practice. However, often a major deterrent to action is a lack of confidence in the analysis that has been developed. By increasing your skill at defining problems and testing your expectations for various solutions to operating problems, we believe you will increase your confidence in your analysis. If this is true then you will increase your willingness to take action as a manager.

There are three chapters in this section entitled "Process Analysis," "Tradeoff Analysis," and "Types of Processes." In the first chapter we introduce the idea of a process flow diagram as an easy way to describe an operating system. We define the various types of inputs that enter a process and categorize the activities within the process in terms of tasks, flows, and storages. There is a section devoted to output measurement that defines cost, quality, and timeliness as three useful output measures. A set of process characteristics are introduced and defined; namely, capacity, efficiency, effectiveness, and flexibility. Finally, an example of a process analysis is presented to help you understand the definitions. This chapter *will give you a vocabulary for describing a process and will begin to define some relationships for you to use in developing reasonable expectations about operating systems. The cases in this chapter will give you practice in problem definition and description and will allow you to develop plans of action for discussion in class.*

The second chapter, "Tradeoff Analysis," will increase your awareness of operating problems. The focus is on the output of the process and the fact that you can increase the value of this output only with a corresponding cost increase. The net effect of this tradeoff may be beneficial and may be desired by you as a manager. However, you should be aware that very seldom does any increase in value come without a cost. The cases in this chapter provide the opportunity for you to practice process analysis as well as to develop your skill at tradeoff analysis.

The final chapter, "Types of Processes," is designed to allow you to begin to classify processes into categories. In a course on biology you learn that animals can be classified according to general characteristics. Once you have learned these categories and their characteristics you can better understand the animal kingdom. The same is true for operating systems. At one extreme we define a job shop and at the other we define a line or flow operation. Each of these processes have some unique characteristics that are important to managers. Once you have learned the various types of processes and their characteristics you will be able to better understand the management problems of operations, and thus, should have better expectations about the reasonableness of proposed solutions to these problems. The cases in this chapter tend to focus on problems that occur when the process is evolving from one type to another. However, as in the first two chapters these cases also allow you to practice a full range of skills from problem definition to analysis leading to management action.

1

Process Analysis

INTRODUCTION

THE AIM of this chapter is to present a simple analytical framework for defining and understanding the operating system of an organization. You should keep in mind that the main reason for understanding the operating system is to allow you as a manager to diagnose problems and develop a reasonable plan of action for the solution of these problems. You will have the opportunity to test this analytical framework on cases after you have read this material. It may be only after this case analysis that you will have an understanding of some terminology and definitions. In fact, most students find it easier to understand a concept after they have encountered a concrete example in a case. For this reason you may want to reread this chapter after you have done the case analyses.

You should also remember that our goal is for you to develop your own approach to analyzing operating problems. Thus the procedure described in this chapter should be modified and expanded by each student to suit his or her own needs.

WHAT IS A PROCESS?

Throughout this text you will see the word "process" or the phrase "operating system." Both of these terms will be used to mean any part of an organization that takes inputs and transforms them into outputs of greater value to the organization than the original inputs. In some cases this definition could include the entire organization; however, in most situations we will focus on a subset of the entire organization that is transforming a set of inputs into useful outputs.

4

Consider some examples of processes. An automobile assembly plant takes raw materials in the form of parts and components. These materials along with labor, capital equipment, and energy are transformed into automobiles. The transformation is called final assembly and the output is an automobile. A fast-food restaurant takes inputs in the form of unprocessed or semiprocessed agricultural products and energy. To these labor is added (the cook) and capital equipment (a stove) and the output is a hamburger or other edible food.

Both of the processes mentioned above had products as an output. However, the output of some operating systems is a service. Consider an airline. The inputs are capital equipment in the form of airplanes and ground equipment, labor in the form of flight crews, ground crews, and maintenance crews, and energy in the form of fuel and electricity. These are transformed into a service, namely, a means of transportation between widely separated points. Another process with a service output would be that found in a hospital. Here capital, labor, and energy are applied to another input, the patient, in order to transform this patient into a healthier or more comfortable person.

The following is a more formal definition of a process. A process is a collection of tasks connected by a flow of goods and information that transforms various inputs into useful outputs. A process has the capability to store both the goods and information during the transformation. In order to analyze a process it is useful to have a simple method of describing the process and some standard definitions for its components. One way to describe an operating system is a *process flow diagram*.

Figure 1–1 show the process flow diagram for a hypothetical process. The operating system is represented by the large rectangle. Inputs enter at the left and are converted into useful goods or services that leave the system as outputs at the right. Tasks in the process are shown as circles,

Figure 1–1
PROCESS FLOW DIAGRAM FOR A HYPOTHETICAL PROCESS

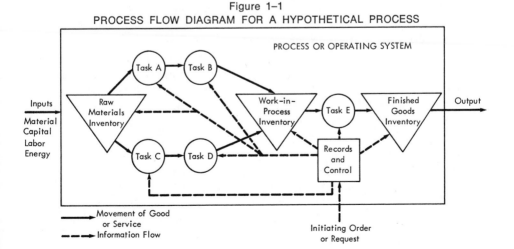

flows as arrows, and the storage of goods as triangles. Information is shown stored in the square in the lower right-hand corner. In this hypothetical process some good is being produced. Raw materials flows to Task A and Task C from a storage called the raw materials inventory. Task B cannot start until Task A is completed. Two such tasks are defined as being in a series relationship. You can see that Tasks C and D are also in series. Task D and Task B are not dependent on each other and as such are defined as parallel tasks. Task E cannot be started until all the others are finished, thus a work-in-process storage is shown before Task E in case Tasks B and D are not completed simultaneously. Task E flows into a finished goods inventory and from there the output flows out of the system.

Once you have been able to describe a process using a process flow diagram you must then analyze its components. After that analysis it should be possible to draw some conclusions about the process as a whole. In the following sections we will discuss each component and some of the problems you will encounter when you try to measure and analyze them. This will be followed by a section discussing some characteristics of the entire process and then we will give a specific example of a process analysis.

INPUTS

The inputs to a process can be divided into at least four categories: Labor, materials, energy, and capital. In order to analyze an operating system it is necessary to measure these inputs and to determine the amount of each input needed to make some amount of output. It would be possible to use physical units to measure the inputs like man-hours for labor, and BTUs for energy. However, it is often more convenient to measure the input in dollars by determining how much it would cost to purchase these units. Thus, in most analyses, it will be necessary to consider the economic conditions that influence the cost of labor, materials, energy, and capital. The problem of measuring the cost of inputs becomes more difficult and requires more care as the time horizon of the problem lengthens.

There are varying degrees of difficulty in determining how much of any input is needed to make a given output. Some inputs such as direct labor and materials are fully consumed to produce an output and are thus easy to assign to that unit of output. For example, it is easy to measure how many minutes of labor a barber uses in producing a haircut or how many ounces of beef are used in making a hamburger. Other inputs are utilized in the production of an output, but are not fully consumed—for example, the chef's stove or the barber's chair. The capital input is often the most difficult of the four to assign to specific output because it is almost impossible to measure how much capital is consumed at any point in time. It is important to be able to determine the amount of each input consumed if we are to calculate the cost of providing a desired output, and we will return to this problem in a later section.

OUTPUTS

The output of a process is either a good or a service. The process flow diagram in Figure 1–1 shows a storage before the output leaves the system called a finished goods inventory. In some organizations this finished goods inventory is kept at zero units and the process produces directly for distribution into the environment. In fact, this is an important characteristic of processes that provide a service as their final output because it is often difficult to store the service for later distribution. In some organizations the finished goods inventory is kept apart from the operating system that produces the good and is managed by a separate group, usually the sales organization. For purposes of analysis it is more useful to treat inventories, if they exist, as though they were within the process, regardless of organizational responsibility.

A meaningful measurement of outputs is often quite difficult to obtain. It is a simple matter to count the number of units produced by some manufacturing organization, or to count the number of patients served by a hospital. It is much more difficult to place a value on this output. The question of valuing the outputs can be approached from an economic point of view if a market will place a value on the output through the pricing mechanism. Thus, if we know the revenue that can be obtained from selling the good or service this should serve as a measure of its value. For this reason it is necessary to have a good understanding of the economic environment within which the process must exist. "What are the market conditions?" and "What is competition doing?" are two important questions to address when analyzing a process.

The question of what price will be paid for the output is difficult to answer unless some other information is known about the output. For our purposes three output characteristics will be useful to consider: The *cost* of providing the output; the *quality* of the output; and, the *timeliness* of the output. Often none of these measures are easily obtained, but they can serve as a checklist in your analysis of operating systems. It is also quite possible that other characteristics for measuring the output of a process will be useful in some specific situations.

TASKS, FLOWS, AND STORAGE

So far we have discussed what goes in and what comes out of a process. It is also necessary to understand what goes on inside a process. The specifics of every process are different, but there are three general categories for all activities within the process. These are tasks, flows, and storage.

A task results when there is an addition of some input that makes the product or service more nearly like the desired output. Some examples of tasks are: (1) operating a drill press to change a piece of metal; (2) inspecting a part to make sure it meets some standard; (3) flying an airplane; and (4) anesthetizing a patient before an operation. A task quite often takes the form of added labor to the product with or without the use of capital. In cases where some form of automation of the process has occurred, capital and material may have been substituted for the labor in a task.

There are two types of flows to be considered in each process: The flow of goods and the flow of information. Figure 1–1 shows the goods flow in solid lines and the information flow in broken lines. The first one results when goods are moved from task to task or from some task to storage or vice versa. Labor or capital are added during a flow because it requires workers or equipment to move the goods. The difference between flows and task is that flows merely change the position of a good or service in the process while a task changes its characteristics. The flow of information initiates and aids in the production of a good or service. This flow results when the necessary records or instructions move from their point of inception or storage to the task, in time to be used in the task. Quite often the information will physically move through the process with the good or service. This happens when a routing slip[1] is attached to the physical good. In other situations workers must go to some central location to obtain the information before performing the task or they may carry the necessary information in their heads. In yet other situations the information arrives by a flow independent of the flow of the good or service being processed. It is important in analyzing a process to consider the information flows in addition to the physical flow of goods or services.

The final of the three activities within a process we will define as storage. A storage results when no task is being performed and the good or service is not being transported. In other words a storage is everything that is not a task or flow. In Figure 1–1 we have shown the storage of goods as triangles. Technically, there should be a triangle beside every task. If there is no delay in starting the task after the flow has been finished the storage will have zero units in it. If there is no storage between two connected tasks there must be a planned continuous flow between these tasks or the receiving task cannot operate continuously. Figure 1–1 shows only one in-process storage (commonly known as work-in-process inventory).

It is also possible, and in fact necessary, to store information. This storage is shown as a box in Figure 1–1, with an arrow coming in from the environment labeled information. There are two labels on the box: records and control. Records will be used to refer to general instructions such as blueprints and maintenance documents. Control will be used to indicate

---

[1] A routing slip describes each task to be performed, where the task is to be performed, and the sequence of these tasks needed to make the output.

information specific to a given order such as the due dates and routing procedure for this particular order, or special instructions that make this order different from the generally accepted procedures explained in the records.

THE ENVIRONMENT

There are two major areas of the environment that will be useful to consider as you analyze operating systems. We have already explained that the *economic conditions* in the environment are important and that an analysis of them is necessary if you are to determine the costs of the inputs and the value of the output. The second environmental area we will call the *state of technology* and is more difficult to explain. Technology can be defined as the set of knowledge regarding processes, methods, techniques, and capital goods by which products are made or services rendered. In less precise terms technology is what determines the nature of the tasks and flows within the process and how they relate to each other. It is often possible to choose among a number of technologies when designing a process. The choice of process technology will determine the relationship between the tasks and flows and determine the inputs needed to provide the process output. For example, consider two alternatives for providing copies of some information, one using a printing press and the other using a Xerox machine. The press requires several tasks to produce the information; typesetting, proofreading, and press operation are some examples. The Xerox machine on the other hand requires only an operator and an original document containing the information. The cost of providing the information also is different for each technology. The Xerox has a small cost per copy but this cost is about the same for each copy regardless of how many are produced. The printing press has a very high setup cost but each additional copy is very cheap. Thus for large numbers of copies the press has an economic advantage.

As the state of technology changes it may be possible to change the process and achieve the same output with less inputs or to use the same inputs to achieve more output. This will alter the costs of inputs and may improve the quality and timeliness of the output. Changes in technology may allow a process to make entirely new outputs. For these reasons it will be necessary to give consideration to the state of technology when analyzing a process.

CHARACTERISTICS OF A PROCESS

So far we have defined the process in general terms and given names to various components of the process, namely the *inputs,* the *output,* and the *tasks, flows,* and *storages* within the process. We have also stated that the process must exist in an environment. The economic conditions will influence the values of inputs and outputs and the state of technology will influence the nature of the tasks and flows. Using these concepts as a base we can now discuss some process characteristics. We will concentrate on four characteristics of the process: *capacity, efficiency, effectiveness,* and *flexibility.*

Capacity

Capacity is the rate of output from the process. This characteristic is measured in units of output per unit of time. For example, a steel mill can produce some number of tons of steel per year, or an insurance office can process some number of claims per hour. Capacity is easy to define and hard to measure. It is often possible to determine the theoretical maximum capacity of a process—the most output it could generate under ideal conditions over some short period of time. For planning purposes and management decisions it is more useful to know the *effective capacity* of a process. To measure effective capacity it is necessary to know a great deal about the process, and to carefully analyze the particular situation at hand. Quite often managers believe that the capacity of a process is an absolute fixed quantity, such as the height of a person. This is not true. The capacity of a process can change for many reasons and we will encounter several cases where this is a key factor in the problem facing the manager. In our example above, for instance, a steel mill may be designed for some ideal capacity of x tons of steel per year. However, the actual capacity may be more or less than x due to such factors as: the nature of the raw materials being utilized, the mix of products in the output, and the quantity and nature of the labor input.

Efficiency

Efficiency is a measure that relates the value of the output of the process to the value of the input. The concept of efficiency is widely used to measure physical processes. Every engine has an efficiency and it is expressed as a ratio of output energy to input energy. For example, an engine with 75 percent efficiency can deliver 75 percent of the input energy as useful output energy. The energy efficiency of physical systems does not exceed 1.0; i.e., the useful output energy is always less than the input. This is not true of economic processes. The value of the output should exceed the value of the input if the process is going to generate sufficient resources to support its own continued operation. If we measure the value of output by the price or revenue it will bring in the market and if we measure the value of inputs by their costs, the measure of efficiency is profit. Profit which is simply revenue less cost is the value of output minus the value of input. Profit is a very simplistic definition of efficiency and for any real problem the measurement of efficiency may be very complex.

You should realize that one of the main difficulties in measuring efficiency is determining what inputs were used to produce what outputs. Earlier we discussed the problem of determining how much capital input was consumed in producing a given output. In order to deal with this problem the accounting profession has developed very elaborate rules to guide managers in assigning capital costs to production. These guides usually assume that capital is consumed evenly over time and each unit of production produced in a given time period consumes an equal amount of capital. Such an allocation scheme requires an assumption be made about how long an asset will be productive and this is very difficult in many cases. It is not our purpose to comment on how well the accounting profession has succeeded in this attempt to assign capital input to final output, but rather to point out the difficulty of this job. In any process analysis you must attempt to deal with this problem.

In some analyses it will also be difficult to measure the value of the output. For example, in many markets it would be possible for a company to initially sell a product of low quality at a standard price. However, over time the general reputation of the company may be hurt and other products produced by that company would be discounted in the market. This latter loss in revenue should have been considered when the decision was made on the original product.

In your analyses you should attempt to take into account long-run effects of the current decision alternatives. When you need to determine the efficiency of the process you should look at long-run profitability not just the profit generated from any short-run action.

Effectiveness

Another characteristic we are interested in is the effectiveness of the process. *Effectiveness* is a measure of actual output against planned output. Determining effectiveness requires that some plan or standard be established before the process begins to produce output. The actual output is measured in some way and compared to the plan. This measurement may be along many dimensions; three of the dimensions we will be interested in are cost, quality, and timeliness.

Efficiency and effectiveness are often confused. Some plant managers will state that they have reached X percent efficiency in a given week. When questioned about this they will often explain that the output that week was X percent of what they had been given as a standard. According to our definitions they are describing effectiveness. The distinction between these two characteristics has a practical value for managers. Efficiency is difficult to measure accurately and involves calculation about both output and input. Effectiveness on the other hand is easier to measure if some standards have been established. We believe that effectiveness is more a management concept since it involves the setting of goals and the measurement of performance relative to these goals.

Flexibility

A final characteristic we will want to consider in analyzing a process is its flexibility. This is a measure of how long it would take to change the process so that it could produce a different output, or it could use a different set of inputs. *Flexibility* is the characteristic that allows a process to respond to changes in its environment. It is the least precise and hardest to define of all characteristics we have considered. Often it will be necessary to describe this characteristic in qualitative terms; however, this does not make it any less important to managers.

A SIMPLE EXAMPLE OF PROCESS ANALYSIS

The XYZ Company supplies a component to several large automobile manufacturers. This component is assembled in a shop by 15 workers working an eight-hour shift on an assembly line that moves at the rate of 150 components per hour. The workers received their pay in the form of a group incentive amounting to 30 cents per completed good part. This wage is distributed equally among the workers. Management believes that they could hire 15 more workers for a second shift if necessary.

Parts for the final assembly come from two sources, the XYZ molding department makes one very critical part and the rest come from outside suppliers. There are 11 machines capable of molding the one part done in house, but historically one machine is being overhauled or repaired at any given time. Each machine requires a full-time operator. The machines could each produce 25 parts per hour and the workers are paid on an individual piece rate of 20 cents per good part. The workers will work overtime at a 50 percent increase in rate, or for 30 cents per good part. The work force for molding is flexible and currently only six workers are on this job. Four more are available from a labor pool within the company. The raw materials for each part molded cost 10 cents per part and a detailed analysis by the accounting department has concluded that 2 cents of electricity is used in making each part. The parts purchased from the outside cost 30 cents for each final component produced.

This entire operation is located in a rented building that rents for $100 per week. Supervision, maintenance, and clerical employees receive a payroll of $1,000 per week. The accounting department charges depreciation for equipment against this operation at $50 per week. The company has been shipping 6,000 parts per week to customers under a long-term agreement for $1.40 per part.

In order to analyze this process it is necessary to describe it. A useful way to do this is to construct a process flow diagram similar to the one in Figure 1–2.

The tasks are shown as rectangles and the storage of goods (or inventories) as triangles. We do not know how much is kept in inventories,

Figure 1–2
XYZ COMPONENT OPERATION

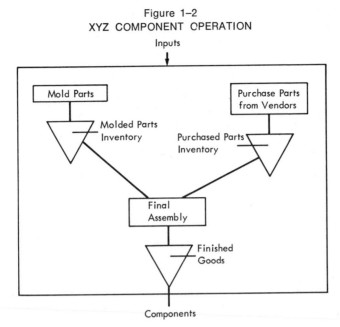

but we can guess that they are not empty. The size of inventory depends on many factors, however, one important consideration in determining inventory size is how much is needed to allow other tasks to operate without interruption. Thus it is reasonable to assume that in order to have an uninterrupted final assembly there will be some molded parts and purchased parts in the respective work-in-process inventories.

Once the process is described, it is useful to determine how big it is, or in other words to measure its capacity. It should be obvious that the capacity of the entire process is dependent upon the capacity of each task. We will assume that the task of purchasing parts has unlimited capacity; i.e., it can provide any reasonable number of parts each week. The plastic molding task as currently designed can produce 6,000 parts per week according to the following calculation.

Molding Capacity = 6 machines × 25 parts per hour per machine
    × 8 hours per day × 5 days per week = 6,000 parts per week

The assembly task is also operating at 6,000 parts per week:

Assembly Capacity = 150 components per hour
    × 8 hours per day × 5 days per week = 6,000 components per week

Thus, we can conclude that the entire process has a capacity of 6,000 components per week and that the capacity of all tasks are balanced.

If the molding task were increased to ten machines the workers could produce 10,000 parts per week. If no change is made in the final assembly task, however, the entire process still has only a capacity of 6,000 per week *because in the long run the overall capacity cannot exceed the rate of the slowest task.* XYZ could operate their process out of balance if they were willing to build up the inventory of molded parts. They would not want to do this unless they had plans to stop the molding task for some period of time or to eventually increase the capacity of the final assembly task.

Assume that XYZ went to a second shift on assembly. This would increase assembly capacity to 12,000 components per week. Now the overall process capacity would be 12,000 per week until the inventory of molded parts was exhausted and then it would become 10,000 per week because the molding machines would be the limiting task. If some molding machine operators went onto overtime to increase that rate to 12,000 per week, the entire process could again be put in balance at 12,000 per week. It should be clear that capacity is not easy to define without stating your assumptions about the availability of inputs, the sequence of tasks, the size of inventories, and many other factors.

One assumption we made implicitly was that only ten molding machines were available. For long-run planning this is reasonable if the maintenance record is as stated. For a short period of time it might be possible to use all 11 machines and increase the molding task capacity. Twenty-four-hour operation of all 11 machines would represent the theoretical maximum capacity of the molding task. The effective capacity is less than this amount because of the long-run need to overhaul and repair the equipment, even if they are scheduled for use 24 hours per day.

So far we have not focused on any decisions that management might make. We have only described the system and placed some limits on its capacity. In order to define some economic alternatives it is necessary to determine the value of the inputs and the value of the outputs.

In this case XYZ has a long-term agreement to deliver 6,000 parts per week at $1.40 per part. Clearly every good part that comes out of the system is worth $1.40 as long as there are 6,000 per week delivered. If management were interested in soliciting orders for more than 6,000 per week the value of new output might be different than $1.40 per part. However, for the sake of illustration we will assume that XYZ management felt it could get $1.40 per part for any amount up to 20,000 per week and that all parts will be of adequate quality.

Table 1–1 is a summary of the costs of inputs.

This listing is an adequate summary of input value. However, the key question is how do the inputs relate to the output? In other words how efficient is this operation.

One measure of this efficiency is the dollars of input cost per dollar of output value produced. It should be clear from Table 1–1 that there are two major types of cost: Those that vary with the amount of output,

Table 1–1
COST FOR XYZ COMPONENT

Purchased parts	$0.30 per component
Raw material molding	$0.10 per component
Electricity for molding	$0.02 per component
Labor for molding	$0.20 per component regular time
Labor for molding	$0.30 per component overtime
Labor for assembly	$0.30 per component
Rent	$100 per week
Supervision, maintenance, clerical	$1,000 per week
Depreciation	$50 per week

and those that vary only with time. These later costs that vary only with time are often called fixed costs. This name refers to the fact that they do not change with the amount of output produced. Fixed costs have to be allocated to output units; i.e., some portion of the total fixed costs has to be attributed to each unit of output. In this example, the equipment in this operation may have cost a total of $26,000 and have a 10-year life and each week $50 of capital is "used up." How much of this is "used up" by each unit of output will vary with the number of units produced per week (in the case of 6,000 units it is $\frac{\$50.00}{6,000}$ or $0.0083 per unit). Thus, in order to allocate all input costs to output we must state how much output will be produced in some period of time. Table 1–2 is a calculation

Table 1–2
TOTAL INPUT COST FOR VARIOUS VOLUMES OF OUTPUT PER WEEK

Output per Week	3,000	6,000	10,000	12,000
Parts and materials	$1,200	$2,400	$ 4,000	$ 4,800
Electricity	60	120	200	240
Molding labor	600	1,200	2,000	2,600*
Assembly labor	900	1,800	3,000	3,600
Rent	100	100	100	100
Supervision	1,000	1,000	1,000	1,000
Depreciation	50	50	50	50
Total Cost	$3,910	$6,670	$10,350	$12,390
Cost per Unit of Output	$ 1.30	$ 1.11	$ 1.04	$ 1.03

* $0.30 per unit for all over 10,000.

of these input costs per unit output for various assumptions about the amount to be produced in one week.

The last row in Table 1–2 gives the average cost of inputs for every unit of output produced. This can be compared to $1.40, the value of a unit of output, and the average profit per unit produced can be determined.

If XYZ were not sure of the value the market would pay for each unit of output it would be difficult to measure the efficiency. However, it would still be possible to measure the effectiveness of the process. If the company planned to make 10,000 units in a given week it would be logical to plan to spend $10,350 in total or about $1.04 per unit of output. This could be called the standard cost per unit. After the week's production it would be possible to determine with some effort how many components were produced and how many resources were consumed.[2] From this information it would be possible to calculate the actual cost per unit produced. This cost could be compared to the standard cost. If these costs were the same they could conclude that the process was going according to plan. If the costs were not nearly the same, they could perform further analysis to determine why.

In measuring effectiveness you should remember that you only know the plan has been met; you do not know how good the plan was.

AVERAGE COST VERSUS MARGINAL COST

Table 1–2 gives the cost per unit output for various levels of output. This cost is an average cost and as such it assigns some of the fixed costs to every unit of output produced.

Sometimes it is more useful to consider how much it would cost to produce an additional unit of output once you are in operation. For example, suppose that XYZ has an opportunity to sell an additional 4,000 components to a parts dealer for $1 per component. Looking at Table 1–2 you can see that at the current rate of operation, 6,000 units per week, the average cost of input needed to make a part is $1.11. These costs make the opportunity seem unattractive. Even if you look at the column headed by 10,000 the average cost is $1.04 per unit.

A closer analysis could be made to determine the incremental cost of the extra 4,000 units. XYZ would not need to input more rent, supervision, or depreciation to the process to obtain the additional 4,000 units. In fact the total cost of 10,000 units is $10,350 and for 6,000 it is $6,670. Thus, the extra cost needed to produce the 4,000 would be $3,680. This means $0.92 per unit for the additional output. The $0.92 cost is called the *marginal cost* or *incremental cost* of the extra unit of output given that they have already decided to produce 6,000. This marginal cost makes the $1 price offered by the dealer a reasonable proposal. XYZ may still reject the opportunity for qualitative reasons, or because they do not believe it represents a large enough profit per unit produced.

We have now described two ways to measure the cost of a unit of output: marginal cost and average cost. Both of them can be calculated if you know the total input cost for various levels of output. The necessary

---

[2] Collecting such data usually requires a very good information system and it is often a very difficult job in practice.

cost and volume information is shown in Table 1–2 and can also be sum-marized in a break-even graph like the one shown in Figure 1–3.

The solid line in Figure 1–3 is drawn through the total costs points from Table 1–2 for various levels of output. This cost line has a slope of $0.92

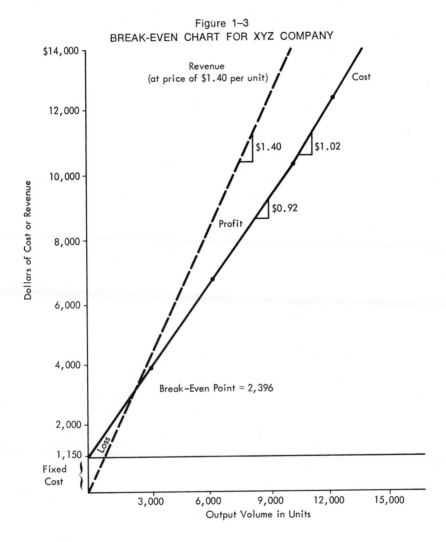

Figure 1–3
BREAK-EVEN CHART FOR XYZ COMPANY

per unit until volume reaches 10,000 units. Above this volume the slope is $1.02 per unit. This slope is the marginal cost of output. The average cost is found by dividing the total cost by the total volume at any point on the line.

The broken line starting at the origin is called the revenue line. It in-creases at the rate of $1.40 per unit of output. The difference between the revenue line and cost line is the loss or profit. The two lines are equal at 2,396 units. This is called the break-even point and can be found by dividing the profit per unit into the fixed costs. In this case profit per unit is ($1.40 — $0.92) = $0.48. The fixed costs are $1,150 per week. Therefore break even is 1,150 ÷ $0.48 = 2,396 units.

FLEXIBILITY

In the XYZ example we were not given any information on how flexible the process might be. If we want to know something about flexibility it would be useful to know how long it would take to recruit and train workers for the second shift of the assembly task. It would also be useful to know what other parts could be made on the molding machines. Both of these facts, and many others, would allow us to determine how quickly this process could respond to changes in the demand for its output and how costly such a change might be.

SUMMARY

In this example we have not tried to address any management problem. In any real case it is clear that the nature of the problem should focus your analysis. Instead, we have tried to show several steps that might be useful in an analysis. These steps are summarized below.

1. Define the process.   Determine the tasks and the flows of information and goods. Also, determine where it is possible to store goods in the process. This effort can be recorded in a process flow diagram.
2. Determine the range of capacity for the process.   This will require an analysis of each task and a comparison of how these tasks are balanced. In addition determine the effect of storage in the system on the capacity of tasks and flows. Inventories may allow the process to operate out of balance for some time, but in the long run the capacity of the process is limited by the capacity of its slowest task.
3. Determine the cost of inputs and relate these costs to the output. This will result in the calculation of the average cost of a unit of output or the marginal cost of a unit of output or both. Once this is done it may be possible to determine the value of the output in some market by comparing the cost, quality, and timeliness of this output to the needs of that market.

CASES IN THIS CHAPTER

There are four cases in this chapter all of which provide the opportunity for you to do an exhaustive process analysis. Once your analysis is complete you should have an understanding of the problems facing the managers in these situations and be able to recommend some action to these managers. The Blitz Company is a small manufacturer of printed circuit boards that has been experiencing rapid growth. The National Cranberry Cooperative is having trouble meeting the highly seasonal demand for its processing facilities. The Lowell Steel Corporation is an integrated producer of steel products and must decide if it should increase its steel making capacity by 10 percent. The Office of Senator Ronald R. Kenmore provides a description of the mail handling and information processing in the office of a U.S. senator and gives you an opportunity to try your skill at a process analysis for a service producing organization.

Blitz Company[1]

In October 1961, Mr. Alfred Jodal, president of the Blitz Company, was reviewing the company's position prior to planning 1962 operations.

The Market

The Blitz Company manufactured electrical circuit boards to the specifications of a variety of electronic manufacturers. Each board consisted of a thin sheet of insulating material with thin metal strips (conductors) bonded to its surface. The insulating sheet acted as a structural member and supported electrical components and fragile conductors which connected the components into an electrical network. A typical example of the products produced by the company was a circuit board consisting of a $4 \times 2 \times \frac{1}{16}$-inch plastic plate with 18 separate conductors bonded on its surface, as shown in Exhibit 1. In the customer's plant, assemblers positioned electronic components in the holes on the board, soldered them in place, and installed the assembly in final products such as two-way radios, electronic instruments, and radar equipment. Because circuit boards reduced the labor required in assembling and wiring electrical components, lessened the chances of human errors in assembly, and reduced the size of completed assemblies, the market for circuit boards had grown rapidly since World War II.

Competitive Advantages

Since the start of operations in 1959, the Blitz Company had specialized in making circuit boards for experimental devices and for pilot production runs. Earning statements and a balance sheet are shown in Exhibits 2 and 3. Most of the company's managers were engineers with substantial experience in the electronics industry. Mr. Jodal and the firm's design engineer,

---
[1] All figures have been disguised.

Exhibit 1
A TYPICAL CIRCUIT BOARD IN ITS STAGES OF FABRICATION

Figure a. The raw material is a plastic sheet with a copper veneer.

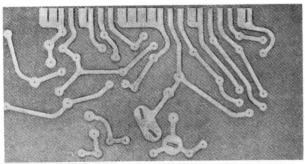

Figure b. After etching and shearing, only plated conductors are left on the plastic sheet.

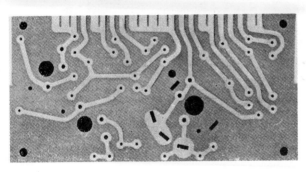

Figure c. The finished circuit board has been shaped to final dimensions in a stamping operation and drilled.

Mr. Krebs, had invented several of the company's processing methods and had patented applications, processes, and modifications of some commercial machinery. The president believed that the Blitz Company was therefore more adept than its competitors in anticipating and resolving the problems inherent in new designs and production techniques.

MANUFACTURING PROCESS

The manufacturing process was divided into three stages: preparation, image transfer, and fabrication. In the first stage, patterns, jigs, and fixtures

Exhibit 2

SUMMARY OF PROFIT AND LOSS STATEMENTS

	September 1961		August 1961		July 1961		January–June 1961		1960	1959
Net sales*	$33,201	100%	$34,689	100%	$16,089	100%	$78,585	100%	$93,837	$50,778
Direct material:										
Beginning in-process inventory	$ 8,277	24.9	$ 4,743	13.7	$ 3,906	24.3	$ 3,162	4.0	$ 2,511	$ 1,209
From stock and purchases	5,766	17.4	12,462	35.9	4,557	28.3	22,971	29.2	25,947	14,136
Chemicals, film, and supplies	2,325	7.0	3,627	10.5	2,418	15.0	10,044	12.5	6,603	3,999
Shop wages and foreman's salary	6,231	18.5	5,859	16.9	3,906	24.3	22,692	28.9	29,016	16,275
Overtime wages	279	0.8	1,023	2.9	0	0	1,023	1.3	n.a.	n.a.
Other expenses†	1,488	4.5	1,116	3.2	930	5.8	6,231	7.9	7,254	3,534
Total	$24,366	73.4%	$28,830	83.1%	$15,717	97.7%	$66,123	84.1%	$71,331	$39,153
Less closing in-process direct material	(6,603)	19.9	(8,277)	23.9	(4,743)	29.5	(3,906)	5.0	(3,162)	(2,511)
Cost of goods manufactured	$17,763	53.5%	$20,553	59.2%	$10,974	68.2%	$62,217	79.2%	$68,169	$36,642
Gross profit	15,438	46.5	14,136	40.8	5,115	31.8	16,368	20.8	25,668	14,136
Company overhead:										
Salaries (administrative, engineering, and office)	4,836	14.6	5,487	15.8	4,278	26.6	25,482	32.4	26,784	11,346
Other (rent, interest, telephone, utilities, etc.)	837	2.5	930	2.7	651	4.1	4,371	5.6	7,812	2,883
Profit or (loss) before taxes	$ 9,765	29.4%	$ 7,719	22.3%	$ 186	1.2%	($13,485)	(17.2%)	($ 8,928)	($ 93)

* Recorded on day of shipment.
† Includes water, heat, power, payroll taxes, group insurance and depreciation ($279 month in 1961).
n.a. = Not available.
Source: Company records.

Exhibit 3

BLITZ COMPANY

Balance Sheet, September 30, 1961

Assets				*Liabilities*		
Cash			$13,299	Accounts payable . . .		$24,180
Accounts receivable.			53,196	Commissions.		6,231
				Taxes payable		3,069
				Notes payable		14,229
Inventory:						
Raw material	$ 2,976					
Supplies	2,232					
In-process	6,603	11,811				
Prepaid expenses . . .		2,325				
Current assets			$ 80,631	Current liabilities		$ 47,709
		Depre-				
	Cost	*ciation*				
Buildings	$14,880	$ 1,953		Long-term notes.		2,604
Machinery	15,531	3,162				
Small tools.	2,325	2,232				
Office equipment . . .	3,627	651				
	$36,363	$ 7,998				
Fixed assets			$ 28,365			
				Net worth:		
				Capital stock	$63,519	
				Deficit 1–1–61. . . .	(9,021)	
				Profit for year. . . .	4,185	58,683
Total			$108,996			$108,996

Source: Company records.

were produced and raw material was prepared for processing. The next step, image transfer, yielded a sheet of plastic with appropriate conductors bonded on the surface. In the final stage, this material was transformed into shaped, drilled, and finished circuit boards. The most common sequence of operations is listed in Exhibit 4.

Preparation Stage

The pattern used in the image transfer stage was made by photographing the customer's blueprint and producing a "panel" negative showing a number of the circuits in actual size, side by side, on a 12 × 18-inch film. This negative was then used in conjunction with a light-sensitive chemical (KPR), as described later in the case. In other preparatory steps, simple drilling jigs and fixtures and routing fixtures for the fabrication operations were made using bench drills, a circular saw, a band saw, and hand tools. Stamping dies, when required, were obtained from subcontractors.

The principal raw material used by the company consisted of plastic panels with a thin sheet of copper facing bonded to one surface. This material was usually purchased in sheets of desired thickness measuring approx-

Exhibit 4

Operation	Standard Production Times (in minutes)		September's Production			September's Total Standard Production (in minutes)		(in hours)
	Setup	Run	Orders	Cir-cuits	Setup	Run	Total	Total
Photograph	29	0	59	4,690	1,710	0	1,710	28.5
Inspect and shear	20	.5*	60	5,740	1,200	360	1,560	26.0
Drill (location holes)	10	.5*	60	5,740	600	360	960	16.0
KPR	1	10*	60	5,740	60	7,200	7,260	121.0
Touch up and inspect. . . .	10	3*	60	5,740	600	2,750	3,350	45.8
Plate	10	5*	52	5,616	520	3,510	4,030	67.2
Etch	10	4*	59	5,739	590	2,870	3,460	57.7
Shear (into circuit boards) .	10	.5*	56	5,828	560	360	920	15.3
Drill (location holes)	10	.5†	53	5,709	530	2,855	3,385	56.4
Configuration:								
Rout	50‡	1†	49	2,380	2,450	2,380	4,830	80.5
Punch press	150	.6†	4	3,329	600	2,000	2,600	43.3
Drill holes:								
Green pantographic . . .	50‡	.05 per hole‖	8	1,879§	400	9,400	9,800	163.3
Manual	15	.10 per hole	40	494	600	4,940	5,540	92.3
Epoxy painting	50‡	1†	8	1,000	400	1,000	1,400	23.7
Stake:								
Eyelet	20	.07 per eye	14	487	280	340	620	10.3
Terminals	20	.15 per term	3	257	60	40	100	1.7
Solder	30	1.5†	8	1,233	240	1,850	2,090	34.8
Inspect and pack	10	1.5†	60	5,740	600	8,610	9,210	153.5
Total			713	67,341	12,000	50,225	62,225	1,037.3

* Per panel.

† Per circuit board.

‡ Includes time for jigs and fixtures.

§ Only lots of more than 100 boards were drilled on this machine.

‖ This time is for each board. It was estimated by assuming more than one board would be drilled at a time.

Assumptions: 8 circuit boards per panel; 100 holes per circuit board; 10 eyelets and 1 terminal per circuit board.

Source: Prepared by case writer from company production records and standard times estimated by Mr. Jodal.

imately 48 × 36 inches. In the preparation stage, these sheets were inspected visually for flaws, and were then cut on a shear into smaller panels measuring approximately 12 × 18 inches. The panel's exact dimensions were chosen by the operator so that the maximum number of circuit boards could be obtained from the sheets. Location holes, used to facilitate positioning in later processes, were then drilled in each panel.

Image Transfer

In the image-transferring process, the panels were washed, dipped into a solution of a light-sensitive chemical (KPR), and baked. A panel negative was then laid over the KPR-coated copper surface and the assembly was exposed to ultraviolet light for two minutes. A finishing dip in a solvent removed that portion of the KPR coating which had been covered by the dark portions of the negative and had not been exposed to the ultraviolet light. After this step, the areas of the panel's copper surface corresponding to the desired conductors remained bare.

Next, the bare surfaces (conductors) were protected with a metal plating. The plater inspected each panel, touching up voids in the remaining KPR coating and removing any excess, and then inserted it into a 50-gallon plating tank where a .001-inch-thick coating of lead-tin alloy or other metal was deposited on the panel's bare surfaces. In the following etching operation, the plated panels were placed in rubber-coated racks and successively submerged in a coating solvent, a rinse solution, an acid bath, and another rinse. The acid ate away the unprotected copper, thus producing a sheet of plastic with a pattern of plated conductors on its surface.

Fabrication

Subsequently, the etched panels were cut into individual circuit boards on the same shear used previously to cut the plastic sheet into panels. Two location holes were then drilled in each circuit board on a bench press.

Each individual board was then reduced to the desired final size and shape either by die-stamping in a 20-ton punch press or by shaping on a routing machine. The operator of the routing machine (which was similar to a vertical milling machine) placed each circuit board on a fixture which controlled the way it was fed into the cutting tool.

On the average, 100 holes were drilled in each circuit board using either ordinary bench drill presses or the company's modified Green pantographic drill press.[2] An operator using the pantographic press could drill as many as three circuit boards simultaneously by stacking them on top of each other in a fixture positioned on the machine's worktable. The location of all the drilled holes was controlled by a master pattern (a plastic plate with the proper hole pattern drilled in it) mounted alongside the worktable. To position the tool and drill the circuit boards, the operator simply inserted the machine's follower stylus successively into each of the pattern's holes.

After drilling, some circuit boards were coated with an epoxy resin in a painting process to inhibit damage caused by corrosion, scratching, and rough handling.

To assemble eyelets and terminals in the holes of the circuit boards, an operator sat before a simple staking machine and placed the hole to receive an eyelet or terminal on the machine's anvil. Eyelets were fed and positioned automatically and terminals were positioned manually.

In the soldering operation, each circuit was dipped into a vat of molten solder for a few seconds.

---

[2] Occasionally these holes were punched out in the preceding stamping operation.

In final inspection, any production employee who had run out of his ordinary work visually checked each finished board for omitted operations, scratches, and poor workmanship. Items passing inspection were wrapped in kraft paper and deposited in a shipping container.

Although the work normally progressed through the sequence of operations described, some orders by-passed two or three operations. For example, some initial operations were omitted when the customer supplied pre-cut boards or negatives; others were omitted when the customer preferred to do them in his own shop. Occasionally an order was sent ahead and then returned to continue through the normal sequence of processes.

Supervision

Supervisory responsibility for various phases of production was shared by three men: Joseph Hadler, the expediter; Alexander Krebs, the design engineer; and Michael Beck, the shop foreman. Messrs. Hadler and Krebs reported to the president; Mr. Beck reported to Mr. Krebs.

Mr. Hadler had been hired in August 1961. He kept track of orders in process and initiated action if an order failed to progress through manufacturing satisfactorily. When the foreman's daily progress report (showing the last operation performed on each order) indicated a delay, Mr. Hadler investigated and usually secured the missing supplies or instructions, told the foreman to start the job moving again, or called the customer and advised him of possible late delivery. On average, Mr. Hadler investigated from two to three slow orders each day. In addition he conferred with the sales manager and president to determine how many small special orders (usually having a four-day delivery date) should be sent into processing.

Mr. Krebs' primary duties were to inspect the customer's blueprints and requirements in order to locate design errors, to determine the best means of processing, and to identify unusual production problems. In addition he commonly spent 10 hours a week talking with shop employees about these problems and others that cropped up in processing.

Mr. Beck, the foreman, was in charge of all other aspects of manufacturing from the time he received a shop order and blueprints until he shipped the order. In total, Mr. Beck supervised the activities of 20 production employees. Four of these were lead men who spent about 10 percent of their time instructing people in their areas or advising the foreman on various problems.

The Shop Employees

The shop was nonunion and employees were paid an hourly wage averaging $1.72 per hour. They used simple, manually controlled apparatus to perform light, short-cycle, repetitive tasks and commonly performed two or three different operations every week. Only the photographing, plating, and etching operations were not traded among a number of workers. The photographer alone used the company's camera and darkroom to produce and develop negatives used in image application. The plater and etcher exchanged jobs between themselves, but not with other employees. The usual pattern of work was such that most workers interrupted their tasks from seven to nine times a day to secure more work from another room, to seek advice on a problem, or to deliver completed work to the foreman's desk or other storage area.

Judgment and experience were important in the photographing, plating, and etching processes since the operators had to compensate for such factors as changes in the shop's temperature and the slow deterioration of the chemical action in various solutions. In the other operations, some care was required to position both tools and work pieces accurately and to prevent scratching or marring of the circuit boards. To reduce the chance of damage in transport, panels and circuit boards were moved and stored between operations in racks holding as many as 15 pieces. Some typical operations are shown in Exhibit 5.

Order Processing

As the first step in the preparation of a factory order, Mr. Jodal and Mr. Krebs estimated material and labor costs. These estimates were then used in preparing a bid for the customer. If the customer subsequently accepted the bid, the Blitz Company would promise delivery in three weeks for orders of less than 1,000 boards and five weeks for larger orders. The estimate sheet and blueprint were then pulled from the files by a secretary and delivered to Mr. Krebs, who wrote out detailed material specifications (there were 30 types used by the company) and a factory order showing the delivery date, the number of circuits, the material specifications, and the sequence of operations. The order was then sent to the treasurer, who required one or two days to locate the needed raw material at a low price and to order it. (The materials used in September are shown in Exhibit 8.) A secretary then entered the order in a log and sent the blueprint and factory order to the foreman. Most orders reached the foreman about four days after the bid had been accepted.

Occasionally the president or sales manager promised delivery within four days in order to satisfy the customer's urgent need. These rush orders were expedited by Mr. Krebs. As soon as the order was received, he wrote material specifications, gave the foreman a factory order and a blueprint, and instructed the treasurer to secure material for delivery on the same or following day.

When the foreman, Mike Beck, received a factory order, he used his own judgment in scheduling preparatory work. Usually Mr. Beck delayed

Exhibit 5
TYPICAL SHOP OPERATIONS

Figure a. The photographer is inspecting and retouching a panel negative before sending it on to the image transferring operations.

Figure b. The plater is examining a panel during the plating operations. Panels in-process appear behind him.

Exhibit 5 (*Continued*)

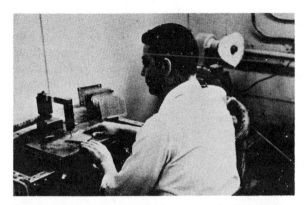

Figure c. An operator is shaping some circuit boards to their final configuration and dimensions on the routing machine.

Figure d. Two employees are drilling holes in circuit boards on bench drill presses.

his scheduling decision for several days until the raw material arrived from the vendor. He then estimated the labor required in each step, examined the work in process at critical points, estimated the difficulties in meeting the new order's shipping date, weighed the sales manager's priority on orders already in process, guessed at the possibilities of these orders being held up, and then decided when to schedule the order. The foreman spent much of his time determining when to move jobs ahead of others during process and when to shift workers from one operation to another.

Until a job was shipped, the factory order and blueprints were kept by the foreman, who gave them to any worker requiring information. A ticket denoting the factory order number was kept with the first rack of material as it moved through processing.

Facilities and Layout

When the company moved to its present location in January 1960, Mr. Jodal had chosen a production layout which he felt minimized installation costs, preserved the life of expensive machines, and isolated the operations' diverse environments (see Exhibit 6).[3] Cost had been an important con-

Exhibit 6

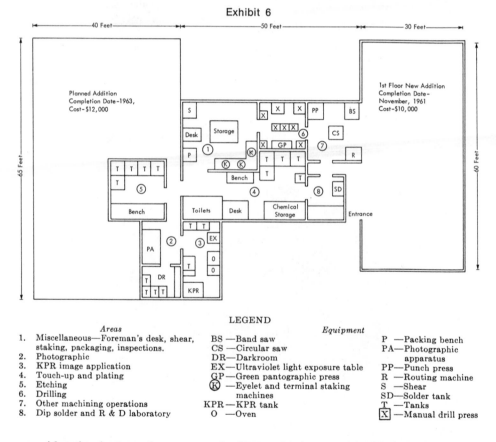

LEGEND

Areas		*Equipment*	
1. Miscellaneous—Foreman's desk, shear, staking, packaging, inspections.	BS —Band saw	P —Packing bench
2. Photographic	CS —Circular saw	PA—Photographic
3. KPR image application	DR—Darkroom	apparatus
4. Touch-up and plating	EX—Ultraviolet light exposure table	PP—Punch press
5. Etching	GP—Green pantographic press	R —Routing machine
6. Drilling	Ⓚ —Eyelet and terminal staking	S —Shear
7. Other machining operations	machines	SD—Solder tank
8. Dip solder and R & D laboratory	KPR —KPR tank	T —Tanks
	O —Oven	⊠ —Manual drill press

sideration because the company had committed most of its funds for equipment and had not been able to attract outside capital. The plating apparatus had cost about $5,000, while the photographic equipment, the Green pantographic drill press, and the punch press were purchased for approximately $1,500 each. The company had paid an average of $300 apiece

---

[3] This plan shows the location of the addition to the plant due for completion in 1961 as well as a possible second addition projected for 1963.

for the shear, eight bench drill presses, the routing machine, band saw, and circular saw; and less than $3,000 (total) for all the other equipment.

Mr. Jodal had spent $1,000 to install the partitions for isolating the production processes. (Recent inquiries indicated that removing these and putting up six other ones would cost about $3,000). The plating and etching processes, which released acid vapors, had been located far from the machining operations to prevent excessive corrosion of the machine tools. Similarly, the machining operations, which created dust, had been separated from the photography, KPR, plating, and etching processes, which were sensitive to dust and dirt. After a year and a half, neither the machine tools nor the photographic equipment exhibited signs of corrosion. Similarly, dust from the machining areas had not contaminated other processes although no doors had been installed to seal the passages between the process areas. In October 1961, the company was fully utilizing the space in its existing plant. An 1,800-square foot addition was due to be completed in November.

CURRENT OPERATING PROBLEMS

In assessing the company's operating position, Mr. Jodal was most concerned about the current difficulties which he described as bottleneck, performance, quality, and delivery problems.

Production Bottleneck

The bottleneck was perplexing because it shifted almost daily from one operation to another, without pattern. Anticipating where work would pile up in the shop on a given day had proven difficult because individual orders imposed varying work loads on each operation. These variations stemmed from difference in order size, from orders by-passing some operations, and from differences in circuit designs. Also contributing to fluctuations were the four-day rush orders (usually three a week), orders requiring rework at one or two operations, and work delayed in process pending a customer's delivery of special eyelets and terminals or a design change (one to nine a week). Approximately a fourth of the jobs delayed in process were held as a result of telephone calls from the customers' engineers who had encountered a problem. Then, any time from one day to two weeks later, the customer would relay permission to complete the order as originally specified or give new specifications. About an equal number of jobs were stopped as a result of processing problems or mistakes made in operations which could be overcome by a specification change. These orders were held until Mr. Krebs could secure permission to deviate from the customer's original specifications.

During the past several months the foreman had found compensating for these variations increasingly difficult because he had no accurate way of predicting where work would pile up or run out, or of assessing the future effects of any corrective action. A recent Wednesday's events were typical. Early in the morning, three men engaged in manual drilling had run out of work. The foreman, therefore, shifted them to other tasks until other boards could be expedited to the drilling operation. In this case, the foreman decided to meet the situation by expediting two orders which required work in only one or two operations preceding drilling. By midmorning one of the men transferred away from drilling had completed his new assignment and had to be given a different job. In the afternoon, by which time the expedited orders had reached the drilling operation, the foreman found that two employees assigned to certain of the steps which had been by-passed by the expedited orders had run out of work.

Only the small orders (ten circuit boards or less) seemed to pose no scheduling problems. Such orders were always assigned to a senior employee, Arthur Dief, who carried each order from step to step, doing the work himself or having someone else perform it. Dief consistently met delivery deadlines, even on four-day rush orders, and his reject rate was usually zero.

Performance and Methods

Mr. Jodal realized that it was impossible to evaluate shop productivity precisely. However, during his daily trips through the shop he had noticed that several of the machines were idle more often than he would have expected. In commenting on the summary of productive labor shown in Exhibit 4, the president noted that total standard man-hours did not include time which was spent reworking or replacing circuits which failed inspection or were returned by customers. In addition, he believed that the time required to move boards from one operation to another and between elements within an operation was not adequately reflected in the standards. The time standards used in Exhibit 4 were based in part on a synthesis of what they knew to be the standards applied in competing firms (from whom they had hired various workers and supervisors) and in part based on judgments made by Mr. Jodal and Mr. Krebs after long experience gained in performing and observing those jobs in the Blitz Company. In preparing time estimates for bid preparation, Mr. Jodal actually used figures which were substantially above those standards.

The president felt, however, that the job methods in use were far from ideal and that the standards did not reflect improvements which could probably be made in almost any job in the shop. As a specific example, he cited the plating operation. The plater worked at a desk inspecting (touching up) panels and then carried the panels to plating tanks 18 feet away, inserted them, and returned to inspect more panels. He interrupted his work at the desk every three or four minutes to inspect the panels in one of the tanks. Mr. Krebs thought that the plater sometimes spent

15 percent of his time simply walking between the desk and the tanks.

Mr. Jodal suspected that methods improvements were not being introduced because the current pressure for output, the constant shifting of men from job to job, and other immediate problems inhibited experimentation with new ideas. Furthermore, job improvements often seemed, in retrospect, to have created more problems than they solved. For example, those infrequent cases in which improvements had substantially increased production at one station often resulted in work piling up at the following operations. The foreman was then forced to reschedule orders and reassign workers, thus adding to the general confusion and occasionally creating personal friction.

Quality and Delivery Problems

Mr. Sacks, who joined the company as the sales manager in April 1961, was concerned about recent failures in maintaining quality standards and in meeting promised delivery dates. Since August, customer returns had increased from 4 percent to about 8 percent and shipments had averaged nine days late. Mr. Sacks felt that a continuation of these conditions would impede his hope of increasing the present sales volume and achieving the company's sales goals. The sales goals shown in Exhibit 7 had been devel-

Exhibit 7
BLITZ COMPANY
Pro Forma Profit and Loss Statement
Prepared by Rothchilde and Rommel, Inc.—Management Consultants on November 21, 1960
(in thousands of dollars)

	1961		1962		1963		1964	
Net sales	$199	100%	$336	100%	$521	100%	$823	100%
Direct material	45	22.4	75	22.4	116	22.3	181	22.0
Chemicals, film and supplies. .	17	8.4	32	9.4	56	10.7	74	9.0
Wages and foreman's salary . .	50	25.2	88	26.3	135	25.9	214	26.0
Other expenses*	11	5.6	18	5.3	28	5.4	47	5.6
Cost of goods sold	123	61.7	213	63.4	335	64.3	516	62.6
Gross profit	76	38.3	123	36.6	186	35.7	307	37.3
Company overhead:								
Salaries (administrative, engineering, and office) . .	42	21.0	56	16.6	79	15.2	130	15.8
Other overhead (rent, interest, utilities, etc.) . . .	13	6.5	20	5.8	28	5.4	42	5.1
Profit before taxes	21	10.8	47	14.1	79	15.2	135	16.4

* Water, heat, power, depreciation, etc.
Source: Company records.

oped by a local consulting firm in November 1960, after a month's study of the potential market. The sales manager predicted that volume would reach only $600,000 in 1964 if he began promising four-week deliveries on small orders, as four competitors were quoting. If, on the other hand, the company were able to regain its pre-August delivery performance, Mr. Sacks felt sales should exceed $1.5 million in 1964. Both Mr. Sacks and Mr. Jodal believed that the company should continue to bid only for low-volume, special circuit board business. Their sales estimates, therefore, were based on an order-size profile similar to that actually produced in September 1961, as shown in Exhibit 8.

Exhibit 8
THE ORDER SIZE AND NUMBER OF ORDERS PROCESSED
DURING SEPTEMBER 1961

Order Size (number of circuit boards in each order)	Raw Material Code Letters	Number of Orders	Total Number of Circuit Boards
1.	A,B,D,E	7	7
2.	A,B,F,H	8	16
3.	B,D	2	6
4.	A,B,C,F,H	10	40
5.	A,D	2	10
6.	B,C	2	12
10.	B,D,E	3	30
11.	D,F	2	22
12.	A,J,K	3	36
14.	A,E,G	3	42
20.	D	1	20
40.	B,K	2	80
50.	C,E	2	100
60.	C	1	60
84.	J	1	84
100.	C	1	100
113.	E	1	113
136.	C	1	136
140.	F	1	140
154.	A	1	154
200.	D	1	200
229.	E	1	229
252.	A	1	252
800.	G	1	800
1,000.	D,M	2	2,000
1,050.	A	1	1,050
		61	5,739

Source: Company records.

Quality

Mr. Jodal was also concerned about the present inspection system in which formal inspections of raw material and finished boards were supplemented by each worker's informal examination of the units as they moved through processing. The president felt that any effort to specify quality standards more exactly and to enforce them more rigorously might not be feasible because the standards varied from customer to customer and even from order to order. For example, in one recent episode a customer's engineers had praised the quality of the Blitz Company's work on one order even though the boards were scratched and marred and had one or two holes located out of tolerance. A week later, other engineers at the same company had rejected 25 apparently perfect boards because one conductor on each had a single .005 $\times$ .010- inch nick in it.

A tenth of the boards returned were damaged or out of tolerance. The remainder were returned because the Blitz Company had failed to perform one or two required operations. These boards were reprocessed and shipped within one or two days. The company's preshipment reject rate in September amounted to 7 percent of which 4 percent were total losses and 3 percent were missing operations.

Deliveries

Mr. Jodal had always emphasized a shipping policy aimed at clearing all the work possible out of the shop prior to the end of each month. As a result, substantially fewer shipments were made in the first half of each month than in the second half, as shown in Exhibit 9. Actual deliveries

Exhibit 9
VALUE OF ACTUAL SHIPMENTS IN SEPTEMBER 1961

Date	Daily	Cumulative
1	$ 2,957	$ 2,957
4	(316)*	2,641
5	1,079	3,720
6	451	4,171
7	592	4,763
8	2,242	7,005
11	637	7,642
12	(182)	7,460
13	681	8,141
14	1,576	9,717
15	(39)	9,678
18	1,051	10,729
19	3,515	14,244
20	2,678	16,922
21	1,479	18,401
22	605	19,006
25	47	19,053
26	(353)	18,700
27	(2,121)	16,579
28	4,771	21,350
29	11,851	33,201

* Negative shipments, shown by parentheses, indicate that receipts returned for rework or refabrication exceeded shipments.
Source: Company records.

in August, September, and the first part of October had averaged ten, eight, and nine days late, respectively. During the period, the company had continued its historical practice of quoting three weeks' delivery on orders of less than 1,000 circuit boards and five weeks on larger orders. In August, when deliveries climbed to a volume of $34,700, eight new people had been added to the production force. Mr. Jodal observed that these eight workers had developed some skill by the second week in August, but believed that they would require three months to become as skilled as the company's more senior employees.

National Cranberry Cooperative

ON FEBRUARY 14, 1971, Hugo Schaeffer, Vice President of Operations at the National Cranberry Cooperative (NCC) called his assistant, Mel O'Brien, into his office.

Mel, I spent all day yesterday reviewing last fall's process fruit operations at Receiving Plant No. 1 (RP1) with Will Walliston, the superintendent, and talking with the coop members (growers) in that area. It's obvious to me that we haven't solved our problems at that plant yet. Even though we spent $75,000 last winter for a fifth Kiwanee dumper at RP1, our overtime costs were still out of control this fall, and the growers are still upset that their trucks and drivers had to spend so much time waiting to unload process fruit into the receiving plant. I can't blame them for being upset. They are the owners of this cooperative, and they resent having to lease trucks and hire drivers to get the berries out of the field, and then watch them stand idle waiting to unload.

Will Walliston thinks that the way to avoid these problems next fall is to buy and install two new dryers ($25,000 each), and to convert our dry berry holding bins so that they can be used to store either water harvested or dry berries ($5,000 per bin). I want you to go out there and take a hard look at that operation and find out what we need to do to improve operations before the 1971 crop comes in. We're going to have to move quickly if we are going to order new dryers since the equipment and installation lead times are in excess of six months. By the way, the growers in that region indicated that they plan on about the same size crop this year as last. But, it looks like the percentage of water harvested berries this year will increase to 70 percent of total process fruit from last year's 58 percent.

NCC AND THE CRANBERRY INDUSTRY

NCC was an organization formed and owned by growers of cranberries for the processing and marketing of their berries. In recent years 99 percent of all sales of cranberries had been made by the various cooperatives that are active in the cranberry industry. NCC was one of the larger cooperatives and had operations in all the principal growing areas of North America: Massachusetts, New Jersey, Wisconsin, Washington, Oregon, British Columbia, and Nova Scotia. Exhibit 1 contains industry data for U.S. production and sales of cranberries.

Exhibit 1
UNITED STATES* CRANBERRY CROP
Acreage Harvested, Yield per Acre, Production/Utilization,
Season Average Price, Five-Year Averages and Annual

Crop Year	Acreage Harvested (acres)	Yield per Acre (barrels)	Production/Utilization†			Average Price (All Uses)‡ (dollars per barrel)
			Production (barrels)	Fresh Sales (barrels)	Processed (barrels)	
5-Year Average:						
1935–39	26,022	23.7	615,100	466,844	148,256	11.06
1940–44	25,434	24.9	634,300	380,965	253,335	15.50
1945–49	26,205	31.3	822,580	381,320	436,060	17.15
1950–54	24,842	39.8	983,660	439,170	532,070	11.71
1955–59	21,448	51.2	1,096,160	427,520	543,860	9.79
1960–64	20,778	62.6	1,300,120	468,340	755,760	10.90
1965–69	20,988	73.7	1,546,120	327,980	1,169,360	15.88
Annual:						
1965	20,640	69.6	1,436,800	389,600	1,033,200	15.50
1966	20,760	77.0	1,598,600	328,000	1,249,600	15.60
1967	21,220	66.2	1,404,300	278,300	1,034,900	15.50
1968	21,135	69.4	1,467,800	301,900	1,111,200	16.50
1969	21,185	86.1	1,823,100	342,100	1,417,900	16.30
1970§	21,445	95.1	2,038,600	367,000	1,418,600	12.90

* Five states: Massachusetts, New Jersey, Oregon, Washington, and Wisconsin.
† Differences between production and utilization (fresh sales and processed) represent economic abandonment.
‡ Beginning in 1949 the series represents equivalent returns at first receiving station, fresh and processing combined. Years prior to 1949 represent season average prices received by growers for all methods of sale, fresh and processing combined.
§ Preliminary figures for 1970.
Source: Annual reports of Crop Reporting Board, Statistical Reporting Service, USDA.

Some significant trends are observable in the data of Exhibit 1. Probably the most important of these trends is the growing surplus of cranberries produced over those utilized. This surplus was serious enough by 1968 for the growers to resort to the Agriculture Marketing Agreement Act of 1937. Under this act growers can regulate and control the size of an agricultural crop if the Federal Government and more than two-thirds of the growers by number and tonnage agree to a plan for restriction. In 1968 this act was used to create the Cranberry Marketing Order of 1968, which stipulated that no new acreage was to be developed over the next six years and that each grower would have a maximum allotment at the end of six years that would be equal to the average of his best two years from 1968 through 1973. Eighty-seven percent of all growers voted in favor of the order making it binding on all cranberry growers.

In 1970 the growers resorted to the Agriculture Marketing Agreement Act once again. Under the Cranberry Marketing Order of 1970, the growers and the government agreed that 10 percent of the 1970 crop should be "set aside." The "set aside" berries (berries that are either destroyed or used in a way that will not influence the market price) amounted to more than 200,000 barrels. (A "barrel" of cranberries weighs 100 pounds) Handlers physically set aside 10 percent of the berries before harvesting under the supervision of a committee of growers, and representatives of the Department of Agriculture.

Another important trend was the increasing mechanization of cranberry harvesting. "Water harvesting," in particular, was developing rapidly in the vicinity of Receiving Plant No. 1. Under traditional "dry harvesting," berries were hand-picked from the bushes. In water harvesting the bogs were flooded, the berries were mechanically shaken from the bushes, and the berries then were collected easily since they floated to the surface of the water. Water harvesting could result in yields up to 20 percent greater than those obtained via dry harvesting, but it did cause some damage and it did shorten the time that harvested fruit could be held prior to either its use or freezing for long-term storage. Water harvesting had developed at a remarkable rate in some areas. Receiving Plant No. 1 received 25,000 barrels of water harvested fruit in 1968, 125,000 barrels in 1969, and 350,000 barrels in 1970.

Water harvesting was not the preferred harvesting method for fruit that was to be sold fresh since fresh fruit must be undamaged and have as long a shelf life as possible. It was also necessary to ship fruit that was to be sold fresh to receiving plants in "field boxes" that contain about $\frac{1}{3}$ barrel of berries rather than in bulk (trucks holding up to 400 barrels) in order to avoid damage. Fresh fruit was inspected berry-by-berry prior to packaging. Altogether, fresh fruit production remained a very labor-intensive process.

RECEIVING PLANT NO. 1 (RP1)

RP1 received both fresh fruit and process fruit during a season that usually started early in September and was effectively finished by early December. (See Exhibit 2.) The fresh fruit operation was completely separate from the process fruit operation and took the fruit from receiving through packaging. This operation involved more than 400 workers during the peak of the season. Most of the workers were used to inspect berries as they moved by on teflon-coated conveyors. Packaged fresh fruit was shipped from RP1 directly to market by truck. No problems had been experienced in fresh fruit processing in the past.

Exhibit 2
DAILY DELIVERIES OF BERRIES (BOTH FRESH AND PROCESS) TO RP1

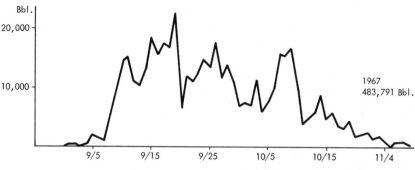

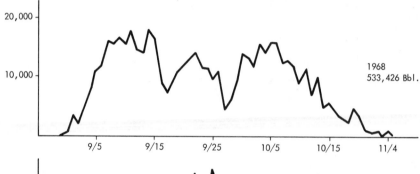

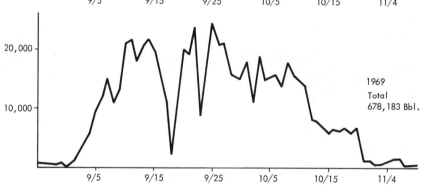

Note: A "barrel" of cranberries weighs 100 pounds.

Handling of process fruit at RP1 was highly mechanized. The process could be classified into several operations: receiving and testing, dumping, temporary holding, destoning,[1] dechaffing,[2] drying, separation, and bulking and bagging. The objective of the total process was to gather bulk berries

---

[1] Destoning was the separation of foreign materials (such as small stones) which might be mixed in with the berries.

[2] Dechaffing was the removal of stems, leaves, etc., which might still be attached to the berries.

and prepare them for storage and processing into frozen fresh berries, sauce, and juice.

PROCESS FRUIT RECEIVING

Bulk trucks carrying process berries arrived at RP1 loaded with anywhere from 20 to 400 barrels. These trucks arrived randomly throughout the day as shown in Exhibit 3. The average truck delivery was 75 barrels. When the trucks arrived at RP1 they were weighed and the gross weight and the tare (empty) weight were recorded. Prior to unloading, a sample of about 30 pounds of fruit was taken from the truck. Later this sample would be run through a small version of the cleaning and drying process used in the plant. By comparing the before and after weight of this sample it was possible to estimate the percentage of the truck's net weight made up of clean, dry berries. At the same time, another sample was taken to determine the percentage of unusable berries ("poor," smaller, and "frosted" berries) in the truck. The grower was credited for the estimated weight of the clean, dry, usable berries. In 1970, on the average, the growers were credited for 94 percent of the scale weight of dry deliveries and 85 percent of the scale weight of wet deliveries.

At the time the truck was weighed the truckload of berries was graded according to color. Using color pictures as a guide, the Chief Berry Receiver classified the berries as 1, 2A, 2B, or 3, from poorest color (No. 1) to best (No. 3). There was a premium of 50 cents per barrel paid for No. 3 berries since color was considered to be a very important attribute of both juice products and whole sauce. Whenever there was any question about whether or not a truckload was 2B or 3 berries the Chief Berry Receiver usually chose No. 3. In 1970 the 50 cent premium was paid on about 450,000 barrels of berries. However, when these berries were used, it was found only about half of them were No. 3s.

In order to improve this yield, Mr. Schaeffer was considering the installation of a light meter system for color grading. This system was projected to cost $10,000 and require a full-time skilled operator at the same pay grade as the Chief Berry Receiver.

TEMPORARY HOLDING

After a truckload of process berries had been weighed, sampled, and color graded, the truck moved to one of the five Kiwanee dumpers. The trucks were backed onto the dumper platforms which then tilted until the contents of the truck dumped onto one of five rapidly moving belt conveyors. Each of the five conveyors took the berries to the second (upper) level of the plant and deposited them on other conveyors which were capable of running the berries into any one of 27 temporary holding bins. Bins 1–24 held 250 barrels of berries each. Bins 25, 26, and 27 held 400 barrels

Exhibit 3

LOG OF ALL DELIVERIES FOR 9/23/70

Time*	Color	Wet or Dry	Weight	Time	Color	Wet or Dry	Weight	Time	Color	Wet or Dry	Weight	Time	Color	Wet or Dry	Weight
411	3	D	33940	594	3	W	13500	897	3	D	11420	1140	3	D	9020
413	3	D	9980	597	3	W	11560	900	3	W	7160	1140	3	D	9020
416	3	D	10020	599	3	D	18340	904	3	D	17600	1140	3	W	8240
428	1	D	12200	601	3	D	20340	916	3	D	8780	1140	2	D	7660
439	3	D	8980	604	3	D	9600	922	3	D	3660	1140	3	D	3960
445	3	D	7520	609	3	W	13020	924	3	W	14840	1140	3	D	4100
446	3	D	4140	625	2	D	2680	937	3	W	9160	1140	2	W	11860
448	3	D	11730	630	2	D	11460	942	3	W	15960	1140	3	D	11460
451	3	D	6580	633	2	W	3600	945	3	D	1280	1140	2	W	11840
456	3	D	1480	634	2	D	7280	947	3	D	10300	1140	3	D	1980
459	3	W	12660	636	3	W	9840	949	2	W	11540	1140	3	D	10480
460	3	D	31640	638	3	W	12700	954	3	W	12580	1140	2	D	11600
462	3	W	11920	640	3	W	28780	957	3	D	11040				
463	3	D	2060	645	2	D	18000	959	3	W	7740				
468	3	D	6020	648	3	D	8240	961	3	D	12500				
471	3	W	12640	650	3	W	13820	962	3	W	7000				
472	3	D	3940	651	2	W	11280	968	3	D	7340				
477	3	D	6060	655	3	D	1280	969	3	D	4260				
480	3	D	4660	660	3	D	500	975	3	D	1660				
482	3	D	1880	663	2	D	29560	977	3	W	4980				
485	3	D	7260	664	2	D	9720	980	3	D	12640				
495	3	D	4860	665	3	W	8800	982	3	D	6420				
498	2	D	3160	666	3	W	24640	984	3	D	11200				
499	2	D	3320	671	3	D	1880	996	3	D	11920				
500	3	D	17820	673	2	W	12760	1000	3	W	12320				
508	3	D	3360	674	3	D	9980	1005	3	W	8860				
511	3	D	10420	677	3	W	12980	1008	2	W	7140				
512	2	D	5780	678	2	D	7860	1010	3	D	7180				
513	3	W	5500	681	3	W	11480	1011	2	D	11220				
515	3	D	8880	684	3	D	12680	1012	2	D	6840				

Totals for Day 9/23

Total lbs. 1834020
Wet. 768600
Dry. 1065420
Color 1. 34460
Color 2. 401080
Color 3. 1398480
Total no. of trucks 243

Time	n	Type	Weight
519	3	D	17880
522	3	D	1580
524	3	D	6440
527	3	W	7860
528	3	W	33720
533	2	W	11340
534	2	D	6480
535	3	D	5280
538	3	D	11640
543	2	W	11180
551	3	D	2900
560	3	D	3580
565	3	D	8400
567	3	D	3920
570	3	D	1200
572	3	D	3480
577	3	D	3680
580	3	W	8440
581	3	D	8500
584	2	D	7560
586	3	D	4540
587	3	D	6040
588	2	D	3360
591	3	D	2820
698	2	D	5640
780	3	D	2220
790	2	W	11500
791	3	W	9460
793	3	W	12660
809	2	W	5620
811	2	D	2540
817	3	D	11760
818	2	D	7720
823	2	W	7080
825	2	W	20400
838	3	D	12200
841	2	D	7420
842	2	W	3140
843	3	D	13740
845	3	D	2840
846	3	D	15240
848	2	D	11540
850	3	W	31460
865	3	W	9300
862	1	D	4580
874	3	W	11280
876	2	W	12720
877	2	D	14140
878	3	D	26700
879	3	W	11820
882	3	D	12800
887	2	D	7980
895	3	D	8900
1022	3	D	9600
1040	3	D	11100
1043	3	W	11080
1046	1	W	11020
1047	1	W	11240
1050	3	D	35060
1051	3	W	31580
1056	3	D	7420
1061	3	D	4500
1064	2	D	5700
1068	3	D	4940
1073	2	D	2420
1079	3	D	9440
1081	2	D	11620
1082	3	D	8360
1084	3	D	10500
1085	3	D	3240
1090	3	W	10280
1091	3	D	8140
1092	2	W	2440
1095	3	D	13720
1101	3	W	13180
1111	3	W	13420
1116	3	D	7400
1126	3	D	7260
1127	3	D	6240
1129	2	W	13120
1132	3	D	8340
1134	3	D	6160

* The time recorded is *minutes from (after) 12:00 A.M.* That is, the recorded time of 411 is equivalent to 6:51 A.M.
Note: All weights are in pounds.

each. All of the conveyors were controlled from a central control panel. Since the man running the control panel could not see all of the conveyors, he relied on others working in the plant to help him by shouting necessary information up to the control room.

It usually took from 5 to 10 minutes to back a truck onto a Kiwanee dumper, empty its contents, and leave the platform. However, at times some trucks had to wait up to 3 hours before they could empty their contents. These waits occurred when holding bins became full, and there was no place in the receiving plant to temporarily store berries before further operations.

The holding bins emptied onto conveyors on the first (lower) level of the plant. Once the bins were opened (a manual operation) the berries flowed onto the conveyors and started their way through the destoning, dechaffing, drying (for water harvested berries only), milling (quality grading), and either bulk loading or bagging operations. The rate at which berries flowed from the holding bins was determined by the degree to which sliding doors on the bottom of the bins were opened.

DESTONING, DECHAFFING, AND DRYING

Holding bins 25–27 were for wet (water harvested) berries only. Holding bins 17–24 could be used for either wet or dry berries. Wet berries from these bins were taken directly to one of the three dechaffing units (destoning was unnecessary with water harvested berries) that could process up to 1,500 barrels per hour each. After dechaffing, these wet berries were taken to one of the three drying units where they were dried at rates up to 200 barrels per hour per dryer for berries that were to be loaded into bulk trucks, and approximately 150 barrels per hour per dryer for berries that were to be bagged. Wet berries that were to be bagged had to be drier than bulked berries since the bags tended to absorb moisture, and would stick together when frozen.

Holding bins 1–16 were for dry berries only. Berries from these bins were routed through one of three destoning units which could process up to 1,500 barrels of berries per hour before going through the dechaffing units. Frequently, both wet and dry berries were processed at the same time through the system. The wet berries would be processed through the part of the system that included the dryers, while the dry berries were processed through different machines.

MILLING (QUALITY GRADING)

After destoning, dechaffing, and drying (when necessary) berries were transported to one of three large "take-away conveyors" that moved berries from the 1st level of the Receiving Building to the third level of the adjoining Separator Building. Here these same conveyors were called "feed conveyors" (see Exhibit 4) as they were now feeding berries into the

Exhibit 4
SEPARATOR BUILDING—ELEVATION VIEW

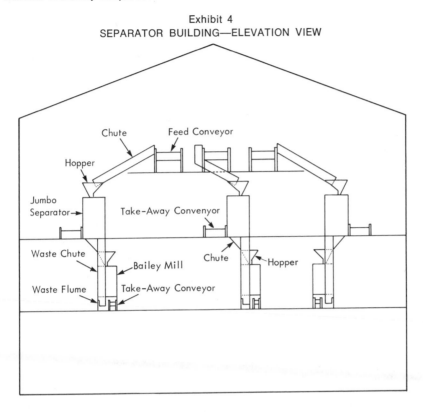

Jumbo Separators. There were nine Jumbo Separators along each of the three feed conveyors. The Jumbo Separators identified three classes of berries: first-quality berries, *potential* second-quality berries and unacceptable berries. The separation process was a simple one that was based on the fact that "good" cranberries will bounce higher than "poor" cranberries. (See Exhibit 5 for an explanation of the separation process.) The first-quality berries went directly onto one of three take-away conveyors on the second level and were transported to the shipping area. The unacceptable berries fell through waste chutes into water-filled waste flumes on the first level and were floated off to the disposal area. The potential second-quality berries fell into the Bailey Mills on the second level of the building. The Bailey Mills separated the stream of incoming berries into second-quality berries and unacceptable berries. The Bailey Mills operated on the same principle as the Jumbo Separators. Over the years the percentage of second-quality berries had consistently been close to 12 percent.

Each of the three separator lines could process up to 450 barrels per hour, but the rate of processing declined as the percentage of bad fruit increased. It was estimated that the average effective capacity was probably slightly less than 400 barrels per hour for each line.

Exhibit 5
SEPARATOR OPERATION

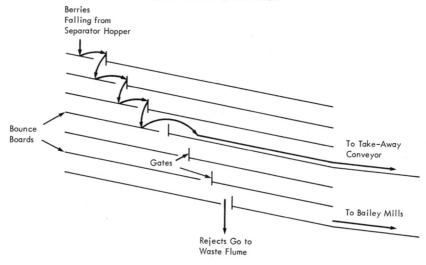

The sketch above illustrates a cross sectional view of the heart of a Jumbo Separator and the path a particular first-quality berry might take through the separator. The separator operation was based on the fact that "good" cranberries are more resilient than "poor" cranberries and thus the good berries will bounce higher than the poor berries. Berries that failed to bounce over any of the seven gates in a Jumbo Separator were considered rejects. Berries that bounced over any of the first four gates were considered first-quality berries. Berries that jumped over gates 5, 6, or 7 went to the Bailey Mills where they would be classified as either second-quality berries or rejects. The Bailey Mills are essentially the same as the Jumbo Separators, but somewhat smaller.

The gates in the separators could be raised or lowered to control the fraction of berries that were classified first-quality berries. When it was known that berries coming into the separators were high-quality berries, then the gates were lowered to speed up the separation process. Two women working in the separator area took three cup samples every 15 minutes from each separator to determine the actual quality of the berries that were bouncing over the first four gates. If the quality was not up to first-quality standards, the gates were raised to reduce the fraction of berries that would be classified first quality. Raising the gates did, however, slow down the separation process.

BULKING AND BAGGING

Six conveyors carried berries from the separator building into the shipping building: three from the Jumbo Separators and three from the Bailey Mills. Each of those six conveyors could feed berries onto any one of the three main flexible conveyors in the shipping area. Each of the three conveyors in the shipping area could be moved to feed berries into any one of four bagging stations, any one of four bulk bin stations, or any one of two bulk truck stations. The berries left RP1 in bulk trucks for shipment directly to the finish processing plant, in bins for storage at freezers with bulk storage capability or for storage in freezers which could handle only bagged berries. These frozen berries were then held for year-round usage by one of the NCC processing plants. Some processing plants could receive only bagged berries while others could receive either bulk or bagged berries.

A maximum of 8,000 barrels could be bagged (60 pounds of berries per bag) in a 12-hour period. To attain this output three five-man teams ran three of the bagging machines and stacked bags in trucks. A fourth bagging machine was kept as a spare in case there was a jam or a breakdown of one of the three operating machines. A study had shown that it cost about $0.05 more in direct labor per barrel for bagging than for bulk loading and the cost of bags was $0.12 each. In 1970 four commercial freezers were under contract with NCC to accept bagged fruit according to the rate and capacity schedules shown in Exhibit 6. Trucks were under

Exhibit 6
FREEZER RATES AND CAPACITIES (1970)

	Freight (dollars per barrel)	Initial* (dollars per barrel)	Continuing (dollars per barrel– month)	Total Capacity (barrel)
I. Bulk Berries				
Frostway†	$0.25	$0.81	$0.22	280,000
Inland	0.30	0.76	0.23	25,000
NCC freezer.	0.23	–	–	30,000
NCC process	0.23	–	–	–
Total				335,000
II. Bagged Berries				
Farmers	0.29	0.76	0.23	75,000 ·
Northern (5½ day week)	0.29	0.80	0.22	‡
American (6 day week)	0.60	0.75	0.22	‡
Freeze-Rite (6 day week)	0.70	1.24	0.34	‡
Total				‡

* Initial cost included in and out handling cost and freezing cost.
† The contract with Frostway included a guarantee that at least 280,000 barrels would be put in the Frostway freezer. For every barrel less than 280,000, NCC would pay a penalty of $0.81.
‡ Total capacity was not a constraining factor.

contract with NCC to haul berries to the freezers at the freight rates also shown in Exhibit 6. They were available 24 hours per day and there was rarely a holdup for want of a truck. Freezers were generally open 24 hours per day seven days per week.

Exhibit 6 also shows the rate and capacity schedules for those freezers

Operations Management: Text and Cases

that were equipped to handle bulk berries. Included are NCC's own freezer and the local NCC processing plant which converted the bulk berries to finished products. The local processing plant utilized an average of 700 barrels daily from bulk bins that could be filled at the rate of about 200 barrels per hour at each of the 4 bin stations. Berries could be loaded directly into bulk trucks at two stations each capable of loading up to 1,000 barrels per hour. One man ran both stations. There was normally about a ten-minute delay between the time when one truck was filled and the time when another truck was in position ready for filling. This is one instance where the station operator had to shout up the line that the flow of berries coming to one of his stations should be slowed or stopped. Others relayed the information to the control room.

MANNING

During the harvest season (September 1–December 15), the process fruit side of Receiving Plant No. 1 was operated 7 days a week with either a 27-man workforce or a 53-man workforce, depending on the relative volume of berry receipts. (See Exhibit 7.) When the volume of berry receipts was expected to be low, the plant operated with six men in

Exhibit 7
1970 DELIVERIES OF PROCESS BERRIES

Day	Scale Weight Total Deliveries (barrels)	Percent Delivered Wet	Percent Color 1	Percent Color 2	Percent Color 3
9/1–9/19	44,176	54	6	72	22
9/20	16,014	31	0	44	56
9/21	17,024	39	0	35	65
9/22	16,550	39	0	22	78
9/23	18,340	42	0	22	78
9/24	18,879	41	0	21	79
9/25	18,257	36	0	14	86
9/26	17,905	45	0	10	90
9/27	16,281	42	0	18	82
9/28	13,343	38	0	15	85
9/29	18,717	43	1	11	88
9/30	18,063	59	1	9	90
10/1	18,018	69	1	11	88
10/2	15,195	60	2	18	80
10/3	15,816	60	3	12	85
10/4	16,536	57	5	21	74
10/5	17,304	55	2	26	72
10/6	14,793	46	7	32	61
10/7	13,862	61	3	39	58
10/8	11,786	56	0	36	64
10/9	14,913	54	0	33	67
10/10–12/10	238,413	75	0	22	78
9/1–12/10	610,040	58	1	25	74

receiving (two three-man teams operating one Kiwanee dumper each), ten men in the milling area (one five-man team per feed conveyor), eight men in shipping (one five-man team on a bagging station, one man operating the two bulk stations, and two men together operating a bulk bin station), one man supervising the destoning, dechaffing, and drying operations, and two men (one on each of two shifts) in the control room. Exhibit 8 shows the planned daily manning schedule for the low volume periods which were anticipated before the 1970 harvest season began.

Exhibit 8
27–MAN SCHEDULE
(9/1–10/1 and 11/15–12/15)

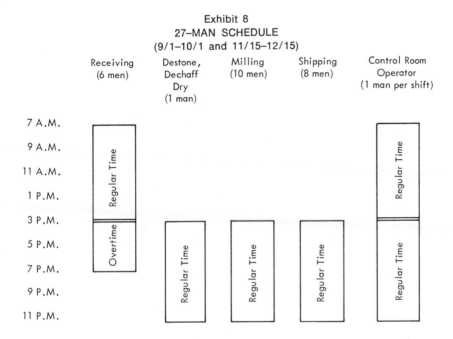

During the peak of the season, the 53 men who operated the process fruit side of Receiving Plant No. 1 were assigned as follows: 15 men in receiving (five three-man teams, each assigned to one dumper), 15 men in milling (three five-man teams, each assigned to one of the feed conveyors), 20 men in shipping (three 5-man teams each assigned to one bagging station, 1 man operating the two bulk stations, and two 2-man teams each assigned to one bulk bin station), 1 man supervising the destoning, dechaffing and drying operations, and 2 men (1 on each of two shifts) in the control room. Exhibit 9 shows the planned daily manning schedule for the high volume periods anticipated at Receiving Station No. 1 before the 1970 harvest season began.

There were 27 employees at RP1 who were employed for the entire year; all others were hired for the season only. The 27 nonseasonal employees were all members of the Teamsters Union, as were 15 seasonal

Exhibit 9
53–MAN SCHEDULE
(10/1–11/15)

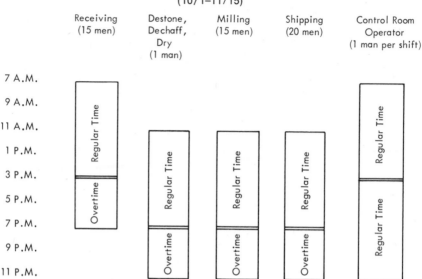

workers. Seasonal workers could work only between the dates of August 15 and December 25 by agreement with the union. Most seasonal workers were employed via a state employment agency that set up operations in a trailer adjacent to the plant each fall. The employment agency helped in placing seasonal workers in the receiving plant and in harvesting jobs with the local growers. The pay rate for seasonal workers in the process fruit section was $2.25 per hour. Many of the seasonal workers worked 12 to 16 hours per day, seven days a week. They were paid the overtime rate of 1½ times their straight-time rate for anything over 40 hours per week. The straight-time pay rate for the full-year employees averaged $3.75 per hour.

The amount of overtime used in a day or week depended on how effectively workers could be scheduled. If it were known, for instance, that the plant would have to run beyond the normal 11 P.M. shutdown time, then it would be desirable to have some men report for work at 6 P.M. or later, but it was not always possible to find men who would do this. There was also the problem of absenteeism, which caused Will Walliston to carry more men on the payroll than he really needed. He had to have "20 on the payroll in order to be reasonably sure I'll have 15 on hand." Higher than expected absenteeism, of course, often resulted in overtime for those who were there. For the 1970 season the process fruit operation at RP1 utilized about 22,000 man-hours of straight-time direct labor and about 12,000 man-hours of overtime.

When it was necessary to work beyond 11 P.M. a crew of only eight or nine men was required to run the holding bins empty and do bulk loading. Although dry fruit could be held in the bins overnight, it was considered undesirable to hold wet fruit in the bins any longer than necessary, so wet fruit was always run out before shutting down. The plant never ran more than 22 hours a day since at least 2 hours were required for cleaning and maintenance work. Downtime due to unscheduled maintenance was very small: "We ran 350,000 barrels through the wet system in 1970 and we were down a total of less than eight hours."

Lowell Steel Corporation

THE LOWELL STEEL CORPORATION, a major producer of steel in the United States, was located in a small town on the Shenango River about 16 miles from Youngstown, Ohio. The company and its subsidiaries manufactured and sold hot and cold rolled carbon steel strip, stainless and alloy steel strip, steel sheets, carbon and alloy seamless tubing, galvanized and other coated products, and certain miscellaneous items.

In 1955, the company began an extensive program of expansion and integration. The program was designed: (1) to enlarge the company's steel ingot producing capacity, and (2) to secure manufacturing subsidiaries which could further process steel the company had been selling as hot rolled strip and thereby enable the company to "take its products to market at higher levels of price." In April 1956, management was considering possible directions of further expansion. In addition, they were trying to decide whether to increase the operating rate by 10 percent.

MANUFACTURING FACILITIES

The Lowell Works had blast furnaces, steelmaking and rolling mill facilities on a single site (see photograph in Exhibit 1). The two 800-ton blast furnaces had rated annual capacities in excess of 500,000 tons of hot metal. Fourteen open hearth furnaces could produce a million tons of steel ingots in a year. A 36-inch blooming mill, 24-inch bar mill, and 18-inch bar mill reduced the ingots to billets, blooms, and slabs for further processing at Lowell, or shipment to a subsidiary mill or a customer. All of these facilities had been constructed before 1940.

At the end of March 1956, the two blast furnaces at the Lowell Works were being operated as close to capacity as was possible and together were producing from 45,000 to 46,000 tons of pig iron per month. This metal was charged hot to the open hearth furnaces. The company was operating ten open hearths, each of which had an output of about 7,000 tons of

Exhibit 1
PHOTOGRAPH OF LOWELL WORKS
(blast furnaces and open hearth shop are in the background)

steel ingots per month. The hot metal and scrap charge to the open hearth furnace was made up of about 58 percent pig iron and 42 percent scrap metal. Each furnace was tapped every 10 to 11 hours and produced slightly over 100 tons per heat.

The company had found that the optimum ratio of molten iron in the metal charge for the open hearth furnace was somewhere between 62 percent and 65 percent, a higher proportion of molten iron resulted in certain process difficulties; a lower proportion increased the time per heat because of the larger amount of cold scrap which had to be melted. Under normal circumstances the furnaces were never operated with less than 50 percent or more than 70 percent molten iron in the charge. Above 70 percent, the furnace reaction became so violent that it was somewhat uncontrollable. Below 50 percent, the furnace reaction removed too much of the carbon from the metal, and it became necessary to go to the cost and trouble of adding carbon to the melt. Moreover with more than 50 percent cold scrap in the charge, the melting times became excessively long.[1]

The Lowell Company's sales of ingots and semifinished steel products (plates, slabs and bars) averaged approximately 17,000 tons per month in the spring of 1956. Most of the company's semifinished steel output, however, was converted to hot rolled strip at the Lowell Works. In 1956, the company was operating four hot strip mills. The continuous mill was used for strip ranging between 5 inches and 22 inches in width. The 8-inch hand-fed mill was used for strip between $\frac{3}{8}$ inches and $1\frac{1}{4}$ inches in

---

[1] 1.12 tons of hot metal and scrap input were needed for 1 ton of steel output regardless of percentage scrap.

width, the 9-inch mill for strip between 1 inch and $2\frac{1}{4}$ inches in width, and the 10-inch mill for strip between 2 inches and $5\frac{1}{4}$ inches in width.

More than half of the hot strip was further processed on the company's cold finishing equipment at Lowell or in subsidiary plants. About 11,500 tons per month were being cold rolled at the Lowell Works and another 9,000 tons were transferred to subsidiaries. The remaining strip was sold to customers in many different industries for fabrication into a very wide range of end products. In a typical month the tonnage of hot rolled strip might be sold as follows:

9,000 tons to other converters for processing into cold rolled sheet and strip.

1,800 tons to manufacturers of automobile parts, accessories, and supplies.

1,300 tons to manufacturers of heavy industrial machinery and equipment.

1.500 tons for use in contractor's products.

1,300 tons for use in cooperage, box strapping, and containers.

1,100 tons to manufacturers of agricultural machinery.

1,400 tons to steel jobbers.

1,300 tons to manufacturers of appliances, utensils, and cutlery.

SUBSIDIARIES

The activities carried on by the several subsidiary companies may be summarized as follows:

The Perkins Tube and Steel Company operated a tube plant in Detroit and a cold rolling mill in Dearborn. The tube plant secured about 20 percent of its requirements of semifinished steel rounds[2] from the Lowell Works and purchased the remainder on the open market. Requirements from all sources in early 1956 averaged 7,500 tons per month. The Lowell Works did not have sufficient equipment to produce all of the different sizes and types of rounds required in the tube plant. Additional equipment was to be installed for rolling rounds, but it was anticipated that the tube plant would always buy some of its steel from other companies. The output of the tube plant was sold primarily to the automobile and oil industries.

The cold rolling plant in Dearborn secured all of its requirements of hot rolled strip from the Lowell Works. Monthly shipments to Dearborn were averaging 5,000 tons of hot rolled strip in early 1956. About 80 percent to 90 percent of the output of this plant was sold to customers in the automobile industry and the remainder to miscellaneous steel stamping companies.

The Maynard Steel Corporation operated cold reducing and cold finishing mills in Cleveland. The requirements of hot rolled strip 4,000 tons

---

[2] These rounds did not go through the hot strip mill.

per month, were secured from the Lowell Works. The finished products of the company were sold to a large number of relatively small customers in all sections of the country. The most important item in the company's line was box strapping.

MANUFACTURING COSTS

The Lowell Steel Corporation was not a "low-cost producer of tonnage steel" in the same sense as were the larger concerns in the industry. The company's production operations in 1956 were integrated to a greater degree than were those of the other specialized, small independent steel producers. It did not, however, own sources of raw materials, ore mines, ore boats, loading docks, or railroads; ownership of these properties was quite common among the United States Steel Corporation, the Bethlehem Steel Corporation, the Republic Steel Corporation, and other large producers. In some instances, the Lowell Steel Corporation purchased its raw materials from the larger concerns (or their subsidiaries) and used their transportation facilities to assemble the materials at its plants. Moreover, the equipment in its plants was smaller in size and operated at slower speeds than the equipment maintained by some of the big steel companies. Illustrative manufacturing costs for the winter of 1956 are presented in Exhibit 2.

As a result of these circumstances, the Lowell Steel Corporation operated at somewhat of a cost disadvantage with respect to the big steel producers on large tonnage orders for standard grades of steel. The company was in a favorable position to compete, however, for small volume orders on certain specialty items. It was thus necessary for the company to "discriminate" in its selling activities; that is, to seek out customers whose particular requirements were such that the company could capitalize on the flexibility of its small plant, the capabilities of the particular equipment it operated, and the "know-how" it had acquired over a great many years for handling certain special grades of steel.

For example, a customer might wish to buy hot rolled strip 18-¼ inches in width and .090 inches in thickness. The Lowell Steel Corporation could roll such steel in its continuous hot mill at a rate of perhaps 500 tons per 8-hour shift. A big producer with large equipment, however, would probably be able to roll the same steel in 37-inch or 54-inch widths at a rate of perhaps 1,000 to 2,000 tons per 8-hour shift. The large widths could then be quickly slit to the desired dimension of 18-¼ inches. In a situation of this type the conversion costs of the big producer would unquestionably be lower than those of the Lowell Steel Corporation.

The Lowell Steel Corporation was in a favorable position to compete, however, if the customer wished to buy in a quantity which was too small to justify the large producer in setting up his mills. The company was also in a favorable position if the customer insisted on having "mill" rather

Exhibit 2
MANUFACTURING COSTS—MARCH 1956

Blast furnace operations
Materials charged (to furnace no. 2 during March)

	Tons	*Cost per Ton*	*Total Cost*
Iron ore	39,683	$ 9.04	$ 358,734
Scrap, dust, cinder, miscellaneous.	5,547	–	35,167
Limestone	9,445	2.80	26,446
Coke	23,096	19.53	451,065
Subtotal			$ 871,412
Labor and other direct operating costs			
(not including depreciation).			142,592
Total Cost.			$1,014,004
Tons of hot metal produced			22,971
Net cost per ton of hot metal			$ 44.14

Open hearths
Cost per ton of ingots
(based on 10 furnaces producing 70,000 tons per month)

Metals Charged	*Tons Charged per Ingot Ton Produced*	*Cost per Ton of Charge*	*Cost per Ton Ingots Produced*
Hot metal from blast furnace	.650	$44.14	$28.69
Steel scrap	.470	48.00	22.56
Ore and miscellaneous metals	.060	–	1.74
Subtotal			$52.99
Cost above metal (labor, operating expenses,			
molds, fluxes, etc., excluding depreciation) . . .			19.78
Net cost per ton of ingots			$72.77

Blooming billet and bar mills
Cost per ton of slabs produced

Gross Metal Input (84.7% yield)	
1.18 ingot tons × $72.77 per ton.	$85.87
Scrap credit (13.7% salvaged, at $48 per ton)*	(7.76)
Net metal cost	$78.11
Cost above metal	7.24
Net cost of slabs	$85.35

Continuous hot rolling mill
Cost per ton of hot rolled strip

Gross Metal Input (93.6% yield from slabs)	
1./936 tons × $85.35	$ 91.20
Scrap credit (6% salvaged, at $48 per ton)†	(3.08)
Net metal cost	$ 88.12
Cost above metal	14.43
Net cost of hot rolled strip	$102.55

* 13.7 percent of input is salvaged—1.18 × .137 × $48.
† 6 percent of input is salvaged—1.07 × .06 × $48.

than "sheared" edges on the steel,[3] because then the big producer could handle the order only by running it in single thickness with his equipment operating at less than full capacity. Similarly, if the customer wished a very high-carbon steel or unusually close tolerances on the gauge, the Lowell Steel Corporation might be in a favorable position to handle the order, because high-carbon steels were difficult to roll in wide widths and the problems in controlling tolerances tended to increase as the width of the strip increased.

Circumstances analogous to those noted for hot strip existed in the case of the many other different grades and finishes of steel which the company sold. As a result, it was the policy of the company to seek out customers and markets where the manufacturing requirements were such that it would enjoy a competitive advantage or at least compete on equal terms with the larger producers. Conversely, the company made no attempt to solicit business in such markets as automobile sheet steel where the contracts were let for very large tonnages of standard grades and finishes.

During early 1956, steel prices were such that the Lowell Steel Corporation could have met competitive prices and secured a fair rate of return in almost any market. In the long run, however, the executives believed that the company's interests would best be served by developing those markets which the large producers were not too well equipped to serve. As a result of its sales policies, the company had established a position as one of the most important producers in the field of special and coated steels. It was a major producer of high carbon steel and ranked as perhaps the largest producer of cutlery and cooperage steels in the United States.

SITUATION IN APRIL 1956

The steel market was strong in early 1956 and the Lowell Company benefited from the high operating rate and firm product prices. In early April, management was considering whether to authorize the start-up of Open Hearth Furnace No. 11, which would add 7,000 ingot tons to monthly output. Steel scrap prices had recently risen to $50 per ton in the Shenango Valley and many observers were expecting a further rise of 5 percent to 10 percent in the next 30 days. The management was certain that any additional production could readily be sold in ingot form for further processing by other mills at or near the prevailing market price of $80 per ton. The market for semifinished steel seemed strong and it seemed likely that existing customers would be interested in additional tonnage during the summer. The Lowell Company was presently realizing an average revenue of $95 per ton on semifinished steel sales. The most attractive market was for hot rolled sheet and strip. Sales revenues averaged $140 per ton of strip, but the sales manager was uncertain whether addi-

---

[3] A "mill" edge was the edge resulting from normal hot rolling operations; a "sheared" edge was the edge left after shearing operations.

tional volume for these products could be generated within the next few months.

A furnace that is ready for start-up must be heated for about 24 hours before the first steelmaking heat can begin. Three heats are usually required to reach the normal cycle. Cost of the light-up is $2,200, of which one half is for fuel. Once a furnace has been started up, it is kept in operation for a campaign of 450 heats. This campaign is divided into two parts. After approximately 250 heats, the furnace roof must be rebuilt. This entails shutting the furnace down and relining the roof with refractory materials. The furnace is fired up again and run for another 200 heats. It is then shut down and completely rebuilt—end walls, sides, and roof. The floor is not rebuilt; it is patched after every heat, and will last about 20 years. The checker chamber (where air going to the furnace is heated) is cleaned of soot and its top layer of bricks is replaced. To rebuild the roof of a 100-ton furnace after 250 heats takes 5 days around-the-clock, from gas off to light-up, and costs $60,000. The cost of completely rebuilding a furnace is $150,000 and takes 9 to 10 days.

Furnace No. 1 at the Lowell Works had been completely rebuilt and was ready for start-up in early April. The Lowell Company's practice was to amortize the costs of starting and rebuilding furnaces by a per ton charge against all ingot production. This charge was included in the "cost above metal" for the open hearths.

The Office of Senator Ronald R. Kenmore

In May of 1971 Mr. Ted Powell learned of his upcoming promotion to administrative assistant on Senator Ronald Kenmore's personal staff. In his current position as assistant counsel on the staff of the Senate Committee on Banking, Housing and Urban Affairs, Mr. Powell's primary responsibilities had been to represent the Senator on the Committee. In his new position he would be responsible for managing the Senator's office operations.

Immediately after learning that he would be changing jobs, Powell called in a team of management consultants to discuss changes which he felt might be called for in the office operations. In an initial discussion with the consultants, Powell expressed his ideas as follows:

> With my background, which is entirely in law, I have little expertise on how to set up efficient office operations. But I don't think it takes an expert to see the need for improvement in the way this office runs. We anticipate that in about two months we may be moving to new offices. Before that time comes, I want to have an optimal system developed to handle the work of Senator Kenmore's office. That way we'll be able to make the move and the operational changes all at once. That is why I called you in; I feel we need modern methods. The senator is coming up for reelection in three years and I would like to have the mail system highly responsive to our constituency before that time.
>
> I have prepared a brief summary of our personnel and their job responsibilities to help you get started. [See Exhibit 1.]

* * * * *

Exhibit 1
MR. POWELL'S SUMMARY OF OPERATIONS
5/12/71

INTRODUCTION

In as much as Ted Powell will be assuming responsibilities as Senator Kenmore's Administrative Assistant and Ken Graham will become a member

Exhibit 1 (*Continued*)

of the Senate Committee staff, some of the information will undoubtedly have to be altered. Our present state of operations are set forth since the functions described must be carried out in each case.

Personnel Responsibilities

Chandler Arnold—Administrative Assistant to Senator

Responsibilities include patronage, miscellaneous special projects, (e.g., state economy issue). Problems with government agencies. In addition Mr. Arnold will be given administrative responsibilities which relate to meeting important constituents regarding business activities, etc.

Kay Beaver—Legislative Secretary to Ken Graham

General secretarial responsibilities in addition to specific projects relating to environment problems.

Connie Chevalier—ROBO Assistant

Work machines which are located in basement of building for mass mailings on legislative matters and occasionally special projects. Runs mimeograph machine.

Phyllis Coleman—Secretary to Chandler Arnold

General secretarial work. Handles White House political clearances. Answers mail from constituents seeking government jobs.

Fran Collins—Secretary

General secretarial responsibilities which will possibly include work with MTST.

Ken Graham—Legislative Assistant (see Exhibit 4)

Ruth Hagen—Caseworker

Responsible for military cases as well as selective service matters, social security problems and veterans' cases.

Lois Hawkins—Mail Assistant

Responsible for counting and sorting all mail. Categorizes mail and marks for form response if applicable. Divides remaining mail according to issue and gives to person handling particular area. Handles all major filing of letters in our master file.

Karen Jenkins—Personal Secretary to RRK and Office Manager

Acknowledges Senator's personal mail, handles personal financial matters, miscellaneous mail (e.g., letters of sympathy). In her capacity as Office Manager, she is responsible for all administrative matters including interviewing secretarial staff personnel, possible interns, overseeing office expenditures, office scheduling and supervision of work flow.

Peter Johnston—Press Secretary/political advisor to RRK

Mr. Johnston will be going to the home state in the near future to handle press matters in the state. He will head and coordinate press matters both in the home state and in Washington.

Paul Katz—Paid intern (See Exhibit 4)

His responsibilities will be shifted to the press operation shortly after a new press secretary is hired. They will include responsibility for operation of press releases, statements and other numerous PR activities.

Exhibit 1 *(Continued)*

Arlene Kelly—Secretary to Ted Powell
General secretarial work. Appointments, phone calls, etc.

Eleanor Kendall—Press Secretary's assistant
Responsible for production of press releases, scheduling Senator's press conferences. Notification to all press in the home state of such press releases. Handles correspondence of PR division. Up-to-date information on all grants, contract awards and makes determination of press value.

Jane Lodge—Head Receptionist
Handles major phone calls and directs to proper person. Greets constituents and sets up White House tours and other government tours. Answers mail on requests for material.

Lynn Middleton—Legislative Assistant (See Exhibit 4)
In addition, Miss Middleton serves as the Senator's primary speech writer.

Susan Miller—Legislative Secretary to Mr. Morse
Responsible for answering constituent mail relating to Mr. Morse' Committee assignments as well as handling the flow of legislative mail.

Carl Morse—Legislative Assistant (See Exhibit 4)
In addition, Mr. Morse is responsible for certain special projects such as a summer camp for underprivileged children in the home state.

Frank Mullen—ROBO Assistant
Responsible for maintenance and addition of names to mailing list. Oversees production of mass mailings.

Ted Powell—Assistant Counsel—Committee on Banking, Housing and Urban Affairs
Responsible for the development of legislation relating to banking, securities, international trade and housing. Oversight function limited to Committee activities, with responsibility for mail relating to these subjects.

Don Russell—Caseworker
Responsible for federal contracts, grants, awards and services which includes communication with "governmental agencies" and follow up on federal assistance programs.

Mary Teeling—Legislative Secretary to Lynn Middleton
Handles correspondence relating to committees which Lynn oversees. Does special work on the Arts and Humanities. General secretarial work for Lynn.

Barbara Thompson—Scheduling Secretary to RRK
Handles all mail regarding invitations, appointments, speaking engagements. Makes daily schedule for Senator. Receives all calls not related to personal financial matters which Karen handles.

Carol Woolten—Caseworker
Responsible for problems relating to immigration, Post Office matters, Civil Service problems, Federal Aviation Administration problems, auto repairs, and miscellaneous casework.

RICHMOND OFFICE

Jeanette England—Administrative Assistant for Richmond
Personal representative of Senator as well as office manager. Performs casework functions as well as public relations responsibilities.

Exhibit 1 *(Concluded)*

Irene Orlando—Secretary/Receptionist

Responsible for all incoming calls. Initially opens mail. General secretarial work for Richmond as well as miscellaneous casework.

Mary Sullivan—Caseworker

Handles major casework in Richmond office. Responsible for problems relating to Administration, veterans, Small Business, and federal employment. Immigration matters and military matters which can be handled in Richmond.

FRANKLIN OFFICE

Jean Laplante—Secretary and caseworker

Responsible for local community matters which our office can assist in, i.e., contact local federal agencies. Some casework and general run of office.

Bob Lendzion—Administrative Assistant for Franklin

Part-time office manager and caseworker with public relations responsibilities.

* * * * *

I have briefed all the staff to expect you to be talking with them about their jobs. I'm sure they will be most open with you.

Mr. Powell had also outlined the following "obvious problems" which he wished the consultants to consider.

1. The primary problem facing office personnel involved the flow of mail. In this respect, thought should be given to the microfilming of records and the retention of useful information in a computer data base (e.g., for campaigns, state-wide surveys). The mailing list should be integrated into office procedures and machine produced letters used to the maximum extent possible.

2. The foregoing primary areas of concern must be accommodated within existing budgetary resources.

To amplify on this list of problem areas, Powell offered, in response to the consultants' questions, the following description of the problems as he saw them:

Our biggest problem is mail. Our incoming letters in a normal week run from 2,000 to 4,000 pieces. We make a point of replying to every piece individually, though in some cases the reply is a general letter outlining the Senator's views on the issue addressed by the constituent. National emergencies create huge irregularities in this mail count. For instance, after the Cambodian invasion of 1970 we received 150,000 pieces of mail on that subject alone. One of those pieces of mail was a petition containing over 5,000 names and addresses of signers. We sent our reply to every signer. You can imagine the kinds of problems we have. Letters are answered very late, and too much of our staff's time is spent reading and answering mail. I would especially like to free up the legislative assistants' time. These are the people who help the Senator carry on the business of the Senate. They are professionals of very high calibre. By forcing them to spend about 50 percent of their time answering constituents' letters we are keeping them from more important work.

One of the consultants asked Mr. Powell to be specific about his objectives in improving the mail answering problem, or if he would consider alternatives to their present objective of answering all mail. Powell replied as follows:

> My objectives are, first, to get mail answering work off the backs of the legislative assistants, second, to find a way to get the flow of mail under control (right now no one seems to know what's going on), and third, ideally, to have a *Manual of Operations* detailing systematic methods of handling paper and information.
>
> I'd like you to develop an optimum system. I'll worry about implementation myself.
>
> I guess the only other thing I should mention is our budget. The Senator is allocated exactly $341,400[1] per year to run his offices. This money is available in twelve monthly chunks, and we can't carry over one month's savings to apply the next month. Once unspent budget is gone, it's gone for good.

In reply to a final question regarding equipment alternative, Powell answered:

> We can't get any equipment unless it is on the "approved list" issued by the Senate Rules Committee. IBM's Magnetic Tape Selectric Typewriter (MTST) has just been approved, and we would consider using that system in place of our present ROBO[2] machines. Eliminating all these space-consuming desks and file cabinets by installing carrels and a central filing system has also come to mind as a possibility.
>
> If you have any problems or need any more information, see Karen Jenkins. Karen is our office manager, and knows everybody pretty well.

THE PRESENT OFFICE OPERATIONS

The Senator's office suite was located on the second floor of the Old Senate Office Building. The suite consisted of five rooms, all opening onto the central hallway; however, only the reception room door was kept open to the hallway. In addition to the Senator's Washington office he maintained offices in his home state towns of Richmond (the capital) and Franklin for the purpose of providing contact with his constituency.

---

[1] See Exhibit 2 for a breakdown of the office budget.

[2] ROBO was the office nickname of the Friden Flexowriter automatic typewriters used to type form letters. Both ROBO and MTST could produce letters which were indistinguishable from hand-typed letters.

Exhibit 2

	Yearly
Budget*	**$341,400**
Salaries	
†Chandler Arnold.	$ 20,400
Kay Beaver	7,900
Connie Chevalier	8,100
Phyllis Coleman	7,600
Fran Collins	8,100
Ken Graham.	11,300
Ruth Hagen	10,300
Lois Hawkins	7,300
Karen Jenkins	10,800
Peter Johnston	16,400
Paul Katz	6,100
Arlene Kelly	9,600
Eleanor Kendall	9,100
Jane Lodge	9,800
Lynn Middleton.	14,500
Susan Miller	9,800
Carl Morse	12,000
Frank Mullen	4,000
Ted Powell	24,000
Don Russell	10,300
Mary Teeling	8,600
Barbara Thompson	12,500
Carol Woolten	10,300
Jeanette England	13,500
Irene Orlando	7,300
Mary Sullivan	8,300
Jean Laplante	8,400
Bob Lendzion	4,000
Total salaries	**$290,300**
Available for miscellaneous purchases	$ 51,100

* Budget was for salaries and miscellaneous purchases. Office operating costs (such as utilities and maintenance) and much of the supply costs were paid directly by the Senate.

† Mr. Powell was replacing Mr. Arnold who was going to the Senate Banking Committee.

The purpose of the office was to aid the Senator in all aspects of his job as an elected representative of the United States Senate. The functions of the Senator's staff were to:

1. Keep the Senator current on information related to issues on the Senate floor and in Committee;
2. Develop legislative issues and programs;
3. Assist in writing speeches; and
4. Handle contacts with a great majority of the public resulting from
   a. Visits to the offices.
   b. Letters involving case work and answers to legislative problems.

THE GENERAL OFFICE OPERATION

The operation of the Senator's office staff could be divided into five areas. They were:

1. Handling visitors.
2. Secretarial service.
3. Press service.
4. Case work.
5. Legislative work.

The reception room was occupied by two receptionists and the Senator's scheduling secretary. Visitors entered the Senator's office suite through the reception room. Although some of the visitors were individuals who had business and/or personal appointments with the Senator himself, a large majority of the visitors (15,000 to 20,000 a year) were visiting constituents, tourists and even curiosity seekers. The receptionists supplied information about the Senator's activities, Washington tourist information, and various other services which visitors might request.

Occasionally, when a group of constituents made their plans to visit known in advance, the Senator would be on hand to have a few words with the group. Individuals who had appointments, or were seeking appointments with the Senator were referred to Barbara Thompson, the Senator's scheduling secretary.

Secretarial service to the Senator was divided into two general functions—those of the scheduling secretary, Barbara Thompson, and those of the personal secretary, Karen Jenkins. As described above, Barbara was responsible for the Senator's daily schedule involving appointments, invitations, and speaking engagements. Karen handled the Senator's personal mail and financial matters and took care of the Senator's personal secretarial requirements, such as dictation, typing, and many other miscellaneous tasks which were often required. In addition, Karen was responsible for the administrative matters of the office—overseeing office secretarial staff, office expenditures and supervision of work flow.

The Senator's press secretary was Peter Johnston. Peter and his assistant Eleanor Kendall were responsible for keeping the Senator abreast of current issues and the editorial positions of the various news media; and providing the media with information on the Senator and his activities. Peter's desk was always piled high with home state and national newspapers and magazines which he reviewed daily. The press secretary was responsible for the physical preparation of the Senator's speeches (although Lynn Middleton served as the Senator's primary speech writer), production of a newsletter to the Senator's constituency, development of press releases, and compilation and evaluation of federal information on grants and awards to the Senator's state.

Exhibit 3
OFFICE LAYOUT
(not to scale)

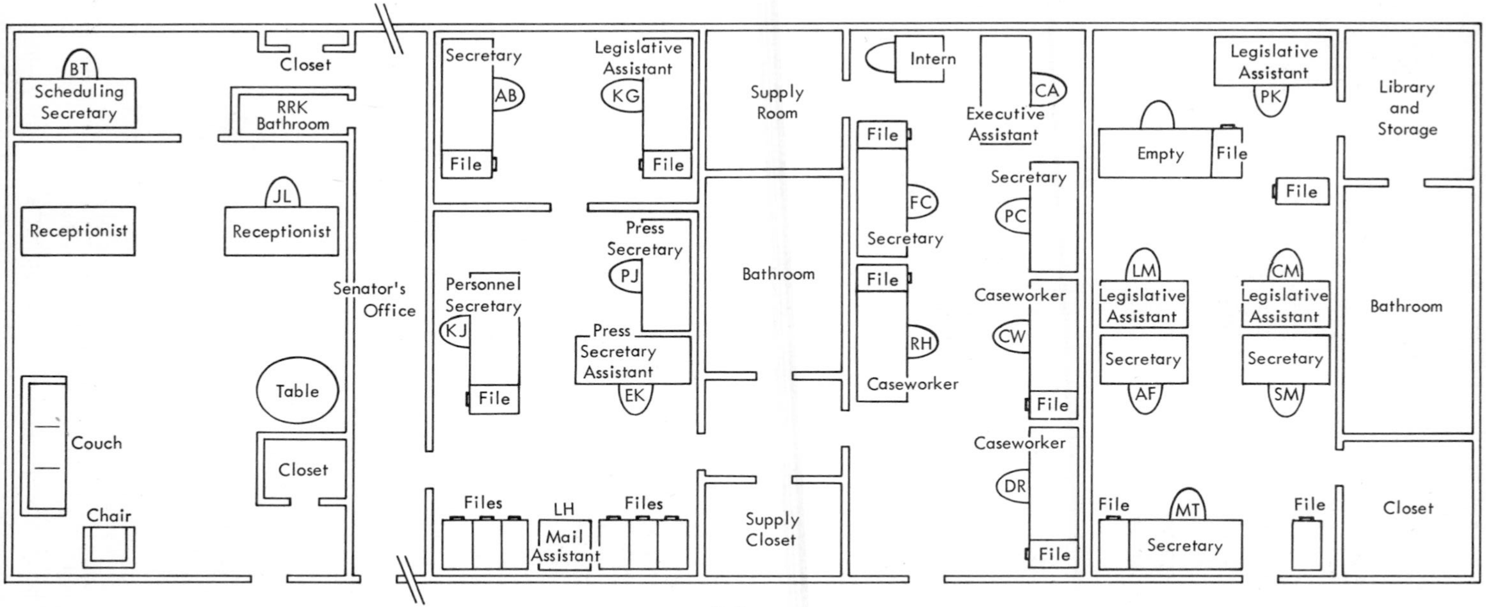

One of the many ways in which the Senator's staff provided services to his constituency was by assisting them with problems about which they had written to the Senator. This service, called casework, was handled by Ruth Hagen, Carol Woolten, and Don Russell, with the secretarial assistance of Fran Collins. Case work involved a wide variety of inquiries from both constituents and non-constituents. Although inquiries which were not from the home state could be classified as being from non-constituents, they could often be related to a constituent or constituents who find themselves temporarily displaced for one reason or another. Such was often the case when inquiries came from colleges, military installations or tourist towns. The volume of mail handled by the case workers was multiplied by the fact that a single case often required the writing of many letters of inquiry and follow-up to the inquirer and government organizations (such as an inquiry to the State Department on a case involving a passport or visa problem).

Exhibit 4
LEGISLATIVE COMMITTEE ASSIGNMENTS
(assignment covers both authorization and appropriations)

Lynn Middleton
Foreign Relations
Armed Services
Atomic Energy
Rules
District of Columbia
Government Operations/Government
    Reorganization
Welfare—Family Assistance

Ken Graham
Commerce
Finance (Taxes, Trade)
Interior (National Energy)
State Economy
Commissions of which RRK is a
    member

Paul Katz
Space
Post Office and Civil Service
Veterans Affairs
Judiciary (assisting Carl)
Campaign Spending

Carl Morse
Labor and Legal Services
Judiciary
Public Works
Agriculture
Interior
Domestic Action
Special Committee on Aging (Social
    Security)
Equal Educational Opportunity

Susan Miller
Education
Drugs

Mary Teeling
Arts and Humanities

Exhibit 4 shows the areas of responsibility of the various legislative assistants. The legislative assistants (LA) were responsible for:

1. Being informed on their respective areas.
2. Keeping current with the committees for which they were responsible.

3. Drafting legislation at the request of the Senator or on their own initiative.
4. Answering legislative inquiries from constituents.
5. Drafting speeches related to their area of concern.

Normally the greater part of the legislative assistants' time was spent reading and auditing committee meetings. When assigned to draft a piece of legislation or a speech, almost 100 percent of the LA's time was spent in researching and writing. These demands left little time for handling legislative inquiries from constituents.

Exhibit 5
LEGISLATIVE MAIL COUNT FOR 1970

TOTAL MAIL COUNT			
1968			81,799
1969			98,591
1970			149,591
Total Casework and Miscellaneous		57,490	
Total Legislative		92,101	
Average legislative mail per week		1,771	
Senate legislation	610		
House legislation	370		
Responses to our letters	247		
Thank you's for positions	120		
Other	397		
Total signatories answered			261,739*
Issues, 1970†			
Military and the war			182,125
Cambodia		168,566	
Individual communications	56,418		
Petition Signatures	112,148		
Other		13,559	
Imports and trade			3,522
Taxes and tax reform			99
Banking and housing			1,062
Health, education and welfare			3,681
Labor and business			744
Pollution, environment and interior			3,675
SST		2,211	
Other		1,464	
Post Office			1,207
Foreign Affairs			3,818
Arab-Israel conflict		2,865	
Other		953	
Crime, unrest, justice and legal matters			3,528
Carswell nomination		2,031	
Other		1,497	
Transportation			370
General			418

* The legislative mail included a number of petitions with more than one signatory. Since each signatory was answered individually the petitions necessitated 112,148 answers in excess of incoming pieces of mail.

   † Number of issues (1970) 165; (1969) 213.

THE MAIL SYSTEM

A good part of the office activity centered around the flow of mail—which was generated by the receipt of approximately 400 pieces of casework and 1,600 pieces of legislative mail each week. Exhibit 5 shows the legislative mail count for 1970 and Exhibit 6 shows a typical weekly mail

Exhibit 6
MAIL COUNT, MARCH 20–26, 1971

TOTAL MAIL COUNT 4,394
LEGISLATIVE MAIL 3,207

132	Susan & Paul		100	Ken Graham
	69 Cigarettes			27 SST
	38 Miscellaneous			21 Miscellaneous
	8 Social Security			11 Trade
	6 FAP/Welfare Reform			7 Transportation
	5 National Health Plan			6 Taxes
	4 Title 29/Apprenticeship Training			6 National Energy
	2 Busing			5 Communications
				3 Airport Noise
				4 Alaskan Native Land Claims
93	Lynn Middleton			3 Revenue Sharing
	35 Draft			3 Fisheries
	35 Vietnam; 5 Other			2 Railroad
	5 POW's			2 Defense Conversion
	5 Middle East			
	5 ABM/MIRV/SALT		59	Carl Morse
	1 Greece			8 Law
	2 Africa			8 Pollution
2,823	ROBO			7 Aging
	SST			7 Agriculture
	1,217 Con SST			4 White River Valley
	1,307 Pro SST			4 Interior (land, parks)
	82 Vietnam			4 Legal Services
	42 Draft			4 Environment
	26 Davis/Bacon Con Suspension			3 Co-sponsorships
	25 POW's			3 Food Stamps
	42 HEW Funds			2 Drugs
	16 Abortion			1 Courts
	14 Nursing–Manpower Training Funds			1 Public Works
	8 Russian Jews			1 Indians
	7 H.R.5375–Protect Wild Horses			1 DDT
	6 Pollution			1 Consumer
	5 Animal Protection			
	4 Military Funding			
	3 Social Security			
	3 Vocational Education Funds			
	3 Alaskan Pipeline			
	3 Soil Conservation Service Funds			
	2 Israel			
	2 Deaf-Blind Funds			
	2 Seal Harvest			
	2 Imports			
	2 Jetport Proposal			

count during 1971. Total mail count in these exhibits include legislative, casework, and miscellaneous mail. There was no mail count available on casework mail.

Mail delivery was made to the Senator's office three times per day. All of the mail (including letters and telegrams) was delivered to Lois Hawkins, who opened and sorted the mail according to a procedure she had developed over the period of time she had worked in the Senator's office.

1. All mail which appeared to be personal in nature was delivered to Karen Jenkins.
2. Requests for assistance from constituents were placed in the mail boxes of the responsible caseworker. The individual caseworkers periodically picked up their mail.
3. Legislative inquiries were placed in the mail boxes of the responsible LA's as specified in Exhibit 4. All legislative mail was picked up periodically by Susan Miller.
4. Particular legislative inquiries (e.g., SST) which were received in volume often had a standard reply letter which was typed by "ROBO" equipment (Friden 2303 Flexowriters). These inquiries were placed in a mail box for Connie Chevalier, the ROBO operator.
5. Outgoing mail was accumulated at Lois' desk for pickup by the mail deliverers.

Exhibit 7 diagrams the legislative mail flow.

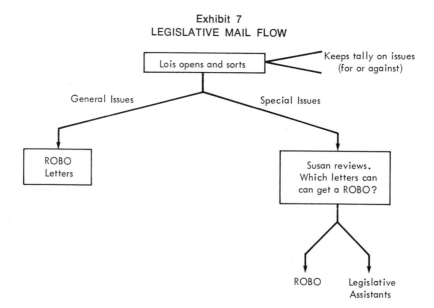

Exhibit 7
LEGISLATIVE MAIL FLOW

CASEWORK MAIL

Mail going to the case workers was divided into three groups, with Ruth Hagen handling military, selective service, social security and veterans problems; Carol Woolten being responsible for immigration, civil service, aviation, and miscellaneous problems; and Don Russell responsible for problems related to federal contracts, grants, awards, services, and assistance program.

Ruth described herself as a military caseworker:

> My job is to serve the people. All of our cases are initiated by a letter to the Senator. The cases I handle deal mostly with the relationship of an individual to the military. The letter itself usually comes from one of three people: the individual himself, his wife, or his mother. About 50 percent come from wives and mothers. Whenever we get a request from a wife or mother we must first investigate the desires of the individual involved.
>
> There are two broad types of military cases—those involving people already in the military and those involving people subjected to Selective Service. The first type normally deals with a man's relation to the military structure such as assignment or promotion. The second type is concerned with an individual's rights and obligations under the Selective Service laws. Most of these are requests for aid in acquiring a draft deferment or exemption.

Ruth explained that she received 75–125 letters a week. These included 7–12 new cases and the balance were related to cases she was already working on. The letters relating to old cases were either from the individuals involved or from government departments and were responses to Ruth's inquiries. She kept an alphabetical file of cases pending. This file contained about 200 cases. The number of pending cases tended to hold steady because new incoming cases tended to balance closing cases. The average case went through roughly five steps.

1. A letter was received from the constituent.
2. An acknowledgement was sent.
3. A letter of inquiry was sent to the agency concerned.
4. A reply was received from the agency.
5. A cover letter, with the reply, was sent to the constituent.

Some cases tended to continue because of the need for further investigation of other departments or because of a follow-up inquiry from the constituent, but these cases were rare. Ruth did not use any form letters because she felt that her work required personalized communication.

Ruth expressed enthusiasm for her job:

> The work is very enjoyable. We work on our own. I decide how to handle each case, which ones to refer to the Senator, or which depart-

ment should handle the problem. The job involves a lot of letter writing and communication with people.

Carol Woolten also seemed enthusiastic in describing her work:

> I wouldn't consider any other job. In this job I really get a chance to help people. Take immigration for example. Immigration laws are very restrictive and this has caused the development of waiting lists from many countries. In order to circumvent the existing laws for a particular individual a private bill must be introduced into the Congress. Thirty percent of all the bills in the Senate are private immigration bills. We get several requests a week for private bills and in 1970 the Senator introduced eleven such bills.

Carol described her job as understanding and communication. Typically a case involved simply a clarification of a constituent's understanding of the law. This often involved guiding them through the governmental "red tape." In handling constituent letters, Carol processed the easy things first, such as requests for information.

Miss Woolten stated that she received 150–200 letters per week. Her file contained approximately 250 cases pending. In order to insure that they were not forgotten she reviewed her file once a month and took follow-up action on those which had been waiting for a reply for longer than a month. Carol's casework often included some unusual problems.

> Many times people are in an emotional state by the time we hear from them. One family was trying to get their son's body back from the Middle East for burial in their home town. For health reasons the State Department was blocking shipment. A member of the foreign govenment told the parents that unless the body was shipped out soon they would have to stick it in a basket and bury it in an unmarked grave. Well, you can imagine the state the mother was in after that. In another case we received a card from an out of state prison with the single word HELP! written across it. Someone was going to throw it out but I was able to intercept it. Upon inquiry I found that the man needed immediate psychiatric help.

Don Russell's mail ran from 50 to 75 letters per week; he did not find difficulty handling his mail load. Because of the nature of his area of responsibility Don spent a good deal of his time away from the office dealing with people on a face-to-face basis.

LEGISLATIVE MAIL

Susan Miller picked up all legislative mail from Lois' desk, reviewed and distributed it to the various responsible individuals. Susan explained why she reviewed the mail before distributing it.

> I have a better idea than Lois about the work load of the legislative assistants. Often I can have some mail answered by the secretaries. Also if a particular piece of legislation is getting 10 inquiries or more

a week we can compose a standard letter and send it down to ROBO. We have to type individual copies for everything under 10 a week. I also try and flag VIP's for special handling. The VIP's are often sent to Eleanor for Peter's response. The letters going to ROBO I put in a file for Connie. You can see it has gotten pretty thick since she hasn't picked it up for a week or two.

Often a letter was received which had comments about more than one legislative subject. These letters had to be answered individually even though there might have been ROBO letters on the individual subjects. Periodically, a petition was received with thousands of signatures; a ROBO response was written and a typed copy sent to each signatory. Once the legislative inquiries were answered by a legislative assistant, the answers, with the inquiry attached, were filed alphabetically by the addressee. This file was used if another letter was received referring to a previous correspondence. Inquiries answered by ROBO were filed by date answered for a period of about a month and then destroyed. Occasionally a letter was lost for a period of time but all the office staff believed that eventually 100 percent of the mail was answered by a letter with the Senator's signature.

Each legislative assistant had his or her own way of handling these inquiries. Lynn allowed her mail to stack up, sometimes for two to three weeks, before putting aside some time for answering the inquiries. She would then type drafts for all the letters and give them to Arlene to have finished copies typed. Carl spent one or two hours once a week dictating answers to Susan who would then type up and mail the responses. Paul Katz, who was a part-time intern, answered the letters as received. According to Paul:

> I have no trouble answering my mail but then I often have a lot of time. I often have to look for things to do. This will change as I gradually take over more of Peter's responsibility for handling press information and releases.

Since their main task was to develop and shape new legislation, all of the legislative assistants considered the legislative letter-answering task as something which detracted from their work.

A large part of the legislative mail was not really handled by the legislative assistants but by the secretaries to the legislative assistants—Susan Miller, Arlene Kelly, and Mary Teeling, and the ROBO operator, Connie Chevalier.

THE ROBO OPERATION

Each senator was supplied with certain services for the administration of his office. Utilizing his available budget, a senator could purchase various pieces of office equipment which he might need. This equipment became the property of the Senate but was for the exclusive use of the individual Senator. The Senate provided a work area and maintenance for the equipment. When the Senator left the Senate his equipment became a part of a pool which could be drawn upon by any Senator. Senator Kenmore's office had purchased three Friden 2303 Flexowriters. The Flexowriters, located in the basement of the Old Senate Building, were the responsibility of Connie Chevalier.

A Flexowriter was a typewriter which produced individually typed letters from punched paper tapes. These machines were useful when it was necessary to send a single letter to a large number of individuals. By the use of two paper tapes, this machine could provide multiple copies of a letter with the same text but different addresses and salutations. These tapes were key punched by Connie on the Flexowriter; one tape contained the text of the letter, and the other contained a listing of the individual addresses and salutations. These two tapes were then mounted on the Flexowriter. The Flexowriter sequenced each address on the address tape to type the heading and salutation of the letter. After each salutation the text was typed by the other tape loop. The result was a series of individually addressed standard letters.

The three Flexowriters were used to produce responses to petition letters and large volume inquiries on a particular subject. One Flexowriter was used exclusively for the cutting of letter and address tapes. Using this machine an operator could cut a tape of 45–50 addresses in 30 minutes. The other two were used for the actual typing. The Flexowriters printed at a speed of 100 words per minute (a word averages seven characters). Once the tapes were cut, little time was required to set up the machines; regardless of the number of addresses on the tape it took less than five minutes of down time to introduce new letter and address tapes into the machine.

In explaining the ROBO operation, Connie stated that she had a problem keeping up with the mail flow.

> We don't have much of a backlog now but that is because Fran was down here helping me last week and we pretty much caught up. It's quiet now but it is usually pretty noisy because both machines are going. I guess I send out about 300 letters a day. I have 200 here now ready for the Senator's signature; Karen is sending Fran down to help me sign them so we can mail them.

Connie picked up legislative mail which could get ROBO responses from Lois and Susan whenever she was getting low on work. Each inquiry was put into a folder designated by a ROBO letter number. In all there were about 160 standard letters. These letters averaged about 22 lines of text (a line contained approximately 80–85 characters). Each new standard letter had to have a punch tape cut. Occasionally an LA decided to revise an existing ROBO letter. The folders containing inquiry letters were kept in a file on a small table next to the Flexowriter used to cut tapes. The folders were in no particular order and contained letters as much as three weeks old. The folders were entered into the ROBO system in random order. Upon choosing a folder to do, Connie pulled a copy of the designated letter and its tape out of the file or cut a tape if it was a new ROBO letter. She then cut an address tape which contained all of the addresses in the folder. The two tapes were mounted on another Flexowriter which typed the individual letters by automatically processing the complete text tape after each address and salutation. When the address tape was completely run and all the letters typed, the finished letters (typed on a continuous strip of letterhead stationery perforated above each letterhead) was torn off the Flexowriter after the last completed letter. The stationery was then folded on the perforations and Connie carried the pile of letters to a distant office where they were separated and the guide holes cut off the side of the letters. The result was a pile of individually typed letters on $8\frac{1}{2}$ inches $\times$ 11 inches letterhead stationery. Connie then returned to the ROBO office, signed the letters, folded them and inserted the letters in window envelopes. The address tapes were then thrown into a cardboard box which was disposed of when full. At the request of one of the consultants Connie tallied the completed letters for May 13th; that tally came to 209. The Flexowriters were loaded with tapes in the order the address tapes were cut by the operator. If at the end of the day a Flexowriter was working on a tape it was allowed to continue after Connie had left so that the tape would be completed by morning.

One of the steps being considered by Mr. Powell was the replacement of the Flexowriters by MTST equipment. This equipment had the advantage of storing up to 48 individual paragraphs. A letter could be constructed using any combination of these paragraphs. It would then be feasible to construct letters in response to multiple subject inquiries. This would result in a decrease in the mail load of the legislative assistants.

To acquire MTST equipment, Ted would have to either use part of the operating budget ($341,000 per year), or turn in the Flexowriter equipment to the Senate office equipment pool in trade for MTST equipment if it became available. Upon investigation, one of the consultants obtained the following costs for this equipment.

	Purchase Price	Monthly Rental
IBM MTST	$11,700	$265
Friden 2303	$ 4,000	$125

MAILING LISTS

The Senate also provided each senator with a mailing service. This service could be utilized for bulk mailing such as reports to constituents.

The mailing service incorporated the use of the Senate's IBM 360–40 to provide updated mailing lists and address labels. The tapes from the MTST or Flexowriter could not be used as input without additional coding. The Senator's mailing lists were being developed by the acquisition of existing mailing lists from professional and other organizations. The service of the 360–40 was limited to a mailing system and could not be used for information storage and retrieval. The service was further limited to providing each Senator with storage of up to 500,000 addresses on magnetic tape and up to 220,000 mailings per month. These services were administered under the Senate Rules Committee through the Senate Sergeant at Arms and any changes in the services, such as increased storage allowances, had to be approved by the Rules Committee.

At the present time, Senator Kenmore's office had approximately 29,000 addresses on file. It was presently the job of Frank Mullen, a part-time intern, to increase this mailing list.

2

Tradeoff Analysis

IN THE LAST CHAPTER we presented the idea that an operating process can be described using a process flow diagram and that useful measurements can be made of the process once it has been described. The purpose of this chapter is to present a framework for using these measurements to make a tradeoff analysis. Most of you are very familiar with the idea of a tradeoff even though you may not use that name to describe the concept. We all know the old adage: "You can't get something for nothing"—that is a concise way of saying you must make a tradeoff. Barry Commoner in his book *The Closing Circle*[1] has postulated four laws of ecology. The fourth law states, "There is no such thing as a free lunch." Commoner goes on to state that this law was derived from the literature of economics and it implies that all gains are achieved at some cost.

The idea that all gains have some cost is one that most of us accept intuitively as a generalization yet we can often ignore it when we consider a specific problem. We like to believe that we have found that unique case where we are getting something for nothing. In organizations this is often true when a problem is analyzed in a superficial way. As an example, the manufacturing department of an organization may decide to use a less expensive type of raw material to make a product. This will reduce their material costs and allow them to show a savings relative to their budget. The use of this cheaper raw material will in all probability have one of two effects. The product produced will be of lower quality and thus, may bring a lower price in the market, or may cause increased customer complaints. The other possibility is that the lower cost material will require

---

[1] Barry Commoner, *The Closing Circle* (New York: Alfred A. Knopf, Inc., 1971).

77

increased capital or labor costs to maintain the quality. In the first instance the price of the increased savings is paid by the marketing department. What at first appeared to be a "free lunch" for the manufacturing department had a cost for the marketing department. In the second case the cost of low-quality raw materials is shifted to another input. The company may in fact want to use the less expensive raw material, but the analysis leading to such a decision should consider both the *gain* and *cost* resulting from such a decision. With such an analysis, the company can "trade off" the gains against the cost and decide if the net benefit is positive.

In general it is easy to describe how to make a tradeoff analysis.

1. Recognize that the potential for a tradeoff exists.
2. Identify the possible actions available to the management.
3. Determine all the costs of each action.
4. Determine all the benefits of each action.
5. Translate the benefits and costs into a common denomination (if possible).
6. Take the action with the highest net gain.

The first step should be axiomatic for managers. The second step requires some imaginative thinking on the part of the analyst. Steps 3 and 4 are much more difficult than they sound. In this chapter we hope to give you practice in identifying costs and benefits in several cases. Step 5 is in some cases impossible. It is usually possible to measure costs in terms of dollars, but benefits are often in some other unit of measurement. The easiest situation is where someone is willing to pay a price for the benefits. In other cases you will not be able to measure the benefits in dollars. For example, many decisions can be made by a hospital administrator that cost money and result in greater patient comfort. How much is this benefit worth in dollars? The fact that benefits cannot be translated into dollars should not cause you to abandon a tradeoff analysis. In these cases it requires more management judgment in step 6 to decide which action has the greatest "net gain." A good tradeoff analysis makes the costs and gains associated with each management action explicit.

The text of this chapter will describe some typical tradeoffs that often occur in the operations department of an organization. Next a specific tradeoff will be analyzed in detail. Finally, some generalization will be presented on how to perform a tradeoff analysis. This text is followed by six cases that should give you experience in making tradeoff analyses.

TRADEOFFS IN OPERATIONS

There are two major types of tradeoffs that frequently occur when decisions are made about the operating system of an organization. The first involves tradeoffs within the operating process. The second involves tradeoffs between the operating process and the rest of the organization.

Both situations can be analyzed by following the six steps outlined above. However, the first case is usually easier to analyze because in most instances the benefits can be measured in terms of reduced costs. For example, it may be possible to reduce the labor costs if some part of the operation is subcontracted; however, such a decision will increase the amount of dollars spent on materials and purchased parts. It may be a difficult job to isolate all of the costs associated with this decision and often some approximations are required, but once this has been done the tradeoff between costs and benefits is straightforward, since management will want to take the action with lowest total costs.

In the second situation, where the tradeoff is between the operating process and the rest of the organization, the tradeoff analysis is more complex. Often the cost is to be carried by one part of the organization and the benefit to be received by another. Such a tradeoff often revolves around the characteristics of the output being produced by the operating process. Specifically, the cost, quality, and timeliness of the output from the process are all subject to change by management decision and action. It is possible to increase quality, by increasing inspection cost. It is often possible to reduce costs by postponing delivery dates. The key to analyzing such tradeoffs is being able to assign a value to the benefits. This will require an understanding of the organization beyond operations because this is where the benefit has value. In addition these types of decisions require that the rest of the organization has an understanding of the costs associated with the benefits. These costs are often in the operations and should be recognized by the other parts of the organization and not considered a "free lunch."

Wickham Skinner has developed the data shown in Table 2–1 for use in a seminar with nonmanufacturing executives. We have included it here as a useful summary of some types of tradeoffs that occur between the operating department and the rest of the organization.

AN EXAMPLE OF A TRADEOFF ANALYSIS

A company plans to use a new part in one of their main products. This product has been sold for many years and its sales pattern is quite stable. It sells about 50,000 units per year and there is no seasonal pattern to the demand. The company will use one part in each product and is confident that the modified product will work as well as the old model. This new part cannot be manufactured in the company's machine shop because of capacity limitations. They have received a price quotation from a local machine shop that they believe has the ability to manufacture this part at the quality standards required. The machine shop has agreed to supply the part at $4 a unit plus an $800 charge for each time an order is received. The machine shop is unwilling to carry any inventory of the part,

Table 2–1

TRADEOFFS IN MANUFACTURING SYSTEM PERFORMANCE

Assume that manufacturing performance in some base situation is generally acceptable; it is considered "good" in terms of company strategy, marketing requirements, competition, and financial objectives.

Then, something changes the "manufacturing task." Referring to the table below:

Case A Costs must be lowered.
Case B Quality must be improved.
Case C Delivery times were too high and had to be reduced.
Case D Delivery reliability was too low and had to be raised.
Case E Top management felt that return on investment was low and wished the investment base reduced.
Case F We need to introduce many more new products quickly.
Case G Business turns down and we must lower the break-even point.

Below, in each hypothetical case, we improve on one criterion, are able to hold others steady, and weaken on one or more of the others. (There is no significance in the absolute numbers used; the purpose is to illustrate some typical responses among criteria relative to each other.)

TRADEOFFS IN MANUFACTURING SYSTEM PERFORMANCE
(hypothetical case)

	Criteria of Manufacturing Performance						
	Cost	*Quality*	*Delivery*	*Delivery Reliability*	*Invest-ment*	*New Product Capability*	*Break-even Point*
Base situation	$3.00 per unit	95%	22 days	90%	$5 million	3 per year 12-month cycle	$18 million
Improving on One Criteria:							
Cost	$2.80	91%	*	*	$5.5 million	*	$20 million
Quality.	$3.10	98%	24 days	*	$5.3 million	3 per year 14-month cycle	$20 million
Delivery	*	*	19 days	85%	$5.5 million	*	*
Delivery reliability . .	$3.05	*	*	96%	*	*	$19 million
Investment.	*	*	25 days	*	$4.5 million	*	*
New product	$3.05	*	23 days	87%	$5.4 million	6 per year 6-month cycle	$21 million
Volume flexibility . .	$3.10	*	*	*	*	*	$15 million

but is willing to set up to manufacture this part as often as the company requests if they receive the $800 setup payment. All the shop needs to know is how often the part will be ordered during the year. The company believes this procedure is fair and has agreed to buy the part and let the shop know the manufacturing schedule it desires.

At first glance this may look like a simple problem. If the company wants to spend the smallest amount in material costs, it should buy all 50,000 parts at one time and spread the $800 setup charge over the largest number of parts. The total material cost would be $200,800, and the average cost per part would be $4.016. Any order size less than 50,000 would result in more than one set up charge being paid. Table 2–2 summarizes the material cost for various order sizes, Q, under these assumptions.

Table 2–2
COST OF MATERIAL FOR DIFFERENT ORDER SIZES

Order Size, Q	5,000	10,000	25,000	50,000
Number of orders per year.	10	5	2	1
Setup cost per year	$ 8,000	$ 4,000	$ 1,600	$ 800
Part cost per year	200,000	200,000	200,000	200,000
Total material cost	$208,000	$204,000	$201,600	$200,800
Average cost per part	$ 4.16	$ 4.08	$ 4.032	$ 4.016

Unfortunately, the material cost is not the only cost affected by the decision on the ordering policy and thus, the tradeoff analysis is not yet complete. The company must carry the parts in its inventory until they are assembled into the final product. This will require an increase in the working capital required to support the operations. Such an investment will have costs that the company must recognize in its analysis. The most obvious cost is the cost of obtaining the funds for the inventory investment. Most companies assign an opportunity cost to funds tied up in inventory because these funds cannot be used in other activities of the organization. In fact, this company has chosen 12 percent as the opportunity cost of its funds. This means that they believe that each dollar of investment in inventory could earn 12 cents in other activities.[2]

There are many other costs associated with carrying inventories in addition to this opportunity cost. It is necessary to provide space to store the inventory, and in many situations property taxes must be paid on inventory investment. Labor must be provided to move parts into and out of inventory and finally inventory is often damaged or becomes obsolete while it is in storage. Most of these costs vary proportionately with the amount of the investment in inventory. For the basis of this analysis the company

---

[2] The other activities need not be manufacturing. In fact, the other activity may be to reduce the company borrowings.

felt that all of these costs were approximately equal to 8 percent of the investment in inventory.[3]

Thus, the company feels that it would cost 20 cents per year in carrying costs for every dollar increase in the average inventory level. In order to determine the average inventory the company needs to know the usage pattern and delivery schedule for the part. Figure 2–1 is a diagram of the

Figure 2–1
INVENTORY LEVEL ASSUMING A PERIODIC ORDER OF Q UNITS AND A DEMAND RATE OF D UNITS PER YEAR

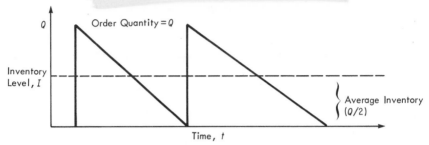

inventory level over time if the company ordered Q units in each order and the usage rate is constant throughout the year.

From this figure you can see that the inventory level starts at Q right after an order arrives and falls at a constant rate until it reaches zero. We assume that a new order of Q units arrives just as the old inventory is gone and thus, the company has *on the average* one half of the order on hand during the year. Therefore, it is easy to calculate the average inventory resulting from a decision to order the entire yearly demand of 50,000 parts. It would be 25,000 parts at $4 per part or $100,000. Recognizing that each dollar investment in inventory costs 20 cents in carrying costs gives a total carrying cost of $20,000 per year for this order policy. Table 2–3 summarizes the carrying cost associated with different order sizes

Table 2–3
ANNUAL CARRYING COSTS ASSOCIATED WITH DIFFERENT ORDER SIZES

Order Size, Q	5,000	10,000	25,000	50,000
Average annual dollar investment at $4 per part	$ 10,000	$ 20,000	$ 50,000	$100,000
Annual carrying cost at 20%.	$ 2,000	$ 4,000	$ 10,000	$ 20,000
Total material cost (Table 2-2)	$208,000	$204,000	$201,600	$200,800
Total cost	$210,000	$208,000	$211,600	$220,800

---

[3] The determination of the storage, taxes, handling, obsolescence and shrinkage cost is an important part of any analysis involving inventory size and requires careful consideration. A useful reference to this subject is John F. Magee, "Guides to Inventory Policy," *Harvard Business Review*, January-February 1956.

based on the cost assumptions stated above. This table also shows the material costs for different order sizes from Table 2–2.

As you can see the benefit of larger order size is a decreasing material cost while the cost of larger order sizes is increased carrying cost. Since the benefit and cost are both in dollars they can be added to obtain the total cost associated with any given order size. From Table 2–3 you can see that the best action is to order 10,000 units which will result in five orders being placed each year.

THE ECONOMIC ORDER QUANTITY

The problem we have just described is a very common one. In fact, many people have studied it and have developed a general formula that provides the best order size based on the specific economics of the particular problem. If you were to draw a diagram of the costs in our example for all possible order sizes it would look like Figure 2–2. In this figure we have excluded $200,000 of the material cost spent for the 50,000 parts since this cost cannot be altered by a change in the order size. Thus, Figure 2–2 shows setup charge and carrying cost as a function of the order size Q.

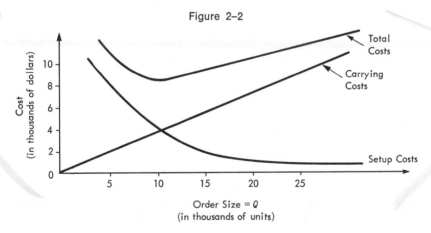

Figure 2–2

The nature of the tradeoff should be very clear from this diagram. The carrying costs are increasing with order size and the setup costs falling with increasing order sizes. The total cost curve which is the sum of the other two falls and then increases. Where the total cost curve goes through its lowest point is the best order size if we have correctly included all costs. This point can be determined using the EOQ or Economic Order Quantity formula. This formula is shown in Table 2–4 and the EOQ for our example problem is calculated.[4]

---

[4] For a detailed derivation of this formula, see Magee, "Guides to Inventory Policy."

Table 2–4

THE ECONOMIC ORDER QUANTITY FORMULA

I. General formula:

$$EOQ = \sqrt{\frac{2Ds}{Ci}}$$

where:

D = Yearly demand for the product.
s = Setup cost per order.
C = Unit variable cost of the product.
i = The cost of carrying inventory as a fraction of inventory investment.

II. Specific example:

D = 50,000
s = $800 per order.
C = $4 per unit.
i = 20 percent.

$$EOQ = \sqrt{\frac{2 \times 50,000 \times 800}{(4 \times .2)}}$$

$EOQ = \sqrt{100,000,000}$

$EOQ = 10,000$

The use of the EOQ formula is a short cut to performing the entire tradeoff analysis shown above. In many cases it is useful, but in other situations it may not apply. As an example in many parts ordering decisions, the transportation costs, or the discounts available from ordering large quantities far exceed both the inventory carrying costs and the setup costs. In such cases the EOQ formula is clearly inappropriate because it ignores both of these costs.

You should be careful to remember the assumptions behind the EOQ formula. A list of these assumptions is given in Table 2–5. If you are not sure about when to use the EOQ equation, you should spend the time to do the entire tradeoff analysis. This means identifying the setup costs, carrying costs, and all other relevant cost associated with each order size and calculating the total cost for each decision. The best decision will have the lowest total cost.

Table 2–5

ASSUMPTIONS IN EOQ FORMULA

1. Demand known with certainty.
2. Demand at a constant rate all year—e.g., no seasonal pattern.
3. Setup costs are the same for every order.
4. Variable costs of manufacture are constant regardless of order size, e.g., no economies of scale or volume discounts.
5. Cost of carrying inventory is directly dependent on inventory investment and can be estimated accurately.
6. Delivery and production times known with certainty.

GENERALIZATIONS ABOUT TRADEOFFS

The economic order quantity is only one example of a formal tradeoff analysis. It is worth reviewing this example to draw some generalizations.

First, it is necessary to isolate a decision variable that can be used to measure cost changes. In other words, what is it that management must decide and how will this decision influence costs? In the EOQ model this decision variable is the order size, Q. In a quality control problem the decision variable could be the size of a sample to be set aside for detailed inspection. In a construction project it could be the number of workers assigned to a job within the project.

Second, it is necessary to determine all of the costs that change as management increases or decreases the decision variable. Any costs that do not vary with the decision variable can be ignored for the tradeoff analysis. In the EOQ example, the $200,000 paid for parts is not influenced by the order size decision so it could be ignored. In all cases you will find that some costs increase and some decrease with changes in the decision variable. Summing all of the relevant costs will give the total cost. The value of the decision variable that gives minimum total cost is a candidate for implementation. The reason that this point is only a candidate is because we have only considered items than can be expressed as costs.

Next, it is necessary to consider if there are benefits other than reduced costs that might result from a change in the decision variable. In the EOQ example, it might be possible to use a better machine to manufacture the part if the lot size were large enough. The setup costs and variable costs of using this machine could be incorporated in the total cost curve, but how would you account for increased quality of the part? There are two approaches to this problem. First, it may be possible to assign a value to the increased quality. If the product that used the part could be sold for a higher price this change in price could be assigned as a value to the better quality. It might be possible to make some other component of the product more inexpensively because of the increased quality and this savings could be assigned as a value. Both of these approaches have used a more detailed economic analysis to assign a dollar value to the increased quality. This in general should be your first attempt to assign value to benefits in a tradeoff analysis.

Occasionally, you will be frustrated in your attempt to assign a dollar value to all benefits. When this happens you should make this fact explicit. You can calculate total costs and then calculate total benefits in whatever units the benefits are measured. If you do not do this last step and ignore all nondollar benefits you have assigned a value of zero to them. This often happens even when every party to the analysis agrees there is *some* value to the benefits. A story is told of a citizen's committee trying to assign a value to an old school building when writing a report for the school committee. There was no active market for this type of building and thus, they concluded it would require them to make judgment. There was heated discussion about whether the building was worth $50,000 or $100,000 with no hope of resolution. Finally, they voted unanimously to delete any mention of this building from the report. In reality, the school committee was presented with a document claiming no value for the building when in fact every member of the citizen's committee felt it was worth at least $50,000. When preparing tradeoff analyses, don't get caught in this "zero trap." If there are benfits they should be considered even if there is no clear method for assigning a dollar value.

The final step in any good analysis is a recommendation for action. This recommendation should be based on the analysis and should give careful consideration to both quantifiable and nonquantifiable benefits.

CASES IN THIS CHAPTER

In this chapter we have included six cases that should be viewed in pairs. Each pair addresses a different type of tradeoff. Gentle Electric Company and Blanchard Importing and Distributing Co., Inc., look at tradeoffs related to inventory. Reynolds Construction Company and the PLANETS II Exercise consider the tradeoff between project costs and the completion date of the project. Benson Electronics, Inc. and The Ferdanna Company (A) consider the problems associated with the cost of improving quality.

Gentle Electric Company

ROBERT EDISON, general manager of Gentle Electric Company (GEC), was contemplating several recent developments in the power transformer market. Mr. Edison was concerned because in its production of control units for passenger and freight elevators, GEC used five large transformers each working day of the month. (GEC operated on a 20-day per month schedule.) For several years the transformers had been produced in only two locations in the United States, one in New England and the other on the West Coast. Luckily for GEC, the New England producer was located several miles away and offered free delivery to GEC within hours.

Several months earlier Mr. Edison had compiled the following information about the transformers:

Information		*Source of Information*
Total annual usage	1,200 units	Purchasing
Requisitions per year	48 times (weekly)	Purchasing
Units per requisition	25 units	Purchasing
Inventory carrying cost	20%	Controller
Weight per unit	500 pounds	Shipping and receiving
Cost of unloading into warehouse	$0.10 per hundred weight (100 pounds)	Warehouse manager
Clerical cost per requisition	$10	Purchasing
Expediting cost per requisition	$15	Shipping and receiving
Warehouse capacity	200 units	Warehouse manager
Outside warehouse costs	$12 per unit per year*	Warehouse manager

* There is existing space in the warehouse for 200 units. Additional space must be leased for a year. As a result, if an order of more than 200 units arrives, part of the order must be stored in leased space.

Several months after compiling this information, Mr. Edison was informed by his purchasing agent that GEC's local supplier had followed his West Coast competitor in announcing a new price structure:

Units per Order	Unit Price
First 100	$500
Next 100	$490
All over 200	$475

Just recently, GEC's local supplier announced that he was discontinuing production of transformers, forcing GEC to deal with the West Coast supplier whose prices are the same as the local supplier except that they are f.o.b., California. The traffic department informed Mr. Edison that the transportation cost per hundredweight is $6 for carload lots of 50,000 pounds. The LCL (less than carload) rate is $10. per hundredweight. The replenishment cycle will normally take one week.

Mr. Edison wonders what effects these new developments will have on his cost structure.

Blanchard Importing and Distributing Co., Inc.[1]

UPON COMPLETING his first year at the Harvard Business School, Hank Hatch accepted summer employment with Blanchard Importing and Distributing Co., Inc., a Boston firm which dealt in the processing and wholesaling of alcoholic beverages. Early in June 1972, Hank had met with Toby Tyler, the general manager of the company, who was a recent graduate of the Harvard Business School. Toby had described the initial tasks which he wished Hank to perform as follows:

> Hank, during your first few days at Blanchard, I'd like you to become familiar with the general scope of operations of the firm. As you investigate our various product lines, I think you will find that the most rapidly expanding demand for alcoholic beverages is in the wine market. At the present time we estimate that we can earn a before tax return of 20 percent on any money we put into wine merchandising. However, to date, Carmen Petrillo, our Wine Division Manager, and Dave Rubin, the Sales Department Manager, have been unable to exploit this trend due to lack of funds needed to hire experienced wine salesmen and build up an adequate inventory of wines. Here is a recent balance sheet [see Exhibit 1] which shows that we have just about reached the limit of our borrowing capability. It appears that a reduction in inventory level is the only substantial source of funds available to us. That's where you come in.
>
> After you've become acquainted with our operations, I'd like you to spend some time analyzing the inventory situation and recommend ways in which we can economize in that area. Initially, you can look into the method we use in scheduling production runs of those beverages which we bottle ourselves. The current scheduling system, which was initiated in October 1969, calls for bottling of an Economic Order Quantity (EOQ) of an item when the stock level of that item falls below

---

[1] The figures given in this case have been disguised for teaching purposes and do not represent actual operating data of the company.

Exhibit 1

BLANCHARD IMPORTING AND DISTRIBUTING CO., INC.
Balance Sheet as of January 31, 1972
(in thousands)

Assets			*Equity*		
Current assets:			Current liabilities:		
Cash	$	24	Payroll withheld.	$	1
Accounts receivable (net)		483	Unsecured notes payable.		809
Inventory*.		1,050	Accounts payable.		173
Prepaid expenses		32	Federal distilled spirits taxes		
Total current assets.		$1,589	payable		337
Fixed assets:			Accrued taxes.		40
Plant and equipment, net of			Accrued expenses.		11
depreciation.		287	Total current liabilities.		$1,371
Registered trademarks		8	Long-term debt		64
Total fixed assets	$	295	Total liabilities		$1,435
Total assets		$1,884	Stockholders' equity:		
			Capital stock		100
			Retained earnings.		349
			Total equity		$1,884

* Inventory was subdivided into the following categories:
Finished case goods (uncontrolled stock)   311
Finished case goods (controlled stock).   362
Customs bond (raw bulk and uncontrolled
finished case goods stock)   171
IRS bond (raw bulk)   175
Miscellaneous (bottles, cartons, labels, flavors, etc.)   31

a fixed Re-order Point (ROP). This Re-order Point trigger level is equal to 3½ weeks' worth of the average weekly demand throughout the year ending October 31, 1969. I suspect that many of the EOQ and ROP quantities calculated in 1969 should be recalculated based on changes in annual demand over the past 2½ years. As a first assignment you can update the EOQ and ROP figures. While you're at it, keep thinking about ways in which we can reduce expenses and cut back on unnecessarily high stock levels—any cash which can be made available for wine merchandising will be greatly appreciated by Carmen and Dave.

BACKGROUND

Product Lines

During the first week of June, Hank learned that Blanchard was a full-line alcoholic beverage house which distributed both imported and domestic goods including wine, beer, distilled spirits, cordials, and pre-mixed cocktails. Blanchard purchased pre-bottled goods (called "uncontrolled stock") for resale to retail outlets at wholesale prices. Uncontrolled stock accounted for 45 percent of the firm's annual sales. The remaining 55 percent of Blanchard's revenue was attributed to sale of "controlled stock," those items which Blanchard bottled and sold under its own brands and private labels.

In June 1972, controlled stock consisted of 158 products which Blanchard processed in its own bottling facility. These 158 items were differentiated by bottle size, type and proof of beverage, and brand label. Blanchard produced 25 items in half gallons, 63 in quarts, 42 in fifths, 12 in pints, and 16 in half-pints.

History of the Firm

The Blanchard name was originally established as a chain of retail liquor stores, the first of which was opened in 1938 by John D. Corey. In 1957, Mr. Corey became interested in the wholesaling of alcoholic beverages and began distributing case goods to retail outlets. In order to devote his full efforts to this new venture, he transferred ownership of the chain of Blanchard retail outlets to other members of the Corey family. In 1964, the present warehouse and office facility was completed, and in 1966, equipment was installed to permit the conversion of raw bulk spirits to bottled goods for sale under the firm's own brands and private labels. When Mr. Corey died in 1968 his son John D. Corey Jr. assumed responsibilities as president and treasurer of the company. As of June 1972, the firm's annual revenue was $4 million, of which $3 million represented sales to the seven Blanchard retail stores owned by other members of the Corey family.

Warehouse Layout

Exhibit 2 depicts the layout of the recently completed Blanchard warehouse. Most of the warehouse space was set aside for stocks of bottled case goods. These areas included a large margin for future growth, and actual finished goods inventories had never occupied more than 50 percent of the reserved space.

In addition to the areas set aside for storage of finished case goods, space was occupied by two U.S. bonded warehouses and the rectification and bottling equipment used for processing controlled stock. The government required that all products imported to the United States by Blanchard, including both pre-bottled goods and raw bulk spirits, enter the Blanchard facility by way of the Customs Bonded Warehouse. In addition, all the raw bulk spirits which Blanchard purchased for processing in its bottling operation were required to pass through the IRS Bonded Warehouse prior to rectification. The flow of goods into and out of the two bonded warehouses was closely monitored by federal officials to insure that the required tax and customs duty obligations were met by the company.

Exhibit 2
WAREHOUSE LAYOUT

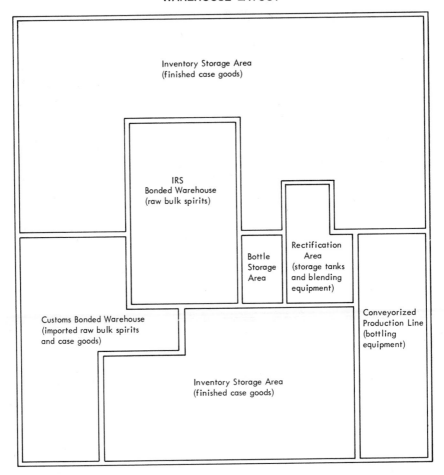

CONVERSION OF RAW BULK SPIRITS INTO BOTTLED CASE GOODS

In preparation for his first assignment, Hank made a thorough study of the method used by Blanchard to process controlled stock. Hank learned that two salaried employees, Bob Young and Eliot Wallace, were in charge of this operation. Bob Young, a skilled machinery operator, had worked for Blanchard since 1969, and Eliot Wallace, a chemistry expert with a degree in food technology, had worked for Blanchard for seven years. The combined annual wage of these two employees was $23,000. Bob and Eliot explained that the conversion process followed three steps: withdrawal of raw spirits from bulk storage, rectification of the spirits, and bottling of the finished product.

Withdrawal from Bulk Storage

Raw bulk was purchased by the barrel and stored either in the Customs Warehouse or the IRS Warehouse depending on whether the spirits were imported or domestic. When a bottling run called for use of a particular type of raw bulk, Bob and Eliot withdrew the spirits from one of the two bonded warehouses and pumped it into mixing tanks for rectification; imports were withdrawn from the Customs Warehouse via the IRS Warehouse, incurring both a customs duty and federal distilled spirits tax liability, while domestic spirits incurred only the federal distilled spirits tax liability upon withdrawal from IRS Warehouse storage.

Rectification

Rectification of withdrawn bulk consisted of diluting the spirits with distilled water to attain the desired "proof," mixing several different types of spirits to form combinations such as blended whiskey, and adding non-alcoholic ingredients to yield cocktails such as screwdrivers and whiskey sours. Eliot Wallace was responsible for performing chemical tests on each rectified beverage to verify that the appropriate ratio of ingredients had been established before releasing the beverage to the bottling line.

Bottling

The bottling operation utilized a fully automated conveyorized line of equipment including machines which filled each bottle, screwed on a cap, attached a brand label, and affixed the government seal which protected the consuming public against unauthorized opening of a container following bottling. Since 1966, the demand for controlled stock items had required operation of the bottling line less than one out of every three available working days. Thus, the capacity of the bottling line equipment was more than adequate to support the current level of sales. Bob Young was responsible for maintenance and repair of this equipment and verified the setup of each machine prior to initiating a bottling run.

Bob Young and Eliot Wallace worked together in completing all preparations for a bottling run, including the withdrawal and rectification of spirits and the setup of the bottling equipment for each size and label combination. When preparations were complete, Bob and Eliot were joined by five part-time workers drawn from the local area who were each paid $2.50 per hour. While Bob and Eliot supervised overall operation of the bottling line, these five laborers packed filled bottles into cartons, labeled and stamped each carton with appropriate information, and stacked the cartons on pallets for transfer to the controlled stock case goods storage area. The five temporary laborers were paid soon after completion of the bottling run.

Tax and Customs Duty Considerations

It was the practice at Blanchard to delay withdrawal of bulk spirits from storage in the two bonded warehouses until just before the start of a bottling run to avoid incurring tax and custom duty liabilities earlier than necessary. Consequently, the length of time between withdrawal of bulk spirits from storage and transfer of the bottled product to finished case goods storage never exceeded one week.

In addition to the federal distilled spirits tax and customs duty charge, two other taxes were levied against alcoholic beverages: a federal rectification tax was incurred during blending of certain items, depending on the mixing process, and a state tax was incurred upon sale of the finished product by Blanchard. Federal and state regulations required the company to pay the customs duty charge, federal rectification tax, and state tax within a few days after these liabilities were incurred; however, payment of the federal distilled spirits tax was not required until one month after sale.

FORMAL EOQ/ROP SCHEDULING SYSTEM

Before making corrections to the EOQ and ROP figures for each of the 158 items bottled by Blanchard, Hank located the documents showing how the formal scheduling system was developed in 1969. These records, which are reproduced in Exhibit 3, indicate the general method used to determine EOQ and ROP quantities for each Blanchard product. During his review of the system, Hank made the following observations about the inputs to the EOQ calculations:

Setup Costs, S

Blending setup cost was based on the annual salaries of Bob Young and Eliot Wallace and the length of time required for these men to withdraw the appropriate spirits from bulk storage and complete rectification for a given item.

Size changeover cost equaled the cost of resetting all machinery for a change in bottle size divided by the average number of different items of a given size processed between size changeovers.[2] The cost of resetting all machines for a change in bottle size was based on the annual salaries

---

[2] In a typical year, Blanchard operated the bottling line for 77 days during the year. The bottling equipment was adjusted approximately 35 times during the year for a change in bottle size; however, an average of 10 different items of a given bottle size were processed between size changeovers, resulting in about 350 separate item-bottling runs during the year.

Exhibit 3
EOQ AND ROP CALCULATION METHOD

$$\text{EOQ} = \sqrt{\frac{2RS}{CK}} \qquad \text{ROP} = \frac{3.5}{52} \times R$$

Where:

Annual demand, R: Demand for an item for year ending October 31, 1969, in cases of bottles.

Setup cost, S: Setup cost per bottle run of an item.

S = blending setup cost + size changeover cost + label changeover cost + order processing cost.

Blending setup cost = actual cost of labor for blending during rectification and is different for each item.

Size changeover cost = average cost of labor to reset all machines for a change in bottle size and is a constant $8.85 for all 158 items.

Label changeover cost = average cost of labor to reset labeling machine for a change in labels and is a constant $11.78 for all 158 items.

Order processing cost = average cost of administrative labor to process an order for a bottling run and is a constant $51.43 for all 158 items.

Unit cost, C: Cost per case of bottles of an item after bottling and packaging.

C = materials cost + bottling labor + fixed overhead allocation + variable overhead + customs duty + federal distilled spirits tax + federal rectification tax.

Materials cost = cost of raw bulk, bottles, caps, and labels.

Bottling labor = cost of part-time bottling line labor per case of bottles produced and is a constant $0.10 per case for all 158 items.

Fixed overhead allocation = total company fixed overhead for the year divided by the number of cases sold per year and is a constant $1.31 per case for all 158 items.

Variable overhead = total direct expense (other than material and direct labor costs) resulting from production of one case of an item and is a constant $0.50 per case for all 158 items.

Customs duty = charge on imported spirits and varies with the alcoholic content of the beverage.

Federal distilled spirits tax = IRS tax on all spirits sold in the United States and varies with the alcoholic content of the beverage.

Federal rectification tax = IRS tax on certain mixed beverages and varies with the alcoholic content of the item.

Carrying cost percentage, K: Percent of average inventory value which represents annual cost of carrying inventory of an item.

K = cost of capital + other carrying costs.

Cost of capital = 9 percent for all items.

Other carrying costs, including estimated costs of obsolescence, shrinkage, insurance, and year-end inventory tax = 2.5 percent for all items.

of Bob and Eliot and the fact that it took these two men one full day to complete all the machinery adjustments required for a size changeover.

Label changeover cost was based on the average length of time that the bottling line was shut down to change from one label to another label of a given bottle size. This idle time was assumed to be 30 minutes, which included 20 minutes to reset the labeling machine and 10 minutes to restore the labeling machine to continuous error-free operation following the change in labels. Since the part-time bottling laborers remained idle during the label changeover, the cost of this 30 minutes of down-time was based on both the hourly wage rate of these five workers and the annual salaries of Bob and Eliot.

Order-processing cost equaled the yearly cost of two office workers who earned a combined annual salary of $18,000 divided by the total number of separate item-bottling runs per year. These two clerks worked full-time processing the customs duty forms, federal tax forms, state tax forms, and other paper work required to support the bottling operation.

Unit Cost, C

Blanchard used a standard form titled "Cost and Price Data" to determine the wholesale price per case of each item. This price was based on a "full unit cost" figure which included all direct expenses incurred in producing and selling an item plus an allocation of the total fixed expenses of the company. Since the state tax liability was not incurred until sale of the finished product, the "unit cost" used in the EOQ formula was determined by deducting the state tax from the "full unit cost" figure shown on the Cost and Price Data form.

Carrying Cost Percentage, K

The only substantial component of the inventory carrying cost was the cost of capital. Equity was not considered as a source of funds since all common stock was privately held by John D. Corey, Jr. who wished to maintain full control of the company. As a result, the cost of capital was assumed to be 9 percent, the prevailing interest rate for debt available to Blanchard. Components of the carrying cost percentage other than cost of capital were small and amounted to only 2.5 percent.

ACTUAL SCHEDULING SYSTEM IN USE

Hank decided to make his first corrections to EOQ and ROP figures for the items to be produced during an upcoming bottling run. He learned that Bob and Eliot planned to bottle the following items during the last week in June:

Number of Cases to Be Bottled	Item	Number of Cases on Hand as of June 20, 1972
1,000	Blanchard's 80 proof vodka (quarts)	144
600	Blanchard's 80 proof gin (quarts)	55
60	MacCoy & MacCoy 86 proof scotch (quarts)	54
120	Triple 7, 86 proof blended whiskey (quarts)	301
50	Blanchard's 80 proof Ron Cores rum (quarts)	45

Hank then located the Cost and Price Data and the original EOQ and ROP Calculation Sheets for these five items and summarized the data in tabular form (see Exhibits 4 and 5). Hank compared the annual demand for the year ending October 31, 1969 (see Exhibit 5) with the monthly

Exhibit 4
SUMMARY OF COST AND PRICE DATA
(in dollars per case)

	Blan-chard's 80 Proof Vodka	Blan-chard's 80 Proof Gin	MacCoy & MacCoy 86 Proof Scotch	Triple 7 86 Proof Blended Whiskey	Blan-chard's 80 Proof Ron Cores Rum
Wholesale price	$43.99	$43.99	$57.39	$49.87	$47.39
Materials—beverage	0.93	1.08	4.46	2.52	2.74
Materials—packaging	1.27	1.27	1.27	1.27	1.27
Direct labor	0.10	0.10	0.10	0.10	0.10
State tax	10.08	10.08	10.08	10.08	10.08
Federal distilled spirits tax	25.20	25.20	27.09	27.09	25.20
Federal rectification tax				0.76	
Customs duty			1.55		
Variable overhead	0.50	0.50	0.50	0.50	0.50
Fixed overhead allocation	1.31	1.31	1.31	1.31	1.31
Full unit cost	39.39	39.54	46.36	43.63	41.20
Profit before income tax	4.60	4.45	11.03	6.24	6.19

sales summary report for the fiscal year ending January 31, 1972 (see Exhibit 6) and noted significant shifts in demand between the years ending October 1969, and January 1972, especially for the MacCoy & MacCoy scotch and Ron Cores rum products.

On June 21, Hank finished recalculating the EOQ and ROP figures and decided to find out how the schedule for the upcoming bottling run had actually been determined. He found Bob and Eliot in the blending area where they were withdrawing corn spirits from the IRS Warehouse prior to rectification of Triple 7 blended whiskey and questioned them about the schedule:

HANK: How did you decide on these particular items for next week's run, Bob?

Exhibit **5**
SUMMARY OF EOQ AND ROP CALCULATION SHEET DATA

	Blending Setup Cost	All Other Setup Costs	Total Setup Cost (S)	Annual Demand (R)	Carrying Cost, Percent (K)	Unit Cost (C)*	EOQ $\sqrt{\dfrac{2RS}{CK}}$	ROP $\left[\dfrac{3.5}{52} \times R\right]$
Blanchard's 80 proof vodka	$1.15	$72.06	$73.21	2,455	11.5%	$29.31	327	165
Blanchard's 80 proof gin	1.08	72.06	73.14	1,421	11.5	29.46	248	96
MacCoy & MacCoy 86 proof scotch . .	3.24	72.06	75.30	800	11.5	36.28	170	54
Triple 7 86 proof blended whiskey .	2.62	72.06	74.68	3,096	11.5	33.55	346	208
Blanchard's 80 proof Ron Cores rum	2.33	72.06	74.39	449	11.5	31.12	137	30

* Unit cost (*C*) = full unit cost (see Exhibit 4) – state tax (see Exhibit 4).

BOB: Well, every week the computerized inventory control system issues us a card for each item that has dropped below the 3½ week ROP stock level. As of yesterday, we had several half-gallon and quart items which have dropped below their ROP levels, including the vodka and gin quart products scheduled for bottling next week.

HANK: Why don't you bottle both the half-gallon and quart items next week?

BOB: It takes Eliot and me just about one full day to make all the adjustments to the bottling equipment required for a size change. Consequently, we limit each bottling run to a single size and process several combinations of beverages and labels in the size during the run. Since quarts are our most popular size, we plan to bottle only quarts next week. We'll try to make a run of half-gallons in three weeks. Hopefully, the 3½ week advance notice will keep us from stocking-out of any half-gallon items.

HANK: What about the rum, whiskey, and scotch quart products: How did they get added to the schedule?

ELIOT: After we decided to bottle quarts based on the low gin and vodka inventories, we checked the stock level for each of the remaining 61 quart items. We're going to try to make a run of quarts every four weeks for the next two months. So the June 20 stock level of any quart item which we *don't* schedule for bottling next week has to last at least six weeks until the following run is completed at the end of July. The stocks of MacCoy scotch, Triple 7 whiskey, and Ron Cores rum were all below the six-week level when we checked yesterday, so we added them to the list.

HANK: How do you minimize the length of time that the line is idle when you shift from one item to another?

ELIOT: We process the lighter beverages first so that we can switch from one item to the next with only a few bottles of distilled water in between to rinse the bottling machine. As a result, the bottling machine is ready after about only eight minutes of rinsing. We have sixteen tanks for storing rectified

Exhibit 6
MONTHLY SALES SUMMARY DATA (in cases of quart bottles)
(February 1971–MAY 1972)

		Feb-ruary	March	April	May	June	July	Au-gust	Sep-tember	Oc-tober	No-vem-ber	De-cem-ber	Janu-ary	Year Total
Blanchard's 80 proof vodka	(1971)	128	136	233	219	284	343	368	230	162	246	252	114	2,715
	(1972)	210	303	275	463									
Blanchard's 80 proof gin	(1971)	51	52	74	157	150	257	179	83	72	89	181	42	1,387
	(1972)	166	142	133	213									
MacCoy & MacCoy 86 proof scotch	(1971)	79	82	151	66	127	96	85	61	67	103	131	39	1,087
	(1972)	82	68	66	38									
Triple 7 86 proof blended whiskey	(1971)	163	180	198	183	217	207	186	171	205	266	257	654	2,887
	(1972)	177	163	162	256									
Blanchard's 80 proof Ron Cores rum	(1971)	10	34	44	26	33	35	51	16	15	26	43	22	355
	(1972)	11	28	61	55									

beverages prior to bottling which have a combined volume equivalent to 10,000 cases of half-gallons, quarts, pints, or half-pints. This is more than enough storage capacity for all items scheduled for a single bottling run. Since Bob and I finish rectification of all beverages during the week before a scheduled bottling run, each item is always ready when the schedule calls for bottling to begin. No adjustment for bottle shape is necessary since we only run one size at a time and each size has a standard shape. That leaves label changeover as the controlling item, right Bob?

BOB: Yes, every time we shift from one item to the next, I have to adjust the labeling machine and load in a stack of labels for the new item. This takes about 20 minutes, and during that time, the five part-time workers are idle. Once in a while the labels for two items in a row are the same shape, which permits me to make the change in about three minutes. At any rate, Eliot usually finishes purging the bottling machine and completes the shift to the new blending storage tank well before I have the labeling machine ready to resume bottling.

HANK: Once you have decided on the items you intend to bottle and the order in which you intend to bottle them, how did you determine the number of cases of each item to process? Did you use the EOQ figure that was calculated in 1969 when the scheduling system was originally developed?

BOB: Not exactly, Hank. Since we'll probably be bottling quarts every four weeks for a while, we tried to predict what the demand for each item will be between runs; then we took into account the inventory on hand and scheduled production of enough cases to last until the next scheduled bottling run for quarts.

HANK: How did you go about predicting what the demand for each item will be?

BOB: We used the data from the monthly sales summary [see Exhibit 6] to see what the demand was last month. Then we adjusted this May 1972 sales figure by adding a safety factor to offset any difference between sales in May and July.

HANK: Then the planned production volume for each of the five items scheduled for bottling next week represents your predicted demand for July, with an adjustment made for the current inventory on hand?

BOB: Yes, except for the gin and vodka. We're finding it difficult to accurately predict demand for these two items because sales are up substantially from last year. So we've decided to bottle enough gin and vodka to last us *two* months, through the end of August. If our predicted sales volumes for gin and vodka are correct, we can omit production of these products during the July bottling run of quarts and save the cost of blending and label changeover for these two items. However, if demand continues to spiral and exceeds our prediction, we can add these items to the July schedule and avoid a stock-out.

CONCLUSION

The day after Hank's discussion with Bob Young and Eliot Wallace, Toby Tyler asked Hank to report what he had accomplished on his first assignment and to recommend appropriate action based on his findings. Hank realized that the scheduling system in use bore little resemblance to the formal EOQ/ROP system developed in 1969. In preparation for his meeting with Toby, Hank decided to evaluate the disadvantages of both the original scheduling system and the improvised system developed by Bob and Eliot. Based on this analysis, Hank felt that he could determine if improvements could be made which would warrant adoption of one of the two systems on a permanent basis.

Reynolds Construction Company

IN 1973, Reynolds Construction Company had received a contract to construct a water purification system for the city of Oakmont. By the fall of 1974, work was nearly complete on the main system, however it was apparent that work on a special remote control building would have to be finished earlier than originally planned if the main system was to be completed on time.

Mr. James Alison, field construction supervisor for Reynolds had arranged a meeting with Mr. Henry Phillips, project engineer, to restudy the arrow diagram of their critical path schedule for the construction of the remote control building in an effort to determine the shortest possible time in which the job could be done without spending more money than necessary.

Reynolds used the Critical Path Method as a tool to assist in project planning and control. Two documents are used in this control system, an activity network and a cost table. A list of the activities for the remote control site are in Exhibit 1. The activity network, Exhibit 2, shows all the activities and the sequence in which they can be performed. No activity can begin until all the previous ones on its path have been completed. The Cost Table, Exhibit 3, lists the activities and their duration along with

Exhibit 1

Job Label	Job Description	Immediately Preceding Jobs	Normal Time
A	Procure materials	Start	3
B	Prepare site	Start	6
C	Prepare request for Oakmont Engineering Department approval	Start	2
D	Prefabricate building and deliver to site	A	5
E	Obtain Oakmont Engineering Department approval	C	2
F	Install connecting lines to main system	A	7
G	Erect building and equipment on site	B, D, E	4

102

Exhibit 2
CRITICAL PATH DIAGRAM FOR REMOTE
BUILDING PROJECT

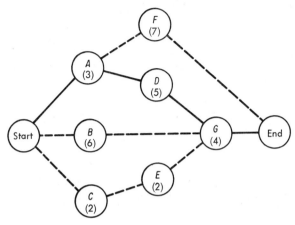

( ) = Planned duration of activity in weeks.

— = Critical path.

Exhibit 3
COST TABLE FOR REMOTE CONTROL BUILDING PROJECT

Activity	Normal		Crash*		Cost Slope, Dollars per Week
	Weeks	Dollars	Weeks	Dollars	
A	3	$ 5,000	2	$ 10,000	$5,000†
B	6	14,000	4	26,000	6,000
C	2	2,500	1	5,000	2,500
D	5	10,000	3	18,000	4,000
E	2	8,000	2	8,000	—
F	7	11,500	5	17,500	3,000
G	4	10,000	2	24,000	7,000
Total		$61,000		$108,500	

* Crash weeks shown represent the minimum possible time for the given activity.
† This is the cost of gaining one week over the normal time by use of "crash" methods.

the cost needed to complete them in this "normal time." The Cost Table also lists the minimum amount of time for each activity, called the "crash" time; and the costs needed to achieve this minimum time. In addition, a final listing in the Cost Table showed how much it cost to shorten each activity one week. The sequence of consecutive activities requiring the longest time to complete before the end of the project is known as the "critical path" for that project. The path is considered "critical" because any delay in the particular sequence will delay the completion of the entire project.

Mr. Alison had the original arrow diagram for the remote control build-ing project (Exhibit 2) in his office. It was, of course, considerably simpler than the similar diagrams for the control of the entire construction job.

It was apparent to Mr. Alison that the critical path for this project fol-lowed the sequence of activities A-D-G and would require 12 weeks. The original project cost was estimated at $61,000. Mr. Alison could lag as much as four weeks behind schedule without affecting the planned time for the completion of the project.

Although a computer was necessary for the rapid solution of critical path problems in larger projects, Mr. Phillips had manually worked out a schedule for this project which indicated that the job could be completed in nine weeks at a total cost of $77,000. The additional cost of $16,000 was largely attributable to the cost of extra shift operations necessitated by a "crash" program. It will be noticed that in his revised schedule (Ex-hibit 4), three paths had become critical to the completion of the project as rescheduled.

In their conference, Mr. Alison and Mr. Phillips concluded that a further speed up of the job was both necessary and possible.

Exhibit 4
REVISED—PROGRAM SCHEDULE FOR REMOTE
CONTROL BUILDING PROJECT

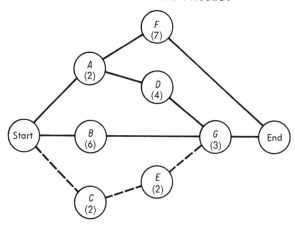

( ) = Duration of activity in weeks.

—— = Critical path.

Path	Time	Additional Cost
ADG ..	2 + 4 + 3 = 9	$5,000 + 4,000 + 7,000 = $16,000
AF ...	2 + 7 = 9	
BG ...	6 + 3 = 9	
CEG ..	2 + 2 + 3 = 7	
Planned cost + additional cost = $61,000 + 16,000 = $77,000		

PLANETS II[1]—PLAnning and NETwork Simulation II Manual

INTRODUCTION

PLANETS is a project management exercise which simulates the progress of a development project currently scheduled for completion in six months. Successful completion of the project requires careful planning and scheduling of a variety of interrelated activities under severe time and cost constraints. The educational objectives of the exercise include:

Introduction to the nature and significance of time/cost trade-offs for the achievement of project objectives.
Familiarization with the problem of planning under time constraints.
Development of skill at working with a network representation of a project.
Experience in the use of a computer simulation model for testing alternative management decisions in an uncertain environment.

Approximately three players will be assigned to each project management team. Although several teams play simultaneously, an individual team's decisions do not affect any other team's performance. However, since the objective is successful completion of the project—that is, completion at minimum cost—there is a definite element of competition between teams. Final time and cost results for a team's performance can be readily compared with other teams' results.

---

[1] Adapted from CAPERTSIM—Computer Aided PERT Simulation—which was developed by the U.S. Army Logistics Management Center, Fort Lee, Virginia. The basic CAPERTSIM program is available from the IBM SHARE library. The PLANETS program was adapted from a version of CAPERTSIM programmed by North American Aviation, Inc., Autonetics Education and Training Department. PLANETS II is a modification of PLANETS.

THE PLANETS PROJECTS

PLANETS is based on a sequence of design, testing, and plant setup activities for a large component of an electronic system. The project has been broken down into 43 activities: these activities and their interrelationships are described in the Appendix. Each activity is identified by an "activity code" consisting of its starting and ending events. For instance, Activity A–B starts at event A and ends at event B.

A network representation of the 43 activities which comprise the PLANETS project is shown in Exhibit 1. The network uses an "activities

Exhibit 1
PLANETS NETWORK

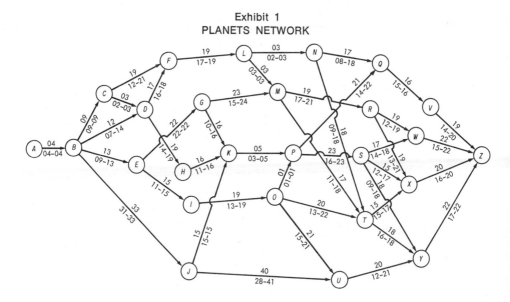

on arrows" notation; that is, each arrow represents a time-consuming activity. The nodes represent events—start and/or completion of activity. A basic network rule requires that *all* activities coming into a node must be complete before any activity leaving the node can begin.

The structure of the network shown in Exhibit 1 will remain unchanged throughout the exercise. This differs from normal practice in which networks are often changed substantially as the project progresses; such changes can be an important method of shortening critical paths.

Each of the 43 individual activities shown on the PLANETS network must be completed to complete the development project and these must be completed in a sequence which does not violate the precedence relationships shown in the network diagram. As in real life, the activities which make up the total project do not have a single, fixed duration, but can vary with the amount of resources management expends. The primary task for a project management team is to decide on the activity times (durations) to be scheduled for each activity, taking into account costs and project completion time implications. In addition to management's plan there are factors beyond the control of management that can influence the length of an activity. During the project, occurrences such as strikes or acts of nature may cause some activities to be delayed beyond their planned duration. On the other hand, "fortune" may smile and result in an earlier than planned completion of some activity.

The PLANETS network shows the original plan for the project. The times *above* the arrows represent the time originally planned (in days) in each activity. The times *below* each arrow represent the upper and lower limits between which the project management team may vary the planned duration of each activity. For example, activity H–K (the mechanical breadboard) is scheduled to take 16 days at the start of the exercise; this time can be rescheduled by player decision to any integer duration from 11 to 16 days.

$$(H) \xrightarrow[11 - 16]{16} (K)$$

Original plan at start = 16 days
Minimum possible duration = 11 days
Maximum possible duration = 16 days

The original planned activity duration decisions which have already been made have resulted in an expected completion time for the project, as well as a total cost for completing the project. The expected completion time is obtained by adding up the total time to complete the activities along the critical path in the network. The critical path here is path A–B–E–G–K–P–S–Y–Z, which totals *123* days. The project is assumed to start on July 1; therefore, the expected project completion date at the start of the exercise is December 24, 123 working days after the project starts. Note that no work is planned for *weekends or holidays*.

Total project cost is made up of the sum of the *delay cost* (described below) and the planned *task costs* for each of the 43 tasks. These task costs are derived from Exhibit 4 which shows, for each activity, the cost associated with each possible planned duration. As shown in Exhibit 3, the total task cost for the original set of durations (the initial plan in Exhibit 1) is $382,022.

Player decisions will establish new planned duration times for some activities and will therefore change both the planned completion time of the project and its total cost. Decreasing activity duration times will increase costs. The maximum task cost, $433,007, for the project would result if all activities were planned at their shortest duration. Minimum task cost, $378,954, on the other hand, results when all activities have their longest duration. The difference between these two costs, $54,053, is the amount of resources that can be influenced by the management team's decisions.

The simulation begins on July 1. The *expected* completion date, based

on the plan in Exhibit 1, is December 24. A new target completion date
has been established for December 2. This is 16 working days earlier than
originally planned. If the project is *not* complete by December 2, a $*500
penalty will be imposed for each day of overrun.* The expected delay cost
for the current plan is therefore $8,000. Shortening the entire project to
bring the final event to completion by December 2 may be accomplished
by the expenditure of resources where necessary to shorten various activities throughout the network. The way money is spent—for overtime, for
additional men, for extra machinery and the like—is not specified in this
exercise. The assumption is made that manpower and resources are available to accomplish activities within any planned duration which does not
fall outside the limits in Exhibit 1. Each project management team is thus
responsible for planning activity durations, so that the project is completed
at the lowest possible total cost, where total cost is the sum of task costs
and delay costs.

During this exercise the management team must submit six decisions.
After a decision has been submitted the computer will simulate the passage
of 20 working days and will provide management with a list of all activities
completed in that time period. In addition the computer will provide an
explanation of any delays or early finishes that may have caused an activity
to take a different amount of time than was planned by the project team.
Before any decision the management team can change the planned duration for any activity that has *not* been completed. Obviously, the duration
of a completed activity can no longer be altered by management decision.

Because of the large number of activities and complexity of the planning
task the computer can be used to help in your analysis. At any time before
a decision is submitted the management can ask for a trail run. The computer will provide a list of all tasks and their current planned duration
along with the amount of slack in that task. A sample of this printout
is shown in Exhibit 2. More detailed instructions on this and other computer options will be provided by your instructor.

STARTING INFORMATION

Each project management team will begin play with the same information and proceed independently to the objective end event. Group starting
information will include the following items found in the exhibits.

1. A master network showing the starting position and limits on activity
    duration times. (Exhibit 1.)
2. A computer printout of a trial simulation run under the starting condi-
    tions. This printout shows the starting and ending events for each ac-
    tivity, planned project duration, and slack in days. (Exhibit 2.)
3. A full computer printout of the starting position. (Exhibit 3.)
4. Cost data for each activity in the network. (Exhibit 4.)

Exhibit 2
TRIAL RUN—
COMPLETE REPORT
(starting decisions)

Exhibit 3
ACTUAL RUN REPORT FORMAT

CPM REPORT   7- 1-69

TSK	DUR	SLK
A-B	4	-16
B-E	13	-16
E-G	22	-16
G-K	16	-16
K-P	5	-16
P-S	23	-16
S-Y	18	-16
Y-Z	22	-16
G-M	23	-15
M-R	19	-15
R-W	19	-15
S-W	17	-15
W-Z	22	-15
B-J	33	-13
J-K	15	-13
R-X	19	-13
X-Z	20	-13
B-C	9	-12
B-D	12	-12
C-D	3	-12
D-H	19	-12
H-K	16	-12
J-U	40	-12
M-T	17	-12
T-Y	18	-12
U-Y	20	-12
S-X	15	-11
P-Q	21	-9
Q-V	16	-9
V-Z	19	-9
D-F	17	-8
E-I	15	-8
F-L	19	-8
I-O	19	-8
L-M	3	-8
O-P	1	-8
C-F	19	-7
O-U	21	-7
T-X	15	-7
L-N	3	-6
N-T	18	-6
O-T	20	-4
N-Q	17	0

PROJ FINISH 12-24-69
DELAY COST   8000
TASK COST   382022
TOTAL COST 390022

CPM REPORT   7- 1-69

TASK	DUR	ACTUAL FINISH	EXPECT FINISH	LATEST FINISH	SLACK
A-B	4		7- 8	6-13	-16
B-E	13		7-25	7- 2	-16
E-G	22		8-26	8- 4	-16
G-K	16		9-18	8-26	-16
K-P	5		9-25	9- 3	-16
P-S	23		10-28	10- 6	-16
S-Y	18		11-21	10-30	-16
Y-Z	22		12-24	12- 2	-16
G-M	23		9-29	9- 8	-15
M-R	19		10-24	10- 3	-15
R-W	19		11-20	10-30	-15
S-W	17		11-20	10-30	-15
V-Z	22		12-23	12- 2	-15
B-J	33		8-22	8- 5	-13
J-K	15		9-15	8-26	-13
R-X	19		11-20	11- 3	-13
X-Z	20		12-19	12- 2	-13
B-C	9		7-21	7- 2	-12
B-D	12		7-24	7- 8	-12
C-D	3		7-24	7- 8	-12
D-H	19		8-20	8- 4	-12
H-K	16		9-12	8-26	-12
J-U	40		10-20	10- 2	-12
M-T	17		10-22	10- 6	-12
T-Y	18		11-17	10-30	-12
U-Y	20		11-17	10-30	-12
S-X	15		11-18	11- 3	-11
P-Q	21		10-24	10-13	-9
Q-V	16		11-17	11- 4	-9
V-Z	19		12-15	12- 2	-9
D-F	17		8-18	8- 6	-8
E-I	15		8-15	8- 5	-8
F-L	19		9-15	9- 3	-8
I-O	19		9-12	9- 2	-8
L-M	3		9-18	9- 8	-8
O-P	1		9-15	9- 3	-8
C-F	19		8-15	8- 6	-7
O-U	21		10-13	10- 2	-7
T-X	15		11-12	11- 3	-7
L-N	3		9-18	9-10	-6
N-T	18		10-14	10- 6	-6
O-T	20		10-10	10- 6	-4
N-Q	17		10-13	10-13	0

PROJ FINISH 12-24-69
DELAY COST   8000
TASK COST   382022
TOTAL COST 390022

THE COMPUTER PRINTOUT

The computer printout in Exhibit 3 shows the starting position for the project and identifies:

1. Starting and ending events for each activity.
2. Planned activity duration.
3. Actual date of activity completion (these dates will be entered by the computer as activities are completed during the simulation).

4. Expected date or earliest date that an activity can be expected to be completed.
5. Latest date that an activity can be completed without missing the scheduled completion date for the project.
6. Slack in days showing the extent to which an activity is ahead of or behind schedule.

The computer printout used in PLANETS is a *Slack Sort*. In this type of report, the most critical activities are printed at the top of the list. Since the most critical activites of a network comprise the critical path, the first entries on the PLANETS printout along a path from event A to Z identify the critical (longest) path for this project. Subsequent entries on the printout show subcritical paths in the order of their criticality. When an activity has negative slack the entry will be preceded by a minus sign. (Note in Exhibit 3 that the minimum slack is minus 16 days. This can be explained by the fact that the initial expected project completion date, December 24, is 16 working days behind the scheduled completion date of December 2.)

PLANETS COST DATA

Cost data in Exhibit 4 shows the change in cost associated with a change in planned activity duration. Cost data is furnished for all changes that are permitted between the upper and lower time limits for each activity. Time changes that are not within the limits will be rejected by the computer.

PRELIMINARY ANALYSIS

Each project management team should study the starting position date, considering alternative courses of action for meeting the required project

Exhibit 4

The following are differential and/or absolute cost matrices for each of the 43 project activities.

Determine the change in cost for change in an activity duration by referring to the *differential* cost matrix for that activity. Determine the total cost for an activity set at a particular time by referring to that activity's *total cost* list (at the far right of the differential cost matrix).

For example, activity B–D is currently planned to take 12 days. This has added $3,450 to the total cost of the project. If you wish to reduce this activity to 10 days the differential cost would be $150. The total cost activity for B–D for 10 days would thus be $3,450 + $150 = $3,600. Once the project plan for activity B–D is fixed at 10 days you may wish to make another change. For example, increasing this time to 14 days. The differential cost is −$258 which would make the total cost $3,600 − $258 = $3,342.

Exhibit 4 (*Continued*)

Activity A–B

Days	Total Cost
4	$1,000

Activity B–C

Days	Total Cost
9	$500

Activity B–D

Differential Cost Matrix

From (days) \ To (days)	7	8	9	10	11	12	13	14	Total Cost
7	0	−160	−285	−385	−467	−535	−593	−643	3,985
8	160	0	−125	−225	−307	−375	−433	−483	3,825
9	285	125	0	−100	−182	−250	−308	−358	3,700
10	385	225	100	0	−82	−150	−208	−258	3,600
11	467	307	182	82	0	−68	−126	−176	3,518
12	535	375	250	150	68	0	−58	−108	3,450
13	593	433	308	208	126	58	0	−50	3,392
14	643	483	358	258	176	108	50	0	3,342

Activity B–E

Differential Cost Matrix

From (days) \ To (days)	9	10	11	12	13	Total Cost
9	0	−133	−243	−333	−410	3,033
10	133	0	−110	−200	−277	2,900
11	243	110	0	−90	−167	2,790
12	333	200	90	0	−77	2,700
13	410	277	167	77	0	2,623

Activity B–J

Differential Cost Matrix

From (days) \ To (days)	31	32	33	Total Cost
31	0	−282	−548	19,032
32	282	0	−266	18,750
33	548	266	0	18,484

Exhibit 4 (*Continued*)

Activity C–D

Differential Cost Matrix

From (days) \ To (days)	2	3	Total Cost
2	0	−167	650
3	167	0	483

Activity C–F

Differential Cost Matrix

From (days) \ To (days)	12	13	14	15	16	17	18	19	20	21	Total Cost
12	0	−77	−143	−200	−250	−294	−333	−368	−399	−428	4,000
13	77	0	−66	−123	−173	−217	−256	−291	−322	−351	3,923
14	143	66	0	−57	−107	−151	−190	−225	−256	−285	3,857
15	200	123	57	0	−50	−94	−133	−168	−199	−228	3,800
16	250	173	107	50	0	−44	−83	−118	−149	−178	3,750
17	294	217	151	94	44	0	−39	−74	−105	−134	3,706
18	333	256	190	133	83	39	0	−35	−66	−95	3,666
19	368	291	225	168	118	74	35	0	−31	−60	3,631
20	399	322	256	199	149	105	66	31	0	−29	3,600
21	428	351	285	228	178	134	95	60	29	0	3,571

Activity D–F

Differential Cost Matrix

From (days) \ To (days)	16	17	18	Total Cost
16	0	−74	−139	3,750
17	74	0	−65	3,676
18	139	65	0	3,611

Activity D–H

Differential Cost Matrix

From (days) \ To (days)	14	15	16	17	18	19	Total Cost
14	0	−119	−223	−315	−387	−460	8,785
15	119	0	−104	−196	−278	−351	8,666
16	223	104	0	−92	−174	−247	8,562
17	315	196	92	0	−82	−155	8,470
18	387	278	174	82	0	−73	8,388
19	460	351	247	155	73	0	**8,315**

Exhibit 4 (Continued)

Activity E–G

Days	Total Cost
22	$750

Activity E–I

Differential Cost Matrix

From (days) \ To (days)	11	12	13	14	15	Total Cost
11	0	−3,788	−6,993	−9,740	−12,121	50,454
12	3,788	0	−3,205	−5,952	−8,333	46,666
13	6,993	3,205	0	−2,747	−5,128	43,461
14	9,740	5,952	2,747	0	−2,381	40,714
15	12,121	8,333	5,128	2,381	0	38,333

Activity F–L

Differential Cost Matrix

From (days) \ To (days)	17	18	19	Total Cost
17	0	−327	−619	10,382
18	327	0	−292	10,055
19	619	292	0	9,763

Activity G–K

Differential Cost Matrix

From (days) \ To (days)	10	11	12	13	14	15	16	Total Cost
10	0	−910	−1,667	−2,308	−2,858	−3,334	−3,750	20,000
11	910	0	−757	−1,398	−1,948	−2,424	−2,840	19,090
12	1,667	757	0	−641	−1,191	−1,667	−2,083	18,333
13	2,308	1,398	641	0	−550	−1,026	−1,442	17,692
14	2,858	1,948	1,191	550	0	−476	−892	17,142
15	3,334	2,424	1,667	1,026	476	0	−416	16,666
16	3,750	2,840	2,083	1,442	892	416	0	16,250

Exhibit 4 *(Continued)*

Activity G-M

Differential Cost Matrix

From (days) \ To (days)	15	16	17	18	19	20	21	22	23	24	Total Cost
15	0	−1,041	−1,961	−2,778	−3,509	−4,166	−4,762	−5,303	−5,797	−6,250	19,666
16	1,041	0	−920	−1,737	−2,468	−3,125	−3,721	−4,262	−4,756	−5,209	18,625
17	1,961	920	0	−817	−1,548	−2,205	−2,801	−3,342	−3,836	−4,289	17,705
18	2,778	1,737	817	0	−731	−1,388	−1,984	−2,525	−3,019	−3,472	16,888
19	3,509	2,468	1,548	731	0	−657	−1,253	−1,794	−2,288	−2,741	16,157
20	4,166	3,125	2,205	1,388	657	0	−596	−1,137	−1,631	−2,084	15,500
21	4,762	3,721	2,801	1,984	1,253	596	0	−541	−1,035	−1,488	14,904
22	5,303	4,262	3,342	2,525	1,794	1,137	541	0	−494	−947	14,363
23	5,797	4,756	3,836	3,019	2,288	1,631	1,035	494	0	−453	13,869
24	6,250	5,209	4,289	3,472	2,741	2,084	1,488	947	453	0	13,416

Activity H-K

Differential Cost Matrix

From (days) \ To (days)	11	12	13	14	15	16	Total Cost
11	0	−189	−349	−487	−606	−710	7,772
12	189	0	−160	−298	−417	−521	7,583
13	349	160	0	−138	−257	−361	7,423
14	487	298	138	0	−119	−223	7,285
15	606	417	257	119	0	−104	7,166
16	710	521	361	223	104	0	7,062

Activity I-O

Differential Cost Matrix

From (days) \ To (days)	13	14	15	16	17	18	19	Total Cost
13	0	−1,373	−2,564	−3,605	−4,525	−5,342	−6,073	31,730
14	1,373	0	−1,191	−2,232	−3,152	−3,969	−4,700	30,357
15	2,564	1,191	0	−1,041	−1,961	−2,778	−3,509	29,166
16	3,605	2,232	1,041	0	−920	−1,737	−2,468	28,125
17	4,525	3,152	1,961	920	0	−817	−1,548	27,205
18	5,342	3,969	2,778	1,737	817	0	−731	26,388
19	6,073	4,700	3,509	2,468	1,548	731	0	25,657

Activity J-K

Days	Total Cost
15	$3,750

Exhibit 4 (Continued)

Differential Cost Matrix

Activity J–U

From (days) \ To (days)	28	29	30	31	32	33	34	35	36	37	38	39	40	41	Total Cost
28	0	-863	-1,667	-2,420	-3,125	-3,788	-4,412	-5,000	-5,556	-6,082	-6,579	-7,052	-7,500	-7,927	35,000
29	863	0	-804	-1,557	-2,262	-2,925	-3,549	-4,137	-4,693	-5,219	-5,716	-6,189	-6,637	-7,064	34,137
30	1,667	804	0	-753	-1,458	-2,121	-2,745	-3,333	-3,889	-4,415	-4,912	-5,385	-5,833	-6,260	33,333
31	2,420	1,557	753	0	-705	-1,368	-1,992	-2,580	-3,136	-3,662	-4,159	-4,632	-5,080	-5,507	32,580
32	3,125	2,262	1,458	705	0	-663	-1,287	-1,875	-2,431	-2,957	-3,454	-3,927	-4,375	-4,802	31,875
33	3,788	2,925	2,121	1,368	663	0	-624	-1,212	-1,768	-2,294	-2,791	-3,264	-3,712	-4,139	31,212
34	4,412	3,549	2,745	1,992	1,287	624	0	-588	-1,144	-1,670	-2,167	-2,640	-3,088	-3,515	30,588
35	5,000	4,137	3,333	2,580	1,875	1,212	588	0	-556	-1,082	-1,579	-2,052	-2,500	-2,927	30,000
36	5,556	4,693	3,889	3,136	2,431	1,768	1,144	556	0	-526	-1,023	-1,496	-1,944	-2,371	29,444
37	6,082	5,219	4,415	3,662	2,957	2,294	1,670	1,082	526	0	-497	-970	-1,418	-1,845	28,918
38	6,579	5,716	4,912	4,159	3,454	2,791	2,167	1,579	1,023	497	0	-473	-921	-1,348	28,421
39	7,052	6,189	5,385	4,632	3,927	3,264	2,640	2,052	1,496	970	473	0	-448	-875	27,948
40	7,500	6,637	5,833	5,080	4,375	3,712	3,088	2,500	1,944	1,418	921	448	0	-427	27,500
41	7,927	7,064	6,260	5,507	4,802	4,139	3,515	2,927	2,371	1,845	1,348	875	427	0	27,073

Exhibit 4 (Continued)

Activity K–P

Differential Cost Matrix

From (days) \ To (days)	3	4	5	Total Cost
3	0	−166	−266	966
4	166	0	−100	800
5	266	100	0	700

Activity L–M

Days	Total Cost
3	$2,000

Activity L–N

Differential Cost Matrix

From (days) \ To (days)	2	3	Total Cost
2	0	−167	650
3	167	0	483

Activity M–R

Differential Cost Matrix

From (days) \ To (days)	17	18	19	20	21	Total Cost
17	0	−78	−148	−211	−269	6,411
18	78	0	−70	−133	−191	6,333
19	148	70	0	−63	−121	6,263
20	211	133	63	0	−58	6,200
21	269	191	121	58	0	6,142

Activity M–T

Differential Cost Matrix

From (days) \ To (days)	11	12	13	14	15	16	17	18	Total Cost
11	0	−159	−294	−409	−509	−597	−674	−743	4,909
12	159	0	−135	−250	−350	−438	−515	−584	4,705
13	294	135	0	−115	−215	−303	−380	−449	4,615
14	409	250	115	0	−100	−188	−265	−334	4,500
15	509	350	215	100	0	−88	−165	−234	4,400
16	597	438	303	188	88	0	−77	−146	4,312
17	674	515	380	265	165	77	0	−69	4,235
18	743	584	449	334	234	146	69	0	4,166

Exhibit 4 (Continued)

Activity N–Q

Differential Cost Matrix

From (days) \ To (days)	8	9	10	11	12	13	14	15	16	17	18	Total Cost
8	0	-334	-600	-819	-1,000	-1,154	-1,286	-1,400	-1,500	-1,589	-1,667	8,000
9	334	0	-266	-485	-666	-820	-952	-1,066	-1,166	-1,255	-1,333	7,666
10	600	266	0	-219	-400	-554	-686	-800	-900	-989	-1,067	7,400
11	819	485	219	0	-181	-335	-467	-581	-681	-770	-848	7,181
12	1,000	666	400	181	0	-154	-286	-400	-500	-589	-667	7,000
13	1,154	820	554	335	154	0	-132	-246	-346	-435	-513	6,846
14	1,286	952	686	467	286	132	0	-114	-214	-303	-381	6,714
15	1,400	1,066	800	581	400	246	114	0	-100	-189	-267	6,600
16	1,500	1,166	900	681	500	346	214	100	0	-89	-167	6,500
17	1,589	1,255	989	770	589	435	303	189	89	0	-78	6,411
18	1,667	1,333	1,067	848	667	513	381	267	167	78	0	6,333

Activity N–T

Differential Cost Matrix

From (days) \ To (days)	9	10	11	12	13	14	15	16	17	18	Total Cost
9	0	-244	-444	-611	-752	-873	-978	-1,069	-1,150	-1,222	12,444
10	244	0	-200	-367	-508	-629	-734	-825	-906	-978	12,200
11	444	200	0	-167	-308	-429	-534	-625	-706	-778	12,000
12	611	367	167	0	-141	-262	-367	-458	-539	-611	11,833
13	752	508	308	141	0	-121	-226	-317	-398	-470	11,692
14	873	629	429	262	121	0	-105	-196	-277	-349	11,571
15	978	734	534	367	226	105	0	-91	-172	-244	11,466
16	1,069	825	625	458	317	196	91	0	-81	-153	11,375
17	1,150	906	706	539	398	277	172	81	0	-72	11,294
18	1,222	978	778	611	470	349	244	153	72	0	11,222

Activity O–P

Days	Total Cost
1	$150

Activity O–T

Differential Cost Matrix

From (days) \ To (days)	13	14	15	16	17	18	19	20	21	22	Total Cost
13	0	-127	-236	-332	-417	-492	-559	-619	-674	-724	9,269
14	127	0	-109	-205	-290	-365	-432	-492	-547	-597	9,142
15	236	109	0	-96	-181	-256	-323	-383	-438	-488	9,033
16	332	205	96	0	-85	-160	-227	-287	-342	-392	8,937
17	417	290	181	85	0	-75	-142	-202	-257	-307	8,852
18	492	365	256	160	75	0	-67	-127	-182	-232	8,777
19	559	432	323	227	142	67	0	-60	-115	-165	8,710
20	619	492	383	287	202	127	60	0	-55	-105	8,650
21	674	547	438	342	257	182	115	55	0	-50	8,595
22	724	597	488	392	307	232	165	105	50	0	8,545

Exhibit 4 (*Continued*)

Activity O–U

Differential Cost Matrix

From (days) \ To (days)	15	16	17	18	19	20	21	Total Cost
15	0	−79	−149	−211	−266	−316	−362	7,266
16	79	0	−70	−132	−187	−237	−283	7,187
17	149	70	0	−62	−117	−167	−213	7,117
18	211	132	62	0	−55	−105	−151	7,055
19	266	187	117	55	0	−50	−96	7,000
20	316	237	167	105	50	0	−46	6,950
21	362	283	213	151	96	46	0	6,904

Activity P–Q

Differential Cost Matrix

From (days) \ To (days)	14	15	16	17	18	19	20	21	22	Total Cost
14	0	−71	−134	−189	−238	−282	−321	−357	−390	7,571
15	71	0	−63	−118	−167	−211	−250	−286	−319	7,500
16	134	63	0	−55	−104	−148	−187	−223	−256	7,437
17	189	118	55	0	−49	−93	−132	−168	−201	7,382
18	238	167	104	49	0	−44	−83	−119	−152	7,333
19	282	211	148	93	44	0	−39	−75	−108	7,289
20	321	250	187	132	83	39	0	−36	−69	7,250
21	357	286	223	168	119	75	36	0	−33	7,214
22	390	319	256	201	152	108	69	33	0	7,181

Activity P–S

Differential Cost Matrix

From (days) \ To (days)	16	17	18	19	20	21	22	23	Total Cost
16	0	−111	−209	−297	−375	−447	−512	−571	10,875
17	111	0	−98	−186	−264	−336	−401	−460	10,764
18	209	98	0	−88	−166	−238	−303	−362	10,666
19	297	186	88	0	−78	−150	−215	−274	10,578
20	375	264	166	78	0	−72	−137	−196	10,500
21	447	336	238	150	72	0	−65	−124	10,428
22	512	401	303	215	137	65	0	−59	10,363
23	571	460	362	274	196	124	59	0	10,304

Activity Q–V

Differential Cost Matrix

From (days) \ To (days)	15	16	Total Cost
15	0	−75	9,200
16	75	0	9,125

Exhibit 4 (*Continued*)

Activity R–W

Differential Cost Matrix

From (days) \ To (days)	12	13	14	15	16	17	18	19	Total Cost
12	0	−224	−416	−583	−729	−858	−972	−1,074	12,916
13	224	0	−192	−359	−505	−634	−748	−850	12,692
14	416	192	0	−167	−313	−442	−556	−658	12,500
15	583	359	167	0	−146	−275	−389	−491	12,333
16	729	505	313	146	0	−129	−243	−345	12,187
17	858	643	442	275	129	0	−114	−216	12,058
18	972	748	556	389	243	114	0	−102	11,944
19	1,074	850	658	491	345	216	102	0	11,842

Activity R–X

Differential Cost Matrix

From (days) \ To (days)	13	14	15	16	17	18	19	20	21	Total Cost
13	0	−76	−143	−201	−253	−299	−340	−376	−410	6,576
14	76	0	−67	−125	−177	−223	−264	−300	−334	6,500
15	143	67	0	−58	−110	−156	−197	−233	−267	6,433
16	201	125	58	0	−52	−98	−139	−175	−209	6,375
17	253	177	110	52	0	−46	−87	−123	−157	6,323
18	299	223	156	98	46	0	−41	−77	−111	6,277
19	340	264	197	139	87	41	0	−36	−70	6,236
20	376	300	233	175	123	77	36	0	−34	6,200
21	410	334	267	209	157	111	70	34	0	6,166

Activity S–W

Differential Cost Matrix

From (days) \ To (days)	14	15	16	17	18	Total Cost
14	0	−109	−205	−290	−365	13,642
15	109	0	−96	−181	−256	13,533
16	205	96	0	−85	−160	13,437
17	290	181	85	0	−75	13,352
18	365	256	160	75	0	13,277

Activity S–X

Differential Cost Matrix

From (days) \ To (days)	12	13	14	15	16	17	Total Cost
12	0	−109	−202	−283	−354	−416	9,916
13	109	0	−93	−174	−245	−307	9,807
14	202	93	0	−81	−152	−214	9,714
15	283	174	81	0	−71	−133	9,633
16	354	245	152	71	0	−62	9,562
17	416	307	214	133	62	0	9,500

Exhibit 4 *(Continued)*

Activity S–Y

Differential Cost Matrix

From (days) \ To (days)	9	10	11	12	13	14	15	16	17	18	Total Cost
9	0	−144	−263	−361	−444	−516	−578	−632	−680	−722	7,444
10	144	0	−119	−217	−300	−372	−434	−488	−536	−578	7,300
11	263	119	0	−98	−181	−253	−315	−369	−417	−459	7,181
12	361	217	98	0	−83	−155	−217	−271	−319	−361	7,083
13	444	300	181	83	0	−72	−134	−188	−236	−278	7,000
14	516	372	253	155	72	0	−62	−116	−164	−206	6,928
15	578	434	315	217	134	62	0	−54	−102	−144	6,866
16	632	488	369	271	188	116	54	0	−48	−90	6,812
17	680	536	417	319	236	164	102	48	0	−42	6,764
18	722	578	459	361	278	206	144	90	42	0	6,722

Activity T–X

Differential Cost Matrix

From (days) \ To (days)	15	16	17	Total Cost
15	0	−625	−1,177	25,000
16	625	0	−552	24,375
17	1,177	552	0	23,823

Activity T–Y

Differential Cost Matrix

From (days) \ To (days)	16	17	18	Total Cost
16	0	−92	−174	7,562
17	92	0	−82	7,470
18	174	82	0	7,388

Activity U–Y

Differential Cost Matrix

From (days) \ To (days)	12	13	14	15	16	17	18	19	20	21	Total Cost
12	0	−160	−298	−417	−521	−613	−695	−768	−833	−893	9,083
13	160	0	−138	−257	−361	−453	−535	−608	−673	−733	8,923
14	298	138	0	−119	−223	−315	−397	−470	−535	−595	8,785
15	417	257	119	0	−104	−196	−278	−351	−416	−476	8,666
16	521	361	223	104	0	−92	−174	−247	−312	−372	8,562
17	613	453	315	196	92	0	−82	−155	−220	−280	8,470
18	695	535	397	278	174	82	0	−73	−138	−198	8,388
19	768	608	470	351	247	155	73	0	−65	−125	8,315
20	833	673	535	416	312	220	138	65	0	−60	8,250
21	893	733	595	476	372	280	198	125	60	0	8,190

Exhibit 4 (*Concluded*)

Activity V–Z

Differential Cost Matrix

From (days) \ To (days)	14	15	16	17	18	19	20	Total Cost
14	0	−62	−116	−164	−206	−244	−278	3,928
15	62	0	−54	−102	−144	−182	−216	3,866
16	116	54	0	−48	−90	−128	−162	3,812
17	164	102	48	0	−42	−80	−114	3,764
18	206	144	90	42	0	−38	−72	3,722
19	244	182	128	80	38	0	−34	3,684
20	278	216	162	114	72	34	0	3,650

Activity W–Z

Differential Cost Matrix

From (days) \ To (days)	15	16	17	18	19	20	21	22	Total Cost
15	0	−208	−392	−556	−702	−833	−953	−1,061	9,333
16	208	0	−184	−348	−494	−625	−745	−853	9,125
17	392	184	0	−164	−310	−441	−561	−669	8,941
18	556	348	164	0	−146	−277	−397	−505	8,777
19	702	494	310	146	0	−131	−251	−359	8,631
20	833	625	441	277	131	0	−120	−228	8,500
21	953	745	561	397	251	120	0	−108	8,380
22	1,061	853	669	505	359	228	108	0	8,272

Activity X–Z

Differential Cost Matrix

From (days) \ To (days)	16	17	18	19	20	Total Cost
16	0	−129	−243	−347	−439	16,187
17	129	0	−114	−218	−310	16,058
18	243	114	0	−104	−196	15,944
19	347	218	104	0	−92	15,842
20	439	310	196	92	0	15,750

Activity Y–Z

Differential Cost Matrix

From (days) \ To (days)	17	18	19	20	21	22	Total Cost
17	0	−82	−155	−220	−280	−334	7,470
18	82	0	−73	−138	−198	−252	7,388
19	155	73	0	−65	−125	−179	7,315
20	220	138	65	0	−60	−114	7,250
21	280	198	125	60	0	−54	7,190
22	334	252	179	114	54	0	7,136

completion date approximately 6 months away. While a complete analysis of the network is not essential at this point, the group should at least identify critical and subcritical paths, and consider carefully activities that are likely to be completed during the first 20-day report period. Remember once a decision is made, activities completed during that period cannot be changed.

APPENDIX: PLANETS II

The first activity establishes the project organization and identifies and locates the technical staff who will be drawn from other project teams, as well as from the corporate R&D staff:

A–B   Organization and Staffing

When the organizational activities are complete and the technical staff has been assembled, four major activity sequences can begin.

       1. Recruitment and orientation of hourly employees who when trained, will process and inspect purchased equipment and then receive further technical training:

B–C   Employee Recruiting
C–F   Orientation Training
F–L   Equipment Processing and Delivery
L–N   Inspection and Report
N–T   Technical Equipment Orientation

       2. Process design and layout for inspection equipment. The layout must wait on completion of a report which includes a list of hourly employees and their skill classifications:

B–D   Design Study
C–D   Report Preparation
D–F   Layout Design

       3. Design, procurement, testing and installation of power and safety equipment:

B–E   Power Source Study
E–G   Power Equipment Procurement
G–M   Install Power Equipment
G–K   Testing (can be concurrent with installation [G–M])
M–R   Install Safety Equipment (must be preceded by setup [L–M])
R–W   Trial Run—Power and Safety Equipment
R–X   Machinery Adjustment (can be concurrent with trial run [R–W])

       4. Design, programming and testing of computer software for the project; these activities are performed by Data Processing personnel and do not require project personnel:

B–J   ADP Systems Design
J–U   Simulation Testing
J–K   Control Application Testing (can be concurrent with simulation testing [J–U])

When the purchased equipment has been processed, some hourly employees will be free to set up the jigs and fixtures required for the installation of the safety equipment (M–R). After the setup and after installation of the power equipment (G–M), the customer must inspect the facilities:

L–M   Setup
M–T   Customer Inspection

Completion of the power source study (B–E) also triggers the start of following sequence:

E–I   Site Modification
I–O   Preliminary Model Design
O–T   Design Translation
O–P   Report Preparation (can be concurrent with design translation [O–T])
O–U   Theoretical Testing (can be concurrent with report preparation [O–P])
U–Y   Concurrent Testing (Theoretical Testing [O–U] and Simulation Testing [J–U] must be complete)

Methods work can begin as soon as the process design study (B–D) is finished; a mechanical breadboard can begin when the methods study is through:

D–H   Methods Study
H–K   Mechanical Breadboard

When the breadboard is built (H–K) and both the power equipment (G–K) and the control application software (J–K) have been tested, a test report can be prepared, trial runs can be made with the breadboard, and technical literature can be developed for the customer:

K–P   Report Preparation
P–S   Trial Run—Breadboard Components
P–Q   Literature Development (can be concurrent with trial run [P–S])

Completion of the inspection report on purchased equipment allows the start of a three-activity sequence involving the writing, review and distribution of a specification study:

N–Q   Specification Study
Q–V   Review and Approval
V–Z   Printing and Distribution

After trial run of the breadboard components (P–S), these activity sequences can start:

  1. Preliminary production of customer's production prototype, including inspection:

S–W   Preliminary Model Production
W–Z   Inspect and Adjust Customer Prototype (trial run of power and safety equipment [R–W] must precede [W–Z])

  2. Adaptation and adjustment of components for volume production:

S–X   Component Adaptation

3. Layout and design of control reports

S–Y   Control Report Design

The completion of activities N–T, M–T, and O–T unblocks fabrication of a preliminary model and stress-testing development:

T–X   Preliminary Model Fabrication

T–Y   Stress-Testing Development

Now the last two activities—preliminary production run and final simulation—can begin and the project can be completed:

X–Z   Preliminary Production (must be preceded by [T–X], [S–X], and [R–X])

Y–Z   Systems Simulation (must be preceded by [U–Y], [T–Y], and [S–Y])

Benson Electronics, Inc.

In June of 1973 Phil Davidson, Operations Manager for the Integrated Circuit Division at Benson Electronics, voiced some thoughts concerning Benson's present situation. As a producer of components and subassemblies for the computer industry, Benson's fortunes are closely tied to the computer manufacturers who purchase much of Benson's production.

The computer industry has continued to grow during the past five to ten years while it has undergone a significant shake down. The period of radical product change has been replaced by one that seeks reliable, compact, but sophisticated and cost competitive equipment. Although a number of large companies have left the industry, there have also been some basic changes in the way we must conduct business, so that competition is now actually much keener and demanding than before. The increasing cost competition in computer systems is passed down to the market for computer components even though the rate of technological advance here has probably continued at a pace that is greater than for the computer system itself. As a major manufacturer in the computer industry and as an aggressive bidder for government subcontracts, Benson has been very successful so far, but success is becoming more and more expensive. Reflecting a continuous effort to develop and apply the most advanced technology possible to the design and manufacture of computer products, Benson spent well above the industry average, for research and development last year and expects to spend more this year. With the new market environment within this industry, however, simply spending more on research and development isn't enough. Effective product and production process design as well as strict cost controls are becoming more and more important.

As far as Benson's thin-film integrated circuit division is concerned, we continue to be among the industry leaders in thin-film technology, a fact which has enabled us to meet industry requirements for progressively smaller, more complex and more reliable electronic circuitry. However, we haven't been able to make any money. Let me explain that further. Most of the production actually shipped out of the plant is in the form of subassemblies. My division manufactures the thin-film IC components for these subassemblies and transfers these components to other departments at a standard cost. So far we have been unable to consistently produce our integrated circuits at or below these standards, so, in effect, I am producing at a loss. Our quality requirements are rigid and are set for us by the customers we supply, whether they are other Benson divisions or outside companies. Consequently, we have to look at the production process itself in our efforts to cut costs without sacrificing quality. Most of the areas in our operation have been examined thoroughly; new equipment and techniques are constantly being evaluated for ways to increase yields and reduce costs.

I feel one area we should be investigating more closely is our present inspection structure. Ideally, the costs of inspection to weed out faulty components in the process should be balanced against the cost of processing these faulty components further, and rejecting them later. I'm not confident that our current arrangement achieves this balance.

BACKGROUND

At present, thin-film circuits are manufactured at Benson by depositing thin layers of metal on a ceramic substrate about 3 inches wide, $4\frac{1}{2}$ inches long and one-thirtieth of an inch thick, etching away parts of the different layers of metal to form the conductor and resistor circuits, and attaching "chip" capacitors, small silicon integrated circuits (SICs) and other "active" elements to the surface of the circuit. The finished circuit is encapsulated in a protective insulation, leaving only the leads exposed. Exhibit 1 shows the integrated circuit (IC) at various stages in the manufacturing process.

Benson's principal manufacturing plant is modern and well designed. Thin-film integrated circuit production occupies only a small amount of the plant's floor space but turns out some 15 different integrated circuit designs in large volume.

The labor force is relatively stable and well trained. Should additional labor be needed, the supply is ample. At present the IC Division is running two shifts. A third shift is possible with only a minimal addition to overhead, should an increase in volume warrant a third shift. Also, if for any reason it is necessary, different stations in the manufacturing process can go to third shift operations or overtime on an individual basis. This has happened in the past to remove temporary bottlenecks, which can shift from one station to another when yields at different stations change as the result of new techniques or temporary problems with a particular operation.

At present, all major equipment is depreciated over a ten-year period. In general, such equipment is replaced by technically more advanced machines and techniques because it has become obsolete or uneconomical, not because it has worn out.

Exhibit 1
A TYPICAL INTEGRATED CIRCUIT (IC IN VARIOUS STAGES OF PRODUCTION)

A. Ceramic substrate after pattern generation of 9 identical circuits (actual size $3\frac{2}{3}'' \times 4\frac{1}{3}''$)

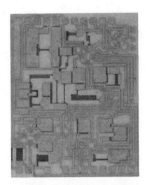

B. Single IC after scribing (actual size $1'' \times \frac{3}{4}''$)

C. IC mounted on frame with leads attached and after mounting .of "chip" capacitors

D. Enlarged photo showing close up of one of the SICs mounted on the IC besides capacitors 241 & 300 (actual size of SIC approximately .03" × .03")

In examining the manufacturing methods used in the production of thin-film integrated circuits, the casewriter followed the production sequence for one particular IC, the H–39, a circuit fairly typical of Benson's IC operations.

THE INSPECTION STRUCTURE

In the production of the H–39, each IC passes through a series of operations on its way to completion. Each operation is closely monitored through sampling, instrumentation and supervision to ensure that the chemical or electrical process itself is functioning properly. Over the past year and a half Phil Davidson's division has pursued an aggressive and systematic program to increase the effectiveness of the "process" inspections and to reduce the lead time between detection and subsequent correction of a misfunctioning operation. This program has substantially improved the yields at each stage of the production process, but it has by no means eliminated defective circuits. There are several reasons for this. Several of the delicate operations are performed manually through the aid of a microscope, and the IC, prior to encapsulation, is very vulnerable to damage from handling. However, principal causes of the rejects in many cases are the technological limitations present in the production processes themselves. Not all circuits processed through a particular operation will conform to specifications, despite the fact that the process itself is functioning "perfectly." In other words, even under ideal conditions the yield will not be 100 percent. For this reason, there are also "100 percent inspections," or "part" inspections, in which every single circuit is examined, and tested, at various stages in the process to isolate and, if possible, repair defective circuits.

PRODUCTION PROCESS FOR THE H–39

A standard size ceramic substrate is purchased from an outside source at a unit cost of $1.40. In the case of the H–39, each substrate will eventually be divided up into nine identical integrated circuits. At the first station a metal called tantalum, chosen for its resistance and stability, is evenly deposited on the "raw" ceramic substrate in a very thin-film by an operation called "sputtering." In this process the substrate is bombarded by individual tantalum atoms in a carefully controlled environment. Each tantalum-covered substrate is valued at $1.90 and the added cost can be broken down as follows: 10 cents in direct labor, 10 cents in material and 30 cents in allocated overhead. (An overhead rate of 300 percent of direct labor is assigned at present volume. Actual overhead expense is composed almost entirely of fixed costs consisting of depreciation, research and development, and general administrative costs.)

Following the sputtering operation the electrical resistance of each substrate is measured to ensure that the layer of tantalum is of the correct thickness. In the past this inspection has averaged about 90 percent yield (90 percent of the substrates pass the inspection). However, the engineers involved indicated that as they continue to learn more about the sputtering technique itself, this yield figure should improve. Each substrate requires about 14 seconds to test, adding about 3 cents in direct labor to the value of the substrate. All rejects are unrepairable, and are discarded.

After testing, the surviving substrates are transferred to a controlled access room where a thin layer of gold is "evaporated" onto the substrate (much less expensive than sputtering, this process is impractical for tantalum, which has an extremely high vaporization point, even in a near vacuum). Evaporation adds 10 cents in direct labor and 70 cents in materials to the value of the substrate. No inspection occurs here other than to ensure that the chemical process itself is functioning correctly.

The substrate then proceeds to the pattern generation area, where the conductor circuit will be fashioned from the layer of gold and resistors will be shaped from the tantalum. First, the substrate is sprayed with a chemical called photo-resist, which reacts when exposed to photographic light. The substrate is then carefully aligned with a transparency containing the circuit pattern for the H–39, and photographically exposed. Following exposure, the substrate is washed, dissolving the exposed photo-resist, and then baked, leaving a hard, protective covering over those areas that were underneath the pattern. These areas will form the conductor circuit. The substrate is then placed in a hydrochloric acid solution, which etches away the unprotected gold, leaving the desired conductor pattern. This entire process is repeated, using a different pattern, to form the tantalum resistors. Pattern generation adds an additional 6 cents in materials and $1.04 in direct labor to the cost of the substrate.

After pattern generation the substrates are baked under pressure for a predetermined amount of time, oxidizing a thin layer of the tantalum resistors. This layer serves as a protective barrier to uncontrolled oxidation, which would raise the resistance level of the tantalum resistors. The resistors are then anodized to bring them up to their specified resistance level. This chemical process is regulated by a small computer and adds about 21 cents in direct labor and 2 cents in materials to the cost of each anodized substrate.

The substrate is then cleaned, scribed by a laser, and "broken" into nine identical circuits, an operation which adds about 9 cents in direct labor cost to the value of the substrate.

At this point the circuit undergoes another electrical resistance test and a visual inspection. The purpose of the resistance test is to isolate circuits which contain resistors which are out of tolerance. Resistors whose values are high are not repairable, and circuits containing such resistors are discarded. Resistors whose value is low are repaired. In the visual inspection cracked substrates, faulty laser scribing, peeling circuitry and bad scratches are looked for. None of these defects are repairable and all circuits containing one or more of these defects are discarded. Including those circuits successfully repaired, the final yield from these two inspections is 84 percent. An average cost of 7 cents in direct labor is added to the value of each *circuit* entering the inspection and testing sequence. This figure includes the cost of all attempts at repair. No material worth noting is added.

At this stage, a frame holding the required leads is bonded to all circuits surviving test and inspection. The lead frames are purchased for $1.00 a piece, and about 3 cents in direct labor is required to attach the frame to the IC. Eight small "chip" capacitors are then attached to the IC by the "solder reflow" method, in which solder previously placed on the capacitors is melted again, firmly attaching the "capacitors" to the integrated circuit. The chip capacitors cost about 50 cents each and about 14 cents worth of direct labor is needed to attach all the capacitors.

Following capacitor attachment, three silicon integrated circuits (SICs) are bonded to the thin-film IC. Each SIC costs about $1.00, and 16 cents in direct labor is needed to attach all three SICs to a circuit.

Following SIC bonding, 16 cross-over circuits made of gold are also bonded to the IC to complete the conductor circuitry. Each cross-over is purchased for 20 cents and 27 cents in direct labor is required to attach all the cross-overs.

Technological considerations demand that the capacitors be placed on the circuits before the SICs are bonded, and handling considerations require that the cross-overs be put on after the SICs have been bonded.

At this point all ICs undergo a rigorous, computer regulated functional test which completely checks the electronic circuitry for each IC.

Seventy percent of the ICs initially pass this test. Ten percent of the circuits tested (or one-third of the rejects) are sound with the exception of one or more cross-overs, which have failed as a result of either faulty bonding or handling. An attempt is made to repair these rejects. The cost of attempted repairs averages about $2.70 in materials and direct labor for each fautly IC and about 60 percent of these ICs are successfully repaired. Ten percent of the circuits being tested fail solely as a result of a faulty SIC bond and are discarded, although a possibility exists that in the future these circuits can be repaired. The remaining 10 percent fail for a variety of reasons—usually a combination of reasons—and are not repairable. The direct labor cost of this functional test is about 6 cents per circuit tested.

At this point the lead frames are trimmed on each surviving circuit exposing the leads themselves. Then, the circuits are encapsulated in a protective insulating material. The variable cost of these two operations is 6 cents in direct labor, and 14 cents in material for each circuit encapsulated. The encapsulated ICs are then given a second functional test, identical to the first except for the diagnostics. Ninety percent of the ICs pass this test and are readied for transfer or shipment. (Ten percent are damaged as a result of the encapsulation operation.) Once the ICs are encapsulated no repair is possible and the rejects are discarded. The direct labor cost of this second functional test is also 6 cents per circuit tested.

Seated with the casewriter after a tour of the H–39 production process, Phil Davidson continued to express some of his thoughts concerning thin-film production.

FUTURE INVESTMENT

It's difficult to pigeonhole our IC production here at Benson. Our operation is an anomaly of sorts. It has developed almost out of necessity into a highly capital intensive process using expensive specialized equipment despite the fact that, as I mentioned earlier, the technology associated with integrated circuitry continues to change at a rapid rate, often leading to major process changes as well as product changes.

In fact, capital investment decisions take up a great deal of my time. For example, in the case of the H–39, we are currently considering the purchase of a new piece of equipment to test the circuit after the SICs are in place but before the cross-overs are bonded. A considerable amount of value is added at the cross-over operation and it might be economical to isolate bad circuits before the cross-overs are bonded. With this equipment we feel we could isolate virtually 100 percent of the circuits defective for other reasons. Such a test would of course eliminate all faulty—and presently unrepairable—circuits before the cross-overs are installed.

This piece of test equipment would be similar in nature to the equipment we presently use for our functional test and would cost about $180,000 with an additional $100,000 involved in installation costs and other start-up expenses. The test equipment would be used only for the H–39 circuit.

Analysis has indicated that such a test would cost about 4 cents in direct labor per circuit tested and would have a yield of 80 percent. Since we feel that currently 7 of 8 circuits successfully go through cross-over bonding, and, as I mentioned earlier, 60 percent of those rejected for bad cross-overs can be successfully repaired, our percentage yield for the first functional test would improve, although the actual number of finished circuits suitable for shipment would remain unchanged.

AN ALTERNATIVE

On the other hand, our familiarity with the production process for the H–39 has developed to the point where we feel we could isolate 80 percent of the circuits containing faulty SIC bonds through a visual inspection immediately after the SIC bonding operation. We know that 7 of 8 circuits successfully undergo SIC bonding; therefore, the visual inspection would reject 10 percent of the circuits inspected. Not all circuits surviving this inspection would be sound, of course. In fact, our analysis indicates that while 20 percent of the circuits entering the visual inspection would be faulty for one reason or another, only half of these would be caught and rejected at such an inspection, allowing the remaining 10 percent to proceed through cross-over bonding to the first functional test, where they would be discovered and rejected.

In summary, if visual inspection were undertaken, the first functional test would have an initial yield of 77.8 percent with half the rejects being sound except for one or more faulty cross-overs (again, an attempt would be made to repair these rejects). We feel that it would cost about 10 cents in direct labor for each circuit visually inspected; however, the only investment would be two high power microscopes, which cost about $1,000 a piece and are good for about 5 years of two-shift operations.

The trick is to decide whether either of these process innovations would be worthwhile, and if they are *both* worthwhile which one should we choose? Is such an expensive piece of equipment worth the investment? What are the risks involved? We're not yet confident that we have the answers to these questions.

At present, Benson Electronics produces about 80,000 H–39 circuits a year.

The Ferdanna Company (A)[1]

In early February 1960, Mr. Stanley Newland, Vice President for Research and Development for the Ferdanna Company, was troubled by a series of eight civil suits filed against Ferdanna during the preceding four years. A suit was filed in January which asked over $1 million in compensatory and punitive damages. The injuries were claimed to have been received as a result of the explosion of a supposedly unopened can of Clear, one of Ferdanna's leading products.

Mr. Newland knew he would be asked to comment on his department's quality control methods and procedures. He felt his department had done all that was possible to ensure Ferdanna's outgoing product would meet their rigid specifications and felt hard-pressed to understand how any explosions could have occurred under the conditions alleged.

COMPANY BACKGROUND

Founded in 1905, the forerunner of Ferdanna began operations as a selling agent for a number of manufacturers in the Cleveland, Ohio area. In 1912, the company began its own manufacturing operations, specializing in drugs and household cleaning products. Its early product line included such items as bulk chemicals (sales only), lye, chlorinated lime and epsom salt (packaging and sales).

In 1918, Mr. M. J. Ferdanna, a Chemical Engineer and one of the company's early leaders, decided the company should diversify and expand its scope of operations. To aid in meeting this objective, he selected Clear, a household drain unclogger, as the product to bring visibility to the company and provide profits on which to base future growth. In 1922, Clear was marketed for the first time on a national level and enjoyed consistent growth in sales and in contribution to total company profit. In 1931,

---

[1] This case was prepared from public documents. All names, however, have been disguised.

Ferdanna chemists developed the formula for Seethru, a household window cleaner. After national marketing was begun in 1934, Seethru, like Clear, enjoyed a consistent record of sales growth and, together with Clear has formed the backbone of the Ferdanna product line.

By the late 50s, Ferdanna marketed a broad line of household products. Exploiting the discoveries of its own research lab and giving national exposure to the products of a number of companies Ferdanna acquired during this period, the company's product line included: Clear, Seethru, an air freshner, silver cleaner, a sink and tub stain remover, a bowl cleaner, moth repellants, a garbage can deodorant/disinfectant, plastic sprayers, pumps and dispensers.

Company officials credited two main areas for the success Ferdanna enjoyed: the achievements of their Research Department and the impact of a vigorous national advertising effort in virtually every media. In particular, the company placed great emphasis on pioneering new fields, preferring not to imitate products already on the market. Quality Control was considered a vital part of the firm's operations. In 1954, for example, one-fourth of the company's lab personnel were engaged in work "guarding the quality of our products and of the materials that go into them."[2] The other three-quarters were involved in basic research. Financial data for the period 1952–1959 can be found in Exhibits 1 and 2. Background information on certain company personnel are contained in Exhibit 3.

CLEAR

The Ferdanna Company introduced Clear as a product to be used in the home to solve a long-standing household problem: clogged drains. After normal use of a kitchen sink, oily substances have a tendency to gather and congeal on the top of water left standing in the typical U-shaped kitchen drain pipe. With carelessness (i.e., failure to run scalding water through from time to time), the congealed fat and materials (such as hair, garbage bits, etc.) tend to grow into a mass large enough to impede smooth flow of water. This blockage can range from partial (i.e., water gurgles and flows slowly while draining through) to total. Drain cleaners, such as Clear were designed to unclog drains in a minimum of time and with less mess than the use of a "plumber's snake." This was done by generating enough heat to dissolve the fat and grease thus allowing the other substances trapped in the plug to flow out of the blocked pipe. Clear was one of the first such products developed, and by 1951, it was reported that over half of all families using some kind of drain cleaner used Clear. During the 50s other drain-cleaning products were introduced; however, in 1960, Clear continued to dominate the market, due to Ferdanna's vigorous national advertising campaign and protection by three key patents.

---

[2] Annual Report, 1954.

Exhibit 1

THE FERDANNA COMPANY (A)
Ferdanna—Income Statements
(000)

	1959	1958	1957	1956	1955	1954	1953	1952
Net Sales	$28,400	$29,498	$26,689	$24,683	$19,454	$21,651	$27,871	$27,726
Cost of Goods Sold	14,186	9,730	18,716	17,614	13,396	17,282	23,610	23,119
Gross Profit	$14,214	$19,768	$ 7,973	$ 7,069	$ 6,058	$ 4,369	$ 4,261	$ 4,607
Depreciation and Amortization	—	—	—	—	—	—	—	—
Selling and Administration	—	—	—	—	—	—	—	—
Selling, research, general and Administration	(9,631)	(6,768)	(5,776)	(5,237)	(4,288)	(3,044)	(2,854)	(2,752)
Interest expense	—	(31)	(119)	(104)	(84)	(125)	(199)	(201)
Other income and deductions	149	160	(23)	(15)	(29)	(1)	(27)	(201)
Profit before tax	$ 4,732	$ 3,129	$ 2,055	$ 1,713	$ 1,657	$ 1,199	$ 1,181	$ 1,453
Tax (federal and state)	2,398	1,593	1,060	864	872	611	601	740
Profit after Tax	$ 2,334	$ 1,536	$ 995	$ 849	$ 785	$ 588	$ 580	$ 713
Number of common shares outstanding	869	706	706	706	706	706	706	706
EPS (after preferred dividends)	$2.58	$2.02	$1.24	$0.96	$0.94	$0.68	$0.67	$0.86
Dividend per common share	$1.00	$0.75	$0.50	$0.45	$0.40	$0.40	$0.40	$0.40

Exhibit 2
THE FERDANNA COMPANY (A)
Balance Sheets
($000)

	1959	1958	1957	1956	1955	1954	1953	1952
Current Assets:								
Cash	$ 1,447	$ 1,385	$1,216	$ 1,674	$ 1,124	$ 2,692	$ 2,440	$ 2,964
Marketable securities	3,971	3,370	3,162	998	1,497	400	0	0
Accounts receivable (net)	1,927	1,270	1,002	1,477	1,424	974	1,054	1,319
Cash advance-soybean K's	0	0	0	317	235	40	266	191
Inventory	2,735	1,874	1,501	2,061	2,344	1,207	1,437	1,266
Other current assets	0	0	0	0	0	0	0	2
Total Current Assets	$10,080	$ 7,899	$6,881	$ 6,527	$ 6,624	$ 5,313	$ 5,197	$ 5,742
Net plant and equipment	3,082	2,019	1,516	4,766	4,683	4,836	5,042	4,762
Investments (at cost)	1,013	1,012	1,027	1,020	1,020	16	11	5
Prepaid expenses	171	205	248	363	127	160	150	131
Trademarks and patents (net)	0	0	0	0	0	0	0	0
Other intangible assets	0	0	300	0	505	0	0	0
Other assets	0	0	0	0	5	65	74	84
Total Assets	$14,346	$11,135	$9,972	$12,676	$12,964	$10,390	$10,474	$10,724
Current Liabilities:								
Accounts payable	$ 1,304	$ 872	$ 789	$ 813	$ 677	$ 380	$ 478	$ 467
Accounts liability	515	396	205	232	264	153	191	180
U.S. and foreign tax payments	1,899	1,671	91	795	863	610	595	882
N/P W/I 1 year	0	0	250	250	250	150	150	150
Other current liabilities	448	0	150	0	0	0	0	18
Total Current Liabilities	$ 4,166	$ 2,939	$1,485	$ 2,090	$ 2,054	$ 1,293	$ 1,414	$ 1,697
Notes payable	0	0	875	1,875	2,125	1,650	1,800	1,950
Other long-term liabilities	65	0	0	0	0	0	0	0
Total Liabilities	$ 4,231	$ 2,939	$2,360	$ 3,965	$ 4,179	$ 2,943	$ 3,214	$ 3,647
Minority interest	91	65	44	30	24	0	0	0
Common stock	869	706	706	706	706	706	706	706
Preferred stock	1,280	2,326	2,700	3,250	3,724	2,700	2,700	2,700
Capital surplus (paid-in)	2,005	223	185	185	157	157	157	157
Retained earnings	5,870	4,876	3,977	4,540	4,198	3,883	3,696	3,515
Total Net Worth	$10,024	$ 8,196	$7,612	$ 8,711	$ 8,761	$ 7,446	$ 7,259	$ 7,078
Total Liabilities and Net Worth	$14,346	$11,135	$9,972	$12,676	$12,964	$10,390	$10,474	$10,724

Exhibit 3
KEY FERDANNA PERSONNEL

Frank Ferdanna—*President*—(*Chairman, Ferdanna Products Co.*)
Undergraduate major: Engineering and Marketing (some chemical engineering training), MBA (Chicago), 1932. Worked at Ferdanna in chemical research and control, market research, selling and advertising, budgeting, purchasing, manufacturing, traffic and in personnel. Asst. to the president, 1941. Executive vice president, 1943; president, 1948.
Stanley T. Newland—*Vice President in charge of Research and Development*
A.B., University of Cincinnati, Major: chemistry; LLB (Bachelor of Laws); admitted to the Ohio bar.
Brian M. Landon, Jr.—*Vice President, Marketing & Advertising*
Employed at Ferdanna since 1934.
P. L. Sather—*Vice President, Manufacturing*
Richard M. Evans—*Plant Manager*
(In charge of the manufacturing department)
Undergraduate degree in Mechanical Engineering (Purdue 1939)
George Kleinman—*Section Head of the Quality Control Program*
(Under the direction of Mr. S. T. Newland)
Bachelor's Degree, Chemistry
(Eastern Michigan University)
James Hawkins—*Assistant to George Kleinman*
Arthur P. Bell—*Technician—QC & Research Departments*
A.B., Chemistry (Wittenberg College).

Maintaining essentially the same form from 1949 to 1960, Clear was a dry, granular substance comprised of 54.5 percent sodium hydroxide (NaOH),[3] 30.5 percent sodium nitrate ($NaNO_3$), 4.2 percent aluminum particles, and 10.8 percent sodium chloride (NaCL, or regular salt). Each ingredient retained its particulate integrity within the can and reacted only when coming in contact with water.

Clear, when added to water, generated heat. This is accomplished through a number of steps in the overall chemical reaction. First, on contact with water, the sodium hydroxide and the sodium nitrate dissolve. The aluminum particles then react with the sodium hydroxide in solution, the aluminum thereby dissolving, giving off a fair amount of heat. Hydrogen gas is formed but is almost immediately oxidized by the sodium nitrate, giving off more heat, and a vapor is formed comprised of: ammonia, ammonia hydroxide, ammonia gas, and steam. Ferdanna personnel were aware that if water was added to a beaker containing Clear, enough heat would be generated that the beaker could not be picked up without burns resulting. It was also common knowledge at Ferdanna that Clear, when mixed with water in a closed container, could generate so much vapor the resultant pressure could be sufficient to rupture the container.

---

[3] All figures by weight.

Two factors were key in determining the degree of heat generated and, therefore, the effectiveness of any one usage of Clear. First was the size of the aluminum particles. On one hand, the smaller the particle, the faster the reaction, thereby generating the greatest amount of heat. If, however, the particle was too small, it had a tendency to rise to the surface of the water in a clogged pipe or in the sink basin itself, thereby generating heat far from the greasy plug. In 1959, the aluminum particle size varied from 110 to 130 particles per gram. The second factor determining effectiveness was the concentration of aluminum in any one portion of the total mixture. One out of every twenty-five particles was aluminum and if these particles aggregated in one part of the can, the remaining portions might prove relatively ineffective while the aluminum-concentrated portion could be highly volatile.

In a dry state, most of the ingredients in Clear were relatively harmless. However, one prime ingredient, sodium hydroxide (also known as caustic soda or lye) was known to burn human tissue. While it could not damage a steel pipe, it was nevertheless classified by chemists as a corrosive.[4] While Ferdanna chemists had not conducted specific tests regarding the effects of Clear (or sodium hydroxide alone) contacting human tissue, the company had established safety procedures to be followed by employees working with Clear (see Exhibit 4).

Company officials were sensitive to a major packaging problem resulting from the inherent nature of Clear. Standing inert, Clear was hydroscopic, i.e., it would absorb moisture from the air. This property often caused two undesirable effects. First, it allowed rust to build-up inside and around the can opening. Second, it would cause lumping or caking of the Clear itself. Over time, the lumpy or pasty Clear would harden and become extremely difficult to remove from the can. If the caking were pervasive enough, the consumer might be forced to discard the can altogether. Company officials therefore recognized the need for tight can closure to keep moisture out.

Prior to July 1958, Clear was packaged in a can employing what was termed a "friction cap." This type of cap was "pressed into" an opening at the top of the can (most cans of house paint utilize a form of friction cap). The company had always used a metal friction cap with a metal can. Unfortunately, consumers were not always careful in opening the friction cap, often using a screwdriver and damaging the ring on the can itself. Once this happened, it was nearly impossible to obtain a tight reseal and moisture would get into the can. In some cases the hydroscopic property of particles left on the rim would result in a sort of self-sealing effect (i.e, the particles swelled and dried, sealing off any opening) but more often the contents of the can became caked. In June 1958, after a number of meetings where such factors as tightness of seal, potential internal pressure

---

[4] "Corrosive" is a term used to describe the ability of some substances to "eat away" and destroy all but the hardest of materials, usually through chemical reaction.

Exhibit 4
EXCERPTS FROM DIRECTIVES TO EMPLOYEES RE: SAFETY PROCEDURES

Clothing

Workmen should wear cotton clothing, which is more resistant to caustic soda than wool, rubber, heavy canvas or moleskin gloves, high brimmed hat to keep the caustic from going down the face and neck, either low acid proof rubber shoes or a canvas shoe with rubber soles and heels, and goggles properly adjusted to the contour of the face.

First-Aid, General

Caustic soda coming in contact with the skin tends to penetrate into the flesh tissues rapidly, producing severe burns unless prompt action is taken. Therefore, the prerequisite would be a drinking fountain and a shower bath or its equivalent located near where the material is to be handled. Also, a first aid cabinet containing a liberal supply of 5 percent magnesium sulfate solution labeled "For external burns, mouth and ears," and also a 5 percent magnesium sulfate solution labeled "For eyes only."

Contact with Eyes

Quick action is required when the eyes burn. It should be thoroughly flushed with plenty of water immediately. If a drinking fountain is available hold the eye open and flush thoroughly. Flush out with 5 percent solution of magnesium sulfate to neutralize the remaining caustic. Follow it by further flushing with water to remove the magnesium sulfate.

Contact with Ears

Ears. First thoroughly flush the ear out with the 5 percent solution of magnesium sulfate, followed by sterile oil. If the external part of the ear is burned, wash with 5 percent solution of magnesium sulfate, then apply ice compresses followed by the application of a bland ointment.

Contact with Mouth

Mouth. Thoroughly rinse the mouth out with cold water, and wash with a 5 percent solution of magnesium sulfate. After this procedure, hold sterile oil in the mouth until relieved. If there is a swelling of the tongue, hold a small piece of ice in the mouth. If there is a swelling of the lips, apply ice compresses, also a bland ointment.

General Remarks

General Remarks. We cannot over-emphasize the necessity for immediate action in the treatment of caustic burns, as the caustic must be washed out and neutralized immediately to avoid serious injury. All caustic burns in the eye or ear or severe body burns should receive prompt and competent medical attention immediately following first aid treatment.

build-up and consumer convenience were considered, it was decided to adopt a plastic cap which would screw on to a relatively narrow protruding opening on the can. This "pour-spout" was chosen to provide a long-lasting tight seal (to avoid spillage and moisture contamination). It was also easier to pour Clear out of the can than to spoon it out.

In 1959–60, Clear was marketed in containers of two different sizes: the traditional 12-ounce and the newer economy-sized 18-ounce can (production began on that size on 12/16/58).[5] Throughout 1958 and 1959, the ratio of 12-ounce cans to 18-ounce cans produced remained at about two to one.

THE MANUFACTURE OF CLEAR
AT THE CLEVELAND FACILITY

All of the chemical raw materials used in Clear were certified[6] by Ferdanna's suppliers. The Ferdanna laboratory also conducted its own tests to determine strength, purity and other chemical properties. The sodium chloride and sodium nitrate were received in bulk in boxcars and shovelled into screw conveyors which carried the materials to a storage area on the plant's third floor. The sodium hydroxide arrived in 55 gallon drums (weighing 500 pounds each) and were kept in a storage area on the first floor. Aluminum was received in ingots, averaging 6 feet in length, as a special alloy prepared according to Ferdanna's specifications. The aluminum was also stored in an area on the first floor.

The cans, with the label lithographed on them but without tops, were received from boxcars in cardboard containers. The Perkins Can Company, a long-time supplier of Ferdanna, manufactured the metallic can components according to Ferdanna specification. While not consulted before the design change in 1958, Perkins representatives did consult with Ferdanna officials on the subject of can feasibility after the change-over decision had been made.

The four basic raw materials were weighed out carefully in a batch process and then poured through a screen (to eliminate over-size particles or caked pieces) into a mixer, cylindrical in shape (similar to a concrete mixer) about 10 feet in diameter and 6 feet wide. The material was mixed for 8 minutes (to ensure a relatively even distribution of the four chemicals). The mixed product was then dropped into a feed hopper connected to the filling machine.

The empty cans were put into a hopper which automatically picked them up and placed them in an upright position. The cans were then fed onto a stainless steel conveyor belt. They moved to the filler where they entered the circular rotating device. The Clear itself passed through a hollow cylindrical filling spout into the cans below. The cans then left the filler and continued down the conveyor belt where they were agitated, to settle the material into the can. After agitation, a gap usually existed between the top of the Clear and the top of the open can, amounting to three-quarters plus or minus three-eights of an inch. When the pour spout, itself three-quarters of an inch high, was finally added, the gap amounted

---

[5] Based on tests, it was believed that these two cans were structurally identical and the same Clear formula was used regardless of can size.

[6] Certification indicated that the materials met specifications such as purity and/or particulate size established by Ferdanna.

to roughly an inch and a half. The top was then seamed[7] onto the open can by a seaming machine purchased by Ferdanna. The as yet uncapped cans moved to a separate capping machine which had a rotating head. This head came down over the plastic cap and twisted it on.[8]

Immediately after this operation, the cans passed a worker stationed on the line, whose job was to determine whether or not the machine had put a cap on the can, and to visually inspect the caps for defects such as fill-out failure and flashing. The caps, made by an independent supplier, were fabricated in a mold. Sometimes too little plastic entered the mold and the resultant cap was missing certain areas. When this occurred it was said to have failed to fill out. At other times, too much plastic entered the mold and excess plastic would be protruding from the rim of the cap itself. When this occurred, the defect was termed flashing. These problems, however, were sporadic. More consistently, once or twice daily, this worker would remove cans which had failed to receive a cap from the line.

After capping, the filled cans moved through a spray washing device, approximately 3 feet long, 3 feet high and about 18 inches wide. The purpose of having the cans run through this bath was to remove any sodium hydroxide sticking to the can and to remove any oil or other foreign substance which existed on the label. Occasionally, dirty cans were discovered during the packaging operation and these were sent back to the line to be washed again.

The finished cans then moved to the end of the conveyor where a packing machine loaded the cans into cases. The filled cases then went through a gluer and afterwards the sealed case was stacked on a platform. When the platform (also called a flat or pallet) was loaded with the appropriate number of cases, it was taken by fork truck either to the warehouse area or to a carrier for shipment to some store. There were no particular instructions given either to Ferdanna employees or to carriers or retailers regarding storing or handling the finished product since it was felt these were essentially unnecessary. There were either 12 or 24 cans per case, depending on whether 18-ounce or 12-ounce cans were being produced and there were about 90 cases per flat. At a minimum, 5,000 cases per day were produced. On December 22, 1958, sixty-nine 500-pound drums of sodium hydroxide were used in making 23 batches of Clear during normal one shift operations.

Mr. Evans, Ferdanna plant manager estimated the longest period any case of the new 18-ounce size Clear would be held at the plant was about one month during late 1958 and much of 1959.

---

[7] Seams are double crimps at the top, side and bottom of the can. The side and bottom seamings were performed by Perkin before shipment to Ferdanna. The top seaming was done by Ferdanna. Both edges of the metal to be seamed together were in a U-shape. They fit together, in what children would describe as an "Indian-grip." The seaming action rolls this over and flattens it resulting in a double crimp.

[8] One company official estimated the elapsed time between filling and final capping at 3–4 minutes.

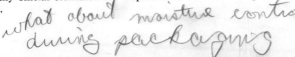

RETAILER HANDLING OF CLEAR

Ferdanna shipped sealed cases of Clear to retailers by truck and by railroad car. While particular methods used to handle Clear at the retailer level varied among stores and chains, the experience of one large (170–180 store) grocery chain in the New York area, the Grand Tea Company, was illustrative.

Grand received shipments of Clear at its central dry grocery warehouse. Fruits, vegetables and meats were handled in an entirely separate warehouse and dairy products were received in still a third warehouse. The Grand dry grocery warehouse was a windowless oblong-shaped building, about 1,200 feet long and 600 feet wide and it covered 16¼ acres all under one roof. Goods were received at a totally roofed truck dock which stood over 4 feet above ground level. Because of the nature of the goods received there, every precaution was taken to ensure dry unloading, storage, and reloading. Grand never experienced trouble with water in their warehouse.

The delivering trucker loaded his goods onto 48 $\times$ 40 inch pallets which were lifted by fork lift trucks and carried to what were termed reserve aisles. He then loaded the cases of Clear into the appropriate aisle. Clear was kept roughly in the center of the warehouse in the household goods section. After unloading all the pallets, the truck operator would attach a color coded rotation tag to the last pallet he unloaded, stamped the date and signed his initials. There were three colors: red, green and yellow. These colors were used in rotation during successive four-week periods. Since the pallets were removed from the other side for shipping to individual stores, the system in effect employed a first-in-first-out method for turning over merchandise. One spokesman for Grand noted that any one shipment remained in the Grand warehouse a maximum of 3 months with average turnover time being 3 weeks. Grand receipt and shipment of Clear in the 18-ounce size is contained in Exhibit 5.

The demand from any individual store was known to vary to a considerable degree. A quarterly full stock inventory was taken by a crew sent out from the chain headquarters, and was used as one basis for reordering goods. More often, however, the store manager ascertained restocking needs after making his daily store inspection. When an order was received at the warehouse, the appropriate amount was pulled and shipped by truck to the particular branch. Shipping records were retained at the warehouse but only for a short time.

When a shipment arrived at the branch store it was typically unloaded at the grocery receiving area by means of conveyors and rolled into the back room of the store. There, it was stacked in regular commodity sections (i.e., cereal, coffee, household cleaners, etc.) on pallets. The store manager or assistant manager marked the price on the cases. Regular store personnel then reloaded the cases, one at a time, onto trucks for stocking

Exhibit 5

GRAND RECEIPT AND SHIPMENT OF 18-OUNCE CLEAR DURING MOST OF 1959

	Receipt of Clear (Cases)		Deliveries to Stores		
Date	Number	Cumulative	Week ending	Number	Cumulative
2/12	400	400			
3/3	300	700			
3/20	200	900			
3/24	530	1,430			
4/2	1,000	2,430	3/27	163	163
			4/3	482	645
			4/10	28	673
4/17	650	3,080	4/17	367	1,040
			4/24	351	1,391
5/1	550	3,630	5/1	297	1,688
5/6	250	3,880	5/8	292	1,980
			5/15	283	2,263
			5/22	280	2,543
5/25	400	4,280	5/29	275	2,818
			6/5	277	3,095
6/8	450	4,730	6/12	263	3,358
6/17	230	4,960	6/19	232	3,590
6/25	300	5,260	6/26	247	3,837
			7/3	230	4,067
7/7	400	5,660	7/10	263	4,330
			7/17	251	4,581
7/20	350	6,010	7/24	233	4,814
7/29	600	6,610	7/31	255	5,069
8/7	350	6,960	8/7	261	5,330
			8/14	275	5,605
8/20	600	7,560	8/21	312	5,917
			8/28	313	6,230
9/3	650	8,210	9/4	286	6,516
			9/11	301	6,817
			9/18	286	7,103
9/21	700	8,910	9/25	266	7,369
9/24	300		10/2	261	7,630
10/2	300	9,210	10/9	244	7,874
			10/16	267	8,141
10/14	600	10,110	10/23	259	8,400
			10/30	271	9,671
10/27	495	10,605	11/6	251	9,922
11/5	200	10,805	11/13	281	10,203
11/12	300	11,105	11/20	237	10,440
11/24	400	11,505			

in the store, having cut the top off the cases to ready the goods for individual price-stamping. A stamper, working at a stamping table, marked each item, usually on the top or side, with the appropriate price.

When part-time stockboys arrived at the store after school they took the loaded trucks into the sales area. They then removed old stock from the shelf, cleaned the shelf off, and dusted off the old stock using a standard feather duster. They loaded the new stock onto the shelf first and finally replaced the older stock at the front of the shelf, so that customers would remove this old stock first. Also, just before closing, the store personnel "faced" the shelves, meaning they dusted once again and turned all labels to the front. During stamping, restocking, and facing, store personnel visually inspected the cans for defects. Damaged cans were removed. They would not, however, check the cans for tightness of capping.

After a customer made a selection and finished shopping, a checker processed the goods out and determined the total cost. During this process too, all goods were visually checked for damage, and if damaged, removed. One store manager, whose store experienced typical demand patterns for Clear, estimated that, at most, any one can would remain in the store for about two weeks before being sold.

QUALITY CONTROL PROCEDURES FOR CLEAR

As head of research and development it was Mr. Newland's responsibility to develop new products, to improve existing products and to be in charge of quality control activities. Organizationally, the R&D Department was divided into two sections, the Research Lab and the Control Lab (QC). The Control Lab was headed by Mr. George Kleinman and was staffed by his assistant and a number of technicians and chemists (ranging from 4 to 6 from 1958 to 1960). The Lab was charged with the responsibility to establish standards and to see that Clear lived up to the design specifications. The Control Lab has absolute authority over quality at all phases of the production process—it determined whether or not in-bound raw materials were accepted and used, and could reject anything production made. The Lab determined what corrections would be made and how they would be made.

Quality Control activity began when the raw materials arrived. Laboratory samples were taken and tests made to determine purity, strength and other specific chemical properties. (One spot test conducted was the determination of the moisture content of the sodium nitrate.) A sample of aluminum was periodically sent out for analysis of the alloy to check against the certificate received from the supplier. If the material was satisfactory, the laboratory released it to the production department. If found to be unsatisfactory in any respect, materials were held and the Purchasing Department was notified. The empty cans were checked mechanically and visually for obvious defects such as poor seaming or dents by an inspector before reaching the filling machine.

The Lab also periodically audited the mixing department and production mixing logs. The mixing process was checked to ensure the scales were in control, that employees at the mixer were logging properly, and that Clear ingredients were being mixed for the appropriate amount of time. A daily raw material report showed the time of the mix per batch, the pounds of raw materials by ingredients that were entered into the batch, the size container in which the caustic soda was received and the number of drums used that day. A separate record entry was made for each batch.

After the first few cans in any one batch were filled, these cans were pulled, emptied and checked for "screen size," to determine if the ingredient particles were of the right size. This was done to ensure particularly that the hydroscopic sodium hydroxide was not lumping up prior to or during filling which would result in an imperfect in-can distribution of the chemical ingredients. This test, performed routinely by production personnel, was audited by the Control Lab.

After filling, but before final seaming, a number of other tests were performed. Almost constantly, one inspector would remove cans from the line, visually inspect them, check them for proper weight and replace the cans on the line. Also, 2 out of about every 4,000 cans were pulled for the purpose of conducting a heat-of-reaction test. This test essentially duplicated actual usage in a household drain. The recommended amount was placed in a tube, a normal amount of water was added, and two thermocouples measured the heat at the top and bottom of the reaction. The results were recorded mechanically on a graph and were checked against what was considered an acceptable range of temperatures.

After the ring and spout (can top without cap) were seamed on, a leakage test was performed by the Lab. The product was emptied out of the can and the can itself was immersed in water where it was subjected to an air leakage test. The leakage test was relatively new and probably not performed prior to mid-1959.

After top seaming but before capping, the cans were coded on the bottom showing where and when the particular can was manufactured. Another operator then systematically check-weighed a number of cans, recording the results on a chart for later use by the Lab. The principal purpose of this test was to ensure the consumer received the appropriate amount of Clear in each can. This data was the only instance where written records were kept of checks performed by production personnel.

After capping, samples of the finished product were tested again for heat of reaction and for proper weight. Other tests were made which measured or recorded temperature rise, stirring action, caustic heel, quiescent layer, and foam. The results were compared with specification and retests made if necessary. Also, from 100 to 300 cans out of every shipment (usually numbering several thousand) would be chosen for an examination of outward appearance, weight, scratches, or some other deformity.

One further test was conducted before the Lab would finally allow a shipment to be released. Because of the importance attached to obtaining a tight closure, Ferdanna's Production Department conducted what was called a torque test on the caps of the Clear cans. By use of a special testing machine, the Lab determined how much force was required to open the closure made by the cap. The test was conducted on a small sample of each batch. In 1958 and 1959, the average that the Lab required before allowing shipment was six inch-pounds.[9] The Ferdanna Lab felt that six inch-pounds was a reasonable objective—they knew that ten inch-pounds would provide a reasonably waterproof can. They also knew that it was virtually impossible to achieve moisture-proofing and/or air-tightness with a screw-on can. The obvious difficulty of providing a can which is extremely tight is the problem that the average user would have in getting the can open.

Most interdepartmental communication regarding QC matters were in writing. Should some defect be found either by the Lab or by the production operators on the line, the line would first be stopped and any production that had gotten beyond the end of the line would be held. The defective or suspect goods would then be "blue-tagged" by Lab personnel. A control technician physically placed a tag on the material in question. This tag could not be removed until whatever corrective action the Lab directed had been taken, under their supervision. No material that had a tag on it could be shipped until the tag was removed. Only Lab personnel could remove tags. The removed tags were kept for a short time, usually for no more than a year or two, for reference. Tags which were thought to be of little permanent value (i.e., relating to appearance defects only) were destroyed.

When a defect was discovered, one of the Lab technicians would write a report concerning its nature and extent on what was termed a "Form 111." It would be addressed to Mr. Kleinman who in turn would forward it to the appropriate personnel. Whenever a Form 111 was written up, an entry would be made in a chronologically ordered logbook which was permanently retained. Based on reports from his staff, Mr. Kleinman would, from time to time, issue memoranda explaining a particular problem and containing his recommendations as to how the problem should be dealt with. In general, these memoranda were sent to, at most, the 4 or 5 men who would be most concerned: Mr. Newland, head of R&D; Mr. Evans, plant manager; Mr. Sather, head of sales; Mr. Randall, plant foreman; or Mr. Gilbert, head of the shipping department. When follow-up action was necessary, a route slip was often attached to the memorandum with room for the addressee to comment, in writing, about progress that had been made on the particular problem. These memoranda, with route-slips (if any), were retained for reference purposes. Generally, check sheets were used for routine testing but they were discarded shortly after use. There were no daily reports of routine inspections—the only records the company retained were ones pertaining to perceived problems and were found either on the Form 111 or in the retained memoranda.

---

[9] Six inch pounds of torque could be obtained by applying one pound of pressure to the end of a wrench that was six inches long and attached to the cap at the other end. Likewise, two pounds of pressure on a three-inch wrench would yield six inch-pounds.

The Control Laboratory supervised remedial action performed by the Production Department. In most cases, when a defect was found, inspection for other possible problems was also performed in addition to correction of the specific defect. Both the results of the reinspection (if no further defects were found) and notice of compliance with QC's orders were communicated verbally to the Control Laboratory. They in turn removed the hold tags and verbally notified the shipping dock of their authorization for the release of the previously held goods.

Mr. Newland and the Control Laboratory were principally concerned with abnormal mixtures, lumps, hot cans, and excessive aluminum. However, company officials were aware of a difficulty they had experienced in 1958 and 1959 regarding loose caps. After standing for 24 hours the caps of certain batches had demonstrated a tendency to loosen somewhat. Mr. Newland admitted that the looseness could have been caused by machinery wear. Ferdanna changed its capping machine in the spring of 1959.

THE JANSE SUIT

Based on the depositions of Mary Janse, her husband Frank and a neighbor, Mrs. Lois Day, the three witnesses to the occurrence, Mr. Newland was aware of the following alleged facts surrounding the incident leading to the current suit:

On November 21, 1959, Mrs. Janse purchased an 18-ounce can of Clear from a Grand Tea Company store in Brooklyn.[10] She had used the product many times in the past, and said she noticed the can had a screw-on cap. She said this particular can remained beneath the sink in her kitchen until approximately 9:30 A.M. the following day. On the morning of November 22nd she took the can of Clear, which until then had remained unopened, went into the bathroom and set the can down on the side of the sink.[11] As she reached across to turn on a cold water faucet, in her own words: "there was a sound of an explosion and I had a terrific burning in my eyes."

Mr. Janse was in the dining room at the time he heard an explosion and seconds later saw his wife in the kitchen trying to splash water on her face. She told him that a can of Clear had exploded. He said he saw crystals laying all over the bathroom: in the tub, in back of the toilet and in the sink. He also found the can of Clear with the cap still on, in the bathtub and saw that it had burst apart at the seams. Mr. Janse called for an ambulance and took his wife to the hospital. Mrs. Janse subsequently lost the sight of both eyes.

Mrs. Lois Day, a family friend, said that she came to the Janse home at 10:00 A.M. on the morning in question and observed "crystals, sort

---

[10] Coding on the can indicated it had been processed on December 22, 1958.

[11] She said her normal procedure was to first put cold water in the drain and then to add two tablespoons of Clear.

of a grayish crystal, in the bathroom." She said she saw the Clear can and asserted that the cap was on.

The Janse's were suing the Ferdanna Company, The Ferdanna Products Company,[12] the Perkin Can Company, and The Grand Tea Company. Mrs. Janse was suing to recover $1,200,000 in compensatory damages (i.e., for medical bills and pain and suffering) and an equivalent amount in puni-

Exhibit 6
SECOND RESTATEMENT OF TORTS, SECTION 402 A

§402A. Special Liability of Seller of Product for Physical Harm to User or Consumer

(1)   One who sells any product in a defective condition unreasonably dangerous to the user or consumer or to his property is subject to liability for physical harm thereby caused to the ultimate user or consumer, or to his property, if

(a)   the seller is engaged in the business of selling such a product, and

(b)   it is expected to and does reach the user or consumer without substantial change in the condition in which it is sold.

(2)   The rule stated in Subsection (1) applies although

(a)   the seller has exercised all possible care in the preparation and sale of his product, and

(b)   the user or consumer has not bought the product from or entered into any contractual relation with the seller.

The rule stated in this Section does not require any reliance on the part of the consumer upon the reputation, skill, or judgment of the seller who is to be held liable, nor any representation or undertaking on the part of that seller. The seller is strictly liable although, as is frequently the case, the consumer does not even know who he is at the time of consumption. The rule stated in this Section is not governed by the provisions of the Uniform Sales Act, or those of the Uniform Commercial Code, as to warranties; and it is not affected by limitations on the scope and content of warranties, or by limitation to "buyer" and "seller" in those statues. Nor is the consumer required to give notice to the seller of his injury within a reasonable time after it occurs, as is provided by the Uniform Act. The consumer's cause of action does not depend upon the validity of his contract with the person from whom he acquires the product, and it is not affected by any disclaimer or other agreement, whether it be between the seller and his immediate buyer, or attached to and accompanying the product into the consumer's hands. In short, "warranty" must be given a new and different meaning if it is used in connection with this Section. It is much simpler to regard the liability here stated as merely one of strict liability in tort.

Note: While the law regarding strict liability can vary somewhat from state to state, the formulation contained in the Restatement is purported to represent the rule of law in a majority of states.

Source: 38 *University of Chicago Law Review*, p. 17, Products Liability, McKean.

---

[12] The Ferdanna Products Company sold all Ferdanna products.

tive damages, alleging that Ferdanna, Grand, and Perkins had acted wantonly and willfully in allowing the circumstances to exist which she said led to the explosion. Mr. Janse was suing to recover $50,000 in compensatory damages and an additional $50,000 in punitive damages for his medical expenses in caring for his wife and for the loss of "the services, companionship, society, affection, and consortium" of his wife.

Mr. and Mrs. Janse were suing to recover the compensatory damages under three legal theories: (1) strict liability, (2) breach of implied warranty of safety for intended use and (3) negligence. Mr. Newland knew that under the doctrine of strict liability the Janses, in order to recover, needed only to prove that a defect, either real or latent, existed in the can of Clear when it left Ferdanna or Grand's hands; that with the defect, the product was inherently dangerous; and that the defect did in fact cause the injuries suffered (see Exhibit 6). Recovery under the breach of implied warranty theory was very closely related to strict liability. Here, the court

Exhibit 7
UNIFORM COMMERCIAL CODE (U.C.C.)

Section 2–314. Implied Warranty: Merchantability, Usage or Trade.

(1) Unless excluded or modified (Section 2–316), a warranty that the goods shall be merchantable is implied in a contract for their sale if the seller is a merchant with respect to goods of that kind. Under this section the serving for value of food or drink to be consumed either on the premises or elsewhere is a sale.

(2) Goods to be merchantable must be at least such as
  (a) pass without objection in the trade under the contract description; and
  (b) in the case of fungible goods, are of fair average quality within the description; and
  (c) are fit for the ordinary purposes for which such goods are used; and
  (d) run, within the variations permitted by the agreement, of even kind, quality and quantity within each unit and among all units involved; and
  (e) are adequately contained, packaged, and labeled as the agreement may require; and
  (f) conform to the promises or affirmations of fact made on the container or label if any.

(3) Unless excluded or modified (Section 2–316) other implied warranties may arise from course of dealing or usage of trade.

Section 2–315. Implied Warranty: Fitness for Particular Purpose.

Where the seller at the time of contracting has reason to know any particular purpose for which the goods are required and that the buyer is relying on the seller's skill or judgment to select or furnish suitable goods, there is unless excluded or modified under the next section an implied warranty that the goods shall be fit for such purpose.

Note: At the present time, all states but one have adopted all or part of the Uniform Commercial Code as state law.

could assume a warranty[13] (i.e., promise or guaranty) had been made by Ferdanna and/or Grand that the product was safe for its intended use. If so held, the Janses needed to prove the breach of warranty and defend against possible claims of misuse in order to recover. (The defendants would be denying that there was any breach by them; in a sense they would blame Mrs. Janse for some action which led to the alleged explosion.) (See Exhibit 7.) The Janses also alleged numerous acts of negligence in their complaint. Proof of any one act and of causation would entitle them to recovery (see Exhibit 8). The last counts of their complaint alleged that the acts of negligence contained in the 5th Count were performed willfully and wantonly by Ferdanna and the other defendants to enable the Janses to receive double compensation for their alleged losses in the form of punitive damages.

Mr. Newland knew that Ferdanna had been sued three times previously for injuries resulting from explosions of allegedly unopened cans of Clear with the screw-on caps. He also knew that a number of memoranda had been circulated during the past year and a half regarding problems encountered with the Clear manufacturing process. He knew that any of these that might be even in the least incriminating would probably be introduced at trial and he was well aware that the Janse's attorney had subpoenaed any and all documents pertaining to Clear from the Production and Laboratory Departments. As he reflected on Ferdanna documentation procedures, he wondered how to best use the documents he had, how to guard against future losses in other product liability litigation, and how to avoid incidents such as the Janse accident altogether.

Exhibit 8
COUNT V

Now comes the plaintiff Mary Janse, complaining of the defendants, Grand Tea Company, a corporation, Ferdanna Products Company, a corporation, The Ferdanna Company, a corporation, and Perkins Can Company, a corporation, and says:

1. That on and prior to November 22, 1959, the defendant Grand Tea Company, a corporation, operated certain retail stores in the City of New York, State of New York, and in the said stores sold a product known as Clear for home cleaning purposes, which it knew or ought to have known had explosive and dangerous propensities and could cause injury to the vendees or members of their households.

2. That the defendant Perkins Can Company, a corporation, manufactured and sold to the defendant The Ferdanna Company, a corporation, or to the defendant Ferdanna Products Company, a corporation, a can which it knew was to contain a certain product known as Clear, the chemical components

---

[13] Often courts, in the interest of public policy, assume the existence of certain provisions in both unwritten and written contracts.

Exhibit 8 (*Continued*)

of which were of such nature as to be dangerous and explosive in character when used by third persons.

3. That the defendant Ferdanna Products Company, a corporation, and/or the defendant The Ferdanna Company, a corporation, manufactured and placed Clear into a can manufactured by the defendant Perkins Can Company, a corporation, or in the alternative manufactured the said can in which the Clear was contained; that Clear was to be sold to the public for use in cleaning parts of the home, and the defendants, and each of them, had knowledge of the dangerous characteristics of Clear as well as its explosive propensities.

4. That the plaintiff Mary Janse, prior to and at the time of the occurrence complained of on November 22, 1959, was in the exercise of ordinary care for her own safety; that while the said plaintiff was undertaking or preparing to use the said Clear, the said can and the Clear exploded, causing injury to her.

5. That the defendant Grand Tea Company, a corporation, was then and there guilty of one or more of the following wrongful acts:

a. Carelessly and negligently sold a product which it knew or should have known could cause injury;
b. Carelessly and negligently failed to examine the said product to ascertain its condition before selling it to its customers;
c. Carelessly and negligently failed to test the said product to ascertain its condition before selling it to its customers;
d. Carelessly and negligently stored the said product so that it built up internal pressure;
e. Carelessly and negligently permitted and allowed the said product to be and remain in a damp storeroom prior to distribution of the said product, which made the said product more susceptible to explosion;
f. Carelessly and negligently failed to warn the plaintiff Mary Janse of the dangerous characteristics of the said product;
g. Carelessly and negligently sold to the public a product which was dangerous in character without proper labeling of the product.

6. That the defendant Perkins Can Company, a corporation, was then and there guilty of one or more of the following wrongful acts:

a. Carelessly and negligently manufactured the component parts of the said can containing Clear;
b. Carelessly and negligently failed to inspect the said can to ascertain whether or not it was safe for the purpose for which it was to be used;
c. Carelessly and negligently failed to test the said can in question before leaving its place of manufacture to determine whether or not it was reasonably safe for the purpose for which it was employed;
d. Carelessly and negligently employed an improper design in the manufacture of the can for a product having the propensities of Clear;
e. Carelessly and negligently furnished a container for the said Clear which was insufficient and insecure, considering the character of the components of the product known as Clear;

Exhibit 8 (*Concluded*)

7. That the defendant Ferdanna Products Company, a corporation, and/or the defendant The Ferdanna Company, a corporation, were then and there guilty of one or more of the following wrongful acts:

a. Carelessly and negligently prepared for sale to the public a preparation known as Clear composed for the most part of caustic soda which would cause injury immediately upon contact with a human being, of which characteristics the defendants, and each of them, knew or ought to have known;

b. Carelessly and negligently failed to test the said completed product to ascertain whether it was safe and proper for the purpose for which it was sold, although they knew or ought to have known that further testing was necessary;

c. Carelessly and negligently failed to properly inspect the said completed product to ascertain whether it was proper or safe for the purpose it was to be sold, although they knew that such an inspection was necessary;

d. Carelessly and negligently failed to heed the admonitions of their quality control department;

e. Carelessly and negligently sold Clear to the public with loose caps, although they knew this presented a hazard;

f. Carelessly and negligently prepared for sale to the public Clear with lumps, indicating the presence of moisture, although they knew that the said condition was dangerous;

g. Carelessly and negligently employed an improper design for the manufacture of the can for a product of the propensities [sic] of Clear;

h. Carelessly and negligently employed an improper type of container for the said Clear;

i. Carelessly and negligently employed a container which in the event of any internal pressure would give at the seams and allow caustic soda to be spread into the area;

j. Carelessly and negligently failed to properly label the said product so that the public would know of the dangerous characteristics of the said product.

8. That as a direct and proximate result of one or more of the aforesaid wrongful acts on behalf of one or more of the aforesaid defendants, the plaintiff Mary Janse sustained injuries alleged in paragraph 5 of Count I of this complaint.

Wherefore, the plaintiff Mary Janse asks judgment in compensatory damages against the defendants, and each of them, in the sum of One Million Two Hundred Thousand Dollars ($1,200,000.00).

3

Types of Processes

In the first two chapters of this section we have discussed some tools for analyzing operating systems. In Chapter 1 we indicated that it is possible to describe an operating system with a process flow diagram containing all the tasks, flows, and storages in the system. Once this has been completed it has been possible to measure some characteristics of the system and its output and to analyze how these characteristics could be modified by management action. In Chapter 2 we described the idea of making tradeoffs between various output characteristics of the operating system.

In these chapters we have treated every process as though it were unique, however, you may have noticed some similarities between the various processes. For example, in Lowell Steel Corporation and the National Cranberry Cooperative, the good being produced flowed from task to task on a continuous basis with no storage except at the beginning and end of the process. In the Blitz Company and Senator Kenmore's Office, there was a dominant flow pattern through the process; however, any specific job might move through some tasks and not others. In addition, there was much storage within these two operations.

As you might expect it is possible to group operating systems in categories based on their similarities and differences. It is useful to make such categorizations if you are to develop reasonable expectations about operating systems. This process of generalization is typical in the study of sciences. For example, in biology, the animal kingdom has been classified according to similarities and differences. If the classification of a specific animal is known, it is possible to make some reasonable judgment about that animal wtihout performing a detailed analysis.

In this chapter we will describe three major types of processes: *A line or flow shop,* a *job shop,* and a *project.* We will try and relate some characteristics that are associated with each process type and give you some idea of the potential problems and opportunities associated with them. These categories are idealized and seldom in practice will you find an organization with only a single type of process. However, you will be able to isolate parts of many operations that correspond closely to one or another of our categories and your understanding of them will be aided if you look for their basic characteristics.

LINE OR FLOW SHOP

In a line or continuous processing system the tasks are arranged by the sequence of operations that are needed to make the product. The automotive assembly line, and the induction physical examinations in the "old" Army are two examples of line flow processes. There is a single flow and all products follow a definite progressive sequence from one task to the next. They all require that the same tasks be performed and consequently on the average take the same amount of time at each task. A simple line operation of seven tasks is shown below in Figure 3–1. In addition to the

Figure 3–1
A LINE

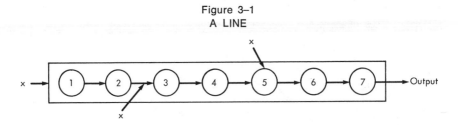

raw materials introduced at the beginning of the sequence, various materials, parts, or component inputs may be introduced along the line, shown as *x*s in Figure 3–1. However, every product follows the same path, uses the same inputs and neither skips tasks nor loops back. Although each task is connected directly to the preceding task by a single flow, it is not necessary that tasks be physically next to one another. Through the use of transportation methods, adjacent tasks can be physically remote from one another. The location of the tasks and nature of the flows do have important management implications. For instance, if the line is paced by mechanical conveyors, management must see that the work done at each task is completed at the same rate, otherwise, a single task can disrupt all the other tasks and flows in the process. Also, because of the continuous nature of the operation, there is little need for work-in-process storage under normal operations.

The capacity of a line operation is controlled by how long the operation runs. Because of the high degree of interrelation between the tasks they cannot be operated for long in isolation. Therefore, all tasks usually start and stop together. It is quite easy to calculate the capacity once the line is designed and its length of operation is known.

Most line operations are highly specialized and are not flexible. They usually produce only a small range of products. If a different product mix is desired, the operation must be replanned and the tasks balanced for this new output.

JOB SHOP

A job shop process is characterized by a large number of different products, each using a different set or sequence of tasks. The product flow in many general-purpose metalworking shops, and the flow of patients through special treatment units in a hospital are typical job shop processes. A given product will utilize only a few of the different tasks that are available in the system, and the tasks that are used as well as the sequence of flows will differ from one product to another. Typically, some tasks are specialized and often require large capital inputs (like heat-treating facility in a machine shop, or X-ray facility in a hospital). These tasks can only be economically operated when they serve many product lines. The resulting flow pattern in a job shop is one that varies from product to product or job to job. Figure 3–2 diagrams a job shop with the flow

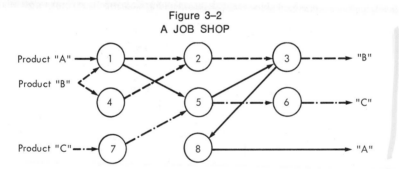

Figure 3–2
A JOB SHOP

patterns for three typical products. Product A goes through task 1, 5, 3, and 8. Product B goes through task 1 and 4 in parallel and then to 2 and 3 in a series. Product C goes to tasks 7, 5, and 6 and is done.

A job shop must provide a large amount of in-process storage. If two products need to have the same task performed on them simultaneously, clearly one must wait until the other is finished. The implication of this characteristic is that it is often difficult to precisely know the location of any product at any time. In addition, the time to complete the entire process is usually much longer than the sum of the processing times at each task. Both of these features make it important to have a good control system to keep track of jobs and provide data to estimate completion times.

Most job shops are very flexible and can produce different types of outputs with short notice. The capacity of a job shop is difficult to calculate because it depends on the particular product mix existing at any one time. As an example, a hospital operating room can handle many more patients if the operation is a tonsillectomy rather than open heart surgery.

PROJECT

A project organization is often related to unit production. It is concerned with the production of a unique, one of a kind, product or service that requires the coordinated inputs of large amounts of resources never before organized into a single process.

Because the product is a one-shot production, the usual separation between direct production process activity and so-called indirect functions like planning, marketing, purchasing, design, and other indirect functions is not meaningful. A project, therefore, is a process in which *all* activities that impinge on performance—technical, managerial, direct labor, or otherwise are managed as a total system. In projects the resources required for performance of project objectives are devoted to project purposes for the required periods of time. The project management problem then is one of marshaling these resources in time-phased sequence to best achieve goals. The project management scheduling problem is frequently represented as a network, as shown in Figure 3–3, showing the timing and prece-

Figure 3–3
A PROJECT NETWORK

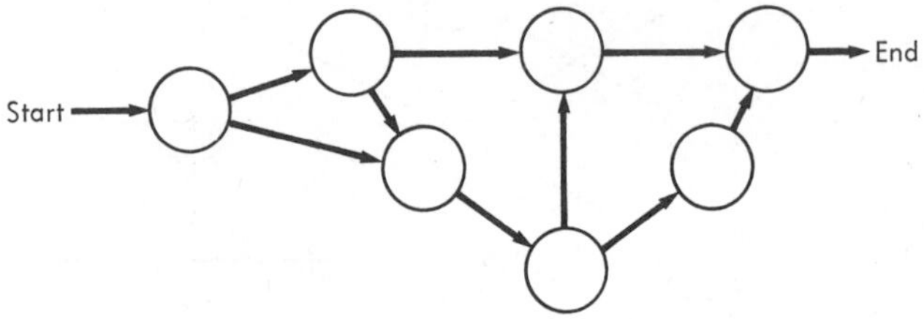

dent interdependence of all required tasks to the achievement of the planned outcome.

Construction, technological development, and the management of new products provide a few examples of activities that are frequently managed as projects.

IMPLICATIONS OF CHOICE OF PROCESS ORGANIZATION

By describing the "ideal" process organizations, we are able to highlight some performance characteristics of each particular type of process. For example, from the description of a line process we can see that there is a continuous flow of a single product from this process. What are the implications of having this type of process? Normally a continuous flow process will:

1. Require a continuous input of raw materials.
2. Have the capability of producing a high-volume output at low cost.
3. Have little flexibility to change products.

On the other hand a job shop operation will:

1. Require a large variety of different raw materials and often special order materials.
2. Have low-volume output capabilities and be a high-cost operation (because of idle machines not in a particular process).
3. Have a great deal of flexibility to change products.

Because of the nature of these differences in the performance characteristics of different process organizations, the choice of a type of process is often one of the most pervasive decisions that an organization makes. Although this decision involves the technology of the process, it is more a management decision than a technical one because it affects:

a. The overall economics of production—the cost of the product and the potential for future cost reduction.
b. Capital requirements—through direct investment implications and secondary implications for working capital requirements (through effects on inventory, direct and indirect work force structure and labor skills).
c. Product quality and reliability—the process design sets limits on the type of quality levels that can be attained and the need and opportunity to manage these.
d. Work environment—the basic structure of supervisory subordinate relationships (as well as nontask social relationships) between direct labor employees and supervisory personnel are influenced by process choice.
e. Opportunities for automation or other productivity enhancing improvements—standardization of tasks, specialization of labor, and systemization of product and information flows.
f. Labor relations—the role that organized labor plays in the organization, the issues of concern and frequently the specific union are influenced by the kind of process and the technology.
g. Market response—the ability to respond to market needs, in terms of variety, timing, product innovation, and cost are all process derived characteristics.

Table 3–1 highlights and compares some of the principal features of the three types of process organization and their effect upon performance characteristics.

Table 3–1
TYPICAL CHARACTERISTICS OF PROCESSES

	Line	*Job Shop*	*Project*
Suitability to Type of Product:			
Volume	Suited for high-volume standardized product.	Suited for product line that has low volumes of identical products and considerable variety in product characteristics.	Suited to large high-cost products with little standardization and low volume.
Product change	Change is costly since entire process must be changed or balanced with each product change.	Product changes are easily accommodated.	Well suited to continuous change—unique products.
Demand variation	Best suited to stable demand without heavy cyclicality.	Lumpy or uncertain product demand easily accommodated.	Wide variation in product demands are accommodated with labor variations.
Market type	Standardized mass-marketed product usually produced for inventory.	Production is usually to order or specialized for a market segment.	Production to customer specification or design.
Suitability to Method of Production:			
Task characteristics	Tasks with high specificity—well defined, divisible, teachable and of known duration.	Tasks with low specificity are accommodated. Difficult to acquire skills and uncertain or variable completion times.	Mixtures of task types are accommodated.
Capital embodied technology	Permits process automation via specially designed equipment often unique to product or industry and requiring technological development.	Permits capital intensity via general purpose equipment that can be purchased from several suppliers.	Relies on inexpensive general-purpose tools and equipment. Difficult to automate due to product variety, lack of standardization, and product size.
Human Inputs:			
Labor skills	Manual dexterity and tolerance for repetition.	Trade skills or craftsmanship.	Task flexibility depending on job.
Work environment	Highly visible paced performance, product-oriented teamwork, repetition, tightly coupled achieving unit.	Unpaced individual work, craft-skill specialization, fixed workplace and long-term assignments.	Changing work assignment and location. Variety in performance requisites.
Labor characteristics	Workers become highly proficient but only in one type of operation.	Valuable trade skills, trade union-oriented labor attitudes.	Industry-oriented skills, "shipbuilders, aircraft or construction workers."

Table 3–1 (Continued)

	Line	Job Shop	Project
Production Characteristics:			
Raw materials inventories	Low relative to the quantities consumed. Ideally the material is scheduled to arrive as needed.	Relatively high because buffer inventories are needed due to demand uncertainty and many types are required due to product variety.	Typically low but purchasing cost is high since it is ordered as needed and cannot be stocked due to unique nature of products.
Material handling	Usually automated and routine requiring little management control.	Extensive and demands much management control.	Relatively low but large equipment often required due to size.
In-process inventories	Very low because wait times between operations and material handling movements are short.	High because of movement delays and wait time before processing at each operation.	Typically high because large expensive units are produced and must be held during long periods of production.
Productivity	Typically high when demand is stable due to division of labor, specialization, and learning that occurs with scale. Little setup cost and, much opportunity for automation.	Labor tends to become efficient in machine operation for a variety of tasks but per unit productivity is lower than line operation due to setups and little repetitive learning opportunity.	Productivity is hard to control and dependent on individual motivation, as well as scheduling efficiencies.
Production control	Control is straightforward under stable conditions but indirect support in the form of maintenance, material supply and supervision is critical to avoid *complete* shutdown.	The variety of different jobs, uncertain completion times and large amounts of in-process inventory make job control necessary and complex.	The complexity of scheduling can vary considerably depending upon the responsibility assumed by the work force.
Capacity control	Capacity is well defined but expensive to change in even a moderate degree due to pervasive effects of change throughout the production system.	Capacity is ill defined but flexible within broad limits. As demand approaches capacity in-process inventory tends to become very large and out of control.	Capacity is rather flexible and easily varied.
Throughput time (manufacturing cycles)	Short. From start to finish, a given item is in-process only a short time.	Often quite long.	Moderately long due to time required to manufacture one unit.

CASES IN THIS CHAPTER

The four cases in this chapter will give you an opportunity to develop the skills of recognizing the various types of processes. You can also use these cases to improve your skills at process analysis and trade-off analysis.

The Fabritek Corporation is a machine shop that has just taken on a large new contract. Art-Tone Cards (A) is considering a new method for filling greeting card boxes. In both of these cases you should give careful consideration to the problems of worker attitude and motivation. The New Process Rubber Company (B) must balance their assembly line for a new rate of operation. After solving this line-balance problem, think about the management implications of this *technical job*. Finally, the Max-Able Medical Clinic (A) is considering the adoption of an automated testing center for examining patients and performing a series of standardized tests on them.

Fabritek Corporation

ONE AFTERNOON in March of 1969 Frank Deere, milling department foreman of the Fabritek Corporation, was approached by Stewart Baker,
Fabritek's automotive products manager.

> Hi, Frank. I hope that you've got good news for me about this
> week's Pilgrim order. I don't think that my nerves can take a repeat
> of last week.

Fabritek Corporation was organized in 1938 and in its early years had
specialized in machining castings for the packaging machinery industry.
In recent years the company had developed a strong position in the high
quality machined parts market. In 1968 Fabritek sold $15 million worth
of parts to 130 machinery and equipment manufacturers in several different industries. The Fabritek plant and offices were in Columbus, Indiana,
in a modern, single-story building with 150,000 square feet of floor space.

The company had worked hard to develop a reputation for rapid, on-
time delivery and competitive prices for its high quality machine work.
The president (the son-in-law of Fabritek's founder) stressed four key elements of the company's strategy for meeting these objectives: (1) a highly
skilled and well-paid work force; (2) a large number of general purpose
machine tools, readily adaptable to a wide variety of precision machinery
operations; (3) an engineering department capable of developing imaginative approaches to machining problems to produce quality parts at low
cost; and (4) a strong emphasis on inspection and quality control at several stages of the machining operations.

The company employed 250 workers, 200 of whom were engaged in
production and maintenance activities. The United Auto Workers represented Fabritek workers. In 1952, the U.A.W. had waged an intensive
organization drive at a nearby diesel engine plant; the union had subsequently signed an agreement with Fabritek without a vote by Fabritek
employees. Relations with the union had been cordial, due in part to the

fact that Fabritek's wage level had been consistently higher than those of other companies in the area.

Stewart Baker had joined the marketing department of Fabritek in June 1968, following his graduation from a graduate school of business. He had personally obtained Fabritek's first automotive parts contract early in January, after learning that one of the suppliers to the Pilgrim Corporation (a major auto manufacturer) was having delivery problems because of labor difficulties. The contract with Pilgrim required delivery of 17,000 units of a major engine part over a period of about six months. Specifically, weekly shipments of 650 units were to be made each Friday, starting January 31 and continuing until the contract was fulfilled. The part required machining a purchased casting to close tolerance since it was to be assembled into an engine where high temperature and friction stresses would occur.

Pilgrim officials had made it clear that this was a trial contract: if Fabritek's quality and delivery performance were satisfactory, larger and more permanent contracts were likely to follow. In mid-January, Mr. Baker was designated automotive products manager and given responsibility for establishing Fabritek in the automotive market.

Most of the company's machine tool operators were paid on incentive piece rates based on stop-watch time studies. In the event that an operator failed to meet standard performance he was paid at a base rate equal to the piece rate times the standard output rate. However, when an operator exceeded standard pace his earnings increased in direct proportion to his output. Actual experience with the incentive plan over a period of years showed that Fabritek machinists, on the average, performed at about 133 percent of standard. Most operators were able to earn considerable premium pay above their base rates, in some instances well over the 133 percent average. As a result the company assumed operation at 133 percent of standard for scheduling production and for balancing machine time and operator time.

Fabritek executives were anxious to prevent "machine interference" (forced idleness while an operator waited for a machine to complete its operation) from limiting the productive effectiveness of any operator who was capable of exceeding the standard. If there was machine interference on a job, any time saved by a proficient operator on his own operations would merely result in increased idle time per cycle for the operator, rather than in increased production. To avoid this, company executives had adopted a policy of attempting to assign enough machines to each operator to prevent machine interference from limiting an operator's productivity, even if the operator would thus exceed standard work pace by a considerable margin. In this way workers were assured that, within broad limits, their ability to earn premium pay would be determined by their own ability and willingness to maintain a premium work pace, and would not be impeded by machine interference.

At normal operating volume, sufficient numbers of the various machine-tools were available to allow this policy of assigning a liberal ratio of machines to men. When the volume of production rose, however, additional operators had to be hired to permit tighter scheduling of machine capacity. Under such circumstances the demands on setup men were heavy. When Stewart Baker obtained the Pilgrim contract in early 1969, the overall plant volume was well above normal. Specifications for the Pilgrim part required eight operations:

1. Unpack and visually inspect purchased casting.[1]
2. Rough mill bearing surface.
3. Finish mill bearing surface.
4. Mill face.
5. Mill keyway.
6. Drill eight holes.
7. Finish grind bearing surface.
8. Final inspection and pack.

Because of design characteristics, it was essential that all four milling cuts be made in fixed sequence (cut no. 1 before cut no. 2, etc.). At the time the job was undertaken there was considerable demand for milling machine capacity in the shop and the engineering department believed that it would not be possible to assign more than four milling machines to this sequence of operations without seriously disrupting the scheduling of other work in the milling department. It was anticipated that the demand for milling machine capacity would remain extremely high for some time to come, and that this fact would prevent even a subsequent assignment of more than four milling machines to this order. The four available machines were located in close proximity to each other and since they were equipped for automatic feed, it was possible for a single operator to run all four of them.

The method which the engineering department developed for the four milling operations required that each of the four milling machines be set up to make one of the required cuts. Other possibilities, such as combining cuts by using specially formed milling cutters or changing the design of the casting, were explored but were rejected on technical grounds. Setup time averaged two hours for each milling machine; setup men were paid $4.20 per hour.

Exhibit 1 shows the type of milling machine used for each of the four milling operations. The setup men mount the appropriate cutters, adjust the table for proper depth of cut, and set cams and stops which determine the direction and limits of table movement. Feed and speed rates (see footnote†, Exhibit 2) are set by moving levers to point to appropriate readings on indicator dials. In practice these levers are often missing and adjustments are made with a wrench.

---

[1] Castings which contained pits, scars, or excess flash, or which failed to meet other quality criteria were returned to the vendor.

Exhibit 1
DIAGRAMMATIC SKETCH OF A MILLING MACHINE

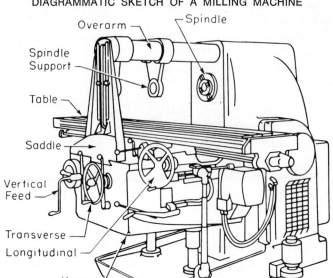

This sketch is of a general-purpose milling machine of the type used on the Pilgrim part. Fabritek generally uses this type of machine for production work rather than depending on higher speed, special-purpose machinery.

Three table movement hand controls are shown. Each of these movements is also provided with power feed in either direction. The table can be set up to follow an automatic cycle when it is to be used for a production job. The speed of table movement and the rotational speed of the cutter are set on indicator dials on the back of the machine.

The piece to be milled is clamped to the table. Cutters are mounted on a horizontal shaft which is rigidly supported by the spindle and spindle support. Table movement then feeds the work into the rotating cutters.

The machining processes to produce the Pilgrim part were set up in January 1969. A drill press and a grinder were moved close to the four milling machines. Two inspector/material handlers and two experienced machine operators, all of whom had been working together on another order, were transferred to the new job. One operator was assigned to the four milling machines, the other to the drilling and grinding operations. On their previous job the two machine operators had been paid on an individual incentive basis: the inspector/material handlers had been paid an hourly rate. These pay arrangements were continued on the new job. Since it was often difficult to trace the responsibility for quality problems or rejects, workers were paid on the basis of total output, rather than total good output.

The standard was set at 100 completely milled pieces per day for the milling operations. However, since an experienced worker was assigned to the milling machines, an output of at least 133 percent of standard was expected. Assuming the 133 percent output, a small cushion of 15 pieces per week would exist. Stewart Baker thought this was a bit tight, but was reluctant to add more men to the job because of the limited profit margin on the order.

Soon after production started, a smooth flow of material was obtained and no unacceptably large in-process inventories accumulated between operations.

The first shipment of 650 pieces was made on schedule on January 31. The group settled down to an average performance of 135 percent of standard. Frank Deere reported to Stu Baker that the group was continuing to work as well on this product as they had on their previous job. The group took rest and lunch breaks together as they had before moving to the Pilgrim part job.

After two deliveries had been made to Pilgrim the milling machines operator was involved in a weekend automobile accident. He was hospitalized with severe injuries and, although the exact time of his return could not be predicted, it was clear that he would be unable to return to work for several months.

On Monday morning, Frank Deere assigned a particularly skilled operator, Arthur Moreno, to the milling job. Moreno started the Pilgrim job after lunch. This assignment meant transferring Moreno from another job on which he had been earning substantial premium pay. His typical weekly takehome pay on that job—where he worked alone—had been $215 of which approximately $85 was premium pay attributable to working in excess of standard pace. The foreman believed, however, that production on Moreno's present job was coming to an end and that it would work out well to transfer him to the new job which would continue for several months.

Frank Deere and Stu Baker were pleased that the group had little difficulty in meeting the February 14th delivery. Moreno had learned the job well by the middle of the week and, except for an occasional build-up of inventory ahead of the drill and grinder, the transition seemed to be smooth and successful.

On Thursday, February 13, Moreno had mentioned to Frank that he thought he wouldn't be able to make as much money on the milling job as he had been making on his last job. Frank felt this mild discontent was to be expected from someone who had recently changed jobs.

On Tuesday, February 18, Arthur Moreno received his pay for the first full week's work on the new job. He burst in on Frank Deere waving a check for $174.14. "I told you this was a bum job, Frank, and here's the proof. I just can't go fast enough to make out on this job."

Frank thought that Moreno simply was used to working faster than the other members of his group, but realized that Moreno had raised a strong enough objection to have the job checked.

Just before lunch on Wednesday a time study man evaluated the milling job. Moreno, the foreman, and the time study man agreed that this study indicated that the original study (shown in Exhibit 2) was technically

Exhibit 2

CYCLE ANALYSIS FOR MILLING OPERATIONS ON PILGRIM PART NO. 37906
(all times in minutes—operation at the rate shown results in standard production of 100 pieces per day*)

	Total Cycle Time	Machine Time	Total Operator Time†	External Time†	Internal Time†
Milling Cut No. 1	3.594	2.600	1.139	.994	.145
Milling Cut No. 2	2.964	2.220	.992	.744	.248
Milling Cut No. 3	3.301	2.420	1.244	.881	.363
Milling Cut No. 4	1.725	1.118	1.035	.607	.428

* The operator has allowances of 39 minutes per day for personal time, fatigue, etc.

† Total Operator Time for each milling cut was divided between "Internal Time" (i.e., the time required for operations which the operator was expected to perform during the machine cutting time) and "External Time" (i.e., the time required for operations which the operator was not expected to perform or could not perform during the machine cutting time). Load and unload operations, for example, always required External Time. Total Cycle Time equalled Machine Time plus External Time. The operator times shown are summaries of observed element times (adjusted for pace). Machine times shown are derived from standard shop feed and speed tables. Feed rate is the rate at which the work piece is fed against the milling cutter. Speed rate is the rotational speed of the milling cutter. Setting the machine at the proper feed and speed rates was important for several reasons—to minimize undue stress, wear and tear on the motor and drive mechanism of the machine, to prevent rapid wear and damage to the cutting tool, and to insure a proper finish by preventing "tool chatter" or skips and jumps of the tool which would leave a rough, scratched, or bumpy surface finish on the piece being milled.

sound. Even though Moreno agreed with the figures shown in Exhibit 2, he restated to Frank that he was annoyed at not being able to make more than a 33 percent bonus. Frank admitted that all jobs in the line had been balanced for average work rates and told Moreno, ". . . . Don't worry about piling up work ahead of the next operation. If you want to go faster, go ahead."

By Thursday afternoon Moreno was upset again. He had run out of work and couldn't find the inspector/material handler who prepared the work pieces for the milling operations. The inspector had other duties as well as the Pilgrim auto part castings job, and was working in another part of the plant. The other workers told Moreno they didn't know where he was.

The next day, the Pilgrim shipment was made on schedule and, although work was beginning to pile up ahead of the drilling and grinding operation, there appeared to be no problems.

During the next week a new problem developed. The final inspector, who checked the parts before packing, rejected 38 pieces of Monday's and

Tuesday's output. Since the critical bearing surface on the part was out of tolerance and rough, the problem seemed to lie with the grinding operation. Frank Deere asked the drill and grinder operator, Paul Clark, to work three hours overtime on Wednesday to regrind some of the defective pieces and to cut into the accumulated backlog ahead of his machines. Clark was delighted with the opportunity for overtime work, but made it clear to Frank that he felt he was *not* responsible for the unacceptable bearing surfaces, commenting, "If you want to find trouble, ask Moreno. He's feeding me a lot of crap, and I've got to slow down the grinder feed to get a decent finish."

Moreno was now producing milled castings at a rate of 167 per day (167 percent of standard).

The February 28 shipment was made, but the company truck was delayed for an hour waiting for the last few parts to be finished, inspected, and packed.

By Tuesday, March 4, it was clear to Frank Deere that the quality problem was not solved and that, even with considerable overtime for Paul Clark, they were going to have difficulty making the Pilgrim shipment on Friday. During the afternoon Stewart Baker came to check on the Pilgrim run.

"Stu, we've got a real problem. It looks as though I'll have to add more

Exhibit 3
CHRONOLOGY

Jan.	31	Friday	First shipment
Feb.	3		
	4		
	5		
	6		
	7	Friday	Second shipment
Feb.	10	Monday	Moreno assigned to milling operations
	11		
	12		
	13	Thursday	Moreno's first complaint
	14	Friday	Third shipment
Feb.	17		
	18	Tuesday	Moreno's first paycheck for this job
	19	Wednesday	Time study re-evaluation
	20	Thursday	Moreno runs out of work
	21	Friday	Fourth shipment
Feb.	24		
	25		
	26	Wednesday	38 pieces rejected—Clark works overtime
	27		
	28	Friday	Fifth shipment—truck delayed
March	3		
	4	Tuesday	Discussion between Baker and Deere

people, replace someone, work overtime, or put on another grinder. Of course, I'll have to talk with the superintendent before I decide what I'm going to do here."

"Wait a minute," Stu replied. "We don't know what's causing those rejects yet. If we sweep this problem under the rug with something like overtime, we'll lose our shirts on this order."

"What else can I do, Stu? You want that order out on time, don't you?"

"Well, we were doing all right until a week or so ago. I think that Moreno must have something to do with it. It must bother Clark to see that pile of work ahead of him getting bigger every day. And Moreno's rushing may mean that Clark's grinding operation is slowing down. You know, I've never seen Moreno with that group except when they're on the job."

"I suppose you want me to take Moreno off the job. He's one of my best men. Look, Stu, you'll get your Pilgrim order on time. Now I've got other things to do. I've got 23 other millers to keep busy, you know."

Art-Tone Cards (A)

DURING THE first week in January of this year, workers in the Boxing Department of Art-Tone Cards were using three new methods for packing greeting cards and their envelopes prior to shipment to customers. Two of the methods had been installed in the department during the last two weeks of December by Bob Hayes, the company's only industrial engineer, who left the company on December 31 to take a higher level position with another company.

Mr. Conrad Rorick, the plant manager, had received a four-page memorandum from Mr. Hayes on December 31. The memorandum outlined the methods work which Hayes had done and gave production figures in the Boxing Department for December 28, 29, and 30. This memorandum, along with Mr. Hayes' working notes, constituted the written records of Mr. Hayes' work which were available to Mr. Rorick.

COMPANY BACKGROUND

Art-Tone Cards was one of several medium-sized companies in the greeting card industry. Its plant in Detroit, Michigan, produced greeting cards and also a small amount of gift wrapping materials. Art-Tone was an integrated producer; it designed, printed, and distributed greeting cards to retail outlets.

In recent years, Art-Tone's sales had been in excess of $10 million. Approximately half these sales were from "seasonal cards," such as those for generally recognized holidays. Christmas cards accounted for one-half of all the seasonal sales. The balance of sales were "everyday cards," such as birthday and get-well cards, which exhibited no seasonal sales pattern. At any one time, the company offered for sale about 4,000 different card designs.

The predominant distribution method in the greeting card industry was direct sale to retail outlets. Like Hallmark Cards, the largest company in the industry. Art-Tone sold exclusively to retail outlets. Most retailers sold the cards from display racks. It was customary for the rack spaces to be allocated to several card manufacturers, with the retailer deciding what percentage of the rack would be supplied by each manufacturer. It was generally conceded in the industry that sales depended on the rack space allocated to a company by retailers.

THE DETROIT PLANT

Art-Tone's Detroit plant was its only production facility in the United States. The two-story plant building was two years old and was located in a suburban area. The second floor housed the art and verse departments, the photographic department, and some of the administrative offices. Printing and other production departments and the main offices were located on the ground floor.

The production of cards began in the art and verse departments where the creative part of the process took place. Cards were printed on offset presses, using plates prepared by a photographic process. After printing, some cards were embossed, and then all the large sheets on which the cards were printed were cut to obtain the single, unfolded cards. The cards were then sorted by design and automatically folded. After folding, the cards were transported to another area where workers applied special effects and tied ribbons where required. Throughout these operations and those that followed, the operators continually inspected the cards, as they handled them, for dirt, oil smears, off-registered colors, wrinkles, process defects and other faults.

After the cards were completed, they were packed in wooden crates, each of which contained about 2,000 cards. These wooden crates of cards were held in storage before the final counting and packing. Envelopes were held in a separate inventory. Art-Tone's major supplier of envelopes was located nearby and could deliver envelopes of a requested size within one week after an order was placed. The envelopes were bundled by the supplier in packs of 12, fastened by a paper band.

Mr. Rorick supervised all the production activities on the ground floor. Approximately 1,000 people worked in the plant. Three subordinates reported directly to Mr. Rorick, each responsible for one part of the production process. Bert Suvalle, one of the three subordinates, had been hospitalized in December with a heart attack. By early January his condition had improved enough for him to leave the hospital, but it was uncertain when he might be able to return to work. Mr. Suvalle was in charge of the Finishing Section which included the operations from special effects application through the final shipment. Slightly more than 300 workers worked in the finishing Section. Six section heads reported directly to Mr. Suvalle. In January, they were being supervised by the plant manager. One of these section heads, Miss Hudson, was in charge of the Boxing Department.

THE BOXING DEPARTMENT

The Boxing Department prepared both everyday and seasonal cards for the order-filling department. The cards were received in the Boxing Department in the wooden crates. Envelope bundles were delivered to the department in sizes corresponding to the cards to be processed. The workers in the department counted the cards and placed them in piles of 12. A bundle of envelopes was placed with each pile. The combined stack of 12 cards and 12 envelopes was then placed in a container, which in turn was placed in a corrugated paper box. The corrugated boxes, called shippers, were used for delivery to the order-filling department.

When the shippers went to the order-filling department they contained only one card design. The order-fillers made up shipments to customers by taking containers of card designs from various shippers as prepared by the Boxing Department and placing them in a shipper which would go to the customer. Orders typically contained as many as 30 different card designs.

A large inventory of cards was kept in the order-filling department so that the Boxing Department seldom was required to rush through an order of a particular card. The company manufactured seasonal cards far enough ahead so that the total volume of cards through the Boxing Department was nearly constant throughout the year. This total volume of cards was expected to approximate 800,000 cards per day during the current year. About 48 percent of the cards processed through the Boxing Department in a year were seasonal cards and the balance were everyday cards. This proportion was closely maintained throughout the year.

Because of the even volume of cards passing through the Boxing Department, the work force was held at about 43 people throughout the year. In January 22 of these laborers were working on everyday cards. In addition to the 43 workers the department had five materials handlers. The department worked a seven and one-half hour day, with two ten-minute breaks, which brought actual production time down to 430 minutes per day. The plant workers were members of a union.

Up until July of last year, the Boxing Department had used a small cardboard box as the container in which the pile of counted cards and the bundle of envelopes were placed. The boxing operation had been accomplished through the use of a conveyor belt with six work positions. The first worker placed the small open box and its cover on the end of the conveyor belt. The next two workers took cards from wooden crates, counted them into stacks, and placed the stacks on the belt. The next worker on the belt placed envelope bundles on top of each pile of cards. The fifth worker placed the combined pile of envelopes and cards into the box and put the lid on the box. The sixth worker removed the boxes from the conveyor and stacked them.

The stacks of filled boxes were then taken to another area in the department where labels were applied to the ends of boxes. These labels indicated the number and type of cards in the box. Since most orders were very small the 12-card box provided an acceptable basic shipping quantity for one card design. The small boxes were packed into shippers for delivery to the order-filling department.

THE PAPER PACKER

In an effort to reduce costs, Art-Tone introduced a paper "packer" as a substitute for the cardboard box to contain the everyday cards. This packer was used for all everyday cards starting in the previous summer. The packer was a manila envelope, with a flap on the long side. One size packer, eight and one-half inches long, accommodated 90 percent of the cards in the everyday line, and the balance of the designs fitted in a second size packer, ten inches long, except for about ten designs which required a box because of their unusual thickness.

By adopting the packer on everyday cards, Art-Tone was able to replace 102 sizes of the small boxes with two sizes of packers. Whereas the boxes had required 47 sizes of shippers, the packers could be fitted into two sizes of shippers. Art-Tone also realized savings by eliminating the hand labelling operation for everyday cards. The packers could be printed within 24 hours to meet the requirements of runs scheduled in the Boxing Department.

The packers were not introduced in the seasonal line because Art-Tone feared retailer resistance. When the dealer received everyday cards, he withdrew the cards and envelopes from the packer, placed some in his display rack, placed the balance into numbered files in rack drawers, and threw away the packer. In seasonal cards, however, the dealers purchased ahead in quantities larger than could be displayed or stored in the drawers in the display rack. The retailer could easily stack the small boxes in his storeroom, but the paper packers would be more difficult to store. Hallmark had introduced packers in its everyday line before the last summer, as had other manufacturers, but Hallmark had not experimented with packers on its seasonal line until its Fathers' Day cards in June. Even though Art-Tone's dealer survey indicated this innovation was successful, Art-Tone felt that Fathers' Day cards were too low a volume seasonal card to serve as a fair test of dealer acceptance.

When the packer was introduced in the Boxing Department in July, the method used for packing was a slight adaptation of the method used previously with the boxes. Two of the department's four conveyors were changed to accommodate the packers. The new worker arrangement is shown in Exhibit 1.

The first worker on the belt inserted a bundle of envelopes in a packer and placed the packer on the belt. The next two workers counted out stacks of cards and placed them on the belt. The fourth worker placed

Exhibit 1
LAYOUT FOR THE SIX-OPERATOR BELT METHOD

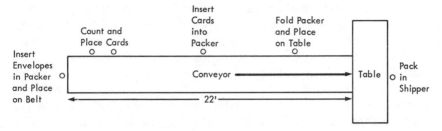

a stack of cards in the packer and the fifth worker folded over the packer flap, removed the packer from the belt and put it on a table. The sixth worker took the filled packers from the table and packed them in a shipper.

At the time the packers were introduced in the Detroit plant, Art-Tone's Canadian affiliate was using the same packer in its Boxing Department. The Canadian plant was averaging 175 packers per hour for each worker on the line, using the same six-operator method and layout shown in Exhibit 1. Since Art-Tone had been getting 212 boxes per hour for each worker in the Boxing Department before shifting to packers, Art-Tone management was concerned that increased labor costs might offset the savings in changing to the packer. The number of cards contained in either a box or packer was the same.

As the result of a study made by a management trainee, the plant manager authorized two measures intended to reduce costs for filling the packers; one of them based on a simplified manual operation, and the other using a mechanical aid to filling the packers. The first measure was to assign the plant industrial engineer, Bob Hayes, the job of improving the six-operator belt method which was then being used with the packers. The method he developed as a result of this assignment is described below as the "single-operator method." The second measure was the placing of an order for a Tele-Sonic machine. The salesman representing the manufacturer of the Tele-Sonic machine claimed that his company could adapt the machine for use with the packers and that it could produce at a rate of at least 26 packers per minute. On the basis of this claim and the experience of Art-Tone personnel with other models of the machine, an order was placed for one machine in July of the past year.

THE SINGLE-OPERATOR METHOD

As Bob Hayes worked to improve the packing methods, he decided to experiment with a single-operator method. In this arrangement, each laborer worked at a separate table, with all materials supplied to the table by the materials handlers. The materials handlers also took away the finished shippers. Each operator arranged the materials on a table and then filled the packers and placed them in the shipper. Packers, envelopes, and cards were placed by the materials handlers in open boxes along the rear of the table. The worker first arranged enough packers on the table to fill one shipper. The operator then placed the same number of envelope bundles in a loose pile on the right of the packers. The operator reached under the table to get a shipper from the stack stored there and placed one open shipper on the table to the left. The operator next reached into the container of cards, took a handful, counted them into stacks of 12, and placed the stacks on the table beside the envelopes. The operator was then ready to fill the packers and pack them in the shipper. In his memo and throughout his training of the operators, Mr. Hayes emphasized the necessity of arranging the materials on the table neatly to achieve high output.

Exhibit 2 shows the workplace layout developed by Bob Hayes for the

Exhibit 2
LAYOUT FOR THE SINGLE-OPERATOR METHOD

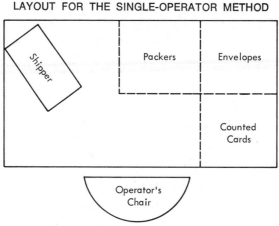

single-operator method, and Exhibit 3 is Hayes' calculation of the total time required to fill one shipper, including the operations which were performed only once in the filling of a shipper. These times were all derived from MTM standard data. (See footnote to Exhibit 3.)

Hayes used the standard times he calculated to set goals for the five workers he trained in the single-operator method. He began training the five workers on December 14, and he had given each about six hours of instruction when they began to use the single-operator method in the Boxing Department on December 21. Hayes kept no records of their learning progress during the training, but he estimated that on the last day of training the slowest operator was producing at the rate of 1,000 packers per day and the fastest, 1,700 packers. The only production figures which

Exhibit 3
TIME STANDARD FOR SINGLE-OPERATOR METHOD

Element	Element Time* (minutes)	Frequency per Shipper	Normal Time per Shipper
1. Get packers	.0384	1	.0384
2. Get envelopes	.0425	1	.0425
3. Get shipper	.1088	1	.1088
4. Count cards	.0025	360	.9000
5. Fill and pack	.0698	30	2.0940
6. Aside shipper	.1088	1	.1088

3.2925 minutes per shipper
+ 15% personal and fatigue allowance
= 3.7825 minutes per shipper
divided by 30 packers per shipper
= .1261 minutes per packer

* All the times were developed using Methods-Time Measurement (MTM). This is a method of developing "synthetic" time standards by breaking down the work into elements, to which predetermined times are assigned. The time assigned to each work element is intended to represent the time required by an average proficient worker at a normal pace without allowance for unavoidable delay, fatigue, or personal time.

were kept for the five workers were for December 28, 29, and 30. On those three days the average production per operator was 1,415, 1,332 and 1,610 packers per day.

THE TELE-SONIC MACHINE

On December 24, the Tele-Sonic machine was delivered to the Art-Tone plant in Detroit. The billed price to Art-Tone was $800, but the manufacturer said he would not deliver another machine for less than $1,500 because of the difficulties encountered in adapting it to take the Art-Tone packer.

The Tele-Sonic machine was a flat table, approximately three feet by four feet, under which were mounted two small fans. The air blast from the fans was directed through a tube to the top of the table. Seventy-five packers were held in a recess in the top of the table so that the packer on top of the pile was just flush with the surface of the table. The packer's open side was pointed toward the air jet. The packer was held in place by two small metal arms inserted into the packer from the open end. The blast of air held the packer open so that, with one hand, a person could slide a stack of cards and bundle of envelopes into the open mouth of the packer. By continuing the motion, the hand could push the packer and its contents off the two metal arms. The other hand could then take the packer and place it on another table at the side of the Tele-Sonic machine. As the packer left the two metal arms, a spring-loaded device raised the pile of packers to bring the next packer even with the metal arms. The blast of air opened the packer and the arms again engaged the edges of the packer. The machine was thus automatically ready for another cycle. An MTM study by Bob Hayes produced an estimated time of .0374 minutes to perform this cycle given that envelopes, cards, and packers were available when needed.

Bob Hayes had worked out the layout for the Tele-Sonic machine shown in Exhibit 4 before the machine was delivered, so that he was able to start

Exhibit 4
LAYOUT FOR TELE-SONIC MACHINE

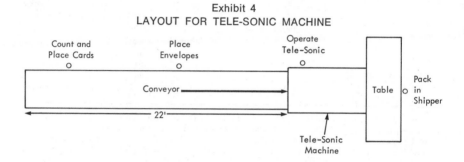

training the four operators on December 24. The machine was put in production in the Boxing Department on December 28. In the first three days of production the four operators on the team using the machine produced 4,065, 6,700, and 6,178 packers per day.

Bob Hayes had estimated (using MTM) that it would take .042 minutes to place one bundle of envelopes on the conveyor in the Tele-Sonic method. Similar calculations indicated a time of .03 minutes to count and place 12 cards on the conveyor, and .024 minutes to place a filled packer in a shipper. From these calculations, Hayes decided that the first worker on the conveyor would count cards and the second worker would place envelopes.

THE FIRST WEEK IN JANUARY

After the New Year's holiday, Miss Hudson had 12 laborers working on the single-operator method. Since Mr. Hayes was gone and she felt incapable of training the seven workers, she had directed the five operators already trained to teach the others. The operators were deviating from the method developed by Hayes. They were using the same general hand motions, but none of the workers was carefully laying out the work area as planned by Hayes. The workers were particularly sloppy in placing the stacks of counted cards. Occasionally one of the counted stacks of cards would fall over or become entangled with another stack. As a result, the operators lost time when reaching for stacks of cards.

Everyday cards were being processed not only by the twelve single operators, but also by one belt running on the Tele-Sonic machine, and by a second belt which was used with the six-operator method. The six-operator line had never exceeded production of 9,400 packers per day, and its production had been as low as 6,202 packers on December 28. Average production for the belt during December was 9,100 packers per day. These three methods handled all the everyday cards for the Boxing Department. One materials handler was serving the two belts and a second materials handler was able to support the twelve single operators. The Boxing Department's other two belts were being used for the seasonal cards. Six operators worked on each of these belts with the remaining nine workers labeling the boxes and placing them in shippers.

In January, Art-Tone was considering introducing packers in the seasonal cards. Hallmark had used packers with their entire Christmas line and Art-Tone was awaiting results of a survey of dealer reaction to determine whether they would go to packers on the seasonal cards. If dealers accepted the Hallmark packers, Art-Tone anticipated all the card manufacturers would follow Hallmark's lead to avoid mixed types of containers for the retail dealers.

Mr. Rorick had recently discharged Miss Hudson's assistant in the Boxing Department and he had no replacement in mind. In the absence of Mr. Suvalle, Mr. Rorick realized he would have to continue to take responsibility for activities in the Boxing Department.

If production per minute increases may get seasonal cards done to quick & may hav to lay off workers.

New Process Rubber Company (B)

THE NEW PROCESS RUBBER COMPANY manufacturers a wide line of rubber footwear, waterproof wearing apparel, and industrial gas masks for other concerns. Its Standards Department makes continual revisions in time standards as product designs are changed, new materials are introduced, and new methods are developed. For new products, the department participates in preparing bids, planning production methods, and establishing final production standards and piece rates. Typical of the new products was a face blank assembly for an industrial mask. The Standards Department was instructed to revise the production layout for the assembly of gas masks so that there would be a 50 percent increase in output.

The assembled face blank for the gas mask is made up of 10 parts: a face blank, a lens blank, two transparent plastic lenses, a valve stay, four buckles, and a join strip (see Exhibit 1). The face blank, the lens blank, the valve stay, and the join strip are cut with dies from sheets of rubber stock on blanking presses, the lenses are stamped out of sheets of plastic, and the buckles are purchased from another manufacturer. In the assembly of the mask the lenses and lens blank are cemented to the inside of the face blank in such a manner than the lenses are held in position between the face blank and the lens blank. The vent stay is also cemented to the inside of the face blank where it serves as reinforcement for the hole punched in the mask to permit attachment of the exhaust valve. The four buckles are attached by forming a loop in the straps and cementing down the ends. The two chin straps are cemented together in a butt joint which is covered inside and out by the join strip. The assembled mask is then vulcanized in large ovens, packed, and shipped.

A year ago, when New Process decided to begin manufacture of the gas mask, the Standards Department assisted in preparing bid prices and determining output schedules. In making these estimates, the Standards Department studied the blueprints and specifications and broke down the job into operations by drawing on past experience with similar products

Exhibit 1

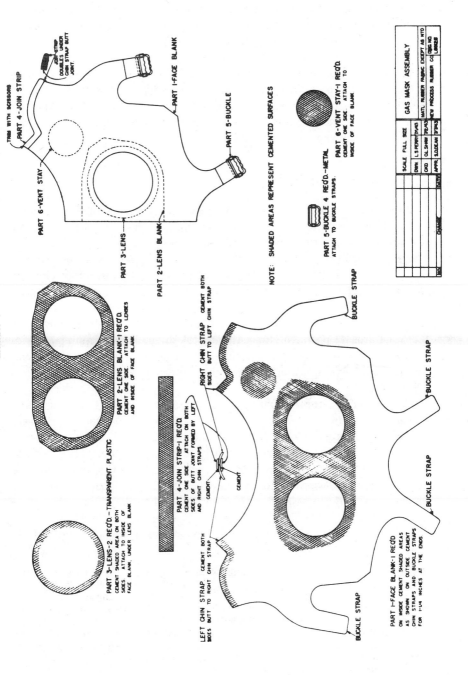

and by visualizing the work that would have to be done at various stages of construction. It then estimated the direct labor time that each operation would require. The time estimates were determined from past experience, by comparison with similar operations on other products, and by use of constants for certain common elements. The sum of the time estimates for each operation provided a basis for calculating the maximum output of the unit. Moreover, the department could readily convert the total direct labor time into a direct labor cost. To this figure it could apply standard overhead rates and estimate the total cost by adding material costs, which were calculated from blueprints and design specifications.

PRODUCTION PLANNING

After the company received the contracts it began production planning by dividing the entire job into major sections, such as preparation of the raw rubber, calendering, cutting out, assembling, vulcanizing, and shipping. The superintendent of each division then became responsible for deciding the best method of doing the job in his area. In the assembly division, for example, the superintendent had to decide whether the gas mask would be assembled on a table, a swivel jack, a conveyor, or a conveyor belt.[1] In reaching decisions on such points the division heads drew heavily on the Standards Department for estimates of direct labor requirements for each of these setups. For the gas masks the decision was to arrange assembly operations along a flat conveyor belt approximately 60 feet long and 4 feet wide.

Certain other service departments also assisted the division superintendents. The Technical Service Department constructed several of the masks by hand and experimented with different rubber compositions, cements, gums, and technical processes. Similarly, the process engineers aided the division heads in deciding on machines, jigs, fixtures, and tool design. The process engineers worked closely with the Standards Department because in many cases the advisability of installing a particular jig or other piece of equipment depended largely on the direct labor time it would save.

Following completion of the production planning for all phases of the

---

[1] A table was a stationary bench fitted with appropriate tools and jigs where the assembly work could be performed by a single operative or crew of operatives. A swivel jack was a rotary piece of assembly equipment so arranged that a last or other holding device could be loaded by an operative at one station and then rotated in a circle to one operative after another for successive operations until the completed unit returned to the starting point. A conveyor was any mechanical system of material transport such as an overhead train of moving hooks which would carry an article from the operative performing the first operation to the one performing the second operation and so on until the unit was completely assembled. A conveyor belt was a moving, flat canvas belt. As each operative completed work on a unit, it was placed on the belt, which carried it to the operative farther down the line who performed the next operation.

job, the conveyor belt for the assembly of the gas masks was installed and the required equipment arranged along it. The Standards Department gave the Assembly Department a rough estimate of the way in which the assembly work along the conveyor should be divided into operations and the number of operatives which should be assigned to each job in order to secure the desired output of approximately 2,000 units per day. In making this preliminary lineup, the Standards Department was influenced largely by the natural divisions between operations, but at the same time it attempted to divide the work on the basis of rough time estimates so that each operative would have approximately the same amount of work to do. Instructors in the Assembly Department then worked out at experimental tables an efficient routine for performing each operation. After the operatives had been hired and trained on these routines, the belt was started in operation.

MEASURING THE JOB

In the initial stage of operation the conveyor belt was badly out of balance. Some laborers had to work at an excessive rate of speed to keep pace with the belt, while people on the other operations were working slowly or were idle a portion of the time. From observation alone it was impossible to tell how underloaded or overloaded each operative was and what a proper division of the work should be. Moreover, there was no basis for accurately calculating the daily output that could be expected from the assembly crew. The Standards Department was, therefore, called in to measure the job and, thus, provide a basis for obtaining a more satisfactory balance, determining production requirements, and calculating standards for payment.

The Standards Department had three procedures at its disposal for measuring a job or operation.

1. Time-study with a stopwatch.
2. Motion-time analysis using constants for basic muscular movements.
3. Comparison with similar job elements and application of constant values.

In the first procedure, a stopwatch timed one of the workers performing the operation. In the second method, the operation was broken down into basic muscular movements to which standard values could be applied. The sum of the times for these basic movements gave the time required for a complete operation or one of its elements. In the third procedure, the time for an element of an operation was determined by comparison with a similar element of some other operation for which a standard time had previously been established by one of the first two methods. Regardless of the procedure used, the objective was the same: to determine the time in minutes that an average operative working at normal rate of speed would require to complete a particular operation on one unit.

The method of measurement selected by the Standards Department in a particular instance depended on the nature of the job. If the product were radically different from anything the company had ever made, the extent to which standards could be established by the use of basic data would be limited. Nevertheless, the company had found that in almost any new job there were handling elements, such as loading and unloading a fixture, which were of sufficient uniformity to permit the use of established values. The time-study procedure was faster than motion-time analysis and was used where circumstances required that standards be set quickly. The motion-time analysis, however, had an advantage in that the extensive motion analysis which it involved often yielded valuable improvements in the method of doing the work.

For the assembly of the gas masks, the operations were measured by time studies with a stopwatch and standard times were determined for each element of each operation. The Standards Department used the element times in drawing up plans for balanced conveyor operation. These plans were subsequently submitted to the Assembly Department by means of a "standards letter" (Exhibit 2). Copies of this letter were also sent to the timekeeping section, the Cost Department, and the ticket office, which was responsible for making out production schedules. (Exhibit 3 shows a rough sketch of the conveyor belt laid out to operate in accordance with these plans, and Exhibit 4 gives a more detailed explanation of the various operations. These two exhibits were not a part of the standards letter as prepared by the company.)

THE IMPORTANT CONSIDERATIONS

In developing plans for the gas mask conveyor lineup the Standards Department first grouped the job elements into operations and determined the number of workers to be assigned to each operation. Several considerations were important.

1. The balance of work between operations. The more evenly balanced the division of labor was, the more efficiently and economically the line functioned.

2. The natural split-up of the work. A perfect balance could be obtained on any lineup if elements were grouped without regard for natural divisions between operations. Such a procedure, however, usually distrubed the regular cycle of the work, created secondary operations that would not otherwise be necessary, or made it impossible to trace back defective work to the operative responsible. In the assembly of the gas mask, for example, it was clearly impractical to have an operative apply cement to one side of the face blank and a second operative to the other side, because that would have required locating each face blank in two separate jigs.

Exhibit 2
STANDARDS LETTER
STANDARDS FOR DEPARTMENT 511—GAS MASK MAKING 17 OPERATIVES

Base Rate	Operation	Number of Operatives	Standard per Mask
A	*Cement Lens Blank*	1	0.33 min.
	(.16) Dip brush, cement lens blank		
	(.06) Separate and aside to vellum		
	(.06) Vellum and blank to belt		
	(.005) Position new pile of blanks		
	(.035) Clean vellum under blanks		
	(.01) Clean hands		
A	*Cement Face Blank*	4	1.27
	(.16) Blank to jig		
	(.11) Close and lock jig		
	(.22) Cement lens blank area		
	(.17) Cement chin straps		
	(.06) Cement vent reinforcement area		
	(.03) Turn jig over		
	(.20) Cement chin straps and buckle straps		
	(.09) Turn jig over, unlock, open		
	(.11) Face blank from jig to drying rack		
	(.09) Face blank from drying rack to belt		
	(.015) Refill cement pot		
	(.015) Change jig		
A	*Assemble Mask*	2	0.59
	(.07) Two lenses from rack to table		
	(.20) Get face blank from belt, apply to lenses, turn over		
	(.16) Lens blank and vellum from belt, aside vellum, apply lens blank		
	(.055) Get valve stay from paper and apply		
	(.04) Aside mask to belt		
	(.02) Turn lens rack around		
	(.01) Aside empty valve stay paper		
	(.005) Aside and arrange pile of vellum		
	(.015) Lens rack to service person		
	(.015) Full lens rack to position		
A	*Assemble Buckles*	2	0.49
	(.05) Mask from belt to table		
	(.39) Get supply of buckles and attach		
	(.05) Aside to belt		
A	*Press Mask**	2	0.52
	(.05) Mask from belt to bench		
	(.16) Stitch each buckle strap close to buckle and at end of strap		
	(.03) Open press		
	(.08) Remove vellum from mask previously in press, mask from tray to belt		
	(.20) Place new mask in tray in press, cover with vellum and to press		

Exhibit 2 *(Continued)*

Base Rate	Operation	Number of Operatives	Standard per Mask
C	*Join Mask*	5	1.56
	(.20) Get join strip and last to horse		
	(.23) Get mask from belt, apply right chin strap to join strip		
	(.17) Apply left chin strap to join strip		
	(.15) Roll joint, stitch throat		
	(.07) Fold down top of join strip		
	(.19) Roll strip, stitch across throat and along edges of strip		
	(.10) Remove work from horse and place on horse other side out		
	(.19) Roll strip, stitch across throat and along edges of strip		
	(.10) Remove mask from horse		
	(.02) Swab horse		
	(.13) Get scissors and trim off excess join strip, aside mask to form		
	(.01) Clean horse		
C	*Inspect, Redeem, and Rack Gas Masks*	1	0.28 min.
	(.06) Inspect one mask, removing blisters and wrinkles in join strip as necessary		
	(.08) Walk to and from rack truck		
	(.03) Place masks on tray		
	(.005) Record		
	(.005) Rip defective join strip from mask		
	(.01) Rip defective mask apart completely		
	(.015) Move out full trucks		
	(.015) Move in empty trucks		
	(.01) Return bad mask to operative, explain mistake		
	(.014) Consult instructor		
	(.005) Move trays in truck		
	(.03) Take full board of join strips to joining operatives, remove and aside empty join strip board		
	(.001) Pick up masks fallen from form		

Peak	Total Work Conveyed	Balance Delay	Unit Standard Time	Ticket	Belt Speed
0.33	5.04	0.30 minutes (5.6%)	0.314	1880	13.4 sec. per space

* A mask had to remain in the press a little over 7 seconds, or about 0.12 minutes.

Similarly, if one operative attached one lens to the face blank and left the other to be attached by an operative farther down the line, extra operations and an unnatural break in the work would have resulted.

3. The number of operatives desired by supervision.

4. The daily production required. This consideration is closely related to the preceding one. The normal procedure in making conveyor line-ups is to use the maximum number of operatives for which work space is available and for which a well-balanced lineup can be devised. This practice secures the highest possible output from production equipment.

Exhibit 3

CONVEYOR LAYOUT IN ACCORDANCE WITH STANDARDS LETTER

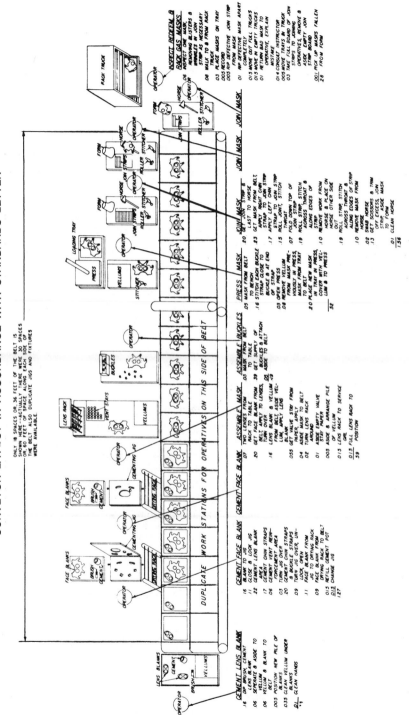

ONLY 18 SPACES OR 36 FEET OF THE BELT IS
SHOWN HERE—ACTUALLY THERE WERE 30 SPACES
OR 60 FEET OF SPACE ALONG EACH SIDE OF
THE BELT ALSO DUPLICATE JIGS AND FIXTURES
WERE AVAILABLE.

DUPLICATE WORK STATIONS FOR OPERATIVES ON THIS SIDE OF BELT

Exhibit 4
DETAILED DESCRIPTION OF OPERATIONS

Cement Lens Blanks

This operation was performed by a laborer working at a flat table at the head of the conveyor belt. The lens blanks were supplied in piles of 20 or 30 at a time. Adhering lightly to one side of each blank was a brown paper duplicate which came from a paper sheet placed under the rubber stock at the time the lens blanks were stamped out. The worker dipped a brush in a can of cement, applied the cement to one side of the lens blank, separated the lens blank from the paper duplicate, and placed it on a flat sheet of paper or vellum about 18 inches square. The vellum was then placed on the conveyor belt. The vellums were used to carry the parts in order to keep the cement from coming directly in contact with the belt. They were used over and over again, and it was the duty of the operative at the head of the belt to see that they were kept relatively clean and did not accumulate an excessive amount of cement.

Cement Face Blank

Workers performing this operation stood in front of small jigs, two on each side of the belt. The jigs consisted of two flat boards hinged at one edge so that they could be opened and shut like the covers of a book. In both boards certain areas were cut away so that when a face blank was inserted between them the top half of the jig would expose the surfaces to which cement was to be applied on one side of the face blank and the bottom half, the surfaces to which cement was to be applied on the other side of the face blank. The face blank was properly located between the two halves, and the jig was closed and locked. The operative applied cement to the areas exposed through the top half of the jig, turned the jig over, and repeated the procedure for the underside of the jig. The jig was then turned over again, unlocked, and opened. Since the face blank had cement on both sides, it was hung on an adjacent rack for a few minutes to allow the cement to dry slightly before it was placed next to the lens blank on one of the vellums coming down the belt from the first operative. There were three sizes of face blanks, small, medium adult, and large adult, and the operatives had to change their jigs every time a different size was run.

Assemble Mask

The two laborers performing this operation worked at flat tables, one on each side of the belt. Lenses which had previously been given a coat of cement about ¼-inch wide around the circumference on both sides and arranged in special racks were supplied by service workers. The operative took two lenses and placed them the proper distance apart on a table, then took a face blank from the belt, centered it properly over one of the lenses, and pressed it down. This process was repeated for the other lens. The worker then turned over the face blank with the two lenses adhering to the underside and laid it flat on the table. The operative next took the vellum and the lens blank from the belt, laid the vellum aside, and pressed the lens blank down over the lenses. Finally, the operative pressed a valve stay down in the proper

Exhibit 4 (*Continued*)

place and returned the assembled mask to the conveyor belt. The valve stays were supplied to the operatives on square sheets of paper, each containing about 36 stays.

Assemble Buckles

This operation was performed by two workers sitting at flat tables one on each side of the belt. The supply of buckles was contained in an ordinary shoe box on the table in front of each operative. From time to time the operative secured a handful of buckles from the box and spread them out on the table in a convenient position. In assembling the buckles, the operative first took a mask from the belt and laid it flat on the table. The worker then slipped the end of a strap under the end rung in one of the buckles, folded it back, and pressed it down so that the buckle was held in the loop thus formed in the end of the strap. The other three buckles were attached in an identical fashion. The mask was then returned to the belt.

After this operation, the conveyor belt carried the masks under a roller which ran across the width of the belt and served to press the cemented parts firmly together.

Press Mask

The two workers performing this operation were equipped with small presses which were nothing more than a device for pressing the masks between two flat boards. The masks were loaded into the press on a tray which had raised bosses to distribute the pressure in the proper places. The press was opened and closed by means of a foot pedal. It was necessary that the mask remain in the press for about 7 seconds, and in order to make use of this time, the operation was performed in the following manner. While one mask was in the press, the operative took another mask from the belt, placed it on a bench beside the press, and stitched down the buckle straps by running a small roller with a dull edge on the circumference along the edges of the cemented joints. The worker next opened the press and moved the tray back into the loading area. The vellum covering the mask during the pressing operation was removed and the mask returned to the belt. The operative then located the mask which had just been stitched on the loading trap, covered it with a piece of vellum, and moved it into the press.

Join Mask

This operation was performed by five workers grouped around the end of the belt, two on each side and one at the end. Each operative worked with a small wooden "horse," about 5 inches long, 2 inches wide, and ¾-inch thick, which was supported at a convenient height on a wooden pole (see Exhibit 3). These horses were covered with a special rubber compound so that the cement on the masks would not adhere readily to them. In performing the joining operation, a worker picked up one of the join strips, which were supplied on flat boards containing about 12 strips each, and "lasted" or pressed it down along the upper edge of the horse. The join strip ran the length of the horse and projected for about half its length over the end of the

Exhibit 4 (*Concluded*)

horse. The operative next took a mask from the belt and pressed the right
chin strap down on the join strip so that the edge of the strap followed
the center line of the join strip. The edge of the left chin strap was then
brought up to meet the edge of the right chin strap and pressed down on
the join strip. The operative rolled the joint with a small roller and stitched
it across the ends or throat. The projecting end of the join strip was next
folded back on top of the joint, rolled down, and stitched along the edges
and across the throat. In the next part of the operation the mask was removed
from the horse and replaced inside out. Again the strip was rolled and stitched
across the throat and along the edges. Finally, the projecting end of the join
strip was cut off with a scissors, and the mask was placed on an aluminum
form ready for the next operation.

Inspect, Redeem, and Rack Gas Masks

This person worked in and out among the five other workers performing
the joining operation, picking up the completed masks, inspecting them, and
removing any wrinkles or blisters that might appear in the join strip. The
operative then placed the masks on flat trays in a large rack truck which
was used to carry them to the vulcanizing room. When one truck was full,
it was rolled out and another one brought in. This operative kept a record
of production and was responsible for ripping apart any defective work discovered. When the defect was traceable to a laborer on the belt, this operative
took it to the laborer and explained the mistake. In connection with this
work it was occasionally necessary to consult the instructor or supervisor.
Additional duties included keeping the joining operatives supplied with join
strips and removing the empty join strip boards.

*   *   *   *   *

5.   Other products to be assembled on the same equipment.   If a conveyor was to be used for more than one product, an effort was made to
keep the variation of both duties and the number of operatives at a minimum. It was usually impossible, however, to achieve both these objectives
at the same time. For example, if a shoe with a foxing was made on the
same equipment as a shoe of the same construction without a foxing, it
was possible to keep the number of operatives constant, but the balance
could be preserved only by changing the duties of all the operatives. The
alternative was to leave the duties as they were and to add an operative
to perform the additional elements. The usual practice in this respect is
to make the conveyor as efficient as possible for the first of a new line
of products and to adapt subsequent items to it as closely as possible.
Whenever standards for a whole style group are revised, production lineups
are, of course, based on the particular items for which the largest volume
was expected.

6.   Equipment and layout limitations.

7.   Base rate limitations.   Whenever an assembly process involved elements requiring high skill and a high base rate of pay, an effort was made

to group these elements as closely as possible in order to keep the number of highly paid operatives at a minimum. Moreover, for maximum efficiency it was desirable that the high base-rate operatives performed only those operations that required high skill. So many other factors entered into the problem, however, that it was usually necessary to fill out a high base-rate operative's job with elements that could be performed by other operatives.

BALANCING OPERATIONS AND CREW

In grouping the job elements for the assembly of the gas masks the Standards Department first added together all of the standard times to secure the total direct labor time of 5.04 minutes (see Exhibit 2) required to assemble one mask. This figure was then multiplied by 2,000, the desired daily production, to obtain an estimate of the total direct labor minutes required per day:

$$2,000 \times 5.04 \text{ minutes} = 10,080 \text{ minutes per day}$$

It was planned to operate the conveyor seven hours each day, and hence division of this total by 420 minutes would have given an approximate figure for the number of average operatives that should have been assigned to the conveyor. Actually, however, the workers assigned to the assembly of the gas masks were considerably above average and were rated as an 84 point-hour[2] crew, capable of doing 84 minutes of work in each hour. Accordingly, the total of 10,080 minutes was divided by 7×84, or 588, which represented the number of minutes of work each crew member would be able to do during the seven-hour day.

$$\frac{10,080}{7 \text{ hrs.} \times 84} = 17.1 \text{ operatives required}$$

Dividing the number of operatives in the crew into 5.04, the total work content of the process for assembly of one mask, gave the number of minutes which each operative would work on each mask if the conveyor were in perfect balance.

$$\frac{5.04}{17} = 0.296 \text{ minutes}$$

Keeping in mind these general considerations, the Standards Department attempted to group the elements into operations in such a manner

---

[2] In the point system used by the company one point was the amount of work an average operative could do in one minute. Hence, an average, or 60-point operative, completed 60 points or minutes of work in one hour; ad 84-point operative completed 84 points or minutes of work in one hour; and so on for all other point ratings. Operatives were paid a certain amount for each point or minute of work completed during the day. The base rate, or amount paid per point, varied for different types of jobs depending on the skill, training, and experience required.

that each one would require 0.296 minutes or some multiple thereof. Accordingly, the Standards Department took several elements out of the operations of which they had originally been a part when the belt was started up and incorporated them in other operations. The "stitching" down of the buckles to the face blank was one of these.[3] The Standards Department found that a better balance could be obtained if this operation was done by workers farther down the line who pressed the cemented parts together in a flat press. Moreover, this arrangement got part of the stitching done during the "dwell time" when one mask was in the press and the operative would otherwise have been idle (see Exhibit 2). Similarly, the operatives who joined the two chin straps together had originally replenished their own supply of join strips. A beter balance was obtained by shifting that element to the person who did the inspecting at the end of the belt.

Where a satisfactory balance could not be secured by rearrangement, the Standards Department occasionally removed an element from the belt altogether and had it done separately by a service worker who might do several such jobs. For example, service workers gave the lenses a ¼-inch coat of cement around the circumference on both sides and arranged them in racks ready for assembly. Similarly, they applied cement to the join strips before the workers at the end of the belt delivered the strips to the joining operatives.

Another device employed to acquire a better balance was to study the method in a troublesome element in order to reduce its standard time or to eliminate it from the job altogether. The workers attaching the buckles, for example, had originally been supplied with buckles from special sloping bins. Replacement of these bins with an ordinary shoe box from which they could take a handful of buckles as needed eliminated some of the elements required for loading and refilling the bins and reduced the time on other elements. Again, operatives at the head of the belt applying cement to the lens blanks had originally used a blanking mask which covered all areas except those to which cement was to be applied. Further study of the method showed that with a little practice they could do the job faster without any blanking mask at all. The times for swabbing and cleaning the horse in the joining operation were likewise reduced by covering the top half of the horse with a special rubber compound to which the cement would not adhere readily.

TIME PER MASK AND SETTING OF LOAD

After the most satisfactory balance possible had been obtained, the Standards Department next determined which was the "peak" operative or the one who was required to do the most work on each mask. In this case the first operative, who had to do 0.33 minutes of work on each mask,

---

[3] Stitching consisted of running a little roller with a dull edge on its circumference along the edge of the joint.

was the most heavily loaded (see Exhibit 2). It was the policy of the company that no one would be required to do work more than 5 percent faster than the standard time allowed for an average operative without receiving additional compensation. Accordingly, the figure of 0.33 minutes was divided by 105 percent to determine the minimum time in which an average peak operative would be expected to complete work on one mask.

$$\frac{0.33}{105 \text{ percent}} = 0.314 \text{ minutes per peak}$$

Since all other operatives were less heavily loaded than the peak operative, it was evident that the speed of the belt for an average crew could be set to require the completion of one mask every 0.314 minutes, or 171 masks per hour.

$$\frac{60}{0.314} = 191 \text{ masks per hour}$$

The crew selected for the assembly of the gas masks, however, was an 84-point crew capable of doing 84 minutes of work in each hour. Hence, the belt was set to operate at the rate of 268 masks per hour instead of 191.

$$\frac{84}{0.314} = 268 \text{ masks per hour}$$

From this figure of 268 masks per hour, the speed of the belt in seconds per space[4] (see Exhibit 2) could readily be determined.

$$\frac{3,600 \text{ seconds}}{268} = 13.4 \text{ seconds per space}$$

The next step in the preparation of the standards letter was to determine the extent to which the belt was out of balance. Since one mask was completed by an average crew every 0.314 minutes, the total standard direct labor minutes per mask assembled could be computed by multiplying 0.314 times the number of operatives.

$$0.314 \times 17 \text{ operatives} = 5.34 \text{ minutes per mask}$$

The difference between this total required time and the sum of the standard times for the separate operations, 5.04 minutes as shown in Exhibit 2, indicated the time lost per mask as a result of imperfect balance, in this case 0.30 minutes. This amount was referred to as the balance delay, and often was expressed as a percentage of the direct labor time, at standard, required to assemble one unit as the line was designed. For a conveyor

---

[4] A space was an area marked off on the belt designed to accommodate the parts for one mask.

in good balance it usually amounted to 3 to 7 percent. In the case of the gas mask conveyor belt, it amounted to 5.6 percent.

$$\frac{0.30}{5.34} = 5.6 \text{ percent}$$

Since an average crew was allowed 0.314 minutes to assemble a mask on the belt, that figure became the average pay standard for the entire crew. This meant that for each completed mask that came off the belt, each operative was credited with 0.314 points or minutes of work. As a result, everyone earned exactly the same wages with the exception of workers performing the last two operations, who had a slightly higher base rate and, thus, received more for each completed point.[5] If a crew worked at above average speed, it completed more than 60 points, or minutes of work, in an hour and was paid accordingly. As noted previously the speed of the belt for the 84-point-hour crew was set so that operatives could assemble enough masks to earn 84 points per hour.

Since the average pay standard for the crew was taken as the peak operative's load divided by 105 percent, it followed that the peak operative on an 84-point-hour crew would actually work at the rate of 88 points and receive payment for 84 points while others less heavily loaded might work at the rate of 60 points or 70 points and also received payments for 84 points of output. In the long run these discrepancies averaged out, because the peak operative on one lineup be one of the most lightly loaded operatives on the next lineup. The only problem presented by the wage payment system lay in the fact that it was sometimes difficult for the workers to understand why a job element of substantial amount might be added to the duties of an operative who had a light load without any change in the daily output or earnings of the crew, while the addition of even a small job element to a peak operative's duties was reflected immediately in daily output and earnings.

The final computation made in preparing the standards letter was the determination of the exact daily output that could be expected from the assembly crew. Since the belt was set to travel at the rate of 13.4 seconds per space or piece, the daily output was determined by dividing 13.4 into the number of seconds in the working day.

$$\frac{7 \text{ hours} \times 3,600 \text{ seconds}}{13.4} = 1,880 \text{ masks per day}$$

Since it was expected that workers would be able to operate at a slightly higher rate of speed as their familiarity with the product increased, the figure was regarded as sufficiently close to the desired rate of 2,000 units per day, and no further adjustments were made.

---

[5] The difference in base rate categories is indicated by the letters A and C in the first column of the standards letter. People working at the C rate earned an extra 10 cents per hour.

During the first six months of the year the conveyor belt operated quite satisfactorily in accordance with the plans developed by the Standards Department. For the latter half of the year, however, an increase in demand was anticipated, and the Standards Department was requested to draw up a new standards letter which would provide for operation of the conveyor belt at a rate of 3,000 units per day. By this time workers had gained enough experience so that they could be expected to operate on the new lineup at the rate of 90 points per hour.

Max-Able Medical Clinic (A)

HARRY D. EUGENE, M.D., felt a growing sense of concern for the Automated Multitest Laboratory project, as he reread the memorandum from his close associate Dr. George Johnson, a radiologist in the Max-Able radiology department (Exhibit 12). As head of the medical systems technology department he had worked closely during the past year with Drs. George Johnson in radiology, Roy Burns in internal medicine, and members of the executive committee at Max-Able, such as Dr. Long to develop plans for an innovative automated multiphasic testing laboratory at the Max-Able Clinic. He reminded himself that he must take concerns such as those expressed in memo into account as he prepared the final proposal for the project to the Executive Committee.

The Max-Able Medical Clinic was a private, multi-specialty group-practice clinic. It was located in a relatively affluent urban region in the southeast, where it had spacious modern facilities and laboratories. It was organized as a partnership with more than 130 affiliated physicians.[1] (See Exhibit 1). Individual salaries and participation in earnings were closely proportional to the revenue each physician generated. Revenue from patient charges at Max-Able was generated from three sources: physician visits, tests and other procedures performed by the attending physician during the visit, and procedures ordered by the attending physician. These categories accounted respectively for 37 percent, 42 percent, and 21 percent of the revenue overall but they varied from 70 percent, 7 percent and 23 percent for general practice in internal medicine, to 10 percent, 85 percent

---

[1] In typical usage the term "multi-specialty group practice" refers to an affiliated group of physicians who largely practice in the medical specialties. They typically treat patients with acute, difficult to diagnose or complex health problems, who they attract by referral from a primary care physician or by reputation. In contrast, the primary care physician (including general practitioners, internists in general practice, family practitioners, and pediatricians) typically treat the full range of health problems they encounter and assume much of the responsibility for preventative medicine and education.

Exhibit 1
THE MAX-ABLE MEDICAL CLINIC STAFF

Executive Board	Administration
6 M.D.s	5 administrators
Internal medicine	General and thoracic surgery
	1 M.D.
Cardiology—4 M.D.s	General and vascular surgery
	2 M.D.s
Chest diseases—6 M.D.s	Plastic and reconstructive surgery
	2 M.D.s
Endocrine and metabolic diseases—	Neurosurgery
5 M.D.s	1 M.D.
Gastroenterology—3 M.D.s	Orthopedic surgery
	6 M.D.s
General medicine—5 M.D.s	Orthopedic surgery and athletic
	medicine
	1 M.D.
Hematology and oncology—2 M.D.s	Urology
	3 M.D.s
Infectious disease and immunology—	Ophthalmology and optometry
1 M.D.	7 M.D.s
Nuclear medicine—1 M.D.	Otolaryngology
	3 M.D.s
Peripheral vascular diseases—1 M.D.	Obstetrics/gynecology
	6 M.D.s
Renal diseases—1 M.D.	Anesthesiology
	5 M.D.s
Rheumatology—2 M.D.s	Environmental medicine
	2 M.D.s
Allergy	Environmental medicine/
2 M.D.s	industrial surgery
	1 M.D.
Neurology	University health service
3 M.D.s	9 M.D.s
Dermatology	Radiology
2 M.D.s	7 M.D.s
Pediatrics	Laboratory medicine
7 M.D.s	1 M.D.
Pediatric cardiology	Pathology
1 M.D.	1 M.D.
General practice	Medical electronics
7 M.D.s	1 M.D.
Psychiatry and clinical psychology	Medical systems
3 M.D.s	1 M.D.
2 Ph.D.s	
General surgery	
3 M.D.s	

and 5 percent for radiologists (X-ray). All major specialties and subspecialties were represented in the clinic, and almost all the clinic's physicians also held appointments as "clinical" faculty at a nearby well-known university school of medicine. Max was one of the early models of "group practice" and had a national reputaton for its innovations in community health care and health program organization.

Consequently, it was not surprising that when a firm in the health services industry—now AML International—had developed an automated health testing service characterized by modular design and a "carousel" configuration of patient flow, it had brought the design to Max for consideration.

Dr. Eugene was currently facing the problem of deciding whether to proceed, what tests to include in the automated laboratory (lab.), how the tests would be scheduled in a process flow, proper design of test sequences, pricing and how to handle possible resistance among the clinic's physicians.

BACKGROUND ON AUTOMATED LABORATORIES

With the recent focus on the nation's health care delivery system, automated multiphasic laboratories were being heralded as an important breakthrough. The basic idea underlying the automated health testing concept was that a battery of critical medical tests could be administered to patients receiving medical checkups through the use of a special facility employing advanced technology and operated by medical technicians rather than physicians. In this way a comprehensive sequence of carefully designed, standardized tests whose quality was carefully controlled could be effectively administered to a large number of patients at low costs and without the use of scarce and costly physicians' time. Such a facility promised to provide better quality information for diagnosing the health status of patients and the early detection of diseases than was typically available for the traditional health checkup.

In traditional medical practice a checkup involved an initial visit to a physician, typically a general practitioner or internist (practicing general medicine). In the course of the visit the physician would write up a lengthy medical history, examine the patient and perform a number of routine tests depending upon the patient's history, condition, symptoms, the equipment available in the office, and the physician's customary procedures. The patient might then be sent for further tests, laboratory procedures, X-rays, etc., often in other locations and following the receipt of results, scheduled for another visit with the physician. If medical difficulties could not be diagnosed by this physician or if special procedures were required, then the patient might be referred to a specialist such as a cardiologist for heart diseases, or a surgeon in any one of several specializations.

As planned, the multiphasic testing laboratory would be used at Max-Able, to short cut many of these time consuming steps and improve the effectiveness with which physician and patient used their time. The patient would visit the multiphasic laboratory at his own convenience before the initial visit to the physician and results would be available before the initial physician visit. In this way the physician would have a strong information base even at the initial visit and could make the best use of his time and knowledge in exploring particulars and making judgments rather than on the mechanics of testing procedures. The patient would be assured of a thorough and comprehensive checkup at a low cost and with a minimum waste of time in making repeat visits. Dr. Eugene thought the new laboratory would prove useful in several ways: In providing important diagnostic data for patients that came for general checkups, as a source of base line data on patients with specific medical problems that came to the specialists at Max; as a service to nonaffiliated physicians in the community that might wish to have such a good work-up on their patients, and it might provide a resource for Max physicians who wished to innovate in establishing new programs, like executive health checkup programs, etc.

Multiphasic health testing laboratories had been introduced several years earlier, and successfully used in several major institutions. They were currently being introduced in many others. Pioneering work had been carried out, among other places, at Kaiser Permanente in California and the Mayo Clinic in Minnesota. Kaiser was world famous for the success which it, as a private institution, had achieved in providing a rather complete program of health care to several million persons in California at a reasonable predetermined annual charge. Because it provided complete health services at a fixed annual charge and was highly integrated, Kaiser had the incentives to seek the health improvement as well as labor-saving benefits of a multiphasic testing concept. It would experience the direct economic consequence of any improvement in its patients' health condition (or deterioration) that influenced the rate with which costly acute hospital facilities were utilized. It was therefore not surprising that Kaiser had been an innovator in this type of program. The Mayo Clinic, renowned for specialty care and not heavily involved in prepaid comprehensive care, had strong governance and instituted the multiphasic concept as a matter of policy.

In some of the early applications the multiphasic testing laboratory concept was used to screen patients, that is, to separate the "worried well" from the sick and thereby determine which should receive the immediate and serious attention of a physician. Critics sometime compared such facilities with military induction physicals where service is impersonal, and patients are denied privacy, being required to dress and undress at several stations during the test sequence. There was also concern with use of multiphasic automated tests to screen patients, since it might lead to the denial of appropriate medical care.

The multiphasic lab, as proposed for Max-Able, differed in important respects from some of the earlier approaches. It would complement rather than replace the initial physician-patient contact. Furthermore, it would emphasize personalized services with many patient amenities.

It was technically feasible to include many tests in the lab but the mix of tests would largely determine the potential demand. Most tests under consideration were costly. Dr. Eugene realized that the facility would have to offer profitable operations before the directors of the clinic would approve its implementation, yet the price for the battery of tests would greatly affect the usage of the facility. He also knew that gaining the support of the physicians before the lab was implemented was especially important in a group practice. Poor acceptance by physicians and their patients would not only cause problems at Max-Able but would also delay the widespread application of the concept elsewhere. AML International was anxious that the system be accepted at Max, because recovery of its development costs required broad adoption of the AML design in many practices. Failure of the design at Max-Able would mean an almost certain end to potential sales.

PROPOSED LABORATORY DESIGN

The modular "carousel" design proposed by AML International promised to offer all the benefits of previous automated testing labs at Kaiser and Mayo:

More information for the physician's use in diagnosis.
No need for the physician to perform the tests himself.
Less need for the physician to refer the patient to a laboratory for general tests and for the patient to schedule another visit to the doctor.
A sophisticated base of medical data for comparative analysis of long-term health trends.
Use of paramedical and nonmedical personnel to staff the AML.
Substantial decrease in medical costs and improvement in quality of testing.
Early diagnosis of certain diseases at a stage when they are most responsive to therapy.

The new design offered two additional benefits:

Convenience: no long waits, travel between test areas, or multiple dressing and undressing.
A personal touch: one technician assigned to a patient for the whole sequence of tests.

The general layout of the laboratory as proposed is presented in Exhibit 2. The entire sequence of patient movement through the facility would consist of five stages of activity: (1) Pre-test arrangements; (2) medical history and patient preparation; (3) initial stationary tests; (4) carousel tests; and (5) final stationary tests. Tests for all stages except the carousel had been tentatively decided.

Pre-Test Arrangements

Patient processing at the facility would begin when an appointment was made with the laboratory. Only patients referred by a physician could

Exhibit 2
MAX-ABLE MEDICAL CLINIC (A)
Facility Design

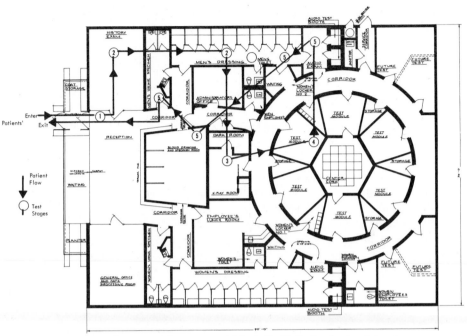

Floor plan for AML International's Automated Multiphasic Health Testing Services Laboratory
* Reg. U.S. Patent No. 3,470,671. Other patents pending.

make an appointment, although for self-initiated patients the facility might suggest the names of several physicians to sponsor the tests. The patient would then be assigned an appointment time and asked to fast for five hours beforehand. Except in the case of rush appointments, the patient would be sent a questionnaire to be completed before the appointment. Upon arrival at the lab, the patient would give the questionnaire to the laboratory appointment secretary, who would assign a number to the patient to be used for test identification. The information from the questionnaire would be fed through an on-line terminal into a computerized patient record.

Medical History and Patient Preparation

The patient would then be instructed in the use of a computerized medical history terminal consisting of a back-projected filmed questionnaire and simple answering device. The patient would be presented a sequence of questions with several logical branches. If, for instance, the patient answered a question indicating a prior known medical condition the terminal would branch to present a special questionnaire section to explore this condition. These answers would also be automatically fed into the patient's stored computer record.

Upon completion of the history portion of the exam, a patient would be given a large amount of glucose and shown to the males' or females' dressing area, where disposable garments would be issued for wearing during the tests. (The patient flow can be visualized from the layout in Exhibit 2 where major testing activity groups are indicated by numbers in circles.)

Initial Stationary Tests

The next stage of tests would involve those performed in stationary rooms in the facility before the patient entered the carousel. A technician would be assigned to the patient and stay with the same patient throughout this and the next test stage.

The first test in the initial stationary stage would consist of an X-ray. This would be followed by a digitally displayed measurement of the patient's height and weight. The X-ray test required a shielded X-ray room. After these procedures the patient would be led into one of the modules of the carousel, accompanied by the AML technician for the next stage of testing.

Carousel Tests

The carousel consisted of a "core" room which provided space for a large amount of test equipment, with six patient testing rooms, "modules" in a circle around it (see Exhibit 2). The wall of the core, which was the inner wall of each module, turned to present the connections for various tests to each module. The patient would stay in his assigned module throughout this stage of the testing. Although the carousel could accommodate up to six modules, not every module had to be operable and furnished. Also, the carousel could be operated, if necessary, without having patients in all operable modules. For instance, only three modules might be equipped to handle patients. On any given cycle all three modules might not be full, but each module with a patient would still face, in turn, each side of the central core which paced the test sequence. Large expensive equipment would be located in the core of the carousel and connected through the wall to sensors and input devices in each module. (See Exhibit 2), while less expensive equipment for other tests would be located in or on the wall of each module. Only the central wall rotates with respect to the modules according to the sequence of test operations.

The technician would perform the appropriate tests or connect electrical leads to the core through input jacks located in the exposed section of the core wall. In fact, if a test were being given which did not require connection to the central core, the rotation of the wall merely served to pace the testing sequence. In fact the real affect of the moving center was more an organizational aid than a rigid technological constraint. It would provide a privacy shield between the modules and the center cove, where expensive units of equipment would be kept (spirometer, electrocardiograph, and blood pressure analyzer). There was even an opening between the core and module so that with minor modification the connecting leads could be passed through, no matter which face of the core wall faced a particular module.

The movement of the core wall would help to organize and smooth the testing sequence insuring orderly service to patients and effective use of equipment. The plan for handling patients was to have each patient arriving at the carousel, enter the most recently vacated module, imparting a smooth flow to the service of patients. Given morning startup and evening shutdown constraints, about seven hours of operation of the carousel was considered maximum for each of the five days per week the AML would be open.

Final Stationary Tests

After the sequence of tests in the module, the patient would be directed to an audiometer room for a hearing test. Two audiometers each could be located next to the males' and females' dressing areas. After completing the hearing test, the patient would be directed by the AML technician to return to the dressing room and then to proceed to the blood drawing and specimen room, the blood sample and the urine specimen would be taken and the examination would be over. One-way doors would prevent the patient from returning to the carousel or test areas.

PLANNING FOR THE LABORATORY

The staffing plans for the laboratory were to have it headed by a registered nurse. The number of supporting personnel would largely be a function of the number of active modules per day, i.e., the number of filled modules per cycle around the core, the number of scheduled cycles to fulfill demand, and the general technology of the facility. A computer operator would be required to update the automated records and complete the medical history records in a batch mode using as input the results of the AML tests. The proposed AML staffing requirements, job specifications, and salary requirements are presented in Exhibits 3 and 4.

PROPOSED TESTS

The medical planning committee for the lab had decided that the X-ray, height and weight test, audiometer hearing test, and blood and urine tests should be included in any test sequence. However, the number of duplicate

Exhibit 3
STAFFING REQUIREMENTS AND COSTS

Personnel Requirements

Assuming one or two test sequences per half hour:

Supervising nurse	1
Technicians:	
Front desk.	1
Test sequence	1 per operative module
Back-up/core	
equipment operator	
Computer operator.	⅓ part time

Job Descriptions

Supervising Nurse.   Responsible for directing, supervising, and counseling staff members of the AML. Must arrange for ECKs and X rays to be sent to a cardiologist and radiogists for reading and interpretation and then returned to the AML to be forwarded to the referring physician. Responsible for the purchase of laboratory supplies and the detection and reporting of any malfunction in equipment.

Technician.   Under the general supervision of the supervising nurse, and ministers a battery of medical tests to patients and performs clerical duties. Must be able to record test measurements and operate testing equipment.

Computer Operator.   Must be able to operate a small computer in batch-mode to complete the medical records with the results of the AML tests.

Suggested Wage Structure

Supervising nurse	$12,000 average wage
AML technician	6,100 average wage
Computer operator	3,600 part time cost

units of each type of test equipment and the complete testing sequence were as yet undetermined. Dr. Eugene realized that each test was expensive and consequently was concerned that the total cost might exceed the level acceptable to a large number of patients. A certain test might also add too much time to the cycle of the carousel, thereby limiting the number of patients that could be handled in a working day.

The committee, including Dr. Eugene and representatives from many departments at Max had examined a number of technically feasible and medically proven tests, and had found that the quality of each testing procedure was acceptable:

Spirometry.   A test of lung capacity that required the patient to exhale
through a mouthpiece into a device measuring the volume and pres-

sure of the exhalation. Results contribute to the diagnosis of heart disease and lung diseases such as emphysema.

Mamography. A test for cancer of the breasts, an appropriate testing procedure only for females in the mid-forties to early fifties.

Electrocardiography (EKG). A test for heart disorder or weakness performed with the patient connected electrically to a device measuring the electrical impulses of the heart. Results had to be interpreted by a trained cardiologist.

Vision. A test for corrected vision (reflecting mirrors would provide the standard distance for the test within the confines of the module).

Ocular Tension (*Tonometry*). A test for the indications of glaucoma (a serious eye disease usually occurring in late middle age or later) performed by placing a rubber probe against the surface of the eye. To facilitate the test, the eye must be anesthetized; consequently, the test must be performed after the general vision test, and the patient must be observed for at least twenty minutes afterwards until adequate vision is regained.

Blood Pressure. A test for blood pressure performed by a device measuring the Doppler Effect associated with the changes in pressure.

Pap Smear. A test for cancer of the cervix performed on most adult women.

This menu of tests was developed for possible inclusion in the lab on the basis of medical importance, quality of automated equipment, and the precedents established in earlier automated test labs. Test applicability varies substantially for patient groups that differ by age, sex, income level, and race, as illustrated by the 10-year death risk profile given in Exhibit 13 for just two factors, age and sex. All tests had been included in existing automated labs previously established for screening. For instance, monography was included in the Kaiser testing facility. The Pap Smear test for cervical cancer (an inexpensive and effective test, especially in particularly susceptible socio-economic categories including many of Max-Able's patients) was often included, too. This test required professional training, however, because the set-up was similar to a general gynecological examination. Several committee members wondered if many physicians would feel that the Pap Smear should be an integral part of the doctor-patient relationship. Even though the test might uncover some incidence of the disease, he questioned whether it should be included in the module in the face of such possibly adverse reaction.

As part of the AML International proposal, variable and fixed costs as well as the duration of each test under consideration were provided. The committee had updated these figures and thought they represented the costs he should use in reaching a decision. (See Exhibits 5 and 6.)

Exhibit 4

General Cost per Annum

1.	Office supplies	$ 350
2.	Utilities	$ 1,500
3.	Maintenance and repair	$ 1,800
4.	Telephone	$ 850
5.	Insurance and miscellaneous	$ 1,100
6.	Taxes	$ 1,850
	Total	$ 7,450

Exhibit 5
COSTS AND TEST DURATION

Capital Costs and Test Duration

Test and Necessary Equipment	Cost*	Duration
1. History documentation: 5–6 terminals and computer . . .	$80,000	15–45 minutes
2. Chest X-ray: Odelca camera and darkroom facilities	$22,220	2 minutes
3. Height and weight: load cell, linear potentiometer, and digital read-out	$ 4,200	1 minute
4. Audiometer: Rudmose Model ARJ-4A	$ 1,800 per set	5 minutes
5. Blood sample and urine collection	$ 1,200 per station	5 minutes
6. Spirometer: Electro-Med Model 780 and Pulmodigicomp Model 1000	$ 8,180	2–3 minutes
7. Electrocardiograph: Hewlett-Packard 1513A (3 channel recorder)	$ 4,600	15 seconds to 5 minutes
8. Ocular tension: MacKay-Marg Electronic Tonometer	$ 2,000 per module	5 minutes
9. Vision: American Optical Project-O-Chart	$275 + $500 per module	3–5 minutes
10. Blood pressure: Godart Model 151-CC	$ 3,600	4 minutes
11. Mamography: several types available	$25,000 per module	9–11 minutes
12. Pap smear: no capital equipment necessary		2 minutes
13. Miscellaneous (dressing, rotation, instruction)		10 minutes
14. General module equipment . . .	$ 1,000 per module	

* Represents total test equipment capital cost for up to six modules except where cost per module is specified.

Exhibit 6
VARIABLE COSTS OF THE AML

Expendable Supplies per Patient	*Cost per Item*	*Subtotal*
a. Appointment procedures		
1. Appointment brochure	$0.06	
2. Confidential Medical Information Form	0.02	
3. AML letter size envelope	0.02	
4. Stamp (postage)	0.08	
5. AML appointment scheduling chart	0.02	
	$0.20	$ 0.20
b. Computer processing		
1. Storage envelope	$0.05	
2. Labels (identification)	0.07	
3. Labels (ECG)	0.01	
4. Computer paper	0.08	
5. AML medical report folders	0.10	
6. Cardboard storage boxes	0.01	
7. Computer ribbons	0.01	
	$0.33	$ 0.53
c. Main desk		
1. Glucose drink (100 Gm carbonated cola)	$0.25	
2. Cups for glucose	0.02	
3. Disposable thermometer tip	0.04	
4. Exit brochures	0.05	
	$0.36	$ 0.89
d. Laboratory		
1. Urine specimen cups	$0.05	
2. Urine specimen cup lids	0.05	
3. Bili-Labstix	0.12	
4. Testuria	0.28	
5. Pre-Packed	0.02	
6. Vacutainers (2 tops, holder, and needle)	0.40	
7. Serum tubes	0.04	
8. Alcohol wipe	0.01	
9. Bandaid	0.01	
10. Wood applicators	0.01	
11. Glass beads	0.02	
12. Dispo pipets	0.01	
	$1.02	$ 1.91
e. Dressing booth		
1. Gown	$0.25	
2. Slippers	0.06	
3. Plastic bag	0.02	
	$0.33	$ 2.24
f. X-ray department		
1. Chest X-ray film	$0.83	
2. Envelope	0.05	
3. Developing chemicals	0.02	
4. Radiological interpretation	1.00	(by contract with radiologists)
	$1.90	$ 4.14

Exhibit 6 *(Continued)*

Expendable Supplies per Patient	Cost per Item	Subtotal
g. Test modules		
1. Tonometry		
a. Ophthaine	$0.02	
b. Tissues	0.01	
c. Tonotips	0.10	
d. Wetting agent	0.01	
e. Recording paper	0.05	
	$0.19	$ 4.33
2. EKG		
a. Electrolyte cream	$0.02	
b. Alcohol wipes	0.02	
c. Tissues	0.01	
d. Cardiological interpretation	1.00	(by contract with cardiologists)
e. Interpretation–Abnormal ECGs (25% occurrence)	5.00	
$20	$6.05	$10.38
3. Blood pressure		
no supplies		
4. Vision		
Visual field pattern card	$0.01	$10.39
5. Spirometry		
Spirotubes	0.05	$10.44
6. Mamography	9.50	$19.94
7. Pap smear	4.00	$23.94
h. Miscellaneous		
1. Paper head protectors	$0.04	
2. Paper towels	0.02	
3. Tissues	0.01	
4. Soap	0.01	
5. Technical supplies	0.21	
	$0.29	$24.23

PROCESS UTILIZATION

One of the most difficult problems in designing the lab was determining its potential utilization. Dr. Eugene was able to find little published data that might help him in reaching a conclusion.

The committee approached the problem of obtaining data in several different ways. He believed that ultimate demand would be based on several factors:

1. The number of patients coming to Max-Able for a checkup or for general health care, not for follow-up or "routine" visits.
2. The applicability of the lab for any specialty. Many patients seeing a physician or specialist might not need the sequence since they have a well-defined health problem or because the general tests might not be as thorough or exact as special tests performed in the laboratory.
3. Age and sex of patients.
4. The price of the sequence.

It was felt that demand could be estimated from data on these factors.

Two statistical samples were taken, one that represented all Max-Able patients during a typical "composite week" and the second was a study of new patients only. Fortunately Max-Able used a computer-based billing system; these records contained the patient's name and information about the attending doctor and his services—his name, specialty, charges, and some of the laboratory procedures performed during the visit or subsequently ordered. Using these sources, Dr. Eugene randomly drew a day's history for each day of the week to make up a composite week at Max-Able that was free of seasonal variations. From this composite week he determined the number of eligible patients by types of diagnosis and laboratory procedures. Patients for whom the lab tests were completely inapplicable, such as those returning for follow-up visits, were excluded. Exhibit 7 gives the number of visits to Max-Able by eligible patients during

Exhibit 7
WEEKLY COMPOSITE STUDY

Visits by Specialty	*Total Visits*	*Men*	*Women*	*Percentage for Whom AML Was Applicable*
Internists.	1,357	556	801	75%
General practice.	531	232	299	75%
Environmental medicine	118	39	79	10%
Obstetrics/gynecology	487	–	487	5%
Subtotal	2,493	827	1,666	
Other specialties.	4,983	2,413	2,570	1%
Total.	7,476	3,240	4,236	

this composite week by selected medical specialty and a subjective estimate of the percentage of eligible patients for whose diagnostic and treatment regime the lab tests might be applicable.

The 7,476 visits in the composite week were further examined to determine visits that were equivalent to a comprehensive initial physical examination or regular annual checkup, but not necessarily as comprehensive as the lab. Approximately 10 percent or 781 of the visits fell in this category. Exhibit 8 gives the age/sex distribution of these patients.

The best judgment suggested that the highest potential utilization of the lab would come from the groups of patients who were properly most concerned about their health, those over, say, forty years old. Even though a doctor might prefer that all patients have a comprehensive test sequence like the lab's, the basic good health of young people and the cost of the lab sequence might induce him to omit such a sequence for lower age groups and rely instead on detection during the normal office visit.

To obtain further data, the treatment patterns of new patients at Max-Able were examined. Of the 1,685 new patients seen during a week's time, 14 percent or 235 were considered candidates for the lab.

Exhibit 8
GENERAL PHYSICAL EXAMINATIONS BY SEX AND AGE
(from the composite week sample)

Age Group	Males		Females		Total	
	Number	Percent	Number	Percent	Number	Percent
Infants (0–11 months)	35	8.5	24	6.5	59	7.6
Children (1–12 years)	45	10.9	28	7.7	73	9.3
Teens (13–19 years)	22	5.3	25	6.8	47	6.0
Twenties (20–29 years).	35	8.5	39	10.6	74	9.5
Thirties (30–39 years)	55	13.3	44	12.0	99	12.7
Matured (40–49 years)	98	23.7 ⎫	56	15.2 ⎫	154	19.8
Middle aged (50–69 years)	100	24.2 ⎬ 53.6	103	28.0 ⎬ 56.5	203	26.0
Elderly (70 years plus)	23	5.7 ⎭	49	13.3 ⎭	72	9.2
Totals	413	100.1	368	100.1	781	100.1

Further analysis was performed to obtain the distribution of current total testing fees for these 235 patients at Max-Able. Undoubtedly, the price of the lab facility would be compared by both patients and physicians to fees for similar tests performed by existing laboratory facilities, either at Max-Able or elsewhere. Since Max-Able physicians would not be constrained to refer patients to the lab even if it were built, the price would have a great effect on demand. The present fees for laboratory testing are summarized in Exhibit 9.

Each test under consideration for the lab would have a different usefulness to a physician depending on his specialty. The committee ranked each test's usefulness for each specialty from "very useful" (an integral part of most diagnoses) to "generally useful" (related only to the physician's concern for the overall health of his patient). (See Exhibit 10.)

Dr. Eugene initially felt that the maximum potential demand might be quickly approximated as the 1,068 patients per week that were represented by an adjusted sum of the composite week group plus the new-patient potential. These adjustments involved weighing the composite week demand by patient age percentages and the applicability factor for each specialty. Based on these calculations (presented in Exhibit 11) Dr. Eugene revised his estimate of the maximum potential demand upward to almost 1,100 patients per week. Finally, this demand was adjusted for each price range that might be charged by multiplying the cumulative percentage of all laboratory procedures that cost more than a given price for the new lab. For instance, only 7 percent of new patients were currently charged more than $60 for laboratory tests by existing laboratories. Consequently Dr. Eugene assumed that only 7 percent of the total weighted potential demand would desire the AML tests at a cost of $60 in lieu of Max's regular laboratory tests (even though they may not have been as comprehensive as the new lab sequence).

Exhibit 9
ACTUAL LABORATORY COSTS FOR SAMPLE OF
INITIAL PATIENTS

Billing (dollars)	Number of Patients out of 235	Billing (dollars)	Cumulative Frequency (percent)
$0–9	55	over 0	100
10–19	12	over $ 9	77
20–29	58	over $19	72
30–34	9	over $29	47
35–39	10	over $34	43
40–49	43	over $39	39
50–59	31	over $49	21
60 or over	17	over $59	7

EKG (without interpretation)	$17.50
Spirometer	10.00
X-ray	12.00
Blood and urine tests	25.00
History (done by physician)	7.00
Visual test (done by optometrist or ophthalmologist)	3.00
Audiometer	10.00
Mamography	10.00
Pap smear	5.00
	$99.50

THE REPORT TO THE EXECUTIVE COMMITTEE

As he prepared to draw up final recommendations for the automated lab, Dr. Eugene reviewed the basis for his interest in the project and the origin of resistance to the project within Max-Able. The impressive stack of reports on his desk from the Public Health Service and elsewhere, provided convincing evidence that such a lab, if properly implemented and supported, both could and had: improved the rate of condition finding in diagnosing patients, helped to reduce morbidity in the population of patients that were processed and reduced the cost of health care.

He felt that it was important to draw up a final plan specifying the exact tests that would be included, the number of units of test equipment that should be purchased, the patient flow through the facility and a pricing recommendation. The recommendations should be so carefully thought out that potential opponents would find no basis for criticism in these specifics.

At the same time he recognized some very real sources of resistance to aspects of the new project. There was very little doubt but that the tests would be of high quality but in many instances they would present established physicians with new and unfamiliar sources of evidence upon which to base their diagnosis. These would represent documentary evi-

Exhibit 10

USEFULNESS OF TESTS BY MEDICAL SPECIALTY

	Internists: General Medicine, Gastroenterology, Cardiologists, Sub-Specialties	General Practice	Environmental Medicine	Obstetrics/ Gynecology	Other Specialties	Radiologists
History	Very useful	Very useful	Very useful	Very useful	All tests generally useful for diagnosis, but tests often too broad in scope, or doctor has complete medical record when he first sees patient (i.e., patient has been referred, so tests have already been performed)	Only X-rays appropriate; 50% of work done on chest x-rays for routine physicals
Chest X-ray	Very useful	Very useful	Very useful	Generally useful		
Height and weight	Very useful	Very useful	Very useful	Very useful		
Blood and urine	Very useful	Very useful	Very useful	Very useful		
Audiometry	Generally useful	Generally useful	Very useful	Generally useful		
Spirometry	Very useful	Very useful	Very useful	Generally useful		
EKG	Very useful	Very useful	Very useful	Generally useful		
Blood pressure	Very useful	Very useful	Very useful	Generally useful		
Vision	Desirable for patient	Desirable for patient	Generally useful	Generally useful		
Tonometry	Very useful	Very useful	Generally useful	Generally useful		
Pap smear	Very useful	Very useful	Generally useful	Very useful		
Mamography	Very useful	Very useful	Generally useful	Very useful		
Applicability factor (for patients over 40)	75%	75%	10%	5%	1%	—

Exhibit 11
TOTAL WEIGHTED POTENTIAL DEMAND

A. Weighting by Patient Age Percentages over 40.
   (Weekly demand from composite study [Exhibit 7] weighted by percent of patients over 40 [Exhibit 8].)

   Male = 53.6 percent over 40   Female = 56.5 percent over 40

	Male	*Female*	*Total*
Internists	556 × 53.6% = 300	801 × 56.5% = 450	750
General practice	232 × 53.6% = 124	299 × 56.5% = 170	294
Environmental medicine	39 × 53.6% = 21	79 × 56.5% = 44	65
Obstetrics/gynecology. .	0 × 53.6% = 0	487 × 56.5% = 275	275
Specialties (other)	2,413 × 53.6% = 1,300	2,570 × 56.5% = 1,460	2,760

B. Weighted by Specialty Applicability Factor
   (From Specialty Applicability Factor [Exhibit 10].)

Internists	750 × 75% = 562
General practice	294 × 75% = 222
Environmental medicine	65 × 10% = 7
Obstetrics/gynecology.	275 × 5% = 14
Specialties (other)	2,760 × 1% = 28
	833

Total Potential Weighted Demand = 833 + 235 new patients = 1,068 patients per week or 55,536 per year for a 52-week year.

C. Weighted by Price

	Cumulative Percent
If AML costs over $29.	47% × 55,536 = 26,000
If AML costs over $34.	43% × 55,536 = 23,800
If AML costs over $39.	39% × 55,536 = 21,600
If AML costs over $49.	21% × 55,536 = 11,600
If AML costs over $59.	7% × 55,536 = 3,900

dence, which the busy, established physician would have to interpret fully if he used the facility at all. Otherwise he would be exposed to the risk of a malpractice suit in the event that a medical problem was overlooked.

There were physicians who claimed that a standardized battery of tests were inappropriate in the first place since patients differed enormously in the conditions that warranted exploration. This line of reasoning led to the argument that the new concept would actually raise health costs since it induced unnecessary testing.[2]

---

[2] It would not be unusual for the results from a particular test to be far outside a normal range for a particular patient when he was otherwise apparently healthy. This anomaly might result from prior diet, emotional conditions, drugs taken or unexplained reasons, but involve considerable retesting to insure that medical problems were not the source of the test result.

Finally, while results from the lab report would undoubtedly save a great deal of time during the patient's visit, it might also result in a reduction of physician fees for tests that would otherwise have been done in the office. Since each physician's fees were ultimately related to the procedures he performed, the introduction of the lab into the group practice might redistribute fees among physicians and between physicians and the lab. For instance, both the electrocardiograph and X-ray tests would be interpreted by specialists before being sent to the physician who referred the patient. Although Dr. Eugene had negotiated a low $1 interpretation fee, these might run normally from $5 to $25.

Dr. Eugene was sensitive to the large investment that AML International had made for technical, architectural, and system development and realized that if the AML facility were built, Max-Able would have to invest over $250,000 in land and another $500,000 in the building. All the partners of Max-Able would be very concerned with the lab's economic viability, because Max-Able expected to obtain a reasonable net contribution on any investment.

In large part, the executive board of Max-Able would decide the general feasibility of the facility on its merits as a potential investment. Since the project had the strong support of Dr. Long, an eminent national figure in medicine as well as at Max-Able, Dr. Eugene felt confident that a sound proposal would be accepted, provided that affiliated physicians would not be required to use it for their patients. Given the type of resistance that was evident in Dr. Johnson's memo he still wondered if there was other action he should take.

Exhibit 12
RESISTANCE TO AML
MEMO

To: Harold D. Eugene, M.D.
From: George P. Johnson, M.D.

Re: Automated Multitest Laboratory

If a vote were held in the X-ray department on the acceptance of an AML, I calculate that it would lose, 4 to 2. Some of the department members are disturbed that there was not more research into the value, patient acceptability, and cost of such an endeavor. Furthermore, there is a genuine desire to practice episodic medicine rather than encourage mass surveys of essentially well patients. There are some reservations against entering into a project with a commercial company [AML International]. The department as a whole would prefer to exclude chest films from the AML and retain the present system of hjving the individual physician request the films and interpretation from us as indicated.

Exhibit 13

DEATH RISK PROFILES WITH MODIFYING CONDITION

(specifies probability of death within 10 years by four principal causes for each
age sex group in percentage terms)

	White Male Age 20–24	White Female Age 20–24	White Male Age 40–44	White Female Age 40–44
*,†,‡ Motor Vehicle Accidents	0.58%	0.12%	0.28%	0.10%
With seat belts 75%–100% of time	0.46	0.09	0.23	0.08
Heavy social drinking–definite excess.	2.90	0.60	1.42	0.51
‡,*,† Suicide.	0.13	0.04	0.26	0.09
† Chronic rheumatic heart disease	0.02	0.03	0.17	0.13
†,‡,§ Vascular lesions affecting central nervous system (hemorrhage)	–	0.02	0.22	0.20
* Homicide	0.06	0.02	–	–
* Accidents, drowning.	0.04	–	–	–
‡,§ Arteriosclerotic heart disease	0.03	–	1.88	0.30
1 or more packs cigarettes per day.	0.04	–	2.81	0.62
Cigarettes plus 75% overweight and high cholesterol level	0.23	–	10.56	2.34
With success in prescribed exercise, weight reduction, stopped smoking	0.02	–	1.26	0.33
‡ Cirrhosis of liver	–	–	0.22	0.13
With heavy social drinking–definite excess . .	–	–	1.11	0.66
§ Cancer of breast	N.A.	–	N.A.	0.35
If mother or sister had C.B..	N.A.	–	N.A.	0.70
With regular self-exam and mammogram . . .	N.A.	–	N.A.	0.17
§ Cancer of cervix	N.A.	–	N.A.	0.14
Jewish	N.A.	–	N.A.	0.01
Low socio-economic status with teenage marriage or sex relations	N.A.	–	N.A.	0.60
With three negative Pap smear tests in last five years.	N.A.	–	N.A.	0.01
Over-all probability of death from all causes in percent.	1.58	0.60	5.56	3.02

No entry indicates cause was not included in top 14 causes of death for group in question.
* Four principal causes of death for white males 20–24 years of age.
† Four principal causes of death for white females 20–24 years of age.
‡ Four principal causes of death for white males 40–44 years of age.
§ Four principal causes of death for white females 40–44 years of age.
All probabilities are approximations.
Source: Based upon data in Lewis C. Robbins, M.D., MPH and Jack H. Hall, A.B. M.D.,
How to Practice Prospective Medicine, Methodist Hospital of Indiana, 1970.

SECTION TWO

Capacity Management

INTRODUCTION

Thus far, the text and cases have been primarily concerned with the analysis of operating systems in a static environment. The emphasis has been on understanding and evaluating the operations of a firm given a fixed level of demand, stable markets, and a well-defined process technology. The next three chapters are concerned with capacity management, where the focus shifts to adapting the firm's operations to a dynamic environment. Here, the emphasis is on planning and implementing changes in the size, location, utilization, and makeup of the operating system in response to variations in demand, changing markets, and innovations in process technology.

The major issues in capacity management revolve around five questions which any firm must ask itself as it looks into the future:

How much capacity should we have?
When should capacity be acquired?
What kind of capacity should we use?
How should this capacity be utilized?
Where should capacity be located?

These questions seem straightforward. The challenge of capacity management however, is to resolve and integrate them for a continuum of futures—the future of a week hence, the future of a month from now, and the futures one, two, and more years away. For each of these futures, the questions above remain the same, but because of the various lead times involved in implementing different kinds of change, the set of feasible answers, and the tradeoffs involved in obtaining them, are different.

215

For example, consider the problems of a multiplant, multiproduct company looking first three months, then two years, and finally three years into the future. Suppose that three months from now, the company predicts a large, but temporary, increase in sales volume—an increase which would make monthly sales greater than monthly capacity. The company's first problem then, is to determine how much capacity to add to meet these sales, when to add it (how far in advance of the predicted increase), where (at which of their locations) to increase capacity, what kind of capacity to obtain (a longer workweek or additions to the work force) and how the capacity is to be used (for which products). Obtaining additional capacity by adding a new plant in a new location is out of the question in this instance. Feasible solutions are restricted to those that can be implemented within three months. These may include (1) working overtime at Plant X, (2) adding a second shift at Plant Y. (3) building inventories in anticipation of the increase in sales, (4) subcontracting, (5) foregoing the production and sale of low-profit items in favor of high-margin products, or (6) trying to influence demand in such a way as to delay or smooth out the surge in sales.

The final solution to this three-month capacity management problem will depend upon the economic, organizational, and marketing consequences of each alternative. Working overtime, for instance, may be quite costly both in terms of dollars, and the morale of the work force. But this alternative may be more economical than building inventories, because of the high financing costs required to support the inventory buildup. The least cost solution in the short term may involve foregoing the production of low-profit items, but this alternative may degrade the marketing image of a company which emphasizes its reliability as a source of supply to its customers, and its full line of products.

The same company, looking two years into the future where it foresees a general increase in sales in excess of available capacity, is faced with the same problem: how much capacity to add, when to add it, where, what kind, and how to use it. But with two years to effect the changes required to solve this problem, the number of alternative solutions increase, perhaps including an expansion of Plant X, or upgrading Plant Y from an old to a new technology, or building a new plant at a different location. In this instance, the financial impact of economies of scale, reduced transport costs, or higher productivity may be the decisive factors in choosing from the available alternatives.

Looking even further into the future, the company may recognize several alternative process technologies in various stages of development. If the company sees that it will take three years to effect an efficient changeover to one of these new advanced technologies, it must again consider: what kind (which technology) of capacity, and when, where, how much, and how to utilize it. In this instance, the number of alternatives may be quite small, but the analysis extremely complex. The capacity management problems in this time frame can often significantly alter the cost and capital structure of the entire firm, and impact the fundamental business strategy which guides it.

The organization of the following three chapters reflects the impact of various planning horizons on capacity management decisions. The text and cases in Chapter 4, "Aggregate Planning, Scheduling, and Dispatching," emphasize the decisions and implementation problems which are relevant in adapting to changes in the environment which are expected to occur within a year, or less. This includes an examination of the costs and benefits of various strategies for making short-term shifts in capacity, as well as the major policies which affect capacity management decisions; e.g., inventory policies, distribution policies, work force policies, and certain marketing policies.

Chapter 5, "Facilities Planning," focuses on the capacity management decisions which arise when we anticipate the environment one to two years in the future. These decisions are usually concerned with various strategies for adding physical capacity (facilities and equipment). As the cases in this chapter will illustrate, facilities planning is an important input into the capital budgeting process. However, other considerations including the effect of alternative facilities plans on the basic business strategy of the firm, and its competitive posture, are also of fundamental importance.

Chapter 6, "Technology Planning," is concerned with the process by which new product and process technologies are evaluated and implemented. The planning horizon relevant to these issues is generally quite lengthy; three, four, or even ten years in some instances. The length of this planning horizon emphasizes the special problems which arise in managing and planning major changes in the operating system under a high degree of uncertainty.

As you read and study these three chapters, you will have the opportunity to apply many of the techniques and concepts you acquired in studying previous cases. In addition, you will learn to understand many more. But you should be aware that some of the most important of these new concepts will become apparent as you reflect on the interrelationships between the issues raised in various cases and different chapters. This exemplifies a basic premise involved in almost all capacity management decisions: the way one chooses to solve the problems of today, determines the way in which one is able to solve the problems of tomorrow.

4

Aggregate Planning, Scheduling, and Dispatching

In many firms, three activities are critical to the process of adapting capacity levels and utilization plans to short-term shifts in demand. The first, aggregate planning, involves forecasting product demand 6–18 months into the future and deciding on the size of the work force, and the amount of inventories, overtime, and subcontracting that will be required. These decisions are generally formalized in a production budget, which can be used to derive personnel plans and policies, warehousing needs, purchasing plans, and cash requirements (payrolls, and so on) for financial purposes. The second activity, scheduling, involves allocating the resources acquired as a result of aggregate planning to specific products in specific time periods. Dispatching, the third activity, is concerned with adjusting the schedule to reflect last minute changes in demand or production capabilities, and implementing it.

The purpose of this chapter is to describe the important decisions and tradeoffs commonly involved in each of these hierarchically related activities, and to illustrate them with examples. In doing so, our objective is to provide a basis for examining and analyzing short-term capacity management problems, and related operating policies.

AGGREGATE PLANNING

Aggregate planning involves the preparation of not one, but a series of interrelated plans which provide a guide for production in the short term. These plans include: a *production plan,* which specifies the total amount of production (or subcontracting) to be accomplished within each of a series of future periods (typically months); an *input plan,* which specifies the inputs to the production plan by detailing the size of the work force, the length of the workday, and materials requirements; and an *output plan,* which indicates the disposition of production output into sales channels or inventories.

As with most activities in capacity management, aggregate planning begins with a forecast of future demand. This forecast, in effect, provides a series of goals (demand in a particular period) which must be met by carefully coordinating the production, input, and output plans. These three plans must be coordinated since we know from our work on process analysis that the rate at which inputs are acquired (specified for labor and material inputs by the input plan) affects the rate at which the process can produce (specified by the production plan) which in turn affects the rate and disposition of the outputs (specified by the output plan). The problem in aggregate planning is that there are a number of alternative ways that the input rates, production rates, and output rates can be juggled to meet forecasted demand, and each alternative is likely to have different cost and operating consequences.

For example, consider the simple process shown in Figure 4–1. If fore-

Figure 4–1

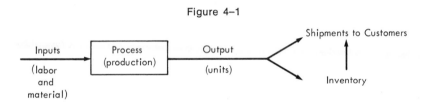

casted demand is 100 units in month 1 and 200 units in month 2, how can the input, production, and output rates be varied to meet these forecasts? One alternative is to change the input rate, production rate, and output rate simultaneously in moving from month 1 to month 2. In month 1, enough materials and manpower can be acquired to produce exactly 100 units. In month 2, the number of workers, the amount of material, and the rate of production can be doubled to produce 200 units of output. Another alternative is to keep the labor inputs (in terms of the number of workers) constant over the two months, and double materials inputs, production rates, and outputs. This could be accomplished by working overtime during the second month. A third alternative is to keep all the inputs and the production rate constant over both months. When input rate and production rate are fixed, the output rate is also fixed, but the disposition of the output may vary. If inputs and production rates were held constant for both months at a level sufficient to supply 150 units of output per month (300 in two months), 50 units of output would be inventoried in month 1 and 100 units shipped to customers, while in month 2 all of the output would be shipped along with the 50 units in inventory.

The advantage of one of these plans over another depends upon the relative magnitude of the costs associated with changing input and production rates, and the cost of the various ways of disposing of the output. These costs are likely to be both tangible and intangible. For example, the tangible costs of varying labor inputs from period to period would be the cost of advertising, interviewing, and training when new workers are hired, and severance and unemployment insurance charges when workers are laid off. The intangible costs of changing labor input levels may be reflected in a poor community image for a company, and labor unrest. The tangible costs of changing material inputs may be the costs associated with odd lot purchases of raw material, raw material inventory costs, and clerical order costs. The intangible costs may result from a disruption of supplier relationships. The tangible costs of changing production rates, given a work force of a certain size, show up in higher labor costs when overtime is used to increase production, or in even higher unit costs when labor is allowed to stand idle, to decrease production rates. The intangible costs here are those associated with disrupting the normal rhythm of work. The tangible costs of changing the disposition of output are generally reflected in inventory carrying changes. The intangible costs (or benefits) may be associated with the degree of flexibility to meet unexpected surges or drops in demand from forecast levels. All of these costs must be considered in developing a coordinated aggregate plan.

The aggregate plan and its components may be quite detailed, delimiting the production dates for specific products and work centers. However, it is frequently stated in general terms, a concession to the difficulty of planning with large quantities of data. For example, instead of planning the production of units of apples and units of oranges, an aggregate measure (tons of fruit) may be used. Likewise, labor may be planned using aggregate statistics such as the ratio of total labor-hours to sales dollars of output, rather than breaking down labor inputs by component work centers. The use of aggregate data (from whence the appellation aggregate planning) means that many detailed interactions in production are ignored. As a manager you will often have to decide whether a more detailed set of plans is worth the time and effort involved in obtaining them, or to fine tune a rough plan after "getting in the ballpark."

A SIMPLE EXAMPLE

To illustrate the process of aggregate planning and the tradeoffs involved in it, consider the ABC Company, a producer of appliances. Faced with the 12-month forecast shown in Table 4–1 (in equivalent appliances, an aggregate measure) the company must decide on an aggregate plan which will minimize costs. The relevant costs in this example are the costs of holding inventory ($1 per equivalent appliance per month); the cost of hiring a new worker ($500 per worker, based on expected training ex-

Table 4–1
ABC SHIPMENT FORECAST
(in equivalent appliances)

Jan.	Feb.	March	April	May	June
7,000	9,000	10,000	16,000	18,000	17,000

July	Aug.	Sept.	Oct.	Nov.	Dec.
8,000	8,000	7,000	6,000	5,000	5,000

penses); the cost of laying off a worker ($500 per worker including sever-ance pay and contributions to state unemployment insurance programs), the straight-time cost of an employee ($800 per month, 40-hour week), and the cost of utilizing overtime (1.5 times the straight-time labor cost). With the forecast, this cost data, and the knowledge that each worker can produce 50 equivalent appliances per month on straight time, that the pres-ent inventory is 600 appliances, that the present size of the work force is 150, and that the maximum physical capacity is 20,000 appliances per month, the ABC Company can evaluate various aggregate planning strate-gies. Because material inputs can be obtained on short notice, they are controlled separately. A materials plan is not included in the ABC Com-pany aggregate plan.

One strategy which the ABC Company can follow is called a "chase" strategy. Here, production levels "chase" demand by varying to the same extent that projected shipments do. One way this strategy can be accom-plished is by maintaining a constant work force, just large enough to pro-duce shipment requirements for the average month on regular time. Using this kind of labor-input plan, production levels can be changed by varying the length of the workday. That is, overtime can be used in peak months while enforced idleness can be used during slack periods. An aggregate plan consistent with this strategy is shown in Table 4–2. This plan was devised by noting that the average forecasted shipment rate is approxi-mately 10,000 units per month. Since each worker is expected to produce 50 units per month, a work force of $10,000 \div 50 = 200$ is required, which necessitates 50 hires in the first month. This work force level is more than adequate for producing requirements in most months on a regular time basis. However, in April, May, and June, projected shipments are greater than 10,000 units per month and overtime must be used. The amount of overtime required in these months can be calculated by finding the number of worker months of production required, and subtracting this figure from the planned size of the work force. For example, in April shipments are expected to be 16,000 units. This equates to $16,000 \div 50 = 320$ worker months of production. Since only 200 workers will be available in April, 120 $(320 - 200)$ worker months of overtime must be used.

Table 4–2

AGGREGATE PLAN 1: VARYING PRODUCTION—CONSTANT WORK FORCE

	Jan.	Feb.	March	April	May	June	July	Aug.	Sept.	Oct.	Nov.	Dec.
Shipment forecast*.	7,000	9,000	10,000	16,000	18,000	17,000	8,000	8,000	7,000	6,000	5,000	5,000
Production plan*.	6,400	9,000	10,000	16,000	18,000	17,000	8,000	8,000	7,000	6,000	5,000	5,000
Output Plan:*												
Shipments.	7,000	9,000	10,000	16,000	18,000	17,000	8,000	8,000	7,000	6,000	5,000	5,000
Inventory.	—	—	—	—	—	—	—	—	—	—	—	—
Input Plan:												
No. of workers.	200	200	200	200	200	200	200	200	200	200	200	200
Hires-layoffs (±).	+50	—	—	—	—	—	—	—	—	—	—	—
Overtime (Worker/months).	—	—	—	120	160	140	—	—	—	—	—	—

Cost of Plan 1:

Inventory cost. . . . . $ —

Hiring cost. . . . . 25,000 ($500 × 50 hires)

Labor cost:

Straight time . . . . $1,920,000 (200 workers × $800 per month × 12 months)

Overtime. . . . . 504,000 (120 + 160 + 140 = 420 worker months of overtime × $800 × 1.5)

Total Cost. $2,449,000

* In equivalent appliances.
† Inventory level at end of month. Note that 600 units initially in inventory were used with the 6,400 units produced in January to satisfy January demand.

The cost of this plan is $2,449,000. As might be expected, the largest portion of these costs are labor costs. These reflect overtime costs, and more importantly, the loss in productivity associated with maintaining a large work force during periods of low shipment volume. Note, for example, that during the month of December, labor productivity with this plan will only be 20 equivalent appliances per worker month.

Alternate ways of planning production, output, and input are reflected in the aggregate plans shown in Tables 4–3 and 4–4. Aggregate plan 2 (Table 4–3) is also based on the chase strategy, but it varies production rates by hiring and laying off workers rather than using overtime or undertime. In both of these variations on the chase strategy, however, production equals projected shipments in each month. The total costs of plan 2 are lower than for plan 1, reflecting the advantage of making the tradeoff between hiring and layoff costs and overtime/undertime costs. The total cost of plan 2, $2,103,400, represents an incremental advantage of almost $400,000 over the first.

Aggregate plan 3, shown in Table 4–4, reflects a different strategy. It seeks to maintain labor productivity and a stable work force by leveling production and building inventories. This "level production" strategy was developed by noting that in order to meet forecast demand in the last of the peak months, as well as in previous months, cumulative production must equal cumulative requirements up to that point. That is, cumulative production through June must equal 77,000 units (7,000 + 9,000 + 10,000 + 16,000 + 18,000 + 17,000). This can be accomplished by producing an equal amount in each of these first six months. The average production rate over this time span is thus about 13,000 units per month (77,000 units ÷ 6 months). Production at this constant rate requires 260 workers on regular time (13,000 units ÷ 50 units per worker per month. This production plan will allow inventories to accumulate in periods in which shipments are less than 13,000 units per month, and will result in their depletion when shipments are greater than 13,000 units per month.

Figure 4–2 shows a graphical method for developing a level production strategy. It illustrates the growth in cumulative shipments and production over the year with aggregate plan 3. The space between the cumulative shipments and production lines at a particular point in time indicates the amount of inventory on hand at that time. By way of contrast, cumulative production with a "chase" strategy is also shown in this graph. Of course, inventories are not created with a chase strategy. But since inventories can buffer the production plan from unexpected changes in shipment requirements, the level production strategy may be more flexible and thus more desirable, than the less costly "chase" plans.

These three aggregate plans represent but a few of many feasible alternatives. There are innumerable hybrids between the level and chase strategies. You should be able to identify several alternatives with lower costs than any of the three plans presented above.

Table 4-3
AGGREGATE PLAN 2: VARYING PRODUCTION—VARYING WORK FORCE

	Jan.	Feb.	March	April	May	June	July	Aug.	Sept.	Oct.	Nov.	Dec.
Shipment forecast*	7,000	9,000	10,000	16,000	18,000	17,000	8,000	8,000	7,000	6,000	5,000	5,000
Production plan*	6,400	9,000	10,000	16,000	18,000	17,000	8,000	8,000	7,000	6,000	5,000	5,000
Output Plan:*												
Shipments	7,000	9,000	10,000	16,000	18,000	17,000	8,000	8,000	7,000	6,000	5,000	5,000
Inventory†	—	—	—	—	—	—	—	—	—	—	—	—
Input Plan:												
No. of workers	128	180	200	320	360	340	160	160	140	120	100	100
Hires-layoff (±)	-22	+52	+20	+120	+40	-20	-180	—	-20	-20	-20	—
Overtime (worker/months)	—	—	—	—	—	—	—	—	—	—	—	—

Cost of Plan 2:

Inventory cost.	—
Hiring cost.	$ 116,000 (52 + 20 + 120 + 40 = 232 hires × $500)
Layoff cost.	141,000 (22 + 20 + 180 + 20 + 20 = 282 × $500)
Labor cost:	
Straight time.	$1,846,400 (128 + 180 + 200 + . . . + 100 + 100 = 2,308 worker months × $800)
Overtime.	—
Total Cost.	$2,103,400

* In equivalent appliances.
† Inventory level at end of month. Note that the 600 units initially in inventory were used with the 6,400 units produced in January to satisfy January demand.

Table 4-4
AGGREGATE PLAN 3: LEVELED PRODUCTION—CONSTANT WORK FORCE

	Jan.	Feb.	March	April	May	June	July	Aug.	Sept.	Oct.	Nov.	Dec.
Shipment forecast*	7,000	9,000	10,000	16,000	18,000	17,000	8,000	8,000	7,000	6,000	5,000	5,000
Production plan*	13,000	13,000	13,000	13,000	13,000	13,000	13,000	13,000	13,000	13,000	13,000	13,000
Output Plan:*												
Shipments	7,000	9,000	10,000	16,000	18,000	17,000	8,000	8,000	7,000	6,000	5,000	5,000
Inventory†	6,600	10,600	13,600	10,600	5,600	1,600	6,600	11,600	17,600	24,600	32,600	40,600
Input Plan:												
No. of workers	260	260	260	260	260	260	260	260	260	260	260	260
Hires-layoffs (±)	+110	—	—	—	—	—	—	—	—	—	—	—
Overtime (worker/months)	—	—	—	—	—	—	—	—	—	—	—	—

Cost of Plan 3

Inventory cost.	$ 182,200	(6,600 + 10,600 + . . . + 40,600 = 182,200 unit months × $1)
Hiring cost.	55,000	(110 hires × $500)
Layoff cost	—	
Labor cost:		
Straight time	$2,496,000	(260 workers × $800 per month × 12 months)
Overtime.	—	
Total Cost.	$2,733,600	

* In equivalent appliances.
† Inventory level at end of month.

Figure 4–2
GRAPHICAL METHOD FOR LEVELING PRODUCTION

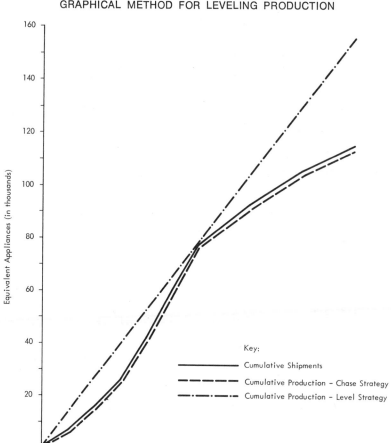

Key:
——————— Cumulative Shipments
– – – – – Cumulative Production – Chase Strategy
–·—·—·— Cumulative Production – Level Strategy

A number of mathematical methods[1] exist for determining the optimum (least cost) aggregate plan under the conditions described in the example. However, aggregate planning involves far more than determining a least cost plan by manipulating manpower levels and inventory policies. It also involves a consideration of the underlying production, financial, and marketing policies which give rise to the problem in the first place. An analysis of these policies in the light of environmental realities, can either eliminate a number of alternative aggregate plans, reducing the complexity of the problem, or admit ingenious solutions which transcend the manipulation of work force and inventory variables. For example, one such policy may

[1] See, for example, E. Buffa and W. Taubert, *Production Inventory Systems* (Richard D. Irwin, Inc., 1972).

involve a commitment to a stable work force, perhaps as a result of union pressures, tight labor markets, or quality considerations. This policy effectively limits the number of feasible aggregate plans by fixing the input plan. Marketing policies can also affect aggregate plans. The strategic timing of advertising and promotional campaigns can serve to smooth out demand over the year to help stabilize the production system. If these policies result in leveled demand patterns, the level and the chase strategies become one and the same. Similarly, financial policies can be used to smooth demand. Many firms in seasonal businesses use delayed billing and extended payment terms to encourage early buying. Policies such as this can effectively push the effects of seasonality out of the production system and into distribution channels. These are but a small sampling of the policy implications of aggregate planning.

USING THE AGGREGATE PLAN

Aggregate plans, production programs, budgets, or whatever they are called in a particular company, find wide usage both within the functional area of production, and without. This is true whether "production" takes place in a manufacturing or service business.[2] Their potential for usage in functional areas other than production are obvious. Marketing provides a basic input to the plan (the forecast), and can use it to gauge the amount of flexibility the business has to meet unexpected surges in demand. Finance uses the plan, in conjunction with other plans such as a marketing plan, to formulate budgets and project profits and cash flow requirements for inventories and payrolls. Service staff organizations, such as personnel, distribution, and purchasing also use the plan; personnel to carry out the hiring and laying off of workers, and as a basis for planning training programs; distribution to calculate derivative shipping and warehousing plans; purchasing as a basis for negotiating purchase contracts and delivery dates on raw materials.

Within the functional area of production, the aggregate plan serves as a basic road map from which more detailed plans can be drawn and implemented. The process by which the aggregate plan is decomposed into action plans, and then implemented during the consummate act of production, involves scheduling and dispatching.

SCHEDULING

The primary concern of scheduling is planning the utilization of available resources. It involves specifying the time, place, and personnel required to produce specific products. Thus, a schedule will ideally consist

---

[2] Note that an aggregate plan for a service business such as an airline, restaurant, or hospital, is essentially identical in form to that of a manufacturing enterprise. It is composed of a production plan, an output plan, and an input plan. However, it is frequently impossible to store a service in inventories. Thus, the production plan and the output plan will be essentially identical, and the labor input plan becomes the most critical component.

of instructions such as "Joe, Sam, Ollie, and Ellen will produce toasters on assembly line 7 from 10:00 A.M. to 4:00 P.M., on Monday, September 8. Then, Will, Larry, Harry, and Thelma will produce steam irons on assembly line 7 from 4:00 P.M. to 5:00 P.M. on Monday September 8." Rarely are schedules as detailed as these, for frequently people are permanently assigned to facilities or machines, thus requiring only the specification of the product and the time or quantity. In service operations, where the product line (the service) associated with a set of facilities is homogenous, it is only necessary to specify the time at which individuals are to work at the facilities. But a schedule always states, directly or inferentially, the location and timing of the production of a good or service.

The scheduling process itself remains one of the most challenging tasks in managing operations on a day-to-day basis. At the level of detail involved in scheduling, one is confronted directly with the problem of setting multidimensional priorities for allocating scarce resources; the priority of one product over another based on its profitability; the priority of one customer over another based on considerations of customer goodwill; the priority of one worker over another based on productivity standards or union work rules; the priority of one machine over another; or the priority of machine set up costs over inventory holding costs. In other words scheduling involves facing up to the multitude of tradeoffs so necessary in accomplishing any business function—important tradeoffs which are obscured when products, people, customers, and facilities are phrased in aggregate terms.

A Simple Example

The process of scheduling in a particular firm is influenced by a number of environmental factors, such as the nature of the market, the technology, and cost structures. The following example, however, illustrates the characteristics they hold in common, including the specification of the time and place of production, and the tangle of priorities and tradeoffs involved in arriving at a schedule.

Returning to the ABC Company, we may find that an important family of appliances is assembled on one of two assembly lines. Table 4–5 shows the current inventory position, unit profitability, economic order quantity (reflecting the assembly-line setup cost and inventory holding cost associated with each product), and a forecast of shipments for each of these products. As a result of an aggregate plan which was formulated in a previous period, enough workers have been hired to operate each of the assembly lines on a one shift basis. Emergency overtime, of course, can be used to extend the current regular time capacity of 100 units per line per week (20 units a day). The aggregate plan, made at the beginning of the year, does not call for any appreciable buildup of inventories or usage of overtime over this time horizon.

Table 4–5
ABC COMPANY PRODUCT LINE

Product	Inventory	Profit*	EOQ	Unit Forecast by Week					
				1	2	3	4	5	6
A	10	$10.00	100	80	20	20	30	30	30
B	10	8.00	300	20	40	20	20	50	50
C	200	8.00	200	20	20	40	20	20	20
D	20	11.00	200	60	50	30	20	20	20
E	200	14.00	100	30	40	80	50	40	40

* Profit contribution per unit.

ABC's scheduling problem is to allocate products to assembly lines (assuming that the crew at each line is fixed) over time. In performing this task, they must take into account several considerations. First, they would like to meet forecasted shipments. Failure to have enough on hand for shipments may mean lost sales at the retail level, or at the least, angry distributors. Second, they would like to produce in lot sizes that are as close as possible to the EOQs, to keep setup and inventory costs at a minimum. Third, they would like to maintain a high level of utilization for the assembly lines to keep labor productivity up, and avoid emergency overtime to keep costs down.

Figure 4–3 shows one possible schedule which the ABC Company can follow. It is in the form of a Gantt Chart, a helpful scheduling device which plots the usage of a key resource (in this case assembly lines) over time. This schedule was derived by recognizing the important deadlines and cost parameters, and using trial and error. First, the runout dates for each of

Figure 4–3
GANTT CHART SCHEDULE

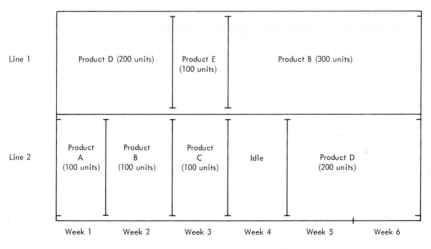

the products was derived. A glance at Table 4–5 shows that the demand for product A will exceed the inventory balance in week 1. The same is true for products B and D. The inventory of products C and E, on the other hand, will not "run out" until weeks 8 (approximately) and 4, respectively. This observation immediately places products A, B, and D on the high priority list. Using this knowledge, and the profitability of these products and their EOQs as a further guide, the production of specific products was allocated to the time periods and assembly lines shown on Figure 4–3.

The schedule shown in Figure 4–3 does not meet all the criteria we have stated. It allows product B inventory balances to fall below demand in week 1 for instance. This deficiency might be repaired by making an alternate schedule, or by calling a distributor and charming him into taking a shipment of product B a few days late. In several instances, the schedule plans production in lot sizes significantly different from the EOQ. Moreover, a week of idle time appears in the schedule for line 2 in week 4. These undesirable characteristics of the schedule may be eliminated by making any number of combinations of alternative schedules, marketing moves, or cost tradeoffs.

Using Schedules

Schedules like the one illustrated in the previous example serve two purposes. The first is as a communications document which notifies personnel in other functional areas when to expect the availability of certain products. In this regard, marketing is usually the most interested party. The schedule tells them if they will be late in meeting promised deliveries and allows them to take corrective action. Sometimes, schedules are sent intact to customers, so they can gauge the arrival of materials in planning their own production or inventories. These external uses of schedules explain why marketing personnel are often deeply involved in the process of scheduling.

The second major purpose of a schedule is as a foundation for derivative production and purchasing schedules. This function is particularly important in multistage production or service operations, where one factory or work center feeds parts to another. Suppose, for instance, that product E is assembled from two parts, one of which (part 1) is produced by another company and which must be ordered two weeks in advance, and another (part 2) which is produced within the ABC Company with a one-week lead time. Part 2, moreover, is produced with parts 3 and 4 which are purchased from outside suppliers with a one-week lead time. Noting the planned production of product E in the third week (see Figure 4–3), this information can be used to schedule the delivery of parts 3 and 4 at the beginning of the second week, the delivery of part 1 at the beginning of the third week, and the production of part 2 at the beginning of the

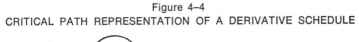

Figure 4–4
CRITICAL PATH REPRESENTATION OF A DERIVATIVE SCHEDULE

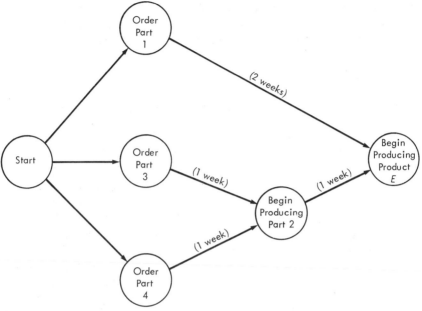

second week. Figure 4–4 is a critical path representation of this derivative schedule.

DISPATCHING

The final step in the sequence of short-term capacity management activities is dispatching, which involves implementing the production schedule. This should be a relatively easy task. *If* the forecast is correct, *if* the materials ordered as a result of the derivative scheduling procedures arrive on time, *if* the production of a product previously scheduled on a line is completed on time, *if* all the workers on the line are present, dispatching would be reduced to the simple act of writing a production authorization and handing it to the line supervisor so he can start producing. It doesn't happen that way. Materials are late, or sometimes lost, workers are absent, machines break down, and a whole host of random occurrences can make the schedule nothing more than a wish. Because of these uncertainties, dispatching involves taking corrective action—coercing vendors into speeding the delivery of needed materials, appeasing customers while telling them their order will be three weeks late, expediting the production of component parts, switching people around to operate vacant machines, making snap decisions on overtime—that's dispatching!

It is only in the light of this critical and inventive activity that one can fully understand the meaning of the word flexibility as it applies to the precursor aggregate plans and schedules. Realistically, one does not plan production in aggregate planning, nor schedule it in scheduling. One only sets the stage for this final stage where plans are transformed into action.

CONCLUSION

Dispatching, scheduling, and aggreggate planning are illustrated in the cases which immediately follow. They present the managerial problems associated with these activities and further illuminate the important economic and policy tradeoffs involved in solving them.

In the Kool King Division case, the effect of various aggregate plans on costs, marketing, quality, and labor relations are important concerns. In formulating an aggregate plan for Kool King, you will also be required to consider potential scheduling and dispatching problems. The second case, Productos de Concreto S.A. (D), presents the production, marketing, and financial problems of a Central American concrete block manufacturer. Many of these problems derive from the firm's method of scheduling. The third case, Eastern Airlines—December Schedule, illustrates the problems of dispatching and scheduling in a service business. Here, prior plans have been obsoleted by unpredictable weather conditions, and the formulation and implementation of a new December schedule must be accomplished. The last two cases in this section, Sunshine Builders, Inc., and Chaircraft Corporation, consider the whole complex of aggregate planning, scheduling, and dispatching issues which arise when one takes a broad strategic view of a company.

An important issue which links these cases together is the design of a planning and control system which integrates aggregate planning, scheduling, and dispatching together over time. The examples of aggregate planning, scheduling, and dispatching given in this chapter may be misleading in this regard. The functions these activities perform in terms of specifying how much, where, what kind, when and the how to's of short-term capacity management will remain the same. However, the timing and sequence in which such tradeoffs are made are not necessarily the same in all situations. These functions may be collapsed into one overall planning activity, or telescoped into more than the three common ones we have discussed. In different types of operating systems, these activities may also assume varying degrees of importance. For example, dispatching may be of primary importance in job shops, aggregate planning in seasonal assembly operations, and scheduling in the process industries, such as paper making or chemicals. Thus, in passing from this note which has stressed the similarities in short-term capacity management among businesses, you should slowly make the transition to analyses which consider individual differences.

Kool King Division

ON THE MORNING of September 4, 1964, Mr. Tom Stanley, Marketing Manager for Kool King air conditioners, called Mr. James Lewis, Vice President of the Kool King Division, and requested he schedule a meeting with key division personnel to discuss the latest forecast for fiscal 1965.[1] This group had already met several times during the past three months to discuss forecasts and production plans for the coming year.

Later in the day, Mr. Stanley drove to the Kool King plant in Melrose Park, Illinois, from corporate headquarters in Chicago and the meeting began in Lewis' office. Mr. Lewis, as division Vice President, was responsible for manufacturing, engineering, and product development. Others at the meeting were:

Mr. Robert Irwin—Plant Manager
Mr. Earl Williams—Division Controller
Mr. Russell Frank—Materials Control Supervisor
Mr. John Victor—Personnel Manager

"I've just finished a careful review of the final figures for fiscal 1964," Mr. Stanley stated. "I've also spent four days in the field talking with three of our key distributors and one of our largest retail accounts."

"We lost far more sales this past year than any of us realized. We knew about the stockouts of 208 volt models that hurt us in New York City and we discussed them at our last meeting, but it now looks like we underestimated the total effect of those stockouts."

"As a result of this kind of information and other data that I've pulled together, I've raised the forecast for the coming year to a little over 120,000 units." (See Exhibit 1.)

"You've got to be kidding, Tom," replied Mr. Irwin. "Just three weeks ago we all sat around this table and talked about 114,000 units."

---

[1] The fiscal year ran from September 1 to August 31.

Exhibit 1
SALES HISTORY AND FORECASTS

Fiscal Year	Actual Sales
1961	65,034 units
1962	64,636
1963	70,272
1964	102,874

	Fiscal 1964 Forecast Sales	Beginning Inventory Sept. 1, 1963	Fiscal 1964 Actual Sales	Ending Inventory Aug. 29, 1964	Latest Fiscal 1965 Forecast Sales
Midget	30,000	0	36,482	0	46,500
Mighty Midget.	13,000	753	8,499	1,420	11,000
Breeze Queen	33,000	6,136	38,620	2,165	41,000
Breeze King	4,000	1,320	6,647	0	8,000
Islander.	7,000	2,049	4,215	2,604	5,000
Super.	3,000	102	779	312	1,500
Slim Line.	10,000	9,144	7,632	1,512	10,000
Totals	100,000	19,504	102,874	8,013	123,000

"That's right, Bob, but I'm telling you that our stockouts hurt more than we realized. Also, this year's early delivery orders[2] are running well ahead of what we expected. I'm pretty sure of these figures now."

"While I have the floor," Mr. Stanley continued, "I want to report that many of our distributors say that, in addition to losing sales because retailers won't wait for factory shipments, they're getting an increasing number of quality complaints."

"I've heard some of these complaints myself," said Mr. Lewis. "You don't seem too worried about our product quality, Bob, but I'm concerned about our performance and about the possible negative effect of our quality on the image of other divisions."

Mr. Irwin addressed James Lewis: "I don't think quality is a big problem, we're doing as well as we ever have. The quality complaints I've heard are mostly nickel and dime oversights by new people on the line—getting the name-plate on crooked, not tightening the knobs, leaving the operations manual out of the carton, stuff like that. Our basic quality is still very good. Last year less than 0.5 percent of our production was returned for repair on warranty."

Tom Stanley broke into the conversation: "Look, what's important here is our increase in market share. Let's not kid ourselves. Sure, total sales have increased nicely lately, but the whole market is growing. We've got to do better than our competition in all respects. Crooked name plates and loose knobs don't build a market."

---

[2] Kool King's discount plan for distributors is discussed later in the case.

Mr. Irwin turned to Mr. Stanley: "The discount policy is helping us level out production to some extent, but your forecasts don't help. If we stuck to your figures as a basis for production, we'd have to buy a new warehouse to cover for the mix and timing variations which we always have to deal with."

COMPANY HISTORY

Kool King was a division of The TIA Corporation (Television Industries of America). TIA, headquartered in Chicago, Illinois, was organized in the early 1930s to manufacture radios. After World War II, the company diversified into other electronics products including television sets.

In 1953, through an acquisition, TIA expanded its line to include oil and gas burners, room air conditioners, and central cooling systems. The acquired company was sold in 1959 but the room air conditioner portion of the business and the Kool King brand name were retained. In 1960, the Kool King Division was established in a new plant in Melrose Park, Illinois. Growth of this division was a source of pride to TIA executives. Unit sales for the division for four years are shown in Exhibit 1. The division produced seven model lines of air conditioners shown in Table 1.

Table 1
KOOL KING PRODUCT LINE

Chassis Series	Cooling Capacity BTU^1	Voltage Rating	Mounting Hardware[4]		
			A	B	C
Midget	4,000	115		*	*
Slim Line[2]	5,500	115		*	
Mighty Midget.	6,000	115		*	*
	6,200	115 ⎫			
Breeze Queen[3].	8,000	115 ⎬	*	*	*
	9,300	208 or 230 ⎭			
Breeze King	9,000	115 ⎫	*	*	*
	11,000	208 or 230 ⎭			
	11,000	115 ⎫			
Islander.	14,000	208 or 230 ⎬		*	
	17,000	208 or 230 ⎭			
Super.	24,000	208 or 230		*	

[1] BTU (British Thermal Unit) was the standard cooling capacity unit used to rate air conditioners. Manufacturers' ratings of their units were checked by representatives of the National Electrical Manufacturers Association (NEMA) at frequent intervals. Earlier methods of rating air conditioners (tons, horsepower, etc.) were no longer used in 1964.

[2] Slim Line Units were designed to fit casement-type windows which in general were narrower than double-hung windows. The Slim Line Units were also frequently sold for installation in double-hung windows too narrow to accommodate the regular units.

[3] The Breeze Queen series was available with a reverse cycle feature allowing the same unit to operate as a heater or an air conditioner.

[4] Mounting hardware was available in three different designs. Available hardware shown by an asterisk.

All marketing of Kool King products was handled by TIA marketing people. TIA distributors in several large cities sold Kool King air conditioners as part of the full TIA line. Kool King products were also sold through TIA's field sales force to independent jobbers and to large retail accounts. Mr. Stanley had been with TIA for four years. He had assumed marketing responsibility for the Kool King product line, his first major responsibility in the firm, in December 1962. He was concerned primarily with marketing planning and advertising. Field sales for Kool King were headed by a colleague of Tom Stanley—both individuals reported to a marketing vice president who was responsible for a product group of which Kool King was a part.

PRODUCTION FACILITIES

The division production facilities in Melrose Park were located in a modern, one-story building with 100,000 square feet of floor space. The division had no facilities for manufacturing any of the components used in its air conditioners—all component parts were purchased from outside suppliers. A typical room air conditioner had 200 parts, a dozen of which represented 85 percent of the material cost of an individual unit. Ten per-

Exhibit 2
LAYOUT OF ASSEMBLY LINE

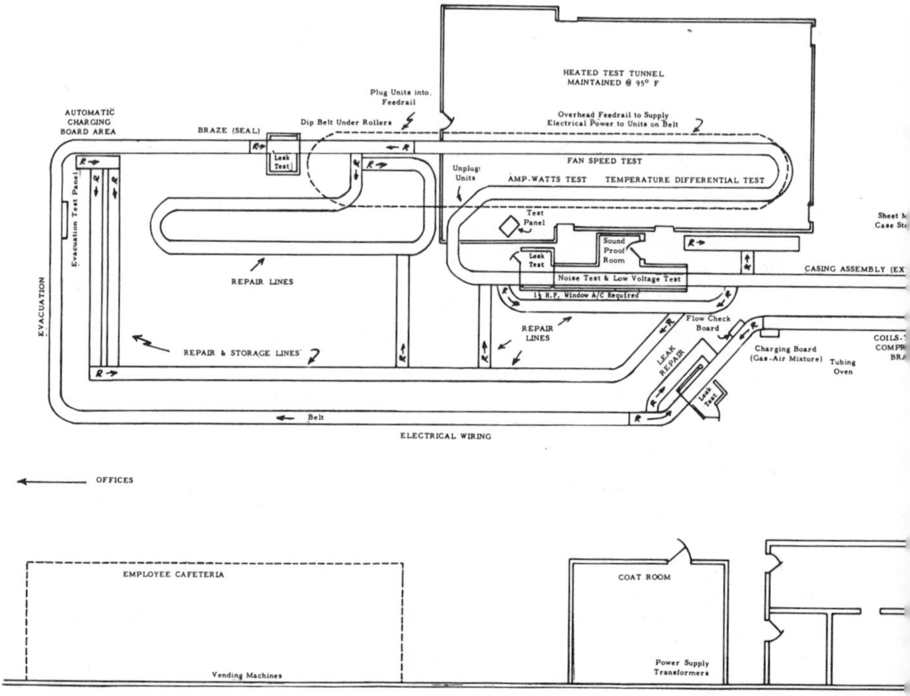

cent of the component parts were common to different chassis series. Within a given series, however, 75 percent of the parts were common.

Most models were assembled on a single assembly line. Differences in construction dictated that only one chassis type could be produced at a time. A large portion of the line consisted of a waist-high, roller conveyor along which partially assembled units riding on plywood pallets were pushed manually. Other portions of the line had a moving belt which moved the units along automatically at a preset speed. Most of the parts were screwed or bolted to the chassis by hand tools or small air-powered wrenches. Motors, compressors and cooling coils, purchased already assembled, were easily mounted and wired to the chassis. The compressed gas charge required careful handling and frequent checking for leaks. Exhibit 2 shows the layout of the assembly line and describes the operations performed along its length.

SEASONAL SALES AND DISCOUNT STRATEGY

The sale of air conditioners involved a marked seasonal trend. In the early days of room air conditioners, the sales year ran from June 1 to August 1. As the industry developed, the sales year for room air condition-

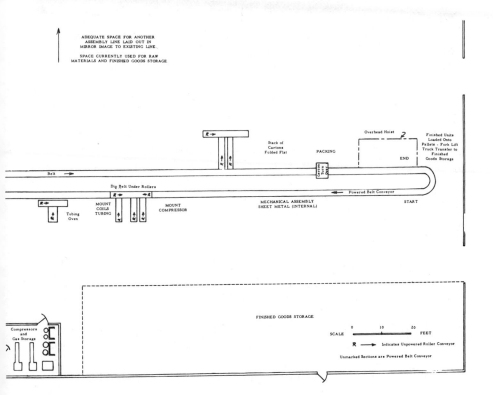

ers lengthened. The company had attempted to broaden the production year by offering substantial discounts to distributors if they took delivery of air conditioners between October and February rather than March to June. Discount and deferred payment plans had been recommended for several years by Mr. Irwin and Mr. Lewis. In fiscal 1964, their suggestions had been adopted, and the following plans were again in effect for 1965.

I. Early Order Discount Plan

All orders received after September 1, 1964, but before November 1, 1964, will receive an early-order discount off the regular manufacturers F.O.B. Melrose Park, Illinois, prices. Deliveries on such early orders will be scheduled as follows:

One-quarter of the order in October.
One-quarter of the order in November.
One-quarter of the order in December.
One-quarter of the order in January.

II. Deferred Payment Plan

Payment for any orders received before February 1, 1965, will be due in three equal installments—May 10, 1965, June 10, 1965, and July 10, 1965.

Sixteen thousand units had been ordered in fiscal 1964 under the early order discount plan. Mr. Stanley estimated that 24,000 units would qualify for early order discounts in fiscal 1965.

A growing consumer attitude that air conditioning was a necessity helped to lengthen out the sales year. With one out of eight homes in the United States having at least one air conditioner, replacement sales were beginning to rise; these were made from early April to early September. The small, quick installation Midget unit was introduced in 1963 and sold for $100 retail. An entirely new market was expected to open up for this unit characterized by multiple purchases, impulse buying, capturing a portion of the market for large fans, and an extended buying season. In contrast, the 24,000 BTU unit, selling for $400 and requiring professional installation, would typically be purchased in April or May. Seasonality was influenced somewhat by weather, but mainly at the extremes. A chilly April would reduce sales significantly, whereas a hot April led to very brisk sales.

PLANT WORK FORCE

In 1964, the Kool King Division employed 150 people of whom approximately 100 were classified as "direct labor." Included in the 150 employees was an executive group of six—the vice president of the division, the plant manager, the personnel manager, the accounting manager, the materials control manager and the director of engineering. Four other groups of employees were classed in categories other than hourly employees. These four groups were: the plant foremen (4) the purchasing agents (4), the engineering and design group (16), and the clerical staff (8).

A total of 112 employees were classified in eight grades as follows:

Grade 1   Assembly line workers. No previous skills required. Approximately two-day training period. (70)

Grade 2   Inspectors, janitors, and "spares"—people trained for any position on the line as replacement for absent workers or workers temporarily called away from the line. (10)

Grade 3   Repair men who repaired defective units discovered in the final test area of the assembly line, fork lift truck drivers, station wagon driver, stock clerks, receiving and shipping department employees. (14)

Grade 4   Group leader in the stockroom. (1)

Grade 5   Refrigeration mechanic, employees who sealed the tubing used in air conditioners, mechanical inspector in the receiving area. (8)

Grade 6   Maintenance men (a carpenter, an electrician, and a plumber), quality control spot checkers. (5)

Grade 7   Line supervisors. (3)

Grade 8   A machinist and model maker. (1)

All direct labor was paid on an hourly basis with no incentive. New Grade 1 employees were paid $1.60 per hour, a competitive wage in the Melrose Park area for unskilled labor. The union contract provided regular pay increases for Grade 1 employees over a period of 18 months. After 18 months, a Grade 1 employee reached $2.00 per hour and could increase his hourly rate only by moving to a higher grade. The contract also provided a 30-day trial period for new employees. During this period the company could discharge an employee without consulting the union. The reason for most dismissals during the trial period was that new employees could or would not maintain the relatively rapid pace required on the job.

Mr. Victor, the personnel manager, had estimated the cost of changing the size of the work force.[3] He stated: "The turnover of Grade 1 employees, within the 30-day trail period, is quite large when compared to that of unskilled employees in other plants around here. Although this situation isn't too desirable, it's not serious because assembly line operations are carefully laid out by our industrial engineers. We estimate that new employees are up to peak efficiency within two days."

Turnover of personnel in higher grades was another matter: "Skilled production employees are vital to maintaining our product quality and plant efficiency. We try to keep turnover in Grades 2 through 8 as low as possible by avoiding a varying rate of production, which involves laying off and then rehiring skilled workers."

---

[3] See Exhibit 3.

Exhibit 3

KOOL KING DIVISION

MEMORANDUM

To: Bob Irwin
From: John Victor

Subject: Costs of Changing the Size of the Work Force

As I have previously mentioned, we have no exact data on the costs of changing the size of our work force. Since we cannot change the number of assembly workers on the main line without rebalancing the job assignments, we have not had much experience with more than two or three work force levels on the main assembly line.

The costs involved in hiring a new worker can be estimated as follows:

Application Processing, Interview and Selection (character reference check, etc.)	
3 hours employment office clerical time at $6 per hour	$18.00
1 hour interviewer's (personnel manager's) time at $7 per hour	7.00
Physical examination	10.00
Payroll entry preparation	
30 minutes per new employee at $7 per hour	3.50
For payroll clerk and overhead	0
Training	
Assume 2 days per worker at $13 per day	26.00
Plus lost time for experienced worker-trainer, say 1 day at $20 per day	20.00
Plus lost time for foreman, say ½ day at $30 per day.	15.00
Total.	$99.50

In addition to these costs, any significant increase in the number of employees would require more supervisory personnel, more indirect labor (order clerks, receiving clerks, stock room clerks, materials handlers, etc.) and perhaps extra costs for maintenance and repair.

Decreasing the size of the work force involves costs that are even more difficult to estimate. In some cases, laying off grade 1 employees and replacing them with new workers actually would result in a saving because of the automatic wage increase feature of the union contract. However, our unemployment compensation costs are tied to the stability of our work force. Our maximum contribution is 2.7 percent of the employee's pay up to the first $3,000. This contribution can drop to as low as 0.1 percent if the cumulative amounts of withdrawals from the compensation fund by employees laid off is small for the past 3 years.

Wide swings in our employment level may be costly in terms of bad will in the community and may also adversely affect the quality of our product.

The plant had shut down for a period of 40 working days in 1961, 1962 and 1963. In 1964 this was cut to 30 days.

PRODUCTION PLANNING

Production planning for the Kool King Division had in past years started in May. In a series of meetings, Kool King and TIA executives laid out general guidelines for the division's production for the next fiscal year. The production planning meetings in 1964 had begun with an aggregate forecast of air conditioner sales for the coming year presented by Mr. Stanley. Kool King executives usually questioned some features of the forecast. For example, the 1964 TIA forecast had been based on the assumption that the new Mighty Midget would not only take over a portion of the market of the smaller Midget unit, but also increase total sales volume. Mr. Lewis had believed this assumption to be erroneous, and had pointed out that the Mighty Midget's $150 price opened a new sales market in this price range in addition to the $100 Midget market.

A large chart was prepared to facilitate the development of a production plan for the division (see Exhibit 4 for the plan which has been adopted one year ago for fiscal 1964). The number of units in a given series which could be produced in a week at the normal work force level was determined from the production rates shown in Exhibit 4.

In determining the production plan to be entered on the chart, division executives were guided by three policies which they believed to be very important: (1) the desire to minimize fluctuations in the size of the work force throughout the production year, (2) a preference for a large lot size since model-change-over costs were estimated at $2,000 per change (a 10,000 unit run was considered optimal. If demand for a certain model was 20,000 units, the planners tried to schedule two runs during the year), and (3) a finished goods inventory containing almost all the division's products. Because distributors frequently order in truckload lots to minimize freight costs, most orders were for a mixture of large and small quantities of several different units. Production plans had to account for this product mix requirement.

The production plan (Exhibit 4) was not intended as a production schedule for the whole year. Production plans on the chart were for aggregated groups of product and did not show, for example, the BTU or voltage rating on products, the number of units to be made with or without the heating feature, etc. Detailed production schedules were issued frequently throughout the year by the materials control supervisor, Mr. Frank. These schedules listed the production schedule for a 12-week period and showed in detail the number and type (voltage, accessories, etc.) of each model to be made each week. These schedules were reviewed and reissued at least once a month so the net effect of a series of these overlapping schedules was to reschedule the production for a given period at least three times. As a production year progressed, information was received which tended to force changes in the original production plan. Because such changes were quite frequent, management liked to keep the schedule flexible at all times. Information on actual production and shipments is shown in Exhibits 5 and 6.

Any changes from the original production plan meant a change in the planned pattern of component parts acquisition. In fiscal 1964, Kool King processed $7 million worth of purchased parts. Mr. Frank attempted to

Exhibit 4
PLANNED PRODUCTION BY WEEK—FISCAL 1964

Chassis Series

	Midget	Mighty Midget	Breeze Queen	Breeze King	Islander	Super*	Slim Line†
Estimated 1964 sales	30,000	13,000	33,000	4,000	7,000	3,000	10,000
Inventory, September 1, 1963	0	753	6,136	1,320	2,049	102	9,144
Estimated 1964 production requirements	30,000	12,000	27,000	3,000	5,000	3,000	0
Production rate (units per day)	550	550	325	325	275	65	550
Week ending							
September 7	550						
14	1,000						
21	2,750						
28	2,750						
October 5	2,750						
12	2,750						
19	1,450	1,300					
26		2,700					
November 2		2,000					
9			1,075				
16			1,625				
23			1,625				
30			1,300				
December 7			1,625				
14			1,625				
21			1,625				
28			1,300				
January 4			200	975			
11				1,625			
18				400	975		

Month	Date				
				1,375	
February	8	50		1,275	50
	15	2,200			250
	22	2,750			250
	29	2,750			250
March	7	2,750			250
	14	2,750			250
	21	2,750			250
	28	2,750			250
April	4	2,750			250
	11	500	1,200		250
	18		1,625		250
	25		1,625		250
May	2		1,625		200
	9		1,625		
	16		1,625		
	23		1,625		
	30		1,625		
June	6		1,625		
	13		800		
	20				
	27		CONTEMPLATED		
July	4				
	11		INVENTORY		
	18				
	25		AND		
August	1				
	8		VACATION		
	15				
	22		SHUTDOWN		
	29				

* The Super units were assembled on a small assembly line which was not part of the main assembly line.
† The Slim Line unit was scheduled for a complete redesign in 1964—no production of Slim Line units was contemplated until 1965.

Exhibit 5

ACTUAL PRODUCTION, SHIPMENTS, INVENTORIES (UNITS) AND DIRECT LABOR INDEX BY WEEK—FISCAL 1964

Chassis Series

Week ending	Midget	Mighty Midget	Breeze Queen	Breeze King	Islander	Super	Total Production	Shipments	Finished Goods Inventory	Direct Labor Hours Index†
August 31			* (1)				—	—	19,504	—
September 7			441				441	128	19,817	48.4
14	1,149						1,149	31	20,935	88.4
21	2,005						2,005	292	22,648	95.0
28	2,277						2,277	208	24,717	111.4
October 5	2,568	*					2,568	521	26,764	116.1
12	2,715	*					2,715	660	28,819	120.1
19	2,849	*					2,849	968	30,700	121.3
26	2,831	*					2,831	1,876	31,655	120.3
November 2		2,693					2,693	2,786	31,562	123.2
9		1,298					1,298	441	32,419	76.9(7)
16		301	1,300				1,601	1,503	32,517	112.0
23			1,685				1,685	469	33,733	111.2
30			1,043				1,043	651	34,125	66.7(2)
December 7			1,689				1,689	114	35,700	109.0
14			1,623				1,623	266	37,057	103.5
21			1,587				1,587	1,417	37,227	106.9
28			664				664	2,746	35,145	47.0(3)
January 4			671				671	2,315	33,501	52.5(2)
11			1,155	360			1,515	285	34,731	115.6
18			442	400			842	1,031	34,542	58.9(4)
25				1,401			1,401	1,237	34,706	100.0
February 1				324	967		1,291	1,054	34,943	113.6
8					895		895	1,432	34,406	82.2
15					1,516		1,516	2,698	33,224	116.6
22					1,072		1,072	1,519	32,777	103.4
29			1,125	*	320		1,445	3,561	30,661	97.9(2)

March	7		1,155		480			1,635	1,413	30,883	126.4

Date						Super	Total units		Inventory	Index
March 7			1,155		480		1,635	1,413	30,883	126.4
14			1,684			130(8)	1,814	1,570	31,127	139.4
21			1,431			275(8)	1,706	2,326	30,507	137.4
28			1,237(6)		200	231(8)	1,668	1,830	30,345	121.3
April 4	*			1,582		287(8)	1,869	1,076	31,138	134.4
11	*		1,054	580		66(8)	1,700	2,423	30,415	131.4
18	100		1,540				1,640	3,344	28,711	135.9
25	2,334						2,334	5,613	25,432	134.3
May. 2	2,925						2,925	4,146	24,211	129.0
9	2,917						2,917	2,771	24,357	130.2
16	2,893						2,893	3,694	23,556	129.2
23	2,762						2,762	3,225	23,093	127.4
30	900		1,087				1,987	7,038	18,042	123.8
June 6			1,985				1,985	4,898	15,129	143.9(5)
13	*		2,117				2,117	2,198	15,048	136.1
20	*		1,995				1,995	2,587	14,456	132.2
27	*		1,985				1,985	5,061	11,380	131.4
July. 4	*		2,019				2,019	2,354	11,045	132.7
11	*	1,565	1,114				2,679	3,511	10,213	132.4(5)
18	3,309		136				3,445	3,302	10,356	138.2
25	3,329		45				3,374	4,538	9,192	135.0
August . . . 1	1,928		577				2,505	2,981	8,716	130.1
8			60			60		557	8,219	Inventory
15		3		*	3			105	8,117	and
22	*	*				–		51	8,066	Vacation
29	*	*				–		53	8,013	Shutdown
Totals	36,482	9,166	34,649	5,327	4,770	989	91,383	102,874		

* Stocked out.

† This index was calculated by dividing the actual direct labor hours for each week by the direct labor hours for the week ending January 25, i.e., index = 100 for week ending January 25.

(1) Stocked out of 9,300 BTU model only.
(2) One day holiday this week—holidays often followed by substantial absenteeism.
(3) Two day holiday this week.
(4) Two day plant shutdown—snow storm delayed receipt of parts from a supplier in West Virginia.
(5) One day holiday this week not taken—i.e., overtime paid for working on holiday.
(6) Parts shortage for Breeze Queen units.
(7) Two day plant shutdown—election day and shortage of Mighty Midget motors.
(8) The Super units were not run on the main assembly line.

Exhibit 6

MONTHLY SUMMARY OF PRODUCTION, SHIPMENTS AND FINISHED GOODS INVENTORIES

	Sept.	Oct.*	Nov.†	Dec.	Jan.*	Feb.	March	April*	May	June	July*	Aug.	Total
Monthly shipments	659	6,811	3,064	4,543	5,922	9,210	7,139	16,602	16,728	14,744	16,686	766	102,874
Percent of year's shipments shipped this month	0.64	6.62	2.98	4.42	5.76	8.95	6.94	16.14	16.26	14.33	16.22	0.74	100.00
Percent of year's shipments cumulative	0.64	7.26	10.24	14.66	20.42	29.37	36.31	52.45	68.71	83.04	99.26	100.00	
Average finished goods inventory during month	22,029	29,900	33,198	36,282	34,485	32,767	30,715	27,981	22,262	14,003	9,904	8,104	

* For the months of October, January, April and July, the shipments for the first day or two of the next month were included, e.g., October figures include data from week ending November 2.

† Commitments on the early order discount plan were not met in November due to shortages in the stock of several models.

Exhibit 6 (*Continued*)

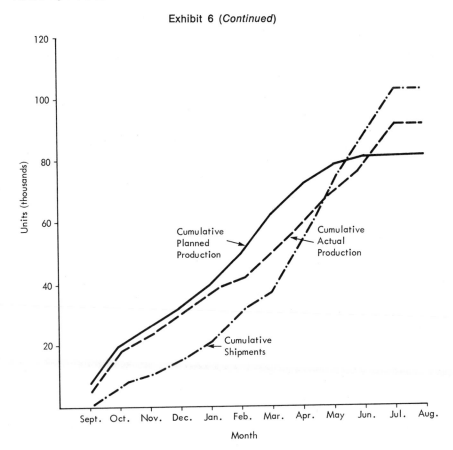

keep no more than two weeks component parts inventory on hand at any one time. For models running on the assembly line the component parts inventory might be as low as one or two days' production requirements, since material was being received regularly. For models which were not being produced currently, component parts inventory could be as much as one or two months ahead of scheduled production. This was particularly true when extreme changes were made in the schedule.

Mr. Frank hoped to plan schedules 12 weeks in advance. In actual practice some planning had to be done more than 12 weeks ahead. The purchasing of steel, for example, required planning up to four months in advance of production. On the other hand, many decisions could not be made and then held for 12 weeks. Developments in the market often forced the company to change the schedule with only one or two weeks' notice. The minimum advance notice required to make changes in the schedule was a function of the lead time of the suppliers of component parts. If all the parts were in inventory or on order, a one- or two-week lead time often

Exhibit 6 (*Concluded*)

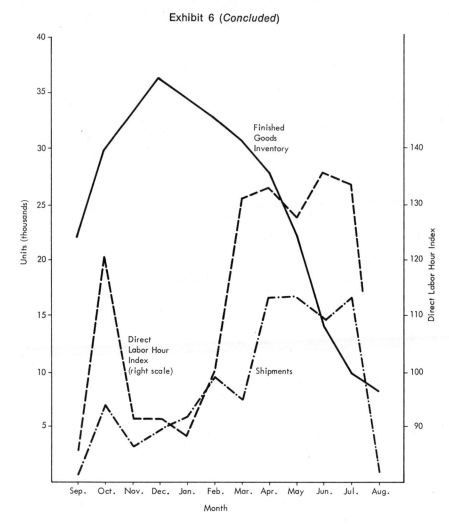

Month

caused no difficulty. If a major change in the schedule was contemplated, however, a number of suppliers could not furnish the required parts without a five-, six-, or sometimes even an eight-week lead time. This was especially true when Kool King attempted to make major changes in the orders for motors or cooling coils.

Mr. Lewis stated, "There are obviously different points of view about what's important here. One thing I'm sure we all agree on is that we need a new plan and we need it fast. What do you think, Bob?"

Mr. Irwin replied, "Frankly, I wonder if we should really run with this new forecast. Tom is planning almost a 30 percent increase in sales of the Midget unit. Keep in mind that we're not the only ones in the market with a $100 unit any more. Also, I think this increase in the forecast will push us beyond one-shift capacity."

"This is a realistic forecast," Mr. Stanley said. "You fellows have to realize that we're in a rapidly growing market and just holding our market share will give us considerable growth."

"We'll have to evaluate this thing carefully," Mr. Irwin replied. "This may cause quite a bit of overtime or perhaps a second shift for part of the year. We've got the space for a second assembly line and I suppose, on a crash program, we could have it installed by Christmas."

The controller, Mr. Williams said, "One of the problems that we face when annual demand begins to push against our capacity is that our finished goods inventories go up. I've got some figures on inventory costs for last year (see Exhibit 7). Even at a 4 percent cost of capital we spent $30,000 to carry excess inventory."

Exhibit 7

ANALYSIS OF INVENTORY CARRYING COSTS—FISCAL 1964
(prepared by Mr. Williams)

I. *Annual Space Cost*

Space cost 9/1/63–8/29/64

$$\frac{\$155,000}{100,000 \text{ sq.ft. plant space}} = \$1.55 \text{ cost per sq.ft.}$$

II. *Warehousing Space*

(1) Sum of weekly inventory $1,308,798 \div 52$ weeks = 25,169 average units
     Less: Basic inventory quantity carried weekly
              as part of manufacturing operations   −15,000*
     Average excess warehousing weekly inventory   10,169 units per week

(2) Average floor space required per unit = .725 sq.ft. (units stacked in pallet loads)
     Add 40 percent for idle space (aisles, etc.)

$0.725 \times 1.4 = 1.015$ sq.ft. per unit (space occupied by average unit)

III. *Warehousing Labor*

1 worker full time 52 weeks at $100 = $5,200 per year

IV. *Cost of Finished Goods*

Standard cost of average unit produced 9/1/63–8/29/64 = $96.80 average unit cost

V. *Total Dollars Tied up in Finished Goods Inventory*

Space $1.55 per sq.ft. × 10,169 units × 1.015 sq.ft. per unit = $	16,000
Labor =	5,200
Finished goods 10,169 units × $96.80 average cost per unit =	984,500
Total dollars	$1,005,700

VI. *Cost of Total Dollars Tied up in Finished Goods*

$1,005,700 × .04 corporate interest rate × $\frac{39}{52}$ (finished goods inventory exceeds 15,000

units on 39 weeks only)   = $30,000

---

* Manufacturing assumes that 15,000 units of finished goods inventory are required to permit long runs and to assist in leveling production. Inventory charges are assessed only against units over 15,000.

Mr. John Victor, Personnel manager, added: "Don't forget though, Earl, that inventory buys us something. The work force can't be counted on to stick with us when we change things around. As a good example, yesterday morning when we opened the plant after our annual shutdown, 30 workers didn't show up. Even though a number of our skilled workers received 2 or 3 weeks of paid vacation during the shutdown, 7 workers from Grades 3 and 5 didn't come back."

Productos de Concreto S.A. (D)[1]

PRODUCTS DE CONCRETO S.A. of San Jose, Costa Rica, Central America, fabricated a wide line of products derived from cement, including concrete pipes for sewers and drains, blocks, floor joists, pillars for electric transmission lines, mosaics and terrazzo blocks for floors, and septic tanks. Because of the weight of cement products, almost all of the company's sales were within Costa Rica. The company's market, however, was in the midst of a boom in public, industrial, and private construction. Company sales for recent years were:

1958	$240,000	1962	$650,000
1959	370,000	1963	740,000
1960	480,000	1964	790,000
1961	570,000	1965	900,000

Sales for 1966 were projected at $1.2 million and at midyear were running ahead of projection.

The company was founded in 1948 by two engineers, Jorge Figuls and Trino Araya. Production began in the backyard of Mr. Araya's home, with two workers producing concrete pipes by hand. Mr. Figuls sold his share of the company in 1950. Subsequently, other companies merged with the original firm to form the present corporation.

In 1966 the company employed 260 persons and was the largest Costa Rican producer in its field. Its engineers had not only assisted in the construction of structures using the company's products in Costa Rica, but also had consulted on construction jobs in Panama, Honduras, El Salvador,

---

[1] This case is a revision of Productos de Concreto S.A. (C). Monetary values have been changed from Costa Rican colones to American dollars (exchange rate = 6.66 colones per dollar) for the convenience of American students. To protect the proprietary interest of the company some of the information in this case has been disguised.

Exhibit 1
ADMINISTRATIVE ORGANIZATION

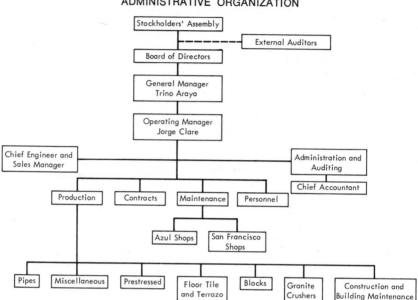

Nicaragua, and other countries. The organization chart in Exhibit 1 reflects the diverse activities of Productos.

The Operating Manager was Jorge Clare, who had formed a partnership in 1952 to manufacture mosaic and terrazzo blocks. His company merged with Productos in 1958, and he was successively in charge of the tile department, Superintendent of Production, and Production Manager before becoming Operating Manager. In his current capacity Mr. Clare was involved in all aspects of management at Productos. For example, in July 1966, he was supervising the installation of two large pipe producing machines and the construction of a maintenance shop in addition to his day-to-day activities. The management personnel included also Eddy Bravo, Chief Engineer and Sales Manager.

CONCRETE BLOCKS

This case focuses on the production of concrete blocks, begun by Productos in 1950. (Part of the line of blocks as of 1966 is shown in Exhibit 2.)

The process consisted of mixing sand, crushed stone, cement, water, and some additives; packing this mixture into molds; removing the molds; and curing the block. In the early days of the company this entire process was done by hand. In 1953, vibrating stands were introduced to improve the packing of concrete into molds. By 1962, 20 workers were producing a

Exhibit 2
SOME OF THE BLOCKS MANUFACTURED

	Block Type	Price
10 × 20 × 40 cm. block	1	$0.125
10 × 20 × 20 cm. block	3	0.060
15 × 20 × 20 cm. block	4	0.150
Pavas type block 12 × 25 × 25 cm.	9	0.099
Pavas type half block 12 × 12 × 25 cm.	11	0.052
20 × 20 × 40 cm. block−2 holes	12	0.180
20 × 20 × 20 cm. half block−1 hole	13	0.125
20 × 20 × 20 cm. crown block	14	0.125
Prestressed floor block, 12.7 kilograms	A	0.300

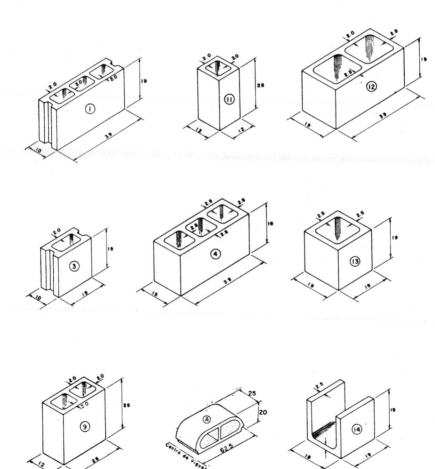

total of 5,000 blocks per day of the large-selling block number 9, using machine-mixed concrete and vibrating stands for packing the molds.

Mr. Clare described the period of 1962 as follows: "We had grown through mergers and we had improved our process, but at the same time we had become a high-cost producer. We had a large overhead, which our competitors did not, and both we and they were basically manufacturing by hand processes. Our biggest selling block was number 9, which I can use as an example. We sold our number 9 blocks at $0.115 each. None of our competitors charged more, and most charged less. We had lost part of our share of the block market and were losing money on blocks. Something had to be done. One alternative was to get out of the concrete block business.

"We chose another alternative. We lowered our price to $0.081 per block and we sought automatic equipment to lower our cost. A U.S. machine designed to make standard sizes of concrete blocks was available for $30,000 but it was not capable of manufacturing a large floor block (block A) which represented roughly 25 percent of our block business. To get a U.S. machine capable of manufacturing all blocks would cost $90,000. A German machine that could make all our blocks—including block A—but was of somewhat lighter construction, had slightly less capacity, and produced a block of not quite as good quality, was available for $30,000. We chose the German machine on the basis of lower cost, and we were able to pay for it without borrowing. Borrowing would cost us at least 9 percent for loans under a year and perhaps as high as 11 percent on long loans. Our purchase made us the only block maker in Costa Rica using automatic equipment.

"At the same time we continued our emphasis on quality. Our blocks are the only Costa Rican blocks that meet the standards published by the American Society for Testing Materials (see Exhibit 3). We achieve this level of quality through care at all steps in the process. For instance, our incoming sand is tested to be sure that it is free of organic material. Next, we make our batches of aggregate according to accurate weights of the components. We visually inspect all blocks for cracks as they leave the molds. Finally, we carry out destructive testing of one block in each thousand. The blocks made by machine have been much more uniform than the blocks formerly made by hand. In addition to reliable quality, we give reliable deliveries. Construction firms have learned that our blocks will arrive at the construction sites as agreed.

"We regained a large share of the market, and we were able to raise our price on block number 9 to $0.099 each. At this price and with our automatic equipment we make a profit."

PRODUCTION OF CONCRETE BLOCKS BY MACHINE

Wall blocks numbers 1, 3, 4, 9, 11, 12, 13 and floor block A were manufactured one-type-at-a-time on the automatic machine using remov-

Exhibit 3
EXCERPTS FROM STANDARD SPECIFICATIONS FOR HOLLOW LOAD BEARING CONCRETE MASONRY UNITS
Specification C 90-52

SCOPE

1. These specifications cover hollow load-bearing concrete masonry wall units made from portland cement and suitable aggregates such as sand, gravel, crushed stone, bituminous or anthracite cinders, burned clay or shale, pumice, volcanic scoria, air-cooled or expanded blast-furnace slag, and other slag.

CINDER AGGREGATE

2. The combustible content present in cinder aggregate shall not exceed 35 percent of the weight of the aggregate.

PHYSICAL REQUIREMENTS

3. At the time of delivery to the site of the work the units shall conform to the physical requirements prescribed in Table I.

Table I
PHYSICAL REQUIREMENTS

	Compressive Strength Minimum, psi (average gross area)		Moisture Content Maximum, Percentage of Total Absorption
	Average of 5 Units	Individual Unit	Average of 5 Units
Grade B	700	600	40

PERMISSIBLE VARIATIONS IN DIMENSIONS

4. No over-all dimension (width, height, and length) shall differ more than 1/8 in. from the specified standard dimensions.

VISUAL INSPECTION

5. All units shall be sound and free from cracks or other defects that would interfere with the proper placing of the unit or impair the strength or permanence of the construction.

MARKING

6. All units shall bear a distinctive mark of the manufacturer or shall be otherwise readily identified as to origin.

able molds. Other blocks were manufactured in lesser quantities by the older, hand method.

The machine process began with the weighing of the materials. Aided by gravity, a worker filled a hoist bucket resting on a scale with sand and crushed stone and then dumped in the contents of cement bags and a proprietary combination of additives. The raw materials were then raised by the skip hoist to the top of a 14-foot steel structure where the load charged a cement mixer. Water was added and the ingredients mixed. The wet concrete was batch-dumped into a holding tank from which it was farther dropped automatically in smaller quantities to fill the mold in use.

The forming of the blocks was carried out near the bottom of the steel structure. In a repetitive, automatic cycle the following took place: a wooden pallet was positioned under the mold; the mold, open at top and bottom, came down on the pallet; the mold was filled from the top with concrete under pressure and the mold and pallet were vibrated together; lastly, the mold was separated from the blocks leaving them standing on the wooden pallet. The pallets moved away from the machine, riding on moving, parallel steel cables which passed over spaced, grooved wheels. A short distance from the machine the blocks passed under a revolving brush which removed excess material from the tops of the blocks. Next, a worker inspected the blocks as they passed, removing any that were cracked or appeared otherwise to be defective. The wet concrete from defective blocks was returned to the machine for reuse. Approximately 5 percent of the blocks were removed. The pallet with good blocks rode with steel cables to two workers who removed the pallets from the conveyor with hoists and placed the pallets in rows for the blocks to dry for 24 hours. (See Exhibit 4 for a diagram of the production area.)

After the 24 hours the blocks were strong enough to stack and they were removed to the curing yard. This task was performed by four workers in one eight-hour shift. They carried the blocks by hand to the edge of the drying area where they stacked the blocks on large pallets. A fork lift truck took the loaded pallets to the curing area. After all of the day's production had been moved to the curing area the same men who had loaded the pallets unloaded them and stacked the blocks. One man kept the stacks of blocks wet for the first two weeks of the curing period, and this was followed by two weeks of drying.

Mr. Clare was concerned about the efficiency of the process of moving the blocks to the curing area. "It costs us as much for labor to move the blocks as it does to make them," he said. "We have studied the possibility of conveyors and machines to move the blocks to the curing area but have concluded that savings in labor do not justify the purchase of machinery. Also, if we had enough of the large pallets we could cure the blocks on the pallets and avoid handling the blocks twice, but the cost of the additional pallets would be $15,000 and pallets would last only two years because the water loosens the nails."

Exhibit 4
LAYOUT OF BLOCK PRODUCTION FACILITY

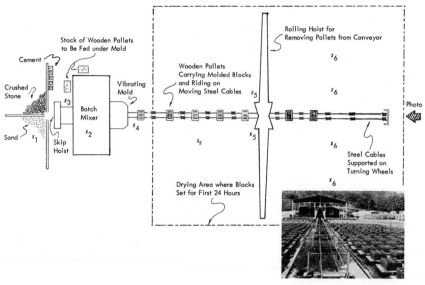

Photo of Block-Making Facility from
Position Marked with Arrow on Layout,
Showing Drying Area in Foreground

Personnel Workers:

x_s—Supervisor.

x_1—Pushes sand and crushed stone towards weighing point.

x_2—Mixes.

x_3—Loads empty pallets; dumps cement bags into skip hoist.

x_4—Looks for cracked blocks and removes when defective.

x_5—Unloads pallets from conveyor.

x_6—Moves blocks from pallets to larger pallets to be taken to the curing area (early shift only).

The four laborers who moved the blocks by hand were paid $0.26 per hour, the men working around the machine, including the men unloading the pallets from the conveyor, earned $0.30 per hour and the man controlling the machine earned $0.38 per hour. It was estimated that social security, fringe benefits, etc., added 33 percent to hourly wage costs. The company's estimated production costs for block number 9 were:

Material	$0.045
Labor.	0.003
Overhead (for maintenance, molds, machine depreciation, etc.)	0.012
General overhead.	0.012
Total.	$0.072

MAINTENANCE

Maintenance of equipment was described by Productos managers as "a considerable problem." They wanted the company to become as self-sufficient as possible and had initiated a policy of installing new equipment with company personnel. "It may take one-and-a-half times as long, but we become very familiar with the equipment in the process," Mr. Clare commented. A new maintenance shop to house machine tools and spare parts was under construction. When the shop was completed, Mr. Clare planned to keep track of maintenance expenses on each machine.

Mr. Clare described the stocking of spare parts as "a pain in the neck. It is hard to determine what parts to have on hand. We try to simplify the problem where possible by our choice of equipment. We want to buy machines with similar electrical equipment, for example, but this is difficult when you buy from different countries."

The German block-making machine was inoperative about 15 percent of the time because of mechanical breakdown or failure of electrical components. The timing device in particular gave trouble; other parts gave way under the strain of weight, pressure, and vibration. The mechanics could make most replacement parts or had them in stock, but seven times during the past three years there were periods from 8 to 14 days during which the machine was rigged to run at half efficiency for lack of a spare part, and once the machine had been shut down completely for two weeks when a pump failed.

LABOR RELATIONS

Mr. Clare commented about the company's labor relations, "I hear a lot of Costa Ricans complain about bad labor. We don't have any problems. Companies that do are guilty of bad management. This company has never had any major labor problems.

"We have a supervisor for every 25 workers and every supervisor but one has been with the company at least ten years. Our workers are so good that other companies try to hire them away from us."

Mr. Clare did not feel that recruiting and training production workers was a problem. The company had an employee recreation facility, including a swimming pool. In addition, it offered an employee savings plan under which a worker could save up to 5 percent of his salary, a sum which the company would match. It also had a policy of sending its managers to courses related to the business with the company paying part or all of the expenses. Productos' managers had attended courses in Europe, the United States, and Central America.

CONTROL OF RAW MATERIALS

Productos used a graphical method of controlling the supply of raw materials. Exhibit 5 shows a sample chart used in controlling number 3 cement purchased from Japan and used in blocks and prestressed concrete products. Cumulative usage was plotted against cumulative receipts, and

Exhibit 5
GRAPHICAL METHOD OF CONTROLLING INVENTORY OF TYPE 3
CEMENT FOR 1966

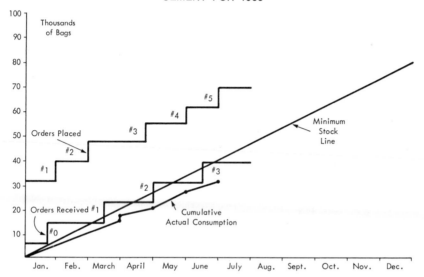

the cement was reordered when the supply available equaled the projected usage in the lead time—in this case two months. The projected cumulative usage was shown as the Minimum Stock Line; the expected rate of usage determined the slope of the Minimum Stock Line. Sometimes delivery took place in one and one-half months and rarely required as long as three months. "If we run out of number 3 cement," Mr. Clare explained, "we can use local cement, which doesn't set quickly, but is cheaper. Since we only move the blocks out of the drying area during one shift per day, we can use local cement each preceding morning and the faster-setting imported cement after noon. This insures that all blocks will be dry when we move them the following day. Imported cement costs us $0.009 extra per block. We figure the reduction in breakage is worth the cost.

"I am going to have to change the slope of the reorder line on the chart for number 3 cement," he continued. "We have not been using cement as fast as we anticipated when we set up the system."

Sand and stone were secured locally and could be obtained on demand.

PRODUCTION SCHEDULING

In April 1966, Productos initiated a new system for scheduling the production of the block-making machine which Mr. Bravo had learned in France. First a Master Schedule (Exhibit 6) had been worked out, based upon past demand and past production rates. (See Exhibit 7 for sales in

Exhibit 6

MASTER SCHEDULE FOR BLOCK MACHINE—MAY–DECEMBER, 1966
(numbers in shaded areas represent days of production)

Block	May	June	July	August	September	October	November	December
No. 9	10 5	23	12	13	12	13	12	13
No. 4	2			3		3		5
Type A	7			7		7		7
No. 1			8		8		8	
No. 12			4		4		4	
No. 11			1		1			1
No. 13	Lasts 13 Months 1							
No. 3			Lasts 10 Months 1					

Basis for the Master Schedule of Production
Production rates, in numbers of blocks per day, were estimated as follows:

No. 9	13,200 blocks	No. 12	4,500 blocks
No. 4	5,950 blocks	No. 11	19,800 blocks
Type A	3,960 blocks	No. 13	5,950 blocks
No. 1	8,570 blocks	No. 3	13,200 blocks

recent months.) It was planned to stick to this schedule except under the following circumstances: when demand deviated markedly from expectations, when there were maintenance problems, when a mold was not ready on time, or when there were special orders.

In order to determine when a change in the master schedule should be made, a perpetual inventory record of "blocks on hand" was maintained. Whenever the "blocks on hand" for a particular style fell below a certain point called the "needed stock level," production of that block was rescheduled. The needed stock level was expected demand for the block in the coming month. Since the required cure time was four weeks, failure to reschedule the production of a block after it hit the "needed stock level" would probably result in a stockout.

Exhibit 7
SALES OF MACHINE-MADE BLOCKS BY MONTH
(number of blocks)

Block Type	Oct. 1965	Nov. 1965	Dec. 1965	Jan. 1966	Feb. 1966	March 1966	April 1966	May 1966	June 1966	Total Oct. 1965–June 1966
1	20,000	20,300	41,750	21,100	52,800	70,500	71,350	57,950	36,200	391,950
3	735	1,600	2,285	1,920	1,755	2,490	3,300	2,450	1,705	18,240
4	6,480	310	7,690	14,270	5,740	6,290	6,420	26,410	16,800	90,410
9	101,000	239,000	100,500	79,400	115,000	145,000	105,300	99,500	133,000	1,117,900
11	5,770	13,900	6,850	4,530	11,000	7,190	6,800	4,630	9,930	70,600
12	8,680	8,110	4,800	13,100	12,700	7,900	11,800	7,030	5,500	79,620
13	–	705	132	700	212	106	1,330	164	367	3,716
A	10,000	12,100	8,700	13,250	7,600	12,200	9,600	13,600	17,400	104,450
Monthly total	152,665	296,025	172,707	148,270	207,007	251,676	215,900	211,734	220,902	1,876,886

It had been necessary to deviate from the master schedule starting in May; actual production for May, June and July was as follows:

Month	Block Type	Number of Days Production	Actual Production
May	9	8	108,000
	A	9	33,000
	4	3	7,250
	4 (grooved)*	4	22,500*
June	4	1	5,300
	9	19	240,000
	1	5	42,400
July	1	3	27,800
(part of month)	12	4	17,200
	1 (grooved)*	3	18,500*

* The grooved blocks were for special orders.

On July 13, 1966, Mr. Clare was scheduling production for the machine. He had the following inventory status report for blocks of each type:

INVENTORY BLOCKS AS OF JULY 13, 1966

Block	Quantity on Hand*	Finished Blocks	Block	Quantity on Hand	Finished Blocks
No. 1	58,000	27,000	No. 11	23,000	23,000
No. 3	3,530	3,530	No. 12	34,500	34,500
No. 4	None	None	No. 13	3,520	3,520
No. 9	74,500	74,500	Type "A"	13,000	13,000

* Both finished blocks and blocks in the curing cycle are counted in the "Quantity on Hand."

"I am going to have to get ten days' production in five with two shifts," Mr. Clare said. "We have not had the speed of reporting sales figures that we need and somehow our production people didn't learn from our marketing staff about a large order of number 4 blocks. According to our Master Schedule we should not need to produce that block again until August, but we are completely out of it and we have an order for 18,000 blocks requiring the delivery of various amounts for the next three weeks. The customer is a good one and late delivery will delay his work and make him mad, but I am not too worried about losing this particular order. On the other hand, I think that for good relations with the customer I should call him and tell him I can't deliver on time and tell him to buy the blocks somewhere else. The order is worth $2,250.

"Floor block A is below the needed stock level and if we are out of stock of the block, we lose sales of the beams, which are used with the floor blocks. The beams are more important to our sales picture than the blocks, but no blocks, no beams. And then block number 1 is below the needed stock level and it is our second largest selling block.

"We do not get any sales forecasts from our sales department. I don't think they can predict demand any better than we can. We just project past figures. There is some advance warning on large orders, however, and, of course, on special orders.

"We lost quite a bit of production since May because we had to make mechanical changes on the machine to make the grooved blocks. Any time we schedule anything other than what is on the Master Schedule we have to reduce production of blocks like number 9. We are barely keeping our heads above water on it."

The machine had been scheduled on the basis of a single 12-hour a day shift, six days per week, but Mr. Clare said he could run two shifts totaling 18 hours per day. The machine ran for full shifts except for two 15-minute breaks per shift, or when it broke down.

The machine was capable of up to 160 cycles per hour of continuous operation, depending on the amount of concrete used per cycle. The number of blocks produced per cycle depended on the number of blocks per mold, which in turn depended on the size of the block. The number of blocks per mold of the major blocks were as follows:

Block Number	Blocks per Mold
9	10
1	6
4	3
12	3
A	2

Although a block was not ready for delivery until 28 days after it was produced—the cure time—it was counted as produced the day it came off the machine.

Length of runs were affected by both demand and the life of a mold. A mold generally lasted about 100,000 cycles at which time it required repair or replacement. All mold work was done at Productos. A thorough repair cost about $600, mostly labor and overhead. A new mold cost $1,000, about 40 percent labor, 40 percent material, and 20 percent overhead. It was considered good practice, where inventory would not be too great in relation to demand, to run the mold until it needed repairing and then change the mold. Alternatively the size of a production run was determined by the charts. Molds were changed at night by a team of three men who were paid $0.60 each per hour for two hours.

Mr. Clare commented about the production planning system. "It seems to work all right, but it is new. We will learn more about it."

Eastern Airlines—December Schedule

ON SUNDAY, December 3, 1972, Captain Mike Fenello, vice president of operational coordination for Eastern Airlines, was still thinking about the meeting that had taken place the previous evening. He and several members of Eastern's Operations Group had been up until 2:30 A.M. working on an air crew scheduling problem which could have a major impact on the company's flight schedule for that month. Events during the past weeks indicated that flight crew utilization for December would be extremely tight, and Captain Fenello was not sure that Eastern had enough total available pilot hours to operate the December flight schedule as it presently stood. If a shortage was expected, it would possibly be to Eastern's advantage to cancel some less-profitable flights during the early part of the month to avoid cancellation of flights toward the end of December when passenger traffic and load factors were always high. On the other hand, flight cancellations of any kind were always dreaded and meant giving up revenues as well as passenger goodwill to Eastern's competitors.

If flights were to be cancelled, Captain Fenello was unsure of how many total pilot hours he should attempt to save. Also, he wondered what criteria should be used for deciding which flights to cancel. As vice president of operational coordination, Captain Fenello was responsible for this decision. However, he knew that he would be expected to justify his actions before a meeting of Eastern's Capability Committee which met regularly on Wednesday afternoons. This committee consisted of the following members (see Exhibit 1):

Colonel Frank Borman—senior vice president of operations group (chairman).
David Kunstler—vice president of schedules and airline planning.
Captain Walter Krepling—vice president and chief pilot.
Captain Mike Fenello—vice president of operational coordination.

Exhibit 1
PARTIAL ORGANIZATIONAL CHART

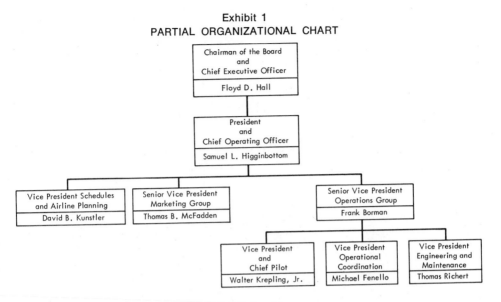

Other members of these departments were also present. To more fully prepare for the meeting, Captain Fenello decided to review once again the
events affecting this situation.

COMPANY BACKGROUND

Eastern Airlines began operations on May 1, 1928, having won a government contract to carry mail by air between New York and Atlanta.
From this base (passenger service was initiated in 1930), the company's
routes quickly expanded to include Daytona Beach, Orlando, Tampa and
Miami, Florida, as well as Newark, New Jersey, Philadelphia, Baltimore
and Washington, D.C. In 1938, Captain Eddie Rickenbacker, World War I
flying ace, and a group of associates acquired control of the company, and
Captain Rickenbacker served as chief executive officer until 1963. After
Eastern encountered a period of economic difficulty at the start of the jet
age, Floyd D. Hall, now chairman and chief executive officer, joined the
company in 1963 as President and chief executive officer. He led a new
management team which guided Eastern back to profitability and growth.

By 1972, Eastern was one of the "big four" domestic airlines in the
United States—the others being United Airlines, Trans World Airlines and
American Airlines. Total operating revenues for the calendar year 1971
were $1,054 million, over 90 percent of which came from the 22.8 million
passengers the airline carried that year. A more complete picture of Eastern's financial history is presented in Exhibit 2.

Eastern's system network comprised 33,080 route miles, linking 101
CAB-designated cities in 29 states plus the District of Columbia (see Ex-

Exhibit 2
INCOME STATEMENTS, 1965–1971
($000)

Income Accounts	1971	1970	1969	1968	1967	1966	1965
Operating revenue:							
Passenger–first class	$ 143,962	$158,544	$154,941	$136,624	$124,888	$ 99,880	$118,661
Passenger–coach	803,519	738,165	633,915	543,485	480,694	355,430	352,329
Mail	13,894	12,206	12,527	10,644	9,876	7,748	8,472
Freight	44,895	44,606	36,222	28,219	21,427	15,185	16,293
Other	47,487	17,528	31,958	25,805	20,919	18,039	11,768
Total operating revenue	$1,053,757	$971,049	$869,563	$744,777	$657,804	$496,282	$507,523
Operating expenses:							
Flying operations	324,848	270,765	253,384	208,018	177,368	134,464	131,503
Maintenance	158,459	149,564	133,482	128,796	108,926	87,277	86,591
Passenger service	97,563	91,641	82,166	72,639	59,247	44,239	42,749
Aircraft and traffic servicing	181,828	163,507	142,830	123,049	103,827	77,839	75,009
Promotion and sales	126,657	123,737	116,558	103,210	88,691	67,947	62,554
General and administrative	49,197	44,610	39,804	36,081	27,386	21,055	19,648
Depreciation and amortization	79,372	83,336	77,494	65,238	48,147	39,209	48,932
Total operating expenses	$1,017,924	$927,160	$845,718	$737,031	$613,592	$472,030	$466,986
Operating profit	35,833	43,889	23,845	7,746	44,212	24,252	40,537
Nonoperating income and expenses:							
Gain on disposition of property	cr 2,431	1,893	cr 2,834	cr 1,062	cr 29	cr 277	cr 342
Interest expense	33,769	37,793	33,331	28,109	15,239	13,089	13,005
Other	cr 2,986	cr 3,138	cr 3,419	cr 3,556	cr 2,856	cr 3,583	cr 1,799
Pretax net income	$ 7,481	$ 7,341	$ (3,233)	$(15,745)	$ 31,858	$ 15,023	$ 29,673
Income taxes:							
Provision for deferred taxes	1,787	1,877	cr 911	cr 3,809	7,741	—	—
Total income taxes	$ 1,787	$ 1,877	$cr 911	$cr 3,809	$ 7,741	—	—
Net income	$ 5,694	$ 5,464	$ (2,322)	$(11,936)	$ 24,117	$ 15,023	$ 29,673
Revenue passenger miles flown (000,000)	15,502	15,493	14,003	12,513	11,225	7,945	8,053
Average yield per RPM (cents)	6.3	6.0	5.8	5.6	5.5	5.9	6.0

Source: Reports filed with the Civil Aeronautics Board.

hibit 3). In addition Eastern provided air service to Canada, Mexico, Puerto Rico, the Virgin Islands, Bermuda, the Bahamas and Jamaica. Including the company's Air Shuttle operation between Boston-New York/ Newark-Washington, scheduled departures averaged 1,526 per day.

Exhibit 3
ROUTE SYSTEM

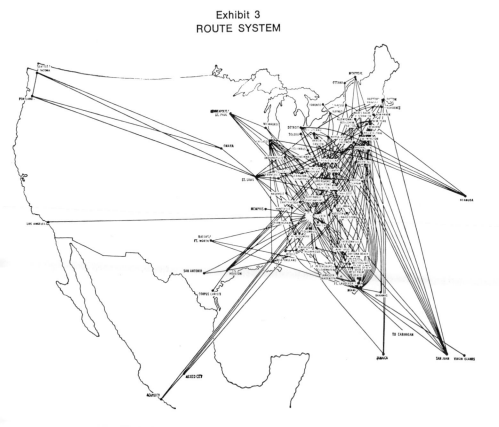

By December 1972, Eastern's jet fleet (summarized in Exhibit 4) consisted of the Lockheed 1011, the company's newest aircraft, the Boeing 727, and the McDonnell Douglas DC-8 and DC-9. The average airspeed for these jets (block to block) was 575 miles per hour.[1] In addition, Eastern owned and operated sixteen Electras which were primarily used as back-ups for the airline's shuttle operations.

The company had been built on a substantial volume of business travel. However, it was very aware of the role of the importance of their customers who were traveling for pleasure or personal reasons. As part of an effort to develop these markets, Eastern had developed a joint advertising

---

[1] Block to block time refers to the time when an aircraft begins to taxi until the time it arrives at its destination terminal. A jet's ground speed (actual speed over the ground) usually exceeds 600 m.p.h.

Exhibit 4
FLEET COMPOSITION, DECEMBER 1972

	Number of Seats per Aircraft (basic configuration)
Jets:　12 Lockheed 1011 Whisperliners	226
16 McDonnell Douglas DC-8-61	203
10 McDonnell Douglas DC-8-21	139
80 McDonnell Douglas DC-9 Whisperjet II	90
75 Boeing 727 Whisperjet	94
34 Boeing 727-200 Whisperjet	163
16 Lockheed Electra (for use strictly as the second sections of the shuttle).	87

On Order:　27 Lockheed 1011 Whisperliners
　　　　　　　7 Boeing 727-200 Whisperjet
On Option:　13 Lockheed 1011 Whisperliners
Reserved Delivery Positions:　6 British/French Supersonic Concorde
Available for Sale or Lease:　10 DC-8-21
　　　　　　　　　　　　　　　16 Electra

program to promote Disney World in Florida and a series of television commercials describing vacation planning services available from the airline. These activities were all part of a program with the slogan "Eastern—the wings of man."

Eastern was recovering from financial difficulties experienced during 1969–1972. Reported profits through November 1972 had increased over the same period in the previous year, and with a good showing in December, Eastern hoped to make record earnings on total revenues of approximately $1,300 million (See Exhibit 5). Crucial to this improvement had been the upsurge in revenue passenger miles (RPMs) experienced

Exhibit 5
NET INCOME (LOSS) AFTER TAXES

	1972	1971	1970	1969	1968
January	$ 4,296	$ (253)	$ 2,781	$(1,937)	$ 1,201
February	1,517	(1,969)	2,514	(2,720)	1,035
March	6,917	(522)	6,656	5,681	2,688
April	7,162	3,835	3,205	1,791	2,246
May	(178)	(844)	991	491	(843)
June	1,463	212	791	(916)	1,051
July	3,437	2,655	1,080	(470)	274
August	4,105	3,684	1,771	2,387	2,154
September	(5,547)	(7,445)	(7,586)	(6,579)	(7,234)
October	(1,853)	(4,478)	(8,559)	(2,754)	(6,981)
November	687	2,697	(2,903)	(1,106)	(7,424)
December		8,118	4,720	3,809	(106)
Total		$5,690	$5,461	$(2,323)	$(11,939)

during the latter part of 1971 and which had continued into 1972. This increase in traffic was expected in light of the improved condition of the national economy during this period.

Eastern's improved performance during the period of 1969 through 1971 had resulted from cost cutting and over-all "belt tightening" by the company. The management had allowed attrition to reduce the level of the work force in nearly every classification. Because flight crews' salaries represented a significant cost item when operating aircraft, Eastern was particularly conscious of the aggregate number of pilots it employed at any one time. Consequently, the company tried to hire and train additional pilots only after careful analysis of the flight schedule indicated that an increase was necessary. Normally, the time required to hire, train and fit an experienced pilot into Eastern's schedule was about six weeks. Variations depended on the type of aircraft the pilot was being trained to fly as well as the availability of flight simulators, instructors and training aircraft. Until July 1972, Eastern had not hired any new pilots for almost two years. As a result, their total number of "line pilots" had been reduced to approximately 2,700. During July and August, the airline had hired 150 pilots in preparation for the increased activity forecast through 1973. Most of these had recently begun flying as second officers aboard the company's B-727s.

EASTERN'S RELATIONS WITH ITS PILOTS

Like most of the larger domestic and international airlines, Eastern's pilots were represented in all wage and contract negotiations by the Air Line Pilots' Association (ALPA). During the last 20 years this organization had been quite successful in improving the hours, pay, and working conditions of their pilots. For example, in 1950 an average commercial pilot might earn an annual salary of $15,000 for working 192 days in the year. By 1970, this figure had increased to around $30,000 and senior captains could earn as much as $65,000 for working approximately 144 days in the year.

Under the terms of the contract in 1972, Eastern's pilots could fly a maximum of 80 "pay hours" per month. Pay hours referred not only to a pilot's actual flying time (block to block) but also included a portion of his time spent briefing and preparing for a flight as well as time traveling to or from a flight. For example, if a pilot based in Miami were scheduled to take a flight from Miami to Chicago to Atlanta and terminate in New York, his pay hours would include all his flight time as well as a portion of the time required to fly him from New York home to Miami. Similarly, if the flight originated in Atlanta, part of the pilot's time traveling from Miami to Atlanta, although he was a passenger, would count towards his 80 hours. For any month this scheduled "dead head" or credit time averaged approximately 25 percent of a pilot's actual block time.

EASTERN'S BID SYSTEM

Eastern's pilots were usually qualified to operate only one type of aircraft, so substitutions of aircraft on a flight (say a DC-8 series aircraft for a B-727 series aircraft) necessitated a change in flight crew. This was the result of the company's bid system covered under the ALPA contract. Under this system pilots could bid twice a year for domicile (or base point) location and type of aircraft within Eastern's fleet they would fly. Results of this bidding were determined by a pilot's seniority within his classification. Eastern's pilots were broken down into three classifications: captains, first officers, and second officers. One of each was required in each of the aircraft operated by Eastern except for the DC-9, which required a crew of only two. The most senior captain necessarily received his first choice as to base location and type aircraft. This was true also for the most senior first officer and the most senior second officer. However, when a pilot advanced his classification, his seniority for bidding purposes was reduced.

When a pilot was assigned to a new type of aircraft, the Federal Aviation Agency (FAA) as well as Eastern required him to undertake simulated and actual flight training in that aircraft. This occurred prior to his first flight carrying passengers. Thus, after every bid, a certain number of Eastern's pilots were taken off the line and put through this training on the company's time. Normally the time required for this training was six to seven weeks, but it was usually spread out among the pilots so as not to interrupt the current flight schedule. Because of the seasonality of Eastern's operations, bids were conducted so that all training would be completed prior to June 1 and December 1 of each year. This would enable maximum utilization of pilots during the peak periods in Eastern's schedule. Once the date for a bid had passed, and a pilot had been trained in his new type of aircraft, under the terms of the contract he could not fly any other aircraft, even though he may have been qualified to do so.

FLIGHT SCHEDULING

As the second largest passenger carrier, flight scheduling for such an operation was an immensely complicated task. According to David Kunstler, vice president of schedules and airline planning, the airline had to look at the feasibility of serving any particular city-pair within the context of the entire system. It was not enough to know that development of a certain market share on a route would yield a lucrative return. Alternative uses of aircraft and flight crews had to be considered along with the possible reactions of Eastern's competitors. Consequently, new ways were constantly being sought to improve Eastern's level of service in a way that would complement the existing operations. The scheduling process was further described as follows:

A perfect schedule is rarely, if ever, attainable. The many varied requirements, many of which are inherently in conflict with one another, simply cannot be simultaneously satisfied. For example, the schedule planner must endeavor to provide adequate ground time for servicing and maintenance, and at the same time keep aircraft in the air for economic utilization. He must provide departure times that are compatible with known customer preference, or build complexes of connecting flights at major gateways, and at the same time avoid excessive peaking of station activity. He must strive for schedule stability for the convenience of both passengers and employees, and at the same time display the flexibility to rapidly adjust to new competitive threats or other developments. He must recognize that public service obligations will sometimes work in the opposite direction from strictly economic considerations, and at the same time remember that his airline could not provide any service at all without a sound financial position. And the conflicts go on and on.

In short, by attempting to optimize the allocation of the airline's principal assets—its aircraft, facilities, personnel and selling resources—considering its route opportunities as well as its route obligations, the resulting patterns must be satisfactory to essentially meet the combined goals of public service, competitive effectiveness, operational performance and profitability. During much of the process, there is very little black or white—but a great deal of gray.

At Eastern, we try hard to insure that the scheduling process is not an "Ivory Tower" approach that disregards the comments, suggestions and recommendations of those responsible for revenue production, operational performance and cost. To the contrary, there is considerable coordination, and in fact, required inputs from each of the involved departments. It is the schedule planner's job to somehow accomplish as many of the justifiable requests as possible.

Normally, Eastern's schedule of flights was written for a year in advance and updated quarterly as passenger forecasts and competitors' schedules changed. This schedule was then used by Eastern's operations and maintenance departments to plan for the delivery and utilization of different types of aircraft and the hiring, training, and scheduling of air crews and flight attendants. In the short run, however, the realities of the airline industry often dictated that this order be reversed. At any one point in time, there was very little flexibility in aircraft and crew availability, and any unexpected change in the condition of one of these factors usually required some alteration of Eastern's flight schedule. For example, if a B-727 which was scheduled to fly from New York to Miami experienced maintenance problems, the company might have another B-727 assigned as a back-up in New York. If so, the substitution was made, and the original aircraft would become a reserve when the repair work was completed. However, if a reserve aircraft was not available in New York, Eastern could either cancel the flight entirely or delay operations until another reserve aircraft could be flown in from another city. This necessitated breaking out another crew of pilots to fly the reserve aircraft into New York where they would either fly that aircraft to Miami or turn it over to the original crew and "dead head" to their next assignment.

OPERATIONAL COORDINATION

Once the schedule for a quarter had been approved, it was turned over to the operational coordination department which was charged with operating the schedule as smoothly and efficiently as possible. Any alteration of the schedule or cancellation of flights past this point due to maintenance difficulties, flight crew problems or for whatever reason was the responsibility of operations coordination, and this department was held accountable for the results.

THE WINTER SCHEDULE

Because of the high demand for travel during the Christmas holidays, Eastern typically scheduled additional capacity during the latter half of December. The impact of this can be seen in the daily available seat miles offered in 1972 in Exhibit 6. It was planned that such a schedule would again be in effect in December 1973 and this was incorporated into the manpower plan in Exhibit 7.

EVENTS PRECEDING THE DECEMBER SITUATION

While there was always some increase in activity in December, and Eastern expected that it was preferable to fall short of available pilot hours at this peak point of the annual operations, rather than carry an excess number of pilots during slack periods. However, this year the situation was worse than normal. ALPA had invoked a clause of the contract that required Eastern to place more pilots into training than had been predicted. This prevented these pilots from being used in December. Compounding these difficulties was the fact that delivery of Eastern's new L–1011 aircraft was running significantly behind schedule. It had been hoped that the company would be able to use these aircraft in December and the allocation of crews had been set based on this expectation. This resulted in not only losing these large capacity aircraft (226 seats each) but also tied up pilots from other assignments under the terms of the ALPA contract.

The operational coordination department had experienced difficulty in meeting the November schedule. Because of these factors and extremely inclement weather, Eastern had exhausted all available monthly pilot hours in the B–727 and DC–9 aircraft categories. Consequently, it had been forced to cancel 40 flight segments between November 28 and 30. Out of the 1,828 passengers scheduled on those flights Eastern

Exhibit 6
FORECAST RPMS, ASMS, AND LOAD FACTOR,
DECEMBER, 1972

Date	Day	ASMs* (000)	Load Factor† (percent)
1	Fri.	130,575	61.4
2	Sat.	131,169	54.3
3	Sun.	132,240	62.7
4	Mon.	128,035	56.1
5	Tues.	125,428	50.7
6	Wed.	126,962	50.6
7	Thurs.	127,537	57.0
8	Fri.	129,084	64.4
9	Sat.	131,127	47.3
10	Sun.	131,948	59.5
11	Mon.	127,984	55.8
12	Tues.	124,979	49.2
13	Wed.	153,215	45.5
14	Thurs.	159,137	51.1
15	Fri.	160,833	59.6
16	Sat.	158,815	57.6
17	Sun.	164,365	48.6
18	Mon.	161,104	48.8
19	Tues.	161,932	53.4
20	Wed.	165,538	68.2
21	Thurs.	165,889	76.2
22	Fri.	165,935	79.1
23	Sat.	166,932	65.4
24	Sun.	160,107	58.3
25	Mon.	150,725	66.9
26	Tues.	159,575	76.0
27	Wed.	158,463	66.7
28	Thurs.	156,414	69.6
29	Fri.	157,941	57.8
30	Sat.	160,682	69.5
31	Sun.	162,918	68.6
		4,597,588	60.3

* ASM stands for available seat mile and is a common measure for capacity in the airline industry. Technically one ASM represents one aircraft seat traveling a distance of one mile.

† Load factor is the ratio of revenue passenger miles (RPMs) to ASMs.

had been able to satisfactorily reschedule 275 passengers on another Eastern flight; 974 were rescheduled on other carriers, while 579 were left "unprotected." Unprotected in this context meant that Eastern was unable to reschedule a passenger from a cancelled flight on another flight to his original destination which arrived within two hours of his original arrival time. Because these November cancellations had all come during the last three days of the month, the percentage of passengers rescheduled on another Eastern flight was extremely low. Captain Fenello thought that had

Exhibit 7
FLIGHT OPERATIONS AND MANPOWER PLANNING
REPORTS FOR DECEMBER 1972–SUMMARY
prepared 11/21/72

	Maximum Capability of Crew Pay Hours*	Allocated Crew Pay Hours	Margin above Allocated Pay Hours
L–1011			
Total.	3,823	3,675	+148
DC–8–60			
Total.	3,500	3,557	– 57
DC–8			
Total.	2,633	2,565	+ 68
B–727			
Total.	43,296	43,780	–484
DC–9			
Total.	29,795	30,127	–332
L–188			
Total.	3,718	3,588	+130
Schedule-Line-A/S			
Total.	86,765	87,292	–527

Prepared 11/28/72

	Maximum Capability of Crew Pay Hours*	Allocated Crew Pay Hours	Margin above Allocated Pay Hours
L–1011			
Total.	3,823	3,675	+148
DC–8–60			
Total.	3,500	3,564	– 64
DC–8			
Total.	2,633	2,558	+ 75
B–727			
Total.	43,296	43,780	–484
DC–9			
Total.	29,795	30,156	–361
L–188			
Total.	3,718	3,550	+168
Schedule-Line-A/S			
Total.	86,765	87,283	–518

* These figures reflected the entire flying operations crew and were not "man hours." For example, the L–1011 required a flight operations crew of 3. The total allocated man hours for December were 11,025 (i.e., 3,675 × 3).
Source: Company records.

he been able to selectively cancel the same amount of flights, he could have rescheduled approximately 50 percent of those passengers inconvenienced on Eastern.

In actuality, the situation was worse than indicated. To complete a number of flights during the last two weeks of November, the operations group had scheduled some supervisory and instructor pilots on regular Eastern flights. While these crews were fully qualified to operate Eastern's aircraft, they were not considered "line pilots" under the terms of the ALPA contract. Thus, they could be scheduled for flights, but they could not take flight time or pay hours from the regularly scheduled line pilots. Whatever flight time they accumulated in a line capacity had to be credited to a line pilot's record for scheduling and pay purposes. Since most pilots had used up their allowed 80 hours for November, this time was then credited on their records for December. The result was that Eastern had started the month of December with some pilot pay hours already expended.

FLIGHT OPERATIONS REPORTS

Eastern made weekly projections of the total pilot hours (block hours and pay hours) required to operate the flight schedule for a particular month. Current records were also kept of the maximum available pilot capacity for the month. These figures were then compared to give an indication of the leeway or cushion existing in this area. So long as the aggregate number of available pay hours for a particular type of aircraft exceeded the allocated number of hours, the schedule was considered manageable. As the two figures approached one another, Captain Fenello knew that things got tight. Once allocated pay hours exceeded the maximum capability, aircraft and/or flights had to be rescheduled to bring the two into balance. One commonly used technique was to try to substitute one type aircraft where excess pilot hours existed on a flight series for another type of aircraft where pilot hours were scarce. For example, it might be possible to substitute a DC–8 for a B–727 run providing that the DC–8 was not already committed or that an alternate adjustment could be made.

By reviewing these figures for the past four weeks, Captain Fenello had become increasingly concerned. Compiled only five days earlier, the last Flight Operations and Manpower Planning Report for December indicated a shortage in pilot hours for the B–727 of 484 hours and of 361 hours for the DC–9. (See Exhibit 7.) Even if the aggregate number of pilot hours equalled the hours required, there could be schedule problems. Captain Fenello felt that it was necessary to have a few extra hours (perhaps 1 or 2 percent) to accommodate mislocations of pilots or other problems that tended to arise once specific schedules had to be filled.

The figures shown in Exhibit 7 assumed "poor" December weather conditions. While the company felt reasonably confident in the forecasts as stated in the Flight Operations Manpower Planning Report, the individuals responsible for scheduling were concerned by recent long-term weather forecasts. If good weather were to occur, the demand for pilot hours would be substantially lower and Eastern would just meet the required hours.

WEATHER

General flying conditions up and down the East coast had been the worst in years during November and had caused considerable delays as well as stranded crews at all major airports. Eastern's meteorologists were forecasting continued fog along the Middle Atlantic States and considerable sleet and icing around the Northeastern airports. These monthly forecasts had been accurate approximately 70 percent of the time and were taken into account in Eastern's Manpower Planning Reports. In other words, Eastern felt that there was 70 percent probability that the November 28 manpower requirements summarized in Exhibit 7 would be what they would experience, while there was approximately a 30 percent probability that there would be weather that would allow the company enough pilot hours to avoid schedule failure.

The use of supervisors as pilots in a pinch in December would do little more than accommodate Captain Fenello's desire for a 1 to 2 percent margin of safety in good weather.

COMPETITION

Captain Fenello was concerned as to what effect the actions of Eastern's competitors would have on this situation. Delta Airlines, the nation's fifth largest carrier and Eastern's chief rival along the East coast, did not normally add as many flights to the winter schedule as Eastern. This was because Delta's route system was more diversified than Eastern's and subject to less seasonality regarding the over-all demand on the system. Moreover, Delta had recently completed a merger with Northeast Airlines; and, under the terms of the merger agreement, Delta had assimilated all of Northeast's pilots as well as most of their routes into their system. Because of extensive rescheduling following the merger, Delta found that they had inherited a larger cushion of pilots than originally had been anticipated. While attrition would eventually reduce this cushion, there would be increased flexibility regarding pilot scheduling for the next few months.

On the other hand American Airlines, which was experiencing relatively poor pilot relations at this point in time, had announced that pilot hours for the month were already known to be particularly tight. Nevertheless, American was expected not to cancel any flights during the early part of December, and would probably try to operate their entire schedule as published.

Sunshine Builders, Inc.

IN THE five years since its founding, Sunshine Builders, Inc. had grown to be one of Florida's larger home builders. In the opinion of the company's management major credit for Sunshine's growth and success was due to customer-oriented service and guarantee policies which, in combination with good construction, reasonable prices, and on-time completions, had enabled the firm to acquire an excellent reputation.

The founders of the company, Charles and Arthur Root, had come to Florida in 1953 at the ages of 28 and 26 respectively after five years in the furniture business in Chicago. Charles Root had majored in economics at the University of Chicago and Arthur Root in chemical engineering at Northwestern. While their furniture business had been moderately successful, they felt that the potential margin of profit was becoming increasingly narrow and that the personal time and effort required was out of proportion to the return attainable.

The Root brothers were attracted to Florida as a state which offered rapid growth and above-average business opportunities. They spent their first several months becoming familiar with the metropolitan area which included a population of nearly 500,000 within a 10-mile radius. During this period, realizing that land was appreciating in value, they bought eight lots for speculation. Shortly thereafter, encouraged by their father, who had had some experience in contracting, they decided to build houses on the lots. These homes were built and sold by early 1954, subcontracting the construction work to different local contractors.

Since this operation had been profitable, population growth was accelerating, land was relatively cheap, and there was some evidence of industrial movement to Florida, the Root brothers became convinced that the home construction business in Florida offered excellent prospects.

CONSTRUCTION OPERATIONS 1954–1958

Following the completion and sale of the first eight homes the Root brothers built a model home and sold 40 very quickly. These homes were located on customers' lots and were entirely subcontracted. Since the customer made regular progress payments as the house progressed, beginning with an initial payment of 15 percent, the net effect of these arrangements was that relatively little capital was required. The company was hard-pressed during 1954 and 1955 to build enough houses to meet the demand.

During this period Charles Root found that his greatest interest was in the development of land and formed a separate corporation (Root Land Development Corp.) for this purpose. Their father took no active part in either Sunshine Builders, headed by Arthur, or the land development operations under Charles. Each brother devoted nearly all of his time to his own operations and only assisted the other as requested or when dealing with major policy issues. A third corporation, Root Associates, was established by Arthur to handle sales for Sunshine Builders. Cooperative selling arrangements were also established with local real estate firms.

From 1954 to 1958 Sunshine expanded each year. Operating data for this period and for the first four months of 1959 are shown in Exhibit 1. During the years 1954–1958 management operations, while extremely hectic and requiring consistently long hours on the part of both brothers, had been essentially simple in concept. With very few exceptions the land on which Sunshine Builders constructed homes was owned by the customer, who had purchased it from either the Root Land Development Corporation, or some other source. All construction work had been subcontracted to local subcontractors who, by mutual consent, had chosen to largely concentrate their efforts on work for Sunshine Builders.

From late 1954 through 1956 Arthur Root was assisted in the job of managing the construction end of the business by Herbert Playford. Mr. Playford had known the Root brothers in Chicago and had come to Florida at their request in September of 1954. Mr. Playford had had a high school education and then had worked successively as a shipping clerk, a neon glass blower, and in his father's junk business. On his arrival in Florida, Mr. Playford, 25, was taken by Arthur Root to visit 13 home sites which were in various stages of construction and given immediate responsibility for their completion with the instruction "Build them." In carrying out this assignment, Mr. Playford acted as superintendent, working with the various contractors, scheduling, coordinating, and supervising their various efforts.

As the business grew, four other superintendents were hired. In 1956 Mr. Playford was moved into the office to serve as an expediter and coordinator of the four superintendents and to take care of the mounting volume of paper work associated with the construction end of the business. In

Exhibit 1
OPERATING PROFIT DATA
(expressed as a percentage of sales)

	1956	1957	1958	1959 (4 months)
Sales*	100.00%	100.00%	100.00%	100.00%
Construction costs†	85.20	86.60	83.33	84.80
Gross profit	14.80%	13.40%	16.67%	15.20%
Expenses:				
Sales expense	5.00	5.00	5.00	5.00
Salaries and wages‡	3.15	3.85	5.23	5.20
Sales promotion and advertising	0.63	0.27	0.78	1.38
Depreciation	0.10	0.21	0.40	0.61
First-year house maintenance ("punch work")	0.13	0.45	0.38	0.37
Auto and aircraft expense	–	0.17	0.33	0.33
Office expenses	0.37	0.18	0.18	0.32
Radio expenses	–	–	0.10	0.19
Production office §	0.37	–	0.16	0.70
Equipment rental	–	–	–	0.36
Maintenance of model homes	0.07	0.10	–	0.02
Maintenance of trucks, tools, and equipment	–	–	–	0.66
Legal and accounting	–	0.04	0.16	0.04
Taxes and licenses	0.46	0.15	0.13	0.69
Travel and entertainment	0.10	0.08	0.20	0.34
Telephone and postage	0.08	0.09	0.10	0.14
Warehouse expense	–	–	–	0.81
Insurance	0.19	0.10	0.09	0.23
Christmas gifts to employees	0.19	0.07	0.09	0.12
Plans and designs	–	0.10	0.08	0.12
Discounts and collection fees on mortgages	–	–	0.04	0.46
Rent	0.10	0.10	0.08	0.21
Miscellaneous	0.08	0.11	0.05	0.11
Total expenses	11.02%	11.07%	13.58%	18.41%
Operating profit ( ) = loss	3.78	2.33	3.09	(3.21)
Number of houses built	124	134	151	52 (4 months)
Average selling price	$13,500	$14,250	$15,000	$15,250
Average number of construction workers	94	114	113	124

(For the years 1956, 1957, and 1958 these figures represent the total of the subcontractors' men working on Sunshine houses. For 1959, the 124 men were on Sunshine's payroll.)

* Based on completed houses. A "sale" was made only when a house was completed and "construction costs" were charged to work-in-process inventory until the home was completed. "Expenses" were charged monthly as they occurred.

† Construction costs include direct labor, material, subcontracting cost, and the salaries and wages of foremen, superintendents, warehousemen, draftsmen, blueprint operators, messengers, and the Service Department, plus fringe benefits for those salaries and wages included.

‡ Includes all other salaries and wages not included under "construction costs."

§ General-purpose production requirements, such as blueprint paper, steel tapes, forms, office supplies, small hand tools.

this capacity he set up the systems of scheduling and cost control described later.

Mr. Playford's assumption of many of the daily details of construction left Arthur Root free for sales work, purchasing, and managing the company's finances. In late 1956 he was joined in the firm by a younger brother, Daniel Root, 25, who until that time had been pursuing graduate studies in history.

On December 1, 1956, Mr. Playford resigned from the company to enter the building business for himself. He founded a new firm, Meadowlark Builders, aided with a substantial investment by the Root brothers. Meadowlark was successful from the start, building a total of 200 low-cost homes in 1957 and 1958. In December 1958 Arthur Root persuaded Mr. Playford to return to Sunshine as treasurer, assistant secretary, and manager of production and service, and the Meadowlark operation was discontinued.

By the end of 1958, Daniel Root, as vice president and secretary, had taken up full responsibility for sales, broker relations, customer relations, advertising, and the developing and merchandising of new models. Arthur Root, as president, handled all financing and purchasing. Charles Root continued to devote his time principally to the Root Land Development Corporation.

The construction work, under Mr. Playford, was handled by eight subcontractors, who performed the following functions:

Plumbing	Plastering
Electrical	Carpentry
Painting	Heating
Masonry	Cleaning

Each contractor sent in a weekly bill for the wages he had paid, plus 8 percent for equipment. His own time was included at an hourly rate approximately 15 percent above his highest paid man. Material was purchased and supplied by the contractor at cost. The contractor hired and fired as he felt necessary, but Sunshine Builders had the right to approve any wage increases. Arthur Root and Herbert Playford made it a practice to question the subcontractors on jobs on which their costs appeared out of line with previous cost experience. Total costs for each contractor were tabulated for each job to furnish this information. Except for the masonry crew the men were not unionized but the wages for each trade were approximately equal to the appropriate general community average.

The contractors each had a number of crews whose activities were arranged and assigned by the four superintendents previously mentioned. The superintendents were paid about the same or slightly more than top construction craftsmen. Each superintendent covered the Sunshine Builders' homes in the geographic territory assigned to him, the bulk of the homes being located within a seven-mile radius.

By late 1958 Arthur Root had become increasingly concerned about the effectiveness of this entire arrangement. In discussions with his brothers and Mr. Playford he made the following observations and criticisms of the existing operation:

1. The superintendents were spending most of their time competing with each other for crews to work on the houses in their territory. They were "high-grade expediters" but made no attempt to coordinate the crew requirements between each other.
2. Seven[1] of the contractors were personally receiving $11,000–$12,000 per year, working solely for Sunshine. In effect, they were acting not so much as independent contractors but rather as foremen, who could be hired for less to perform such work.
3. The subcontractors were not buying labor-saving equipment but tended to "run old equipment into the ground."
4. It should be possible to centralize controls and scheduling and to eliminate conflicts, delays, and superintendents.

After considerable discussion, a unanimous management decision was made to absorb the entire subcontractors' organizations into the Sunshine firm and eliminate the use of superintendents. As planned, the various subcontractor crews would be placed on the Sunshine payroll, with the previous subcontractors as Sunshine foremen.

Individual meetings were held with each contractor in December 1958. The proposed changes were explained and each contractor was offered a salary according to his experience and ability. A reasonable price was to be negotiated for his equipment. In spite of the fact that the salaries offered were 10 percent–25 percent below their recent annual earnings (the masonry contractor, for example, had been making $12,000 and was offered $9,250), the offers were accepted by the entire group. Arthur Root felt that the offers were higher than the men could earn elsewhere and that the men realized they had been overpaid previously and that it was "a gravy train that might stop suddenly any time. They were also glad to be freed of the payroll paper work and to give up some responsibility." Under the new arrangements the foremen were to continue to do the hiring, as necessary. The foremen were also told that they would be given year-end bonuses, dependent on the company's annual operating profit.

The four superintendents were dismissed and the new method of operation was installed on January 1, 1959. Three of the superintendents were rehired as tradesmen on the various crews, and an additional eight construction workers (who had been on the payroll of certain of the subcon-

---

[1] The eighth, the cleaning contractor, had been receiving approximately $5,000 per year.

tractors, performing on jobs other than Sunshine houses) were also absorbed, bringing the construction crew to 124.

OPERATIONS IN EARLY 1959

The Sunshine Builders' organization as of May 1, 1959, is shown as Exhibit 2. The numbers of personnel working in the various functional

Exhibit 2
ORGANIZATION AS OF MAY 1, 1959

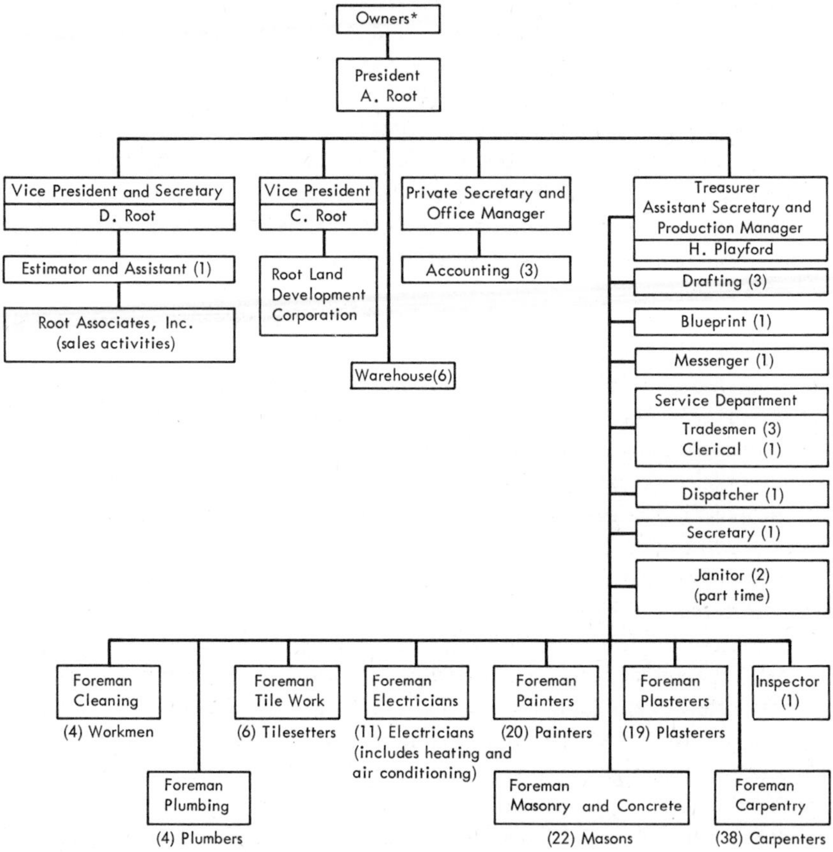

* C. Root, A. Root, D. Root, H. Playford.

areas are shown in parentheses after each descriptive title. Each construction crew consisted of nearly equal numbers of skilled tradesmen and helpers with the exception of the cleaning crew which included only unskilled general labor. The total personnel on the regular payroll at that time numbered 161, of which 124 were direct labor on construction. Following the organizational change, there had been no significant change in construction crew levels during the past four months.

In April 1959 Arthur Root and Herbert Playford both felt enthusiastic about results of the new organization thus far. They stated, for example, that without the superintendents there was "now a closer, more direct line of communication between the office and the crews." Further, fewer mistakes were being made now, according to Mr. Playford. The foremen appeared to be taking a broader point of view which Mr. Root pointed out was demonstrated, for example, by keeping the office better informed as to their own stage of progress on each job.

Herbert Playford ran the production end of the business with an apparent assurance and good humor in spite of a constant rush of decisions and problems to solve. The basic approaches to planning and controlling production employed in April 1959 were essentially the same as those he had set up himself during the years 1955–1956.

The dispatching office and the "production boards" on two walls in that office served as a central nucleus of information in Mr. Playford's system. While no formal scheduling was attempted, the "boards" aided the dispatcher in keeping up to date on where each job stood. The "boards" themselves consisted of wallboard material on which was tacked blueprint-type paper with a two-inch grid. Across the top (along the horizontal scale) were these headings: (*a*) the owner's name, (*b*) the address where the house was to be built, (*c*) the model number of the house, (*d*) the 65 individual steps, operations, or phases of the construction work. These are described in Exhibit 3. The houses were then listed vertically, adding new homes at the bottom as orders were received. The board's appearance is depicted below:

JOBS			CONSTRUCTION STEPS								
OWNER	LOCATION	MODEL	1 SIGN CLEAR LOT	2 DELIVER	3 POWER	4 STAKE	5 DIG	6 POUR	7 ORDER	8 LAY	9 FILL
E.K. Williams	14 Coral St.	69									
D.W. Onan	262 Beach Rd.	14									
A.T. Bovril	69 Hacienda	190	L								

The dispatcher, Mabel Roark, 35, posted the information to the boards. She was an active, personable woman with nearly one year of experience in her job. She placed her initials in the box after she had called the foreman requesting the performance of each construction step. The foreman, of course, knew what work was required for each step but relied on Miss Roark for instructions as to what house and which step should be his crew's next assignment. She wrote in the date when the operation had been promised for completion and noted "O.K." when the step was completed.

Steps of the Construction Job as Used on the Company's Production Boards

Exhibit 3

Manpower and Time Estimates for Dispatcher

Step Number	Operation Required	Explanation	Crew	Normal Crew No. Men	Man-Days of Work	Elapsed Time Allowed (days)	Remarks
1	Sign posted, lot cleared		Masonry	1	–	1	In typical subdivision lot already cleared
2	Deliver stakes, material and steel		Warehouse	–	–	–	
3	Power pole and water meter in	Done by utilities	Power Co.	–	–	–	
4	Stake out		Masonry	3	3	2	Includes a day for checking by foreman
5	Dig footing	Footing only 12"–18" below the surface	Masonry				
6	Pour footing		Masonry	2	1	½	
7	Order sliding glass doors		(Mabel)	–	–	–	
8	Lay foundation	Set reinforcing steel and pour concrete	Masonry	2	1	½	
9	Fill foundation	Fill and pack dirt within foundation for slab	Subcontracted	SC*	–	1	
10	Tie-in foundation	Plumbing for water and sewer connections	Plumbing	2	5	–	Done during No. 11
11	Plumbing rough-in	Set plumbing for slab	Plumbing	3		2½	Includes a day for city inspection
12	Grade slab		Masonry	2	2	2	Includes a day for city inspection
13	Pour slab		Masonry	3	1½	1½	Includes a day after pouring for slab to set
14	Strip for terrazzo	Place strips for sills or sliding doors	Subcontracted	SC	–	1	
15	Pour terrazzo		Subcontracted	SC	–	1½	Includes a day for terrazzo to set
16	Deliver blocks, steel, sills		Vendor and Warehouse	–	–	–	
17	Lay block walls		Masonry	5	10	2	
18	Form and pour lintels		Masonry	2	1	½	
19	First grind, terrazzo		Subcontracted	SC	–	2	
20	Carpenter's frame	Frame up interior wall studs and roof	Carpenters	4	20	5	Must be inspected
21	Order cabinets		(Mabel)	–	–	–	Included in time allowance for #20
22	Dry-in	First layer of lumber on the roof	Carpenters	4	1	–	Done during framing
23	Flue and/or duct work		Masonry	2	4	2	Done during framing
24	Set tub		Subcontracted	SC	–	½	Done during framing (after studs in)
25	Electrical rough-in	Place most of electrical wiring	Electricians	2	4	2	
26	Prime cornice	Paint under overhang of roof	Painters	2	1	½	
27	Order lath		(Mabel)	–	–	1	One day necessary for framing and electrical inspection
28	Lath		Plaster	4	4	1	
29	Order vanity		(Mabel)	–	–	–	
30	Ceiling heat	Electrical radiant heating usually used	Electricians	2	2	–	

Step	Operation	Detail	Responsible				Remarks
31	Roof complete	Pitch and gravel built up roof	Subcontracted	SC	—	⎱2	
32	Scratch for tile	Preparation for tiling	Plaster	2	3	⎰	
33	Brown coat plaster and stucco	First coat	Plaster	4	4	2	Includes a day for drying
34	Second grind, terrazzo		Subcontracted	SC	1	½	
35	Iron Work	Any decorative, iron work	Carpenters	2	—	½	
36	Tile walls	Bathrooms and sometimes kitchen areas	Tile	4	6	1½	
37	Plaster and stucco complete		Plaster	4	4	1	Need two-day notice
38	Install sliding glass doors		Subcontracted	SC	—	1	
39	Glaze	Install window glass	Subcontracted	SC	—	1	
40	Insulation		Subcontracted	SC	—	1	Does not interfere with any other work
41	Clean and rough grade lot	Remove debris and grade	Subcontracted	SC	—	1	
42	Front stoop		Masonry	2	1	½	Usually done while framing
43	Form outside concrete		Masonry	2	2	1	
44	Pour outside concrete		Masonry	2	2	1	Need good weather
45	Outside gravel or asphalt		Subcontracted	SC	—	2	
46	Order trim material	Moldings, door frames, etc.	(Mabel)	—	—	4	
47	Carpenter's trim		Carpenters	5	20	½	
48	Glaze jalousie doors		Subcontracted	SC	—	1	Done by vendor during trim operation
49	Install cabinets		Subcontracted	SC	—	1	
50	Septic tank		Plumbers	2	2		
51	Plumber's trim	Final plumbing work	Plumbers	2	2	1	
52	Heating	Install and/or complete heating system	Electricians	3	6	2	
53	Paint		Painters	4	16	4	Done while carpenters are trimming
54	Install operators and deliver screens	Window mechanisms	Carpenters	1	½	½	Must be alone in house
55	Electrical trim	Install lamps, outlet plates, etc.	Electricians	3	3	1	Now done before glazing
56	Polish terrazzo		Subcontracted	SC	—	2	
57	Clean windows and interior		Cleaning	2	2	1	Must be alone in house
58	Grass		Subcontracted	SC	—	1	
59	Install screens		Carpenters	1	½	½	
60	Painters complete, inspect		Painters	5	15	3	Including time for company inspection, final adjustments and odds and ends
61	Wallpaper and mirror		Painters	2	2	1	
62	Plumbing inspection	By city inspector		—	—	1	City inspection
63	Electrical inspection	By city inspector		—	—	1	City inspection
64	Permanent electrical connection	By power company	Power Company	—	—	1	
65	Production inspection		Co. Inspector	1	1	1	Note also inspection at step No. 60

* SC (subcontracted). In 1959 the average house required $2,500 of subcontracted work.

Miss Roark also used five colored pins to assist in calling her attention to an operation as follows:

Black—indicated "on order."
Red—indicated "did not arrive or get completed as promised."
White—indicated "crew is there, on the job."
Yellow—indicated "Mabel should call."
Blue—indicated "have a question for the foreman."

From the visual standpoint, since the jobs were added at the bottom of the sheet as they were taken on and the construction steps proceeded from left to right, the completed steps made a slightly irregular diagonal line, slanting downwards from right to left. Thus, any house that had fallen behind showed up as an indent to the left in the diagonal line of completed boxes.

By and large, Mr. Playford stated during the last 12 months all houses had been taking the same length of time to complete, namely, 80–85 calendar days from the date construction work was started. Customers were promised delivery in no more than 100 calendar days from the signing of the purchase agreement. Because so many purchasers were new residents moving South and therefore had many moving details to schedule, any delays in house completions were felt to significantly jeopardize customer relations.

In addition to assigning the work to the foremen Miss Roark's activity as dispatcher included maintaining the production "boards" and serving as a communication and recording center for all reports and instructions. In this duty she made full usage of a two-way radio system. Each foreman, Mr. Playford, and the warehouse supervisor had a two-way radio in his car or truck. The radio system had been installed in mid-1958 on a lease basis and cost the company monthly rental of $375.

Miss Roark talked with each foreman intermittently three to six or more times daily. In a typical conversation the masonry foreman might call in and tell her that the footings operation his crew had been working on at the Kelly house was now completed, but that the iron work for the Kent job hadn't arrived and that Mr. and Mrs. Kent had been around that morning and asked if they could change the dimensions of their back patio from 12 feet × 15 feet to 12 feet × 20 feet. He might then ask where Mabel wanted his crew the next day and would she check her paper work to see whether the Larsen house was to have a front planter and whether the plumbers should be through with the O'Leary house so that the slab could be laid by the masons.

Miss Roark independently made the innumerable decisions as to the operations and jobs which would be done next, receiving little or no aid from Mr. Playford, whose office was next door. While he came in to see the "boards" once or twice a week, he did not attempt to participate in the hour-by-hour job of scheduling and directing the crews.

To prevent delays and idle crews Miss Roark had to have a clear understanding of the various operations and their interrelationships. It was essential, for instance, for her to know that the electricians couldn't do their rough-in until the studs were up, that the heating work could be done while the carpenters were trimming, that the electricians and plumbers could go on ahead or behind the painters on certain operations but could not work at the same time in the house with them, etc. Miss Roark stated that "I still make some mistakes but I've learned a lot about house building during this past year."

In scheduling the crews she used the guides of time and crew requirements shown on Exhibit 3. These guides had been established by Herbert Playford and Miss Roark out of their combined experience as to how many men and how much time it was necessary to allow for the completion of each step. They had learned, for example, that it was entirely reasonable to expect a crew of four carpenters to frame up an average house (Exhibit 3, Step No. 20) in five days working at an ordinary pace.

Miss Roark's purchasing function was confined to ordering specific items for delivery from vendors selected previously by Arthur Root. Arthur Root handled all negotiations with suppliers, arranging for prices, delivery, and payment terms. This work occupied a significant portion of his time. He regularly "shopped" for better values in windows, fixtures, lumber, appliances, etc., and had accomplished considerable standardization of purchased items.

In late 1958 Sunshine Builders had leased a 6,000-square-foot warehouse in order to be able to stock various purchased materials. Five men were hired to receive, stock, and deliver items stocked. A sixth employee who had previously acted as a truck driver and errand runner was also assigned to the warehouse group. The arrangement was intended to allow the company to buy in larger volumes at lower prices. It was also intended that this new approach would give Sunshine a direct and closer control over the delivery of items to building sites. Mr. Root estimated that he could negotiate volume purchases covering about 75 percent of the material used (based on cost) which could secure for Sunshine a 4 percent saving in cost if the company would purchase and take deliveries no more frequently than three times per year.

While Sunshine Builders did not attempt to maintain a breakdown between material and labor costs, Mr. Root pointed out that costs had been rising steadily, citing *Engineering News–Record* statistics which showed that on a national basis material costs had been rising at a rate of 2 percent per year over the past four years. Construction labor costs on the same survey showed increases at an annual rate of about 4 percent.

The foremen were responsible for ordering all material from the warehouse with the exception of the staking-out material which Miss Roark ordered. The warehouse truck then delivered the material ordered to each building site.

Sunshine Builders encouraged prospective buyers to make any nonstructural changes which they desired. Daniel Root pointed out that "different models are built in each Sunshine subdivision, making a considerable freedom of choice for the buyer which, coupled with the further variations which Sunshine offers at a nominal price, results in a low-cost house with considerable individuality." The exceptions and additions to a typical contract, shown on Exhibit 4 were not unusual either as to nature or quantity.

Exhibit 4
EXCERPT FROM BUILDING AGREEMENT WITH CUSTOMER

Third: All details of material and construction will be identical with those used in the model home located at

    . . . Lot #4, Belle Lake Subdivision . . . with the following exceptions:

1.	Model 190L	$10,990
2.	Place wrought iron shutters, with oak leaf design on kitchen windows, front bedroom windows and left side bedroom window. Retain stucco decoration.	90
3.	Substitute screen patio with terrazzo floor at house level, full foundation, 1 waterproof electric outlet, light fixture centered over sliding glass doors. Floor area 16 feet × 10 feet. Roof to extend 2 feet past floor area with screening to be canted toward floor. Roof to be aluminum with styrofoam insulation.	740
4.	Install glass shower door in bath no. 2.	50
5.	Substitute American Standard Bildor cast-iron tub for present steel tub.	n/c
6.	Erect tile wainscot in bath no. 2 to 3 feet 8 inch height.	145
7.	Install air-conditioning aperture centered under fron windows to bedroom no. 1, with 220V outlet on separate circuit for same.	28
8.	Install tile backsplash above base cabinets in kitchen.	50
9.	Install gutter and downspout over front entrance, left side of bedroom wing, kitchen and garage.	50
10.	Eliminate Walltex in baths no. 1 and no. 2.	
11.	Install bookshelves between living room and dinette in lieu of present planter and wrought iron. Shelves to be placed at 42 inch, 54 inch, and 74 inch height.	n/c
12.	Raise 1 inch × 4 inch pressure-treated drapery hanger above sliding glass doors in living room to ceiling height.	n/c
		$12,143

Miss Roark and the foremen were given copies of each customer's plans, together with the agreed-upon changes. She kept a "customer detail sheet" for each customer which contained this information and the frequent additional changes. Such further changes were written up and priced by the estimator at the time they were requested. A "Customer Request for Extra Work" form was filled out and signed by the customer, with the original copy being sent to the office for the final bill, the customer keeping the second copy, the foreman receiving the third copy, and the fourth being sent to Miss Roark.

Before actual construction could begin on a specific house, about two or three weeks were required to complete the steps shown on the Start Chart (Exhibit 5). Commencing with the signing of the contract, Mr. Playford personally handled the preproduction phase of each job covering steps 1 through 25 on the "Start Chart."

Exhibit 5
START CHART

CUSTOMER'S NAME _____   BROKER: _____
ADDRESS: _____   LEGAL DESCRIPTION: _____

PHONE: _____   _____

1. Contract signed or on file ☐
2. Detail Sheet #1 received ☐
3. Plans ordered ☐
4. Survey ordered ☐
5. Detail Sheet #2 received (if there is more than 48-hr. lag between #3 and #5, report to A.R.) ☐
6. Plans returned ☐
7. Plans inspected (if there is more than a 24-hr. lag between #6 and #9, report to A.R.) ☐
8. Plans returned for correction ☐
9. Corrected plans returned ☐
10. Plans inspected for correction ☐
11. Plans sent to_____ ☐
12. Plans received from_____ ☐
13. Building permit applied for ☐

14. Plans and letter to customer (air mail special delivery w/ enclosed return envelope) ☐
15. Send loan plans ☐
16. Submit plans for subdivision approval (special messenger) ☐
17. Subdivision approval received ☐
18. Survey received ☐
19. Notify supervisor and production to check lot for clearing and for errors in lot line ☐
20. Customer's approval ☐
21. Notify accounting of loan approval and of who holds the loan ☐
22. Construction loan ☐
23. Add name to production chart ☐
24. Building permit picked up ☐
25. Water meter permit picked up ☐

In explaining his methods of managing the production operation Mr. Playford made the following points:

1. Two employees have been added in drafting since the first of the year in an attempt to eliminate the subcontracting of drafting work. The drafting is necessary in order to have separate plans for every house because of the large number of changes usually incorporated for each customer.

2. The major change in operations without the four superintendents is that the various foremen now have responsibility for the construction of the house at different phases. These responsibilities are as follows:

Operations	*Supervisor or Foreman Responsible*
1–2	Mr. Playford
3	Electrical
4	Carpenter
5–10	Mason
11	Plumber
12–18	Mason
19–23	Carpenter
24	Plumber
25	Electrician
26–30	Plasterer
31	Carpenter
32–34	Plasterer
35	Carpenter
36–37	Plasterer
38–49	Carpenter
50–51	Plumber
52–55	Electrician
56–65	Inspector

3. Low-cost construction comes from doing jobs conventionally. The only good approach to cost cutting comes from making operations fast and smooth. Sunshine has cut two weeks off of building homes in recent years and should eventually be able to cut one or two more. I made a study at Meadowlark which showed that ideally a home comparable to Sunshine's $15,000 models could be built in 52 calendar days if everything worked out well.

Our men use the same methods for each step in every house. It's all pretty much standardized—the block work, slab, framing, electrical wiring, plastering—they do each house the same way as the others. We use only the most elementary common tools and equipment, such as power saws and cement mixers, and have very little else.

By and large most prefabbing does not pay unless the customer is allowed to make no changes and if Sunshine adopted that approach we would lose sales. For instance, prefabbed roof trusses so commonly used by other construction firms are more expensive for Sunshine than on-site building of the roof structure, probably because we have so many models. We visited Levittown, Pennsylvania, in 1956 to see if we could pick up any ideas and found that they permit no changes whatever. Building houses block by block they can do more precutting and standardizing than we can since our houses are usually not adjacent.

One way we save time is to get foremen to make suggestions. For instance, our masonry foreman has learned that a mason will lay blocks faster if his helper will keep the blocks piled up ahead of him. And we have discovered that it is a good idea to supply about 10 percent extra material to each job in order to prevent any picking and hunting for material. Any extra material left over is sent back to the warehouse. But the conventional methods of building are cheapest for us.

4. Our men are picked by the foremen. They usually hear about good men in the trade and many they hire are friends or have been

sent by friends. The foreman can hire and lay off as needed. Crews work a five-day week, nine hours a day, which gives them 45 hours of pay per week. The masons are unionized but the others are not. The men tend to work in teams, a journeyman and a helper. They also tend to specialize. For instance, on a carpenter crew the foreman has separate men for door jambs and window frames, for rafter cutting, for cornices for general framing, and a saw specialist. Helpers are paid $1.25–$1.75 per hour. We pay no overtime, just straight time. The wage structure for the craftsmen is masons, $2.75; plumbers, $3.00; carpenters, $2.45; tile setters, $3.00; plasterers, $3.00; electricians, $2.25; painters, $2.40. There is no wage progression, no future, no security, and no benefits other than those required by law, social security, etc., which add up to about 8 percent over these rates. But we've had no major layoffs ever, and have a darn good crew.

5. Up until January Arthur used the six charts on my office wall—which I started—to control costs. These showed the dollar-per-square-foot cost for each phase (corresponding to the foreman's areas of operations) for each house when it was completed, the point being plotted on the horizontal axis by date of completion. This would have revealed any trends and any house that was out of line. No clear trends were shown, though.

Now these charts are discontinued because they were too much work to keep up. Instead, about once a month we spot-check costs by studying the accumulated costs on several completed jobs quite closely and figuring out the total cost per square foot on various operations such as electrical, plumbing, etc. Every three months I'll make a still more detailed check on 12 houses. I control material costs by controlling the amount sent out to each house, depending on its size. Arthur, of course, keeps check on supply sources.

If any costs get looking high, I talk to the foreman. Recently tile costs had moved up about 15 percent–20 percent and upon investigating I found that the foreman was driving 20 miles for supplies every day. I showed him how to order in advance and stock more in our warehouse. He had also guaranteed his crew 10 hours of pay regardless of the actual time worked. And some of his crew were driving to our warehouse instead of getting material delivered.

As long as I'm out watching, and the men are working, and Mabel keeps things moving, the costs will be O.K.

6. We are still too lax in our attitude toward delay. I want more flow and speed, better customer relationships, lower work in process. I am getting out in the field more now that I've got things set up better here, and getting my eyes opened finding jobs where no action is taking place. Mabel gets along fine with the men and they like her, but she is not firm enough with them and with outsiders. She can learn to do her job even better.

7. Crews are instructed to work an extra hour to finish up on a house and wherever possible to make moves to the next house on an overnight basis. If a house really needs only eight hours of plastering it gets nine, because we work on a nine-hour day. However, if it has

what we might consider 10 hours of plastering it is usually done in 9 also, in order to finish it in one day.

Houses were priced by estimating "construction costs" (see Exhibit 1) and then adding 5 percent for "expenses," and 15 percent for selling costs and profit together. The estimating was performed by Daniel Root's assistant, who served as the company's estimator. He had had some architectural training and spent a large portion of his time working with customers on their changes from standard plans. The average house in 1959 included approximately $2,500 of subcontracting. Exhibits 6 and 7 show one-page

Exhibit 6
SALES PROMOTIONAL MATERIAL
(for a two bedroom model)

$10,990 on your lot   With 2-car garage $11,840

Model 190

- 2 master bedrooms
- 2 "decorator" baths
- cement tile roof over 2x8 rafters
- 15 ft. sliding glass wall to patio
- Sunshine kitchen; Coronet cabinets and Nu-Tone ventilating hood; Moen single-mix faucet
- General Electric wall oven, cook top, 40 gallon water heater
- radiant electric ceiling heat—silent, clean, maintenance-free, economical; individual room-thermostats
- 6" Fiberglas insulation for cooler summers, warmer winters
- Minneapolis-Honeywell tap switches; clothes dryer outlet; circuit-breakers (eliminating fuses); 200 ampere service
- Hall-Mack bathroom accessories
- spacious garage plus utility "ell"
- spot sodded lawn
- square footage: living area   1073
  utility   63
  garage   249
  TOTAL   1385
- Sunshine guarantee of satisfaction

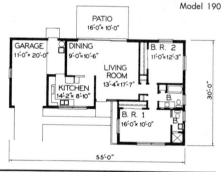

1202 Hacienda Ave. • Minneapolis, Florida • Phone 6-4602

it's a SUNSHINE **home**

Model Home on Poinsettia Rd. — 2 Miles South of Key Drive

brochures on the cheapest and most expensive houses in the line. Once a price was set on a model it was not changed, though its costs tended to rise slightly as new improvements of a minor nature were gradually added. Arthur Root and Herbert Playford agreed with Daniel Root that Sunshine Builders' prices in 1959 could not be increased if Sunshine's product was to remain competitive.

Exhibit 7
SALES PROMOTIONAL MATERIAL
(for a three bedroom model)

$18,500 on your lot

- 3 bedrooms • 3 "decorator" baths
- cement tile roof over 2x8 rafters
- tile foyer entrance with guest closet
- spacious family room with serving bar
- sliding glass walls from living and
  dining rooms to
- 18 ft. screened porch
- 20 ft. free-form patio
- Coronet cabinets in solid maple or solid
  walnut; Nu-Tone ventilating hood;
  Moen single-mix faucet
- General Electric dishwasher, wall oven,
  cook top, 52 gallon water heater
- radiant electric ceiling heat—silent, clean,
  maintenance-free, economical;
  individual room-thermostats
- 6" Fiberglas insulation for cooler
  summers, winter warmth
- Minneapolis-Honeywell tap switches;
  clothes dryer outlet; circuit breakers
  (eliminates fuses); 200 ampere service
- Hall-Mack bathroom accessories;
  "relaxation unit" in master bath
- 2-car garage plus utility "ell"
- spot sodded lawn
- square footage: living area   1656
  porch   180
  garage and utility   505

  TOTAL   2341
- Sunshine   guarantee of satisfaction

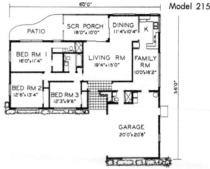

Model 215

1202 Hacienda Ave. • Minneapolis, Florida • Phone 6-4602

it's a      home

Considerable emphasis was placed on customer satisfaction after the house was completed. Sunshine's policy was that during the first year they would repair any item that the customer did not consider satisfactory. As long as the request was in any way reasonable (and often where it did not appear so), they did the work at no charge and with a willing and pleasant attitude. The service department (see Exhibit 2) handled this work. In the Sunshine organization it was referred to as "punch work," meaning that it was to be "punched out, without delay." In April 1959 the "punch work girl" was moved into Mr. Playford's office in order to provide better supervision of her work. The biggest single item requiring punch work was ceiling cracks. In pricing a house, about 2 percent of the expected price was allowed for "punch work" and included in construction cost estimates.

On May 1, 1959, the production "boards" showed a total of 42 houses listed, consisting of 12 different models in a price range of $10,990 to $18,500. Comparable figures for October 1958 and April 1, 1959 showed 35 and 36 houses under construction, respectively. Nine units of the most popular model were under way, five models showed three to six units in process, and the six other models listed three or less units each.

The April rise of houses in process from 36 to 42 was due to a heavy influx of orders received in late March and the month of April. The improved sales results had caused Mr. Playford to gradually increase the houses started each week from three during the first week of April to six in the last week of April. From every indication sales prospects for the balance of 1959 appeared excellent and Mr. Playford expected to be able to continue starting five to six houses weekly. Mr. Playford stated that he liked to make any changes in starts on a gradual basis in order to maintain a smooth flow of work to all crews. "This approach," he said, "paces the whole operation."

Arthur Root stated five principles which he felt represented the key to Sunshine Builders' success and to its future:

1. Our houses must be completely livable.
2. They must have eye appeal.
3. As builders we must develop and hold a reputation for honesty, integrity, skill, and on-time completion.
4. We must offer exceptional value.
5. Our houses must be properly presented and promoted.

"Any one factor that is not up to standard would hurt us badly. We must do a top job on all five."

Chaircraft Corporation

> Frank, I don't want you to feel badly about the remarks that were directed at you and some of your people during yesterday's executive committee meeting, but I don't want you to forget about them either. Several members of the executive committee, myself included, feel that our manufacturing operations are simply not keeping pace with our sales growth and that our declining profit situation is caused in large part by conditions in manufacturing that are almost out of control. We've spent an awful lot of time during the past two years getting our field sales force reorganized and trained. Now that the results of that effort are really beginning to pay off, it appears that we haven't spent enough time looking at manufacturing problems.

The speaker was Mr. Richard Acton, President of the Chaircraft Corporation. He was talking with Mr. Frank Johnson, the company's manufacturing manager.

The Chaircraft Corporation, which was located in a small southern community, manufactured an extensive line of upholstered chairs, platform rockers, and recliners. Sales were nationwide to 10,000 dealers through company salesmen. Sales volume for 1968 was $20 million and a sales growth rate of 10 percent to 20 percent annually had been projected by Mr. Acton. Approximately 700 factory workers were employed. Mr. Johnson was responsible for all manufacturing operations as well as production control, inventory control and shipping.

"My interpretation of the figures you gave us yesterday indicate that frame shop labor costs are going up despite the new equipment you added this year. Your labor and overhead variances were almost double last year's figures and material variance is up, too.

"Charlie Gibson (a region manager who supervised several salesmen) bent my ear for an hour last week in New York about quality complaints from dealers—and your figures show a 20 percent increase in rework costs this year over last.

"What really bothers me though Frank is the $6,000 increase in shipping costs for finished goods. We shouldn't spend a penny on shipping finished goods, but we're now spending over $10,000 per year on it."

"I'll admit we've got some problems, Dick, but I was pretty sore about the manner in which some of our problems were blown all out of proportion yesterday," Mr. Johnson replied. "Our biggest difficulties are in the frame parts and assembly areas and I'm going to look into these areas carefully during the next few months. It may be that the computer can help."[1]

"Good, Frank," Mr. Acton responded. "I'll be in Chicago all next week but I'll check with you again as soon as I get back a week from Monday."

THE MANUFACTURING PROCESS

The Chaircraft company was an integrated manufacturer, converting raw lumber, cotton, cloth fabric, and other materials into upholstered chairs. An upholstered chair is an assembly of three major elements: the frame (itself an assembly of a dozen or more wooden parts); upholstery materials (primarily springs and cotton, foam rubber, or foam plastic); and a cover fabric. The company produced seven lines, or general types, of upholstered chairs on as many assembly lines; the other manufacturing activities of the company supplied the required components to the assembly lines.

Lumber Purchase and Storage

Chaircraft frames were produced from solid southern hardwood lumber of varying species. Lumber was purchased by an independent commission broker. The company purchased three principal grades: first grade, number one common, and number two common. Five thicknesses were used: one inch, one and one-quarter inch, two inch, two and one-half inch, and three inch. About three-quarters of the lumber used was one inch or one and one-quarter inch thick. Lumber costs about 15 cents per board foot.[2]

Lumber was stacked upon receipt to form loads of a single grade and thickness. A load was a stack of boards forming a cube roughly 12 feet in each dimension and containing about 10,000 board feet. As the boards were stacked, each layer was separated from adjacent layers by slats which created spaces through which air could circulate during the drying process. Typically, the equivalent of six months' requirements of undried lumber was stored outdoors.

---

[1] Chaircraft owned a small second-generation computer which was programmed to run payrolls, billing, accounts receivable records and other conventional accounting applications. These programs required only a portion of the computer's capacity.

[2] A "board foot" is the amount of lumber equal to 12 inches × 12 inches × 1 inch.

Lumber Drying

Operations connected with lumber drying occupied a rectangular area roughly 350 feet long and 100 feet in width, with one end abutting the factory. The lumber loads were moved through this area on wheeled platforms which rode on steel tracks. The area was divided across its length into three sections of about equal size with the company's three dry kilns (ovens, each 100 feet long) occupying the center section (see Exhibit 1).

Exhibit 1
DIAGRAM OF PLANT AREA

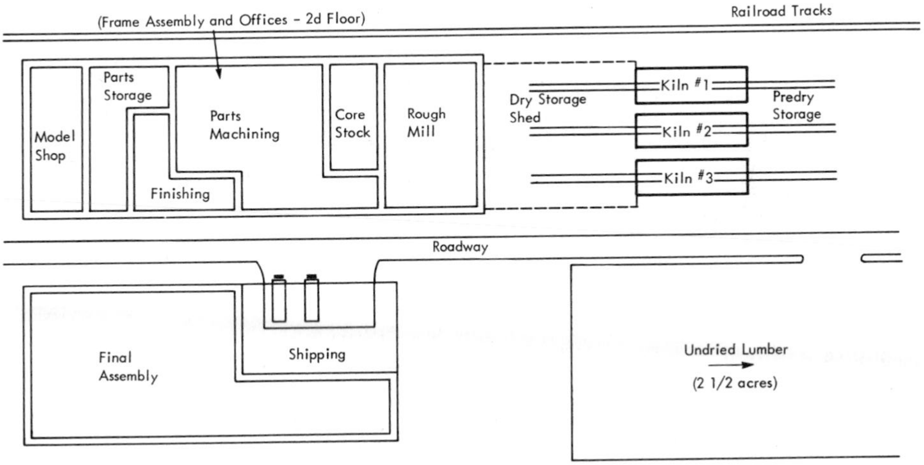

The section farthest from the factory was used as pre-dry storage. Here the loads from the inventory of undried lumber were lined up awaiting entry to one of the kilns. A full "charge" for each kiln was assembled before the kiln became available in order to minimize time spent in "recharging" an empty kiln. Drying time in the kilns varied considerably with species, grade, and moisture content of the lumber and with the season of the year. Exact drying time, therefore, could not be predicted. Average drying time for a charge was about one week.

Subsequent to kiln drying, the lumber moved into the third section—a covered dry storage area. Both the pre-dry and the dry storage areas had a capacity of about 300,000 board feet; an amount roughly equal to the total charge capacity of the three kilns. The size of the dry storage area was limited by the location of the kilns, the factory wall and by property lines. The cost of extra handling prohibited the use of other areas for storing dried lumber.

Maximum use of the kilns depended upon availability of space in the dry storage area to receive the dried lumber promptly upon completion of the drying cycle. But a rapid and orderly use of dried lumber to free storage space was dependent upon the degree to which the mix of sizes, species, and grades available in the dried lumber storage corresponded with the factory requirements at the moment.

Parts Manufacture

After being removed from storage the dried lumber was processed through the frame shop to produce frame parts. The frame shop had two departments: the rough mill department which cut the incoming lumber into "core stock," and the parts machining department which processed the core stock to produce finished frame parts which went into parts inventory.

In December 1968, the frame shop employed 54 men on the day shift and 32 men on the night shift. A full crew of 17 worked each shift in the rough mill while there was only a partial second shift in parts machining. Both shifts were working five 10-hour days a week.

Rough Mill Department

In the rough mill, lumber was brought in a full load at a time and processed on a conveyorized production line operated by a nine-man team. Boards in a given load varied in quality, width, and length, but were of uniform rough thickness. Along the production line, boards were cut to one of three standard lengths, planed, and jointed.[3] After these operations, the boards were sorted on carts according to length. Boards were produced in 70 standard length/thickness specifications.

Lumber from the conveyor line was then cut to width on a ripsaw to form core stock. A piece of core stock was a finished oblong board of determined dimensions which had been set by adding a standard allowance (e.g., $\frac{3}{8}$ inch) to each dimension of the intended finished part. The ripsaw was operated by a four-man team. The saw was set to cut to a few selected widths. The cut pieces had to be sorted as follows: boards of desired width onto handling carts according to size; oversize boards returned to the operator on the "feed" side of the saw for another pass; undersize pieces set aside to be moved to another department where they would be glued up into larger boards; and scrap pieces onto a special conveyor for removal. The ripsaw operation called for special skills because of the rapid pace and the sorting decisions to be made. The rough mill manufactured core stock in approximately 250 specifications.

Parts Machining Department

In the parts machining department core stock was shaped to form finished parts ready for assembly into frames. Most of the 500 parts pro-

---

[3] The planing operation smoothed the top and bottom surfaces of the board and determined its thickness. The jointing operation smoothed the sides of the board.

duced were of relatively simple shapes. For "straight-stock" (parts which were essentially rectangular in shape, usually containing dowels or dowel holes), the machining operations were simple. Principal operations were a double-end cut off to finished length, rip to finished width, and any necessary boring. Parts with more complex shapes were formed on band saws or shapers. The few parts which would be visible in the finished chair were sanded after machining.

Material moved through the parts machining shop in lots, each lot traveling on one cart and containing pieces for one part specification. Each machine was tended by a specific operator who was paid a piece rate and who was also responsible for moving material to his work place and for performing any required setup on his equipment. When an operator completed work on a lot he informed the department foreman and was assigned another job.

During 1968 the company purchased two automatic machines. Shaped parts now could be produced on an automatic shaper at a much higher rate than on the band saw or hand shaper. The new machine required more than an hour to set up, however, whereas the manually controlled machines required at most a few minutes of setup time. A high-speed transfer machine combined the cutoff, boring, and dowel insertion operations for straight-stock. With one operator this new machine operated at a rate faster than the previous method which required three operators using three machines.

Parts Storage

After the last machining operation, four stock handlers moved the completed pieces to bins in the frame parts storeroom. About 500 different parts were required to build the 50 different "frame styles" which made up the seven product lines. A few of the parts were used in more than one line.

Parts Withdrawal and Frame Assembly

Frames were assembled to meet the schedule of the final (upholstery) assembly line. A small buffer stock of assembled frames was used to "uncouple," or separate, the assembly of frames from the final line. Each assembler built complete chair frames, customarily in lots of 25 frames (lots often included two or more chair styles). Space limitations prevented locating more than the parts requirements for 25 chair frames near one assembler. The frame parts were wheeled on carts to the assembly operators by six "stock pickers." The pickers, working from lot tickets which listed the frame styles and the quantity of each style to comprise a lot of 25, called on their memory to determine what parts to remove from the stockroom shelves.

PRODUCTION CONTROL SYSTEM

The control of frame parts manufacturing was tied closely to the company's final assembly and shipment plans. The rate of production varied seasonally and was matched to customer delivery needs (see Exhibits 2

Exhibit 2

CHAIR ORDERS RECEIVED, PRODUCTION, AND SHIPMENTS BY MONTHS—
1965 THROUGH 1968

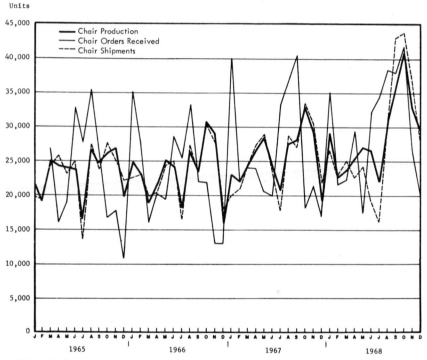

Note: This is a graphic presentation of the figures given in Exhibit 4.

through 5). In general, chairs were shipped within two days after completion of final assembly. A long-standing company policy against carrying finished goods inventories had been modified only twice during the last ten years. At these times Chaircraft had built an inventory of no more than 10,000 chairs in a few popular standard items.[4] In both cases the entire inventory had been sold by the end of the year at regular prices.

The production rate was set by the manufacturing manager who specified the daily production goal, in units, for each of the seven final upholstery assembly lines. Production rates for all contributing departments were then set to match this rate.

---

[4] To cover its 50 different styles of frames, Chaircraft offered over 500 different fabric pattern/color combinations and other choices such as springs or foam rubber upholstery. As a result of these options, the variety in the final product numbered several thousand.

Exhibit 3

PRODUCTION ACTIVITY BY MONTHS—JULY 1966 THROUGH DECEMBER 1968

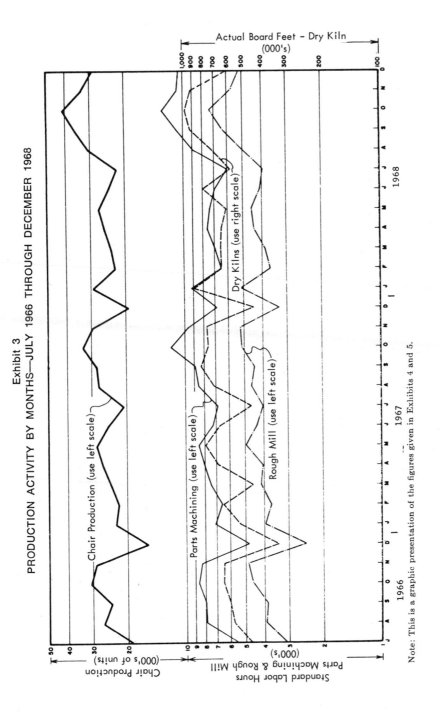

Note: This is a graphic presentation of the figures given in Exhibits 4 and 5.

Exhibit 4
SOURCE DATA FOR EXHIBIT 2
(units in 000s)

	1965			1966			1967			1968		
	Orders Received	Chairs Produced	Chairs Shipped	Orders Received	Chairs Produced	Chairs Shipped	Orders Received	Chairs Produced	Chairs Shipped	Orders Received	Chairs Produced	Chairs Shipped
January	n.a.*	21.9	19.7	35.1	24.8	22.5	39.9	22.9	19.9	35.1	29.2	26.6
February	n.a.	18.8	19.3	27.4	23.0	22.9	21.9	22.0	21.0	21.7	22.6	22.8
March	26.8	25.0	24.2	15.9	18.8	19.9	23.9	24.1	24.3	22.3	23.7	25.1
April	16.0	24.2	25.8	20.2	21.4	20.4	23.8	26.6	27.3	29.3	25.4	22.7
May	18.3	23.8	23.1	19.4	25.1	24.3	20.6	28.4	28.9	17.4	27.1	24.3
June	32.7	23.7	25.0	28.6	24.1	25.0	19.9	24.8	24.8	32.2	24.1	19.3
July	27.7	16.3	13.7	25.3	18.3	16.6	33.2	20.7	17.8	34.4	21.9	16.2
August	35.4	26.8	27.3	33.2	26.3	27.3	36.9	27.6	28.8	38.3	30.6	30.6
September	26.8	24.6	23.7	21.9	24.0	23.4	40.3	28.2	27.2	37.9	35.7	43.1
October	16.6	26.2	27.7	21.8	30.6	30.7	18.1	33.1	33.6	41.8	41.1	43.8
November	17.7	26.8	25.1	12.8	28.8	27.8	21.5	29.3	30.5	26.6	32.9	36.8
December	10.5	19.8	22.2	12.9	15.7	18.0	16.9	19.3	21.9	20.0	29.0	28.0
Total	n.a.	277.9	276.8	274.5	280.9	278.8	316.9	307.0	306.0	357.0	343.3	339.3

* Not available.

Exhibit 5
PRODUCTION ACTIVITY

	Dry Kilns (actual board feet)	Rough Mill (standard labor hours)	Parts Machining (standard labor hours)
1966			
July	467,200	3,064	5,432
August	571,000	3,911	7,897
September	599,900	3,835	7,957
October	646,500	4,596	8,620
November	624,400	4,857	8,347
December	339,600	2,467	4,741
	3,248,600	22,730	42,994
1967			
January	532,600	3,959	7,107
February	650,700	3,680	6,549
March	456,000	4,139	7,459
April	685,800	4,058	8,074
May	793,800	4,973	8,601
June	670,300	4,331	7,235
July	463,700	4,026	6,828
August	718,500	4,625	8,682
September	732,000	4,440	8,907
October	768,000	5,197	11,709
November	775,600	5,208	9,615
December	448,500	3,294	6,802
	7,695,500	51,930	97,568
1968			
January	897,400	5,181	9,171
February	649,500	3,632	6,462
March	657,300	3,870	6,974
April	645,200	4,409	7,619
May	609,800	4,520	7,387
June	795,500	4,093	6,918
July	579,300	3,966	5,879
August	723,700	5,043	8,990
September	928,600	6,327	10,746
October	981,300	7,360	12,863
November	917,700	5,793	10,798
December	610,500	5,092	10,471
	8,995,800	59,286	104,278

Customer orders specified delivery in a given month and upon receipt were added by line to that month's backlog. When the backlog for a given month reached the available capacity for the month (on the basis of the planned production rate for that month), a decision had to be made to increase the production rate (a common event) or to stop booking orders for that month. A report of orders received, backlog, and available capacity for each of the next three months was prepared daily. Orders to be shipped during a given month were normally on hand by the 15th of the prior month. Only exceptional orders were processed for shipment in less than three weeks.

The monthly production schedule was broken down into daily production schedules dependent upon shipping load plans, i.e., lists identifying each chair to be shipped in a given load on a given date. This conformance to shipping load plans reflected the magnitude of freight costs. Customers normally paid full freight costs on all shipments of their orders. To hold down their freight costs, customers expected that items ordered together would be shipped together and expected also that their shipments would be pooled[5] with others destined for the same geographical area. If some chairs on an order were not ready for shipment on the scheduled date, these were shipped separately at the Chaircraft company's expense. To satisfy customers' delivery expectations and to avoid freight charges to the company itself, the Chaircraft company shipped complete orders by pool cars and trucks and emphasized planned production to meet such shipments.

The translation of customers' orders into shipping load plans was the responsibility of the traffic control clerk. He planned each day's shipping loads three weeks in advance of the shipping date. Then, each Friday morning he turned over to the production control section the planned shipping loads for the five days ending on a Thursday three weeks hence. (See "Planning Time Cycle" below.)

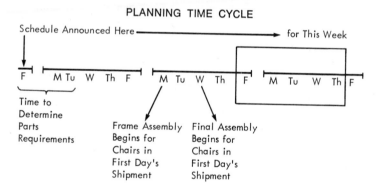

PLANNING TIME CYCLE

The production control section, consisting of a manager and three clerks, used the shipping plans to determine the corresponding frame parts requirements. This was done with the use of the standard parts list for the frames to be built. After parts requirements for a week were accumulated, these figures were compared with frame inventory balances.

Although shipping plans, by day, were established three weeks in advance, the "lead time" at which parts requirements were determined in advance of assembly was reduced considerably by these factors:

The shipping plans were accumulated each week until Friday. This achieved a "batching" of requirements but cut lead time.

---

[5] Shipments occupying part of a truck or rail freight car cost considerably more than would the same shipment "pooled" or combined with other shipments to fill a "pool" car.

Final (upholstery) assembly began two days before the planned shipping date and frame assembly two days[6] before that. This reduced lead time by nearly a week.

Production clerks were occupied from Friday until Tuesday in determining parts requirements and in comparing parts requirements with availabilities.

The net effects was that the actual requirements of parts to be assembled in any week were not known until Tuesday of the preceding week.

To compensate for the limited advance notice of known parts requirements, the production control manager forecast parts requirements each week for one week beyond the two weeks' requirements known. This one-week forecast was, in general, an extrapolation of a simple "visual" average of recent weeks' actual requirements.

In determining what parts to order from the frame shop, the production control manager used the following formula: Parts needed equals the requirements for three weeks (as established above) less the current book inventory and less any quantity currently on order and not received into inventory. If this calculation showed a parts shortage, an order was placed on the shop equal to the standard order quantity (or a multiple of the standard quantity) established for each part. Each standard order quantity was set at 80 percent of the number of pieces of that part that would fit on one of the carts used to move work in the frame shop.

Every Tuesday the production control department issued the week's frame parts orders to the frame shop foreman. These orders were represented by standard order tickets which specified the quantity ordered, the core stock to be used and the standard routing through the parts machining department. Several hundred order tickets were issued each week. Once the core stock had been cut for a given part the order ticket was placed on the cart and remained with the parts in process. The order ticket was returned to the production control department after the parts were stored in the frame parts storeroom.

The frame shop foreman was given complete control in scheduling each order through his shop, subject to one restriction: all parts ordered were expected to be produced and in stock within two weeks of the date of issuance of the order. The foreman tried to schedule orders to balance the load on various machines and operators in the shop. His schedule was dependent also upon the availability of the proper species and quality of lumber in the rough mill. To keep a balance between the mix of lumber being dried and the requirements of the frame parts schedule the frame shop foreman maintained an informal liaison with the dry-kiln foreman. Of the actual orders handled in the frame shop during 1968, 70 percent

---

[6] The required time for a chair to move through final assembly and through frame assembly was considerably less than two days—just a matter of hours. The extra time was used as a buffer and was represented physically by completed frames awaiting the final assembly line and completed chairs awaiting shipment.

were completed within one week of issue, and 90 percent were completed before the two-week deadline.

If all went well, on any Monday the parts inventory would assure the requirements for that week's frame assemblies. The production control manager pointed out, however, that achieving this result depended upon:

1.   The book inventory being correct.
2.   No serious underrun on orders outstanding.
3.   Accurate forecasting for one week beyond known requirements.
4.   Completion of parts within the two-week time.

THE MANUFACTURING MANAGER'S VIEW

Following his conversation with Mr. Acton, Mr. Johnson reflected on the comments which had been made during the executive committee meeting. He felt that the company's production control system for frame parts could be improved and his attention was drawn into three areas—parts ordering, machine loading, and control of the rate of production.

Parts Ordering

Excessive inventories frequently accumulated for some frame parts while other parts were unavailable when needed. This problem was attributed to several factors: the foreman's discretion in scheduling parts for production; lack of central control of overruns and underruns on parts orders; and clerical errors in reporting receipts and withdrawals from stock. The stockroom typically reported from one to three items out of stock daily. Where the production control records indicated inventories of several hundred units, the discrepancy was attributed to failure to record withdrawals or was simply unexplained.

The book inventory record was maintained by the production control department. A new book balance was calculated weekly for each part by adding actual parts production and subtracting standard parts withdrawals. Standard withdrawal figures were arrived at by combining the count of frames actually assembled each week with the list of standard parts for each frame design. If assemblers used nonstandard parts or if they used more than the standard quantity due to spoilage, such use usually went unrecorded. In some instances, assemblers, anxious to increase piece-rate earnings, had found that substituting one part for another speeded assembly. The stock pickers were supposed to report extra withdrawals and to choose only standard parts, but this was difficult to enforce.

Some of the difficulties in parts ordering were related to the job of handling production control information. A standard two-day clerical delay existed between the time shipping load plans for a given week were accumulated and the time corresponding parts requirements could be compared with the record of inventory levels. Standard figures for withdrawals of parts per week were used instead of detailed reports of actual withdrawals to conserve time spent in clerical work.

An out-of-stock condition for frame parts caused difficulty because it greatly increased the chance of missing a shipping load schedule. A lot of the missing parts could be rushed through the shop, but this required special expediting attention by the subforemen and foreman. Frequently they spent time determining why the stock records and actual stock conditions disagreed. They spent time, also, directing the "special handling" of needed parts through the shop and rescheduling parts orders that were displaced. In some instances extra setups were required when rush orders interrupted the machining of a lot already started.

Machine Loading

The foreman and subforemen were given discretion as to what machine to use for each parts order. Mr. Johnson felt this resulted in more machine time being spent than necessary. He believed the loading of some important machines should be centralized in the hands of the production control group. Steps had just been taken to plan loads for the automatic shaper. A production control clerk designated which jobs were to be done on the shaper following two rules. First, the clerk had been instructed to keep this machine fully loaded; and, second, if the available work exceeded the capacity of the machine, the clerk was to select the long-run jobs in order to realize the best return from the higher setup cost of this machine. In the absence of central loading, the mix of parts ordered in a given week frequently overtaxed the time available on one group of machines while leaving other machines and their operators idle.

The chief engineer felt, however, that more data were needed before effective machine load planning could be pursued generally on a centralized basis. Machine loads, he thought, should be scheduled by actual rather than standard times. Hence, it would be necessary to have data on setup times by machine and performance ratios (actual to standard) prepared separately for setups and machining times. Present average output was 125 percent of standard, but performance at individual work stations varied widely.

Production Rate

The seasonal character of sales combined with the Chaircraft scheduling practice led to substantial fluctuations in employment and hours of work. Peak production in the fall of 1968 had strained the dry-kiln capacity,[7] although both the rough mill and parts machining departments could have increased appreciably their volume of work without significant expendi-

---

[7] Throughout 1968 and the immediately preceding years, Chaircraft had the use of two 100-foot kilns and one 50-foot kiln. In December 1968 work was completed to lengthen the 50-foot kiln, giving the company three 100-foot kilns, thus expanding dry-kiln capacity by 20 percent.

tures for additional equipment. Kilns had a replacement value of $27,000. No space existed for adding a kiln adjacent to the factory.

Mr. Johnson preferred to operate the plant on a 45-hour week. He set 36 hours as a minimum work week, and said that this could not be held for more than a month without a great loss in productive efficiency. Similarly, when the work week went above 45 hours, efficiency began to fall. It would be difficult, he believed, to get the men to work more than 50 hours weekly. The average hourly base rate in the frame shop was $2.90, with time and one-half paid above 40 hours per week. None of the attempts by an international union to organize the Chaircraft workers had been successful.

In August 1968 a full second shift had been hired for the rough mill and a partial shift added to break bottlenecks in parts machining. The personnel manager said it was difficult to get skilled operators for the night shift. The cost of hiring was high and the quality and tenure of second-shift operators tended to be low. The personnel manager also indicated his belief that by January 1969 it would be necessary to cut back the work force again to match sales demand.

Training costs in the frame shop were high, although no exact figures could be obtained. It was known that ten of the men hired for the rough mill at the beginning of August 1968 began work at 50 percent of standard. Their production reached 80 percent on November 1, and 100 percent by the first week of December. Similarly, boring machine operators hired in August started at 65 percent of standard and reached 80 percent by late September and 100 percent in October. New employees were paid the full hourly rate until they reached 100 percent productivity and received a bonus above that level.

A STATISTICAL STUDY

In early December 1968 Mr. Johnson had ordered a study of frame parts usage and production. A random sample of 50 of the 500 frame parts was chosen for study and records covering a period of 22 weeks from July through November 1968 were examined to calculate usage, inventory, and production data on the parts comprising the sample. The parts included in the sample accounted for 7.75 percent of lumber consumed and 4.5 percent of standard frame shop labor hours during the 22-week period. On the basis of usage, standard costs, and an assumed inventory carrying cost of 25 percent, an economic order quantity was computed for each part. This was compared with the company's existing standard order quantity (which was equivalent to 80 percent of the number of pieces held on one cart). For the parts covered in this study, the average standard time allowance per lot for setup was 0.46 hours, and the range of allowances was 0.27 to 1.76 hours. The standard cost rate for direct labor and variable overhead in the frame shop was $4.00 per hour. The data of the study appear in Exhibit 6.

Exhibit 6
SAMPLE STUDY OF FRAME PART ACTIVITY
See Exhibit 6 (continued) for Explanation of Column Headings

(1)		(2)	(3)	(4)	(5)	(6)	(7)
				Annual Number of		*Parts Activity*	
				Setups, Based on		*(22 weeks)*	
		Economic		*Economic*	*Actual*		
		Order	*Actual*	*Quantities*	*Quantities*		
Part No.		*Quantity*	*Lot Size*			*Labor*	*Lumber*
1	56	586	450	29	38	20.52	8.28
1	81	2,310	875	15	40	320.20	12.30
2	1	3,310	1,400	20	48	88.80	10.86
2	28	1,940	1,250	19	30	36.90	5.13
3	3	3,065	1,000	36	110	111.65	18.80
3	26	1,480	1,000	8	12	49.20	2.35
4	8	882	1,100	15	12	13.26	2.77
4	35	1,435	1,000	15	22	22.33	3.70
6	16	1,340	450*	1	4	3.59	
6	72	820	215*	3	12	6.73	0.17
7	53	310	110*	4	10	19.70	0.59
7	74	1,071	300*	4	12	8.33	0.24
21	1	1,461	500	13	38	86.83	8.81
21	37	2,110	500	13	54	153.63	13.74
22	4	770	350	20	44	37.84	10.01
22	45	2,285	1,100	11	22	55.55	3.57
22	58	650	300	12	26	17.16	4.35
23	17	316	167*	3	6	1.69	0.16
24	16	3,015	1,000	13	38	45.98	2.14
41	3	1,130	600	13	24	76.68	4.77
41	123	622	275	19	44	216.92	10.22
41	147	2,140	800	14	38	132.24	6.55
41	158	878	200*	2	8	38.84	1.66
41	195	994	350	20	56	155.12	10.44
42	41	1,170	1,250	9	8	9.80	1.10
43	5	1,480	450	17	56	246.40	9.80
43	95	1,935	1,250	10	16	18.24	3.55
43	139	1,165	1,000	5	6	10.65	0.94
43	146	1,360	2,500	3	2	28.10	0.23
43	171	1,076	500*	4	8	8.44	0.45
44	48	2,185	1,750	5	6	21.99	0.70
44	50	377	100*	2	6	2.60	0.17
45	9	838	1,000*	10	8	8.07	0.83
46	30	427	500*	2	2	29.27	0.15
48	46	2,440	625	34	134	229.81	33.61
48	51	806	450	16	28	16.24	4.17
49	87	986	400*	4	10	5.15	0.53
49	98	1,525	600*	3	6	7.03	0.09
51	35	614	625	6	6	9.24	1.28
62	2	786	1,100	9	6	9.75	1.14
62	9	721	1,100	6	4	6.50	0.80
62	25	143	50*	1	2	0.84	0.08
65	1	861	175	61	302	638.73	96.68
66	3	1,950	1,000	13	26	65.00	4.68
81	11	610	1,800	2	—	—	0.13
84	4	2,530	1,500	32	54	27.54	7.14
95	6	790	500	15	24	111.60	5.47
96	6	851	225*	2	8	3.12	0.06
97	78	1,840	750*	2	4	3.93	0.27
97	132	2,850	1,600	9	16	91.52	2.73
99	18	613	325*	4	8	53.76	0.50
					Totals	3,385.—	319.—

* Average parts ordered in smaller than standard quantities.

Exhibit 6 *(Continued)*
SAMPLE STUDY OF FRAME PART ACTIVITY

The data in Exhibit 6 represents the results of a study of production and usage for a sample of 50 frame parts, randomly selected.

The data are based on a 22-week period from July 2 to November 28, 1968. These 22 weeks account characteristically for 50 percent of annual production at Chaircraft.

The data were analyzed to permit comparison between "economic" lot sizes and actual order quantities used by Chaircraft. A corollary aim was to indicate the degree to which lumber usage and shop activity were concentrated on relatively few parts. These data are presented in seven columns of figures in Exhibit 6. The basis of the data in each column is as follows:

Column (1)   Part Number—Identifies part.

Column (2)   Economic Order Quantity—This is a theoretical economic order quantity calculated by the standard formula:

$$\text{Quantity} = \sqrt{\frac{2 \times \text{usage} \times \text{setup cost}}{\text{inventory carrying cost} \times \text{variables unit cost}}}$$

Annual usage was estimated by taking twice the actual usage during the 22-week period of the study.

Setup cost was calculated from standard setup time allowances (on standard cost records) using a variable cost rate of $4.00 per hour and adding a $0.20 allowance for clerical cost of processing each order.

The unit cost is the total variable material, labor, and expense cost from standard cost records.

The inventory carrying cost was taken as an arbitrary 25 percent.

Column (3)   Actual Lot Size—This column shows the quantities actually used for ordering. Figures followed by an asterisk (*) are the average actual lot sizes for parts ordered in lots smaller than the established (80 percent cart capacity) standard quantity.

A comparison of actual and standard order quantities for the sixteen starred items is given in the following table:

Part No.	Average Actual Quantity	Standard Quantity	Part No.	Average Actual Quantity	Standard Quantity
6 16	450	2,000	45 9	1,000	1,400
6 72	215	2,500	46 30	500	1,250
7 53	110	600	49 87	400	2,500
7 74	300	2,500	49 98	600	1,250
23 17	167	1,000	62 25	50	500
41 158	200	250	96 6	225	2,000
43 171	500	1,750	97 78	750	1,500
44 50	100	1,500	99 18	325	1,750

Columns (4) and (5)   Annual Number of Setups—In Column (4) is the number of setups required annually to produce the required volume of each part if orders were based on "economic" quantities presented in Column (2).

Exhibit 6 (*Concluded*)

In Column (5) is the number of setups required annually using actual order quantities from Column (3). This figure is twice the actual number of setups during the 22-week period.

Columns (6) and (7) Parts Activity—These two columns are intended to demonstrate the importance of each part. The "labor" column shows the standard frame shop labor hours required to produce the quantities of each part actually manufactured during the 22-week period.

The "lumber" column represents the standard quantity of lumber (in thousand board feet) required to produce the quantity actually produced in the 22-week period.

5

Facilities Planning

IN THE LAST SECTION of text and cases, we considered the management problems associated with planning and utilizing capacity in the short term. Within the planning horizon relevant to these decisions, changes in the amount of facilities and equipment are generally not feasible ways of adjusting capacity levels because of the long lead times required to obtain them. Thus the emphasis has been on changing capacity by manipulating those variables which can be quickly changed; e.g., the size of the work force, scheduled product mixes, the length of the workday, or the level of subcontracting. This chapter introduces this section on facilities planning. Here, we deal with the larger set of options open to managers when they consider capacity problems with an expanded planning horizon. One of the most important of these new options is the addition or retirement of physical facilities. Facilities planning involves specifying the size, time, and location for these changes. Along with technology planning (considered in the next chapter), facilities planning is the focus for long-range capacity management, and is an integral part of the long-range planning activities for most firms.

An indication of the importance of facilities planning is given by the amount of money U.S. manufacturing firms spend on facilities and equipment—over $113 billion in 1974. The individual capital expenditures of some of our largest companies are equally impressive. In 1973, General Electric spent $5.98 billion on plants and equipment, an amount equal to their net income; in the same year, General Motors spent $1.163 billion on property, plants, and equipment. But facilities planning is important to firms small and large, not only because of the size of the investments involved, but because it frequently entails a consideration of major corporate risks, and can be the focal point of important strategic decisions.

The risks involved in obtaining new facilities are obvious; large sums of money must be committed to an uncertain future two, three, or more years away. It takes over four years to design, construct, and "break in" a new paper mill for example. When a paper company decides to construct such a new facility, it risks millions of dollars that markets and prices four years hence will justify this decision. Strategic considerations can be even more important. Should a company be committed to a few large centralized plants, or many smaller and more geographically dispersed ones. Can an addition of a large increment in physical capacity be used to preempt construction by competitors? These questions can be partially answered by looking at the economics involved. But they also require a penetrating analysis of the total manufacturing strategy, its relationship to the competitive dynamics of an industry, and the impact on the organizational and managerial structure of a business.

In this chapter, we shall discuss the critical steps involved in facilities planning. These steps represent important milestones in many facilities planning projects, and may be helpful to you in approaching the cases which follow. In addition, some of the relationships between cost and volume which are important in facilities planning are described and illustrated. These relationships are useful in making many of the tradeoffs you will encounter. While many strategic relationships can be even more important than the economic ones in facilities planning, we will not discuss them here. The cases themselves provide the most useful medium for discussing these issues.

STEPS IN FACILITIES PLANNING

The steps involved in facilities planning are much like those involved in making a tradeoff analysis (presented in Chapter 2). They include:

1. Determine the need for changes in the level of physical capacity.
2. Generate alternative plans for changing it.
3. Analyze the economic costs, benefits, and risks associated with the plans.
4. Identify the strategic impact of the alternatives.
5. Select a plan and implement it.

The first step, determining the need for changes in physical capacity levels, is a two-stage process. The first stage involves preparing a forecast of demand for future periods and comparing it with present capacity levels. If a significant gap, or difference, between forecasted capacity needs and present capacity levels appears, and it cannot be economically closed by manipulating manpower levels or inventories (as in aggregate planning), the need for a change in physical capacity is indicated. The second stage involves finding exactly where in the process a capacity change is needed.

Rarely are production systems completely balanced; there is generally a bottleneck operation which has a greater need for expansion than others. A process analysis is useful here in indicating the magnitude of required changes in physical capacity at each process step.

To illustrate these stages of analysis, consider the XYZ Company first introduced in Chapter 1. This firm has a two-stage production system. The first stage is where parts are fabricated on XYZ's ten molding machines. The nominal physical capacity of this part of the process is 10,000 units per week. Nominal physical capacity is defined as the maximum sustainable output that can be realized with a full complement of labor on regular time. Clearly, the definition of full complement depends on certain management policies. In the case of the XYZ Company, for instance, we may assume that because of conditions in the local labor market, management has a policy of producing only on a single shift. This assumption is consistent with the nominal capacity of 10,000 units per week discussed above. The actual capacity of the fabrication stage is, however 6,000 units per week because only six workers are currently employed. Full utilization of the ten molding machines, necessary to reach nominal capacity levels, requires ten workers.

The second stage in the process is assembly, which has a nominal physical capacity of 12,000 units per week. Current capacity would also be 12,000 units per week if the fabrication stage were not a bottleneck. The present size of the assembly-line work force is sufficient to handle this volume of production, but because the first stage can only produce 10,000 units per week, then the long-run output of the assembly stage is also limited to this amount.

If a forecast of the demand for current and new products shows that demand is expected to increase by 2,000 units per year over the next five years, future gaps in capacity can be identified. Figure 5–1 plots sales and capacity over time, and graphically illustrates the points at which such gaps occur. Under this assumption, the first gap appears immediately, as demand outstrips current fabrication capacity levels. The chart shows, however, that the nominal physical capacity of fabrication will not be exceeded for two years. This suggests that with an effective aggregate planning and scheduling effort, the physical capacity of existing fabrication facilities is sufficient for the next two years. We can add to the actual fabrication capacity in the interim by simply hiring more people.

Gaps in nominal physical capacity occur in year two, when projected XYZ Company sales exceed fabrication capabilities, and in year three, when assembly capacity becomes insufficient. If it takes two to three years to build a new plant, or to expand fabrication, we have identified the need for action. It is time to plan changes in physical capacity levels.

The second step in facilities planning is to generate alternative plans for changing capacity in accordance with the needs specified previously. This is a creative step. But, the prior analysis already suggests several alter-

Figure 5–1
SALES VERSUS CAPACITY

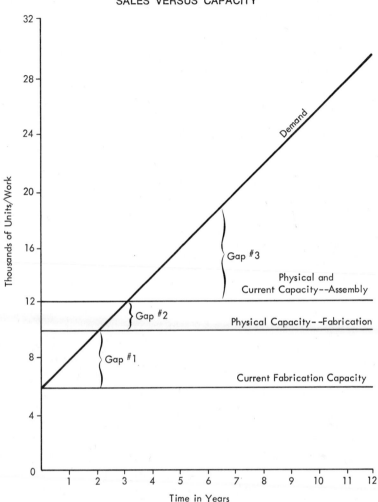

natives. Others can be identified by considering alternative plant sizes, and various locations. A few of these alternatives might be:

1. Expand fabrication capacity by 4,000 units in year two, and assembly capacity by 2,000 units in year three at the present site.
2. Expand fabrication capacity by 12,000 units in year two, and assembly capacity by 12,000 units in year two at the present site.
3. Build a new 10,000-unit fabrication-assembly plant on the West Coast in year two.

The alternative of doing nothing is also generally worthy of at least some consideration. This is particularly true if present facilities are used to produce a broad product line, in which some products are only marginally profitable. In this case, a careful analysis may show that weeding the product line and freeing up existing capacity may be a more profitable alternative than blindly building to a sales forecast.

The third step, analyzing the economic costs, benefits and risks associated with each of the alternatives, involves deriving a quantitative measure of the worth of particular facilities plans. Measures such as ROI (return on investment), DCF% (discounted cash flow percent) and NPV (net present value) are very useful in this regard. The net present value associated with the alternatives for the XYZ Company above, for instance, would indicate the present value of the cash flows for each of them, and would provide a useful basis for comparison.

Since these measures are also used in financial capital budgeting, it is worthwhile to comment here on the important link which exists between it and facilities planning. Capital budgeting involves selecting good projects for investment from a number of alternatives, and planning methods of financing those projects which are selected. Thus, a typical capital budgeting problem may be: Should a company invest in a new computer facility, a new plant for its consumer products division, or a new process technology for the industrial products division? Facilities planning on the other hand, involves coming up with these proposals in the first place; i.e., which of many ways to expand the capacity of the consumer products division is most appropriate for that business? In a sense then, the process of capital budgeting, frequently a corporate problem, is fed by the process of facilities planning, which is usually performed at divisional levels in a large firm. An excellent view of this link is provided in J. L. Bower's *Managing the Resource Allocation Process.*[1]

The derivation of a financial measure for either facilities planning or capital budgeting decisions is a mechanical procedure. A number of computer programs are available, for example, for calculating measures such as net present value (NPV). From a management standpoint, the most important part of the economic analysis is accurately identifying the important costs and benefits associated with alternative facilities plans, so that these measures can be derived. If a manager is to identify or validate these costs and benefits, two things must be understood. First, the manager must appreciate the important tradeoffs involved in running an operation on a short-term basis. Frequently, these tradeoffs must be considered when new facilities are under consideration. For example, a decision to follow a "level production" strategy in aggregate planning may be uneconomical when sufficient facilities are built to allow a "chase" strategy to be followed. An economic analysis must reflect the changes in inventory and labor costs associated with these new facilities.

Second, the manager must have a firm understanding of the relationships of operations costs to the planned volume of output. These cost/volume

---

[1] Division of Research, Graduate School of Business Administration, Harvard University, Boston, 1970.

relationships are very important because they form the basis for predicting future costs as output rises (or falls) over time. You are already familiar with one important cost/volume relationship. This relationship is explained by the interaction between fixed and variable costs, and was introduced in Chapter 1 in the discussion of break-even charts. Recall that in the example of the XYZ Company, the fixed costs of production in their present facility were $1,150 per week, while variable costs were $0.92 per unit. Thus, the total cost of a week's production could be calculated with the simple formula shown below (1), and illustrated in (2) where we calculate expected total cost when weekly volume is 6,000 units.

$$\text{Total cost} = \text{Fixed costs} + \text{variable costs} \times \text{volume} \qquad (1)$$
$$\text{Total cost (6,000 units)} = \$1,150 + \$0.92 \times 6,000 \text{ units} = \$6,670 \quad (2)$$

This fixed-variable cost relationship can be used to derive a graph such as the one shown in Figure 5–2A. With it, the total cost can be determined for a range of weekly volumes. Moreover, we can use the logic behind this relationship to calculate average unit costs, given a certain volume. Table 1–2 in Chapter 1 contains the average unit costs associated with various production volumes for the XYZ Company. These were calculated by totaling all of the costs incurred at a particular volume, and then dividing the resulting total cost by the volume. A faster way of obtaining the average unit cost, however, is given in formula (3), and illustrated for a volume of 6,000 units in (4). Figure 5–2B is a graph of the average unit costs over a range of volumes for the XYZ Company. It was derived by using formula (3) and plotting the results.

$$\text{Average cost} = \text{Variable cost per unit} + \text{fixed costs} + \text{volume} \quad (3)$$
$$\text{Average cost (6,000 units)} = \$0.92 + \$1.150 \div 6,000 = \$1.11 \quad (4)$$

There are two caveats that are important to the manager who wishes to predict costs with volume changes using this well-known relationship. The first is that it is only an approximate predictor of the effect of volume on costs. Like most predictors, the only thing we know for sure about them is that they will produce predictions which are wrong. We can only hope that they are not too wrong, considering the long-term planning horizon involved in facilities planning. This judgment can be made in a particular situation by examining some of the common sources of error in the relationship. For example, one source of error derives from the fact that many costs are semivariable. That is, they are fixed (or variable) over some range of output levels, and fixed at a different level (or variable) thereafter. Labor costs are an example. If one production shift is used, the variable cost of labor may be $0.20 per unit, and the fixed costs (shift supervision) $100 per week. But if two shifts are used, the labor cost per unit may rise to $0.21 per unit because of the shift premiums, generally paid as an incentive for working late hours, and the fixed costs may rise to $150 per week as more supervisors are added. Clearly, the fixed and variable costs are constant over some range of volumes (one or two shifts), and semivariable or semifixed over the whole range. This means that the fixed and total cost lines in graphs such as that shown in Figure 5–1 are usually lumpy and curved, rather than straight. The straight lines are only an approximation of reality. Sometimes, it is important to take the effects of semivariable costs into account in projecting costs as volumes change, but fortunately, these effects are usually so small that they can be ignored for practical purposes.

The second caveat is that the kind of fixed-variable relationships shown

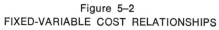

Figure 5–2
FIXED-VARIABLE COST RELATIONSHIPS

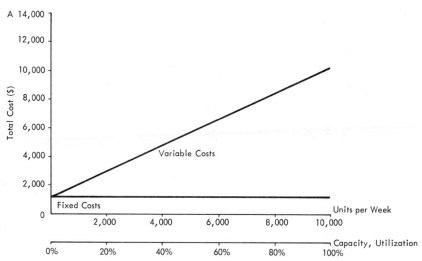

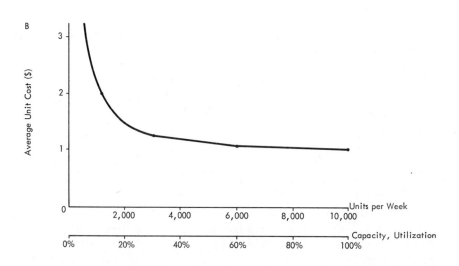

in Figures 5–2A and 5–2B, and formulas (1) and (3), do not hold for all possible production volumes. For example, the nominal capacity of the XYZ operation was given as 10,000 units per week. More than this can be produced in the present facility, but extra costs will be incurred as a result of overtime, or because of poor productivity associated with conjestion on the shop floor. Moreover, production volumes in excess of the nominal capacity may be difficult to sustain. While the minor deviations from the fixed-variable cost relationship caused by semivariable costs may be tolerated in using it as a predictor, the effect of production at levels greater than the nominal physical capacity on costs is usually very important. Average unit costs tend to rise rapidly after this point. This is the reason that we have shown the percent of nominal physical capacity utilization as an alternative axis in Figures 5–2A and 5–2B. Figures 5–3A and 5–3B graphically illustrate the rise in costs associated with overcapacity production.

The fixed-variable cost relationship reviewed above is an important one in facilities planning. For a particular sized facility, it is a very useful input to an economic analysis. But, in order to compare the economic impact of building a facility of one size with that of another size, we also need to know how the *cost structure* changes with different plant sizes. It is very important to know this when deciding how big a facility to build and when to build it.

Suppose, for instance, that the XYZ Company felt there were only three viable alternatives for expanding capacity: (1) Start construction now on a plant with a capacity of 20,000 units per week. This plant would provide sufficient physical capacity for the next 12 years at current growth rates;[2] (2) build a 10,000 unit per week plant now and plan to build a second 10,000 unit per week plant to come on stream in year eight; (3) build a 5,000 unit per week plant now, and plan on building new 5,000 unit per week plants every two and one-half years after year four and a half.

The cost structure of the 10,000 unit per week plant is already known. Assuming that it will be exactly like the existing 10,000 unit per week plant, fixed costs will be $1,150 per week, and variable costs will be $0.92 per unit. Is it reasonable to assume that 5,000 unit per week and 20,000 unit per week plants will have the same cost structure? In all probability, the answer to this question is no. Economies of scale become important.

Economies of scale are the cost advantages associated with managing a large facility over those associated with a small facility; i.e., one in which the "scale" of operations is larger. These cost differences arise from many sources. For example, construction costs are generally proportionately lower for large plants than small ones, because of certain geometric properties, or because the floor space for facilities such as a manager's office

---

[2] 10,000 per week current physical capacity + 20,000 per week more = 30,000 units per week − 6,000 units per week current demand = 24,000 units per week excess capacity − 2,000 units per year annual growth rate = 12 years.

Figure 5-3
FIXED-VARIABLE COST RELATIONSHIPS

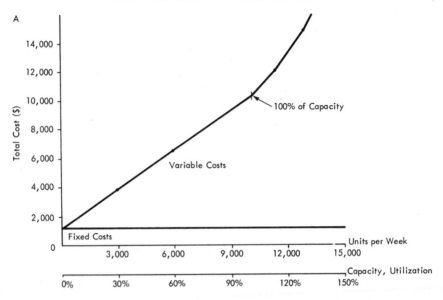

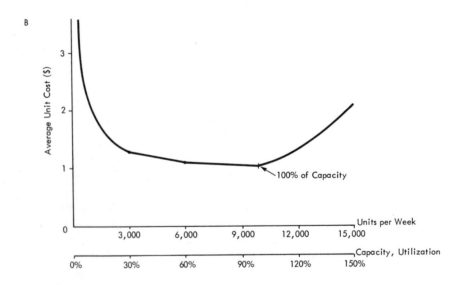

or a cafeteria is the same regardless of plant size. Variable production costs may be lower in large plants because quantity discounts on large volume purchases or shipments can be obtained, or because a large plant can justify a more advanced and more efficient process technology than a smaller plant (more on this subject in the next chapter). Fixed costs may be proportionately lower because a large plant requires about the same amount of supervision as a smaller one. Economies of scale are a dominant eco-

nomic force in industries such as chemicals, petroleum refining, steel production, and complex assembly operations.

Table 5–1 shows the cost structures associated with the different plant

Table 5–1

Plant Size	*5,000 per week*	*10,000 per week*	*20,000 per week*
Fixed costs	$1,000	$1,150	$1,500
Variable costs	$0.95	$0.92	$0.88
Investment	$35,000	$50,000	$80,000
Unit average cost at capacity	$1.15	$1.04	$0.96

sizes being considered by the XYZ Company. These cost structures reflect
the impact of economies of scale in fixed, variable, and investment costs
for each alternative. The average cost curves constructed with this data
(Figure 5–4) show how costs will vary depending on the size of plant and

Figure 5–4
ECONOMIES OF SCALE IN COST VOLUME RELATIONSHIPS

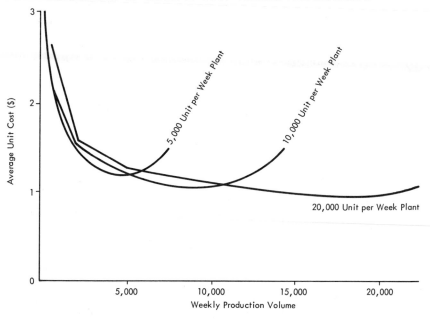

the volume of production. For the XYZ Company, these curves and the
associated investment data present an interesting problem. If they build
a 20,000 unit per week plant now, their investment cost will be $80,000
over the next 12 years, but their average unit costs will be high during
the early years when the plant is operating at low volumes. On the other
hand, if they build a series of 5,000 unit per week plants, their investment
cost will total $175,000 over the same period, but average production costs

will be relatively low for the first five years or so, and higher than those for the 20,000 unit per week plant thereafter. The 10,000 unit per week series of plants offers an intermediate alternative. Which plan would you choose?

The fourth step in facilities planning, a strategic analysis of alternative plans, involves analyzing the important qualitative issues. For example, the XYZ Company may feel that by expanding capacity by 10,000 units per week now, an amount in excess of needs for many years, they can discourage competitors from expanding. This strategy might ensure then a firmer grip on the market. Similarly, a plant built in a new geographical location may give them access to new markets. This kind of strategic analysis emphasizes the impact that facilities planning has on competitive dynamics. But, in addition to such externally oriented strategic analyses an internally oriented view must also be considered. For example, would a large expansion necessitate a change in the work force policy that calls for single shift operations? Would it introduce the need for a fluctuating seasonal work force and a new technology? Would a move to a new location require a reorganization of personnel and their responsibilities? These are important issues which must be faced in analyzing the worth of a plan, and in directing its implementation.

When the time finally comes to select a particular alternative (the last step) the XYZ Company may find that the results of the strategic analysis outweigh the economics derived in the previous step. However, the economic analysis remains the foundation of the total analysis. It provides hard numbers of evaluative purposes, and perhaps of more importance, unveils many new alternatives and reveals subtle problems that would have gone unnoticed.

CONCLUSION

The steps in facilities planning described and illustrated in this chapter are not meant to limit your analyses of the cases which follow. They are intended to focus you on some of the aspects of facilities planning which are common to most situations. In some cases, you will be able to justify a more limited approach. In others, you may want to take an expanded view.

The first two cases in this section, Atherton Division of Litton Industries and North American Rockwell—Draper Division, present problems which emphasize the first two steps in facilities planning. The first deals with identifying capacity needs and generating and evaluating alternatives in a rapidly growing industry. The second with those in a declining business, Gulf Oil, Braniff International, and Distrigas Corporation, are primarily concerned with evaluating alternative facilities plans where economies of scale are important. The last two cases in this section, Zodiac Bros. Toys, Inc. (B) and Carborundum, Inc. are broadly based. They tend to emphasize the strategic issues in facilities planning.

Atherton Division of Litton Industries[1]

IN EARLY March 1973, Mr. William W. George, Executive Vice President of Atherton Division of Litton Industries, was considering whether or not he should submit a request for plant expansion to corporate headquarters for approval. Less than two months ago he had received approval to expand the consumer microwave oven facility from its current floor area of 88,200 square feet to 149,500 square feet. However, recent increases in orders led Mr. George to believe that realistic sales forecasts for the next year and a half might be as much as 40 percent above the January 1973 estimates. Faced with this unexpected increase in projected demand, Mr. George was considering submitting a proposal for an additional 61,300 square foot expansion of the consumer microwave oven plant.

BACKGROUND

History of the Commercial Microwave Oven

In 1946, Raytheon developed and patented the first microwave oven which employs a magnetron vacuum tube rather than conventional electric or gas flame elements, to cook food. The magnetron gives off microwaves which generate heat when absorbed by certain materials. Since the microwaves penetrate food, more energy reaches the interior portion immediately in a microwave oven than in a conventional oven, thereby reducing cooking time considerably. Microwave ovens were first sold in 1959 to commercial institutions such as hospitals, schools, restaurants, and vending machine companies. By 1964, commercial oven sales had reached only 3,000 units, mainly because of the relatively high price which exceeded $2,000.

---

[1] The figures given in this case have been disguised and do not represent actual operating data or sales forecasts of the company.

In 1953, Litton Industries was founded based on the acquisition of a small manufacturer of magnetron tubes. Eleven years later, the Atherton Division was formed by combining personnel from the original magnetron company and a newly acquired Cleveland firm headed by Robert Bruder, who is the current president of Atherton Division and vice president of the corporation. A year later, in 1965, Litton introduced its first commercial microwave oven and within one year had captured 80 percent of the market which had grown to 9,000 units. This spectacular success was attributable in large part to the reliability and low price of the Litton units, which sold for approximately $1,000.

History of the Consumer Microwave Oven

The consumer market for microwave ovens remained relatively undeveloped through 1966 when sales reached 10,000 units. However, in 1967, Amana, a subsidiary of Raytheon, introduced the first 115-volt countertop model, and the demand for consumer units rose to 45,000 by 1969. In that year, Litton began "Phase I" of its long range plan for marketing consumer microwave ovens by producing units for sale under private labels of several well known mass merchandisers and original equipment manufacturers. In 1970, undesirable publicity concerning the hazards of exposure to radiation from microwave ovens coupled with the economic recession held industry sales to 60,000 units. As a result, sales of private brands fell short of projections for Litton's first year in the consumer oven market.

In 1971, in spite of the disappointing results of its entry into the private brand market, Litton decided to move directly into national distribution of the new Litton brand "Minutemaster" microwave ovens. By July 1972, Litton had established full national distribution for its consumer products via 50 distributors and 2,000 dealers and had completed an 88,300 square foot manufacturing facility in Plymouth, Minnesota, a suburb of Minneapolis. This new plant was to be operated separately from the existing commercial oven plant and had a capacity for producing 600 consumer ovens per day.

DESCRIPTION OF ATHERTON DIVISION

Marketing

Litton marketed several variations of consumer table top ovens in 1973. The "300" series, the original line produced by Atherton, included several styles of counter top units priced at $399–$499. The newer "400" series, originally introduced in the summer of 1972, was based on an improved table top design which featured a larger oven interior and retailed for under $400. By early 1973, over half the table top units sold were Series 400 models marketed under the Litton brand name; the remaining table top units were primarily Series 300 ovens sold under private brand names such as Admiral, Sears, and Tappan.

The Series 900 microwave ranges, which combined a conventional electric oven and cooktop with an eye-level microwave oven, were introduced in early 1973. The microwave ovens for these ranges were manufactured at the Litton plant in Plymouth and shipped to the Modern Maid Company in Chattanooga, Tennessee, where the final product was assembled by combining the Litton microwave oven with the electric oven produced by Modern Maid. The bulk of these ranges were then marketed under the Litton "Micromatic Range" brand name as replacement ovens via the Litton consumer oven distribution channels. In addition, ranges were sold by Modern Maid to the kitchen remodeling market under the Modern Maid brand name. The newest products being developed by Atherton were a series of lightweight portable microwave ovens scheduled for introduction in the summer of 1973. Exhibit 1 depicts several models of consumer microwave ovens produced by Litton.

The primary competition for Litton in the consumer microwave oven market came from Amana and Japanese imports. The following table provides data compiled by an independent securities analyst. Industry sales at the factory and retail levels for calendar years 1971 and 1972 are shown:

	1971				*1972*			
	Factory		*Retail*		*Factory*		*Retail*	
	Units	*Percent*	*Units*	*Percent*	*Units*	*Percent*	*Units*	*Percent*
Amana	75,000	43	65,000	43	130,000	28	125,000	30
Litton	50,000	29	45,000	30	125,000	26	125,000	30
Japanese	30,000	17	25,000	17	190,000	40	145,000	35
Other.	20,000	11	15,000	10	30,000	6	20,000	5
Total	175,000	100	150,000	100	475,000	100	415,000	100

The rapid growth in sales between 1971 and 1972 had caused Litton to increase its estimates of future primary demand on several occasions. The following table provides three Litton forecasts of total market size for fiscal years ending July 31:

Date of Forecast	*FY 1973*	*FY 1974*	*FY 1975*	*FY 1976*	*FY 1977*
January 1972	346,000	670,000	900,000	1,100,000	1,225,000
January 1973	579,000	875,000	1,200,000	1,500,000	1,800,000
March 1973	648,000	1,000,000	1,375,000	1,600,000	1,900,000

Exhibit 1
LITTON CONSUMER MICROWAVE OVENS

Model 350

Model 402

Model 933

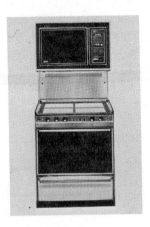

Model 975

Over the next five years, Litton anticipated increased competition from the Japanese and major U.S. producers of household appliances such as General Electric. Firms such as Panasonic, Toshiba, Sharp, and Hitachi had gained considerable experience in manufacturing consumer microwave ovens to satisfy the Japanese demand, which exceeded 850,000 units in 1972. These Japanese companies were now threatening to enter the U.S. market with ovens priced well below those of the leading U.S. producers.

Production

The Atherton production process in use in March 1973 centered around two conveyorized assembly lines. Each line had an output capacity of 300

"equivalent"[2] ovens per day. The company had always found it economically desirable to purchase rather than fabricate most of the parts used
in its products. These parts were receipt inspected before transfer to a
"stores" area which occupied over 21 percent of the 88,200 square foot
floor space of the plant. Parts and components were fed to two sub assembly lines and two main assembly lines which eventually merged into two
conveyorized lines where final assembly of each unit was completed. At
the end of the assembly lines, thorough testing was performed, and repair
and rework were accomplished if necessary. The total assembly area accounted for approximately 29 percent of the plant floor space. At the end
of the production process, each unit was packaged and transferred to a
finished goods storage area which occupied 5,800 square feet of floor
space. The size of this finished goods storage area was sufficient to accommodate two weeks of production capacity.

The established policy of purchasing rather than fabricating parts caused
the material component of the product cost to be quite high, averaging
78 percent of total manufacturing cost for all Litton models of consumer
microwave ovens, while direct labor amounted to only 5 percent. The remaining 17 percent of factory cost covered fixed expenses such as overhead, engineering, quality assurance, and tooling. The contribution to all
fixed costs and profit was about 30 percent of the factory price quoted
to the independent distributors and dealers who handled Litton's products.

The labor force included 150 hourly workers who were represented
by the United Electrical union. About 75 percent of these workers were
women, most of whom were providing a second source of income for their
families. The remaining laborers were mostly young (age 18–21) men. Litton had always had a good relationship with the local union, all of whose
officers were women. However, the current three year contract expired
October 1, 1973, and management was wondering what demands the union
would make given the recent success of Litton's consumer microwave
ovens and the stronger commitment of the company to the Minneapolis
area evidenced by the construction of the Phase I consumer oven production facility.

LONG-RANGE PLANS FOR EXPANSION

Soon after the Phase I production facility was completed, Mr. George
asked Mr. Peter Pirsch, Vice President of Operations to organize a committee to study the long-term manufacturing requirements of the Litton
microwave oven division. In January 1973, a formal report was completed
which forecast the demand for Litton consumer microwave ovens through

---

[2] There was some variation in the assembly time for the different series of Litton
microwave ovens; however, the fact that these variations were small and that the
product mix was fairly stable permitted the output capacity of assembly lines to
be quoted in "equivalent" ovens per day.

Exhibit 2
JANUARY 1973 FORECAST DEMAND FOR
LITTON CONSUMER MICROWAVE OVENS

Fiscal Year	Quarter*	Sales per Day
1973	III	860
	IV	753
1974	I	938
	II	1,250
	III	938
	IV	870
1975	I	1,343
	II	1,617
	III	1,516
	IV	1,396
1976	I	1,962
	II	1,950
	III	1,767
	IV	1,623
1977	I	1,844
	II	2,300
	III	1,797
	IV	1,906

```
*   I = August–October.
   II = November–January.
  III = February–April.
   IV = May–July.
```

fiscal year 1977 (see Exhibit 2). At the time of the report, sales were approaching 750 units per day, straining the 600 unit per day one-shift capacity of the plant to the point that overtime production was required. The report considered various proposals for increasing output to satisfy the rising demand shown in Exhibit 2 in a two step sequence. The first step, Phase II, concerned alternative plans for meeting demand through the end of fiscal year 1974, while Phase III dealt with subsequent long-range plans through the end of fiscal year 1976.

Alternative Proposals for Phase II

The following three courses of action were analyzed in the January study:

1. Begin second shift production at the existing plant and delay facilities expansion until demand exceeds two-shift capacity.
2. Build a second manufacturing plant in another part of the country where wage rates are lower and the potential for labor problems is reduced relative to Plymouth.
3. Expand the existing Plymouth facility by 61,300 square feet to increase the one-shift capacity to 1,200 units per day.

The proposal for enlarging the existing facility called for a 22,000 square foot expansion of the stores area and a 6,400 square foot increase in finished goods storage space; these additions were designed to maintain the inventory turnover rate for parts and completed units at the same level as that established for the 600 unit per day Phase I facility. The proposal also recommended expansion of the oven assembly area by 18,000 square feet to accommodate three new-design assembly lines, each of which would have an output capacity of 400 units per day. The remaining 15,000 square feet of added area were allocated to miscellaneous uses such as receiving, receipt inspection, quality control laboratory space, warehousing, and shipping. As shown in Exhibit 3, the cost per square foot of expansion

Exhibit 3
EXPENSE SUMMARY

	Alternate 1 Expand Current Facility	Alternate 2 Build New Facility	Alternate 3 No Expansion Use Second Shift
Space	61,300 ft.²	79,000 ft.²	–
Facilities cost:			
Rent	$101,865 FC	$131,000	–
Other*	117,735 FC	198,800	$ 82,000
Total expense	$219,600	$329,800	82,000
Staffing expense (addition) . . .	162,700 U	512,000	415,000
Operating expenses	243,400 V	503,000	392,000
Labor inefficiencies.	–	207,000†	85,500‡ V
Outside warehouse	–	–	266,000 FC
Total Operating Cost.	$625,700	$1,551,800	$1,240,500
Equipment expenditure:			
Capital	$144,000	$210,000	$ 25,000
Expense	75,000	90,000	25,000
Total.	$219,000	$300,000	$ 50,000

* Includes utilities, maintenance, outside services, and other fixed costs.
† Year one only.
‡ Ongoing.

space for annual expenses such as rent, utilities, and outside services amounted to $3.58. Also, $406,000 per year in additional staffing and operating expenses would be incurred under this alternative.

The proposal for building a new facility outside Plymouth offered the advantages of manufacturing flexibility, lower wage rates, and reduced potential for labor problems. However, the duplication of common spaces such as the cafeteria and maintenance area put the required floor space for a new facility at 79,000 square feet compared to the proposed 61,300 square foot expansion of the Plymouth facility. Exhibit 3 shows that duplication of effort would also result in a comparatively higher figure for added annual staffing and operating expense, and a $207,000 start-up cost due to labor inefficiency would be incurred in the new plant.

The conservative approach of relying on second-shift operation minimized capital investment and lease commitments but restricted the ability of the plant to meet higher than expected demand. Outside storage space required to accommodate the increased output would cost $266,000 in additional operating costs. The higher turnover and reduced efficiency of second-shift workers, coupled with duplication in line management personnel, would cause the added annual staffing and operating expense to be more than twice that of the proposed alternative for expanding the Plymouth facility. Any reducton in quality of output for second-shift operations was difficult to estimate; consequently, this effect was not included in the expense summary of Exhibit 3.

Based on the cost comparison of Exhibit 3, the January report recommended that the Phase II increase in output be accomplished by enlarging the Plymouth facility. Corporate approval of this plan was subsequently granted, and ground was broken on February 5 with a scheduled completion date of June 1, 1973.

Phase III Considerations

Exhibit 2 shows that sales were expected to exceed the 1,200 unit per day one-shift capacity of the Phase II facility at the beginning of fiscal year 1975. As a result, the January report recommended that preliminary planning be initiated on a second 61,300 square foot addition to the Plymouth facility to raise the one-shift output capacity to 1,800 units. Mr. Pirsch then secured a rental option of $1.13 per square foot for this addition and proposed a tentative completion date of June 1974 for this Phase III expansion.

Other Long-Range Plans

The January study also recommended that Litton consider developing a capability of producing both the conventional electric ovens and the microwave ovens used in the Litton Micromatic ranges. In addition to this forward integration, it was recommended that the feasibility of fabricating rather than purchasing certain parts be evaluated. The report proposed that these two processes be incorporated in a new plant tentatively scheduled for completion in 1975.

RE-ASSESSMENT OF EXPANSION PLANS (MARCH 1973)

By late February 1973, it became apparent that the January forecasts of demand were low. Several factors contributed to this increase in expected sales:

1. New orders for 25,000 units had been received from private label customers for delivery from June through December 1973.

2. Modern Maid Company had tripled its annual requirements for Series 900 units.
3. Current Litton brand orders for the Series 400 and 900 lines were running 30 percent ahead of the January forecast.

The study committee re-evaluated the demand forecasts of Exhibit 2 on the basis of new estimates provided by marketing and sales personnel. As a result, sales projections were increased by 26,700 units for FY 1973 and 95,000 units for FY 1974, as shown in the following table:

Fiscal Year	Quarter	Sales per Day
1973	III	959
	IV	1,104
1974	I	1,328
	II	1,383
	III	1,375
	IV	1,448

Upon receiving the revised sales forecast, Mr. George decided to begin second-shift operation immediately to avoid lost sales during the last half of FY 1973. He realized that, even after the completion of the Phase II expansion in July 1973, the 1,200 unit per day one-shift capacity of the enlarged plant would fall short of the revised forecast for FY 1974 sales. Therefore, he requested that the study committee determine the maximum and minimum expected values for FY 1974 demand in order to set upper and lower bounds on their current estimate of 340,000 units. Based on this range of forecasts, Mr. George asked the committee to evaluate alternatives for increasing output as soon as possible to meet the revised demand forecast. Early in March 1973, the committee completed this task and submitted two Phase III alternatives for increasing output to Mr. George for consideration.

FY 1974 Demand Forecasts (March 1973)

The study committee requested key marketing and sales personnel to provide both pessimistic and optomistic "bottom up" forecasts for FY 1974 sales. Based on the data collected, the committee established upper and lower bounds of 436,000 units and 263,000 units on the range of expected demand for FY 1974. In order to ensure that these limits were realistic, the committee performed its own probabilistic analysis of both the total market potential and Litton's potential share of that market. The results of this internal study indicated that Litton's sales of consumer microwave ovens in FY 1974 had a 75 percent chance of exceeding 210,000 units, a 50 percent chance of exceeding 300,000 units, and a 25 percent change of exceeding 420,000 units.

Alternative Proposals for Phase III

The committee calculated that if no action were taken to expand output and the Phase II plant were operated on a one-shift per day basis during FY 1974, lost sales of 50,000 units would result in a sacrifice of $3.5 million in contribution to fixed costs and profit, assuming the best estimate figure of 340,000 units for demand. For the maximum expected demand of 436,000, lost sales and contribution would rise to 146,000 units and $10.2 million, while the lower boundary of 263,000 units would result in no lost sales or contribution since the Phase II plant could satisfy this smaller demand. As alternatives to this "do nothing" strategy, the committee evaluated the following two methods of increasing output:

1. The Phase II expansion could be completed and a partial second-shift utilized during FY 1974 with additional expansion deferred until July 1974 as previously planned. It was estimated that it would take several months to complete training and set-up of a second-shift operation, and it was expected that the maximum efficiency of second-shift production woud be somewhat less than that of normal daytime operations. As a result, for this alternative, lost sales would be about 43,000 units under maximum expected demand conditions and 14,000 units under best estimate demand conditions. The resulting increase in contribution would have to be balanced against the added expenses of operating a second shift. Since the second shift would be operated only during peak demand periods, this expense would be much less than that shown in Exhibit 3; for example, total additional operating cost would be $876,000 under maximum expected demand conditions, $301,000 under best estimate demand conditions, and zero under minimum expected demand conditions (since second-shift operation would not be needed to meet the lower boundary demand level of 263,000 units).

2. A request for a second 61,300 square foot expansion of the plant to a capacity of 1,800 units per day could be submitted to Mr. Bruder and to Litton corporate headquarters for approval. The enlarged assembly area would accommodate four assembly lines, each of which would have an output capacity of 450 units per day. These lines would be of the same design as those approved for the Phase II expansion; however, the added working space would permit upgrading of the line speed from 400 to 450 units per shift. Exhibit 4 depicts the consumer plant layout after completion of the proposed Phase IIII expansion. The original area of the Phase I facility and the Phase II expansion are also shown for information.

If the request for a Phase III expansion were submitted promptly, Mr. George estimated that construction could be completed by August 1973. If this timetable were met, no lost sales would occur under best estimate demand conditions; in fact, Mr. George was confident that, with careful attention to scheduling, even the maximum expected demand level of 436,000 units could be met without requiring overtime or second-shift

Exhibit 4
CONSUMER MICROWAVE OVEN PLAN LAYOUT (PHASE III)

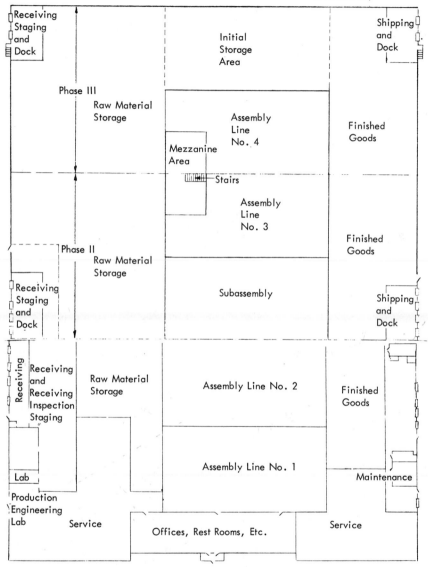

operation. The rental option of $1.13 per square foot of expansion space would apply in addition to an estimated $1.86 cost per square foot to cover other expenses. This facilities cost per square foot would be incurred as a fixed expense even if the added capacity were not fully utilized. However, the added staffing and operating expense would be purely variable since the four assembly lines could be operated selectively to meet fluctuating

Exhibit 5
MINNEAPOLIS TRIBUNE ARTICLE
(March 8, 1973)

Consumers Union doubts safety of microwave ovens

By Jim Fuller
Staff Writer

A Consumer Reports magazine recommendation against the purchase and use of microwave ovens brought a rash of protests Wednesday from the manufacturers of such ovens.

"We are not convinced that they (the ovens) are completely safe to use" the magazine report said. It added that its research has been "unable to uncover any data establishing . . . what level of microwave radiation emission can unequivocally be called safe."

A typical manufacturer's response to the report came from William W. George, executive vice-president of the Minneapolis-based Atherton Division of Litton Industries, Inc.

"We do not feel that it presents an honest or accurate picture of microwave-oven safety," said George. He added that "there never has been an injury from microwave emissions from a microwave oven, and, in fact, all 15 models tested by Consumers Union, by their own admission, meet federal standards." Consumers Union is a non-profit organization that publishes Consumer Reports.

Consumer Reports quoted a Bureau of Radiological Health official as saying "the eye is especially vulnerable to microwaves because of its inability to dissipate heat readily. Animal experimentation has established that microwaves can cause cataracts."

The magazine also said the federal government has warned that even very low-level microwave radiation can interfere with the operation of some types of cardiac pacemakers used to maintain normal heart operation.

Consumer Reports conceded that none of the 15 ovens it tested showed radiation emission levels that exceeded federal standards.

However, the magazine said, "we do not feel we could consider a microwave oven acceptable unless there is no radiation leakage detectable, even under the most severe conditions . . . and until there is sufficient assurance that there will not be any detectable leakage over the life of the oven."

Atherton is the country's largest manufacturer of microwave ovens, with more than 80 percent of the commercial market and about 35 percent of the consumer market. It employs about 500 persons in the Minneapolis

area, up from 400 last November.

George said yesterday that the Consumer Reports article "presents no new facts on microwave-oven safety that weren't already known by government and industry specialists."

He added that federal officials "have said the ovens are safe and that they have no reservations whatever about the safety of microwave ovens."

Atherton products, "and presumably all other manufacturers' products" meet government standards which "provide substantial margins for safety," George said.

He said Consumer Reports testing was done without consulting either government officials or industry experts and maintained that the magazine's testers were not qualified to make the judgement they did.

Representatives of Tappan Company, Raytheon Amana and the Association of Home Appliance Manufacturers echoed George's statements.

Microwave ovens, which use high-frequency radio waves to heat food, have the fastest rate of sales growth among home appliances today.

demand levels; thus, only the fixed facilities cost would have to be netted against the added contribution realized by eliminating lost sales.

Other Considerations

While Mr. George was pondering the options described above, he received a copy of the March 8 newspaper article published by the Minneapolis Tribune which is reproduced as Exhibit 5. This article described a report by *Consumer Union Magazine* which questioned the radiation safety standards set for microwave ovens and recommended against purchase of these appliances by readers of the magazine. Recalling the depressing effect on sales of the 1970 "radiation scare," Mr. George pondered what influence this news should have on his evaluation of the Phase III alternatives. Mr. George was also unsure as to how much effect the expiration of the current union contract in October 1973 should have on his decision since an immediate Phase III expansion would facilitate a buildup of inventories which could partially offset the effects of a potential work stoppage. Finally, Mr. George was wondering if the move into in-house fabrication of parts or production of combination microwave/electric ovens should be undertaken at this time. If these steps toward expanding the scope of the manufacturing task were to be taken soon, perhaps they should be coordinated with a Phase III capacity expansion program in a new plant outside Plymouth, Minnesota.

North American Rockwell— Draper Division

IN OCTOBER 1971, the Draper Division of North American Rockwell (NR) was cited for emitting from its North Foundry gaseous and particle pollutants in quantities exceeding permissible levels under Massachusetts law. Draper responded by promising to eliminate the pollution at its source within two years and to report on its specific plans for action by May 15, 1972. The sources of the pollution were the cupolas used for melting iron in one of its three foundries.

Mr. Robert Mace, President of the Draper Division since January 1970, was being forced to deal with the North Foundry pollution problem at a time when the sales of Draper looms were at their lowest level in many years (3,308 looms in fiscal 1971 versus 18,500 in 1965). Sales of repair parts represented about two-thirds of dollar volume in 1971. In pursuing a course of action on the pollution problem, he was concerned with the possibility of improving the overall foundry operatons of the Division as well as eliminating the pollution problem. Between October and the following April the problem was discussed, alternatives studied, and their implications considered with a view toward reaching a final decision by May 15.

THE COMPANY

The Draper Corporation was founded in 1816 in Hopedale, Massachusetts, as a manufacturer of loom parts. Over the years the company had become one of the world's largest producers of looms for the weaving of textiles. In 1966, Draper was acquired by the Rockwell Standard Corporation which merged shortly thereafter with North American Aviation to become North American Rockwell Corporation. The Draper Division along with the Knitting Machinery Division and two smaller divisions made up the Textile Machinery Division, which in turn was included in the Industrial Products Group of the parent company.

Because Draper's sales had traditionally been largely confined to the

United States, erosion of the American textile industry by increased competition from foreign imports was having a serious impact on Draper's performance. Competition was particularly acute in Draper's market segment—single color cloth. In addition, one foreign manufacturer of textile equipment had made substantial inroads into the U.S. market by competing on the basis of product innovation. This company had introduced new looms which offered U.S. textile manufacturers substantially different features from those offered by Draper, namely, more flexible looms and multicolor weaving capability.

Draper's manufacturing operation involved the casting and machining of metal parts, machining of wood parts, and the assembly of these parts into looms and spare parts. Draper operated several plants in the fall of 1971, as shown in Exhibit 1. An organization chart of the manufacturing

Exhibit 1
DRAPER MANUFACTURING FACILITIES

Location	Principal Products and Operations	Number of Employees	Size in Square Feet
Hopedale.	Looms, spare parts, accessories, sub-contracting, foundries, machine shop and assembly, warehouse, wood parts	1,693	1,826,000
East Spartanburg, South Carolina. . .	Foundry, gray iron machining, spare parts, warehouse	612	320,000
Marion, South Carolina.	Steel machining, wood parts, shuttles, picker sticks	256	119,000
Beebe River, N.H.	Bobbins	209	222,000
Tupper Lake, N.Y.	Wood loom parts, bobbin blanks	62	47,000
Limerick, Ireland	Small loom accessories	50	15,000
Mexico City, Mexico	Shuttles, bobbins, picker sticks, warehouse	80	35,000

operation is shown in Exhibit 2.

The Hopedale plant was the oldest and by far the largest of Draper's seven manufacturing facilities. The plant floor-space of this facility was allocated as follows:

North Foundry	430,000 sq. ft.
West Foundry	70,000
Machine Shop	500,000
Assembly	180,000
Storage	320,000
Offices	200,000
Other	130,000

Exhibit 2
MANUFACTURING ORGANIZATION
(number of employees)

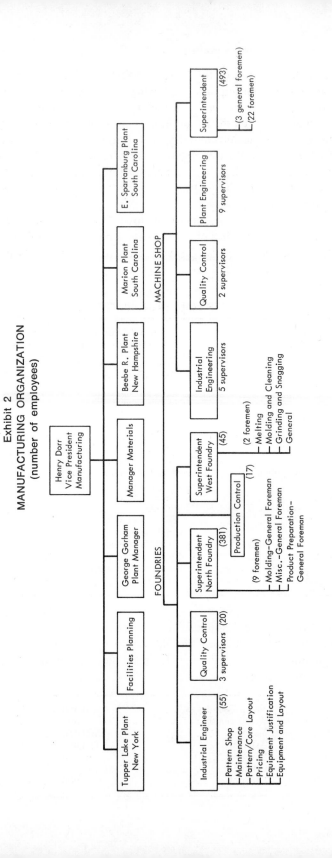

In 1971, total division sales were over $50 million. Most of this volume involved products which used castings. The net book value of Draper's Hopedale buildings and equipment was approximately $20 million of which $2.0 million represented foundry equipment. The plant was operating at a level estimated to be approximately 30 percent of full three-shift capacity in the fall of 1971. Layoffs had been made reluctantly, considering the age and seniority of many employees and the economic dependence of the area on Draper. Termination benefits were considered liberal, costing Draper about $1,000 per employee.

FOUNDRY OPERATIONS

Draper operated the largest foundry in New England at its facilities in Hopedale, Massachusetts. Foundry operations at Hopedale were located in two areas, the North Foundry and the West Foundry, which were approximately one-quarter of a mile apart. The two foundries differed greatly in appearance, operations, capacities, working conditions, and technologies, with the West Foundry being the newer, cleaner, and more modern of the two. The Hopedale facility and a view of the West Foundry are pictured in Exhibit 3. Exhibit 4 shows the floor plans of the foundries, and Exhibit 5 contains sales, cost, capacity, output and employment data.

Exhibit 3
HOPEDALE FACILITIES—WEST FOUNDRY IN FOREGROUND

Exhibit 3 *(Continued)*
WEST FOUNDRY

Exhibit 6 shows employment by departments and Exhibit 7 the 1972 cost plan based on the present operating pattern.

Foundry operations at Draper involved melting a mix of pig iron and scrap metal, pouring the molten iron into sand molds, allowing the iron to cool and solidify, breaking the mold, cleaning the castings by sand blasting, removing the burrs and excess metal (caused by the pour hole and mold crease) by grinding operations, and painting the castings. The manner in which these operations were performed differed radically between the North and West Foundries.

The North Foundry melting operation involved the use of a cupola, a heavily constructed vertical cylinder into which a charge of coke and iron was placed to produce molten iron. The foundry contained two large cupolas with a capacity of 22 tons per hour each, and a small cupola with a capacity of 12 tons per hour. The melt process, based upon a technology which was hundreds of years old, involved the burning of coke in a stream of forced air (much like the hearth and bellows of a nineteenth century blacksmith), and allowing the iron in the charge to melt and trickle downward through the coke. The molten iron collected at the bottom of the cupola and drained off into a collecting tank. The molten iron was poured from the collecting tank into ladles (which could hold about 200 pounds of iron). These ladles, traveling on overhead rails, were pushed to the molding areas where the iron was poured off into sand molds.

The melt process was continuous throughout its cycle by the addition

Exhibit 4

LAYOUT OF FOUNDRIES

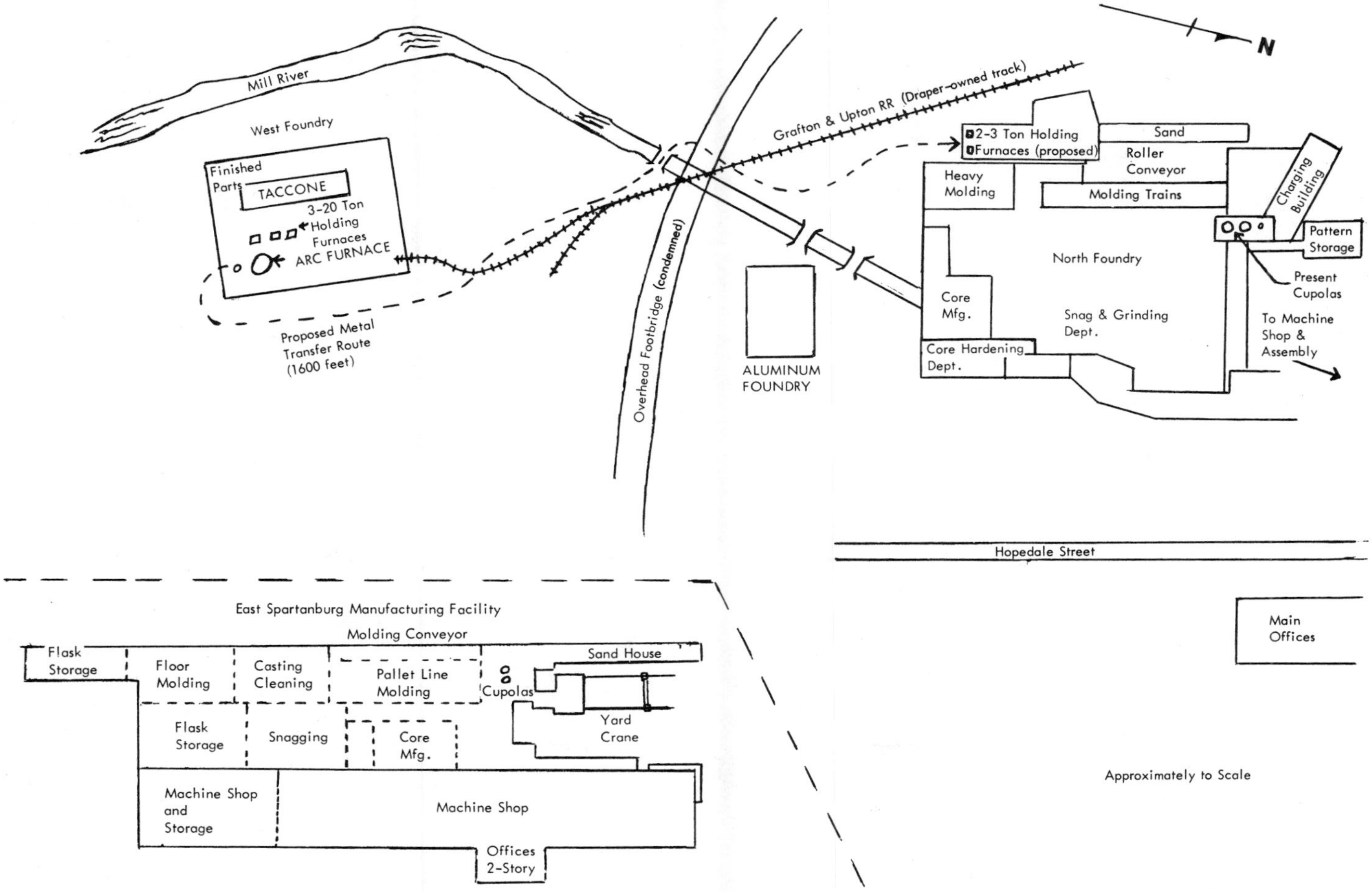

N

Mill River

West Foundry

Finished Parts

TACCONE

3-20 Ton Holding Furnaces

ARC FURNACE

Proposed Metal Transfer Route (1600 feet)

Grafton & Upton RR. (Draper-owned track)

Overhead Footbridge (condemned)

ALUMINUM FOUNDRY

Charging Building

Sand

Roller Conveyor

Molding Trains

2-3 Ton Holding

Furnaces (proposed)

Heavy Molding

Core Mfg.

Core Hardening Dept.

North Foundry

Snag & Grinding Dept.

Pattern Storage

Present Cupolas

To Machine Shop & Assembly

Hopedale Street

Main Offices

Approximately to Scale

East Spartanburg Manufacturing Facility

Molding Conveyor

Sand House

Yard Crane

Cupolas

Pallet Line Molding

Core Mfg.

Machine Shop

Offices 2-Story

Casting Cleaning

Snagging

Floor Molding

Flask Storage

Machine Shop and Storage

Flask Storage

Exhibit 5
DRAPER DIVISION FOUNDRIES—BASIC DATA

	North	*West*	*East Spartanburg*
1972 sales forecast[1]	$5,890,000	$2,177,000	$5,144,000
Ratio Draper work/outside work	55/45	62/38	75/25
Variable costs as a percent of sales			
Direct labor[2]	13%	8%	12%
Material	13	11	13
Overhead[2]	38	21	21
Fixed costs[2]	$ 344,000	$ 766,000	$1,175,000
Book value—buildings and equipment	673,000	2,423,000	761,000
patterns and tools	605,000	203,000	186,000
Melt capacity[3]	300 tons per day	180 tons per day	160 tons per day
Present melt rate[4]	100 tons per day	45 tons per day	120 tons per day
Molding capacity[5]	20,000 molds per day	2,400 molds per day	18,000 molds per day
Present molding rate[6]	7,000 molds per day	550 molds per day	15,000 molds per day
Yield: pounds shipped/pounds melted	48%	46%	46%
Number of employees	[See Exhibit 6]		336
Holding furnaces for hot metal	None	3–20 ton	N.A.

[1] Transfer pricing. Foundry work was priced at 1.15 times full standard cost for Draper jobs.

[2] In addition to these costs there were $2,267,000 in joint service costs for the Hopedale Foundry. See Exhibit 7 for details.

[3] Melt capacity is on a two-shift basis for cupolas (North and East Spartanburg), and three shifts for the West Foundry arc furnace. The small cupola was not considered part of normal capacity for the North Foundry.

[4] Present melt rate was accomplished on one shift in Hopedale and three shifts in East Spartanburg.

[5] Molding capacity is based on three shift operations. A West Foundry mold is equivalent to about four North Foundry molds. The pouring of a West Foundry mold produced, on the average, four parts.

[6] Present molding rate was accomplished on one shift in Hopedale and three shifts in East Spartanburg.

Source: Costs estimated by casewriter. Other data from company sources.

of carefully measured charges of coke and metallics into the cupola at regulated intervals. After eight hours of operation it was necessary to clean out and reline the cupola with a cement-like refractory material. The relining process involved a three-man crew working a total of 21-man hours. Normally one cupola was in use while the second large cupola was being relined.

The melt process could be speeded up or slowed down by regulating the rate of air flow and the quantities of coke and metallics added; however, there was a minimum and maximum operating rate. The maximum rate was determined by the temperature decline of the charge which resulted if metallics were added too rapidly. The minimum rate resulted from the deterioration of the metallurgical properties which occurred if the metallics were added too slowly. The minimum output of each cupola was about 60 percent of its capacity.

Because the operation of the cupolas was, in effect, a carbon burning

Exhibit 6
EMPLOYMENT BY DEPARTMENT
(number of employees—October 1971)

Department	North Foundry	West Foundry	Services*
Melt shop	16	5	
Floor molding	25		
Conveyor molding	124	24	
Cleaning	15		
Snag and grind†	73	13	
Paint	5		
Aluminum foundry	10		
Slinger molding	23		
Flask storage	8		
General		3	42
Pattern shop			33
Quality control			20
Core room			35
Production control			17
Maintenance			17
Industrial engineering			5
Shipping			5
Totals	299	45	174
Total employees			518

* Employees listed under "Services" served both foundries. Organizationally, the structure under which they reported is shown in Exhibit 2.

† Snagging involved removing gates and risers and other excess metal. Grinding involved removing the parting line, i.e., a slight ridge caused by the junction of the two mold halves.

process within a temperature range set by the requirements of the metallics, the process produced an undesirable amount of smoke in the form of noxious carbon oxides, ash particles and iron oxides. In contrast, melting with an arc furnace, as was done in the West Foundry, was virtually a pollution-free process.

The West Foundry melting operation involved the use of an arc furnace in which heat was supplied to a charge of pig iron and scrap iron by an arc between two electrodes. Although the West Foundry contained only one arc furnace, it had been sized to accommodate two. The cycle time to produce a 15-ton batch of molten iron (the capacity of the arc furnace) was two hours. Once melted, the molten iron was poured into a ladle with a capacity of 20 tons. This ladle was carried by overhead crane and poured into one of three, 20 ton insulated, induction heated "holding furnaces," which could hold the iron indefinitely until molds were ready to receive the melt. When ready the molds were filled by the use of buckets (which had a capacity of 1,000 pounds.) The buckets were transported from the holding furnace by a fork lift truck which set them into the pouring equipment, one on each side of the track conveying molds.

The molding techniques employed at the two foundries involved the use

Exhibit 7
1972 COST PLAN
(assumes no change in operations)
($000)

	Direct Labor	Variable Overhead	Fixed Overhead	Total
North Foundry				
Melt shop	0	392	142	534
Floor molding	120	239	21	380
Conveyor molding	263	723	34	1,020
Cleaning	0	164	4	168
Snag and grind	242	477	37	756
Paint	16	53	0	69
Aluminum foundry	31	52	34	117
Slinger molding	119	153	5	277
Flask storage	0	0	68	68
Total	791	2,253	345	3,389
West Foundry				
Melt	0	176	271	447
Mold	138	181	210	529
General	0	12	286	298
Snagging	42	100	2	144
Total	180	469	769	1,418
Services				
General	0	432	730	1,162
Pattern shop	0	383	27	410
Core room	126	262	19	407
Maintenance	0	3	202	205
Shipping	0	83	0	83
Total	126	1,163	978	2,267
Grand Total	1,097	3,885	2,092	7,074

Source: Company data.

of patterns or matchplates, cores, flasks and molding sand. Patterns and matchplates were slightly oversized duplicates of halves of the part to be produced; illustrations of each are shown in Exhibit 8. These could be made out of wood, epoxy or metal.

The basic difference between patterns and matchplates was that patterns were two-piece models of the part (one for the upper and one for the lower halves of the part) and matchplates were single piece models of the part.

In using either matchplates or patterns the part models were mounted on flat metal plates. In the case of patterns the upper and lower halves of the part model were mounted on separate plates. In the case of the matchplates the upper half of the part was molded on one side of the plate (or base) and the lower half on the other side to form a single piece model of the part to be produced. Patterns and matchplates had a life of up to 100,000 parts.

Exhibit 8
ILLUSTRATION OF PATTERN AND MATCHPLATE MOLD MAKING

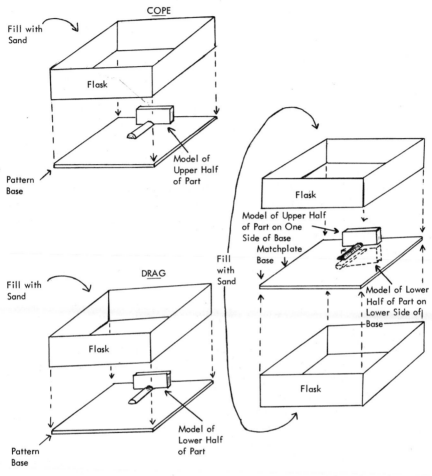

Pattern Molding Process   Matchplate Molding Process

A core was a model of a part cavity and was set in a mold when a hollow part such as a tube was to be produced. Cores were made of a sand and oil mixture which was hardened by baking. Once used a core had to be destroyed in order to remove it from the newly made part.

"Flasks" were square frames. When clamped to a pattern or matchplate the flask formed the sides and the pattern or matchplate formed the bottom of a box into which sand was poured and compressed to form a mold.

Molding sand was a specially prepared sand. This sand was relatively fine and mixed with a damp binding agent. The dampness and texture of the sand were critical to the quality of the part produced. Molding sand was recycled after the production of each part.

A new mold had to be prepared for each part produced. In preparing a mold from patterns each piece (upper and lower half) of the pattern was clamped to a separate flask. The upper half of the pattern with its flask formed a box called the "cope"; the lower half of the pattern with its flask formed a box called the "drag." Sand was poured and compressed into the cope to form the top half of the mold, and into the drag to form the bottom half of the mold. Once the sand was packed, the patterns were carefully removed leaving the sand shaped to the form of the part. A pour hole is formed in the cope, necessary cores placed in the drag, and the cope is gently placed on top of the drag with the pattern impressions face-to-face to form a molding cavity.

In matchplate molding, the matchplate was clamped between two flasks and sand was packed around first one side then the other side of the matchplate to form the two halves of the mold. The top flask was removed from the matchplate to form the cope and the matchplate was removed from the bottom flask to form the drag. Once again the cope was placed on top of the drag to form the mold.

Matchplate molding was usually used to make small parts which were poured in conveyorized line process in the North Foundry. Pattern molding was used for all sizes of parts. Pattern molding was used in the North Foundry in "floor" and "rollover" molding to produce large parts. Pattern molding was used exclusively in the highly automated molding process of the West Foundry.

Molding in the North Foundry consisted of both matchplate, and floor and rollover work, with approximately 70 percent of the tonnage and 95 percent of the number of annual molds produced on matchplate. The matchplate work was done at piece-rate paid individual work stations served by a train conveyor which moved completed molds to the pouring area. The equipment for this process was 20 to 25 years old, with the last major mechanization having taken place in 1945.

The West Foundry had been completed in 1966 around a highly mechanized molding system—the Taccone process. The Taccone unit had been purchased at a cost of $3 million when Draper was making 15,000–18,000 looms per year and wished to set up a mechanized foundry to more economically produce the large, heavy parts required in their looms. It consisted of an integrated system which mechanically and automatically performed the functions of:

a. Placing the cope and drag under a sand chute and delivering a metered amount of sand.

b. Packing and tamping the sand around the pattern in the cope.

c. Packing and tamping the sand around the pattern in the drag.

d. Closing the mold and moving it into position for being poured.

e. Moving the mold through a cooling cycle.

f. Removing the completed cast parts (automatic shakeout).

g. Cleaning out and recycling the flask.
h. Removing and preparing the sand for reuse.
i. Automatic cleaning of completed parts by shot blasting.

Pouring was done after step (*d*) by two pouring machines, one on each side of the conveyor. Each machine was controlled by an operator to position the bucket of molten iron over the mold and tip it for pouring.

Labor operations were required for removing the patterns (after *c*) and for pouring (after *d*). The entire process was linked together by an automatic conveyor that moved the mold from station to station, with each mold moving simultaneously to a different station every 33 seconds.[1] Taccone crew sizes were standard at 24 per shift regardless of volume. Molds were in a standard size flask called a "stool," measuring 48×36 inches which could hold up to 8 patterns each, depending on the pattern size. Though the stool could be set up for 8 of the smallest patterns, 4 was the largest number actually used because only 33 seconds was available for pouring and only two pours from each side of the stool could be made in that time with the present pouring equipment.

In order to achieve its high degree of mechanization, the Taccone process required one standard size flask to hold standardized copes and drags, and relatively expensive special patterns. Taccone patterns cost $2,000–$4,000 (versus $300 for normal matchplates). The higher cost was due to the higher tolerance machining operations required on the Taccone patterns and mounting plates. The higher tolerances were a result of the 1,500 pound sand packing pressure used (versus 80 pounds in manual molding). Castings were limited in depth to 8 inches because of the standard size 12 inches flask. It was considered that the machine was uneconomic for parts which weighed less than 5 to 10 pounds and had an annual usage of less than 4,000 pieces. A total cost of $1,300,000 was estimated to be required to convert North Foundry matchplates so as to be usable in the West Foundry, based on reworking only patterns which suited the size limitations of the automated process. These patterns represented about 36 tons per day of finished parts at current production volumes.

The Taccone process was criticized by Mr. George Gorham, Plant Manager, on several counts:

> First, there are a number of shortcomings to the Taccone system. The process was a good choice when they bought it but when the bottom dropped out of the market, it proved to be costly at low production volumes.
>
> Second, it is inflexible in terms of the standard size flask, the limited casting depth combined with minimum weight castings, and the special patterns required.

---

[1] The conveyor moved intermittently, moving the molds forward to a different station every 33 seconds.

Third, the pouring system is a problem. The two operators (one on each side of the stool) cannot get a smooth enough, accurate enough, or fast enough action due to its inherent mechanical, electrical and hydraulic design. We feel a better pour-off system—which would cost about $68,000—would cut our scrap from 18 percent now to 13 percent and save 40 minutes delay each day. We're now pouring 110 flasks per hour and with a better pour system that could be raised to 120.

Finally, it takes as much manpower to handle 100 tons per day as 200.

The equipment and process technology of the East Spartanburg foundry, built in 1955, was generally similar to that of the North Foundry. Cupolas were used for melting and the bulk of the molding was performed as described for the North Foundry, using mostly matchplates and a conveyorized mold moving setup. A company spokesman described the foundry as follows: "Its strengths are in flexible molding processes, proximity to a good outside market, and high margin outside jobs. Its weaknesses are in marginal working conditions, no pattern making, a tight labor market, limited space for expansion, and pollution complaints are a future threat. It costs about $250 to hire and train a man, but four out of five recently hired quit after a short time."

WORK-FORCE MANAGEMENT

The Hopedale plant was located in a town of 4,000 population about 45 miles southwest of Boston. The town impressed the case writer as unusually attractive. It was neat, laid out with considerable open space, green grass, old trees, and town parks, beautifully wooded, and through it passed a modest stream which had been dammed in the 1800's to form a scenic lake just above the plant site where many in the town swam in the summer and skated in the winter.

Hopedale had been for years a "company town" in the traditional sense. The company had owned a number of houses, a company store, and put in the town sewer system in the early 1900s at its own expense. The Draper family had donated the land and built the clubhouse for a nine-hole golf course, with membership open only to company employees and town residents. Mr. George Draper had built a library and a gymnasium and he and others in his family had, over the years, made dozens of improvements and additions to the town and its facilities. The town had in fact been established in the early 1800s as a Utopian religious community and the several Draper brothers had started the company as one means of providing a living for the members of the religious sect. Thus the relationships between company owners and employees and town residents has been a most unusual one, largely paternal and certainly highly humane according to tenets and values of those times.

In the early 1960s after the Draper Corporation "went public," all of the company-owned houses were sold, the company store closed down, and operations of the country club and other Draper dominated external facilities were turned over to townspeople. In 1971, of the 1,700 employees, about 400 lived in the town of Hopedale itself. Many more lived in Milford, about two miles from the plant beyond Hopedale.

Foundry employees had been unionized under the AFL (International Molders and Allied Workers) since the 1940s but shop employees had not been unionized until 1965, by an AFL-CIO Union. Many NLRB elections had been held in the shop. Until 1965, the Union had always been defeated. In 1965, placing a major emphasis on improving worker productivity, the company brought in a large industrial engineering firm to expand its use of standards to include most of its direct labor work including set-up and machine changeovers. In 1971, the plant manager, George Gorham, felt that this program had been effective in reducing costs but that it was largely responsible for the vote to authorize collective bargaining through the Union. Union-Management relations were entirely cordial and the company had never had a strike. Mr. Gorham, who had been with Draper since 1945 when he started in as a patternmaker, stated that "our people here average about 54 years old. They work. They like to work and they work happily. Morale only goes down when the work load goes down."

An incentive wage plan was used in most production operations throughout the plant. In the foundry, for example, about 140 employees were paid on incentives. There were approximately 65 job classifications in the foundry and some jobs were divided into as many as 6 grades with grading based on seniority. No limits were set on piece rate earnings, and employees were able to produce at up to 150 percent of standard. A sample of average wages is shown below; wages at East Spartanburg were approximately 85 percent of those at Hopedale.

HOPEDALE PLANT—
AVERAGE HOURLY RATE: EARNED

Molder	$4.50
Molding line laborer	3.17
Grinding and snagging machinist	4.45
Grinding and snagging laborer	2.98
Patternmaker	4.30

Foundry workers were difficult to obtain and laborers in the melt and molding operations were hired at the maximum ($3.17) of the job classification in order to attract them. Turnover of these lower grade jobs was high and recruiting difficult in spite of the high unemployment levels (7 to 8 percent) in Massachusetts in 1971. The apparent causes of this problem are described in an interoffice memo (Exhibit 9).

Exhibit 9

INTERNAL LETTER

Date:	January 14, 1972	No.:	
TO:	Mrs. James A. Harvey	FROM:	Mr. Anthony E. Fasano
Address:	Main Office	Address:	Personnel
		Phone:	

Subject: Foundry Personnel

For some time we have been aware of the difficulty in securing foundry help. Although we have been successful in meeting our personnel needs we are now experiencing problems that seriously affect the efficiency of the foundry operations.

Not too many years ago the popular flask sizes were $10'' \times 15''$, $12'' \times 15''$, $10'' \times 17''$, etc. These were of moderate weight and people could work comfortably without excessive strain. Molding was the best paying and the prestige job in the foundry. There was a waiting list of people who had requested such work. To supplement our loom work we turned to outside casting work. In order to become competitive, we were compelled to increase the size of our molds. Weight became an issue and the Union attempted to restrict the size of the flask that a man was required to handle. They were partially successful and the Company established certain limits. However, the so-called "one man jobs" were heavier than previously and men were not so anxious to become molders. The waiting list for molding gradually began to diminish. At present we have no one seeking these positions. Molders are attempting to transfer to other jobs and are willing to accept less wages.

Foundry supervision has been aware of this problem and has expressed great concern. Our younger employees are not interested and are unwilling to train. Our present group is getting older and productivity will undoubtedly suffer. We are experiencing an above normal number of back strains and in many instances must provide adjusted work for these men. This, of course, affects our production schedules and our direct labor dollars. Workmen's Compensation costs are also increasing. Though an employee may return from sick leave, in the case of a back condition, we are faced with the prospect of a recurrence of the injury.

We have been able to hire foundry laborers in sufficient number to meet our present level of business. If we cannot induce men to become molders, hiring of people would be of no avail. I would seriously question our ability to increase our production if future business levels dictated such an increase.

Many foundries have been forced to suspend operations because of their inability to overcome these very problems. We must *look to new and improved methods of making castings or be confronted with a similar decision.*

Anthony E. Fasano
Personnel Manager

AEF/dj

FUTURE DEMAND FOR CASTINGS

In October 1971, loom demand was expected to move back up in the years ahead and Draper sales were forecast to grow at a rate of 6 percent per year over the next five years. The outside market for castings was a mixed picture. Foundry production in New England has been dropping at 6 percent per year from 1966 to 1969, and 15 percent in 1970. Since 1968, 21 foundries out of about 100 had closed. Substantial excess foundry capacity was in existence in the New England area. Some work was being obtained in New York and New Jersey, and some work was being done for other NR divisions and, in particular, for the knitting division where billings for castings were running at about $100,000 per month.

The forecast for future foundry work at Hopedale in 1975 is shown in Exhibit 10.

Exhibit 10
FORECASTS FOR 1975

| | Tons and Thousands of Dollars | | | |
	Outside		Draper	Total Tons
North Foundry				
Matchplates	$2,182	5,400 tons	4,900 tons	10,300
Floor and rollover	766	2,000	1,900	3,900
Total	$2,948	7,400	6,800	14,200
West Foundry	1,235	3,500	4,000	7,500
Total Hopedale	$4,183	10,900 tons	10,800 tons	21,700

Maximum capacity based on present yields 36,000 tons North—2 shift
21,000 tons West—3 shift

Note: Tonnage data represents weight of finished parts

| | Thousands of Molds | | | |
	Outside	Draper	Total	Capacity
North				
Matchplates	970	964	1,934	4,560
Floor and rollover	45	51	96	240
Total	1,015	1,015	2,030	4,800
West	87	138	225	576

Source: Company data.

ALTERNATIVES BEING CONSIDERED

Six alternatives had been proposed and were being considered in April 1972 to alleviate the pollution problem and improve operating costs. Excerpts from a company report concerning these alternatives are as follows:

A. *Install Scrubbers on Cupolas*

A wet scrubber is a mechanical device which cleans exhaust gases by forcing them to impinge on and/or pass through water on their way from a cupola to the atmosphere. Scrubbers require high horsepower blowers, create noise (sometimes at nuisance levels), have inherent maintenance problems, and yield a wet sludge which cannot be discharged into normal sewage channels.

Scrubbers for the North Foundry cupolas have been studied in considerable depth by the Foundry Industrial Engineering Department. They report the following cost/benefit picture based on installing one scrubber, sufficient to allow a maximum melt capacity of 220 tons per day.
One-Time Costs:

New equipment cost	$215,000
Installation and building changes	322,000
New Capital Investment	$537,000

Start-up Costs:
North Foundry production would be interrupted for at least 3 months.
Continuing Effects:

Annual scrubber operating cost	$ 85,000
Annual depreciation added	36,000
Annual profit impact	$(121,000)

B. *Close the North Foundry and Transfer Work*

The concept is to utilize more fully our existing melt and molding capacity at East Spartanburg and in the West Foundry, allowing us to close down all melting and molding in the North Foundry. In operational terms, this alternative implies:

a. Moving all North Foundry matchplate molding jobs to East Spartanburg; 33,000 patterns would be transferred at a freight cost of $6,000. Dispose of North Foundry equipment (net book value, $66,000).
b. Moving rollover and floor molding to the West Foundry. Cost estimated at $41,000.
c. Shipping castings from East Spartanburg to Hopedale for machining. Transportation costs estimated at $80,000 per year.
d. Constructing some new areas in the building at East Spartanburg. Cost estimated at $89,000.

C. *Close the North Foundry and Buy Castings Outside*

The best information available to date, based on quotations received from outside foundries and from other NR sources is that Draper work bought outside would cost 1.5 times the present (full absorption) North Foundry Cost.

D. *Transfer Molten Iron from West Foundry*

By transferring molten metal between foundries, we can maintain our foundry capability in both locations.

Dubbed the "Thermos Bottle Approach," this alternative has been studied and found to have cost advantages. The arc furnace melts more economically than do the cupolas, because it eliminates the need for coke and pig iron and substitutes electricity and scrap metal. A $65,000 per year saving is available in the difference between coke costs and electric melt energy and supply costs. Adding some new operating costs, net savings are expected to be between $20,000 and $30,000 per year. The investment required would be $560,000 for purchase and installation of truck mounted vessels and handling equipment for transferring molten metal. This would include $400,000 for two 30 ton induction holding furnaces.

E. *Install Electric Melt in the North Foundry*

Arc melting and induction melting were considered. Of the two, arc melting is the more efficient at North Foundry volumes.

One-Time Costs:

New Equipment Costs, including Installation:

Arc furnace similar to present West Foundry furnace	$ 460,000
Three induction holding furnaces	600,000
(1) 30T bridge crane	73,000
Building changes	270,000
Move ductile iron operation	40,000
Electric substation	50,000
New Capital Investment	$1,493,000

Continuing Effects:

Annual labor savings	$ 100,000
Annual material savings—pig iron and coke	530,000
Arc power and electrodes	(280,000)
Electric power for receivers	(177,000)
Relining and ladle maintenance	(48,000)
Straight line depreciation	(100,000)
Annual Profit Impact	+$ 25,000

F. *Expand and Improve West Foundry Molding Capability to do all Hopedale Foundry Work*

The West Foundry Expansion was studied in detail in July of 1971. To make the Taccone Machine versatile enough to be reasonably marketable would require a $1 million investment in pouroff, bottom boards, and molding line modifications. To carry out the full expansion program, including the Taccone modifications, would require a total investment of $11.7 million. This proposal would allow complete razing of the present North Foundry building, and would allow a 16 percent reduction in labor costs, or $700,000 per year at present volume.

In April 1972, Mr. Mace faced the necessity of responding to the state government by May 15 with a statement of the company's plans for meeting air pollution regulations. He reviewed these six alternatives and compared their implications to Draper's future operations. In making his final decision he was aware that these six alternatives had been selected from a wider variety of possibilities. He realized that he need not necessarily limit his selection to one of these six but should attempt to develop a plan which would make the best sense for the future of the Division. Views of various process tasks are shown in Exhibit 11.

Exhibit 11
VIEWS OF VARIOUS PROCESS TASKS

1. General view of Taccone process, West Foundry.

3. Patterns about to enter molding cycle.

2. Patterns for Taccone process.

Exhibit 11 (*Continued*)

4. Pouring molds in the Taccone process.

5. Shakeout station in Taccone process.

6. Cleaned castings are off-loaded from conveyor at this end of machine.

Exhibit 11 (*Continued*)

7. Cope flask with matchplate in place. North Foundry.

8. Drag flask and mold with match-plate removed.

9. Cope flask and mold being placed over drag flask and mold. Note cores (light pieces) in mold.

10. Completed molds after flasks have been removed, but before pouring.

Exhibit 11 (*Continued*)

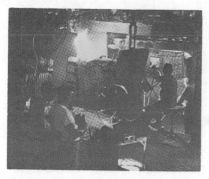

11. Molten iron being received from cupola. North Foundry.

12. Pouring ladle being refilled at cupola. North Foundry.

13 and 14. Pouring molds on train conveyor. North Foundry.

Exhibit 11 (*Concluded*)

15. Shaking out casting from mold after cooling.

16. Completed casting.

17. Grinding casting.

18. "Snagging" (removing burrs) on large casting.

Gulf Oil Company

IN EARLY 1966 the Gulf Oil Company was rapidly approaching a decision regarding its crude oil transportation strategy for the following decade. Although a variety of alternatives had been proposed, they largely represented variations on two basically different strategies. The first would rely on a tanker technology that had already been proven to be feasible, but which promised a relatively low return on investment. The second would require the adoption of bold new approach with attendant high risks but the possibility of a high return.

The latter was referred to as the "transshipment approach": instead of transporting relatively small shipments of Middle East crude oil directly to various European port refineries, this approach called for the construction or several giant tankers and a deep water unloading facility in or near Europe capable of receiving the new supertankers. There the mammoth tankers would transfer or "transship" their oil cargoes into smaller shuttle tankers that could service local European ports too small or shallow to handle the larger tankers (alternatively, there was some support for making these transshipments at sea). Each of these tankers would be more than twice the size of any tanker than in use and at least one-third larger than any then under construction. The economic rationale behind moving towards very large tankers is summarized in Exhibit 6. The Appendix is a more detailed explanation of these economic factors.

Besides requiring the construction of several huge tankers and the European transshipment facility (estimated to cost about $30 million), the transshipment approach would also require a new loading facility offshore Kuwait, Gulf's major source of oil. Bunker and crude oil submarine pipes would have to be extended nearly 10 miles into the Arabian Gulf to a man-made island terminal in 95 feet of water. This terminal would be the only facility in the world capable of loading tankers of more than 250,000 tons capacity. The cost, about $30 million, would be split 50-50 with British Petroleum, Gulf's partner in Kuwait.

THE GULF OIL COMPANY IN 1966

The Gulf Oil Company was celebrating its sixty-fifth birthday in 1966 (Exhibit 1 contains income and financial statements for 1964 and 1965). In 1901 its first (and most famous) well, "Spindletop," had guaranteed the company's immediate survival and put Texas on the oil map. After a period of consolidation in the United States, Gulf made its first foreign production investment in 1912 in Mexico. Twelve years later the company invested in a second set of foreign production facilities in Venezuela. However, it was not until 1934 that Gulf made "the" foreign direct investment that was to play an overwhelmingly decisive role in the company's future

Exhibit 1

GULF OIL COMPANY
Consolidated Statement of Income
(in millions of U.S. dollars)

	Years Ended December 31	
	1965	*1964*
Revenues		
Sales and other operating revenues	$4,185	$3,803
Dividends, interest, and other revenues	48	40
	$4,233	$3,843
Deductions		
Purchased crude oil, products, and merchandise	1,070	1,082
Operating, selling, and administrative expenses	1,252	1,146
Taxes on income and general taxes	1,150	929
Depreciation, depletion, amortization, and retirements	306	266
Interest on long-term debt	15	11
Income applicable to minority interests in subsidiaries consolidated	13	14
	3,806	3,448
Net Income	$ 427	$ 395
Assets		
Current Assets		
Cash	$ 112	$ 90
Marketable securities, at cost, approximating market value	236	183
Receivables, less estimated doubtful accounts	662	614
Inventories of crude oil, products, and merchandise	369	301
Materials and supplies	59	51
Total Current Assets	$1,438	$1,239
Investments and Long-Term Receivables		
Associated and other companies (50% or less owned)	$ 101	$ 79
Other investments and long-term receivables	174	144
Total Investments and Long-Term Receivables	$ 275	$ 223
Investment in subsidiary companies not consolidated	–	$ 215
Properties, plants, and equipment, at cost, less accumulated depreciation, depletion, and amortization	$3,439	$2,948
Prepaid and deferred charges	58	41
Total Assets	$5,210	$4,667

Exhibit 1 (*Continued*)
GULF OIL COMPANY
Consolidated Statement of Financial Position
(in millions of U.S. dollars)

	Years Ended December 31	
	1965	1964
Liabilities		
Current Liabilities		
Accounts payable and accrued liabilities	$ 520	$ 420
Accrued United States and foreign income taxes	189	153
Notes payable and current portion of long-term debt	58	19
Total Current Liabilities	$ 767	$ 592
Long-Term Debt	$ 396	$ 262
Other Long-Term Liabilities.	35	36
Minority Interests in Subsidiaries Consolidated	194	186
Total Liabilities	$1,392	$1,076
Ownership Interest		
Par Value of Shares Issued.	$ 881	$ 881
Other Capital	721	720
Earnings Retained in the Business	2,315	2,080
	$3,917	$3,681
Less Treasury Shares, at cost	99	90
Total Ownership Interest	$3,818	$3,591
Total Liabilities and Ownership Interest	$5,210	$4,667

Source: Gulf Oil Company, Annual Report, 1965.

worldwide operations. In that year, after years of negotiations, Gulf and British Petroleum Ltd. won a concession to explore for oil on a 50–50 joint venture basis in the Middle Eastern Sheikdom of Kuwait.

While commercial production in Kuwait did not commence until after the Second World War, the huge supplies of oil found and produced in the small country soon made Gulf a surplus producer in terms of its refining and marketing capabilities in Western Europe, the principal market for Middle Eastern oil. Fortunately, Gulf was able to sell much of its surplus crude on long-term contract to Shell Oil Company, whose European position was exactly the reverse of Gulf's—that is, too much refining capacity, a plentiful supply of marketing outlets, and too little oil. Gulf also sold over 300,000 barrels of crude per day to Japan, whose requirements were increasing at the rate of about 12 percent per year.

Gulf's surplus supplies of Kuwait oil continued to mount, however. During the fifties, as the Kuwait fields repeatedly increased yearly output, the company produced several times as much crude as it refined and marketed overseas. By 1962 Gulf's share of Kuwait production passed the million barrel per day mark and production was still rising in 1965 (Exhibit 2).

The imbalance created by Gulf's large and growing dependence on

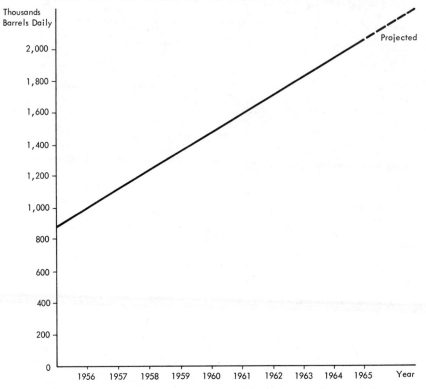

Exhibit 2
WORLD-WIDE NET CRUDE OIL AND CONDENSATE PRODUCED

NATIONAL SOURCES OF GULF CRUDE AND CONDENSATE
(daily averages in barrels)

	1965	1964	Increase
United States	432,100	406,300	25,800
Kuwait	1,260,400	1,182,400	78,000
Venezuela	160,300	158,600	1,700
Iran	99,800	91,200	8,600
Canada	39,200	37,300	1,900
Nigeria	26,500	—	26,500
France	6,900	6,400	500
Totals	2,025,200	1,882,200	143,000

Source: Gulf Oil Company, Annual Report, 1965.

Kuwait crude created several pressures. First, the political instability in the Middle East raised the specter of a possible sudden reduction in the availability of crude from that area. This led the company to increase its exploration for new, alternative sources of crude in other areas of the world.

Second, even though Shell Oil was able to absorb a certain percentage of Gulf's Kuwait crude (700,000 barrels per day in 1965), the Kuwait government's pressure to continually increase production compelled Gulf to increase its own refining and marketing facilities in Europe in order to secure guaranteed markets for its surplus crude. Since Gulf's production of crude was increasing faster than Europe's 7 percent annual growth in the consumption of petroleum products, the company realized that it would aggressively have to seek an increased market share. By 1965 Gulf had acquired two European refineries and expanded its marketing outlets significantly; these refineries were currently operating at capacity. New refineries and capacity expansions of existing refineries were expected to come "on stream" by 1968 (see Exhibit 3).

Exhibit 3
ESTIMATED EUROPEAN REFINING CAPACITY

Location	1966 Capacity (barrels per day)	1968 Capacity (barrels per day)	Ownership Share (percent)
Denmark	31,000	70,000	100
Holland (Europort)	59,000	75,000	100
Wales	—	60,000	100
Spain	—	84,000	50
Switzerland	—	50,000	25
Total	90,000	339,000	
Processed by others for Gulf	100,000	90,000	

Source: Gulf Oil Company.

Finally, as Gulf increased its upstream commitment in European refining and marketing, transportation became an increasingly critical variable in the company's drive to reduce costs and remain competitive. (See Exhibit 4 for a cost breakdown of the different stages of production.) Trans-

Exhibit 4
1966 ESTIMATED UNIT OIL COSTS SHIPPED TO EUROPE
FROM KUWAIT (AROUND CAPE) IN 50,000 TON TANKERS

	Per Barrel
Production costs	$0.30
Taxes	1.00
Crude oil transportation	0.75
Refining	0.50
Distilled products transport to market in Europe	0.40
Marketing	0.41
Marketing overhead	0.18
Total	$3.54
Gross revenue	3.79
Margin	$0.25

Source: Gulf Oil Company.

portation costs crucially affected Gulf's ability to compete because the vast majority of the company's oil was still coming from Kuwait, over 6,000 miles away via the Suez Canal.

In order to improve the company's strategic position, an investment program was launched with projections for large capital expenditures into the seventies. Exhibit 5 provides a rough breakdown of these funds.

Exhibit 5
CRUDE OIL PRODUCTION AND EXPLORATION
ANNUAL CAPITAL EXPENDITURES THROUGH 1965 AND
PLANNED EXPENDITURES THROUGH 1970

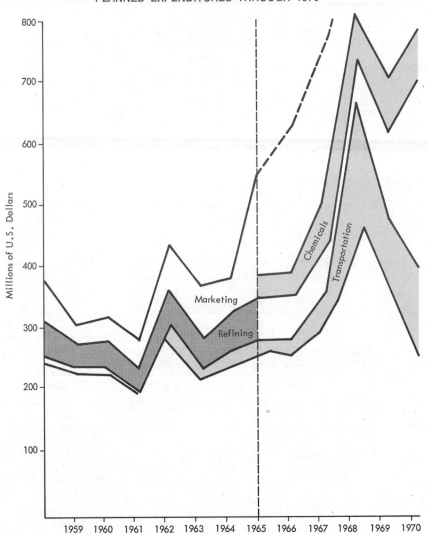

FACTORS INFLUENCING TRANSPORTATION STRATEGY

Gulf officials knew that future shipments of oil through the Suez Canal were both limited and uncertain. The major limitation was the Canal's depth of 38 feet, which would not allow passage to tankers greater than 65,000 tons (fully loaded). The uncertainty was due to the fact that Middle East conflicts had closed the Canal in the past, and future conflicts and blockages of the Suez seemed highly probable. The alternative was an 11,000 mile trip around the African continent.

Gulf's existing system for transporting crude to Europe centered on two sources: its own fleet of leased or long-term chartered tankers, and spot charters from independent shipowners. The Gulf fleet of 86 vessels had a capacity of three million deadweight tons (dwt) in 1965, with an average tanker size of 37,000 tons. Thirty-nine of these ships were owned and the remaining 47 were chartered on a long-term basis. During 1965 Gulf also relied on independent short-term, or "spot," charters to provide an additional 350,000 dwt. of capacity. The company currently was shipping about 70 million barrels of crude a year from Kuwait to its European refineries (both owned and under contract; see Exhibit 3). As a matter of policy it confined itself to transporting only the crude that was destined for its own marketing organization, including that processed for it by other companies' refineries. Companies buying crude from Gulf were responsible for transporting it themselves.

As European demand continued to grow (Kuwait crude was largely cut off from the American market because of U.S. import quotas), Gulf officials knew their reliance on spot charters would also increase unless additional investments were made in new ships. Gulf did not want to increase its dependence or spot charters because rates were uncertain, being influenced by forces of supply and demand outside its control. For example, sudden changes in demand for spot charters by other oil producers for any number of unforeseen reasons could greatly tax the fixed supply of independent tankers, driving rates up. Rates could fall just as quickly as they increased, but Gulf could be hurt badly if high rates were sustained. The main problem was to determine the best way to reduce the company's dependence on independent spot charters.

THE INVESTMENT DECISION

In early 1965, Gulf's chief transportation coordinator made a presentation before the corporate Board of Directors which illustrated the scale economies associated with tankers and pipelines of different capacities (see Exhibits 6 and 7). Both pipeline and tanker transportation offered reduced unit costs for both increased capacity and increased distance.

Comparisons between tankers and pipelines showed that tanker trans-

Exhibit 6
TRANSPORT COSTS OF MIDDLE EAST CRUDE
PERSIAN GULF TO EUROPE VIA CAPE
(dollars per barrel*)

Size of Tanker (deadweight tons)	Direct		Cost of Trans- shipping	Total Cost Transship via Cape
	Via Canal†	Via Cape		
50,000	$0.57	$0.75	–	–
100,000	0.45	0.55	–	–
165,000	0.42	0.45	–	–
200,000	–	0.39	–	–
300,000	–	0.35	$0.05	$0.40
500,000	–	0.30	0.06	0.36

* 1 deadweight ton = 7.3 barrels of crude oil.
† Suez round-trip toll roughly $0.12 per barrel.
Source: Gulf Oil Company and casewriter's estimates.

Exhibit 7
UNIT TRANSPORT COST

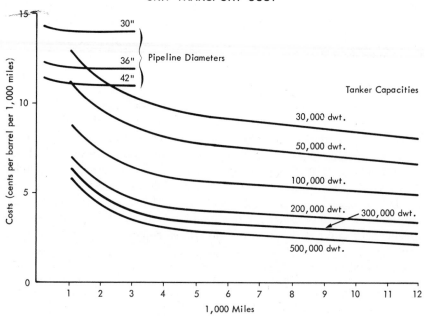

portation had significant cost advantages over pipelines, besides being considerably less vulnerable to disruption and shutdown. Moreover, pipeline unit costs leveled off beyond a certain distance, while tanker unit costs continued decreasing as distance increased, due to the decreasing time spent in port (as a percentage of total voyage time). Given these conditions, Gulf did not consider pipelines a reasonable alternative.

While the economics of tanker transport favored large tankers, the investment decision was complicated by several constraints which inhibited Gulf from quickly opting for an investment strategy calling for building the largest ships possible. The principal constraints were at the European end of the supply line. First, storage facilities for crude at Gulf's European refineries were inadequate to handle huge single deliveries of oil. Second, and more important, tankers above the 165,000 ton class required minimum harbor depths over 60 feet. (See Exhibit 8 for a schedule of tanker

Exhibit 8
WATER DEPTHS REQUIRED FOR CONVENTIONALLY
DESIGNED SHIPS*

Ship Size (000 DWT)	Draft Feet	Required Water Depth
100	44	50
165	54	60 (Europort limit)
200	60	66
275	68	75
350	74	81
500	83	91
1,000	105	115

* "Jersey design."

tonnages and harbor requirements.) Unfortunately, all of Gulf's refineries had harbors with water depths around 40 feet, although their Europort refinery near Rotterdam was expected to have clearance of 60 feet by 1968. Third, uncharted sea wrecks on the bottom of the English Channel increased the possibility of underwater collision for high draft (over 60 feet) tankers passing through this sea lane. The 38 foot depth of the Suez Canal represented a final constraint, but there were plans for deepening it to 60 feet by the mid-1970s.

There appeared to be two alternative ways for dealing with these constraints. The first alternative was to shift radically into the technically unproven shipping method of transshipment. One option under transshipping was to build the largest ship technically feasible given deep water limitations in the Persian Gulf and offshore the European coast. These limitations, plus shipbuilding capabilities, translated into a maximum tanker size of 326,000 tons, equivalent to 21 T–2s. Six tankers of this size would cost about $140 million and be available by early 1968. A second option under the transshipment strategy was to purchase smaller tankers, around 200,000 tons, or 13 T–2 equivalents. These smaller tankers might be able to enter one or two European ports directly in a few years, after ongoing harbor expansion programs were completed. In the meantime, they could transship their cargoes to smaller vessels. Either of these strategies would require the construction of the loading facility in Kuwait.

The second alternative was to continue shipping crude directly from

Kuwait to its European refineries. This would mean investing in tankers 165,000 tons and/or smaller, according to harbor limitations, and expanding storage capabilities. These ships could return from Europe via the Suez Canal (carrying ballast only). Three variations of the direct shipping alternative were available: (1) order all 65,000 dwt. tankers, slightly over 4 T–2 equivalents and small enough to enter the company's shallowest port for complete scheduling flexibility (i.e., any ship could go to any European Gulf refinery and most other ports); (2) order some larger tankers to service exclusively the refineries with the deeper harbors (e.g., the Europort refinery would have the deepest harbor at 60 feet and could service 165,000 ton tankers, but these tankers could not service the other four refineries); (3) order all 165,000 ton ships (11 T-2 equivalents). A dozen of these ships would cost about $160 million. They could only enter Europort directly, and crude would have to be shuttled to the remaining refineries.

All three options offered trade-offs between scheduling flexibility and reduction in unit transport costs. As the ships became larger, costs fell but the number of ports the tankers could enter directly was also reduced. While a premium was attached to scheduling flexibility, the final cost advantage appeared to favor the third method of direct shipping, even after the shuttling costs were included. At this point, the jump from adopting a transshipping strategy emanating from Europort versus transshipping from an even deeper port using larger tankers was an obvious cost-reducing possibility whose merits Gulf officials were debating in 1966. Some interest was also expressed in a compromise strategy in which ships of about 250,000 dwt. would be lightened by drawing off about 70,000 tons of crude at some deep water facility, and would then proceed directly to Europort.

APPENDIX: THE ECONOMICS OF OIL TANKERS (1966)

The oil tanker purchase decision is dominated by two major considerations. The first is that most of the major costs associated with owning and operating a tanker are costs that will be incurred whether or not the tanker is used at full capacity throughout the year; these costs consist primarily of the interest and depreciation costs associated with the capital outlay for the tanker itself, maintenance, overhead and insurance. The second is that these fixed costs do not increase proportionally with the capacity of the tanker. The economies of scale associated with using a single large tanker instead of two small ones will therefore heavily influence any purchase decision.

BACKGROUND

The first ship specifically constructed to transport oil was built in Germany in 1886 to carry oil up and down the Rhine River. Its capacity was

20,000 barrels, slightly less than 3,000 deadweight tons (the term "dead-weight ton" refers to a ship's total carrying capacity, including cargo, fuel, crews, stores and ballast; a deadweight ton of capacity translates into roughly 7.3 barrels of cargo crude). By 1940, tankers having a capacity of 15,000 dwt. were common. The workhorse of the Allied fleet during World War II was the so-called "T-2," which had a capacity of 16,600 dwt. The largest tankers in operation by the end of 1966 were about 150,000 dwt.; however, several 250,000 dwt. tankers were under construction at that time (a 250,000 dwt. tanker is about 1,200 feet long—the height of the Empire State Building—and has a beam of 170 feet and a draft of 65 feet; it will carry almost 2 million barrels of crude).

The appropriate measure of a tanker's "capacity" is not its tonnage but its *annual* capacity, which requires knowledge of its speed, utilization rate (operating days per year), and loading/unloading rate as well. By industry convention, these annual capacities are translated into "T-2 equivalents": the number of T-2s (half of whom were still in operation in 1966) that would be required in order to provide the same amount of annual capacity. Exhibit A-1 provides simplified examples of this calculation of T-2 equivalents, and estimates of the number of T-2s required to haul 10,000 barrels

Exhibit A-1
THE ECONOMICS OF OIL TANKERS (1966)
(definition of T-2 equivalent)

1. *Standard T-2*
   Rated at 16,600 DWT.
   Travels at 14.6 knots (nautical miles per hour).
   Utilization rate 95 percent (348 days per year).
   Four days to load and unload cargo.
2. *Examples* (assume same route, utilization, and loading/unloading time).
   a. 48,000 DWT tanker capable of 17.5 knots

   $$\frac{48,000 \times 17.5}{16,600 \times 14.6} = 3.5 \text{ T-2 equivalents}$$

   b. 170,000 DWT tanker capable of 17 knots

   $$\frac{170,000 \times 17.0}{16,600 \times 14.6} = 11.9 \text{ T-2 equivalents}$$

3. *T-2 Tanker Equivalents to Haul 10,000 Barrels per Day* *
   (Based on 35° API Crude Oil)

From	To	T-2's
Arabian Gulf.	Japan	3.7
Arabian Gulf.	Rotterdam (Suez Canal)	3.6
Arabian Gulf.	Rotterdam (Cape/Cape)	5.7
Arabian Gulf.	Sicily (Suez Canal)	2.5
Sidon (Lebanon)	Rotterdam	2.2
Sidon	Sicily	0.9
Libya	Rotterdam	1.8
Nigeria	Rotterdam	2.8
Venezuela	Rotterdam	2.7

* Takes into account time spent in port.

per day from various representative sources to various representative destinations. Exhibit A–2 describes the changing composition of the world tanker fleet between 1954 and 1964.

Exhibit A–2
FREE FOREIGN TANKER FLEET
(10,000 dwt. and over)

Capacity (dwt.)	*Percent of Total Fleet (year-end)*		
	1954	*1959*	*1964*
10,000–25,000	81.7	59.9	34.8
25,000–35,000	14.4	31.6	29.4
35,000–45,000	3.9	5.5	11.7
45,000–75,000	0	3.0	19.7
75,000 and over.	0	0	4.4
Number of ships.	1,855	2,439	2,532
T–2 equivalents	1,780	2,966	4,394

ON ORDER OR UNDER CONSTRUCTION: JANUARY 1, 1967*

Capacity (dwt.)	*Percent of Total dwt.*	No. of Tankers
Under 50,000	6.2	50
50,000–100,000.	42.0	180
100,000–150,000.	12.8	33
150,000–200,000.	19.0	35
200,000–250,000.	14.3	20
Over 250,000	6.6	5

Total deadweight ton on order or under construction = 32,038,000.

* Approximations based on best estimates available; excludes military tankers.

ECONOMICS OF CONSTRUCTION

The basic law relating tanker size to cost is an outgrowth of simple geometry. Thinking of the tanker as a large cylinder, its capacity will be roughly proportional to the cylinder's volume:

$$\text{Volume} = (\tfrac{1}{4}\ \text{pi}) \times (\text{diameter})^2 \times (\text{length})$$

whereas its cost will be roughly proportional to the cylinder's surface area:

$$\text{Area} = (\text{pi}) \times (\text{diameter}) \times (\text{length})$$

Actually, a conventionally designed tanker is shaped more like a cylinder sliced down the middle, with its length about 7 times its beam (width), and its draft (depth) about two-fifths of its beam. But the basic relationship between its area (roughly proportional to the square of its beam) and its volume (roughly proportional to the cube of its beam) remains the same. Hence, a tanker that has twice the capacity of another will be about 26 percent longer, deeper and wider. Its surface area (and cost) will therefore be about 60 percent greater. Alternatively, a tanker that costs twice as much as another will have about 2.8 times as much capacity. Exhibit A-3 provides rough estimates of the cost of various sized tankers

Exhibit A-3
COST OF NEW TANKERS IN 1966

Capacity	Volume Ratio	Beam Ratio	Cost Ratio	Cost* ($ millions)
50.	1.0	1.0	1.0	$ 5.9
100.	2.0	1.26	1.58	$ 9.3
150.	3.0	1.44	2.08	$12.2
200.	4.0	1.59	2.56	$15.0
250.	5.0	1.71	2.92	$17.1
300.	6.0	1.82	3.30	$19.4
400.	8.0	2.0	4.0	$23.5

* Rough estimate based on formula.

in 1966; actual costs were affected by a number of factors, including the order backlog at the shipyard, the number of ships ordered, special equipment or design characteristics, etc.

In 1965 the cost of a new 200,000 ton tanker was about $15 million. In order to meet its depreciation charges (straightline depreciation over 20 years, typically) as well as earn 10 percent on average investment, therefore, a 200,000 ton tanker should return over $1.5 million every year to its owners after all expenses. Such a tanker, equivalent to about 13 T–2s, would be able to transport about 8 million barrels of oil a year between the Persian Gulf and Western Europe, around the Cape. Hence, the capital cost of the tanker amounted to almost $0.19 per barrel shipped (every 1 percent change in the expected return on investment would change this value by $0.01).

ANNUAL OPERATING COSTS

Representative estimates of the annual direct operating expenses associated with 100,000 and 200,000 dwt. tankers travelling between the Persian Gulf and Western Europe are given in Table A-1 and explained below. The operating costs associated with tankers of different sizes (between 60,000 dwt. and 250,000 dwt.) can be estimated by a straightline interpolation from these figures.

Crew costs are based on the assumption that a 100,000 dwt. tanker will have a crew of between 30 and 35 men (usually Greek, Spanish or Chinese), while a 200,000 dwt. tanker will be crewed by 35–40 men. Wage

Table A–1
DIRECT OPERATING COSTS
(in $000s)

Item	100,000 dwt.	200,000 dwt.
Crew	$ 220	$ 260
Repairs and maintenance.	150	180
Bunkers (fuel).	440	600
Port charges	100	200
Insurance.	120	210
Overhead.	30	40
Totals	$1,060	$1,490
	($0.27 per barrel)	($0.19 per barrel)

rates are expected to increase over the years, but much of this increase is likely to be offset by increased automation.

Repairs and maintenance includes a sinking fund to cover the "special survey" required every five or six years. This cost will probably increase in accordance with the overall rate of inflation. A short-term shortage of repair facilities for tankers over 200,000 dwt. will probably appear in the late 1960s as the number of such ships outstrips the available facilities.

Bunker costs are based on the assumptions that fuel will cost about $11.00 per ton ($1.70 per barrel) and that a 100,000 dwt. tanker consumes about 110 long tons of fuel per day at sea, against 140 tons for a 200,000 dwt. tanker (this assumes normal cruising speed; a change of 10 percent in speed will change fuel consumption by 33 percent). Fuel is generally obtained from the parent company rather than on the open market; hence, the assumed cost of $1.70 per barrel is based on standard cost estimates rather than on world prices. Both costs and prices are expected to increase over time.

Port charges are generally in the range of $0.08—$0.15 per dwt. per visit, and are rising steadily, partly in response to the demand for deeper channels and better navigational aids.

Insurance is the most uncertain of the estimated costs in Table A–1. Insurance cost is obtained by multiplying two factors: an insurance rate, which is based on an estimate of the probability of a catastrophic hull failure during the year (and, to some extent, the cost of the potential external damage occasioned by such a failure), and the estimated cost of replacing the tanker. The costs in Table A–1 assume that the insurance cost for the 100,000 dwt. tanker is 1.1 percent times its replacement cost, while that for the 200,000 dwt. tanker is 1.4 percent times its replacement cost (the higher rate reflecting the fact that the latter carries twice as much cargo).

The uncertainty surrounding the insurance rate arises from the fact that as of 1966 there had been almost no experience with tankers as large as 200,000 dwt. The incidence of catastrophic failures was therefore esti-

Exhibit A–4

TANKER SINGLE VOYAGE RATES 1956–65

(percent above or below London scale*)

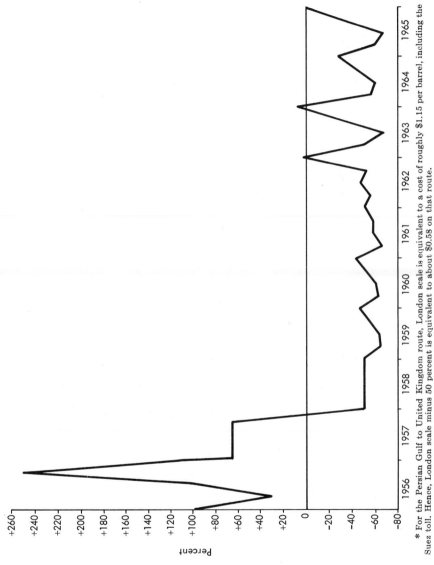

* For the Persian Gulf to United Kingdom route, London scale is equivalent to a cost of roughly $1.15 per barrel, including the Suez toll. Hence, London scale minus 50 percent is equivalent to about $0.58 on that route.

mated to be the same as that for smaller tankers. (The 1.1 percent rate implies that about 1 tanker in every hundred can be expected to be lost in a given year.) The cost of repairing the damage occasioned by an oil spill is also assumed to be proportional to the amount of oil spilled, but some analysts suggest that these costs will go up more than proportionally—that the problems of dealing with an oil spill of 2 million barrels, say, will be considerably more than twice as complex and costly as the problems associated with a 1 million barrel spill.

Finally, the replacement cost of a tanker depends on the extent to which tanker prices rise over the next decade. The insurance costs given in Table A–1 are based on the assumption that this increase will be relatively modest, in accordance with normal inflationary pressures. Increasing automation in the shipyards is also expected to help keep costs down. The shipyard cost per dwt. (currently about $75 per dwt. for a 250,000 dwt. tanker) has been decreasing over the past few years, in fact.

If, as some predict, tanker prices increase rapidly, oil spills are found to be considerably more costly to deal with than expected, and large tankers turn out to have different accident rates than small tankers, then actual insurance costs could easily be double or triple the values given in Table A–1.

COST OF LEASING TANKERS

As an alternative to tanker ownership, many oil companies choose to lease a major portion of their tanker capacity. This can be done in a variety of ways, with the length of the lease being the most critical factor. Long-term leases run for 10 years or more, the most common term being the expected depreciation life of the vessel which is typically 20 years. Such leases offer the closest equivalent to actually owning the tanker, and the lease costs closely reflect the construction and operating costs discussed in this note. Short-term leases, on the other hand, generally run a year or less, or are limited to a single voyage. Their price is based on the current supply-demand relationship and fluctuates widely, almost independent of long-term costs. The recent history of the "spot rate" for tankers is depicted in Exhibit A–4. Medium term leases generally run from 3–5 years, and their price represents a compromise between long-term cost and the short-term supply-demand situation. Hence, these rates tend to fluctuate less rapidly than the spot rate and more rapidly than the cost of long-term charters.

Braniff International

IN EARLY 1969, Harding Lawrence, chief executive officer and chairman of the board of Braniff International Airways (BI), in a meeting with his corporate staff stated:

> There is no question that the wide-body look is the airline look of the 70s. Every trunk airline will have to determine its own approach to securing the wide-body look while maintaining and improving service to every city it serves, primarily in terms of frequent and convenient flight schedules.

BI had recently finished an examination of its equipment strategy in the Latin American Division, and was now considering the strategy to be used for domestic operations during the next several years. The company planned to purchase an average of 1,400 seats of aircraft capacity each year for the next six years.

Since coming to Braniff, Mr. Lawrence had stressed the policy of aircraft "communality." That is, the minimization of the number of types of aircraft operated to promote increased economies in maintenance, crew training, and space-parts inventories. At present, BI operated a number of aircraft types, but it had been suggested that the company might take the opportunity of the recent introduction of wide-bodied aircraft[1] to take steps toward creating a more uniform fleet for domestic operations.

The questions being asked by Lawrence of his corporate staff were:

a. Are wide-bodies inherently more economic than our present aircraft types?

b. Can they be deployed on our domestic route structure profitably?

c. How will they affect our competitive situation in terms of market share and frequency of service?

---

[1] Wide-bodied aircraft include the Douglas DC–10 and Lockheed L–1011 trijets and the Boeing B–747.

COMPANY BACKGROUND

BI was one of 11 major U.S. domestic trunkline carriers[2] providing passenger and cargo services to points throughout the continental United States. BI also served Hawaii, Mexico and South America, operating from gateways on the East, Gulf and West Coast.

The airline, founded in 1928 by T. E. Braniff, had grown to a route structure of 30,000 miles in the United States and Latin America, and was carrying over 6 million passengers annually in 1968.

BI grew through internal development, but major portions of the expansion occurred in 1952 with the merger with Mid-Continental Airlines incorporating 6,241 additional route miles from the Dakotas to Louisiana, and in 1967, with the purchase of Pan American Grace Airways and its routes throughout Latin America (see Exhibit 1).

Exhibit 1
DOMESTIC ROUTE STRUCTURE

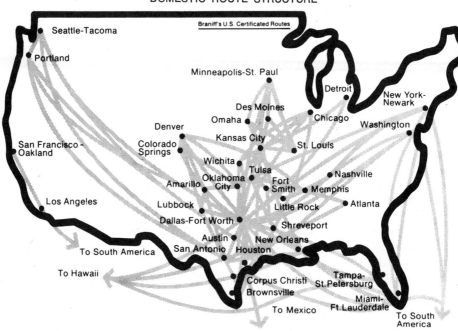

Braniff had a reputation for innovation in the industry, particularly under Harding Lawrence, who took over direction of the airline in 1965. For example, in 1967, Braniff was the first airline to retire its piston-engine aircraft. This left the Lockheed Electra as the only remaining non-

---

[2] The U.S. trunkline industry in 1969 included American, Braniff, Continental, Delta, Eastern, National, Northwest-Orient, Trans-World, Western, United, and Northeast Airlines.

Exhibit 2
COMPARATIVE FLEET MIX AND BRANIFF DOMESTIC CAPACITY 1968

Aircraft Type	Industry Fleet Mix (percent)	Braniff Fleet Mix (percent)	Braniff Fleet Mix (Number of Aircraft)	Domestic Operations		
				Braniff ASM$^\triangle$ Production per Aircraft Type$^\triangle$ (000,000)	Braniff ASM$^\triangle$ Production per Unit— Aircraft Type$^\triangle$ (000,000)	Braniff Average Domestic Stage Length per Type
Electra 188	1.4	11.4	8	595	74.4	210
BAC-111.	1.6	18.6	13	757	58.0	236
B-707	17.4	18.6	13*	752	188.0	661
B-720	11.8	7.1	5	820	164.0	441
B-727	33.8	34.3	24†	2,972	124.0	479
B-737	1.8	–	–	–	–	–
CV-880	3.9	–	–	–	–	–
CV-990	0.1	–	–	–	–	–
DC-8	15.7	10.0	7‡	–	–	–
DC-9	9.2	–	–	–	–	–
Caravelle	0.5	–	–	–	–	–
Fairchild 227	0.1	–	–	–	–	–
Viscount 700	0.2	–	–	–	–	–
Total.	100.	100.	70	5,896	N/A	364.3

* Two flown in Latin American Division, seven flown under Military Air Command Operations.
† All B-727-100s, the annual ASM capacity of the B-727-200 is estimated at 160 million ASMs per year.
‡ All used in Lating American Division Operations.
$^\triangle$ ASM = Available seat miles.

jet aircraft type in service (see Exhibit 2). BI was the first airline to utilize jet assist take-off systems at high altitude airports, and was a pioneer in airborne weather radar. On August 1, 1966 Braniff inaugurated the world's first Boeing B-727 "Quick Change" convertible tri-jet. The B-727 QC could be converted from a "passenger" to an all-cargo or combination passenger/cargo configuration in 30 minutes. This greatly improved aircraft utilization, allowing use of the plane to transport passengers by day and cargo by night. Other innovations included the substitution of Pucci fashions for more conventional hostess uniforms and brightly-colored aircraft rather than the conservative "plain planes."

BI was considered to be a financially healthy member of the airline industry with an above average return on investment during a period of substantial growth. See Exhibit 3 for 1964 to 1968 financial statements and Exhibit 4 for BI operating performance over the same period.

THE AIRLINE INDUSTRY

The U.S. domestic trunk airline group carried approximately 72 percent of all revenue passenger miles flown in the United States during 1968.

Exhibit 3

BRANIFF INTERNATIONAL
Financial Statements—1964 to 1968
(dollar figures in thousands)

Profit and Loss Statement	1968	1967	1966	1965	1964
Operating Revenues					
Passenger	$211,208	$188,487	$156,771	$114,730	$ 96,857
Military contract services	48,207	38,851	14,041	–	–
Express and freight	17,998	16,707	9,973	8,297	7,090
Mail	8,548	6,661	4,492	3,563	2,942
Other	6,688	5,671	2,550	2,675	2,808
	$292,649	$256,377	$187,827	$129,265	$109,697
Operating Expenses					
Flying and ground operations	$155,603	$133,751	$ 89,175	$ 63,124	$ 55,325
Maintenance	41,855	39,459	28,502	21,760	18,377
Sales and advertising	32,157	30,759	23,383	15,545	12,022
Depreciation and amortization, less amounts charged to other accounts	24,992	26,393	15,079	10,014	8,376
General and administrative	12,673	11,553	7,265	5,059	4,300
	$267,280	$241,915	$163,404	$115,502	$ 98,400
Operating income	$ 25,369	$ 14,462	$ 24,423	$ 13,763	$ 11,297
Nonoperating expenses—net	11,971	9,711	3,538	718	938
Income (loss) before provision for income taxes	$ 13,398	$ 4,751	$ 20,885	$ 13,045	$ 10,359
Provision (Credits) for Income Taxes					
Federal					
Current—before investment tax credit	$ 7,317	$ 1,245	$ 4,816	$ 5,424	$ 4,182
Current—investment tax credit	(3,697)	–	(207)	(1,470)	(731)
Deferred	(806)	–	2,305	–	876
Other	168	–	217	148	61
	$ 2,982	$ 1,245	$ 7,131	$ 4,102	$ 4,388
Income (loss) before extraordinary items	$ 10,416	$ 3,506	$ 13,754	$ 8,943	$ 5,971
Extraordinary items	–	1,245	4,062	505	–
Net income (loss)	$ 10,416	$ 4,751	$ 17,816	$ 9,448	$ 5,971
Selected Balance Sheet Items					
Cash dividends paid	$ 1,155	$ 1,474	$ 1,474	$ 295	$ 295
Stock dividends paid	5,441	–	–	–	–
Current assets	$ 78,292	$ 68,658	$ 60,441	$ 29,406	$ 24,131
Current liabilities	56,594	86,411	20,972	13,971	13,164
Net working capital	$ 21,698	$ (17,753)	$ 39,469	$ 15,435	$ 10,967
Property and equipment—net	$270,724	$287,655	$190,844	$ 95,795	$ 65,072
Total assets	372,526	378,082	309,678	130,336	98,806
Long-term debt	213,927	199,000	204,753	51,105	29,600
Shareholders' equity					
Special stock, Class A	$ 7,428	$ –	$ –	$ –	$ –
Common stock	1,561	7,370	7,370	7,370	7,370
Capital surplus	22,208	18,355	18,355	18,355	18,355
Retained earnings	52,607	48,787	45,494	29,151	19,997
Total shareholders' equity	$ 83,804	$ 74,512	$ 71,219	$ 54,876	$ 45,722

Exhibit 4
OPERATING PERFORMANCE, 1964–1968

	1968	*1967*	*1966*	*1965*	*1964*
Revenue Passenger Miles (000)					
Mainland.............	2,846,595	2,499,004	2,236,434	1,580,988	1,342,394
Hawaii	–	–	–	–	–
Mexico..............	121,075	95,163	91,874	44,282	36,461
South America	633,223	562,916	249,705	179,092	136,732
Total scheduled........	3,600,893	3,157,083	2,578,013	1,804,362	1,515,587
Charter.............	1,996,954	1,608,628	481,561	14,339	28,338
Total	5,597,847	4,765,711	3,059,574	1,818,701	1,543,925
Available Seat Miles (000)					
Mainland.............	5,325,356	4,878,538	3,835,376	2,891,069	2,455,523
Hawaii	–	–	–	–	–
Mexico..............	240,407	193,979	184,466	68,041	58,412
South America	1,474,634	1,147,201	575,745	385,181	328,048
Total scheduled........	7,040,397	6,219,718	4,595,587	3,344,291	2,841,983
Charter.............	2,269,668	1,773,510	·554,485	20,176	40,331
Total	9,310,065	7,993,228	5,150,072	3,364,467	2,882,314
Revenue Passengers Carried (000)					
Scheduled	5,749	5,283	4,585	3,372	2,854
Charter.............	386	312	105	13	22
Total	6,135	5,595	4,690	3,385	2,876
System Scheduled Passenger **Load Factor (Percent) .....**	51.1	50.8	56.1	54.0	53.3
Breakeven Passenger Load **Factor on before Tax** **Expense (Percent) ....**	47.6	49.2	48.5	47.5	47.6
Revenue Plane Miles (000)					
Scheduled	71,908	67,862	53,331	40,303	35,847
Charter.............	17,233	13,428	4,846	280	568
Total	89,141	81,290	58,177	40,583	36,415
Revenue Block Hours Flown ..	242,329	231,822	191,628	154,903	146,558
Average Segment Length in **Scheduled Service (Miles) ...**	409	376	317	289	282

Since 1938, which is considered by many to be the beginning of the trunk-line portion of the industry, several trends were discernable. There had been a trend toward concentration through mergers with a general lengthening of route structures and increased number of cities served. Also, there had been increased levels of competition as the overlapping routes and points had intensified.

To maintain productive competition, the Civil Aeronautics Board (CAB) had been created by the Federal Government to regulate the industry to foster its development. The CAB had final approval on fares, routes, mergers, and some aspects of the level of the service. The CAB had set a target of 10.5 percent as a reasonable return on investment (ROI). This ROI was based on a seat load factor (ratio of revenue passenger miles to available seat miles) of 55 percent. In fact, the industry had achieved the target ROI in only two of the ten years prior to 1968. This below-target performance of the industry was due to intense competition between the airlines and the tendency of airline managers to provide excess capacity to gain market share. While the CAB was concerned with this, in a public statement, the board recognized that:

> Schedules constitute the major competitive device of carriers in their efforts to preserve and enhance their participation in the traffic markets which they serve. In any given market, the carrier with the greatest number of schedules will normally carry the largest number of passengers. Thus, the desire to maximize market participation creates powerful incentives to add capacity. The contravailing incentive is supplied only by the imperative of economics: schedules cannot be added indefinitely if the load factor achieved is insufficient, at the prevailing fare levels, to permit the carriers to cover costs and return a profit.

AIRLINE ECONOMICS

The airlines used "available seat mile" (ASM), one passenger seat flown one mile, rather than a "passenger mile" flown, as the unit of production since air carriers *costs* were directly related to the number of *seats* rather than the number of *passengers* flown over a given distance. Once an airplane was scheduled on a particular flight, the total cost of that flight varied only slightly with the number of passengers that the plane was carrying. This characteristic of individual flight operation gave rise to the industry view of itself as having an extremely high percentage of fixed costs.[3]

An industry rule of thumb stated that the variable cost of adding an extra passenger to a flight amounted to only 10 percent of the fare paid by that passenger and that the remaining 90 percent passed directly through as a contribution to operating profit. The cost per unit of production was influenced by a variety of factors, including aircraft type and average length of flights. Given this cost per available seat mile, however, an airline's total operating costs were easily found by multiplying total ASMs by cost per ASM and adding to this "fixed" or ASM-related cost the "variable" cost of 10 percent passenger fares.

Airline costs were, perhaps, less fixed than the industry believed, except in the very short run. Over time spans of a year or more, the industry's

---

[3] For more detail, refer to "Note: U.S. Air Transport Industry," Harvard Business School Case 9-269-017/EA-F-326.

growth rate and inflation tended in effect to make other "fixed" ASM-related costs, such as depreciation and salaries, variable.

While costs were tied most closely to available seat miles, the revenue generated on a flight was directly related to (1) the number of passengers carried, (2) how far they were flown, and (3) how much these passengers paid per mile of flight. The product of the first two factors was revenue passenger miles (RPMs). The third term was commonly called yield per RPM.

Given the high proportion of costs that were fixed, profits were very sensitive to the load factor experienced by an airline.

LOAD FACTORS AND THE EQUIPMENT CYCLE

Since profitability was so sensitive to the load factor, it would seem that the industry would be very concerned with maintaining profitable load factor levels through a policy of restraint in adding capacity.

With the great advances in technology and improved economic performance of aircraft in the 1960s, the airlines undertook massive re-equipment programs. Pressure to keep up with other airlines had resulted in the entire industry going through cycles of buying more capacity than the growth of the market justified.

ROUTE STRUCTURE

Due to the large percentage of fixed costs of a flight associated with take-off and landing operations, the average cost per ASM of longer flights was substanially lower. It was generally believed that the rate structure did not reflect this variation of costs with length of flight, and longer flights were thought to subsidize shorter flights.

ROUTE DENSITY

Another factor in profitability is route density. That is the actual "head count" number of passengers flying between any given city-pair. Over a "monopoly route" this would directly affect the actual load factor for the carrier serving the route. That is, depending on the number of frequencies flown by that airline and the capacity of the aircraft type utilized. Here, the CAB was most vigorous in awarding competitive service in monopoly markets where one carrier had over 80 percent of the traffic. This was most probably due to the fact that the "monopolist" would not be under pressure to expand capacity as traffic grew, i.e., accruing the benefits of high seat load factors. But since seasonal, monthly, weekly and even daily peaks were experienced in air travel, the "public convenience and necessity" demanded moderate average load factors testifying to the carriers' ability to accommodate these peaks in demand.

THE "S" CURVE

The close correlation between an airline's share of passengers flown over a route and the number of seats which the airline flew over the route had long been recognized by the industry. Characteristically, however, on a competitive route served by two carriers, the dominant carrier in terms of seats flown would attract slightly more than its proportionate share of passengers over that route. This relationship may be graphically represented as an S-shaped curve (Exhibit 5). The effect of this curve on in-

Exhibit 5
MARKET SHARE VERSUS ASM SHARE ON A TWO
CARRIER ROUTE

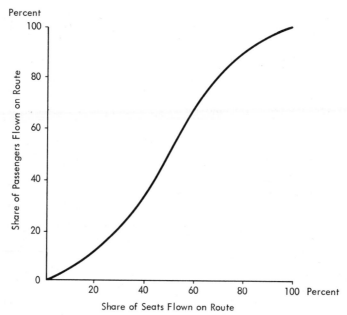

dustry thinking had been so pervasive that it had become known as *the* S-curve and had been the basis for airline capacity decisions.

Historically, there had been a marked tendency for competing airlines to fly similar aircraft over the same routes. This was due to the fact that all carriers were facing similar economics, and that the analyses carried out by planners for different airlines lead them to select similar aircraft. One form of competition over these routes had taken the form of addition of more frequent flights, increasing the share of seats flown, and, following the S-curve, the share of passengers flown. This form of competition, with similar competitive responses, was thought to have contributed materially to dramatic overcapacity situations on many routes.

AIRCRAFT TYPE AND PROFITABILITY

A prominant industry trend had been toward faster and larger aircraft. For example, the average terminal-to-terminal speed in domestic service increased from 314 MPH in 1962 to 413 MPH in 1968. Each aircraft type had its own particular optimization in terms of cost per ASM over a specific range limitation. Generally speaking, total cost per ASM included fixed and variable elements, and decreased on a per unit basis as distance increased. The terminology used in the industry to describe these inherent aircraft costs/ASM were couched in terms of "assignability." This was a delicate transition, since Direct Operating Cost (DOC) should not be confused with "variable costs" because they are not all variable with the amount of ASMs flown. For example, some vary with flight hours, others per departure, and some are arbitrarily assigned, e.g., overhead was estimated to be 40 percent of DOC. Similarly, indirect operating costs (IOC) were not considered "fixed" since the industry's estimate of them was simply 100 percent of the DOC.

In early 1969, the advent of the "era of wide-bodies" was imminent. The Boeing B–747 was to be available by the end of 1969. McDonnell-Douglas and Lockheed were taking orders for the DC–10 and L–1101 to be introduced in 1970 and 1971 respectively. Taken as a group, wide-bodies were expected to have decided economic advantages over presently in-service aircraft types. They were designed to have longer flight ranges with direct operating costs 20 percent below the B–727–200 and 14 percent below DC–8, assuming comparable load factors. They offered unsurpassed luxury, comfort, and passenger appeal with such extras as lounges, piano bars, and increased leg room (pitch between seats). In fact, it was strongly suspected that their introduction into commercial use would stimulate demand by as much as 30 percent in some city-pair markets.

The industry expected the B–747 to be used mainly over transcontinental and intercontinental routes where frequency of service played less of a role in capturing market share. The initial reaction to test flights brought many excited comments from pilots involved. One said "I thought they would never build a better airplane after having flown the 707—But they've done it with the 747!"

The DC–10 and L–1011 were commonly referred to as "airbuses" due to their favorable economics over quite short routes. These wide-body trijets combined the maneuverability and ease of operation of the 747 with the ability to fly in and out of small airports at a lower noise and smoke level than existing aircraft. Terminal expansion was being contemplated at many large airports to handle the increased concentration of passengers although flight congestion was expected to decline as the number of flights decreased.

American and United Airlines presently had over 50 DC–10s on order, and were expected to purchase at least 150 more in the next few years.

They were planning to utilize these aircraft on stage lengths primarily ranging from 1,000 to 1,800 miles.

Because of the resulting backorder situation at Douglas, other trunks were opting for priority delivery position in the essentially similar Lockheed L–1011. Delta and Eastern thought the L–1011 to be more suited to medium and short-range hauls. However L–1011 deliveries were still somewhat uncertain due to the tenuous financial position of Rolls-Royce, the maker of the aircraft's RB–211 jet engines.

The DC–10 and L–1011 compared to the Boeing B–727–200, the mainstay of the BI fleet, as follows:

	B-727-200	*L-1011/DC-10*
Investment (including spare parts)	$7,969,000	$17,503,000
Seats (low-density seating configuration)	125	300
Effective maximum economic range (miles)	1,700	2,800
Direct operating cost per takeoff and landing	$90	$300

ARGUMENTS FOR WIDE BODIES

An engineering-staff member suggested that the "airbus" glamour was an important consideration. Also, the wide bodies were not only likely to stimulate primary demand due to greater flying comfort, they also operated at lower cost per ASM (even on shorter routes) and therefore, they had greater profit potential. He admitted that they used more fuel, but fuel consumed per ASM was actually slightly lower than that experienced with smaller aircraft. "All in all, they are technologically a better aircraft."

This last point was agreed to by the BI pilots who had occasion to test fly the wide-body aircraft. They felt that for their size, they had as much maneuverability as any aircraft in the market, and they were very impressed by the consumer benefits of more space and comfort.

The scheduling and operations group noted that fewer aircraft would be needed to fill the ASM gap, and fewer operations would facilitate computerized scheduling. However, they felt that large aircraft would be less flexible to meet short-term fluctuations in specific city-pair markets. At the same time, these aircraft would help to reduce airport congestion.

Finally, it was mentioned that wide-body aircraft could best provide for BI's faster-than-industry growth. BI was experiencing growth in primary demand and market share in most of the markets it served. This would favor the operation of larger aircraft that were most profitable in dense route operations.

ARGUMENT AGAINST WIDE-BODIES

The marketing department was not entirely anti-wide-body. They were, however, against its application to the Braniff route structure at this point in time. Russ Thayer noted that "in terms of density and length of haul, Braniff cannot economically apply a wide-body." He pointed out that BI's most dense route was ranked 28th on the list of the most dense routes served by the domestic airline industry.

Also, Thayer continued, "In my opinion, people don't ask what aircraft

Exhibit 6
RETURN ON INVESTMENT (ROI) AS A FUNCTION OF
PASSENGERS CARRIED AND STAGE LENGTH
(figures in percent)

WIDE BODY TRI-JET*
Total Operating Cost = 200 Percent of Direct Operating Cost

Stage Length (miles)	Passengers				
	50	*75*	*125*	*200*	*300*
500	−31.7	−22.8	−4.9	21.7	57.3
1,000	−28.7	−16.8	6.9	42.5	89.9
1,500	−26.9	−13.6	13.1	53.1	106.5
2,000	−26.4	−12.3	17.7	62.7	122.6

WIDE BODY TRI-JET
Total Operating Cost = 150 Percent of Direct Operating Cost

Stage Length (miles)	Passengers				
	50	*75*	*125*	*200*	*300*
500	−19.3	−10.4	7.4	34.1	69.7
1,000	−15.6	−3.7	20.0	55.6	103.0
1,500	−13.4	−0.2	26.6	66.5	119.9
2,000	−13.0	2.0	32.0	77.0	136.9

BOEING-727-200†
Total Operating Cost = 200 Percent of Direct Operating Cost

Stage Length (miles)	Passengers				
	50	*75*	*125*	*200‡*	*300‡*
500	−19.8	6.9	45.6	26.2	26.2
1,000	1.1	24.7	76.2	50.5	50.5
1,500	4.8	33.8	91.8	62.8	62.8

Assumptions: · Revenue = $0.06 per passenger mile.
· Utilization = 3,285 block hours per year.
· Block Speed is approximately equal for 727's and wide bodies and:
  500 mile stage length consumes 1.6 block hours
  1,000 mile stage length consumes 2.4 block hours
  1,500 mile stage length consumes 3.2 block hours
  2,000 mile stage length consumes 3.8 block hours.
* Douglas DC-10 and Lockheed L-1011.
† Maximum range of the 727-200 is 1,700 miles. 125 passenger seating configuration.
‡ Multiple flights.
Source: Case writer's estimate based on engineering data.

you're flying. When they call reservations, they ask for departure times. A transportation company serves the consumer by proper scheduling. That's what I've stressed in my advertising program."

Jack Regan, vice president of marketing planning, favored the greater flexibility of scheduling the smaller-capacity B–727–200.

A NEED FOR HARD NUMBERS

Harding Lawrence felt that the Dallas-Chicago market typified the BI situation. Demand over this 811 mile route amounted to approximately 350,000 passengers per year (one way) of which BI carried 144,000. Mr. Lawrence expected demand in this market to grow by about 20 to 30 percent per year over the coming five years. BI and American Airlines each provided roughly half of the ASMs in this market. On weekdays, when the bulk of this demand occurred, BI served this route with five flights in each direction while American operated eight flights in each direction.

Mr. Lawrence believed that it would be possible to finance the necessary investment in new equipment. His staff was asked to calculate the approximate return on investment that might be expected for the B–727–200 and DC–10 or L–1011 for a variety of passenger levels and stage lengths. The conventional practice in the industry was to estimate total cost as 200 percent of the direct operating costs (which include crew, fuel maintenance, depreciation and insurance).

There was some argument that this rule of thumb had been developed

Exhibit 7

ANALYSIS OF MARKETS—65 TOP BI CITY-PAIR MARKETS

City-Pairs with BI 1969 Estimated Market Share <50%

Stage Length (miles)	Average Number Passengers Carried By BI per Day				
	0–100	*101–200*	*201–400*	*401–800*	*>800*
<750	7	4	1	0	0
750–1,249	3	0	2	0	0
1,250–1,750	1	0	1	0	0
>1,750	0	0	0	0	0

City-Pairs with BI 1969 Estimated Market Share >50%

Stage Length (miles)	Average Number Passengers Carried By BI per Day				
	0–100	*101–200*	*201–400*	*401–800*	*>800*
<750	14	17	4	1	1
750–1,249	2	2	2	0	0
1,250–1,750	0	1	1	1	0
>1,750	0	0	1*	0	0

* Dallas–Honolulu.

based on smaller aircraft. Since a significant portion of the indirect costs were related to the number of flights rather than passengers, it might be more appropriate to estimate total costs for wide-bodied aircraft as 150 percent of estimated direct costs. A return on investment calculation based on average fare yield of 6 cents per revenue passenger mile is summarized in Exhibit 6. Exhibit 7 summarizes the city-pair markets being served by BI in 1969.

Distrigas Corporation[1]

In February 1970, Jacek Makowski, the President of the newly-formed Distrigas Corporation, was developing plans to initiate operations as an importer and distributor of Algerian liquefied natural gas (LNG) to Boston, Massachusetts. The imported LNG would be sold to the fast-growing natural-gas distribution utilities in Eastern Massachusetts for peak shaving[2] during the high-demand winter months to supplement natural gas available from domestic pipeline sources serving the area.

The proposed service was scheduled to begin in the winter of 1971–1972. To be prepared for the arrival of the first shiploads of LNG, Distrigas was faced with making several important distribution system decisions within the month. The most pressing concern was the award of the construction contract for the deep-water terminal and the associated tank farm to receive LNG by tank ship at Boston. Construction of this facility would require approximately 22 months.

PEAK SHAVING

The Eastern Massachusetts gas utilities had recently experienced a bitter-sweet problem of unprecedented growth, as summarized by the annual gas "sendout rates" (the amount of gas released to customers) shown in Exhibit 1. This had been the combined result of increasing fuel-oil costs,

---

[1] Selected names and data have been disguised in this case. While all of the material included in the case is based on fact, it has in some cases been liberally interpreted.

[2] Peak shaving is the process of accommodating the extreme demand for fuel, i.e., natural gas, experienced during the winter months. In the past, peak shaving had been performed with a limited degree of success by making use of standby sources of energy such as liquefied petroleum gas (propane). The propane was mixed with air before being delivered to consumers, to provide heating capacities similar to the lower heating capacity of natural gas. This practice, while it had always been expensive, had become increasingly undesirable because of the recent development of alternate markets for propane as feed stock in the chemical industry (detergents, resins, synthetic rubber, and plasticisers). These uses had increased the price of propane to the point where it was no longer practical to be used as make-up gas except in extreme emergencies.

388

compared to declining costs of natural gas service, and the aggressive efforts by the utilities to convert consumers to gas heating.

Exhibit 1
RECENT ANNUAL SEND OUT OF EASTERN MASSACHUSETTS
GAS UTILITIES

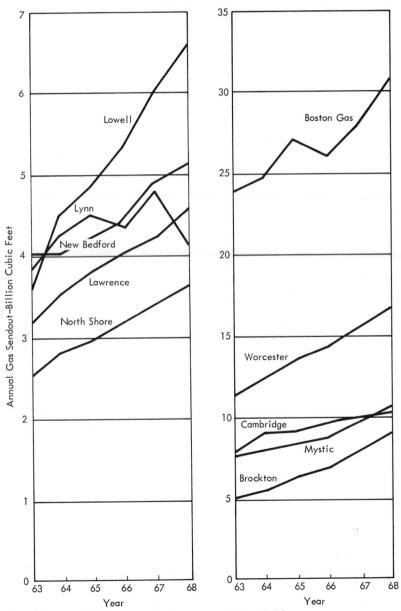

Source: Records of the Massachusetts Department of Public Utilities.

The success of the utilities' programs had resulted in further amplification of the existing seasonal unbalance in gas demand, aggravating the problem of inadequate pipeline capacity to serve the area. Seasonal patterns of sendout rates for Boston Gas, the major distribution utility in Eastern Massachusetts, are shown in Exhibit 2.

Exhibit 2
MONTHLY AND MAXIMUM DAILY (DURING MONTH) GAS SEND OUT
BOSTON GAS—1968

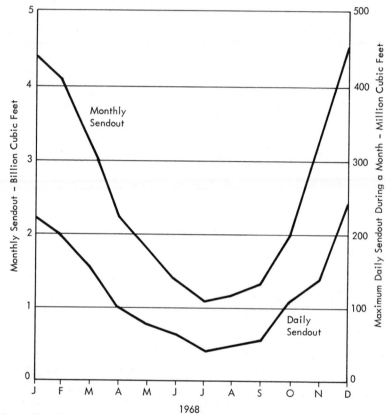

Source: Records of the Massachusetts Department of Public Utilities.

The gas transmission (pipeline) companies that supplied the local distribution utilities (such as Boston Gas) in the region had attempted to establish a rate structure that reflected the cost they experienced in attempting to service peak demands. Specifically, they had developed a two-part rate schedule which included: (1) a "commodity charge" of .3359 per Mcf[3] and (2) a monthly service or "demand" charge. This latter charge was

---

[3] Throughout the case, Mcf = 1,000 cubic feet, with the heating content of 1,000 BTU per cubic foot at standard pressure and temperature. Similarly, MMcf = 1 million cubic feet and Bcf = 1 billion cubic feet.

based on the demand on the maximum-take day in the preceding 12 month period and was equal to \$4.63 per Mcf times the total take during the maximum-take day. Although the monthly demand charge was the result of peak usage on certain days of the month, the utilities converted this cost to an average cost per Mcf as shown in Exhibit 3.

Exhibit 3
CALCULATION OF AVERAGE UNIT COST

The average unit cost per Mcf for a particular month could be calculated as follows:

$$\text{Average cost per Mcf} = \$0.3359 + \frac{(\$4.63 \text{ per month})(\text{demand during maximum-take day})}{(30 \text{ days per month})(\text{daily average demand})}$$

This formula had been standardized in the industry to:

$$\text{Average cost per Mcf} = \$0.3359 \text{ per Mcf} + \frac{\$4.63 \text{ per month per Mcf per day}}{(30 \text{ days per month})(\text{daily average usage as percent of maximum-take day})}$$

For example, if a particular utility had a maximum usage on February 6 of 200 MMcf and an average daily usage 110 MMcf., the average cost per Mcf would be:

$$\text{Average cost per Mcf} = \$0.3359 + \frac{\$4.64}{(30 \text{ days per month})(55\%)}$$

$$= \$0.6169$$

where

$$55\% = \frac{110 \text{ MMcf (average daily usage)}}{200 \text{ MMcf (usage during maximum-take day)}}$$

If the utility made a planning error and took gas from the pipeline to meet a severe peak in a particular day, it would carry that penalty for the next 12 months. Thus taking just an extra Mcf of gas on one cold day might cost the utility \$55.56 (12 × \$4.63). However, it was, of course, considered that such a penalty was modest compared to the onerous situation that might occur if the utility were unable to meet the demand of its consumers on a cold day. Besides the wrath of public opinion, there were serious safety implications (extinguishing of pilot lights, etc.) if line-pack pressure were to drop belof a safe level.

Until the late 1950s, problems of gas storage had restricted the utilization of the off-season pipeline capacity. Natural gas which was 80 to 100 percent methane, unlike propane could not be liquefied at atmospheric (i.e., ambient) temperatures by simple pressurization to achieve the volumetric reduction resulting from the conversion of the product from a gaseous to liquid state. However, in the late 1950s, advances in the field of cryogenics (the science of ultra-low temperatures) resulted in the development of practical and economical processes to liquefy natural gas at its normal boiling point at atmospheric pressure, −259°F. Although the extremely low temperature of the cryogenic LNG[4] presented some substantial handling and storage problems, it provided the very desirable volumetric reduction of approximately 600:1 from the gaseous state.

This had important implications. Through the use of expensive liquefaction plants and elaborately insulated storage tanks, a gas utility could potentially receive gas during the low-demand summer months from the pipeline and hold it in the liquid state to be vaporized and distributed as required during the peak periods. Until this time, all natural gas had been transported exclusively as gas by pipeline. However, the gas now could be stored and transported in liquid form. This was particulary significant because some of the world's largest reserves of natural gas were not accessible to major markets by pipeline (e.g., the Algerian gas fields). This gas was frequently "flared," or burned as a waste by-product of oil production in remote areas. With the development of cryogenic equipment, experimental ocean shipping programs were undertaken. Specially designed LNG vessels were tested, including the "Methane Pioneer" in 1959, and the "Beauvais" in 1961. Three ships were put into regular service from Algeria to England and France in 1964.

During the winter of 1968–1969, Boston Gas was faced with a potential gas shortage because of the delay in the completion of the Algonquin pipeline to their new Commercial Point plant in Dorchester, Massachusetts. The company applied to the Federal Power Commission for permission to import two shiploads of LNG (approximately 85 MMcf each) from Algeria to supplement its pipeline supply. The LNG was unloaded in the Boston Outer Harbor using cryogenic tank trailers rented from a firm in California for the occasion and mounted on barges. While the project costs were substantial it did demonstrate the technical feasibility of trans-Atlantic LNG shipments to the Federal Power Commission and the U.S. Coast Guard, two organizations that previously had expressed concern about the safety of such an operation.

FORMATION OF DISTRIGAS CORPORATION

In October 1969, the Distrigas Corporation was formed as a joint venture of Gazocean (one-third) and the Cabot Corporation (two-thirds). Gazocean, a French firm engaged in the ocean transportation of refrigerated bulk gases in the liquid state, was active in the development of LNG ships. It was the Gazocean ship "Aristotle" that was used in the Boston Gas project. Joint ventures were not unusual to Rene Boudet, the imagina-

---

[4] One gallon of LNG is equal to approximately 83.6 cubic feet of gas at standard temperature and pressure.

tive founder and Managing Director of Gazocean, as demonstrated by the company's 50 percent participation with Sonatrach, the Algerian state petroleum development company, in the creation of a North American LNG sales organization, Alocean. The Cabot Corporation (Cabot) was a Boston-based, world supplier of carbon black founded in 1882. At the time of the formation of Distrigas, Cabot was seeking various opportunities for diversification, and had previously made investments in natural gas ventures, associated with the company's carbon black operations. Only small investments had been made outside of the bulk-commodity industries. Distrigas was conceived by Jacek Makowski while he was Manager of Corporate Development at Cabot, and he was named President when the new company was formed. As of late 1969, he had assembled a staff of five people to develop the Distrigas operation.

OPERATING STRATEGY

Under the proposed plan, Gazocean would deliver for Alocean Algerian LNG to ports on the East Coast of the United States in ship-load quantities (one billion cubic feet) for a price of $0.68 per Mcf to Distrigas which would purchase the landed LNG from Alocean and sell it to gas utilities. The first market area selected for development was the Eastern Massachusetts region.

In February 1970, a formal application for authority was made to the Federal Power Commission, the authority regulating interstate and international movement of sale of natural gas in the United States.

A terminal location in Everett, Massachusetts was selected by Distrigas because of easy deep-water ship access, land availability, and zoning considerations. Although newspaper articles indicated local resistance, it was felt that the zoning petition would be granted by Everett. All plans were based on this assumption.

The role of Distrigas and the overall operating plan was described by Ed Curtis, Director of Corporate Development, as follows:

> Distrigas is in a position to achieve economy of scale not available to individual utilities by serving several customers through the same terminal and distribution facilities. Each utilty will develop satellite storage capabilities and transportation capabilities to a greater or lesser level—primarily depending upon the willingness of individual companies to invest in this high-specialized, single-purpose equipment. Distrigas should be able to achieve a higher level of utilization from transportation equipment than individual customers because of its ability to consolidate the requirements of several customers. For the present, we believe that we should assume that we will have to provide all transportation and satellite storage.
>
> The question to be considered is, where should the LNG inventories be maintained? Great economies of scale and flexibility are achieved

by maintaining a large portion of the inventory at the Everett Terminal. However, this requires a large number of trailers to have the lift capacity to be able to transport the inventory quickly in response to sudden peak demands, as experienced in cold snaps.

Because different customers will require different levels of service, we feel that the Distrigas rates should be divided into distinct functional elements to be most equitable. The liquid, landed and terminaled in Everett, will be sold for $1.00 per Mcf. If the customer desires the liquid to be held in storage at Everett until the beginning of the peak season (December 1–April 1), an additional charge of $0.60 per Mcf will be made.[5] Distrigas will reserve the right to maintain the product in Everett or in Distrigas supplied satellite tanks. The delivery charge to any customer within 75 miles of Everett will be $0.06 per Mcf.

This makes a total price for the full package of services of $1.66, which is competitive with pipeline emergency gas—and is considerably cheaper than what we think the pipeline-gas rates may go to. It is equivalent to the reported costs associated with a utility operating its own peak-shaving liquefying plant. The cost of using a propane-air mixture for peaks is about $1.45 to $2.12 for the equivalent heating capacity of 1 Mcf of LNG. Most utilities estimate the cost to be about $1.80 per Mcf, but anticipate costs will go higher and supplies will be less dependable.

Recent studies published by consultants indicate that the New England market might range from over 4 Bcf if prices are in the $1.50 per Mcf range, down to 400 MMcf at prices as high as $2.00 per Mcf. Just casual discussion with potential customers indicates to me that this is a pretty conservative estimate. I think the potential might be as high as three to four times their estimate.

The Distrigas staff agreed that the actual rate of consumption could be approximated by the pattern shown in Exhibit 4. The season would start on November 15 and last 120 days. Distrigas executives did not feel that they could impose a specific pattern of consumption on their customers, but had decided to agree to be prepared to supply 100 percent of a utility's total purchase commitment in a ten-day period.

ELEMENTS OF THE DISTRIBUTION SYSTEM

The distribution system being considered by Distrigas, shown schematically in Exhibit 5, would utilize an LNG terminal storage tank farm, tank trailers, and satellite storage tanks. Utilities in close proximity to Everett might be supplied by a direct pipeline, thus eliminating tank trailer delivery and satellite for that location.

Pipeline costs in the urban Boston area would be set primarily by the right-of-way and installation expenses. Normally, pipelines would not be sized for the present capacity requirements, but the largest size that might

---

[5] This charge was made whether the LNG was stored at Everett or at satellite facilities.

Exhibit 4
ESTIMATED UTILITY LNG DEMAND PATTERN DURING
NORMAL HEATING SEASON

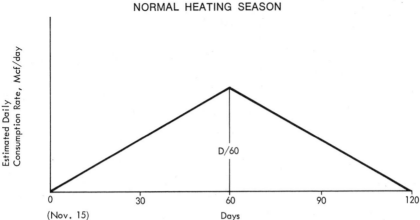

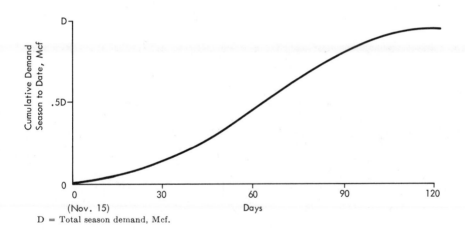

D = Total season demand, Mcf.

ever be required to avoid having to rebuild them. Mystic Gas appeared to be the only candidate for pipeline distribution at the present time. The pipeline would require an investment of approximately $350,000 per mile.

The estimated costs for the erection by a nationally-known tank builder of the terminal tank farm and satellite tanks (not including the cost of the land) are shown in Exhibit 6. It was felt that these costs were known with some certainty. LNG trailers of 1,000 Mcf or 1 MMcf cost $46,000 each. Taxes, insurance, and maintenance on a trailer were estimated to be $4,500 per year. Arrangements with a contract carrier could be made to supply a suitable number of truck tractors and qualified drivers at the rate of $12 per hour.

Exhibit 5
SCHEMATIC OF DISTRIGAS DISTRIBUTION AND SUPPLY SYSTEM

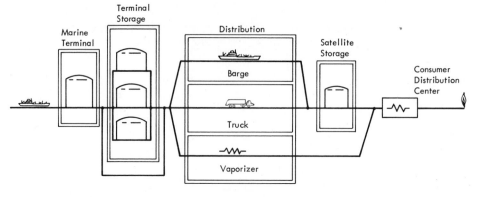

Exhibit 6
ESTIMATED COSTS OF CRYOGENIC LNG TANKS

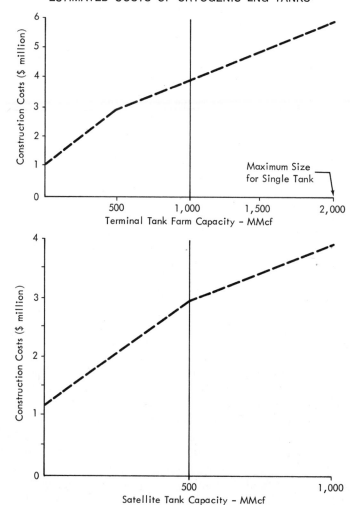

what if only source of oil be cut off

The loading, unloading, and in-transit times required to service potential utility customers are shown in Exhibit 7.

While developing a distribution plan, it was decided that the size of the satellite tanks at the customers' facilities would greatly influence the

Exhibit 7

ELAPSED DELIVERY TIME TO SERVICE NEW ENGLAND UTILITIES
BY TANK TRUCK FROM EVERETT, MASSACHUSETTS

Company	*Elapsed Time-Hours (includes loading, round-trip in-transit, and unloading time)*
Boston Gas	3
New England Electric System	
Lynn	3
Mystic	3
North Shore	5
Lawrence	5
New England Gas and Electric Associates	
Worcester	6
Cambridge	3
New Bedford	5
Springfield	7
Fitchburg	5
Lowell Gas	5
Brockton-Taunton Gas	5

transportation costs. For example, without satellite tanks, it would be necessary to transport the customers' entire demands during the heating season, leaving the highly specialized trailers idle during the remainder of the year. Through the use of satellites, the number of trailers needed could be reduced by building up inventories at the customers' facilities prior to the season.

Preliminary discussions with Boston Gas, Brockton-Taunton Gas, Algonquin Pipeline suggested that it might be possible for a product interchange to be established between the companies. Under this plan, the Brockton-Taunton LNG would be delivered to Boston Gas. Algonquin, which served both utilities, would supply an equivalent quantity of product to Brockton-Taunton. This could consolidate the Boston Gas and Brockton-Taunton satellites for economy of scale, and greatly reduce the delivery distance to serve Brockton-Taunton. The economics of this strategy had not been explored, but it appeared to be worth considering.

The estimated lives and investment leverages available for specific elements of the distribution system are shown in Exhibit 8.

In late 1969, Distrigas had made a preliminary agreement with Alocean for a 20 year supply of LNG. This preliminary agreement could be revised upward as necessary to reflect changes in the New England market. The specific requirements for each year would be estimated in detail in the

Exhibit 8
SUMMARY OF EXPECTED LIFE AND AVAILABLE
FINANCING OF DISTRIBUTION EQUIPMENT

Item	Life (years)	Leverage Debt/Cost*
Terminal storage	25	1.00
Satellite storage	25	1.00
Pipeline	30	0.50
Tank trailer	10	0.80

* Based on Distrigas/Cabot-Gazocean relationship, it
was believed that equipment loans at 9 percent interest
would be possible.

spring prior to the winter being considered. Most of the shipments were
to be made during the summer.

One ship, the "Descartes," would be available for this trade. This vessel
was being constructed by Gazocean on speculation, and had a capacity
of one billion cubic feet gas equivalent of LNG. The scheduled elapsed
time for an Algeria-Boston round trip was 28 days. A charge of $12,000
per day would be made for each day the ship was retained in Boston in
excess of the initial 24 hours of free loading time for each delivery.

According to members of the Distrigas staff, ". . . our terminal unloading rate should be sufficient to unload the 'Descartes' within the free time.
In some cases we may miss the tide change, which would delay departure
a maximum of 12 hours. Of course, if the 'Descartes' arrives from Algeria, and we don't have enough available storage to take the full load
due to a planning error, we are in serious trouble."

CURRENT MARKETING SITUATION

As of February 1970, the LNG market was starting to become firm.
The most significant development had been the signing of a letter of intent
from Boston Gas to Distrigas committing to buy 500 MMcf per year for
20 years, beginning about November 1971, as shown in Exhibit 9.

As an interim measure, during the winter of 1969–1970, Boston Gas
had been successful in securing authority from the Federal Power Commission to import approximately 225 MMcf of LNG to be delivered over a
one-month period from a utility with excess peak-shaving capacity in Montreal. This could only be viewed as a temporary (6 months to 2 years)
source until that utility's demand developed. The LNG was moved from
Montreal to Massachusetts in liquid nitrogen and hydrogen tank trailers
operated by Capitol Truck Line, a Western I.C.C. bulk-liquid carrier that
had specialized in cryogenic liquid transportation. The trailers were of
smaller capacity (about 500 to 700 Mcf) than specially designed LNG

units (1,000 Mcf) and had to be brought to New England from California, and were the same type used in the earlier Aristotle project.

Two other events had occurred as Mr. Makowski was developing his plans. First, Tennessee Gas Pipeline Co. had placed on the market an experimental LNG peak-shaving plant it had built on its pipeline in Hopkington, Massachusetts. Two companies had shown interest in acquiring the facility. Worcester Gas saw it as a peak-shaving plant for their rapidly growing demand, while Lowell Gas was considering entering the peak-shaving business, supplying LNG by tank trailer in direct competition with Distrigas. Worcester was the successful bidder, which neutralized the aggressive Lowell Gas as a competitor but essentially eliminated Worcester as a Distrigas customer. Second, the New England Electric System Group (Mystic, Lynn, North Shore, and Lawrence) had been conducting stormy negotiations with Air Products and Chemicals to erect a cryogenic peak-shaving

Exhibit 9

144 McBride Street
Boston, Mass. 02130
Telephone (617) 522-5600

Distrigas Corporation
125 High Street
Boston, Massachusetts   02110

Gentlemen: December 1, 1969

Letter of Intent

We have reviewed the Distrigas sales brochure sent to us under cover of Mr. R. D. Sullivan's letter of October 31, 1969, setting forth your proposals for the delivery of imported liquefied natural as ("LNG") for peak shaving purposes out of the Distrigas terminal at Everett, Massachusetts.

This will evidence our intent to enter into a formal contract with you in general based on the terms of the Distrigas sales brochure, under which Boston Gas contemplates the purchase from Distrigas of LNG of a 500,000 MMBTU gas equivalent per year for a twenty-year period beginning on or about November 1, 1971. The formal contract will evidence the usual matters pertaining to increases and decreases in quantity, specifications of gas, escalations in the price, the effect of acts of God, and other comparable provisions normally used in contracts for the purchase and sale of gas.

It is anticipated by this letter of intent that a portion of this quantity will be purchased under your Designated Delivery program at $1.06 per MMBTU for LNG delivered between April 1 and November 30 of each year or $1.40 per MMBTU for LNG delivered between December 1 and March 31. It is contemplated that prices in both cases will be FOB our storage facility, Commercial Point, Massachusetts.

It is also contemplated that another portion of our requirement may be delivered as gas vaporized into our mains adjacent to the Distrigas terminal at Everett, Massachusetts, under the terms of your Peak Shaving Plan at a price of $1.06 per MMBTU plus storage charges at an average annual rate of 60 cents per MMBTU.

Exhibit 9 (*Continued*)

Distrigas Corporation
Page Two
December 1, 1969

Boston Gas and Distrigas will proceed promptly with the
preparation and execution of the formal contract referred to
above and it is understood that your agreement to supply
LNG will be subject to your timely receipt of all necessary
government approvals.

If this Letter of Intent correctly states our mutual understanding
with respect to the purchase of LNG, please sign and return the
attached duplicate original of this letter to our office.

                                              Very truly yours,

                                              BOSTON GAS COMPANY

                                              By_____
                                                        Vice President

APPROVED:

Distrigas Corporation

By_____

Dated:_____ *January 29ᵗʰ, 1970*

---

plant for their group. This negotiation was successfully consumated in
February. In 1964, the SEC had ordered the New England Electric
System to divest its natural gas distribution Utilities. Since that time, several extensions of the divestiture order were granted, but on February 24,
the Commission finally acted on a request made five months earlier for a
six month extension. The SEC reluctantly granted a final extension until
April 2, 1970, when separate subsidiaries would be created. The willingness of Air Products to finance the construction of a major plant for the
financially-weaker individual utilities after separation from New England
Electric System was open to question. It was believed that the LNG produced by such a peak-shaving plant would probably cost about $1.90 per
Mcf (including the cost of gas).

The Distrigas forecast of sales to the utilities is summarized in Exhibit
10.

Exhibit 10
FORECASTS OF DISTRIGAS LNG UTILITY SALES

Customer	Quantity MMcf		
	FY 1971*	*FY 1972*	*FY 1973*
Boston Gas ⎱ †			
Brockton-Taunton ⎰ · · · · · · · · · · · ·	900	1,550	2,200
New England Electric System			
Lynn	0	0	100
Mystic	0	0	200
North Shore	0	0	100
Lawrence	0	0	100
New England Gas and Electric Association			
Worcester	0	0	0
Cambridge	200	200	400
New Bedford	0	0	100
Springfield	300	450	600
Fitchburg	0	0	0
Lowell Gas	600	800	1,200
Total	2,000	3,000	5,000

* The Distrigas accounting year began on July 1.

† Deliveries to Brockton-Taunton assumed to be made to Boston Gas under Algonquin interchange agreement.

DEVELOPMENT OF OPERATING PLANS

One operating plan that was considered by the Distrigas staff was to store the maximum volume of LNG at the facilities of the gas distribution utilities. The plan would be to have sufficient LNG to meet the entire winter demand in field storage on the first day of the season. To minimize the requirements for trailers to transport the product from the port to field tanks, a continuous transfer operation would be conducted during the approximately 250 off-season days. This was referred to as the slow-build-up strategy.

The cost of servicing the estimated demand for fiscal year 1973 was prepared (see Exhibit 11). Under this plan, approximately 0.4 percent per day of the total demand would be shipped to the field during the 250 day off-season period. Based on the travel times listed in Exhibit 8, approximately 6 trailers would be required as a minimum to support the operation and to allow for breakdowns and maintenance.

It would be necessary to construct a tank in Everett large enough to receive the contents of a ship as a minimum. This would assume that ships would arrive on a regular schedule throughout the off-season. Also, Distrigas would be required to construct field satellite tanks large enough to hold the winter demand at each gas distributor's facility.

It was believed that this plan minimized the amount of LNG stored at Everett and would offer an attractive 250 day period to deliver the product. This would provide a comfortable inventory for all the distributors in the even of an early winter or unexpected cold snap.

Exhibit 11
SLOW-BUILD-UP STRATEGY, TRAILERS REQUIRED
Trailers Required

Customer Location	Season Demand, MMcf	×	Duration of Trip in Hours	× Fill Factor* =	Trailers Required per Day
Boston.	2,200		3	.00025	1.650
Lynn	100		3	.00025	.075
Mystic	200		3	.00025	.150
North Shore	100		5	.00025	.125
Lawrence	100		5	.00025	.125
Cambridge	400		3	.00025	.300
New Bedford	100		5	.00025	.125
Springfield	600		7	.00025	1.050
Lowell	1,200		5	.00025	1.500

Total Trailers = 5.100
Round up to = 6.

Cost Estimate (million)

	Capital Cost	Annual Cost†
Everett receiving tank	$4.000	$0.16
Field tanks	25.100	1.00
Trailers.	0.276	0.03
Trailer maintenance	—	0.03
Tractor charges (5 trailers × 16 hours per day × $12 per hour × 250 days)	—	0.24
Annual Distribution Cost (excluding interest) . . .		$1.46

* Fill factor = $\dfrac{.004 \text{ of season demand per day}}{1 \text{ MMcf per trailer} \times 16 \text{ hours per day}}$

† 25-year straight-line depreciation with no salvage for tanks and 10 years for trailers.

However, the Distrigas staff was also very concerned that the slow build-up strategy also exposed the company to the maximum capital investment and ignored the potential economy available in the construction of a large central storage facility. One group argued that the company was overly concerned with the cost of trailers. They proposed a storage strategy that would hold all of the LNG in Everett and be prepared to deliver up to 10 percent of a customer's demand in any one day. Such a plan would not require investment in satellites.

The constructon contracts for the Everett terminal had to be awarded within a month. Contracts for the satellite tanks could be delayed as much as six months before being awarded. Trailer deliveries were on a 12 month schedule. A decision had to be made or an entire heating season would be missed.

Zodiac Bros. Toys, Inc. (B)[1]

IN LATE January 1972 Bill Perry, Vice President for Facilities and Planning at Zodiac Bros. in West Bend, Wisconsin, was considering the consequences of recent political unrest concerning the new plant the company planned to build on a nearby Indian reservation (Exhibit 1). This reservation was one of three reservations belonging to the local Indian tribes and was located 45 miles away from West Bend near Baraboo, Wisconsin.

The plant Zodiac Bros. proposed to build would require 55 acres of the 21,700-acre reservation, and would employ 1,000 people at seasonal peak production, many of whom would be from the reservations. Approximately 60 percent of the work force would be women. The local payroll would exceed $5 million per year.

The local Indians were widely respected throughout central Wisconsin as successful businessmen who had simultaneously been able to maintain their cultural identity. In 1964 a federal dam project had taken nearly half of one of the reservations. In compensation the government paid $15 million to the Indians for the land and displacement of families, money which was put towards the development of the economy on the reservations. It was hoped that industry on the reservations would reduce the unemployment rate, estimated to be between 10 and 30 percent, and would bring younger college-educated Indians back to the reservation. In 1966 the Indians had entered into a joint venture with the Henderson Pillow Company, the first industry to locate on the reservation. The work force at this plant at one time reached 125, but by 1972 had been reduced to 20. Henderson Pillow blamed a downturn in the economy for the cut-back.

The Zodiac Bros. negotiations with the Indian leaders had gone smoothly until recently. However, at a recent tribal council meeting, a sizable group of political dissidents had shown up to protest the use of land, the terms of the arrangement with Zodiac Bros., the impact of the indus-

---

[1] The names and figures in this case have been disguised.

403

Exhibit 1
THE PROPOSAL
(January 12, 1972)

Location: On the reservation near Baraboo, Wisconsin.
Ownership: Land and building to be leased by Zodiac Bros. from the
                     Indian Nation.
Size: 500,000 square feet on 55 acres of land.
Cost of Building: $6 million.*
Employment:

	Year 1	Year 3
Total	427	1,014
Indians	119	?

The starting wage is $2.85 per hour (same as other Zodiac
plants) and the labor is non-union.

Finance: The Economic Development Administration, an agency of
                     the Federal Government will supply a $1.5 million develop-
                     ment grant to develop the site (road development, drainage,
                     additional sewers, etc.). The EDA would also loan $3.9
                     million at 6 percent interest to finance construction of the
                     facility. Zodiac Bros. would pay off this mortgage.

Taxes: The Indian land is free of property taxes.
Lease: Length of lease: 25 years
                     Rent:† $40,000 per yr. for first five years
                            $30,000 per yr. for next five years
                            $20,000 per yr. for next five years
                            $10,000 per yr. for next five years
                            Free for last five years

* The net present value of the mortgage repayments and lease costs associated with the building
of this plant was $4.4 million. Zodiac Bros. would pay both the mortgage payments and the lease costs.
    † In addition to mortgage repayment.

trialization policy on cultural values, the possibility that industrializa-
tion would lead to termination or reduction of federal subsidies for reservations, and the leadership of the council members. Local newspapers had
reported the protest. In light of these developments, Bill Perry wondered
if he should reconsider expanding at the Winchester, Kentucky, location or
the year-round level production strategy that had been shelved when
the negotiations with the Indians reached a serious point (Exhibit 2).

COMPANY BACKGROUND

Zodiac Bros., Inc. was founded in West Bend, Wisconsin, in 1930 with
the concept that solid wood blocks decorated with colorful lithographs
would sell as toys for pre-school children. In their first year they produced
and marketed 16 toys which, unlike most toys, were durable and of high
quality. They were to represent value to the buyer as well as be engaging

Exhibit 2
FORECAST OF TOTAL FACILITY REQUIREMENTS TO
MEET 1974 SALES FORECAST
(all locations)

	1971 Facility Requirements		*1974 Forecast Facility Requirements*	
	Present Capacity	*Actual Requirements*	*Expansion Strategy*	*Leveled Production Strategy*
Raw material inventory space . . .	40,000 sq.ft.	40,000 sq.ft.	minor additions	minor additions
Molding presses				
Injection.	53*	109	195†	195†
Blow	20*	33	59†	59†
Molded parts inventory space §				
(000 sq.ft.)	631 (in house)	785 ‡	1,275	507
Number of fab/assembly lines:				
Class I toys	5	5	5	5
Other classes	26	26	40	26
Finished goods inventory space*				
(000 sq.ft.)	442	370	920	3,790
Work in progress inventory cost‖ (molded parts).		$527	$ 810	$ 297
Finished goods inventory cost‖		86	253	1,334
Total inventory cost‖ ($000) . . .		$613	$1,063	$1,631
Labor cost differential for leveling production¶		–	–	$34,000

* Additional molding requirements were subcontracted locally.
† Additional machines could be either acquired for in-house production or the work subcontracted.
‡ Calculated from Exhibit 5 as follows: Inventory on hand in August ($7.85 million) ÷ $100 pallet × 40 square feet per pallet ÷ 4 pallets high = 785,000 square feet.
§ Thousands of square feet required at peak levels.
‖ Cost of capital for financing inventories.
¶ The level production alternative would necessitate an increased amount of second and third shift operations. The labor cost differentials reflect the premium wages paid to second and third shift operators.

and stimulating to children in their early years. Many of these toys have become "classics," enjoyed by successive generations of pre-schoolers.

From the outset, Zodiac Bros. demonstrated an understanding of the inclinations of pre-schoolers. Although the company sustained losses in the first four years of operation, the product line began to generate customer interest and brand loyalty. Avoiding head-on competition with the mainstream of the toy industry, Zodiac Bros. continued to make specialty toys of the wood lithograph variety and by 1947 the company had reached the $1 million sales level.

Under the conservative management of the three company founders, Zodiac Bros. enjoyed moderate but steady growth through the next decade. In 1959, however, significant changes in the product line and pricing policies were instrumental in transforming the firm into a major competitor in the toy industry. Zodiac Bros. became the first successful producer of a line of music box toys that could handle punishment from pre-schoolers and were reasonably priced. The high sales resulting from this new line provided the resources and incentive for further new product introductions. In addition, while management had always advocated price maintenance, the coming of age of large discounters made such a policy impractical. Faced with the threat of losing the growing market share serviced by high-volume discount stores, the company departed from its stringent pricing policies in 1959.

These fundamental product and pricing strategy changes led Zodiac Bros. into a decade of substantial growth in the 1960s (Exhibit 3). In

Exhibit 3
SALES HISTORY OF ZODIAC BROS. TOYS

Year	Dollar Sales
1960	$ 14,000,000
1961	18,000,000
1962	24,000,000
1963	30,000,000
1964	32,000,000
1965	36,000,000
1966	44,000,000
1967	52,000,000
1968	60,000,000
1969	64,000,000
1970	81,000,000
1971	134,000,000
1972	170,000,000 estimated
1973	225,000,000 estimated
1974	240,000,000 estimated

1961 the company purchased a plastics firm and moved it to a new plant in nearby Hartford, Wisconsin, to produce a variety of injection and blow-molded plastic toy parts. During the 1960s the family-managed company set aside the policy of promoting solely from within and began hiring professional management from other industries. William C. Staples, formerly of General Electric, joined Zodiac Bros. in 1966 as President when the company founders retired from active management. Larry Cook, Vice President of Manufacturing, and Bill Perry also joined Zodiac Bros. in 1966.

In 1969, a large conglomerate, impressed by the rapid growth, profitability, and excellent management of Zodiac Bros., purchased the company. While this company tended to be far more aggressive than Zodiac had been under family management, they were hesitant to meddle in the concerns of the toy manufacturer. They did, however, encourage Zodiac executives to adopt a less conservative posture, specifically in their marketing and advertising programs. Zodiac subsequently abandoned its no-TV advertising policy in 1969 and increased the advertising budget substantially. In addition, the conglomerate provided Zodiac Bros. with a secure source of cash to fund expansion.

The result was explosive growth (Exhibit 3). In the stable $3 billion a year toy industry, Zodiac Bros. became one of the industry's fastest growing companies and a major competitor. Of the one thousand firms in the industry, only Mattel, Fisher-Price, and Marx were larger.

While most toy companies produced only one or two successful toys, Zodiac Bros. had eight product lines with a total of 78 toys (Exhibit 4).

Exhibit 4
PRODUCT LINE DATA

Class	Toys per Class	Total Sales in 1971 ($ millions)	Percent of Total Sales	Average Unit Price	Volume (millions of units)
I	10	$ 5.0	3.7%	$1.00	5.00
II	17	15.8	11.8	3.25	4.86
III	4	22.0	16.4	4.80	4.58
IV	4	30.8	23.0	9.75	3.16
V	14	17.1	12.8	2.35	7.28
VI	4	15.8	11.8	6.50	2.43
VII	5	5.1	3.8	1.35	3.78
VIII	20	22.4	16.7	2.15	10.42
	78	$134.0	100.0%	$3.23	41.51

Future sales were expected to increase proportionately in each product class. Overall, the industry was resistant to recession. But product life cycles in other companies were only three to four years, even for successful toys. Consequently, a high turnover of market share was possible.

Each year Zodiac Bros. introduced 12 to 15 new toys. These toys were selected from a larger number of handcrafted samples after the annual Toy Industry Fair, held in New York each February. At this gathering, large retailers placed initial orders for the following Christmas. Based on this preliminary indication, manufacturers selected the toys to be introduced, made sales forecasts, ordered production tooling and molds (this usually took four months) and set production schedules. The investment in tooling, molds, and fabrication/assembly fixtures associated with the manufacture of a new toy is shown in Exhibit 7. Some older toys were produced early in the year, while molds and tooling for new toys were prepared. New toy production typically began in June or July. Final shipments for the Christmas season were made on November 15. Because of the concentration of sales around the Christmas peak, both manufacturers and retailers were gambling on what the consumer would buy far in advance. The tendency was for manufacturers to be more conservative in their estimates than retailers. As Fred Haag, Vice President for Marketing at Zodiac Bros., explained it:

> Success for a toy is empty shelves on December 26. If a retailer sees a toy left over that he will have to mark down, it was a dog. People forget how many they ordered and how many they sold. Next year's repeat sales depend on what is left on December 26.

THE PORTAGE PLANT

In December 1969, Zodiac Bros. purchased a 300,000-square foot facility from the H. J. Heinz Company for $1 million. Zodiac Bros. had greatly underestimated sales in 1968 and 1969 and rapid growth had placed severe strains on capacity. Located in Portage, Wisconsin, 40 miles from West Bend, the facility had once been a cucumber processing plant. With the addition of $5 million worth of equipment, the plant began producing toys in March 1970. A 210,000-square foot warehouse was added to house inventory.

The opening of the Portage facility had an immensely favorable impact on the community that reflected well on Zodiac Bros. throughout central Wisconsin. Like Hartford and West Bend, Portage was a rural village with a population of approximately 6,000 and about 30,000 in the county area. The seasonal peak employment of 1,800 people revived the town's economy.

Zodiac Bros. had always enjoyed good relations with its customers, employees, and the community. The company had consistently aimed for the "quality segment" of the toy market, emphasizing in each toy "intrinsic play value, ingenuity, strong construction, and good value for the money." A leader in the industry, Zodiac Bros. was considered "best to work with" in a poll of toy retailers. Zodiac Bros. employees enjoyed the highest wages in the toy industry and received many benefits, including a generous profit sharing plan. Because the toy industry generally had few environmental problems, the company had been able to locate comfortably amidst fine residential areas.

PRODUCTION AT ZODIAC BROS.

There were three stages in the production process: (1) molding, where parts were first molded from thermoplastic resins; (2) fabrication, where both plastic and wooden parts were decorated and put together into subassemblies; and (3) final assembly, where the toy was completed and packaged for shipment.

Each plant, except West Bend, was organized into molding, fabricating, and final assembly departments (Exhibit 5) under a plant manager. Only the plant at West Bend lacked molding capacity. Purchasing, production scheduling, and inventory storage were centrally controlled under the guid-

Exhibit 5
PRODUCTION FACILITIES AT ZODIAC

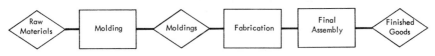

(floor space in thousands or square feet)

	West Bend	Hartford	Portage
1. Molding	none	115	57
2. Fabrication	50 (14 lines)	7 (5 lines)	39 (12 lines)
3. Assembly	50 (14 lines)	14 (5 lines)	43 (12 lines)
4. Work in Process Inventory*	145	115	371
5. Finished Goods Inventory	242†	none	none
	487 thousand square feet	251 thousand square feet	510 thousand square feet

* Plastic resin, the primary raw material, was stored in tank cars on rail sidings. Space required in the plants for RM inventory was quite small (about 40. thousand square feet† total).

◇ Inventory Warehouse

▭ Production Area

† The finished goods inventories at West Bend, New Jersey and Utah were sufficient to warehouse normal inflows, outflows, and in-transit finished goods at the current sales level.

ance of Vice President Larry Cook. Inventories were kept at three stages in the production system (raw materials, molded parts, finished goods) to insulate production levels at different stages from seasonal demand. Toys were often molded in one plant and fabricated or assembled in another.

By late 1971 the company employed the equivalent of 4,500 full-time people at its three plants. About 60 percent of these were employed in fabrication and assembly, about 500 in molding and storage, and the rest were office and supervisory personnel. About 55 percent of the total work force were women, mostly employed in fabrication and assembly. This meant that much of the income generated would be second paychecks for families. The summer seasonal peak meant that sons and daughters of area residents could return home and earn money for college. Molding ran three shifts year round, while fabrication and assembly varied seasonally from one to three shifts.

Zodiac Bros. operated one of the largest thermoplastic molding complexes in the world at the Hartford and Portage plants (Exhibit 6). Because of its technical nature, all blow-molding was done at Hartford, while injection molding took place at both locations. Following the addition of fourteen injection molding presses in 1972 at Portage, floor space for

Exhibit 6
MOLDING DATA

	Injection Molding	Blow Molding
*Presses	67†	20
Direct labor cost per hour per press	$ 6.90	$ 6.85
Full cost per hour per press‡	$17.55	$17.80
Material (pounds per hour) press §	110	80
Pallets per hour produced (capacity)	.35	.5
Subcontracting capacity		
(number of presses within 200 miles)	316	64
Subcontracting cost (dollars per hour)*	22.08	26.14
Price of presses	$87,000	$63,000

     * Exclusive of raw material costs.
     † Including the 14 to be added in 1972.
     ‡ Labor cost plus overhead costs, but excluding material costs.
     § Material costs (plastic) are $0.18 per pound.

molding was completely filled at both plants. Each molding press required approximately 2,000 square feet of floor space.

The molding departments at both Hartford and Portage ran at near three-shift capacity year round. Adding to molding capacity meant either subcontracting or purchasing new machines. In 1971, Zodiac Bros. subcontracted 40 percent of their molding. Expanding molding capacity in existing facilities would require displacement of fabrication, assembly, or warehouse space. Besides, further expansion on the three sites was impossible due to the growth of residential areas surrounding the plants. Construction costs at alternative sites for additional production and office space were estimated at $7 per square foot.[2] Existing warehouse space in the plants could be converted to production at a cost of $3 per square foot.

Fabrication and assembly for class II–VIII toys were performed principally at Portage and West Bend (Exhibit 7). Each fabrication and assembly line could produce $3.75 million in sales value of product per shift per year at full capacity.[3] During slow periods, however, the production rate dropped substantially. By using overtime and additional shifts, capacity could be increased as well. About 3,500 square feet were required for an assembly line. A fabrication line to support the assembly line also required 3,500 square feet of floor space. Only class I toys were assembled at Hartford. The assembly lines there required only 3,000 square feet and the fabrication lines half as much. Each class I line produced $1 million in sales per shift per year at full capacity.

Toys in each class were made of several parts that were produced on different types of molding presses (Exhibit 8). Parts for toys from different classes were often produced on the same molding press and then stored

---

    [2] The construction costs for a plant on the Indian reservation were substantially higher because test borings had shown the ground to be unstable. Substantial additional foundation work was therefore necessary.

    [3] Five-day week, 250 days per year.

Exhibit 7

AVERAGE INVESTMENT COSTS PER TOY OF
TOOLING, MOLDS AND FABRICATION AND
ASSEMBLY LINES
(in $000)

	Tooling Costs	Mold Costs	Fabrication and Assembly Line Costs
Class I	$10	$ 30	$15
Class II	15	45	40
Class III	60	130	80
Class IV	60	120	80
Class V	20	60	40
Class VI	50	40	80
Class VII	7	1	40
Class VIII	1	1	40

The tooling and mold costs are the average investment costs incurred whenever a new toy is produced or parts for an existing toy molded at a new location. The fabrication and assembly line costs are the investment required to build a new assembly line (exclusive of the capital investment in the building) for a particular class of toys. Any (or all) toys (new or old) within a particular class can be produced on these lines.

Exhibit 8

PRODUCTION REQUIREMENTS (1971)

Toy Class	Injection Molding		Blow Molding		Fabrication	Assembly
	A	B	A	B	C	C
I	5.80	29	10.80	54	6.45	22.35
II	8.85	43	7.60	37	19.65	33.00
III	29.95	137	4.75	22	33.70	31.80
IV	66.20	209	3.00	11	108.15	94.10
V	13.95	102	.75	5	15.00	3.15
VI	30.15	73	1.85	5	55.30	72.20
VII	5.10	19	—	—	4.70	24.40
VIII	4.05	42	6.55	68	27.50	37.25
		654		202		

A—Machine hours per 1,000 units.
B—Total machine hours required for 1971 production (000).
C—Man-hours per 1,000 units.

in inventory until fabrication and assembly. Fabrication and assembly lines were designed to accommodate all toys in a single class. Producing toys from a different class involved extensive changeover of the fabrication and assembly lines. Manufacturing costs were about 50 percent of sales. Molding and material costs accounted for one-half of total manufacturing costs. Fabrication and assembly costs made up the other half.

Because of the Zodiac policy of level production and subcontracting in molding, substantial inventories of molded plastic parts built up before the beginning of peak production in the fabrication/assembly stage. Zodiac management felt that they could not obtain reliable subcontracting services on a seasonal basis. Exhibit 9 shows the seasonal nature of product shipments, and the on-hand balances of molded parts inventories through the the 1971 year. In the peak month of July, molded parts inventories of $7.85 million (at cost) were accumulated. It took approximately 800,000

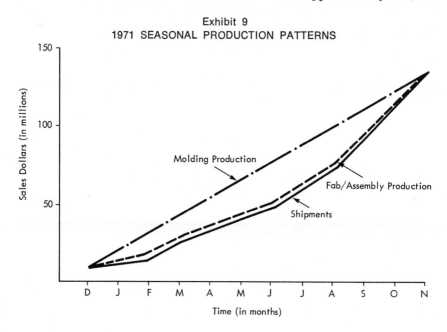

Exhibit 9
1971 SEASONAL PRODUCTION PATTERNS

1971 FINISHED GOODS SHIPMENTS, PRODUCTION, AND INVENTORIES*

	December	January	February	March	April	May	June	July	August	September	October	November
Shipments	9.5	3.6	2.4	9.8	7.2	8.6	7.9	10.9	13.7	19.0	22.9	18.5
Production	8.5	4.0	4.0	8.5	8.5	8.5	8.5	8.5	17.1	17.1	25.0	17.0
Inventory balance.	–	0.4	2.0	0.7	2.0	1.9	2.5	0.1	3.5	1.6	3.7	2.3

* All figures are in millions of sales dollars.

1971 MOLDED PARTS USAGE, PRODUCTION, AND INVENTORIES

	December	January	February	March	April	May	June	July	August	September	October	November
Requirements* . .	8.5	4.0	4.0	8.5	8.5	8.5	8.5	8.5	17.1	17.1	25.0	17.1
Production.	6.8	6.8	6.8	6.8	6.8	6.8	6.8	6.8	6.8	6.8	6.8	6.8
Subcontracting . .	4.5	4.5	4.5	4.5	4.5	4.5	4.5	4.5	4.5	4.5	4.5	4.5
Inventory balance.	2.8	10.1	17.4	20.2	23.0	25.8	28.6	31.4	25.6	19.8	6.1	.3

* Molded parts requirements equal fabrication/assembly production planned for a particular month. All figures in millions of sales dollars.

square feet of warehouse space to hold this inventory. Using a cost of capital of 1 percent per month, the annual capital charges for holding this inventory were about $500,000. In addition, there were charges for using leased and public warehousing.

Zodiac relied heavily on leased and public warehousing to accommodate their seasonal inventories. However, warehouse space was becoming scarce and expensive in the area (Exhibit 10). Additional leasing facilities were

Exhibit 10
LOCAL WAREHOUSING CAPACITY
(in number of pallets)

	Raw Materials/ Work in Process	Finished Goods
West Bend	14,500	24,000
Hartford	11,500	–
Portage	37,100	–
Leased	10,000	20,000*
Public	–	generally available

* Two 10,000 pallet warehouses, one in New Jersey, one in Utah.

THE VARIOUS TYPES OF STORAGE COSTS

	Dollars per pallet per month (Finished Goods)		
	Total	Storage Cost per Month	Capital Cost per Month
In house	$0.50		$0.50
Leased*	1.00	0.50	0.50
Public	1.50²	1.00†	0.50

* The term of the leases was typically no less than one year.
† Exclusive of a $1.00 charge for placing a pallet in storage and $1.00 when the pallet leaves.

not available locally. Presently, the company leased two 10,000 pallet capacity warehouses in Utah and New Jersey to store finished goods. The 4½ foot × 4½ foot pallets, stacked four levels high, required about 40 square feet of floor space for storage, ventilation, and access. A pallet of molded parts represented about $100 worth of material and molding cost.[4] Finished goods inventories were four times the volume of molded parts inventory. The manufacturing cost of a pallet of finished goods averaged $50. The seasonality of the toy business made full year leasing seem uneconomical, and the company was similarly reluctant to build additional warehousing space, which would cost $5 per square foot.

Leased and public storage was all about 25 miles from the West Bend plant, which was 10 miles from Hartford and 40 miles from Portage.

---

[4] See calculation in footnote ‡, Exhibit 2.

Transportation costs between facilities were $0.60 per mile for trucks which could haul 26 pallets, or $0.023 per pallet mile. Transportation on longer hauls (by rail) cost about one-half as much on a pallet mile basis. Freight costs for shipping goods to customers were charged to customers on an FOB West Bend basis, regardless of the distribution point from which they were shipped.

THE WINCHESTER SITE

Even with the additional production from Portage, by late 1970 it seemed obvious to Zodiac Bros. management that more capacity would soon be needed. By 1971 a tentative decision had been made to build additional facilities—a 500,000-square foot plant employing 1,000 people was envisioned. No decision had been made about which products should be produced at the new location or whether a molding facility should be added. Facility requirements for 1974 assuming this expansion strategy are projected in Exhibit 2. The expansion strategy would enable Zodiac to continue their policy of level production in molding, while peaking fabrication/assembly production in the fall. Molding requirements under this expansion strategy could be met by either purchasing molding presses or subcontracting.

Some members of management felt that the alternative of leveling production should also be considered. Additional production could be added in fabrication and assembly by going to second and third shifts earlier in the year. Finished goods could then be distributed to warehouses around the country. No additional fabrication and assembly facilities would have to be built and employment would become less seasonal. A calculation of the 1974 facility requirements for this alternative, which would require two shifts year round and a third shift to be added from July through December, is presented in Exhibit 2. The 1974 pro forma production plans associated with this strategy and the expansion strategy are shown in Exhibit 11.

Because of the desirable characteristics of the toy industry and the good reputation of the company, as soon as it became known that Zodiac Bros. was searching for a new plant site, the management was literally inundated with attractive offers from nearly every state in the nation. Offers of low-cost land, road construction, and tax incentives were made by many communities.

Three areas were selected as potential sites. One was central Wisconsin. As Mr. Perry had stated, "We are a Wisconsin company; we have been since 1930; and we would like to see Wisconsin prosper." At the same time, the distribution of nationwide sales (Exhibit 12) made it more expensive every year to produce and ship solely from Wisconsin. Consequently, Mr. Perry also looked for available sites at the junctures of major market areas. The other two areas selected were eastern Kentucky and the eastern portions of North and South Carolina. In addition to satisfying

Exhibit 11
1974 PRO FORMA PRODUCTION PLANS*

1. Expansion Strategy

	De-cember	Jan-uary	Feb-ruary	March	April	May	June	July	Au-gust	Sep-tem-ber	Oc-tober	No-vem-ber
Fabrication/ Assembly												
Shipments	17	6.5	4.3	17.5	13.0	15.4	14.2	19.4	24.5	34.1	41.0	33.1
Production.	17	10	10	13	13	13	13	26	26	30	39	30
Inventory balance.	–	3.5	9.2	4.7	4.7	2.3	1.1	7.7	9.2	5.1	3.1	–
Molding												
Requirements† . .	17	10	10	13	13	13	13	26	26	30	39	30
Production/ subcontract . . .	20	20	20	20	20	20	20	20	20	20	20	20
Inventory balance.	3	13	23	30	37	44	51	45	39	29	10	–

2. Leveling Production Strategy

	De-cember	Jan-uary	Feb-ruary	March	April	May	June	July	Au-gust	Sep-tem-ber	Oc-tober	No-vem-ber
Fabrication/ assembly												
Shipments	17	6.5	4.3	17.5	13.0	15.4	14.2	19.4	24.5	34.1	41.0	33.1
Production.	17	17	17	17	17	17	17	25	25	25	25	21
Inventory balance.	–	10.5	23.2	22.7	26.7	28.3	31.1	36.7	37.2	28.1	12.1	–
Molding												
Requirements† . .	17	17	17	17	17	17	17	25	25	25	25	21
Production/ subcontract . . .	20	20	20	20	20	20	20	20	20	20	20	20
Inventory balance.	3	6	9	12	15	18	21	16	11	6	1	–

* All figures are in millions of sales dollars.
† Molded parts requirements equal fabrication/assembly production planned for a particular month.

logistical requirements for the distribution system, these locations suited the company's sociological preferences. Zodiac Bros. had traditionally done business in small communities and would like to continue to do so. Since a large portion of the work force needed only minimal training, they felt obliged to locate in those areas where skill levels might not be so high as in the rest of the nation.

By late 1971, a tentative decision had been made to locate in Winchester, Kentucky. Zodiac Bros.' management felt that this was an ideal location for both regional and national distribution. Winchester was 900 miles from West Bend and had a population of 7,500. The population of the area was 15,000, including 3,000 at Winchester State College. Though Winchester was a unionized town, wage rates were about the same as those of central Wisconsin. There were currently no other large manufacturing plants in the town or the county.

Exhibit 12

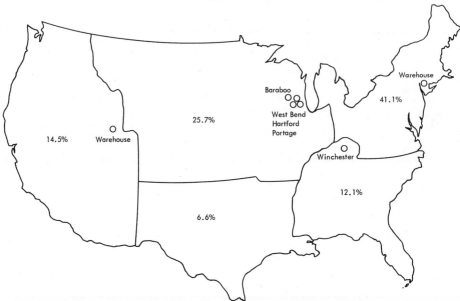

Note: The numbers in each market area represent the percentage of Zodiac Bros. annual sales in that area.

THE INDIAN RESERVATION

It had appeared at this time that there were no sites in central Wisconsin comparably attractive to Winchester. Zodiac could not find a local site which could easily supply a large enough work force for their needs. Even the supply of secondary wage earners was tight. Then, at the annual Milwaukee Chamber of Commerce dinner, Bill Perry met several members of a local Indian tribe, who raised the possibility of a plant on the reservation, a possibility that had not occurred to Zodiac Bros. Serious talks ensued and the Winchester plan was shelved.

But now it appeared that Zodiac Bros. might lose its image as a public-spirited corporation trying to make a contribution to the community. What had started out as business was becoming politics at a time when Zodiac felt that the need for additional capacity was urgent. The Winchester alternative could be reopened. It would now take eight months to complete construction on that site. The reservation plant could also be completed in eight months. The question in Bill Perry's mind was whether he should wait to see if the unrest on the reservation dissipated before starting construction there, or whether he should immediately start construction at Winchester, or try to obtain capacity by leveling production in existing plants.

Carborundum, Inc.[1]

IN MAY of 1969, with the next meeting of the Policy & Planning Council only two weeks away, Group Vice President Tom Grenfield was preparing his position with regard to the expansion of Ceramax production facilities. His assistant, Paul Thomas, working with an outside consultant had conducted analyses of three alternative strategies, and had come out in favor of a small expansion of Carborundum's plant in Lockport, N.Y. His recommendation was based primarily on economic considerations, however, and Mr. Grenfield was weighing in his mind some of the more qualitative considerations affecting this decision to see if they might possibly overrule the economics. The economics themselves, he suspected, might be open to question, as they were based on forecasts and assumptions that were in some cases little more than gut-feel. He wondered how far some of these assumptions would have to be altered before the economics shifted to favor another alternative.

In the back of his mind he mulled over another aspect of the problem. Thomas had worked hard on this project, and appeared to be emotionally committed both to the approach he had taken, which had utilized a rather complicated computer model of the project, and the recommendation he developed. Both to reward him and to give him experience in dealing with some of the most senior executives in the company, Grenfield had asked him to deliver his report to the council. Grenfield knew that these men, like himself, might be more familiar with and heavily influenced by some of the more qualitative aspects of the situation, and he wondered whether this was really the appropriate forum for Paul's presentation. Moreover, he suspected that his initial approval of Thomas' approach and recommendations might have been unduly influenced by the amount of work that Paul had put into it and the glamour of the approach he had

---

[1] This case was prepared with the cooperation of the Carborundum Corporation. The product and certain figures have been disguised, but such disguise does not distort the basic issues contained in the actual situation.

Exhibit 1
CONSOLIDATED FIVE YEAR COMPARISONS

	1968*	1967	1966	1965	1964
Selected Operating Data					
(in thousands of dollars)					
Sales	$255,109	$238,151	$230,602	$202,502	$184,617
Income before taxes	28,692	20,126†	29,693	26,201	22,780
Net income	13,962	11,755†	15,532	13,771	11,710
Cash flow	22,168	20,601†	23,346	21,376	19,070
Dividends paid	4,922	4,732	4,638	3,998	3,442
Spent for properties, plants and equipment	20,404	20,387	27,134	10,361	11,248
Depreciation and amortization	$ 8,206	$ 8,846	$ 7,814	$ 7,605	$ 7,360
Selected Year-End Balances					
(in thousands of dollars)					
Current assets	$129,181	$116,231	$103,384	$ 90,469	$ 86,717
Current liabilities	45,367	32,276	40,419	31,590	29,631
Working capital	83,814	83,955	62,965	58,879	57,086
Properties, plants and equipment, net	100,890	89,863	79,068	59,959	59,332
Total assets	253,017	230,914	202,037	167,479	155,822
Long-term debt	51,754	52,733	25,225	12,000	13,000
Shareholders' equity	$149,009	$139,731	$131,656	$120,683	$110,836
Selected Ratios and Employee Data					
Working capital ratio	2.8:1	3.6:1	2.6:1	2.9:1	2.9:1
Shareholders' equity to long-term debt ratio	2.9:1	2.6:1	5.2:1	10.0:1	8.5:1
Net income as a percent of					
Sales	5.5%	4.9%†	6.7%	6.8%	6.3%
Shareholders' equity	9.4%	8.4%†	11.8%	11.4%	10.6%
Long-term debt and shareholders' equity	7.0%	6.1%†	9.9%†	10.4%	9.5%
Depreciation as a percent of					
Sales	3.2%	3.7%	3.4%	3.8%	4.0%
Average gross fixed assets	4.3%	5.3%	5.5%	5.8%	5.4%
Accumulated depreciation as a percent of gross fixed assets	50.7%	52.5%	52.8%	57.6%	59.6%
Average number of employees	14,443	14,399	13,259	11,614	11,010
Sales per employee	$ 17,700	$ 16,500	$ 17,400	$ 17,400	$ 16,800
Selected Share Data‡					
Common shares outstanding at year-end	3,649,974	3,641,304	3,638,774	3,635,374	3,632,374
On a per common share basis					
Quarterly dividend rate at year-end	$ 0.35	$ 0.32½	$ 0.32½	$ 0.30	$ 0.25
Net income	$ 3.83	$ 3.23†	$ 4.27	$ 3.79	$ 3.22
Cash flow	$ 6.07	$ 5.65†	$ 6.42	$ 5.88	$ 5.25
Dividends paid	$ 1.35	$ 1.30	$ 1.27½	$ 1.10	$ 0.95
Shareholders' equity	$ 40.82	$ 38.37	$ 36.18	$ 33.20	$ 30.51

* See Note 5 to financial statements regarding change in method of computing depreciation.
† Excludes extraordinary income of $972,000, or $.27 per share.
‡ Years 1964–1965 adjusted for 2 for 1 stock split in April 1966.

taken. He needed to address the issue more carefully before he could adequately evaluate the job that Thomas had done.

COMPANY BACKGROUND

In 1968, Carborundum's sales were over $255 million (see Exhibits 1 and 2), making it one of the largest companies in the abrasives industry.

Exhibit 2
CONSOLIDATED BALANCE SHEET*

December 31	*1968*	*1967*
ASSETS		
Current Assets		
Cash, including time deposits of $6,223,000 and $5,346,000, respectively.	$ 16,010,000	$ 13,812,000
Marketable securities at cost and accrued interest, which approximates market.	3,078,000	4,324,000
Accounts receivable, less allowance for losses of $925,000 and $661,000, respectively	46,322,000	40,756,000
Inventories (Note 2).	62,458,000	56,243,000
Prepayments, principally insurance and taxes.	1,313,000	1,096,000
Total Current Assets.	129,181,000	116,231,000
Investments and Other Assets		
Investments and advances 50%-owned companies (Note 1)	4,427,000·	7,108,000
Associated companies and non-consolidated foreign subsidiaries (Note 3).	4,917,000	4,881,000
Patents and processes, net (Note 4).	3,106,000	3,278,000
Non-current receivables, goodwill and deposits.	10,496,000	9,553,000
Total Investments and Other Assets	22,946,000	24,820,000
Properties, Plants and Equipment, at Cost		
Land and mineral rights, less amortization.	3,145,000	2,963,000
Buildings.	66,480,000	60,242,000
Machinery and equipment.	127,890,000	116,297,000
Construction in progress.	7,256,000	9,641,000
	204,771,000	189,143,000
Less depreciation and amortization (Note 5)	103,881,000	99,280,000
Total Properties, Plants and Equipment, Net	100,890,000	89,863,000
Total Assets.	$253,017,000	$230,914,000

* Financial Statement Notes Not Included in the Case.

Although the company had broadened its sales base to the point where it supplied 14 major industries throughout the world—ranging from paper and textiles through electronics, nuclear and pollution control to ceramics—the largest segment of its sales continued to be generated by its Abrasive Systems division. Carborundum defined itself as "a materials and materials systems company" whose major products were "industrial consumptibles" (such as abrasives, filters, resins, etc.) and capital items (such as process and pollution control equipment). Its scope was "multinational, multi-industry, and multi-market; its goals were fast growth, high profits and challenging and rewarding employment opportunities."

Continuing from The President's Letter in the 1968 Annual Report: "To achieve the goals of fast growth and high profits, the Company is dedicated to expansion, both internally and externally, into new businesses interrelated to the wide variety of existing ones. This concept is known as vectored growth. It considers each element of know-how as a vector. For instance, expertise in selling to a specific industry—a vector—leads to a new business for the same market which in turn provides new technological capabilities—a new vector. Additional businesses may then be built around the new vector."

In the ten years prior to 1969, Carborundum's sales and earnings had been growing at a rate of about 8 percent per year. Top management felt that this was much too slow a rate, and the long term objective was to get this growth rate up to 15 percent. Since the bulk of the company's business was in relatively mature markets, whose growth roughly paralleled that of the economy and where competition was well established, Carborundum's top management felt that this faster growth rate could only be achieved by shifting corporate resources as rapidly as possible into either (1) new businesses (obtained through acquisitions or new product development), or (2) those areas already existent in the company whose growth potential was greater and/or whose profitability was higher. The Ceramax business was an example of such an area.

CERAMAX

Ceramax was Carborundum's trade name for a specially-treated high porosity ceramic material which had remarkable filtration properties. It was the principal filtration agent in the high efficiency dust collectors sold by the company, and was being used increasingly in the industrial gas and water pollution control devices produced both by Carborundum and outside companies. The primary markets for Ceramax were in the aerospace, auto, and foundry industries, largely located in the Northeast and North Central States. The company's primary manufacturing source for Ceramax was in Lockport, New York, where gross profit had been in excess of 35 percent of sales. A similar material was sold, under a variety of different names, by five competitors. None of these had a market share over 20 percent.

Total sales of Ceramax by all suppliers had been about 46,000 tons in 1968, with Carborundum having approximately 30 percent of the market. Industry sales were increasing almost 15 percent a year, and were projected to grow at a rate of at least 10 percent over the foreseeable future. Carborundum hoped both to participate in this growth and to increase its penetration to 35 percent of the market within 5 years. On this basis, Carborundum predicted its sales in 1969 would exceed 15,000 tons. First quarter reports indicated that Ceramax orders were up 21.6 percent in tons and 17.5 percent in gross dollar value over 1968. Thomas had estimated that total production capacity in the industry was about 60,000 tons.

Since the maximum annual capacity at Lockport was currently only 14,000 tons, with a 3,000 ton addition coming onstream during the third quarter, the company found itself in the position of having to turn down business. In fact, demand from current customers alone was already consuming Lockport's entire production, with no reserve for new accounts or increased requirements from established users. New facilities were clearly called for as soon as possible.

The location of such new facilities would be influenced by the geographic pattern of demand. In 1968, almost 35 percent of Carborundum's total Ceramax sales were located in the major auto and steel producing region in the U.S.: bounded by Pittsburgh to the east, Chicago to the West, Detroit and Buffalo to the North and Indianapolis to the south (Lockport, N.Y. was in the northeast corner of this region—see map, Exhibit 3). Another 30 percent of sales came from other states in the northeast region. About 20 percent of total demand was located in the southeastern states, and the remaining 15 percent came from the west (of Houston) or from overseas.

Prices were quoted f.o.b. the factory, but in cases where a competitive source of supply was closer to a customer than was Lockport, Carborundum would subsidize his freight costs so as to equalize them with the nearest competitive shipping point.

Three possible alternative sites were under consideration for increased Ceramax capacity.

1. Lockport, N.Y. (5,000 ton increment). The initial cost of expanding production here would be less than at any of the other sites since the land and most of the required additional plant space were already available. Also, annual fixed costs (primarily manufacturing overhead) would be less if one large plant were operated rather than two smaller plants. On the other hand, there was only room available for an additional 5,000 tons of capacity at Lockport. This would only supply forecasted demand through 1971 or 1972, whereas a new plant would probably have an initial capacity of at least 12,000 tons.

Since the new equipment that would be added here would have to be compatible with existing equipment the variable cost per ton would remain essentially the same as at present. As regards freight equalization and ability to compete in various geographic areas, these would be largely unaffected by an expansion of the Lockport plant. The new facilities would be available by mid-1970.

2. Lebanon, Indiana (12,000 ton increment). This location would allow Carborundum to reduce the $12.00 per ton freight equalization that it was currently paying, on the average, in supplying the Chicago, Milwaukee, and St. Louis markets (accounting for an estimated $600,000 in sales

Exhibit 3

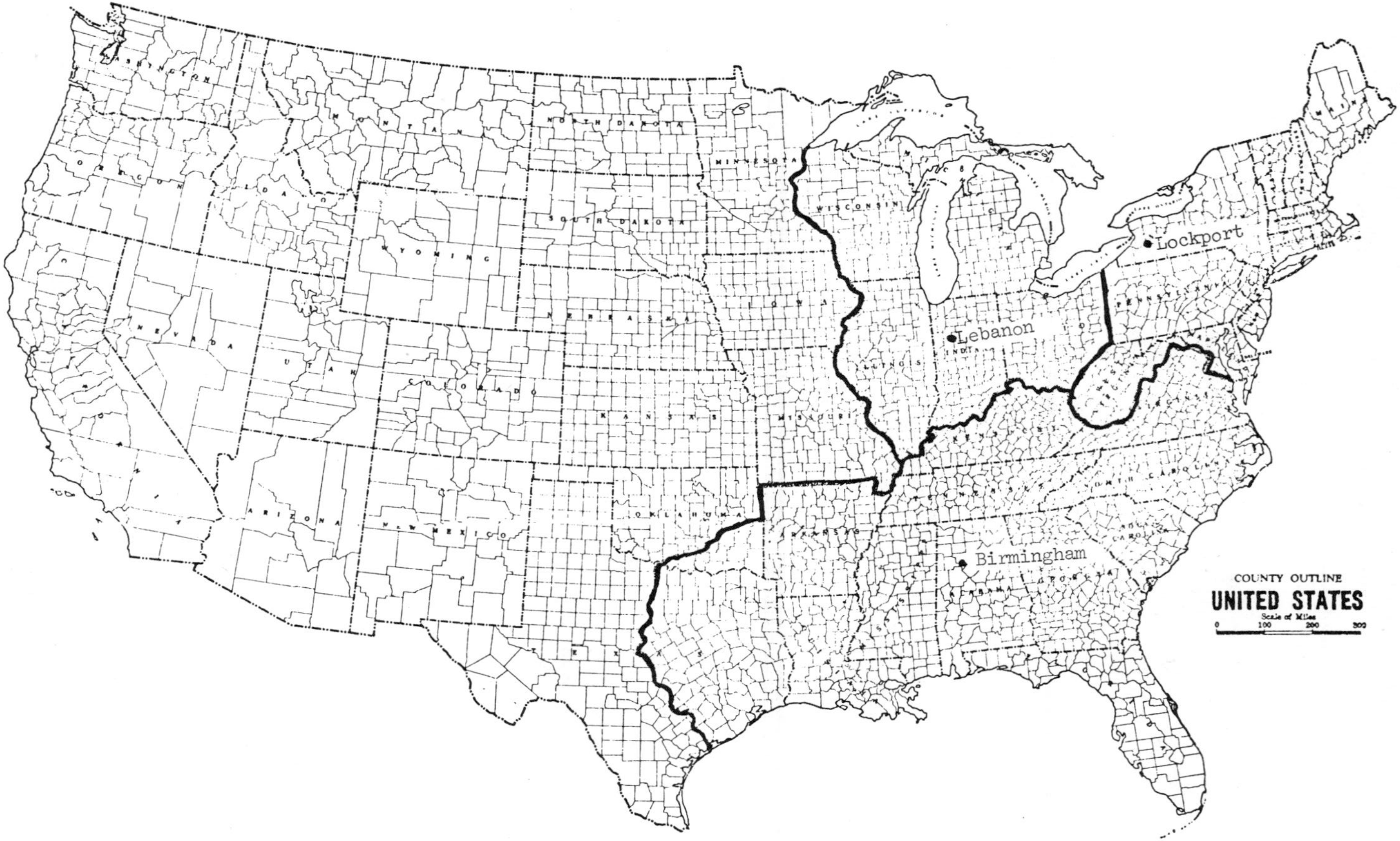
Lockport
Lebanon
Birmingham
COUNTY OUTLINE
UNITED STATES
Scale of Miles
0
100
200
300

in 1969) from Lockport. Freight equalization for the Detroit area and the Southeast region would be unaffected, although freight equalizations to the western region would be reduced slightly. The Lebanon location would have a further advantage in that Carborundum already owned a plant (belonging to another division) in this area that was phasing out its operations, so building and land were already available at a price that was considerably below what the division would have to pay for developing a new site and building a new plant. This would permit production to begin by mid-1970, as would expansion at Lockport. The Lebanon plant was big enough to accommodate an additional 5,000 tons of capacity when it was needed.

3. Birmingham, Alabama (12,000 ton increment). The Birmingham area would provide an estimated $820,000 in sales in 1969, up from $660,000 in 1968, and was regarded as one of the fastest growing market areas in the country. According to one Carborundum executive it was "ripe for development." One competitor was located in the area, and Carborundum was forced to equalize freight averaging $15 per ton. Freight equalization to the Western region would be about the same as Lockport's, but a Birmingham plant would be at a disadvantage as regards the Detroit area.

Other than the previously mentioned disadvantages associated with the splitting up of production among two locations, a Birmingham plant would cost almost $2.4 million for building, land and equipment. Full production could not possibly begin before January, 1971. By building a plant specifically for Ceramax production, however, the company could automate much of the production process and have the lowest cost facility in the industry.

Summaries of the forecasts of various economic variables for each of the four sales regions are given in Exhibits 4 and 5, and for each of the

Exhibit 4
MARKETING REGION COMPARISON
(in 000 tons)

	Northeast	North Central	Southeast	West and Foreign	Totals
1968 industry sales	12.2	17.4	9.4	7.0	46.0
Estimated 1969 industry growth rate	12%	13%	18%	16%	
1968 Carborundum sales. . .	4.5	5.0	2.3	1.8	13.6
1969 average price per ton. .	$310.10	$306.30	$316.20	$319.70	

three alternative plant locations in Exhibit 6. The freight equalization costs are estimates that reflect the *average* subsidy that would be paid by Carborundum to customers in a particular region. The values associated with the Lockport plant are based on historical experience. Sales prices in the four regions were expected to remain relatively constant over the foresee-

Exhibit 5
TOTAL CARBORUNDUM DOLLAR SALES—CERAMAX
(in $000s)

Sales Region	1967	1968	1969 (Est.)
Northeast	$1,280	$1,350	$1,530
North Central	1,360	1,460	1,690
Southeast	560	660	820
West (and foreign)	470	540	630
Totals	$3,670	$4,010	$4,670

Exhibit 6
PLANT LOCATION COMPARISON

	Lockport	Lebanon	Birmingham
Additional capacity (tons)	5,000	12,000	12,000
Available by:	July 1970	July 1970	January 1971
Costs ($000s)			
Land	$ 0	$ 30	$ 55
Building	100	450	600
Equipment	620	1,400	1,700
Total Investment	$720	$1,880	$2,355*
Additional annual fixed cost†	75	190	175
Variable cost per ton‡	129.5	114	106
Freight equalization per ton from plant to: §			
Northeast	0	9.2	16.5
North Central	9.5	2.1	16.5
Southeast	15.2	14.8	3.5
West and foreign	15.9	13.6	17.3

* Total investment required for constructing a new plant having 18,000 tons annual capacity would be about $3.2 million.

† The fixed annual manufacturing costs at the Lockport plant were projected to be $351,000 after the 3,000 ton addition was in operation in late 1969.

‡ Manufacturing costs were expected to increase at a rate of about 4 percent per year. Costs given are as of May 1, 1969.

§ Transportation rates were expected to increase at a rate of about 3 percent per year.

able future; increases in the cost of manufacture and transportation, therefore, would reduce margins.

Projected pro forma revenues, costs, and profits and cash flows for the three plant locations developed by the Thomas' computer model are shown in Exhibit 7 (see Appendix for an explanation of these calculations). They indicated that, on the basis of both a paycheck and a discounted cash flow criterion, the choice of a small addition to the existing plant would be preferable to a larger addition in a new location. Several other considerations gave Mr. Grenfield pause, however. They primarily revolved around the question as to whether this choice would be an aggressive enough strategy for a product which appeared to have unusually high profitability and growth potential. He was mindful of the fact that a new plant not only permitted sales growth to occur, but that it often influenced the magnitude and location of this growth.

For example, a location at Lebanon would not only reduce freight subsidies, but it would introduce Carborundum into a new geographic area and provide an alternative source of supply for the Detroit area, their primary demand center. On the other hand, it would also locate them in the center of most of their major competitors, and Mr. Grenfield had had experience with similar situations where the introduction of a new source of supply into a region that had previously been dominated by a few established competitors had triggered a price war. This might be particularly likely in the case of such a high margin product, and it was conceivable that prices might drop as much as 5 percent for a year or two until the new capacity had been absorbed by demand growth. On the other hand, Lebanon would provide a cheap location for a new facility, and Mr. Grenfield knew that the idle plant space available there would soon be appropriated by one of Carborundum's other divisions unless he acted quickly. Such an opportunity might not present itself again for several years.

The Birmingham location also had several attractive features. It would radically change Carborundum's geographic "center of gravity" in the Ceramax business, and locate them in the midst of what was predicted to be the fastest growing region in the U.S. for Carborundum's products. A new plant there might stimulate demand without instigating a price war.

Finally, although he appreciated the usefulness of the discounted present value criterion, he was uneasy about using it to compare capacity additions of different sizes. Although the Lockport addition appeared to be the most attractive because of the small investment required, it would only satisfy demand for a few years and additional capacity would be required then. The investment necessitated by this "second generation" expansion should somehow be taken into account, he suspected, but he was uncertain as to how this should be done.

APPENDIX: EXPLANATION OF CALCULATIONS MADE IN DEVELOPING CASH FLOW PROJECTIONS

0. Industry Sales (not printed)

Industry sales are projected to grow at different rates in the four sales regions, but the overall annual growth rate is expected to decrease gradually from the current figure of 14.5 to 10 percent. In accomplishing this, the growth rates in the different regions are reduced in the same proportion.

1. Carborundum Sales

Given industry sales in the four sales regions, as calculated above, Carborundum's sales are obtained by applying the market share values. Over time, Carborundum's overall market share is expected to increase

Exhibit 7
OPTION 1: EXPAND LOCKPORT FACILITIES

CARBORUNDUM CERAMAX DECISION

```
PROPOSED NEW FACILITES
LOCATION: LOCK.=1, LEB.=2, BIRM.=3   ? 1
CAPACITY (000 TONS) ?5
NUM. OF YEARS UNTIL AVAIL. ?1.0
COST OF LAND, BLDG. AND EQUIP.   ?0,100,620
ADDNL. ANNUAL FIXED COST ?75
VAR. COST PER TON ?129.5
NUM. OF YRS. TO PROJECT CASH FLOWS ?5
```

	1969	1970	1971	1972	1973
CARB. SALES(TONS)	15.	17.6619	20.6881	22.	22.
CARB. MKT. SHARE	0.285916	0.296351	0.306785	0.289476	0.257835
SALES REVENUE	4666.38	5495.76	6438.95	6343.93	6350.62
COST OF MFG.	2293.5	2782.74	3353.49	3683.93	3831.29
FREIGHT EQUAL.	124.557	152.955	136.846	207.207	216.074
DEPRECIATION	94.3	113.31	132.32	132.32	132.32
PROF. BEFORE TAX	1874.04	2117.01	2374.96	2414.54	2259.9
AFTER TAX PROF.	805.837	910.314	1021.23	1038.25	971.756
INVEST.+W.C. INCR.	119.948	869.289	169.774	73.7957	0.30365
E-0-Y RESID. VALUE (PLANT+WORK. CAP.)	1960.95	2716.93	2754.33	2695.86	2563.34

PRESENT VALUE OF NET CASH FLOWS, DISCOUNTED AT 15 PCT.= 3010.5

OPTION 2: NEW LEBANON PLANT

CARBORUNDUM CERAMAX DECISION

```
PROPOSED NEW FACILITES
LOCATION: LOCK.=1, LEB.=2, BIRM.=3   ? 2
CAPACITY (000 TONS) ?12
NUM. OF YEARS UNTIL AVAIL. ?1.0
COST OF LAND, BLDG. AND EQUIP.   ?30,450,1400
ADDNL. ANNUAL FIXED COST ?190
VAR. COST PER TON ?114.00
NUM. OF YRS. TO PROJECT CASH FLOWS ?5
```

	1969	1970	1971	1972	1973
CARB. SALES(TONS)	15.	17.6619	20.6881	24.1085	27.952
CARB. MKT. SHARE	0.285916	0.296351	0.306785	0.31722	0.327655
SALES REVENUE	4666.38	5495.76	6438.95	7505.34	8704.02
COST OF MFG.	2293.5	2745.82	3323.95	3933.71	4653.77
FREIGHT EQUAL.	124.557	107.223	125.702	154.702	189.721
DEPRECIATION	94.3	140.925	187.55	187.55	187.55
PROF. BEFORE TAX	1874.04	2172.05	2415.42	2779.07	3150.73
AFTER TAX PROF.	805.837	933.98	1038.63	1195.	1354.31
INVEST.+W.C. INCR.	119.948	2029.29	169.774	191.951	215.762
E-0-Y RESID. VALUE (PLANT+WORK. CAP.)	1960.95	3849.31	3831.54	3835.94	3864.15

PRESENT VALUE OF NET CASH FLOWS, DISCOUNTED AT 15 PCT.= 2290.41

OPTION 3: NEW BIRMINGHAM PLANT

CARBORUNDUM CERAMAX DECISION

```
PROPOSED NEW FACILITES
LOCATION: LOCK.=1, LEB.=2, BIRM.=3    ?3
CAPACITY (000 TONS) ?12
NUM. OF YEARS UNTIL AVAIL. ?1.5
COST OF LAND, BLDG. AND EQUIP.    ?55,600,1700
ADDNL. ANNUAL FIXED COST ?175
VAR. COST PER TON ?106.00
NUM. OF YRS. TO PROJECT CASH FLOWS ?5
```

	1969	1970	1971	1972	1973
CARB. SALES(TONS)	15.	17	19.9392	23.2645	27.0046
CARB. MKT. SHARE	0.285916	0.285245	0.295679	0.306114	0.316549
SALES REVENUE	4666.38	5289.81	6205.86	7242.58	8409.
COST OF MFG.	2293.5	2654.6	3156.33	3728.5	4399.76
FREIGHT EQUAL.	124.557	147.223	152.198	183.446	219.736
DEPRECIATION	94.3	94.3	209.3	209.3	209.3
PROF. BEFORE TAX	1874.04	2076.29	2315.68	2686.78	3075.66
AFTER TAX PROF.	805.837	892.806	995.743	1155.32	1322.53
INVEST.+W.C. INCR.	119.948	112.217	2519.89	186.611	209.955
E-0-Y RESID. VALUE (PLANT+WORK. CAP.)	1960.95	1973.87	4289.45	4266.76	4267.42

PRESENT VALUE OF NET CASH FLOWS, DISCOUNTED AT 15 PCT.= 2077.1

OPTION 4: DO NOTHING

CARBORUNDUM CERAMAX DECISION

```
PROPOSED NEW FACILITES
LOCATION: LOCK.=1, LEB.=2, BIRM.=3    ?1
CAPACITY (000 TONS) ?0
NUM. OF YEARS UNTIL AVAIL. ?0
COST OF LAND, BLDG. AND EQUIP.    ?0,0,0
ADDNL. ANNUAL FIXED COST ?0
VAR. COST PER TON ?0
NUM. OF YRS. TO PROJECT CASH FLOWS ?5
```

	1969	1970	1971	1972	1973
CARB. SALES(TONS)	15.	17	17.	17.	17.
CARB. MKT. SHARE	0.285916	0.285245	0.252794	0.223686	0.199275
SALES REVENUE	4666.38	5289.81	5291.97	5292.35	5293.66
COST OF MFG.	2293.5	2654.6	2760.78	2871.22	2936.96
FREIGHT EQUAL.	124.557	147.223	153.537	160.115	166.966
DEPRECIATION	94.3	94.3	94.3	94.3	94.3
PROF. BEFORE TAX	1874.04	2076.29	1964.98	1849.18	1728.71
AFTER TAX PROF.	805.837	892.806	844.943	795.148	743.344
INVEST.+W.C. INCR.	119.948	112.217	0.227516	0.23114	0.234596
E-0-Y RESID. VALUE (PLANT+WORK. CAP.)	1960.95	1973.87	1884.79	1790.72	1696.66

PRESENT VALUE OF NET CASH FLOWS, DISCOUNTED AT 15 PCT.= 3314.46

gradually and the market shares in each region will be adjusted in the same proportion.

Two factors complicate this market share calculation. First, if Carborundum Ceramax capacity is less than the demand, as calculated above, its total sales are reduced to the available capacity and the market shares in each region are reduced by the same proportion. Second, the introduction of a new plant into a sales region may have the impact of increasing Carborundum's market share in that region by as much as 10 percent within the space of a year or two. This is not predicted to happen in the sample calculations given in Exhibit 7.

2. Carborundum Market Share

Obtained by dividing total Carborundum sales (line 1) by industry sales as calculated above.

3. Sales Revenue

Carborundum's sales in the four sales regions, as calculated in (1), are multiplied by the 1969 prices. These prices are assumed to remain constant in the calculations given in Exhibit 7.

4. Cost of Manufacture

Each plant is assumed to supply all the demand in its sales region. If the total excess capacity exceeds demand requirements, the production in each plant is adjusted until overall production equals demand and each plant uses the same proportion of its excess capacity (above that required to service its sales region). Hence, if the excess capacity of plant 1 were 10 million tons and that of plant 2 were 6 million tons, and the total demand in the other two regions were 12 million tons, plant 1 would supply 7.5 tons and plant 2 would supply 4.5 tons. This is roughly in accordance with current procedures in other product lines.

Once the annual production figures have been obtained, the annual fixed costs and variable costs per ton are applied to arrive at the total cost of manufacture. These costs are then adjusted by the annual rate of manufacturing cost inflation.

5. Freight Equalization

The new plant is assumed to divide its shipments equally among the regions not served directly by any plant. The Lockport plant supplies whatever demand remains. The resulting annual shipments are multiplied by the freight equalization figures and then adjusted by the annual rate of transportation cost inflation.

6. Depreciation

The annual depreciation charge for the Lockport plant is $94,300. The depreciation of a new plant is calculated on the basis of straight line depreciation over 30 years for the building, and over 15 years for the equipment. If a plant comes on stream during a year, only the appropriate fraction of depreciation is charged.

7. Profit Before Tax

This is calculated by subtracting sales expenses, manufacturing costs, freight equalization and depreciation from sales revenue as calculated above.

8. After Tax Profit

Taxes are calculated by multiplying Profit Before Tax by 0.43, the current effective tax rate, and are then subtracted from Profit Before Tax.

9. Investment and Working Capital Increase

The amount of plant investment required in a given year is specified by the user's inputs. The working capital required to support that year's sales volume is calculated by multiplying Sales Revenue by 0.18. The change in working capital over the previous year is then determined and added to whatever plant investment is required.

10. End of Year Residual Value

The Book Value of plant and equipment is updated each year by adding whatever new investment is required and subtracting depreciation, as calculated in (6). Book Value is then added to the working capital at the end of the year to obtain residual value.

11. Present Value of Net Cash Flows

The Net Cash Flow for a given year is calculated by adding Depreciation to After Tax Profit and subtracting from this the Investment and Working Capital increase required during the year. These net cash flows are then discounted to the present (mid-1969).

6

Technology Planning

IN CHAPTER 1, we described technology as the set of knowledge regarding materials, processes, methods, techniques, and capital goods by which products are made or services rendered. Up to this point in the text we have considered the technology as a given condition within which we both performed our analyses and made our decisions. While it is true that most short-run and medium-term decisions must be made within the framework of a given technology, long-term decisions, and in particular capacity planning and new product decisions, allow the manager to modify the technology and thus require an understanding of technological alternatives. Even in the short- and medium-term the manager must understand how the given technology will constrain his decisions.

Unfortunately technology is often looked upon as outside the realm of management decision; something which should be left exclusively to scientists, engineers, and technicians. However, as was stated in Chapter 3, decisions which involve the technology of the process are often the most pervasive; they are more management decisions than technical ones because they affect such management concerns as: the economics of production, capital requirements, product quality and reliability, work environment, labor relations, and the capability to respond to market demands. This chapter is designed to improve your understanding of how to deal with existing technology and plan for changing technology.

PRODUCT AND PROCESS

Technology is embodied in both the inputs (labor, materials, capital goods, energy, and information) of the production process and the nature, composition, shape, and performance of the product. In analyzing existing process technology it mut be remembered that there is a very close relationship between product technology and process technology. This is important to both product technology and process technology. On the one hand, the type of product changes which can be made are determined by the existing process. For example, a company producing a metal part cannot change its product to a plastic part without basically changing the entire process technology needed to produce that product. On the other hand, the type of process changes which are sought must be guided by the impact of these changes on the market for the product. For example, by adopting a new and more reliable process of manufacturing critical automatic transmission components, an automobile company was able to reduce service costs and thereby be first in offering an extensive (five-year) warranty on the car's power train with the net result that the company captured a larger market share.

In all cases changes in the way a given process technology is utilized or changes in the process or product technology must take into account the interrelated effect of process and product.

ANALYSIS OF TECHNOLOGY

How much should a manager know about technology? Although some companies require their management group to have formal technical training in the sciences or engineering related to the particular operation the group is going to manage, most often managers have little formal training in the technology for which they are responsible. Even in the case of technically trained managers, it is difficult to have in-depth knowledge in all the technologies which affect the operations for which they are responsible. This is particularly true at higher levels of management where the manager has become responsible for more and more diverse operations. The result of this lack of technical expertise on the part of the manager is often to let the task of managing technology become the exclusive responsibility of technical people.

It is interesting that many managers will deal with technological choices in their private life (choice of automobile, air conditioner, TV, stereo, dishwasher, and other such home equipment) and ignore this responsibility in the workplace. Yet the level of knowledge required and the types of choices which must be made are the same in both cases. For example, in choosing what color TV set to buy you will not want to know whether it was a two-stage or three-stage IF section, but rather what kind of reception it will provide from distant stations; you won't ask what type of pump seals or stator winding are in a dishwasher but rather how maintenance free the dishwasher will be; you won't ask what the "pull down capacity" of a refrigerator is but rather how fast it will make ice cubes.

This same approach can be applied in managing the technology of a process; that is, understanding the *performance characteristics* rather than the *engineering characteristics* of the technology of a given process or a range of technological choices. What are these performance charactersitics? You should have developed an acquaintance with them from reading the previous text and analyzing the previous cases. The following is a nonexclusive list of characteristics one should look at in understanding an existing technology or a choice of technologies.

1. What types of inputs does the process technology require: quality and costs of raw materials; type, quality and quantity of energy; amount and skill level of labor; nature, cost and timeliness of information needed to perform tasks?
2. What are the speeds, capacities, and limitations of individual tasks and flows and how do they combine to affect the capacity of the process?
3. What is the potential efficiency and effectiveness of the process? What is the cost structure and how can the inputs be varied to change that cost structure?
4. How flexible is the process in its ability to change volume, quality, cost, and timeliness of the output?
5. How does the technology of the process and product compare with the environment? What are the competitive characteristics of the existing products and processes vis-à-vis that of other companies in the marketplace? How can the existing process be best utilized to meet market requirements?

Technology planning involves the periodic evaluation of existing technology and technological alternatives in light of forecasted quantity and quality output requirements. Technological planning normally takes place in planning facilities because the purchase of new capital goods provide the opportunity to introduce a whole new set of processes, methods, and techniques. For example, the construction of a new steel mill in the 1960s would probably result in a company purchasing a basic oxygen furnace even though its furnaces at other locations had all been of the older open-hearth type. But, changes in technology are not restricted to major changes in facilities. Technological change may occur through incremental changes in facilities. Technological change may also occur through incremental changes in techniques, skills, and or equipment such as the use of new types of storage bins in National Cranberry Cooperative or packing machines in Art-Tone Cards.

With any given technology there are a whole range of alternatives available to the manager in the terms of the input costs and output characteristics of the process. Within this range of alternatives there is usually one set of alternatives which minimize the input costs for a given output. In Chapter 5, three plants with nominal output volumes of 5,000, 10,000, and 20,000 units were described. The unit cost curves for these three different sized plants utilizing closely related technologies were illustrated in Figure 5–4 and is reproduced in Figure 6–1. If we look at an output of 10,000 units per week in Figure 6–1, we can see that XYZ Company can produce this output using a 5,000 unit capacity plant with low capital

Figure 6–1
ECONOMIES OF SCALE IN COST VOLUME RELATIONSHIP—
XYZ COMPANY

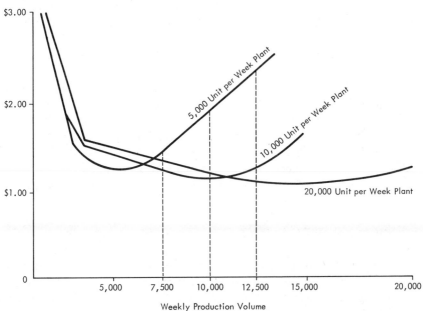

Weekly Production Volume

or facilities cost but high variable (labor and/or materials) cost or utilizing a high volume 20,000 unit plant with high capital cost and low variable cost or a 10,000 unit capacity plant with an optimal mix of fixed (capital) and variable (labor and materials) costs.

Similar comparisons can be made at the 7,500 and 12,500 in a 10,000 unit plant or any other output level. Using his knowledge of the cost structure, the manager, by substituting one input for another, can obtain a "least cost" input mix for any given output. This will be one which utilizes the best mix of inputs for any given output. This is, however, a theoretical "least cost" model and has several limitations in practice. The most obvious limitation is that it is not often easy to substitute one input for another; e.g., it is impossible to change the size of a plant every time there is a change in output volume. This model does, however, provide a theoretical set of minimum input costs to evaluate the existing efficiency of an operating system. For example, Figure 6–1 indicates that with a 10,000 unit plant, unit cost at an output of 7,500 units should be $1.07. However, this is a theoretical optimum cost of input factors for this output. This theoretical optimum (or most efficient utilization of input factors) is often difficult to obtain. When a company adopts a new process technology it takes a good deal of time to reach the optimum input cost since workers and management must learn how to best use the equipment, carry out essential tasks, and so on. The result is that a company improves its input (or factor) cost structure over time as the total volume of production increases.

Looking again at the XYZ Company, we can demonstrate this phenomena by looking at how the company might arrive at the optimum cost structure shown in Figure 6–1. Suppose that the XYZ Company builds a 10,000 unit per week plant in 1972 with the expected optimal costs as shown in Figure 6–1. However the company's demand had not yet reached 10,000 units per week and in fact, it is 7,500 units per week. From the previous calculation, you can see that the optimum cost for this output is $1.07 per unit. In their first week of operation the company finds that its per unit cost is $1.22 per unit. This is much higher than expected. However, as production proceeds a number of improvements occur. Worker skills improve with experience, as they learn to work more efficiently and get the "bugs" out of the equipment; managers and supervisors learn how to improve the utilization of raw materials and develop the necessary support resources such as fixtures, tools, and dies. As a result of these improvements, by 1974 the XYZ Company is able to reduce costs so that they are close to the optimum cost of $1.07 per unit. It takes the company two years while producing at 7,500 units per week to reach this optimum because of the learning required by management and the work force.

This learning effect is a phenomenon which usually affects improvements in all inputs to the production process. As a result, a *learning curve*[1] can be applied to predict the trend that input costs will follow as total production volume increases. A learning curve for the example described above is shown in Figure 6–2 and illustrates the way that total input costs change with cumulative production volume.

The learning curve has been applied in many industries (e.g., steel mills, electronics, wearing apparel, petroleum refining, and so on), where costs have been found to decrease rather smoothly by some consistent percentage each time cumulative production doubles. Thus a new technology usually requires a high input cost relative to the optimum costs. This has major implications for management decision making:

1. The output volume or capacity of a new technology increases over time, this provides inherent opportunities for market expansion.
2. Input costs decrease over time which provides competitive pricing advantages.

---

[1] For a more detailed description of the learning curve and its uses, see F. J. Andress, "The Learning Curve as a Production Tool," *Harvard Business Review,* January–February 1954; W. B. Hirschmann, "Profit from the Leaning Curve," *Harvard Business Review,* January–February 1964; and W. J. Abernathy, and K. Wayne, "Limits of the Learning Curve," *Harvard Business Review,* September–October 1974.

Figure 6–2

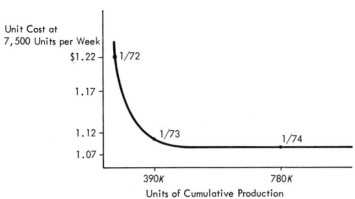

Unit Cost at
7,500 Units per Week

$1.22 — 1/72

1.17 —

1.12 — 1/73

1.07 —

1/74

390K 780K

Units of Cumulative Production

EVALUATING ALTERNATIVE TECHNOLOGIES

In evaluating technological alternatives it is necessary to understand the types of benefits available from new technologies. There are three major types of beneficial technological changes:

1. Societal initiated.
2. Product performance improving.
3. Cost reducing.

The first type of change is often the result of legislative, liability, or other changes in the environment. The Ferdanna Company case in Chapter 2 is a good example of a societal pressure for change in product technology. The need to meet EPA (Environmental Protection Agency) and OSHA (Occupational Safety and Health Act) requirement are examples of pressures for changes in process technology. Or, the desire for improved corporate image could also be a motivating force. (For example, the elimination of potential litter from film processing was cited by company executives as one objective in the development of the Polaroid SX70 system.)

The second type of change, performance improving, is typically the result of recognition of market potential for a higher profit margin product. A change in technology enhances product characteristics which in turn commands higher prices in the market. Introduction of color television by RCA in the 1950s and sophisticated pocket calculators, such as the HP 80 by Hewlett Packard, are examples of such performance improving products. These innovations in product technology seek to increase the value of the product to the customer and often require substantial changes in process technology. Although increasing total cost usually result, the increased revenues more than offset these increased costs as shown in Figure 6–3. An existing product such as a black and white TV, would have a total cost TC_1 and revenues of R_1. Conditions, such as a decreasing margin resulting from price competition, may stimulate a company to develop a new prod-

Figure 6–3
REVENUE IMPROVING TECHNOLOGICAL CHANGE

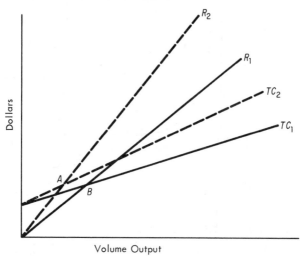

uct such as color TV which may have a higher total cost (TC_2) but can also be priced (because of lack of direct price competition or higher utility) to produce higher revenues (R_2). In Figure 6–3, the new product may start producing profit at a lower point (A) than the break-even point (B) of the older product.

The third type of technology change, cost reducing, is the most prevalent. Cost reduction changes frequently come from the implementation of a process technology which increases the efficiency of inputs by substituting a lower cost input for a higher cost input. Once such substitution is the reduction of one of the direct costs of the process (labor, materials, energy, or capital equipment) through the expenditure of resources on information (research and development).

One of the best known types of process technology changes in the United States to date has been the process of automation which is a substitution of capital equipment for labor. Such capital using technological changes typically result in changes in the cost structure as shown in Figure 6–4. For example, a new plant with more expensive, more advance equipment with fixed cost, FC_2, replaces the older plant which had a lower fixed cost, FC_1. The more advanced equipment results in a lower variable cost providing total cost, TC_2. However, the newer total cost (TC_2) is higher than the total cost of the facility with the older technology for volume of output less than C, but TC_2 is lower than TC_1 beyond volume C.

Capital using technological changes typically require higher volumes to provide lower unit costs, not only because of the higher fixed costs of the capital equipment, but also because fixed operating costs, such as maintenance for the equipment, and higher setup costs must be spread over larger

Figure 6–4
CAPITAL USING TECHNOLOGICAL CHANGE

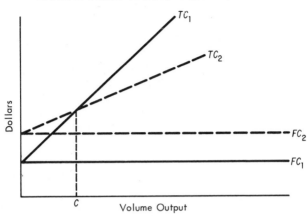

volumes. For example, in the case of the Blitz Company case a number of choices of equipment technologies exist. Two of these choices are between the routing machine and the punch press and the manual drill and Green pantographic machine. Each of these machines have a different capital cost, setup time and run time as shown in Table 6–1.

Table 6–1

	Equipment Cost	Setup Time (minutes)	Run Time (minutes per board)
Manual drill	$300	15	10
Routing machine	$300	50	1
Green pantographic machine	$1,500	50	5
Punch press	$1,500	150	0.6

Three possible process technologies available in the Blitz Company process would be:

1. Use of the routing machine and the manual drill at a capital equipment cost of $600.
2. Use of the routing machine and the green Pantographic machine at a capital equipment cost of $1,800.
3. Use of the punch press and the green Pantographic machine at a capital equipment cost of $3,000.

Because of the differences in setup and run times we get different cost structures (in terms of minutes to produce each circuit board) for the three different technologies. These cost structures are shown in Table 6–2. This

Table 6–2
COST IN MINUTES TO PRODUCE EACH CIRCUIT BOARD
FOR THREE PROCESS
TECHNOLOGIES AVAILABLE IN BLITZ COMPANY
(time in minutes per circuit board)

Number of Circuit Boards per Order	Router and Manual Drill	Router and Green Pantographic	Punch Press and Green Pantographic
1	344.85	374.85	474.45
2	180.6	193.1	242.7
3	125.85	132.517	165.45
4	98.475	102.225	126.825
5	82.05	84.05	103.65
6	71.1	71.9333	88.2
7	63.2786	63.2786	77.1643
8	57.4125	56.7875	68.8875
16	38.35	35.5375	41.3875
24	31.9958	28.4542	32.2208
32	28.8187	24.9125	27.6375
40	26.9125	22.7875	24.8875
48	25.6417	21.3708	23.0542
56	24.7339	20.3589	21.7446
64	24.0531	19.6	20.7625
72	23.5236	19.0097	19.9986
80	23.1	18.5375	19.3875
88	22.7534	18.1511	18.8875
96	22.4646	17.8292	18.4708
104	22.2202	17.5567	18.1183
200	20.8125	15.9875	16.0875
300	20.3433	15.46	15.3933
400	20.05	15.1375	14.9875
500	19.921	14.991	14.791
600	19.7958	14.8542	14.6208
700	19.74	14.79	14.5329
800	19.6687	14.7125	14.4375
900	19.6394	14.6783	14.3894
1,000	19.5925	14.6275	14.3275

cost structure is summarized in Figure 6–5. Note that below an order size of 8 circuit boards per order, point *A* on the graph, the routing machine and the manual drill is the least time cost process technology from 8 circuit boards per order to around 250 circuit boards per order, point *B* on the graph, the routing machine and the Green pantographic machine is the least time cost technology. Above 250 circuit boards per order the punch press and Green pantographic machine is the least time cost technology. Thus, the nature of the business, particularly volume, in terms of order size, is often a determinant choice of alternative technologies. In the Blitz Company case, the company should choose the low capital cost alternative (route and manual drill) if its business is small orders, and the high capital cost alternative (punch press and Green pantographic) if its business is large, volume orders.

Figure 6–5
COST CURVES FOR THREE TECHNOLOGIES IN BLITZ COMPANY

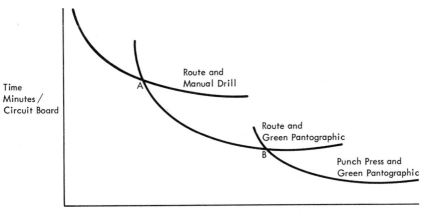

Order Size (number of circuit boards)

Another type of cost reducing technological change is the capital saving technological change as shown in Figure 6–6. The basic oxygen steel furnace, which was developed in Austria as a replacement for the earlier Bessemer converter is an example of such a capital reducing technology. Here a lower cost variable input such as raw materials or direct labor is substi-

Figure 6–6
CAPITAL SAVING TECHNOLOGICAL CHANGE

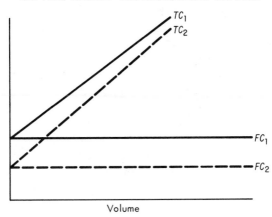

Volume

tuted for a higher cost capital input resulting in a lower fixed cost, FC_2, and lower total cost, TC_2. This type of substitution often occurs in economies with inexpensive labor or raw material and high interest rates. Such has been the case with the location of electronic assembly plants in the Far East to utilize inexpensive labor.

CHOICE OF TECHNOLOGY AND TECHNOLOGICAL STRATEGY

In general technological changes are aimed at:

1. Increasing revenue by the creation of new or improved products.
2. Reducing cost by changing the mix and nature of inputs.

Technological changes aimed at product improvement tend to substitute products less sensitive to price competition for price competitive products, while those aimed at reducing costs tend to substitute inexpensive abundant resources for expensive scarce resources. As a result successful technological planning involves forecasts of future market needs, economic availability of resources and scarce resource saving technologies. Such planning requires both an understanding of the long-term requirements of the operating system and the development of a technological strategy. Normally a technological strategy involves a multiplicity of technological changes, involving societal, revenue improving, and cost reducing changes. The nature of a company's technological strategy must change over time to reflect the effect of environmental changes.

To understand how technological strategy changes over time, we must understand something about the basic nature of the market changes a company's product will face. A wide variety of products or services appear to follow very similar long-term patterns of development. A product or service is first introduced as the result of a major performance improving product innovation. Demand tends to be small and the market uncertain. This may be because of a combination of factors such as lack of market knowledge, high price, and unreliable product performance. However, if the product meets an important market need, demand will start growing rapidly at some point as larger and larger portions of the market become aware of and require the product. As the market becomes saturated, demand starts to level off and tends to remain constant until superceded by a new product. This demand growth pattern, known as the product life cycle, is shown graphically in Figure 6–7.

At t_0 a company brings a new product into the market. In the product introduction stage, from t_0 to t_1 total demand is small. At t_1 demand "takes off" and the market expands very rapidly until it becomes saturated at t_2. Each of these three distinct phases of the product life cycle require different types of technological strategies.

1. Product introduction ($t_0 - t_1$).
2. Growth in market share ($t_1 - t_2$).
3. Mature market (beyond t_2).

In the product introduction stage, a company is initially faced with a product with uncertain quality undergoing much design change being produced by a process which is costly, fragmented, and undergoing numerous changes in process design such as layout, type of equipment and labor skill

Figure 6–7
PRODUCT LIFE CYCLE

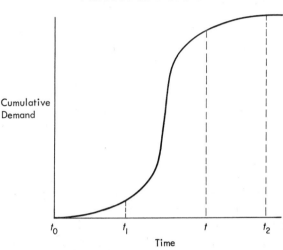

requirements. Changes in both product and process technology are often undertaken during this stage to improve the quality of the product and to standardize both product and process. For example, in the introduction of a new aircraft, tape recorder, or machine tool, it is likely that the new product would be produced on a job shop basis using a high percentage of specialty parts produced by subcontractors and that each of the first 10, 20, or even 100 units might be different. During this period the manager is primarily concerned with problems of understanding what the market really wants, ensuring product performance characteristics, and meeting delivery dates often at the expense of cost and standardization. A high degree of flexibility is demanded of the process to meet product design changes and to overcome errors created by mismatches of product and process designs. The technological change during this period is "performance maximizing" aimed at improving the performance of both product and process.

By the time the life cycle reaches takeoff at point t_1 (in Figure 6–7), most product and process problems have been ironed out. During the second stage $(t_1 - t_2)$ rapid growth in productive capacity is important, in order to capture market share. The market becomes price sensitive as new producers enter the market, but usually demand exceeds the combined capability of all manufacturers.

During this period technological change becomes "capacity maximizing" and is geared to maximizing the utilization of limited resources. Rapid facilities expansion takes place as well as substitution of high-volume equipment for low-volume equipment. Volume processes replace flexible processes; assembly lines replace job shops. The key management concerns during this period are standardization of product and process, changing from a flexible job shop-type process to a line flow, mass-production process, forecasting of sales and capacity requirements, and design of production and distribution networks in terms of size and location of facilities.

By t_2 capacity grows to meet demand and even exceeds demand. Because there is overcapacity, companies begin competing for each other's market share, price competition occurs, and prices and margins fall. Technological change during the mature market stage is aimed at cost minimizing. The ability to minimize costs during this period is restricted by actions taken during the capacity maximizing stage. Often during the second-stage companies lock themselves into technologies with higher costs than those of their competitors. Since these are often embodied in major facility acquisitions, companies with the high cost technologies must make major investments in order to reduce their cost structure. The technological changes during the mature stage may involve incremental changes in the process, such as improvement in techniques to decrease labor costs, reductions in waste and scrap to decrease material cost, relocating plants "offshore" to reduce labor costs, and changes in capital equipment within the process to decrease setup times, energy usages, and maintenance costs. During this stage, management concerns turn more and more to:

1. Materials management.   How reliable are the sources of raw materials? What types of materials to use and from what sources? This decision often results in vertical integration in order to gain control of material sources and reduce delivery uncertainty.
2. Industrial engineering.   Reducing the costs of labor, materials, and capital by changing labor skill requirements, reducing scrap, and modification of existing machines to increase operating speeds of reduce overhead costs (maintainance, setup, and so on.)
3. Tracking the best equipment technology available from equipment suppliers. Also, depending upon the company strategy, there may be a search for a product performance improvement to start a new life cycle.

When you deal with technology planning, it is necessary to know what type of technological changes are required at any particular point in the life cycle and how these changes might constrain future planning.

Following the full life cycle of a product is itself one technological strategy. However, a company may decide a number of other major strategies.

1. A company may deal only in the development of new products and not carry a product through the latter two stages. This company maintains a consistent performance maximizing strategy, introducing a constant stream of new, more advanced products. Hewlett Packard appears to have followed such a strategy in the hand calculator market.
2. A company may let competitors develop new products, letting these companies absorb all the high costs of ironing out the problems during the performance maximizing stage. At takeoff such a company enters

the market and using large market and financial resources, attempts to capture market share. Such companies as GE and RCA appear to have followed this strategy with consumer stereo sound equipment products.

3. A third strategy is to enter a mature market, where a well-established product is being produced in antiquated facilities, acquire the most efficient lowest cost process possible, and erode the market share of existing companies through aggressive price competition. This appears to be the strategy of such companies as Sears and Penneys.

CHANGING PROCESS TECHNOLOGY

No matter what the technological strategy, most managers inevitably come to realize the limitations of their existing process technology. These limitations may be that:

1. The best output of the process does not produce a product of the performance level required by the market or supplied by competitors.
2. Capacity utilization of the process has reached the manageable limits of the existing process technology.
3. Input costs have bottomed out for the process technology.
4. Some input has become a scarce resource (such as labor and materials) and the existing technology has a high utilization of this input relative to other inputs.

Since changing process technology normally requires facilities planning, there is usually a long-time horizon between the recognition of the need for a change and the implementation of the change. Thus, there is a need for technology planning. Technology planning in this instance means:

1. Analyzing the performance limitations of existing process technology.
2. Forecasting performance requirements of the process technology in the future (volume, quality, cost, and so on.)
3. Identifying alternative process technologies and their sources.
4. Evaluate the performance characteristics of alternative process technologies.
5. Choosing for the acquisition and implementation of an alternative technology.

The development of new technology can be described as a transfer system with the following elements:[2]

$$\underset{\text{(discovery)}}{\text{Science}} \longrightarrow \underset{\text{(workable idea)}}{\text{Technology}} \longrightarrow \underset{\text{(product creation)}}{\text{Producer}} \longrightarrow \underset{\text{adoption)}}{\underset{\text{(diffusion and}}{\text{User}}}$$

---

[2] This model is developed from a concept presented in Edward E. Furash, "Problems of Technology Transfer," in A. Bauer and K. J. Gerge, eds., *The Study of Policy Formation* (New York: The Free Press, 1968).

The user in this transfer system is the company or manager who adopts a new process technology. The producer is the manufacturer of the capital equipment, facilities, and/or information system which embodies the technology. This technology can come from any one of a number of sources. The user could be the producer as the case with a production group that develops its own new process. One example of this is the development groups within the manufacturing divisions of Burlington Industries. The producer could be another division or department of the same company, such as the Research and Development (R&D) Division of General Electric. Or, the producer could be one or numerous suppliers of equipment and/or construction services such as the John Deere division which supplies farm and construction equipment, Cincinnati Milling Machine which supply machine tools to industry, or Honeywell Corporation supplying process control computers. Once these companies have identified a process need in their marketplace, they develop a new process technology in their product line. This third source, the equipment supplier industry, is the major source of new process technology.

The manager evaluating alternative technologies should first compile data on the producers that operate in the three sources of technology:

1. Internal (or self) development.
2. Available research and development.
3. Facilities and equipment suppliers.

No matter what the source, the manager should next evaluate the performance characteristics of alternative process technologies and the cost of implementing that technology into an operating process in being. The more uncertain the technology, the higher the cost of bringing it on line. The new technology with the most certain costs and that is the easiest to evaluate is that technology which exists as a product of a supplier and has already operated in competitors' production processes; for example, a textile mill purchasing a new type of loom from an equipment supplier who has already sold thousands of these looms to other textile mills. The manager can *adopt* this technology with fair certainty of the cost of acquiring the physical facilities. However, in spite of the fact that the technology has already been proved in other companies, the company will face uncertain costs in the *start up* of the new process technology. These uncertain costs are a result of implementing the new technology in the existing company environment and adapting the process to the particular environment or vice versa. For example, purchasing a numerically controlled machine to replace a number of different manually operated metalworking machines eliminates a number of work flows and may require radical changes in a company's existing information system. Adaption to such changes are one of the major factors in the learning curve effect. A major disadvantage of being an adopter of a new process technology after your competitors is that the competitors may be well along on the learning curve and thus have a cost advantage over your company until you catch up.

A greater degree of uncertainty is involved when the technology exists only as a workable idea. Here the process has been constructed and tested and no one is as yet utilizing the process technology, but one or more producers have it in their product line. An example is the first use of thin film techniques to produce integrated circuits as described in Benson Electronics, Inc., which was a radical change from a mechanical engineering technology for assembling circuits to a chemical engineering technology for "growing" circuits. This requires the company implementing the new technology to be an *innovator* or first user of the technology. Here again, the cost of facilities is fairly certain or can be made so through contractual agreement between supplier and user. The uncertainty of implementation costs rises dramatically because the new process technology has not been tested under true operating conditions. Problems in organization, operation, and maintenance, which may not have been anticipated will require major modification of the facilities and/or a high degree of user and supplier learning. A major advantage of being an innovator is that after initial start-up and implementation problems are solved, you have a lead on the learning curve over your competitors.

Often required performance characteristics will necessitate the development of an entirely new process technology. This may be because of a product change or because competitors have adopted or potentially can adopt technologies which give them cost advantages which you cannot overcome (because of patents or learning curve effect) without leapfrogging their technology. This will require the creation of a workable idea or *invention* of a new technology. Invention can come from any one of the three sources but is most likely to come from either the internal R&D department or the R&D department of a supplier. With invention, the user is faced with additional uncertainty costs. Here the process technology must be developed from existing basic principles such as the development or invention of laser welders from the basic scientific knowledge about heat-producing laser beams. The uncertain costs in invention are information costs. Often the cost of the invention process itself is so unknown that it requires the expenditure of funds on feasibility research to obtain information on the cost of development so that the manager can trade this information cost off against the benefits obtained in process performance. The inventive activity is very often too high a cost to have offsetting performance benefits in a single operating system. As a result, inventive activities are usually carried out as product development, and thus by selling the new process technology to a number of users, the development costs are absorbed by a number of operating systems.

A striking feature of technological planning is the way that it must be related to the plans that are made within each functional or product area within the firm. It is not just a concern of production, marketing, finance, or engineering. To be successful it must both cut across and integrate the plans made in each separate function. For example, a company's decision whether to follow a particular product through its product life cycle, or as a matter of strategy to concentrate on products that are in the early stages of their life cycle, will have a profound effect on every aspect of the organization. The decision will not only determine future marketing, finance, and production plans, but it will affect the very nature of the company. The viewpoint which must be taken in technological planning is that the firm is a system and that technological decisions are an interface between the strategic plans in all major areas of the company, as well as the operating plans in particular functions.

The cases in this chapter are intended to focus on some of the aspects of technology and its impact on the strategic plans of the company. The first case, P. T. Pertamina—Gulf Industrial Processing, illustrates a choice of technology within a facilities planning decision. The second case, Fawcett Optical Equipment Company, illustrates the impact of the learning curve on scheduling and pricing decisions when an existing operating system is required to produce a new product. In Ampex Corporation (A), a new high technology product requiring a new process technology has difficulty meeting performance requirements. Your experience with the first two cases will be helpful in dealing with the problem of meeting performance and delivery requirements in Ampex. The next two cases are primarily concerned with the introduction of new process technology in established operations. In Berkline Corporation (A), a single new machine is adopted into the process of a furniture manufacturing company with a growing market. Sarepta Paper Company (A), on the other hand, is faced with developing and implementing a major process innovation in a mature industry. The final two cases Mirassou Vineyards (A) and The Kroger Company deal principally with the evaluation of radical new process technologies which have been developed outside the potential using companies.

P. T. Pertamina—Gulf
Industrial Processing

In 1969, Gulf Oil Corporation signed an agreement with the Government of Indonesia permitting Gulf to construct and operate in Indonesia a plant for the purpose of bagging imported fertilizer.

The operation would be a joint venture between Gulf and Pertamina, Indonesia's state-owned petroleum company. Gulf was to hold 51 percent of the shares and would be generally responsible for the management of the operation. The joint enterprise was to be named P. T. Pertamina—Gulf Industrial Processing.

Gulf had long been active in Asia. However, the company did not have other major holdings in Indonesia, although that country had been an important source of oil for the world for many years. In fact, Royal Dutch Shell had its beginning in Indonesia when the area was under Dutch control. Shell began to extract oil from Sumatra before 1900; Stanvac entered Indonesia in 1912; and Caltex began local operations in 1935. After independence, the Sukarno regime (1949 to 1967) took over the Shell properties and required the other oil companies to operate under production sharing agreements with the newly created national oil company.

After the fall of the Sukarno regime in 1967, interest by foreign investors in the opportunities provided by this chain of islands, with a population of 113 million (1968), grew dramatically. Oil firms, mining enterprises, and manufacturing firms made application to the Indonesian Government for permission to invest in the country. Gulf was among these firms.

Gulf was interested in establishing a listening post in this potentially important country, the fifth most populous in the world. The bagging of fertilizer presented a particularly attractive opportunity for Gulf to establish an operation that could fulfill this role. Gulf had conducted similar bagging operations in the United States and the required investment, the size of which would depend partly on the technology chosen, would in any case not be overwhelmingly large. Pertamina would, it was thought, make an ideal partner in this venture. Pertamina had handled most of the fertilizer importing in Indonesia, and would be a likely partner for future operations that Gulf might undertake in the country.

The plant design was handed over to an American engineer who had designed plants for similar processes in the United States. The engineer, Don Myers, was fascinated with his assignment. He realized quickly that conditions in Indonesia were very different from those that he had faced in his previous assignments in the United States. Labor costs were extremely low, for example. An unskilled worker could be hired for Rp.30 per hour.[1] Once hired a worker could not be easily laid off or dismissed. Locally borrowed capital was, on the other hand, very expensive. Five-year loans for equipment could sometimes be arranged from state-owned banks for 12 percent per year, a preferential rate which was generally available only to domestic firms. The normal rate, if funds could be obtained at all, would be at least double this. Working capital from a state bank cost 24 percent per year. Other sources were even more expensive.

Indonesia had gone through a period of rapid inflation. For example, annual price increases had reached a rate of 650 percent in 1966. Over the past two years, however, prices had been rather stable, increasing by not more than 10 percent per year. The history of unstable currency seemed to be changing. The exchange rate had remained stable at about Rp.378 per $1.00 for a number of months, and restrictions on currency transactions had been relaxed considerably.

Mr. Myers set out to learn the rudiments of the Indonesian language and quickly found himself picking up an understanding of local customs. For example, he discovered that the ceremonial burial of five water buffalo heads on the building site had to be accomplished before a building was started, and that a selamatan (ceremonial feast) was always to be held if a workman was killed or injured during the construction of the facilities.

Adjustments to American ways of doing things began early. A likely site was an old coal dump, which had been used previously as a storage area for the port bunkering facility. The excess coal and dust would have to be cleared from the site by hand, without the use of bulldozers, and loaded on to trucks. The building site would then be prepared by packing the residual earth and coal-dust using ancient hand-powered rollers.

Mr. Myers was certain that the plant design would have to reflect local conditions and take into account such local customs and methods.

THE ROLE OF FERTILIZER BAGGING

In Indonesia, agriculture engages about 70 percent of the adult male population. Big, estate-organized agriculture on Sumatra and Java is de-

---

[1] For ease of calculation an exchange rate of Rp.400 = U.S.$1.00 (400 Rupiah equal to U.S.$1) is used in this case.

voted mainly to export; much of the rest is subsistence agriculture. Rice is the staple food and chief crop. Major plantation crops are rubber, tea, coffee, cinchona bark, palm kernels, and sugar. Others are copra, cacao, spices, agava fiber, and kapok. In addition to rice, the chief food crops are maize, cassava, sweet potatoes, peanuts, and soybeans.

Like many other developing countries, Indonesia faces a struggle to increase agricultural productivity in order to feed its large and rapidly growing population. The problem is exacerbated by a tendency for rapid urbanization of the population, which is lowering the agricultural labor force relative to the total population, and creating growing urban unemployment.

One of the methods employed to increase productivity among subsistence farmers is to encourage them to use nitrogenous fertilizers in place of the more traditional methods. The most concentrated solid form of nitrogen available is a white, crystalline, water-soluble compound which is called urea. For use as a fertilizer, urea is manufactured in pellet form.

Indonesian imports of urea have grown rapidly in recent years. Vessels, loaded with bagged urea were berthed at Indonesian ports. The cargo was discharged using ship's gear or shore cranes. Initially, the cargo was warehoused at or near the wharf. Subsequently the bags were dispatched to their field storage location.

In an effort to reduce the costs of importing fertilizer, it was decided to consider importing bulk fertilizer and bagging the product in Indonesia. An estimate of the potential savings from undertaking bagging in Indonesia is shown in Exhibit 1. As shown in the exhibit, the landed cost differential between the bulk and the bagged product (that is, the difference between the cost of a ton of urea, packaged in 20 bags, landed on the wharf at Djakarta, and the cost of a ton of urea still in the bulk-carrier, alongside the wharf at Djakarta) was about $23 per metric ton. The cost of moving bulk urea through an Indonesian port appeared likely to be about one-half the U.S. port cost. Most of this difference resulted from the higher labor costs for stevedoring at the U.S. ports. A further advantage of bagging the urea in Indonesia was that a large portion of the cost of bagging would become a local currency item rather than a foreign exchange cost. Moreover, employment, income and services would be generated at the Indonesian port.

MEETING THE FERTILIZER NEED

Gulf's management thought that certain criteria would have to be met in the design of the plant. Assuming that good, clean, dry urea was delivered on ship alongside the bagging operation, Gulf had to assure that the handling and bagging facilities met high standards. Discharging bulk urea from ocean-going vessels with open holds requires close supervision; synchronization of equipment discharge capacity with receiving, bagging

Exhibit 1

GULF INDUSTRIAL PROCESSING

ESTIMATED COMPARATIVE COSTS PER METRIC TON OF SHIPPING BULK AND
BAGGED UREA FROM U.S. PORTS TO DJAKARTA*

	Vessel	
	U.S. Flag (dollars per ton mile)	*Foreign (dollars per ton mile)*
Gulf Ports		
Bagged		
1. Urea cost FAS (free alongside ship)	$ 45.00	$45.00
2. Stevedoring and bagging, U.S. port†	19.50	19.50
3. Freight cost‡	47.00	20.00
4. Stevedoring and handling, Djakarta	1.75	1.75
5. Landed cost.	$113.25	$86.25
Bulk		
1. Urea cost FAS	$ 45.00	$45.00
2. Stevedoring and handling, U.S. port §	2.00	2.00
3. Freight cost‡	44.00	17.00
4. c and f alongside wharf, Djakarta†	$ 91.00	$64.00
Cost differential‖	$ 22.25	$22.25
U.S. West Coast		
Bagged		
1. Urea cost FAS	$ 45.00	$45.00
2. Stevedoring and bagging, U.S. port†	22.50	22.50
3. Freight cost‡	34.00	15.00
4. Stevedoring and handling, Djakarta §	1.75	1.75
5. Landed cost.	$103.25	$84.25
Bulk		
1. Urea cost FAS	$ 45.00	$45.00
2. Stevedoring and handling, U.S. port §	3.00	3.00
3. Freight cost‡	32.00	13.00
4. c and f alongside wharf, Djarkata	$ 80.00	$61.00
Cost differential‖	$ 23.25	$23.25

* Abstracted from "A Case Study of the Feasibility of Shipping Bulk Urea Fertilizer under Tropical Conditions." Tennessee Valley Authority.

† Includes cost of bags, pallet rentals, service charges, wharfage, storage if any, customs clearance and other incidental charges.

‡ Freight costs are averages based on various sizes and types of ships. Freight rates do not include adjustments for demurrage or dispatch incurred as a result of shipping bagged or bulk urea.

§ Includes cost of labor and incidental charges.

‖ Cost differential represents the gross import substitution potential for local bagging. If the bulk urea can be landed, bagged, and prepared for dispatch for less than the cost differential, there is a potential saving in local bagging.

and storage capacity; precautionary measures against inclement weather; and properly designed equipment, including discharge, bagging and storage facilities.

It was also considered important that too much division of responsibility among various port authority groups should be avoided. It was considered that excessive work stoppages, loss of material, misunderstandings, lower rates of discharge and bagging, and general operating problems would be minimized if the entire unloading and bagging operation was run as a single entity. In view of these several considerations, Gulf approached the project not as merely a bagging plant but as a complete process aimed at performing all operations necessary to transform bulk urea in the hold of a ship into bagged urea ready for dispatch to the farmer. In addition, Indonesian farmers had become accustomed to an imported product. Gulf thought that it was necessary that the bagging of urea in Indonesia produce a comparable product, with uniform, well sealed, clearly marked, and accurately weighed bags.

The logical location for the bagging operation appeared to be Tandjung Priok, the principal port of Djakarta. Land was acquired, including the old coal dump which already had a wharf, and a railroad siding. The plant was to be designed to have an average throughput of 300,000 metric tons per year. Demand was expected to be seasonal, however, with 75 percent of the consumption of fertilizer taking place before or during the wet season (i.e., December through March). The absolute maximum capacity of the contemplated plant would be, it was thought, 400,000 metric tons per year. Mr. Myers estimated that total investment in the bagging operation might amount to $2.5 million, depending on the method of production used.

The approach being considered by Gulf was to operate the joint venture (hereinafter referred to as PGIP) on a tolling basis. That is, the customer would pay the landed price of the bulk fertilizer plus a fee or "toll" for processing the bulk fertilizer from the ship holds into bagged fertilizer loaded onto trucks or railroad cars for delivery to the customer FOB origin. Bulk fertilizer would be packed in bags of 50 kilograms each. Bags would be supplied by either the customer of PGIP in the form of a woven polypropylene exterior with a 1.5 mil. polyethylene liner. When bags were supplied by PGIP, customers would pay a toll of $10.00 per metric ton. The estimated price of $0.20 each for the 50 kilograms bags (including-liner) would be subtracted from this charge when the customer supplied their own bags.

ALTERNATIVE PRODUCTION AND HANDLING METHODS

Bagging could be accomplished in a number of different ways. Plants had been built in Singapore, for example, using very little machinery. They depended primarily on large numbers of workers who would fill bags with shovels and weigh them on simple scales. In the United States, on the other hand, bagging operations were usually highly automated.

PGIP could choose methods at one of these extremes or it could take some middle route.

THE GENERAL STEPS IN THE PROCESS

The activities to be considered could be broken down into five simple sequential steps:

1. Unloading the carrier vessel and movement of product to bulk storage.
2. Removal from bulk storage to the bagging operation.
3. Bagging.
4. Removal from the bagging operation to bagged storage.
5. Dispatch to the customer.

Within the first four steps there was a basic choice of using more labor-intensive or more capital-intensive methods. The process alternatives are described below and are also shown diagrammatically in Exhibit 2.

Exhibit 2

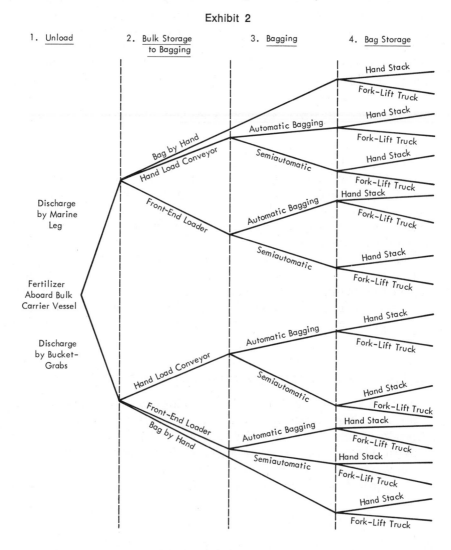

THE ALTERNATIVES

1. Unloading

Bulk carrier vessels would be berthed at the wharf adjoining the plant site. The first step involved removing the fertilizer from the hold of the ship and placing it in a bulk storage area on the plant site. The fertilizer had to be protected from moisture and the important factors determining the choice of unloading method were: the speed of unloading; the relative cost of the alternative methods; the likely waste due to spillage; and the degree of protection from inclement weather. In order to avoid demurrage charges,[2] which ranged from $2,000 to $5,000 per day depending on the size of the vessel delayed, it was necessary to ensure that any method of unloading was capable of removing 3,000 metric tons per day from the ship to the bulk-storage area while the ship was alongside the wharf.

The basic choice faced by PGIP was between emptying the ship by an automatic device attached to a "marine leg," or by means of large buckets attached to the ship's gear. A marine leg is a device that permits the introduction of a probe or leg into each hold of a ship in turn. The leg may carry a bucket conveyor or a sucking head. The leg is mounted on a tower which would, in turn, be mounted on tracks and may be traversed up and down the wharf to provide access to each hold without moving the ship. It was estimated that a marine leg could be constructed at the PGIP wharf, complete with a suitable extraction device, associated conveyor and weigher system to move the fertilizer into the plant, for $150,000. It was planned to store the bulk fertilizer in heaps on the floor of the plant. Storage capacity would be 40,000 metric tons.

Round-the-clock operation of the marine leg conveyor would require four operators at a rate of Rp.100 per hour, one operator for each of the four shift groups necessary to maintain continuous, three-shift availability of labor, seven days per week. In addition, one hatch man on each shift would be required to supervise and guide the unloading head aboard the ship at a rate of Rp.75 per hour. As the marine leg emptied each hold, a crew of eight laborers on each shift would be required to clean out the hold, using shovels, brooms and a bucket attached to the ship's gear. The rate of pay for these laborers would be Rp.30 per hour. Mr. Myers estimated that maintenance and replacement costs for the marine leg would amount to $30,000 per year.

To achieve the required unloading rate, using the alternative method with the ship's gear, would require three automatic grabs at a total purchase and installation cost of $20,000. Each shift would use four winch drivers to operate the ship's gear at an hourly rate of Rp.75. In addition,

---

[2] Charges for having a vessel in port beyond a prearranged period of time.

a gang of 30 laborers at Rp.30 per hour would be needed to service each grab by trimming (i.e., shovelling the product to a position accessible to the grab) in the hold as the unloading operation proceeded. It was estimated that maintenance and replacement parts for the grabs would cost $10,000 per year.

2. Bulk Storage and Removal to Bagging

The second step in the process was to move the fertilizer from the bulk storage area prior to bagging. Each bag had to be filled and sealed. If automatic methods of filling the bags were to be chosen, it would be necessary to provide a system of moving the bulk product from the storage area to some form of elevated hopper. If the bags were to be hand filled, there would be no necessity to elevate the bulk product. If automatic, or semiautomatic bagging methods were to be used, however, and the product had to be elevated, there was a choice among alternative methods of moving the fertilizer from bulk storage to hopper. First, a suitable conveyor would be required so that the product could be raised to the level of the hopper. The alternatives lay in the method of feeding the conveyor. Either the product was to be shovelled onto the conveyor by hand, or it was to be moved to the conveyor by mechanical means. It was estimated that the purchase and installation cost of a conveyor and hoppers would be $50,000 and that maintenance and other costs of operation would be $10,000 per year. If the conveyor was to be hand loaded a crew of 70 laborers would be required for each shift, at an hourly rate of Rp.30. If the product was to be moved by mechanical means, the most suitable machine appeared to be a front-end loader. Two front-end loaders could provide the necessary capacity. Each machine was estimated to cost about $12,000 delivered. A crew of two drivers per shift at an hourly rate of Rp.75 would operate the machines. It was estimated that the two loaders would cost about $12,000 per year in operating, maintenance and replacement costs.

3. Bagging

Three basic alternatives could be considered:

a. A completely automatic bagging operation.
b. A completely manual operation.
c. A partially automated method.

a. Fully Automatic Bagging. In a fully automatic bagging unit, a polypropylene bag, complete with polyethylene liner would be attached by an operator to a conveyor. The bags would be attached by four small clips, the conveyor holding the bag and liner open sufficiently for the penetration of a filler head. The bags would move, suspended from the conveyor, under the filler head which would automatically meter 50 kilograms of product on the arrival of each bag. The bags would then move to a heat-sealing head which would fasten both liner and outer bag. The bag would be dropped onto a belt conveyor, pass through a metallic detection device (to check for foreign matter in the fertilizer) and over an automatic weigher. Bags containing foreign matter or over/under weight would be automatically pushed off the conveyor for rebagging. Passed bags would be piled on pallets and left for removal. Two automatic lines operating continuously would be needed to maintain the required PGIP capacity of around 40 tons per hour. Two men at a rate of Rp.75 per hour would be required to operate each line for a shift. The cost of equipment for each line would be $150,000, installed. Operating, maintenance and replacement expenses were estimated at $60,000 per year for the two lines.

b. Hand Bagging. Gangs of laborers would transfer fertilizer from the storage heaps into hand-held bags, using shovels or small buckets. When the bag was approximately filled, it would be passed to a platform weigher and topped off to the correct weight by the addition of fertilizer; a small trowel or a shovel would be used. The liner would then be tied and the outer bag would be sewn by hand. A crew of 140 laborers on each shift would be required to provide the same bagging rate as the two automatic lines. The rate of pay would be Rp.30 per hour per worker.

c. Semiautomatic Bagging. As in the case of the automatic lines, the bagging line would be fed from hoppers. A polypropylene bag would be removed from a stack of new bags and snapped open. The opened bag and liner would be held to the filling spout of a semiautomatic weigher. The weigher would be activated by pulling a lever, upon which 50 kilograms of product would drop into the held bag. The inner lining of the bag would be tied, using nylon twine. The bag would be visually inspected for damage and faulty tying of the liner. The outer bag would then be sewn, using an industrial sewing machine. The sewn bag would be dropped onto a pallet to await removal. The several positions in the bagging line would be connected by a roller conveyor.

Eight semiautomatic bagging lines would be required to provide the necessary capacity, each line would be operated by a crew of six men on each shift, at a rate of Rp.30 per hour. The installed cost of equipment for each line would be $4,000. Operating and maintenance costs for the eight lines were estimated at $6,000 per year.

4. Bag Storage

After removal from the bagging operation the bags would be stacked. Alternative methods of transporting the bags to the stacks could be considered. If the job was done by hand, a crew of 50 laborers per shift would be required, at Rp.30 per hour, to carry and stack the bags. Alternatively, five small fork-lift trucks, each requiring one driver, and a team of eight laborers could perform the same task. Each truck would cost $5,000 and would require about $2,500 in operating and maintenance costs. The driver's rate would be Rp.75 per hour. In order to use the fork-lift method it would be necessary to place the bags onto pallets. Storage space for the bagged product was limited to 12,000 metric tons.

5. Dispatch

No alternatives were considered in this area. The bags, it was decided, would be loaded to rail or road trucks by contract labor at a cost of approximately $0.10 per ton. This labor would be made available, on demand, by contractors in the port area.

DESCRIPTION OF A "MIDDLE" TECHNOLOGY

Exhibit 3 depicts a possible layout of the PGIP bagging plant using a middle form of technology, between the very labor-intensive and the fully

Exhibit 3
DIAGRAM OF PGIP PLANT LAYOUT FOR "MIDDLE" METHOD

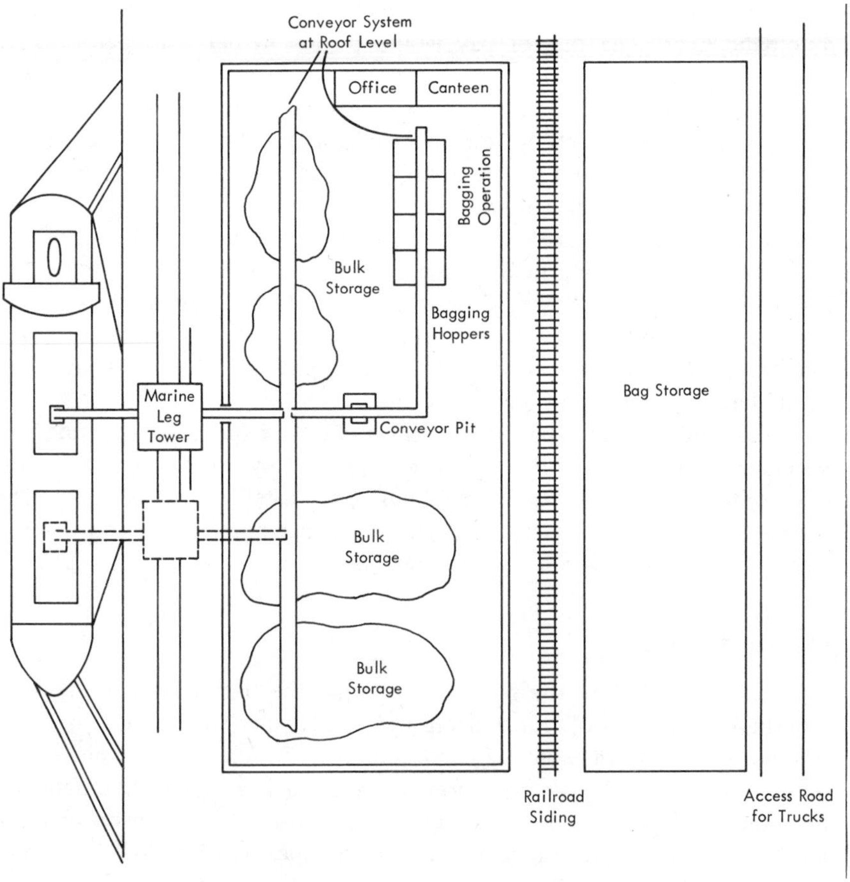

automated extremes. The choices made in adopting this particular solution are indicated by the heavy line path through the decision diagram in Exhibit 2. A summary of the required labor force for this alternative is given in Exhibit 4.

Exhibit 4
SUMMARY OF PGIP WORKERS FOR FOUR-GROUP,
THREE-SHIFT OPERATION
(middle technology alternative)

Total	Per Shift	Task
4	1	Maintenance mechanic*
1	—	Maintenance supervisor*
4	1	Marine leg operator
4	1	Hatch man
21	7	Front-end loader and fork-lift truck operators
32	8	Bag filling
32	8	Liner fastening
32	8	Checkers on bag line
32	8	Sewing machine operator
64	16	Pallet loading
32	8	Pallet unloading
32	8	Sweepers
20	5	Tally clerks*
17	4	Security guards (1 chief)*
1		Works manager*
1		Plant operator (expert)*
329		

Direct workers = 285.

* Overhead personnel.

1. Unloading

Ships, loaded with 8,000 to 15,000 tons of bulk urea, are berthed alongside the wharf. Fertilizer is extracted from the holds by means of the marine leg bucket conveyor. The marine leg traverses up and down the wharf, giving access to each hold. Removal of the residual fertilizer left by the conveyor, and cleaning of each hold of the vessel is carried out by laborers loading one-ton containers which are hoisted to the conveyor by the ship's gear. While the cleaning of the hold is taking place, the marine leg is moved to a full hold to ensure maximum unloading rate.

The marine leg bucket conveyor transports the products to a roof-level conveyor system running to four bulk storage areas and to the bagging hopper.

PGIP is required to unload ships at the rate of at least 3,000 metric tons per 24-hour period. The normal operating speed of the marine leg is 200 tons per hour. For purposes of determining the accountability of product, shrinkage allowance, and processing charges, the shippers' weight of product is used as input tonnage. Intake weight is checked by an electronic Beltvayer automatic scale, incorporated in the conveyor.

2. Bulk Storage

Four areas in the main building are used for the storage of bulk fertilizer. The total bulk storage capacity is 40,000 metric tons. PGIP must ensure that every shipment is stored separately. There is to be no co-mingling of products or shipments in the bulk storage areas. The fertilizer is simply dumped on the floor in separate piles by the conveyor system.

The fertilizer is transported from the bulk storage areas to the centrally located conveyor pit by front-end loaders. Two front-end loaders, each with one operator work round the clock. The two machines would be capable of handling 100 tons per hour, and would provide sufficient excess capacity to cover the expected level of breakdowns. From the pit the fertilizer is carried by the conveyor to the bagging hoppers.

3. Bagging

The bagging weighers are fed from the hoppers. Fertilizer may be fed directly from the marine leg to the hoppers; however, the disparity between the unloading rate necessary to avoid demurrage, and the bagging rate of 40 tons per hour mean that most of the product must be stored in bulk form before bagging.

The bagging operation is carried out at eight "bagging lines." Each bagging line is a simple flow operation consisting of five operator positions. All positions are connected by dead roller conveyor sections. The activities at each bagging line, in order of their occurrence for each bag produced are:

1. One man removes a polypropylene bag from a stack of new bags and tubes the bag by snapping it full of air. The bags have a polyethylene inner lining. He then takes the open bag and holds it to the filling spout of a semiautomatic weigher which deposits a predetermined amount (either 50 kilograms or 25 kilograms) of fertilizer into the bag. The automatic weigher is fed from the bagging hoppers.
2. One man takes the filled bag and ties the top of the inner liner with nylon twine.
3. One man inspects the filled bag and checks for apparent damage or faulty tying of the liner.
4. One man sews the top of the outer bag with nylon twine using an industrial sewing machine.
5. Two men remove the sewn bag from the roller conveyor and place it on a pallet.

4. Bag Storage

The filled pallets containing 20×50 kilograms or 40×25 kilograms bags are transported to the bag storage area by fork-lift truck. Up to five fork-lift trucks, each operated by one driver, may be in use at any time.

Bags are removed from pallets in the storage area. Shortage of pallets prevents stacking of palletized bags. The bags are stacked 25 high in 8 foot $\times$ 8 foot stacks allowing 4 feet around the stack for access. The weight in each stack would be thus 20 metric tons. There is a total capacity for storing 12,000 metric tons of fertilizer in bagged form. Eight laborers per shift are occupied in removing bags from pallets to stacks.

5. Dispatch

Bags are loaded to rail cars or trucks by hand, using contract labor.

Fawcett Optical Equipment Company

ON MAY 25th, Mr. William Thomas, manager of manufacturing of the Fawcett Optical Equipment Company was holding a meeting to discuss and evaluate plans for the assembly activities for the KD 780 photo-reconnaissance Air Force Camera contract. These plans (Exhibit 1) had been

Exhibit 1
ASSEMBLY SCHEDULE

	Assembly Operators Added	Total Operators Available	Effective Man-Hours Available	Cameras Assembled during Month	Cumulative Total Cameras Assembled
June and July	0	4	1,280	2	2
August	25	29	3,440	12	14
September	25	54	7,440	59	73
October	0	54	8,640	120	193
November	0	54	8,640	173	366
December	0	54	8,640	223	589
January	0	54	8,640*	241*	840*

* 665 effective man-hours available in January will not be needed to achieve the total production of 840 units.

Source: Mr. Robert Phillips' KD 780 Camera Assembly Project File.

developed during April and May by Mr. Robert Phillips, superintendent of the assembly of non-commerical products of the Fawcett factory at Cleveland, Ohio. Mr. Thomas and others at this meeting were not at all certain that Mr. Phillips' plans were feasible. The KD 780 camera job was Fawcett's first defense-product contract since World War II, and Mr. Thomas was anxious for the manufacturing division to look good on this job to enhance prospects for more business with the Air Force.

The Fawcett Optical Equipment Company of Cleveland, Ohio, designed, manufactured, and sold optical equipment used in laboratories, factories and medical facilities. Two years earlier the company purchased a factory building and some machine tools, which had been declared surplus property by the U.S. Department of Defense. These new facilities provided about 25 percent more space and machine capacity than was to be required by optical equipment manufacturing, according to a ten-year forecast of sales. However, the price and especially the location of this former government property were so attractive and Fawcett's former plant space had been so inadequate that the added investment in the surplus plant and machines was easily justified. During the ensuing nine months, the move to the new plant had been completed and operations were running smoothly.

The previous September, Mr. J. F. Pickering, president of the company, had decided to solicit government contracts to manufacture and assemble defense products in order to utilize the extra available plant space and machine tools more fully. No commitments were to be made for Fawcett to design or develop new products because Fawcett's engineers were fully occupied with optical equipment design work. Accordingly, a sales engineer and a production engineer had made a series of calls at various military equipment procurement offices. In December, Fawcett was awarded a prime contract to manufacture 840 model KD 780 night-photo reconnaissance cameras for the Air Force. Fawcett had been chosen among competitive bidders as the alternate prime source of supply of these cameras, which had previously been designed and produced by the Sedgewick Instrument Company.

To prepare Fawcett's quotation for this contract, a group comprised of a manufacturing engineer, a tool engineer, a cost estimator, and a purchasing agent had reviewed and analyzed over 600 Sedgewick Instrument Company drawings of detail and assembly parts of the KD 780 camera. After Fawcett was awarded the contract, these drawings were thoroughly checked to insure that Fawcett had drawings showing the latest Sedgewick engineering change information. Then, various make-buy decisions had been made and accordingly materials and tool orders placed with various vendors and/or with the machining and tool-making departments at the Fawcett plant. Air Force procurement officers had stated they desired these cameras as soon as possible. The contract stipulated that Fawcett was to ship the first KD 780 cameras in July, and, by October, Fawcett was to build up its camera output rate to at least 120 units per month until the 840 cameras had been produced and shipped.

DEVELOPMENT OF MR. PHILLIP'S ASSEMBLY PLAN

By February, Mr. Phillips received copies of the parts lists, assembly drawings, and test specifications, after the various procurement and parts manufacturing planning decisions had been made. Mr. Phillips turned these documents over to the assembly methods engineer on his staff, with instructions to plan the layout of the benches in assembly area, to design and order necessary tools and fixtures, and to provide estimates of the standard hours per unit required at each assembly work station deemed necessary. The standard hour estmates were prepared by using predetermined methods and time standard data, and by presuming planned assembly work station layouts, methods, and carefully selected and fully trained assembly operators. Assisting the methods engineer were the project foreman and four "assembly-technicians" assigned as a "nucleus crew" to assembly the first, small production lot of cameras and to "debug" the assembly processing methods. The technicians were later to become working foremen and job leaders of new assembly personnel to be added to the assembly working force, as the assembly output rate was boosted to the minimum rate of 120 units per month. On April 15, the assembly methods planning group advised Mr. Phillips that after the assembly work force were skilled in using the planned methods, each camera would require a total 85 standard man-hours to assemble completely. The 85 standard man-hours was the sum of the standard man-hours per unit for different jobs involved in assembling one camera.

While his assembly methods planning group were engaged in their work, Mr. Phillips concentrated on how to approach the problems of programming the build-up of the assembly work force, and of controlling the rate of build-up in output of the cameras while new personnel were being hired and trained. He anticipated the possibilities of production delays and man-idleness during the entire period of assembling the 840 KD 780 cameras. He had heard of production delay problems in companies producing defense products, in which as much as 95 percent of the units ordered were delayed in shipment to the customer until the last month of a 12-month planned period devoted to producing a particular defense product. This was an experience Mr. Phillips had hoped to avoid. He realized that a desirable approach was one enabling him to anticipate a specific quantitiative pattern of output during the entire period the cameras were being assembled.

While discussing the KD 780 job at lunch one day in March Mr. Phillips heard the sales engineer, who had "landed" this contract, briefly describe "The Manufacturing Progress Function" (otherwise called the "learning curve"), which Air Force procurement officers frequently used as a guide in negotiating price and delivery terms of contracts with manufacturers. Mr. Phillips investigated the literature[1] on this subject and, as a result, decided to adapt the manufacturing progress function as a means for solving his problem of programming and controlling the KD 780 assembly activties. Briefly, the chief premise of the manufacturing progress function was that, just as the effort exerted by a single worker decreased as he acquired experience and skill in doing a set of tasks, so the labor hours or

---

[1] R. W. Conway and A. Schultz, Jr., "The Manufacturing Progress Function," *Journal of Industrial Engineering,* January–February 1959.

labor cost per unit of product produced by a group of workers would decrease as experience was gained by the group in producing the product. Since this learning experinece could be measured quantitatively, Mr. Phillips decided to use this concept as the basis for his assembly operations plans.

As his first step in adapting the manufacturing progress function to his assembly activities, Mr. Phillips listed pertinent conditions that would affect his assembly program.

1. After lengthy discussion with his methods engineer and technicians, Mr. Phillips decided that 90 KD cameras would have been assembled by the time the assembly personnel had developed sufficient skill and experience to meet the standard rate of 85 total man-hours per unit.

2. Starting with the nucleus crew of four assembly technicians, it was decided that additional assembly personnel could be selected, hired, and effectively trained at the maximum rate of 25 new employees per month. To attempt to train more than 25 new operators would overtax training facilities and personnel, Mr. Phillips believed. The personnel manager, Mr. P. D. Kenworthy, had advised that all additional assembly personnel required for the KD 780 job would have to be recruited from the Cleveland area and would require Fawcett company orientation training as well as job methods training. During their first month on the KD 780 job, new employees were presumed to be 70 percent efficient (100 percent efficient meant that an operator completed the job in exactly the standard labor hours set for the assembly tasks assigned for him to complete). After the first month, all operators were presumed to be at least 100 percent efficient.

3. For purposes of developing these plans, Mr. Phillips assumed that there would be 160 assembly operating hours in any calendar month. Since a calendar month contained $4\frac{1}{3}$ weeks, this meant that every third month, a "margin of safety" of one week was available as a reserve for contingencies such as material shortages, quality problems, and other delays interfering with the flow of assembly work.

4. The KD 780 camera contained over 800 parts. Plans for the process specified assembly work to be done at 27 different work stations on four major subassemblies and 35 work stations in the final assembly area. Standard times at these work stations were not uniform, and to insure reasonable continuity of flow of work, buffer stocks were to be provided and certain operators were to be shifted among several work stations. From these plans, Mr. Phillips estimated that the elapsed time for assembling a camera would be four weeks, two weeks for final and test, and two weeks for subassembly work.

5. The initial production-lot quantity planned was two cameras—just enough for the methods engineer and the four assembly technicians to check on the assembly methods, tools and work place arrangements in the assembly area. The Air Force desired to make thorough acceptance tests of the performance of the first two units produced by Fawcett.

6. To use the manufacturing progress function, Mr. Phillips had to make an assumption of the measured rate of progress he could expect the growing labor force to achieve while assembling the 840 KD 780 cameras. He had noted in the literature that an 80 percent learning curve was rather widely used in the aircraft industry. An 80 percent learning rate meant that each time the cumulative number of units produced doubled, the labor hours per unit dropped to 80 percent of its former value. For example, the direct labor cost or time for assembling the 20th unit was 80 percent of the average direct labor time for assembling the 10th unit completed; and the direct labor hours for assembling the 40th unit was 80 percent of the direct labor hours for assembling the 20th unit completed; and so on.

Mr. Phillips had realized that to choose a progress rate parameter of 80 percent, 70 percent, or whatever, he would have to use good judgment in extrapolating from past experiences. He therefore examined blueprints, methods specifications, and labor time tickets for several optical equipment products assembled by Fawcett employees in the past. Each past experience had some degree of similarity with the KD 780 job with respect to such factors as: the numbers of different parts to be assembled; the clearances between parts; the fragility of the parts; the numbers of different assembly operations required and the total assembly hours required per unit. By plotting learning curves for several such similar assembly activities in the past, Mr. Phillips had determined that the assembly progress-rate parameters for these past jobs had ranged from 70 percent to 75 percent.

From this, Mr. Phillips had chosen 72 percent as the expected rate of progress that would be achieved on the KD 780 Air Force camera assembly job.

From these six presumed conditions, Mr. Phillips had developed his assembly production schedule and his manpower build-up schedule, shown in Exhibit 1. The detailed, step-by-step procedure Mr. Phillips followed to determine these schedules is summarized in the Appendix. Mr. Phillips had completed the work of determining these schedules on May 20th.

During a regular KD 780 camera job-progress meeting of manufacturing management personnel held on May 25th, Mr. Phillips had presented his assembly schedules, and had briefly described how he had derived them.

Mr. J. D. Jorgenson, KD 780 Camera Project Cost Supervisor: Bob, using your data on labor hours and total units assembled and some cost figures I have, I estimate that we won't make any money on the KD 780 job until after we have shipped about 600 units. In fact, I don't think we will have absorbed our start-up costs directly incurred on this job until after we've shipped the 400th unit. We're committed to a fixed price on this job you know; we could not get the Air Force to go along with a cost-plus-fixed-fee price. Of course, there is a price renegotiation clause in the contract, but this is a long legal and costly process.

Mr. Phillip D. Kenworthy, Manager of Personnel and Relations: The union has been after me about wage-incentive procedures for this KD 780 camera assembly job. As you know, we put a newly hired man on a straight piecework incentive wage after he has been on the job for one month. As I see this learning curve idea, we have an inevitable "looseness" built into our time standards. I know we regularly use predetermined (synthetic) motion and time standard data, as well as stop watch time studies for the factory floor, to set piece rates. But if we put these KD 780 assembly personnel on an incentive pay basis too soon, their wages will get out of line with other personnel in the same labor class. If we don't put operators on incentives soon enough, the union will gripe. We don't build the same model of optical equipment in quantities compared to the 840 KD 780 cameras, so there isn't the extensive and uninterrupted opportunity for learning on comparable optical equipment assembly jobs. If all your people are put on incentive wage rates by October Bob, and if they progress the way you say they will along your 72 percent progress curve, they will be turning out the 840th camera in less than 30 hours. But if they start pegging rates, say, after the 150th camera (when standard hours are $85/66 = 128$ percent of actual hours), won't this give you some trouble, Bob?

MR. PHILLIPS: There is a possible wage inequity problem, Phil, and all I can say is that we'll have to take a good look at our whole wage payment policy and procedure, in light of this, before our next union contract negotiation. Meanwhile, I'm going to keep my methods engineer alert to keep his methods standards and time standards up to date and to take more initiative in revising methods and time standards. There is nothing in the contract to prevent us from tightening the rates of jobs when we engineer job-methods changes. I'm also going to tell my foreman to encourage our people to exploit this learning opportunity and to assure our people that there will be no tightening of standards when an operator makes methods changes that enable him to beat the rates we have set.

MR. WILLIAM THOMAS, Manager of Manufacturing: Bob, this is quite a program you've planned. I had told Mr. Pickering I thought we wouldn't wind up this KD 780 job until May of next year. Now you show us shipping the last unit in January or February. If you're wrong, and we land another Air Force contract to work on in February, we'll really be in a bind. Are you sure you can make this schedule? Another thing, if you've planned that the standard will be 85 labor hours per unit, and the contract states that we have to ship 120 units per month, then I figure we should have a capacity $85 \times 120 = 10,200$ standard man-hours per month. This is $10,200/160 = 64$ operators. Yet you say you can do the whole job with 54 operators. (If this is true with assembly work, I wonder how this idea would go with our parts machining work.)

MR. PHILLIPS: Bill, I'm convinced we can do this. I'm telling my foremen exactly how I got the 72 percent progress curve, and that I am going to plot their actual progress each week to see how close they come to the curve. All I'll have to do is take the count of cameras coming off the packaging operation, and divide this into the total weekly direct labor hours tallied by the timekeeper. If their actual progress data plot above the curve for direct labor hours per unit, I'll know something is wrong and find out what it is. I'd like to try to carry out these plans, and I hope you will approve them and give me the support I know I'll need.

APPENDIX: FAWCETT OPTICAL EQUIPMENT COMPANY*

1. General Technical Specifications of the Manufacturing Progress Function. When empirical data on direct-labor hours per unit are plotted against the production count of units produced, the resulting curve appears, for example, as shown on the following page for the KD 780 camera assembly operations (Exhibit A–1):

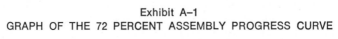

Exhibit A–1
GRAPH OF THE 72 PERCENT ASSEMBLY PROGRESS CURVE

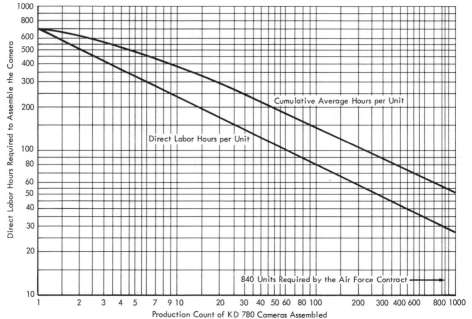

Note: Graphs are plotted on log-log graph paper.
Source: Mr. Robert Phillips KD 780 Camera Assembly Project Files.

The curve depicts a phenomenon which makes strong intuitive sense, that is, *a job requires less effort as more experience is gained and as more methods improvements are made.* As production accumulates progress continues but at a decreasing rate, because further opportunities to improve the job become less and less obvious. This curve is just one of an almost infinite variety of such curves having the same "family-resemblance"; that is the direct-labor hours per unit decrease more or less sharply, but always steadily, as the number of units produced increases.

The algebraic statement of this progress phenomenon is

---

* Summary of the procedure for using the manufacturing progress function to schedule assembly build-up on KD 780 Air Force Night-Photo Reconnaissance Camera. Source: Mr. Robert Phillips' KD 780 Camera Assembly Project File.

$$Y_i = ai^{-b}$$

where

Y_i is the direct labor hours required to produce the ith unit of product.

i is the production count, beginning with the first unit.

a is a parameter of the model which is equal to the labor hours required for the first unit, Y_1 (for $i = 1$, $Y_1 = a(1)^{-b} = a$).

b is a measure of the *rate* at which the direct labor hours per unit are reduced as the production count increases.

When the labor hours per unit and production count data are plotted on logarithmic coordinate graph paper, or when the logarithms of these data are plotted on conventional arithmetic coordinate graph paper, the curve becomes a straight line. Algebraically this fact is stated by taking the logarithmic transformation of the equation above

$$(\log Y_i) = (\log a) - b (\log i)$$

The rate of progress is nominally described by stating the complement of the percentage reduction in labor hours per unit when the production quantity is doubled. This means that if i_2 and i_1 are any two different production counts and if i_2/i_1 always equals 2, then for an 80 percent progress curve, $b \times 0.322$ because $2^{-0.322} = 0.80$; for a 72 percent progress curve, $b \times 0.474$ because $2^{-0.474} = 0.72$.

The *cumulative* number of direct labor hours required to produce n units may be expressed as:

$$T_n = Y_1 + Y_2 + \cdots + Y_n = \sum_{i=1}^{n} Y_i$$

An approximation of this sum is given by the integral:

$$T_n = \int_0^n Y_i \, di = a \int_0^n i^{-b} \, di \cong a \left(\frac{n^{1-b}}{1-b} \right).$$

Dividing this expression by the cumulative number of units (n) gives an approximation for the *cumulative average* number of labor hours:

$$A_n \cong \frac{a}{n} \left(\frac{n^{1-b}}{1-b} \right) \cong \frac{an^{-b}}{1-b} \cong \frac{Yn}{1-b}$$

These approximations typically yield insignificant errors at n values of 100 units or more, but large errors can occur for small values of n.

2.   Method of adapting the manufacturing progress function to plans for assembling the KD 780 camera.

a.   Assumptions made:
(1)   The standard of 85 hours per camera will be achieved on the 90th camera.
(2)   The rate of progress in assembly methods improvements, and in development of skill by assembly personnel would conform to a 72 percent progress function (corresponding to a b parameter value of 0.474).

$$Y_i = a(i)^{-0.474}$$

b.   The assembly progress curve (Direct Labor hours per unit). Using log-log graph paper, starting at 85 hours for the 90th unit, a straight line with a slope of -0.474 was drawn through this point. See Exhibit A–1. This implies that 716 hours will be required to assemble the first camera.

c.   A cumulative Average Direct Labor Hours curve was also plotted on Exhibit A–1 to ease calculations for the assembly output build-up schedule and for the manpower build-up schedule. This curve was developed by calculating the cumulative average hours per unit for a variety of values of cumulative output (n) and then plotting them on the graph (Exhibit A–1). Note that the cumulative average curve becomes asymptotically parallel to the unit curve as the number of units completed increase.

The assembly manpower build-up schedule required that subtotals of the cumulative assembly direct labor hours be related to cumulative production. These subtotals were easily calculated by multiplying the cumulative average direct labor hours per unit by the cumulative number of units assembled. Data on cumulative average direct-labor hours per unit were simply read from the curve. (Without having this curve, calculations for the manpower and output build-up schedules would have been more tedious.) From this curve the following table could be determined (the actual values shown were computer calculated).

Sample Calculations for Assembly Output and Manpower Schedules
June and July
Manpower required for the first two units is approximately 1,240 man-hours.
Manpower available: 4 at 160 hours per month $\times$ 2 months = 1,280 man-hours.
August
Manpower: Add 25 new employees whose efficiency is 70 percent

$25 \times 160 \times 0.70 =$	2,800	
Already available: 4×160	640	3,440 man-hours
Cumulative total man-hours		
through August		4,720

Output:	Comparison of 4,720 with data in column 4 of Table A–1 shows that the 14th unit would have been produced by the end of August. During August 14 — 2 = 12 units would have been completed.	

September

Manpower:	Add 25 new employees—efficiency 70 percent =	2,800 man-hours
	Already available as of September 1: 29 × 160 =	4,640
	Total man-hours expended in September	7,440
	Cumulative total man-hours through August	4,720
	Cumulative total man-hours through September	12,160
Output:	In Table A–1, comparison of 12,160 with data in column 4 shows that about 73 units would have been produced by the end of September. During September 73 — 14 = 59 units would have been completed.	

October

Manpower:	Available as of October 1: 54 × 160 =	8,640 man-hours
	Cumulative total expended through September	12,160
	Cumulative total man-hours expended through October.	20,800
Output:	In Table A–1, comparison of 20,800 with data in column 4 shows that approximately 193 units would have been produced after expending 20,800 man-hours of assembly labor. During the month of October 193 — 73 = 120 cameras would have been assembled.	

From October through January the output schedule was based on the 8,640 man-hours available each month and the data in Table A–1.

Table A–1
TABLE OF CUMULATIVE PRODUCTION AND
LABOR HOUR DATA

Cumulative Production	Hours This Unit	Cumulative Average Hours per Unit	Cumulative Total Hours (Column 1 × Column 3)
1	716	716	716
2	516	616	1,232
10	240	371	3,714
12	221	347	4,165
15	198	319	4,780
20	173	285	5,692
40	125	214	8,564
60	103	180	10,806
75	93	163	12,262
100	81	144	14,412
150	67	120	18,054
200	58	106	21,153
250	52	96	23,903
300	48	88	26,402
400	42	77	30,868
500	38	70	34,830
600	35	64	38,431
700	32	60	41,757
800	30	56	44,864
840	29	55	46,055

Ampex Corporation (A)

TIME: 2:15 p.m.
DATE: Thursday, January 23, 1958
PLACE: Office of the Manufacturing Division, Ampex Corporation

> Andy, I just received the two o'clock status report on the VTR head assemblies. Every one of the "control heads" inspected this week has been a reject. It's clear by now that the changes made by the product engineers haven't solved anything—in fact, they may have created new problems. Furthermore, with all these experiments going on, production has slowed to a crawl. I think that we should develop a new plan of action for you to present to the meeting at 4:30 today in the front office. Get together with Ray to try to work something out, and then we can talk it over at 3:30 here in my office.

With these words Larry Burn, assistant manager of the Ampex Corporation's manufacturing division, asked Charles V. (Andy) Andersen, manager of manufacturing operations, to look for a new approach to solving a problem which had rapidly become the center of attention of the company's operating executives. Mr. Andersen would be working with Ray Heidenreich, general foreman of the assembly department and leader of a special task force which had been organized to coordinate efforts aimed at correcting the situation. At 4:30 that day Ray and others from his special committee would be gathering for their daily meeting in the office of the company's vice president and general manager, Mr. Robert Sackman.

The problem was this. A severe drop in the yield of good units in the manufacture of VTR heads had suddenly occurred early in January. The VTR was the Video Tape Recorder, a machine for magnetic recording of television images and one of the major new products of the Ampex Corporation. The "head" was a small but critical subassembly in a complete system selling for $45,000. After years of development and design work, and enthusiastic acceptance of the product by the broadcast industry, the manufacture of a production model began in November 1957. Production was planned to fill a backlog of orders for 100 systems by the end

471

of April 1958. Seven systems had been completed in November and six more in December. By mid-January, the output rate was expected to reach one per working day. The ouput of heads, however, virtually ceased early in January. Only three systems could be shipped during the first three weeks of that month. On January 23, seven packaged and crated systems sat on the shipping dock awaiting the addition of heads so that they could be shipped. At the same time, eight more systems were undergoing final inspection and would shortly be ready for shipment if heads were available.

COMPANY BACKGROUND

The Ampex Corporation manufactured and sold professional quality magnetic tape recording and reproduction equipment for sound and data recording purposes in the broadcast and phonograph record industries, laboratory instrumentation, many military applications, and industrial control.

Ampex recording equipment, since its introduction in 1948, had represented the accepted standard of quality in the broadcast industry. Instrumentation products introduced in 1950, tapped a substantial market and by 1957 accounted for two thirds of sales volume. The company was the outstanding manufacturer in its field, holding 85 percent or more of the business in most markets in which it competed. The lowest priced product sold to the user for $495, and instrumentation products sold for unit prices averaging $15,000. Most units were sold on a "systems" basis, as a custom designed combination of standard modular sections.

Growth of sales volume resulting from the development of new products had been important throughout the ten-year history of the firm. Sales volume grew from $400,000 in fiscal 1950 to $30 million for fiscal 1958. Personnel and facilities expanded apace. The original facilities, only 9,000 square feet, were abandoned in 1951 for a 25,000 square foot plant. In 1958 operations occupied 14 buildings and a total of 267,000 square feet of space in Redwood City, California. Balance sheets and Income Statements are given in Exhibits 1 and 2.

The company's engineers worked on the frontiers of knowledge in their field, utilizing new technology to develop new and improved products. Nearly $1.4 million had been spent in 1957 on research and experimental expenses. As a result of these research efforts Ampex had developed an advanced line of instrumentation products, a revolutionary machine for recording video images, and an advanced unit for recording digital information to be used in electronic data processing.

Organization

Operations were centered at Redwood City, except that in a nearby community a wholly-owned subsidiary, Ampex Audio, Inc., manufactured certain models for the consumer market. Mr. Robert Sackman, as vice president and general manager, held operational responsibility for all activities in Redwood City. The organization in early 1958, as indicated in Exhibit 3, included six autonomous divisions: two product divisions, the manufacturing and the quality control divisions, a finance division, and a research division.

Exhibit 1

Comparative Consolidated Balance Sheets—Years Ending April 30, 1953–1957

	1957* Pro Forma	1957	1956	1955	1954	1953
Assets:						
Cash	$ 3,993	$ 1,011	$ 704	$ 402	$ 403	$ 103
Accounts receivable	5,561	5,561	2,034	1,583	617	745
Inventories	7,603	7,603	2,742	2,032	2,355	1,065
Prepaid expenses	202	202	107	65	49	36
Total current assets	$17,359	$14,377	$5,587	$4,082	$3,424	$1,949
Investment in OR Radio Industries, Inc.	820	–	–	–	–	–
Equipment and leashold improvements	1,200	1,200	1,033	837	498	295
Depreciation	560	560	398	265	168	104
Net equipment and leashold improvements	$ 640	$ 640	$ 635	$ 572	$ 330	$ 191
Unamortized debenture expense	135	–	80	95	15	16
Total Assets	$18,954	$15,017	$6,302	$4,749	$3,769	$2,156
Liabilities:						
Notes payable	$ –	$ 2,000	$ 850	$ –	$ 735	$ 460
Accounts payable	2,055	2,055	712	512	611	312
Customers' deposits	314	314	125	–	–	–
Accrued liabilities	1,051	1,051	510	365	288	156
Accrued profit-sharing contribution	390	390	–	–	–	–
Federal and Canadian income taxes	1,147	1,147	312	391	57	218
Total current liabilities	$ 4,957	$ 6,957	$2,509	$1,268	$1,691	$1,146
15 year 4½% debentures due November 1, 1969	–	–	1,400	1,500	–	–
10 year 6% debentures due October 1, 1962	–	–	–	–	635	645
15 year 5% debentures due July 1, 1972	5,500	–	–	–	–	–
Capital stock—par value	367	361	267	264	207	120
Capital in excess of par value	6,152	5,721	1,235	1,138	1,023	58
Retained earnings	1,978	1,978	891	579	213	187
Total stockholders' equity	$ 8,497	$ 8,060	$2,393	$1,981	$1,443	$ 365
Total	$18,954	$15,017	$6,302	$4,749	$3,769	$2,156

* The above pro forma balance sheet gives effect to significant financial transactions in the three months subsequent to April 30, 1957, namely: private sale of $5,500,000 of 5% 15-year debentures; payment in full of $2,000,000 bank loan; and acquisition of 28.6 percent of the outstanding shares of common capital stock of OR Radio Industries, Inc. This will be reduced to approximately 25 percent after exercise of outstanding options held by others.

Exhibit 2

Consolidated Income Statement
Fiscal Years Ended April 30, 1953–1957
(thousands of dollars)

	1957	1956	1955	1954	1953
Net sales	$18,737	$10,197	$8,163	$5,418	$3,548
Cost of sales	11,648	6,508	5,446	3,980	2,630
Gross profit	$ 7,089	$ 3,689	$2,717	$1,438	$ 918
Expenses:					
Selling and administrative	$ 3,061	$ 2,045	$1,355	$ 946	$ 447
Research and experimental	1,381	927	502	369	119
Interest–debenture and other	45	109	97	53	50
Total expenses	$ 4,487	$ 3,081	$1,954	$1,368	$ 616
Income before profit-sharing Contribution and before income taxes . .	$ 2,602	$ 608	$ 763	$ 70	$ 302
Profit-sharing contribution	390	–	–	–	–
Income before taxes	$ 2,212	$ 608	$ 763	$ 70	$ 302
Income taxes	1,125	296	397	44	213
Net income	$ 1,087	$ 312	$ 366	$ 26	$ 89

Exhibit 3
AMPEX CORPORATION

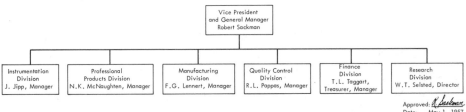

Approved: *R. Sackman*
Date: May 1, 1957

Each product division was responsible for planning, developing, engineering, and selling its line of products. The Professional Products Division managed the line of audio and video recording equipment used in the broadcast and recording industries. The Instrumentation Division sold a variety of standard and specially engineered systems for varied industrial, laboratory, and military applications. Both divisions performed marketing functions, that is, advertising and selling their lines of products, plus engineering functions in the development of new products and the modification of existing models to meet new or special needs. In the normal procedure for development of a new product, the product division held full responsibility for all work from initial conception through completion of approved design blueprints. At this point the manufacturing division assumed responsibility for development of methods and processes, and production of the first units.

In a forecast prepared at the beginning of October 1957, management projected a sales volume of approximately $30 million for the fiscal year ended April 30, 1958. Approximately 55 percent of this volume would come from the Instrumentation Division with the remainder equally split between Professional Product Division and the Ampex Audio subsidiary. Subsequently, however, a sharp reduction in procurement by the Department of Defense had a substantial effect on the volume of incoming orders at Ampex. The backlog of unfilled orders fell from $11.4 million at April 30, 1957, to approximately $7 million at December 31, with the result that 150 production workers were laid off just before the end of the year. A summary report prepared by Mr. Sackman in December offered the following comments: "The initial order upswing in the Instrumentation Division did not continue in November. To meet our year-end shipping goals we're depending upon a substantial expected government order in January plus some upswing in one-at-a-time orders for standard instrumentation products. A very significant downward change in orders received for the Professional Product Division occurred both in professional audio equipment and in orders from Ampex Audio subsidiary. This significant change in our expected product mix has brought a number of risks. Principally, they are that we will be dependent upon shipment of 100 video tape recorders for achievement of goals for the fiscal year and dependent upon certain instrumentation orders for the remainder during this period."

MANUFACTURING DIVISION

The Manufacturing Division, employing 1,100 people, was responsible for methods, fabrication, and assembly in the manufacture of the company's products. The division's organization in 1958 was as shown in Exhibit 4. There were four department managers reporting to the manager and to Mr. Burn, the assistant manager. Mr. Thomas Taggart, treasurer, became acting manager of the manufacturing division on January 1, 1958. Mr. Lennert, the manager, was on an eight-month leave of absence while attending an Advanced Management Training Program at Stanford University. The Manufacturing Division used 145,000 square feet of space in the largest of the buildings occupied by the corporation.

All of the Ampex tape-recording equipment consisted basically of three things: a mechanical tape transport, electronic circuitry, and a recording head. Company policy was to produce these three types of components as standard modular units and store them in a finished goods inventory. The recording systems then were assembled to order and checked out just prior to shipment. In assembly, the modular units were withdrawn from storage and mounted in a cabinet with appropriate electrical and mechanical connections. The manufacturing operations department was responsible for fabrication of parts, assembly of modular units, storage and final assembling of recording systems. Illustrations of modular units and assembled systems appear in Exhibits 5 and 6.

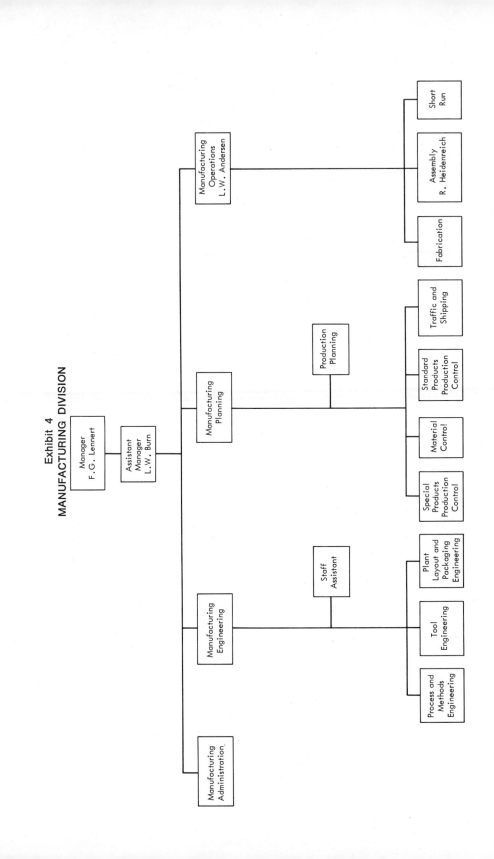

Exhibit 4
MANUFACTURING DIVISION

Exhibit 5
ILLUSTRATIONS OF STANDARD MODULAR UNITS

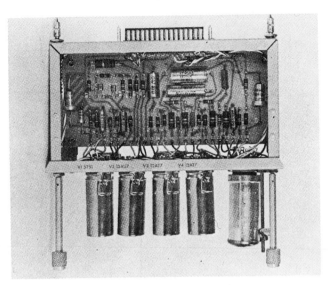

A. Bottom view, plug-in electronic module.

B. Operator aligning standard audio recording heads.

Exhibit 6
ASSEMBLED INSTRUMENTATION RECORDING SYSTEMS

The plant was organized in accordance with the basic processing steps: parts fabrication, assembly of electronic components, mechanical assembly, final assembly, check-out, and shipping. In addition, a special department was devoted to head manufacturing and another to painting and finishing exposed sheet metal parts such as those in the recorder's case. A plan of the layout is given in Exhibit 7.

Engineering Department

The manufacturing engineering department was responsible for processes and methods, tools, plant layout, and product packaging. The department included some 30 engineers and 5 tool designers plus 28 men staffing the tool and die shop on a two-shift basis. The department's functions in the cycle of new product development began after the final design of the product had been approved by the product division concerned. However, prior to that point, one of the manufacturing engineers would work as a liaison man with the product division's design development group. Then, when design blueprints had been prepared, formal responsibility would shift from the product division to the manufacturing engineering department. Manufacturing engineers then prepared bills of material, standard operation sheets, and an assembly manual, designed and constructed necessary tools, and prepared appropriate time and cost estimates. Finally, when the product had been fully tooled and processed, responsibility would shift to the manufacturing operations department.

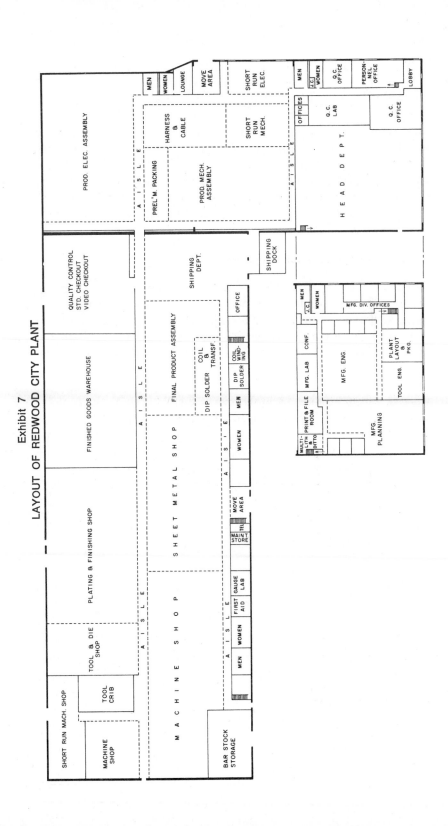

Exhibit 7

LAYOUT OF REDWOOD CITY PLANT

The manufacturing engineering manager felt that his department had to work within a relatively short time period to put a new product into production. Usually the company expected to be ready to ship units four to five months after final design prints had been prepared. To expedite this, the department's liaison man with the product division group would usually become the lead man (or perhaps be the only man) in processing the project when it shifted to manufacturing engineering. According to the engineering manager, one of the liaison man's important functions while working with the design group was to estimate costs and to give advice that would orient design toward economical specifications.

Manufacturing Operations Department

Mr. Charles Andersen was director of manufacturing operations and thus directly responsible for all production activities in the Redwood City plant. Mr. Andersen had joined the company in 1950 as an hourly worker and had been promoted through several supervisory positions. In January 1958 the plant was operating a partial second shift in most production departments. The area and personnel of each department are listed in Exhibit 8. The company paid an average hourly wage of $2 for assembly workers and more than $3 in the machine shop. Two-thirds of the prime cost of production, however, was in purchased material.

Exhibit 8
MANUFACTURING DIVISION—AREA AND PERSONNEL

Department	Area Occupied (square feet)	No. on Payroll, January 1958 First Shift	Second Shift
Administrative	2,500	17	—
Production control	2,500	64	3
Material control and receiving	5,000	63	5
Traffic and shipping	4,000	32	1
Engineering	6,000	59	—
Tool and die	6,600	28	16
Machine shop	13,000	47	38
Sheet metal shop	8,400	28	10
Paint and finish	9,000	49	0
Head assembly	8,400	55	5
Mechanical assembly	6,500	56	—
Electronic assembly	14,000	309	74
System assembly	5,400	19	—
Short run			
Electronic assembly	1,600	50	—
Mechanical assembly	2,200	19	—
Machine shop	2,400	13	12
Stores and warehouse	43,000	—	—

Mr. Andersen described the Ampex plant as "just a gigantic job shop" "We produce hundreds of products and thousands of parts," he said, "but they are all in very short runs averaging, perhaps, 75 units." To do this he felt that the entire organization had to remain very flexible. At the same time, he emphasized that quality was of prime importance in producing Ampex equipment. "That's our only excuse for being in business."

The changing nature of the production operation placed unusual pressure on both supervisor and worker throughout the plant. In assembly operations where a typical line would include 20 to 30 workers, the run frequently would be so short that by the time the last worker got the first piece, the first worker on the line was through with the entire lot. In the machine shops, the workers had to be flexible enough to be able to operate several machines. Mr. Andersen felt that the company couldn't afford to employ just a "mill hand" or a "drill-press operator" because the man had to be able to change his work as the product mix and machine loading changed.

DEVELOPMENT OF THE VTR

Although the development of a magnetic recording technique for television images had for several years been a goal of the broadcast industry, the achievement of this goal represented a great technical challenge for manufacturers of conventional tape recording equipment.[1] The major limitations in the use of tape were in frequency response, since a video signal covered a broad frequency band reaching to several million cycles per second. The most advanced standard model recorders prior to 1956 would not reproduce frequencies greater than 100,000 cycles. Both the Radio Corporation of America and a project supported by Bing Crosby Enterprises had worked to develop a video tape system. Some publicity was given to these projects, both of which were said to be aimed at perfection of a system to permit movement of the tape at speeds sufficient to obtain a frequency of several million cycles with conventional heads.

Ampex Enters the Field

In early 1952 the Ampex Corporation hired Charles Ginsburg, a young engineer, who had been working with a local broadcasting station. Ampex engineers felt at that time that the technical problem involved in moving a tape at several hundred inches per second would prove an insurmountable barrier to the work being done in other companies. They did believe that video recording was an achievable goal, however, and Mr. Ginsburg went to work to develop a system that would move the recording head as well as the tape in order to get the necessary rapid movement of the tape relative to the head. Ampex adapted, under license, an existing patent

---

[1] See the Appendix.

for a rotating drum which swept across a wide longitudinally moving tape. Progress came slowly and in the spring of 1953 the project was temporarily shelved. Work was begun again, however, in 1954 and by 1955 a nucleus of six men was working on the project. In March of 1955 they were able to demonstrate the first working model to the board of directors.

All those concerned with the video project felt that it was necessary to perfect a system that would give a picture indistinguishable from "live" television itself. A number of major technical problems had to be overcome before this could be achieved, and most of them pertained to the recording head itself. The system under development at Ampex employed four separate heads mounted on a drum about two inches in diameter which rotated perpendicular to the tape. Thus the heads were swept at high speed across the two-inch width of the tape. Since the tape itself was moving, the result was a series of slanted parallel lines written magnetically across the tape.

Among the problems faced and surmounted by the development group were: development of a special system to modulate a signal to represent the broad band video signal; a control system to maintain a constant speed in head rotation; manufacturing the heads with the required precision; and controlling the stretch in the tape as it curved around the circumference of the drum in passing the head. Although the initial objectives were to obtain a 2.5 million cycle response at a writing speed of 2,500 inches per second, the final model has a 4.5 million cycle response and a writing speed of 1,500 inches per second. The limiting factor had been the head gap and the achievement was possible only by the use of a gap 0.1 mil across.[2]

A demonstration for the board of directors in March 1955 showed them that the product could perform to the high standards that were to be demanded of it. The project continued with additional funds and was moved to a separate building for reasons of secrecy. Ampex hoped to have a prototype for demonstration to the trade at the April 1956 convention of the National Association of Radio and Television Broadcasters. This goal was met and the first public demonstration was made in conjunction with the Columbia Broadcasting System the day before the 1956 convention at a meeting of CBS affiliate stations. Just three men outside the company had known that Ampex was working on a video recording system although video development projects in other companies had been given a good deal of publicity. In Mr. Ginsburg's words, "When the CBS men saw this machine they jumped and shouted; nobody at Ampex expected this kind of reception but Phil Gundy took out his pad and started taking orders." The machine was formally demonstrated the next day to the entire membership of the NARTB.

One prototype unit was used for all of the demonstrations made in the spring of 1956. Sixteen more prototypes were custom manufactured later

---

[2] A mil is one-thousandth of one inch.

in the year by Ampex engineers; of these 11 were shipped to the television networks, two to the U.S. Government, and three were used within the company. Recordings made on these machines had two important limitations: they could not be edited and they could be played back only on the machine on which they had been recorded. Meanwhile, work proceeded on design and development of a production model of the VTR planned for introduction at the end of 1957. The production model would be equipped with an editing device and tapes made on these models would be interchangeable.

Sales

One sales executive estimated that potential market for VTR systems would probably average two for every United States television station with foreign sales possible to British and German firms which would make the necessary adaptations for their local television systems. Thus, he expected a total potential market in television use of 1,000 to 1,500 units. In early 1958 the 10 direct sales people who handled broadcast equipment coast to coast for the professional products division were concentrating their efforts on the VTR. For each unit sold the company ran a training program for the broadcast station staffs at Redwood City and, in addition, sent two technicians and an engineer to supervise the system's installation. The only competing manufacturer was the Radio Corporation of America with which Ampex entered a cross-licensing agreement for certain patents in January 1958. At that date the production model Ampex system was being delivered at a price of $45,000 with a color television converter priced at an additional $20,000. Lease-purchase plans were available to stations through an independent finance agency. The Radio Corporation of America video recorder was offered at a $49,500 price with the color model costing $14,000 extra, according to the Ampex salesmen, who believed that RCA had not completed its first production model.

NATURE OF THE VTR

The Video-tape recorder was a complex system of electronic and mechanical components weighing more than a ton and occupying a floor console and two equipment racks (see illustrations in Exhibit 9). Eighteen modular electronic units, mounted in the racks, were required for processing the electronic signals in playback and recording. The console contained the control panel for the system and two key elements: the tape transport mechanism (called the "top plate") and recording head.

In operation the transport mechanism moves the two-inch wide magnetic tape past the head at 15 inches per second. The four recording tips are mounted 90° apart on the circumference of a drum two inches in diameter. As the disc rotates at 240 revolutions per second, the tips are

Exhibit 9
PICTURES OF THE VTR

A. System front view.

B. System rear view.

swept across the tape perpendicular to the line of motion of the tape. A vacuum guide chamber helps bow the tape to fit snugly around the circumference of the drum.

The head subassembly, in addition to the rotating drum and four tips, contains a drive motor, vacuum chamber, commutator and other switching apparatus and a photoelectric cell and associated control systems. The entire subassembly is easily demountable as a unit and can be used interchangeably on any system console. The tips themselves had only a limited useful life—about 100 hours—because of the abrasive effect of contact with the tape. When the tips were worn out, the user would return the subassembly to Ampex for rebuilding, which consisted primarily of substituting a new drum. Two subassemblies were shipped as original equipment with each VTR system. Ampex planned to charge $1,500 for the subassembly, plus $300 for each rebuilding.

VTR Production

The Video tape recorder embodied a number of advances in the technology of magnetic recording. With the exception of the head subassembly, however, the component modules presented no unusual problems in manufacture. Three production lots of the modular units had been scheduled to meet the full backlog of orders prior to the April 30, 1958 deadline. The first lot, 25 units of every component but the head, was completed in 1957, and a second lot of 40 units was nearing completion in mid-January 1958. It was expected that the last of these 40 would be in finished goods by early February. The last group of 40 was in the parts fabrication stage and due for assembly in March.

The limiting factor to output of systems[3] was the final check-out procedure. Expensive special-purpose equipment and skilled operators were required to fully check each system. The procedure took six and one-half days, and only eight positions were equipped as of mid-January. Standard head assemblies were mounted on the systems in check-out, thus making it possible to inspect systems separately from the heads with which they were to be shipped.

The VTR Head

The process for assembly of the video head is illustrated in the assembly drawings in Exhibits 10 and 11. In this process the electric motor was mounted on the subplate along with other auxiliary components, the rotating drum subassembly was prepared and mounted on the motor and then the unit was adjusted, the heads polished, and the subassembly inspected. The key element in the head assembly was the drum. Mounted on each

---

[3] The term "system" denotes the console plus two equipment racks of the VTR complete except for the head subassembly.

drum were four "dimes," specially machined metal discs about the size of a 10 cent coin. On each dime were two grooves which held the tips which made contact with the recording tape in operation.

Assembly of the dime is illustrated in Exhibit 12. The tips were made of alphenol metal, a special magnetic material and were only ten mils thick. The two tip halves were aligned on the dime to provide a uniform gap between their facing surfaces. This gap had to be no less than 90 and no more than 120 millionths of an inch across and its width had to be uniform throughout the 16 mil depth of the gap. The gap itself was one of the

Exhibit 10

A. VTR head assembly.

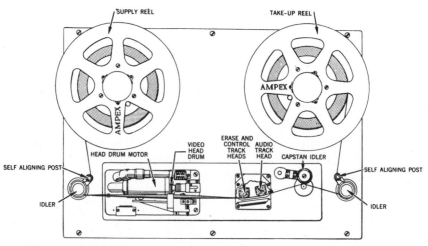

B. VTR top plate layout.

Exhibit 10 (*Concluded*)

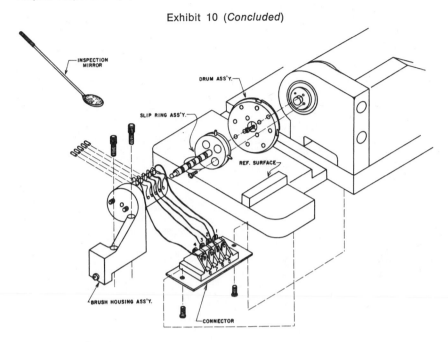

1. Mount drum assembly and slip ring assembly. Minimize
   runoff in both parts with respect to motor shaft.
   Runout cannot exceed .0005.
2. Mount brush housing against reference surface.
3. Install brushes as shown.
4. Position brush housing assembly with adjusting screw
   so that brushes are centered on silver rings on slip
   ring assembly. (Brushes can be viewed contacting slip
   ring assembly by holding inspection mirror under brush
   housing.)
5. Wire slip rings to plug as shown.
6. Fill out assembly tag.

critical determinants of the performance of the entire machine. For greatest
efficiency its walls had to be optically smooth and completely parallel.

The tips were mounted on the dimes with epoxy resin and then the
dime was mounted in the drum on top of a small ferrite coil. This coil
served to convert the magnetic flux in the tip material into electrical impulses. The four dimes had to be situated on the drum with an extremely
high degree of precision. For proper operation the four tips had to be precisely in the same plane with all four gaps parallel to each other on a
standard orientation. The gaps had to be situated at 90° intervals on the
circumference with a tolerance of only 30 seconds of arc.

Two important steps followed the assembly of each head. In the next
operation, called polishing, the head was mounted on a top plate with a

Exhibit 11
VTR HEAD ASSEMBLY DRAWING

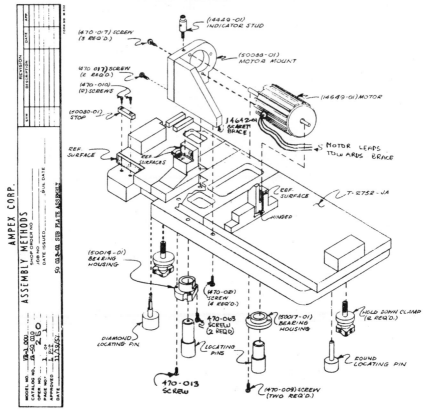

1. Locate and clamp 50 027-01 subplate in T-2752JA fixture tightly.
2. Insert 50 014-01 bearing housing in subplate and position
   with (3) 470-017 screws. (Motor leads towards brace.)
   (3) 470-013 screws)
3. Insert 50 017-01 bearing housing in subplate and
   reference with short locating pin. Fasten bearing
   housing with (2) 470-009 screws.
4. Fasten 50 030-01 stop against reference surface
   shown with (2) 470-010 screws.
5. Loosely fasten 14 649-01 motor to 50 038-01 motor mount
   with (3) 470-017 screws. (Motor leads towards brace.)
6. Loosely fasten motor mount to 14 621-01
   brace with (2) 470-021.
7. Place three parts on subplate and loosely fasten
   with (4) 470-021 screws.
8. Tighten evenly all loose screws holding both ends of
   motor shaft against reference surfaces.
9. Fasten 14 449-01 indicator stud to 50 038-01 motor mount as shown.
10. Invert fixture from position shown to remove assembly.
    Hinged reference surface shown must be rotated to clear
    motor shaft.

Exhibit 12
DRAWINGS OF DIME FOR
VTR HEAD

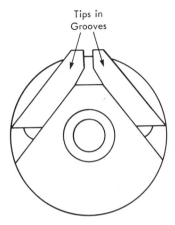

A. Simplified sketch of assembled dime, more than
three times actual size.

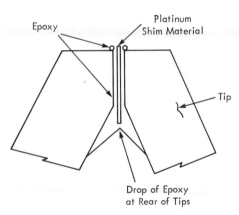

B. Greatly enlarged sketch of tip area
of dimes (corresponds to extreme top of
drawing shown above).

special abrasive tape which was similar to a recording tape. When the unit
was set in operation, the tips were evenly ground as they rotated in contact
with the moving abrasive tape.

After polishing, the head assembly went to final inspection. Although
the subassemblies which made up the head were processed through visual
and mechanical inspections prior to final assembly, it was not possible to
check the electrical performance of the head prior to final inspection. At
this stage the head was mounted on one of three VTR systems available
in the head department and subjected to exhaustive examination. Among
other tests, the head was used to record and play back a standard signal,

and to play back from a standard tape. The output of the head appeared on a TV receiver screen and was closely examined for flaws. Inspection took one hour, and each head was inspected three times, with an overnight delay separating two of the tests.

The Head Department

The VTR head was to be manufactured by a group of 20 hourly workers and 5 inspectors working under the supervision of the head department foreman in one area of that department. Some executives felt that the company's "know how" in producing recording heads had been one reason why Ampex had retained the leading position in its field. The foreman of the head department, who had been in the department for two years, said that "in the past, even when other foremen really got into a stew over some new recorder, we never had any trouble making heads. Everything has been smooth and proper all along in the head department."

For the VTR head, tooling was designed for an output capacity of 20 units per day, on a two-shift basis. The assembly output was planned to rise to the 20-unit capacity by January as the operators acquired the requisite skills. It was expected that 25 percent of output would be rejected and require rework. Performance measured up to expectations during November and December, and 22 heads had been shipped by the beginning of 1958. By that time the early units were being returned for normal rebuilding after the tips had been worn down in use. Until January the department had produced enough heads to meet the shipping schedule for new systems and to service those systems already in the field.

During the first two weeks of January only three VTR heads passed final inspection. Output rose to five new heads and two replacement heads during the week ending January 18 but this was still substantially below needs and expectations. As a result, on January 21, 1958, seven complete VTR systems, which were crated and ready for shipment, lacked the requisite head assembly. On the same date another eight complete systems were ready for check out.

According to Mr. Andersen, the head department had been averaging seven assemblies daily in mid-January, but as he said, "they're lucky to get one through inspection." Of the 40 drums assembled in January eleven had passed inspection, 15 were abandoned, and 14 were in rework on January 22.

Two principal defects had caused most of the rejects. These were: (1) a "waterfall" effect appearing on the picture, and (2) low electrical output. While the engineers believed that waterfall was due to mechanical instabilities in the head, they were uncertain as to the fundamental cause of low output. Mr. Andersen commented: "When a head is rejected for low output on one dime it requires eight hours for rework. It's really frustrating to have that happen when there are three good dimes on the drum. But, there's no way to catch it before final inspection." When a head subassembly was rejected it would not be scrapped. A new drum would be installed and the defective one either scrapped or reworked.

STEPS TO MEET THE PROBLEM

Early in January a special "task force" was established to coordinate efforts aimed at improving the yield in production of VTR heads. Ray Heidenreich, general foreman of assembly was placed in charge of the special group, which included the foreman of the head department and a representative from each of the following departments: manufacturing engineering, quality control, production control, and the video engineering department of the Professional Products Division. Walter Selsted, manager of the Research Division, acted as adviser to the group. The task force set out first to confirm that the manufacturing process was under control and in accordance with specifications. Each operation was reviewed in minute detail. Methods and tools were examined and compared with specifications. Raw materials were analyzed. The progress of several head units in process was followed, and the units examined for mechanical and electrical properties after each operation. The work area itself was thoroughly cleaned to reduce risk of product contamination.

This process of review was completed by January 20, and a few necessary changes made in the methods being used. At that time one of the manufacturing executives stated: "Now we're making heads under much tighter control and we're sure that the process is being executed exactly according to specifications. If these units don't come through, it is a design problem, not a production problem." All units started after this point were marked with red in production records and referred to by the personnel as the "control" heads.

Mr. Burn emphasized that the task force was not the only group working on the problem, and that the line personnel had not in any way been relieved from their responsibilities in the matter. Thus the manufacturing engineering department had assigned three men full-time and one man part-time to the solution of this problem. Furthermore, although the manufacturing division held formal responsibility for the product, the engineers from the Professional Products Division had been requested to assist in troubleshooting. According to Mr. Burn, "manufacturing gave them carte blanche to institute any changes after a thorough evaluation of all techniques."

The View of Top Management

Mr. Sackman, the vice president and general manager, felt that the VTR situation was the prime problem in the company as of mid-January. The problem was an understandable one, he felt, and typical of the difficulties encountered by companies like Ampex working on the frontiers of knowledge in their art. At best, the transfer of a product from the engineering phase to production was a tricky situation. The key element in this situation, as in all problems of this sort, was time—because with enough time all the kinks could be ironed out. "Unfortunately," Mr. Sackman said, "in this business we can't take too much time." He felt that the company's best men had been assigned to the problem, and had confidence that it would soon be overcome. To indicate his personal concern and willingness to cooperate, he began a series of daily meetings in his office with Ray Heidenreich and the department managers concerned. At these meetings the day's developments were reported and discussed.

Mr. Sackman felt that the financial aspects of the problem might be "annoying," but in the short run were inconsequential. The VTR accounted for one-half of the planned monthly billings for the remainder of the fiscal year ending April 30. While not concerned with inventory or billings for the next month or two, he did believe that the year-end figures were important goals—measurements against which the company couldn't afford to fall short.

Market acceptance was an important factor influencing Mr. Sackman's views. Ampex had a commanding lead in this product—probably 6 to 18 months ahead of the nearest competitor. Once Ampex units went into use in the industry, any competition would have to match the standards of the VTR to achieve interchangeability of tapes.

The Product Engineers Role

John Leslie, chief engineer in the Professional Products Division, shared the viewpoint of most Ampex executives toward this problem. Problems had been expected in production of the VTR, but the magnitude of the problem had been underestimated.

"At best, manufacturing VTR heads is an art," Mr. Leslie stated. Engineers had made all of the original and replacement heads for the 16 prototype systems. They had reasoned that a fully tooled production line would have even less trouble than they had had. "It didn't work that way, though," Leslie said, "we didn't realize the inherent artistry of the engineers who built the prototypes. When the line started up in late fall, the engineers nursed it along, and when all went well for the first week, we all relaxed and went back to our other jobs. Then the yield really nosedived," he concluded.

Mr. Leslie felt that you couldn't "inspect quality into the product, you had to build it in." Furthermore, there were several places where that quality would come only as a result of operator judgment. For example, in the polishing operation the head was run against abrasive tape. Since there were no objective standards for the time to be spent on the tape, it was up to the operator to decide in terms of the nature of the unit being polished. In addition the engineers had been able to point out some other aspects of the process requiring extreme care. For instance, handling of the alphenol tips had to be very gentle, as shock would adversely affect the metal's magnetic properties. Furthermore, in mounting the dime on the drum, care had to be taken to insure intimate contact with the ferrite core to insure maximum electrical output.

"We were only called in last week," Mr. Leslie said on January 22. "Solving this one will take time, but it is not unsurmountable. We're re-examining our basic principles now to find the first-order problem. Refinements will come later. So far we've changed several process techniques, but the design is unchanged."

Mr. Burn's Appraisal

At 2:15 P.M. on January 23, after talking to Mr. Andersen, Mr. Burn returned to the latest status report on VTR head production (see Exhibit 13). In thinking through his view of the situation he offered the following

Exhibit 13
VTR HEAD—PRODUCTION AND STATUS REPORTS

	(Units)	
1. *Production*		
Shipments: November	4	
December	18	
Passed inspection:		
Week ended: January 4	2	
11	1	
18	5	

	Jan. 22 (Units)	*Jan. 23 (Units)*
2. *Status of Work (2:00 P.M.)*		
Passed final inspection	2	1
Awaiting final inspection		
"Control" heads*	2	2
Other original equipment heads	2	1
Replacement heads	0	1
Rejects being reworked		
"Control" heads*	6	8
Other original equipment heads	2	5
Replacement heads	7	7

* These were heads produced since manufacturing control was established on January 20.

comments to a visitor in his office: "We have the capacity and proven ability to make 20 new heads per day (10 each shift) if there are no delays. Next week we expect to double capacity by adding a second tool to the bottleneck operation, which is the assembly of dimes in the drum.

This month, we've built 40 new drums—passed 11, given up on 15, and have 14 in rework and inspection today. Thus our yield is 27½ percent, if none of the 14 are good, but allowing for those we ought at least to get a 50 percent yield. We're scheduled to turn out 99 good heads this month, 140 in February, and 200 per month starting in April. We've got to meet the schedule. But how?

"Producing these heads is more of an art than production—people acquire art with practice—we need to accelerate the abilities and increase the artistry of the production operators. Our big mistake was trying to develop the 'art' of manufacturing at the same time that we experimented with the tooling on the line. One thing is sure, however, no below-standard head will leave this plant."

APPENDIX: PRINCIPLES OF TAPE RECORDER OPERATION

During the middle of the 19th century, James C. Maxwell, a British physicist, discovered that a changing electrical current induces a magnetic field surrounding the conductor carrying the current. This simple principle is the basis for all present-day magnetic recording equipment. Tape recorders function by transporting a magnetically coated plastic ribbon, called the "tape," by a "head" which serves to imprint a magnetic signal on the tape.

The head may be thought of simply as a piece of magnetic material, such as iron, with wire wrapped around to form a coil as illustrated below:

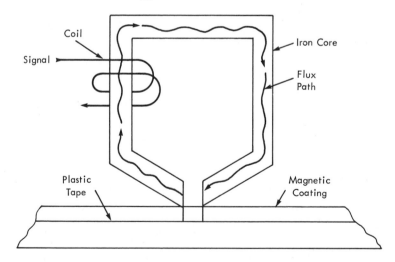

For this to function as a recording or reproducing head there must be a "gap" in the magnetic material. Thus, a very small cross section of the magnetic material is removed and replaced by a nonmagnetic material such as paper. In addition, the surface of the head near the gap is flattened in the vicinity of the gap to conform to the surface of the tape.

If an electrical current passes through the coil, fluctuations in applied voltage will induce a magnetic field in the head. The intensity of that field will change in direct proportion to the fluctuations in the current passing through the coil. As this happens, the magnetic field will try to bridge the gap caused by the nonmagnetic material in order to complete the circuit. Thus, when a recording tape is placed over the gap in a head, the ferrous coating on the tape serves to complete a path for the magnetic field flowing in the head. As this magnetic field passes through the tape coating it influences the orientation of the molecules of iron in the coating. Different field intensities will result in different orientations in the tape. If we pull the tape past the gap in the head while passing a fluctuating current through the coil, the imprint on the tape corresponds to the field present in the head at the instant that section of the tape passed the gap. Thus, if a magnetic recording tape moves steadily across a magnetic head while a current is passing through the coil in the head, the resultant imprint along the tape will be directly related to the signal in the coil with respect to intensity and time sequence. Thus, any fluctuating electrical signal can be represented magnetically on tape.

The signal imprinted on the tape can be "read" from the tape by passing it across the head while there is no current passing through the coil. The changing orientation of the magnetic coating as it bridges the gap in the magnetic head material will set up a slight magnetic field in the head. As this magnetic field fluctuates, it induces corresponding electrical current in the coil. Thus the signal that had originally formed the imprint on the tape is recreated.

The gap in a recording head is an important determinant of the system's performance. A magnetic field will flow into the tape only when there is a gap in the head (that is, when there is no short circuit to provide any easier path for the field). Furthermore, the head will be effective only for signals the wave lengths of which are greater than the length of the gap. In other words, the process works only when the imprint of one wave on the tape is long enough to bridge the gap in the head. A "wave" may be thought of as representing one complete fluctuation, or cycle, in the signal. As the number of fluctuations per unit time increases, the time duration of each must decrease. Since the tape moves at a constant speed, the length of a cycle, in space on the tape, is proportional to its duration in time. Thus, increases in the maximum frequency which can be recorded can be attained only by increased speed of the tape or by a greatly reduced gap dimension. For example:

> In the discussion above it was pointed out that the field in the head is induced by a changing current. If an alternating current changing at a frequency of 100 cycles each second passes through the coil while a tape passes the head at the rate of one inch per second, each inch of tape will bear the imprint of 100 cycles of the signal and each cycle will then require $\frac{1}{100}$ inch along the length of the tape. If the gap in the

head is $\frac{1}{50}$ of an inch, the length of each wave on the tape will be too small to bridge the gap and the system will not function. In order to record this frequency it would be necessary to reduce the size of the gap below $\frac{1}{100}$ of an inch or to increase the speed of the tape above two inches per second so that no more than 50 cycles would appear on each inch.

In practice, there are very definite mechanical limits to both the speed at which the tape can be moved and the size of the gap. So far, it has been impractical to reduce the gap below 0.0001 inch and that dimension is achieved only with difficulty. With conventional heads and tape speeds of 60 inches per second, a maximum frequency of 100,000 cycles per second can be recorded. At this speed of transport, however, a reel of one mil tape 14 inches in diameter is exhausted in 24 minutes.

There are other performance specifications for a tape recording or reproducing system in addition to maximum frequency response. One of these is the dynamic range, which is simply the ratio between the maximum signal loudness and the basic noise level in the system. The maximum achievable dynamic range with current equipment is approximately 60 decibels, which is equivalent to a ratio of 1,000 to 1 between the desired signal and undesired noise.

Another common measure of recording performance is the frequency range, that is, the range between minimum and maximum frequency. Present high-quality equipment will reproduce a frequency range of approximately 10 octaves, or the equivalent of a ratio of 1,000 to 1 maximum and minimum frequency.

Berkline Corporation (A)[1]

EARLY IN JULY 1971, Mr. Jim Griffin, a methods engineer of Berkline Corporation was reviewing the Cost and Variance Statement of July 1, 1971. As project engineer for the Zuckermann SZM88 automatic transfer machine (pictured in Exhibit 1) he was particularly concerned with the ma-

Exhibit 1
ZUCKERMANN SZM88 TWENTY-THREE STATION TRANSFER MACHINE

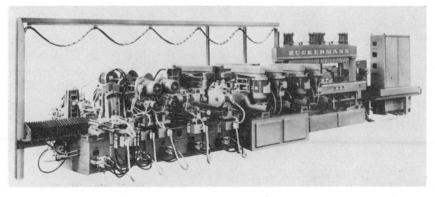

chine's performance. The transfer machine, installed in February 1971 at a cost of $153,000, had been acquired for the primary purpose of cutting labor costs and improving quality in parts production. However, the report had once again shown an unfavorable direct labor variance for the month of June. The statement showed that the Zuckermann work center had a actual direct labor expense of $1,730 against a budgeted expense of $1,057 for the month of June causing an unfavorable variance of $673 for the

[1] Some of the cost and volume data in this case have been changed to protect proprietary information.

month and a cumulative unfavorable variance of $3,579 since operations began. Although an unfavorable variance was expected during start-up while unsolved problems caused down-time and large amounts of maintenance and idle operator labor, the continued unfavorable variance would be viewed by the company's top management as symptomatic of continuing problems of integrating the machine into the factory.

Mr. Griffin felt that this Zuckermann transfer machine should be the first of many such machines in Berkline's production process and he had hoped to use his experience with this installation to anticipate the effects of future installations of new processing techniques.

COMPANY BACKGROUND

The Berkline Corporation manufactured and distributed several lines of upholstered furniture. Berkline's principal product lines were sofas and action chairs.[2] (See Exhibit 2.) These product lines were augmented by correlated furniture pieces to provide complete room "settings." One such setting is shown in Exhibit 3. The product line consisted of several style groups; within each style group there could be as many as 14 different items including recliner and rocker chairs, sofas and tables. In all, more than 200 chair and sofa designs were offered for sale. Sales were nationwide to 6,000 dealers through company salesmen with a sales volume of $26 million in 1970, This volume represented only a small percentage of the $5.1 billion industry sales from 5,214 plants, but it was large enough to place Berkline in the top 20 manufacturers. Although a high percentage of Berkline accounts were small customers, the trend in the industry had been toward mass merchandisers. To meet this trend Berkline's management were directing their efforts towards developing and adding large accounts.

MANUFACTURING PROCESS

The manufacturing facilities were housed in two plant complexes in Morristown, Tennessee; one for the manufacture of frame parts and the second for assembly, upholstery and shipping. The manufacturing process, diagrammed in Exhibit 4, involved the conversion of upgraded lumber, purchased metal parts, cotton and synthetic filling, cotton and synthetic fabrics, and other materials into upholstered furniture. As shown in Exhibit 4, the frame manufacturing process consisted of four basic steps; lumber grading and drying, rough mill, finish mill, and frame assembly. Once the frame was assembled, sewing, upholstery, and covering were required to produce a finished piece of furniture. Buffer inventories were maintained between the lumberyard and the rough mill process, and between finish

---

[2] Action chairs were chairs with moving parts (e.g., recliners and rocker chairs).

Exhibit 2
ADVERTISEMENT SHOWING CUT-AWAY ACTION CHAIR

In comfort T-Cushion Chairs

comparison proves
Berkline Mayfair best...

		Berkline	Competition
1	LIVING ROOM STYLING	YES	?
2	SMOOTH GLIDING ROCKING ACTION	YES	NO
3	QUIET MECHANISM OPERATION (FEATHER-GLIDE)	YES	NO
4	STABILIZER BAR	YES	NO
5	COIL SPRING SEAT	YES	NO
6	LOW PROFILE BASE WITH STEEL SUPPORT	YES	NO
7	PADDED OUTSIDE BACK	YES	SOME
8	PADDED OUTSIDE ARMS	YES	SOME
9	REVERSIBLE "T" CUSHION WITHOUT HANDLE	YES	NO
10	STEEL REINFORCED SEAT FRAME	YES	?
11	EXTERIOR HANDLES*	NO	YES

The most beautiful of all Recliner and Rock-A-Lounger designs are built around comfortable, reversible "T"-Cushions. The distinctive notched-out "T" shape gives the designer a whole new dimension in the creation of a more graceful chair. However, the recliner mechanism for most "T"-Cushion designs required an unsightly exterior handle or lever on the side in order for the chair to be moved into the TV and full recline position until Berkline engineers developed a new "Feather-Glide" mechanism that requires no unsightly outside handles. Berkline owners enjoy many more advantages over competitive chairs beyond a simple superiority of construction features. On all Mayfair Rock-A-Lounger models they'll find styling and construction features rarely found within chairs costing much more. Study the list of Berkline features against those of competitive "T"-Cushion chairs and you will see what we mean.

*All Berkline Rock-A-Loungers are covered by one or more of the following U. S. Patents: 3 163 464, 3 244 448, 3 244 449, 3 279 847, other patents pending.

BERKLINE®

The Berkline Corporation—Post Office Box 100—Morristown, Tennessee 37814

Exhibit 3
ADVERTISEMENT SHOWING ROOM SETTING

A room-full of Berkline.

And you thought we only made recliners. At least that's what we're famous for. But our correlated room groupings are pretty special, too. Talk about mistake-proof decorating. Here it is. By the room-ful. Sure our recliners are part of it. So are sofas. Loveseats. Club chairs and ottomans. Coffee tables. End tables. Lamps. Even a bar. And every piece is in perfect harmony, superb taste. You choose exactly what you like. At a Berkline dealer near you. And write for a color brochure. Send 25¢ to The Berkline Corporation, P.O. Box 100, GH-2, Morristown, Tennessee 37814

BERKLINE®

mill and assembly. The labor content varied from process to process, with direct labor costs comprising one-third of direct manufacturing costs in the lumberyard and kiln area, one-half in the mill department, and two-thirds in assembly and upholstering. In 1971, Berkline employed approximately 900 people in direct labor, including 7 in the lumberyard, 188 in the rough and finish mills, 240 in the assembly (frame and action) area

Exhibit 4
MANUFACTURING PROCESS

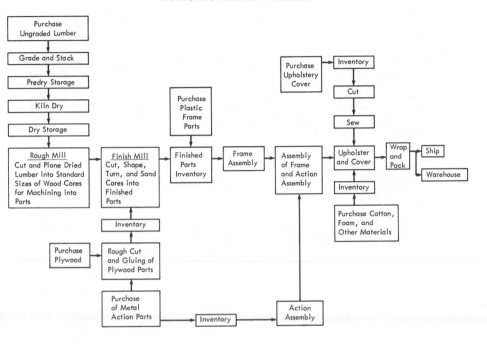

and the balance in the upholstery, cover, and shipping areas. Exhibit 5 contains views of the mill room, frame assembly area, sewing department and upholstery area.

PRODUCTION OF WOOD PARTS

The SZM88 was being integrated into the wood parts manufacturing process. This process began with the receiving of ungraded lumber in five basic thicknesses from one inch to three inches. The lumber was graded and stacked on an automatic handling machine (which required one operator) and stored in the open air. The stacked lumber was processed through a drying kiln to reduce the moisture content of the lumber prior to entering the mill shop. Once dried, the lumber had to be protected from the weather. Extended variation in times between drying and frame finishing could greatly affect the characteristics (size and shape) of the wood as its moisture content varied.

From the dry storage area the wood entered the rough mill where it was cut into "core stock" which was used by the finish mill to produce finished wood parts. Exhibit 6–A shows the layout of the mill department and the location of the machinery. The machinery descriptions and costs are listed in Exhibit 6–B. A piece of core stock was a finished rectangle of

Exhibit 5
VIEWS OF VARIOUS MANUFACTURING AREAS

A. Mill Room

B. Frame Assembly

Exhibit 5 (*Continued*)

C. Sewing Department

D. Chair Upholstery

Exhibit 6-A

LAYOUT OF MILL DEPARTMENT
(not to scale)

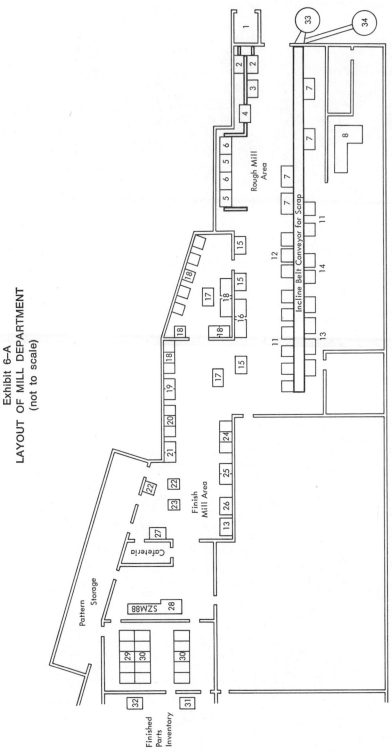

See Exhibit 6-B for definition of number codes.

Exhibit 6–B
EQUIPMENT DESCRIPTION

Code	Name	Use	Cost
1	Lumber elevator	Raise lumber to working height	$ 8,000
2	Cut-off saws	Cut lumber to length	3,500
3	Bursting saw (rip)	Rip or "burst" cupped lumber pieces	7,500
4	Double surface planer	Surface both sides of lumber pieces	32,000
5	Edging (rip) saw	"Joint" both edges of lumber pieces	7,500
6	Canted roll conveyors	Properly direct lumber through edging saws	2,000
7	Rip saw	Cut lumber to widths	7,500
8	Panel flo	Glue pieces into panels	35,000
9	Single surface planer	Surface one side of lumber pieces	12,000
10	Bell 424	Trim, bore, and dowell both ends of piece	32,000
11	Miter saw (variety saw).	Used for making individual miters, trims, or rips	2,500
12	Bell 24	Trim and bore both ends of piece	24,000
13	Band saw.	Saw irregular shapes	3,500
14	Double end trim	Trim both ends of pieces	8,000
15	Profiler.	"Shape" or "profile" one side automatically	20,000
16	Single spindle shaper	Perform light "shaping" by hand	2,500
17	Wide belt sander	Rough and finish sand one side	32,000
18	Soft drum sander	Polish sand pieces	250
19	Disc sander	Polish sand turnings	250
20	Edge belt sander	Sand long lengths	6,000
21	Spindle carve	Perform light hand shaping	450
22	Nash sander	Automatically sand round turnings	15,000+
23	Automatic lathe.	Automatically "turn" pieces	16,000
24	Router	Perform deep cuts	12,000+
25	Finger jointer	"Finger joint" one end of piece	6,000
26	Master carver	"Carve" irregular pieces	18,000
27	Shaper	Automatically shape or profile	20,000
28	Zuckermann 88	Perform various operations & shape both sides, auto.	153,000
29	Vertical boring machines.	Bore holes in vertical plane	9,500
30	Horizontal boring machines	Bore holes in horizontal plane	4,000
31	Double end dowell driver	Dowell both ends of piece automatically	9,000
32	Single end dowell driver	Dowell one end of piece manually	4,500
33	Wood hog	"Grind" wood waste into boiler fuel	15,000
34	Wood chipper	Chip wood into form acceptable for resale to paper industry	25,000+

wood in one of 250 possible stock dimensions slightly larger than the maximum size of the largest finished part which would be produced from the core.

The lumber was first cut, planed, jointed and sawed to a uniform rough thickness on a conveyorized line consisting of equipments 1 through 6 in Exhibit 6–A. The resulting pieces varied in width and length as the operator cut the board to minimize scrappage. These pieces were then sorted on carts according to lengths; widths too thin for making cores were sent to the panel-flow machine to be glued into larger pieces. The sorted lengths were then processed through the line comprising equipments number 7 through 13 to produce the finished core stock which was the starting point for the finish mill operations. Buffer inventories of core stock were established in 1971 for parts machined on the SZM88, but not for other items. Ordinarily, the rough mill operations were scheduled by the foreman to produce core stock need for current finish mill requirements.

Using the core stock and rough cut parts from the plywood shop, the finish mill produced approximately 1,600 different frame parts. Work moved through the mill in varying lot sizes with each lot traveling on one or more carts. The operations performed were sawing, shaping, boring, planing, rough sanding, turning and finishing. The Zuckermann could perform all operations except turning and finish sanding. The orders moved through the finish mill according to the operational sequence specified on the accompanying specification sheet (see Exhibit 14). This specification sheet listed all operations required to produce the finished part, including the operations necessary to produce the core stock. There was no standard order flow through the machine shop. The foreman assigned a job to the machinist responsible for the first operation listed on the specification sheet. The operator would take the specification sheet, draw the core stock, draw any necessary tooling and/or patterns, set up his machine, and run the lot. When he completed the run the operator informed the foreman and was assigned another job. The completed job was then assigned to the machinist for the next operation who sought out the material and proceeded with his operation. When all operations were completed, stock handlers moved the parts to the finished parts inventory area to be drawn on as needed by frame assembly.

Recently Berkline had been replacing some of the interior and exterior frame parts with injection molded plastic parts. These parts were produced by a vendor using molds supplied by Berkline (but purchased from another vendor at a cost as high as $25,000 each). Under normal conditions, only one mold was necessary for any part number, with each mold capable of producing all of Berkline's requirement for a given part at a contract cost of a few cents per part. Molded plastic parts were not a very significant part of the parts inventory, but there were plans to replace other wood parts with plastic where volumes and unit costs made replacement feasible.

PRODUCTION PLANNING AND SCHEDULING

Berkline filled customer orders from both current factory output and from finished goods inventory. Finished goods inventory was maintained in a national system of seven warehouses and was used primarily to provide delivery (at a premium price) earlier than the four-week lead time required by the factory. Although actual factory orders were used to fill customer orders, actual production was based upon a forecast and constrained by a policy of leveling production.

Forecasts of demand were produced by both the Sales Department and a Capacity Planning Committee (which consisted of the vice president of manufacturing, the two plant superintendents, and the production control manager). These two forecasts were negotiated into a merged forecast which became the basis for factory scheduling. The merged forecast for fiscal 1971 is shown in Exhibit 7–A. A recent five-year forecast (by product group) is shown in Exhibit 7–B.

The forecast prepared by sales was judgmental in nature. A history of monthly shipments since 1965 was reviewed to assist in the formation of the estimates. The sales forecast first provided a grand total of units to be sold for the forecast period. A monthly forecast was then made for each geographical market area and adjusted with the grand total forecast. The capacity planning forecast developed a similar monthly forecast. This forecast was also a judgmental forecast, but it was based upon the historical statistics of orders shipped. Both forecasts were revised, extended, and merged each quarter. The sales department then broke the period forecasts down into forecasts of demand for individual styles.

A recent memo described how the Capacity Planning Committee used the merged forecasts.

> The monitoring of forecasts is one of the prime functions of the Capacity Planning section. Sales orders, and their status related to both forecast and capacity, is reflected in an Order Status Report issued weekly.
>
> A monitor report of trade orders received each week is issued to reflect the cumulative orders received as compared to the forecasted period. Each month the internal conditions of manufacturing are constantly reviewed along with the sales potential of the warehouses. Anticipated variances of forecasted ship quantities are noted on the Estimated Monthly Shipping Report.

The forecasts and the monitoring data were used to adjust future operating capacity.

Production rates were developed using the style breakdown of the merged forecast, the available inventory, and a desired closing inventory. The total requirement was divided by the number of production weeks in the forecast period to obtain an average weekly production rate by style. The forecast is then "exploded" to obtain the forecast quantity by frame parts and this was used as a basis for the entry of parts orders into the mill department.

The order scheduling process and its relationship to the forecasting procedure is diagrammed in Exhibit 8. Bill Delozier, the assembly production scheduler released weekly schedules 17 days in advance; e.g., he would release a schedule on July 8 which would cover the production schedule for plant 3 (assembly) for July 19–23 on goods which would ship during the week of July 26. These orders would be a mix of customer and inventory orders. Bob Johnson, Production Scheduler for frame parts, explained how he used Bill Delozier's schedule to order parts.

Exhibit 7–A
FORECAST VERSUS ACTUAL SHIPMENTS, JULY 1970 THROUGH JUNE 1971
(in product units*)

	July	Aug.	Sept.	Oct.	Nov.	Dec.	Jan.	Feb.	March	April	May	June
Trade Forecast†	9,565	14,000	20,500	22,450	18,075	11,225	20,500	18,000	19,500	17,200	16,405	18,950
Actual shipment	8,348	17,092	15,757	15,192	18,227	13,486	22,239	22,795	26,003			
Contract Forecast	1,710	3,000	3,000	2,500	3,000	3,000	2,300	1,400	1,600	2,000	2,000	2,400
Actual	1,980	2,672	3,050	3,533	3,750	3,816	2,435	2,067	2,544			
Total Forecast	23,790	27,470	35,400	40,155	39,095	32,715	32,750	31,500	35,250	27,780	27,570	31,900
Actual	19,094	29,288	33,535	35,163	34,079	34,683	33,337	33,583	40,223			

* A chair was one unit and a sofa counted as two units.
† Sales produced to order are specified as trade. Contract sales are by actual agreement with one customer. Total forecast includes trade, contract and warehouse sales.

Exhibit 7–B
FIVE-YEAR FORECAST—PRODUCT LINE UNIT SALES
(based on five-year plan prepared July 1970)

Product Line*	1970–1971 Planned	1970–1971 Expected†	1971–1972 Planned	1972–1973 Planned	1973–1974 Planned	1974–1975 Planned	1975–1976 Planned
"Sutton"	44,000	26,500	29,200	45,500	57,500	77,000	91,700
Contemporary line	136,000	174,600	190,300	202,700	209,600	216,000	231,600
Traditional	217,000	184,300	191,300	198,400	204,100	205,200	210,400
Total	397,000	385,400	410,800	446,600	471,200	498,200	533,700

* Traditional items were rocker, lounge, and recliner lines which at one time comprised the entire product line. "Sutton" products were more complex, higher priced products which were introduced in the late 1960s. Contemporary lines comprise a related set of groupings introduced at about the same time.
† As of April 1971.

Exhibit 8
ORDER ENTRY PROCESS

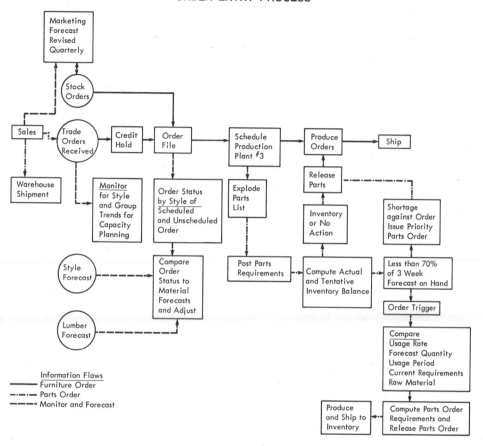

I enter orders into the parts mill once a week based upon parts usage. I know the parts required for each style number and calculate the amount required for each style number. For example, the 184/185 series all require the SA-296 arm which is a part we are making on the Zuckermann. When I get the order release from Delozier I enter the requirement for the week on the Manufactured Parts Inventory Records [see Exhibit 9].

As I release orders I enter the ticket number, date and due date into the Frame Stock Control Ledger [Exhibit 10]. I then keep track of the date the order number is finished and the usage of the stock; that way I have a running inventory of every part number. When the tentative balance gets down to approximately 100 percent of orders entered I enter a factory order for the part. The quantity entered is a multiple of the standard lot size, for example on March 1 I entered an SA–296 order for 5,000, or 20 lots of 250 parts.

Exhibit 9
MANUFACTURED PARTS INVENTORY RECORDS

						Part No. SA-296
Style 185/45 184/80 184/73 184/11 189/24						Part Top Arm
						Std. Order 250
Wood		Thick 5/4		Bd. Ft./Pc		Bd. Ft. Ord.

Week of	Require-ments	Tentative Balance	Quantity Ordered	Quantity Produced	Over/ Under	Tickets Out	Inventory Available
December 1970 . .			3,250			13	2,951
12/28.		2,247	2,500	728	−272	19	5,167
1/4	704	3,931	−	962	−38	15	4,425
1/11	824	2,855	2,500	1,733	−17	18	6,084
1/18	784	4,145	−	498	−2	16	5,298
1/25	1,172	3,302	2,500	1,725	−25	19	6,601
2/1	826	5,034	−	970	−30	15	5,741
2/8	766	4,031	2,500	460	−40	23	7,435
2/15	974	6,113	−	1,085	−165	18	6,296
2/22	388	5,437	−	1,553	+53	12	5,955
3/1	636	4,020	5,000	−		32	10,319
3/8	1,252	8,349	−	995	−5	28	9,062
3/15	718	7,415	−	−		28	8,348
3/22	934	6,554	2,500	1,422	−328	31	9,561
3/29	856	7,956	−	1,945	−55	23	8,639
4/5	1,082	6,582	2,500	1,343	−157	28	9,900
4/12	1,030	8,375	−	−		28	8,863
4/19	652	6,972	2,500	873	−127	34	10,291
4/26	1,246	8,691	−	1,051	+1	29	9,041
5/3	774	7,386	2,500	3,075	−675	24	10,087
5/10	880	9,134	−	159	+159	24	9,366
5/17	748	7,031	−	802	−198	20	8,410
5/24	1,428	6,626	2,500	1,548	−202	23	9,278
5/31	554	7,998	−	495	−104	21	8,828
6/7	928	7,066	−	1,972	−28	13	7,864
6/14	730	6,588	2,500	1,752	−248	15	9,386
6/21	582	7,280	−	−		15	8,800
6/28	1,772	5,630	−	610	+110	13	
7/5	1,402						

Note: As described in the text, "Requirements" are the quantities to be used in assembly operations scheduled for the designated week. The "Tentative Balance" used to determine when to place an order, is updated each week to reflect requirements two weeks ahead, orders issued to the mill during the current week, and any over/under run in the mill during the preceding week. "Inventory Available" is a perpetual book inventory of completed parts actually available in storage—calculated by subtracting current requirements from the previous week's inventory available and algebraically summing this with the quantity ordered and the over/under. (For example, at 1/11 6,084 = 4,425 − 824 + 2,500 − 17.) "Tickets out" is a record of past order tickets still outstanding in the mill.

THE ZUCKERMANN SZM88

The Zuckermann SZM88 transfer machine was developed and produced by Zuckermann, K.G., an Austrian machine tool company. Described by the manufacturer as a "23 station punch card controlled longitudinal and transverse automat," the SZM88 is a follow-on product to the 17 station

Exhibit 10
FRAME STOCK CONTROL LEDGER

Part No.   SA-296

On Hand Plant Balance Max: _____   Min: _____

Item Number	Ticket Number	Date into Mill	Quantity Produced	Date into Storage	Date Transferred into Plant	Date Depleted
1	5473	3/22	200	5/6	5/6	5/20
2	5474		195	5/6	5/6	5/20
3	5475		122	5/6	5/6	
4	6328	4/5	203	5/6	5/6	5/18
5	6329		203	5/6	5/6	5/18
6	6330		293	5/5	5/5	6/3
7	6331		159	5/6	5/6	5/26
8	6332		122	5/6	5/6	
9	6333		159	5/6	5/6	5/26
10	6334		225	5/21	5/21	6/2
11	6335		225	5/21	5/21	6/2
12	6336		86	5/21	5/21	6/2
13	6337		266	5/21	5/21	6/2
14	2114	4/8	218	4/8	4/9	4/21
15	7172	4/19	231	5/27	5/27	6/24
16	7173		231	5/27	5/27	6/24
17	7174		225	5/27	5/27	6/7
18	7175		225	5/27	5/27	6/7
19	7176		247	6/3	6/5	6/29
20	7177		248	6/3	6/5	6/29
21	7178		212	5/25	5/25	6/3
22	7179		212	5/27	5/27	6/30
23	7180		212	5/27	5/27	6/30
24	7181		273	6/8	6/9	6/28
25	8184	5/4	100	6/7	6/7	6/11
26	8185		586	6/7	6/7	6/23
27 . . . . : . .	8186		274	6/8	6/9	6/11
28	8187		189	6/17	6/17	6/23
29	8188		303	6/14	6/15	6/16
30	8189		253	6/8	6/9	6/11
31	8190		253	6/8	6/9	6/11
32	8191		205	6/15	6/15	6/18
33	8192		200	6/15	6/15	
34	8193		183	6/11	6/11	6/14
35	Partial		159	5/13	6/1	
36	9379	5/24	277	6/14	6/15	6/16
37	9380		250	6/10	6/10	
38	9381					
39	9382		172	6/15	6/15	
40	9383		189	6/17	6/17	6/28

SZM77. The SZM purchased by Berkline is pictured in Exhibit 1. The machine was basically designed to hold in position up to three cores, move them past 23 work stations and return a finished part to the operator to be unloaded and replaced with new cores. Since there was only one work holding pallet (which held up to three cores) the SZM88 was not operating

on any work pieces during loading and unloading. After the operator mounted the cores on a design template against pre-set stops, pneumatic pressure arms descended upon the cores from an overhead position to hold the cores in a fixed position. The pieces of wood were then moved in this fixed position along a horizontal rail past the 23 work stations on which were located sawing, boring, mortising, square tenoning, shaping and sanding units. Once at the end of the rail, the work pieces were returned along the same path to the operator's station for unloading. The operating sequence and length of operation of each work station was controlled by a central control unit by means of instructions supplied by a pre-punched metal card. The movement of the machining heads was controlled by settings on the three to seven manual verniers on each work station which positioned each machine head, and by the movement of a guide along the template.

Operating the transfer machine simply required loading and unloading the machine between each operating interval, monitoring the machine's operation, and performing cleaning and minor maintenance. For a part previously produced on the Zuckermann, set-up on the machine required inserting the punch card for sequence control, mounting the templates and setting the positioning verniers for each work station. A typical set-up required four hours for the set-up man to complete. When a part was to be run for the first time on the Zuckermann, it was necessary to design and produce templates, to calculate sequencing time and produce the sequencing card, and to calculate all vernier settings. Production of the punch card, template and vernier settings usually required about 12 man-hours of engineering and 12 man-hours of set-up. In addition, each time a new part number was run there was the possibility that error might exist in the punch card, template or vernier calculation which would only be discovered during the first run of the part. Such an error would necessitate idle time while the error was pinpointed and the set-up corrected.

THE PURCHASE AND START-UP OF THE ZUCKERMANN SZM88

One of the critical problems faced by Berkline's top management was the matching of capacity to sales volume. As sales volume increased, it was the responsibility of the company's Capacity Planning Group to highlight possible capacity problems. One of the problems highlighted by the Capacity Planning Group was the machine capacity of the mill shop. Exhibit 11 shows the results of their report which specified the percentage of existing machine utilization at various weekly sales levels from 7,250 units[3] to 9,000 units.

In addition to specific capacity problems, Berkline was faced with the more general problem of labor shortage. During 1971 it had become al-

---

[3] Each sofa was counted as two units of production and each chair as one.

Exhibit 11
DEPARTMENT 16—RECAP OF CRITICAL MACHINE UTILIZATIONS,* 5-19-71

Machine or Work Station	Code†	Work Hours Scheduled	Percent of Machine Utilization at Various Unit Levels of Production‡							
			7,250	7,500	7,750	8,000	8,250	8,500	8,750	9,000
Router	24	40				85.4	88.1	90.8	93.4	96.1
		45								85.4
		50								
Plane and cut off . .	4	40							86.2	88.7
		45								
		50								
Rip saw	7	40						86.4	88.9	91.5
		45								
		50								
Onsrud profiler . . .	15	40	98.1	101.5	104.9	108.3	111.6	115.0	118.4	121.8
		45	87.2	90.2	93.2	96.2	99.2	102.2	105.3	108.3
		50				86.6	89.3	92.0	94.7	97.4
Automatic lathe. . .	23	40	100.9	104.4	107.9	111.4	114.8	118.3	121.8	125.3
		45	89.7	92.8	95.9	99.0	102.1	105.2	108.3	111.4
		50			86.3	89.1	91.9	94.6	97.4	100.2
Wide belt sander. . .	17	40	130.0	134.6	139.0	143.6	148.0	152.4	157.0	161.4
		45	115.6	119.6	123.6	127.6	131.6	135.6	140.0	143.6
		50	104.0	107.6	111.2	114.8	118.4	122.0	125.6	129.2
Spindle carve	21	40						85.3	87.8	90.3
		45								
		50								
Buff sander	18	40		86.8	89.6	92.5	95.4	98.3	101.2	104.1
		45						87.4	90.0	92.5
		50								
Bell 408	31	40	88.5	91.5	94.6	97.6	100.7	103.7	106.8	109.8
		45				86.8	89.5	92.2	94.9	97.6
		50							85.4	87.9

* In all cases represents two shifts operation of plant. All figures over 100 percent are estimates.
† See Exhibit 6-B.
‡ Weekly requirement of chairs and sofas.

most impossible to find new workers and a recent study of the Morristown area indicated the problem would continue. According to one member of management, the problem was one of quality and not quantity.

The population of our labor pool is expected to be 30 percent higher in 1980. However, the problem is finding enough people with the skills or even the capability we need. In the past year we've had 3,300 people apply for jobs. Twenty-eight hundred of these were deemed acceptable. We hired 900, half of these for the upholstery department. Of those hired for the upholstery department, 80 percent terminated before the end of 12 months and it takes 12 months to train an upholsterer. The mill department has not really been a difficult problem. But even there the 12-month termination rate has been about 55 percent.

Faced with expanding capacity requirements and a diminishing labor market, Berkline had made a concerted effort to increase productivity through automation. In 1968 Howard Westhaver, the manufacturing vice president, had established a methods engineering department to study and implement methods for improving their plant operations. A number of process changes had resulted from these efforts.

1. Cartridge loading systems[4] for some of the manual woodworking machines.
2. A material handling system that separates, facilitates sorting and grading, and stacks purchased lumber.
3. A waste recovery system for wood, scrap, chips, dust, and flour, for resale and use as kiln fuel.

The purchase of the new transfer machine was considered to be a step in the direction of automating the mill shop, a necessary step to handle the labor shortage problem, and a more immediate response to the machine capacity problem.

In July of 1971 the SZM88 was the responsibility of Jim Griffin, a methods engineer in the Engineering Department. Mr. Griffin was a graduate of Tennessee Technical University with a B.S. degree in Industrial Technology. Prior to graduation he had spent four years in the Air Force as an Electronics Technician. Before coming to Berkline in 1968 Jim worked for three years with Republic Steel Corporation as a Production Supervisor. Since coming to Berkline, Mr. Griffin had been involved with the operation of the lumberyard, rough end and mill room. The management of the installation and development of the SZM88 was his fifth project. Prior projects included: layout and construction of a new receiving yard; design, layout and construction of the lumber grader-stacker; layout and development of the plywood dimension plant; and development of the wood waste reuse system.

The chain of events which led to the purchase of the transfer machine began in the spring of 1970. Hans Schneider of Forestry Service Products, U.S. representative for the Zuckermann Company, wrote to Lester Popkin, one of the owners of Berkline, describing the SZM88 and its advantages. Mr. Popkin forwarded the letter to Howard Westhaver, Vice President of Manufacturing who turned it over to Jim Griffin with instructions to evaluate the machine. According to Jim:

> Mr. Westhaver is always interested in types of equipment which could improve factory operations. We briefly discussed the feasibility of the SZM88 for our operation. Because we were faced with a labor and machine shortage in the mill shop, the only question was economics.

---

[4] Cartridge loading was a method for batch loading machines by the operator rather than loading piece by piece.

At Howard's instruction I proceeded to make an economic evaluation of the Zuckermann.

Mr. Griffin's economic evaluation consisted of finding nine high volume high labor parts which could be produced on the transfer machine and calculating labor savings to be realized by producing these parts on the Zuckermann. The results of this analysis were summarized in a letter to Mr. Westhaver in July 1970 (Exhibit 12) and showed a payback of 3.5 years and an internal rate of return of 21.5 percent, based on a cost of $164,500, and assuming full two-shift operation. The estimate of 145 hours of machine time was obtained from the Zuckermann Company on the basis of specifications and monthly requirements (for the nine parts) provided by Mr. Griffin. During the summer of 1970, Mr. Westhaver and others visited two U.S. plants using Zuckermann Model 77 machines and two European installations of the Model 88. Jim Griffin described the events that led to the purchase.

> Everyone was enthusiastic about the machine, but still an expenditure of $165 thousand for a woodworking machine was more than we were used to investing, since the average machine in the mill shop costs about $9,000. We may not have purchased it then except for the fact that we were able to pick one up right away at a lower cost rather than going through all the import problems.
>
> Zuckermann had shipped an 88 into the United States for display at the industry fair in Louisville. Mr. Popkin, Mr. Westhaver, myself and others went to the fair to see it during September. We watched the machine produce parts similar to those produced by Berkline. We negotiated with Hans to buy the display model for less than $109,000 and the decision to purchase was made then and there. We were anxious to try it because it could mean a new direction for Plant One, and Hans was anxious to get one operating in this country. I believe this is still the only one he has sold.

Agreement was reached between Berkline and Forest Service Products, Inc., the U.S. distributor for Zuckermann products, to purchase the display equipment. This arrangement resulted in savings on the cost of freight, reduction in the price of the machinery, and additional savings on tooling and installation to reduce the installed cost to $153,017.

Berkline started constructing the foundation for the transfer machine in early October and all parts of the transfer machine were received in Berkline's plant by the end of October except for the machining units (shapers, saws, etc.) which were not received until early February. By late December, Berkline's tool department had completed the boring knives and cutter heads for the transfer machine's work stations.

During January 1971 Mr. Griffin and Mr. F. M. Stroud, the tool maker who was to become the chief maintenance man for the transfer machine, familiarized themselves with the machine with the aid of an operational

Exhibit 12
ZUCKERMANN "88" ECONOMIC EVALUATION

To: H. Westhaver

From: J. Griffin
13 July 1970

Subject: Summary of Economic Evaluation, Zuckermann "88"

1. Annual Savings:

Based on production of nine parts, two months' requirements of each part produced per set-up.

Process	Machine Time	$\times$	*Direct Labor	=	Labor Cost to Produce
Present Methods:	1,073 hrs.	$\times$	$2.21 per hour	=	$2,370.00
Zuckerman "88":	145 hrs.	$\times$	$2.21 per hour	=	$ 320.00

Direct Labor Savings per month, 1st shift = $2,050.00
Assume second efficiency to be 90 percent of first shifts,
Direct Labor Savings per month second shift = $1,910.00
Direct Labor Savings per month, two shifts = $3,960.00
Indirect Labor Savings per month (one material handler) = 500.00
Total Estimated Monthly Savings, two shift basis = $4,460.00

2. Costs:

   a. One Time Cost

   Machine Cost: $109,500
   Freight Cost :   13,000
   Installation :   33,000 estimated
   Tooling   :   10,000 estimated
                   ——————
                   $165,500

   b. Training Cost: Reflected in first 8-month operation as follows:

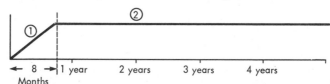

   ① First year labor savings estimated at $34,250.00
   ② Thereafter, annual labor savings estimated at $53,520.00
       (4,460 × 12)
   Training Cost = ② − ① = $19,270.00

   c. Maintenance Cost:

   No available facts or information. General opinion is that it will not exceed the costs involved in maintaining the machines that it replaces.

3. Payback and Long-Term (10 year) Profitability

   a. Payback = 3.5 years, operating the Zuckermann on a two shift basis.

   b. True Rate of Recovery or Equivocal Annual Earning Rate† (Interest rate at which the $165,500.00 would have to be invested in an annuity fund in order for that fund to be able to make payments equal to and at the same time as the receipts from the project) = 21.5%.

* Includes $1.94 (average operator rate) and 14 percent benefits.
   For standard cost purposes, Berkline used a rate of $2.40 per SALH for variable overhead (not including labor fringes) in the Mill Department.
   † Internal rate of return based on ten-year life.

handbook and supervised the setting of the SZM88 on its foundation. Looking back Jim felt that they were able to get the machine up quite rapidly.

> When the first Zuckermann engineer arrived for start-up on February 8th he was amazed to find that we had the machine almost completely set up; they usually had to unpack and set up the machine themselves.
> Much of the reasons for our success with the machine has been Stroud. Howard gave me F. M. Stroud, one of our best tool makers, to handle the actual set-up and maintenance. He has been able to learn the machine very rapidly and by catching minor problems has eliminated the development of major problems.

A Zuckermann engineer remained at Berkline from February 8 until March 22 to provide technical aid during installation and start-up. The first part was run on the machine on February 24 and production was started on a two shift basis on March 20.

Although Berkline experienced no major problems with the start-up of the Zuckermann, a series of minor problems prevented any sizable production until late March; sensitivity to public electric power fluctuations interfered with operation of control relays; improper ventilation resulted in overheating of saw motors; improper gear settings caused rapid wearing of drive belts. All of these problems resulted basically from lack of familiarity of Berkline's personnel with the transfer machine. The following excerpts from Mr. Griffin's log book indicate that other problems resulted from efforts to tool for the first few parts.

3/3/71   Began set-up for part number 43-1221.

3/4/71   Still setting up for 43-1221.

3/5/71   Tried to run a few 43-1221s.

3/6/71   Stroud inventoried tools and copied set-up.

3/8/71   Decided knives for 1221 must be reground—spent all day trying to line adjust vernier settings to no good end. Checked out template cutting units.

3/9/71   Discontinued efforts on 1221. Began set-up for part number SA–296. Had to make drastic changes in the hold-down bars due to the small diameter knives. Took knives to Misenheimen [outside tool and die maker] to be reworked.

3/10/71   Commenced setting back up on part number 51–515. [Part number 51–515 was being run on 3/2/71 prior to attempt to set up part number 43–1221.] Damaged $3\frac{1}{2}''$ spread boring head, took it to Cemco [outside contractor] will not have it until Tuesday of next week.

3/11/71   Cemco has no gear stock on hand. Will be rest of week before boring head is returned.

*   *   *   *   *

3/17/71 Found it to be advantageous for mill room to (1) try new template for part number SA–296, and (2) run a few for production. Set up machine for SA–296. Require extensive template change. Began making new template.

3/18/71 Completed new template and put it on machine.

3/19/71 Ran a few SA–296.

3/20/71 Ran SA–296 for eight hours. Machine ran OK. Trained Leroy Goins for 2nd shift operation.

3/22/71 Ran SA–296 two shifts. Machine performed OK. Tony Schneider, Zuckermann engineer, left.

Initial operations disclosed one significant error in the assumptions used to estimate labor savings expected to result from use of the SZM88. When the first part was set up at Berkline, the Zuckermann engineer pointed out that a single profiler station could not remove all the wood necessary to shape the finished part from available core stock. The depth of cut called for was as much as one inch, whereas the customary European practice was to shape the part roughly on a band saw, leaving one-quarter inch or less to be removed by the profiler knives. The machine hour estimates provided by Zuckermann had assumed the smaller depth of cut, whereas Berkline, consistent with U.S. woodworking practice, would need either to add a preparatory operation or set up additional profiler stations on the SZM. In this case, they chose to use three stations on the SZM, which resulted in lengthening the operating cycle. By March 27, 1971 the new transfer machine was operating on a regular two-shift basis. Exhibit 13 summarizes the production of the SZM88 from March 27 through June 30, 1971. Although production was somewhat sporadic at first, by June most of the bugs had been ironed out and Mr. Griffin felt that production grew as operators became more efficient.

SCHEDULING OF THE ZUCKERMANN

One of the major tasks facing Mr. Griffin was the choice of parts to be made on the Zuckermann. The SZM88 could cut, shape, bore, and sand but it could not finish sand or perform lathe (turning) operations, and had to work from core stock. This necessitated other machines performing operations prior to and after the Zuckermann operations. Since all of the operations listed on the specification sheet prior to the SZM88 operations involved the production of standard core stock, the Zuckermann had a buffer stock of raw material from the rough mill.

In choosing parts that were to be made on the Zuckermann, Mr. Griffin worked closely with Bob Johnson in Production Scheduling. Jim explained this process.

Exhibit 13
SZM88 PRODUCTION 3/27/71–6/30/71

Date	Part Number	First Shift	Second Shift
March 27	SA–296	200	
March 29	SA–296	437	331
March 31	51–515	224	414
April 1	51–515	406	387
April 2	51–515	218	44
April 5	51–515	512	484
April 6	51–515	330	
April 13	SA–296	215	198
April 16	SA–296	250	233
April 19	SA–296	240	
April 28	43–1213+15	*	520
April 29	43–1213+15	800	830
April 30	43–1213+15	775	780
May 3	43–1213+15	820	830
May 4	43–1213+15	900	812
May 5	43–1213+15	818	810
May 6	43–1213+15	210*	
May 6	43–1209	387	138*
May 6	43–1224		416*
May 7	43–1212	525	530
May 8	32–1213	397	
May 9–26	Broken carriage casting		
May 26	43–1213		730
May 27	43–1213	600	775
June 1	SA–296		609
June 2	SA–296		480
June 3	SA–296	435	
June 4	SA–296	673	513
June 7	43–1216	628	690
June 8	43–1216	640	320*
June 8	32–1215		5
June 9	32–1215	701	775
June 10	32–1215	351	732
June 11	43–1209	730	605
June 12	43–1212	380	351
June 14	43–1212	645	250 & 329
June 15	43–1215	700	720
June 16	43–1215	675	607
June 18	51–501	304	320
June 19	51–501	125	
June 21	51–501	300	250
June 22	51–501	250	325
June 23	51–501	342	330
June 24	51–501	295	280
June 25	51–501	331	325
June 26	51–501	121	125
June 28	51–501	330	302
June 29	51–501	231	380
June 30	51–501	296	325
		18,847	19,378

* Set-up change begun during this shift.

The computer explodes the Planning Group's forecast into a six-month parts forecast. I get a copy of this forecast from Bob and look for large volume parts. I check these parts for their labor content and calculate how many of the operations can be sequenced on the Zuckermann and how much labor we can save on these parts. Once I have a group of parts to choose from I get together with Bob and the mill shop foreman and we decide which parts would be best to schedule through the Zuckermann in order to meet requirements and also to level the usage of other machines.

By the end of June, seven parts were being produced on the transfer machine. The specification sheets for four of these parts showing the piece, the woodworking operations, the standard machine hours (SMH) and standard allocated labor hours (SALH) in hours per hundred pieces, and set-up hours (SU) in hundredths of hours per lot, are shown in Exhibit 14.[5] Normally the first operation shown on each sheet, plane and cut-off (P&CO), was the operation performed in the rough mill to produce the cores. The specification sheets shown in Exhibit 14 specify operations and times for normal routing; the operations which are checked in the left hand margin are the operations which can be sequenced on the SZM88 transfer machine. A sample (for two periods) of the computer printout for parts requirements is shown in Exhibit 15.

It was Mr. Griffin's job to decide which parts should be run on the SZM88. In choosing these parts, Jim used a three-step process. First he located part numbers with high requirements. Next he calculated which operations of these high volume parts can be performed on the SZM88. Finally he calculated the SALH which would be required for the SZM88 to perform these operations and compared this with the SALH for the conventional routing shown on the specification sheet to judge if there was a large enough labor savings to justify using the transfer machine to produce the part. Mr. Griffin originally calculated the SALH for the operations to be performed on the new transfer machine as follows:

Part Number	SALH for Normal Routing*	SZM88 SALH† (hours per 100 pieces)
SA–296	5.469	1.666
43–1209	3.255	0.833
43–1212	3.255	0.833
43–1213	2.773	0.833
43–1216	2.773	0.833
51–501	5.232	1.666

* Some of their times vary from those in Exhibit 14 because of changes in specifications, subsequent to the date of Griffin's analysis.

† SALH for SZM88 did not include any set-up time.

$$^5 \text{SALH} = \text{SMH} + \frac{(\text{SU})(100)}{\text{lot size}}$$

Exhibit 14
SAMPLE SPECIFICATION SHEETS

	Orig. by	Ck. by
	BW	

Frame Shop Part Specification Sheet

709-44 FRT. STUMP

Date: 5-14-71

Lumber Species	Core Dimension			Pieces per Core	Finish Dimension			B.F. per Piece	Part No.
	Thick	Length	Width		Thick	Length	Width		
PAU MARFIN	10/4	22 1/2	2 1/2	1	P	21	P	.9766	43-1212 R
									43-1212 L

Set Up At 315	Pieces	R / L	Pieces Ordered	R / L	Pieces Received

Mach. No.	No. Oper.	Quan.	Operation Description	S.M.H.	S.U.	S.A.L.H.
P&CO			Plane and cut off			
✓ RP			Joint 1 edge	.40	15	.188
✓ BP			Strato-Planer other edge	.386	30	.481
✓ BP	(1)		Plane to 2 1/4" width	.168	10	.200
✓ BP	(2)		Plane 1 face (1 pass)	.168	10	.200
✓ DET			Trim to 21 1/2" length sq.	.170	15	.218
✓ WBS	(1)		Sand 2 faces (1 pass each face)	.232	20	.295
✓ WBS	(2)		Sand 2 edges (1 pass each edge)	.232	20	.295
AL			Turn part/patt. (speed 0.5 or 59)	1.847	75	2.085
ROUTER			Route 2 faces on mid stump R&L	2.191	15	2.239
M2			Trim to length @ miter R&L	.302	29	.394
R-170	A-1		Bore 2-7/16" holes in face R&L	.227	63	.427
R-170	B-1		Bore 1-7/16" hole in end R&L	.227	63	.427
PNS			Polish sand R&L	.821	05	.837
BDS			Rough sand	.950	10	.982
BDS			Polish sand	.950	10	.982
			ISSUE #2 4-1-71 E.V.	9.011		10.250

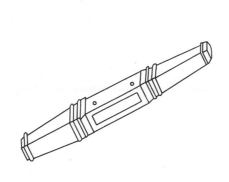

Standard Tolerances
Unless Otherwise Specified

1. Tolerance for Dowel Hole Spread = ± 1/64".
2. Tolerance for Dowel Hole Diameter = ± .005".
3. Tolerance for Dowel Hole Depth = ± 1/16".
4. Tolerance/Maximum Thickness, Width, Length, = ± 1/32";
   Except Stretcher Length = ± 1/64" and ± 1/3°.
5. Tolerance/Maximum Angles or Lead-Off = ± 1°.

Dwn.by	Ck.by	Part No.
g. m.		43-1212

Exhibit 14 (*Continued*)

			Orig. by	Ck. by
			BW	

FRT. STUMP   Frame Shop Part Specification Sheet

Date: 4-27-71

Lumber Species	Core Dimension			Pieces per Core	Finish Dimension			B.F. per Piece	Part No.
	Thick	Length	Width		Thick	Length	Width		
PAU MARFIN	10/4	18 1/2	2 1/2	1	2 1/4	16 15/16	2 1/4	.8030	43-1216 R
									43-1216 L

Set Up At 315	Pieces	R / L	Pieces Ordered	R / L	Pieces Received

Mach. No.	No. Oper.	Quan.	Operation Description	S.M.H.	S.U.	S.A.L.H.
P&CO			Plane and cut off			.472
✓ RP			Joint 1 edge	.140	15	.188
✓ BP			Strato-Planer other edge	.386	.30	.481
✓ BP	(1)		Plane to 2 1/4" width (1 edge) (1 pass)	.168	10	.200
✓ BP	(2)		Plane 1 face (1 pass)	.168	10	.200
✓ DET			Trim to 17 1/2" sq.	.170	15	.218
✓ WBS	(1)		Sand two faces (1 pass each face)	.256	20	.319
✓ WBS	(2)		Sand two edges (1 pass each edge)	.256	20	.319
AL			Turn part/patt. (speed 0.5 or 59)	1.847	75	2.085
ROOT	(1)		Bore 2-7/16" holes in edge R&L	.243	50	.402
ROOT	(2)		Bore 1-5/8" & 4-7/16" holes in face R&L	.243	71	.468
ROUTER			Route grooves in 2 mid faces and 2 top faces	2.497	15	2.545
BSA			Clip off spur	.308	10	.340
PNS			Rough sand top end R&L	.808	05	.824
PNS			Polish sand R&L	1.137	05	1.153
BDS	·		Rough sand	1.200	10	1.232
BDS			Polish sand	1.200	10	1.232
				11.027		12.206
			ISSUE #2 3-24-71 E.V.			

M-2 = .492   CUT FROM CULL STOCK

Standard Tolerances
Unless Otherwise Specified

1. Tolerance for Dowel Hole Spread = ± 1/64".
2. Tolerance for Dowel Hole Diameter = ± .005".
3. Tolerance for Dowel Hole Depth = ± 1/16".
4. Tolerance/Maximum Thickness, Width, Length, = ± 1/32"; Except Stretcher Length = ± 1/64" and ± 1/3º.
5. Tolerance/Maximum Angles or Lead-Off = ± 1º.

Dwn.by	Ck. by	Part No.
gm		43-1216

Exhibit 14 *(Continued)*

Parts	Part No.	Pcs.	Finished Dimension			Orig.by	Ck.by:
Top Arm	41-1061	1	Thick	Length	Width	Date: 4-19-71	
Top Arm End Blank	49-913	2					
			5/4	25 3/8	P	SA-296 R SA-296 L	

			Set Up At 200	Pcs Ordered	Pcs Received		

Mach. No.	No.Oper.	Quan.		S.M.H	S.U.	S.A.L.H.
GR			Glue pcs. together	1.698	06	1.728
√ OP	(1)		Shape 1 edge	.389	27	.524
√ BP			Buss Plane other edge (1 pass)	.168	10	.218
√ DET			Trim to length	.300	15	.375
√ AS			Shape 2 faces R&L	1.793	73	2.158
√ R-170	E-2		Bore 2-7/16" holes in each end R&L	.450	82	.860
DM			Drive 2-7/16" x 2" dowels in each end	.289	26	.419
√ EBS			Sand out saw marks R&L	1.175	10	1.225
SSS			Shape edges R&L	1.300	15	1.375
PNS			Rough Sand R&L	1.963	05	1.988
PNS			Polish sand R&L	1.963	05	1.988
				11.488		12.858
			ISSUE #1 11-3-69 BW			

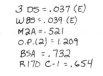

$3 \; DS = .037 \; (E)$
$W \; BS = .039 \; (E)$
$M2A = .521$
$O.P.(2) = 1.209$
$BSA = .732$
$R170 \; C\text{-}1 = .654$

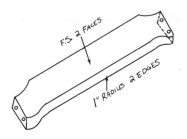

F.S. 2 FACES

1" RADIUS 2 EDGES

Standard Tolerances
Unless Otherwise Specified

1. Tolerance for Dowel Hole Spread = ± 1/64".
2. Tolerance for Dowel Hole Diameter = ± .005".
3. Tolerance for Dowel Hole Depth = ± 1/16".
4. Tolerance/Maximum Thickness, Width, Length, = ± 1/32";
   Except Stretcher Length = ± 1/64" and ± 1/3°.
5. Tolerance/Maximum Angles or Lead-Off = ± 1°.

J. M.		SA-296
Dwn. by	Ck. by	Part No.

Exhibit 14 (*Concluded*)

Orig. by	BW	Ck. by
Date:		6-3-71

185-45 ARM S/R   Frame Shop Part Specification Sheet

Lumber Species	Core Dimension			Pieces per Core	Finish Dimension			B.F. per Piece	Part No.
	Thick	Length	Width		Thick	Length	Width		
ELM FIN. HDWD.	6/4	27	6 5/8	1	1 5/32	26	P	1.8633	51-501 R
									51-501 L

Set Up At 200		Pieces	R / L	Pieces Ordered	R / L	Pieces Received

Mach No.	No. Oper.	Quan.	Operation Description	S.M.H.	S.U.	S.A.L.H.
P&CO			Plane and cut off			1.804
RP			Rip to 3 5/16" width	1.870	15	1.945
RP			Joint to 3 3/16" width	.280	15	.355
PF			Glue 2 pcs. to 6 3/8" width	1.293	02	1.303
BP			Plane 2 faces to 1 3/16" thickness	.436	20	.536
			(1 pass/face)			
✓ WBS			Rough sand 2 faces (1 pass/face)	.396	20	.496
✓ B-424			Trim to length @ miter and bore 2-7/16"	.282	75	.657
			holes in each end and drive 2-7/16" x 2"			
			dowels in each end (select face)			
✓ OP			Shape edge/patt	.375	27	.510
✓ SSS	(1)		Shape curved edge R&L	.386	15	.461
✓ SSS	(2)		Joint and buckshape straight edge R&L	.463	15	.538
✓ ROOT			Bore 4-7/16" & 3-3/16" holes in face	.219	85	.644
			R&L			
R-170	D-1(1)		Counterbore 1-7/16" x 3/16" hole in edge	.382	63	.697
			R&L			
R-170	D-1(2)		Counterbore 1-7/16" x 3/16" hole in edge	.382	63	.697
			R&L			
ROUTER	(1)		Route 2 grooves in face R&L	1.499	15	1.574

ROUTER	(2)		Round 2 grooves R&L	.715	15	.790
WBS			Polish sand 2 faces to 1 5/32" thickness	.632	20	.732
BUFF			Sand around router cuts R&L	.749	10	.799
PNS			Rough sand R&L	1.319	05	1.344
PNS			Polish sand R&L	1.319	05	1.344
				11.704		14.119

ISSUE #4 12-8-70   E.V.

S.C. = .334
E.B.S. = .644

**Standard Tolerances
Unless Otherwise Specified**

1. Tolerance for Dowel Hole Spread = ± 1/64".
2. Tolerance for Dowel Hole Diameter = ± .005".
3. Tolerance for Dowel Hole Depth = ± 1/16".
4. Tolerance/Maximum Thickness, Width, Length, = ± 1/32";
   Except Stretcher Length = ± 1/64" and + 1/3°.
5. Tolerance/Maximum Angles or Lead-Off = ± 1°.

J.M.		51-501
Dwn.by	Ck.by	Part No.

While Mr. Griffin made the original choice of parts to be run on the Zuckermann, the responsibility for seeing that the Zuckermann machine was kept loaded was shared between Griffin, Bob Johnson and Ronnie Perkins (assistant foreman in the mill shop).

In discussing the problems of scheduling the Zuckermann, Mr. Johnson stated that Parts could be divided into 3 groups—A, B, and C. A parts were high use and high (labor) cost parts, B parts were medium use and medium cost while C parts were low cost or low use. A parts represented about 18 percent of the part numbers but 80 percent of the load of the mill shop load. He went on to explain how this was affecting the Zuckerman.

> We are concentrating on putting A parts such as the SA–296 through the Zuckermann but in order to get larger lot sizes for the Zuckermann I am entering orders for eight week's usage based upon forecasts. Thus when we have forecasts for 3,000 185s, I can order 3,000 pairs of arms or 6,000 of the SA–296 parts.

Bill emphasized that there was no clear procedure for scheduling the Zuckermann.

> I coordinate with Jim to see what his loading requirements are as far as meeting operating costs, and Jim and I talk with Ronnie to see how loading the Zuckermann can level the total mill load and help us still meet order requirements. Both Ronnie and I periodically walk down to check the machine's backlog. We don't want that machine standing idle because we didn't provide any orders for it.

One of the problems which Mr. Johnson had with the forecasts was that they were based on aggregates.

> Aggregates are close, but the actual mix of styles and types are something else. When the forecast is broken down by style, we're doing well if we aren't off by more than 25 percent of actual. With the large volumes we are talking about on the Zuckermann, 25 percent is pretty far off.

OPERATING COST AND EVALUATION

Since the machine had been evaluated for purchase on the basis of labor savings, the evaluation of operations was also based upon labor costs. Three direct labor individuals were charged to the Zuckermann. On the first shift the Zuckermann had a full-time operator at $1.88 per hour with no special skill requirements and a full-time maintenance man at $3.30 for die making and set-up. The maintenance man's time was loaned and charged out to other departments when not working on the SZM88. The second shift had one full-time operator—set-up man at $3.06 per hour. Costs of fringe benefits were calculated at 14 percent of base.

The accounting department set up a separate budget allowance for the Zuckermann, based upon the production cost of the Zuckermann, using the SALH the part would have if it had gone through manual machines.

Exhibit 15

SELECTED PARTS REQUIREMENTS

Six Months Requirements 8/27/70 For 8/70 through 1/71 All Part Numbers 43-1210 through 44-0424, and 51-0322 through 52-0147				Six Months Part Requirements 2/25/71 For 2/71 through 7/71 All Part Numbers 43-1210 through 44-0424 and 51-0322 through 52-0147			
Part Number	Quantity	Part Number	Quantity	Part Number	Quantity	Part Number	Quantity
43–1210	412	51–0407	352	43–1210	506	51–0410	450
43–1211	1,672	51–0472	360	43–1211	1,532	51–0425	1,458
43–1212	3,542	51–0473	12,370	43–1212	2,276	51–0439	4,680
43–1213	19,432	51–0474	2,114	43–1213	19,502	51–0442	12,728
43–1215	11,592	51–0476	1,118	43–1215	9,160	51–0449	1,718
43–1216	6,686	51–0477	714	43–1216	5,264	51–0456	1,932
43–1231	1,118	51–0481	1,534	43–1218	22,308	51–0465	262
44–0189	5,788	51–0484	2,344	43–1219	32,216	51–0467	10,650
44–0194	63,580	51–0486	1,581	43–1221	12,298	51–0470	308
44–0235	720	51–0487	548	43–1222	3,924	51–0473	21,658
44–0260	2,942	51–0488	312	43–1223	3,142	51–0474	1,111
44–0261	854	51–0489	11,006	43–1224	1,130	51–0476	11,242
44–0262	5,788	51–0490	246	43–1226	3,520	51–0477	660
44–0265	510	51–0491	4,082	43–1227	1,790	51–0481	1,132
44–0269	1,314	51–0492	9,411	43–1228	1,790	51–0484	230
44–0330	2,554	51–0493	212	43–1229	952	51–0486	526
44–0337	4,002	51–0494	1,130	43–1230	4,466	51–0488	178
44–0358	924	51–0499	364	43–1231	5,842	51–0493	130
44–0395	19,989	51–0500	924	43–1232	1,750	51–0494	524
44–0396	9,620	51–0501	8,094	43–1235	490	51–0499	312
44–0397	18,324	51–0503	7,530	43–1236	490	51–0500	312
44–0398	478	51–0504	7,530	43–1237	770	51–0501	13,018
44–0400	482	51–0505	1,182	43–1228	770	51–0504	5,260
44–0405	13,232	51–0506	1,540	43–1229	952	51–0505	380
44–0423	16,880	51–0507	412	43–1230	4,466	51–0506	996
44–0424		51–0508	820	43–1231	5,842	51–0507	506

Part No.	Quantity		Part No.	Quantity
51-0322	2,554		51-0509	19,432
51-0381	4,002		51-0511	3,702
51-0399	924		51-0512	7,890
51-0400	14,902		51-0513	1,060
51-0401	13,328		52-0006	4,062
51-0402	13,328		52-0054	1,124
51-0405	478		52-0110	924
51-0408	14,902		52-0111	1,314
51-0410	478		52-0113	854
51-0425	4,166		52-0115	7,032
51-0433	720		52-013.	4,088
51-0439	3,714		52-0140	9,524
51-0441	854		52-0141	1,534
51-0442	23,904		52-0142	200
51-0445	1,156		52-0144	480
51-0449	2,942		52-0145	704
51-0456	2,136		52-0146	3,280
51-0465	1,584		52-0147	113,130
51-0466	482			
51-0467	6,014			

Part No.	Quantity		Part No.	Quantity
43-1232	1,750		51-0508	392
43-1235	490		51-0509	19,502
43-1236	490		51-0511	3,968
43-1237	770		51-0512	5,192
43-1238	770		51-0513	8,904
43-1240	720		51-0514	34,776
43-1242	9,908		51-0515	12,298
43-1243	770		51-0516	3,924
43-1245	1,160		51-0517	1,130
44-0189	3,476		51-0518	508
44-0194	33,250		51-0519	3,520
44-0260	1,718		51-0521	490
44-0261	612		51-0524	720
44-0262	612		51-0525	612
44-0265	3,476		51-0529	1,160
44-0269	60		51-0530	720
44-0330	56		51-0531	9,746
44-0337	1,306		51-0534	3,176
44-0358	5,904		51-0006	1,696
44-0396	8,392		51-0110	220
44-0397	4,388		51-0111	56
44-0398	7,376		51-0113	612
44-0400	450		51-0115	690
44-0423	13,122		51-0136	660
44-0424	14,070		51-0137	200
51-0322	1,306		51-0139	2,160
51-0381	5,904		51-0140	4,828
51-0399	220		51-0141	1,132
51-0400	6,162		51-0142	140
51-0401	5,146		51-0144	360
51-0402	5,146		51-0145	564
51-0405	450		51-0146	1,568
51-0408	6,162		51-0147	101,778

Exhibit 16
THE BERKLINE CORPORATION (A)
Morristown, Tennessee
February 26, 1971

TO: Jim Griffin   FROM: David Chambers

SUBJECT: Accounting Procedure for the Zuckermann, Effective March 1, 1971

    I.   The Zuckermann account number will be 9909 in Dept. 16.

   II.   All direct labor (actual milling of parts) will be charged to this account. The employees assigned to this job should be transferred to this account on a permanent basis.

  III.   All set up labor on the Zuckermann will be charged to this account. This may be in the form of one man on a full-time basis. If this man works on any other equipment, that time should be transferred out of this account. If any outside help is required, that time should be transferred into this account.

  IV.   The budget allowance for this account will be the total SALH, for all regular operations eliminated by the Zuckermann, extended by all parts produced on the Zuckermann during the accounting period. The 9901 Account budgeted hourly rate will be used to determine the dollar budget.

Part Number	Regular Operation Eliminated	Regular SALH/L	Pieces	Budget Hours
51-501.	B424	.282		
	Profiler OP. & root	.594		
	Router No. 1	1.499		
	SSS No. 1	.386		
	SSS No. 2	.463		
	WBS	1.028		
		4.252	5,000	212.6
	212.6 × $2.067 = $440			

   V.   The budget allowance for this account will, in effect, be a reduction of the Budget Allowance for both 9901 and 9908 accounts.

  VI.   No parts will actually be routed for the Zuckermann during fiscal 1969–70 or 1970–71. This is a necessity, if the accounting procedure described here is to function properly.

/ rkm

DISTRIBUTION:

Howard Westhaver   Bernie O'Connor
John Rogers   Jim Hammer
Lou Welch   Jim Griffin
Kirtis Bowlin   Ronnie Perkins
Ken Stuckwish   Charles Gantte
                       Gary Freshour

The details of the budget are shown in Exhibit 16. Each month a budget was calculated from the Zuckermann's monthly production and compared to the actual labor cost to give a cumulative yearly control variance. This resulted in the Zuckermann having a deficit variance of $2,274 as of May 1, 1971 resulting from a budget allowance of $914 and actual expenses of $3,188. Mr. Griffin felt that the budgeting procedure set up for the Zuckermann was in error, and the machine's value should be judged on the basis of difference between the normal SALH and the SZM88 SALH for the pieces produced, rather than on a comparison of actual labor costs to SALH for the parts produced. He outlined his accounting procedure for the manufacturing vice president in the letter shown in Exhibit 17.

Exhibit 17
THE BERKLINE CORPORATION (A)
Morristown, Tennessee
May 18, 1971

TO: Howard Westhaver   FROM: Jim Griffin

SUBJECT: Zuckermann 88 Performance Evaluation

1. Machine installation was started February 8 and completed March 20. It began operating, production wise, on a two shift basis.
2. In order to have a monthly evaluation of the machine's performance, for simplicity's sake, it was decided to create a separate account number (9909) on the C&V Statement.
    The labor hours saved by the machine are multiplied by the budgeted direct labor rate (9901) and transferred into the new account to show "Savings." The "Actual Expense" Column, of the C&V Statement is the actual direct labor expense involved in operating the machine
3. In order to arrive at a more accurate "Labor Rate," I will include the following Direct Labor and Expense Accounts; All of which are affected by the operation of the Z-88.

9901	Direct Labor–Measured	$1.820
9905	Trainees	.043
9906	Incentive bonus	.142
99165	Other services	.123
9924	Overtime premium	.458
9925	Shift premium	.033
9928	Fringe benefits	.178
	Total	$2.80

4. *a.* March 10 through 31

SALH of parts, normal routing	250.339	
Labor cost of same (SALH × 2.80)		$ 700.95
SALH of parts, Zuckermann	171.999	
Labor cost of same (SALH × 2.80)		$ 481.60
Savings involved, partial month of March		$ 219.35

Exhibit 17 (*Continued*)

b. April

SALH of parts, normal routing	1,321.108	
Labor cost of same (SALH × 2.80).		$3,699.10
SALH of parts, Zuckermann	957.368	
Labor cost of same (SALH × 2.80).		$2,680.63
Savings involved, April		$1,018.47

5. Operation of the Z-88 made it evident that too much material was being used to produce the top arm, 185 group. A job change, resulting in material and labor savings amounting to .0891 center per piece, has since been instituted on the following parts. Forecasted annual savings are included and should be credited to the Zuckermann.

SA 296	$3,154
309	$2,192
310	$ 700
337	$ 128
339	$1,436
340	$ 694
Total annual savings due to job change equals	$8,304

Mr. Griffin reviewed some of the other problems involved in the evaluation of the Zuckermann.

> Although we should be running high labor parts through the "88," 20 percent of the time we are running "squares" through the machine. That is, we are simply squaring off core stock for the lathe. These are planing and sanding rework operations on parts 43–1209, 43–1212, 43–1213, 43–1215 and 43–1216. Unless these parts are perfectly squared before mounting in the lathe, they turn off center resulting in a nonsymmetrical pattern and the piece has to be scrapped. The operations we do on the squares are of very low labor input but very high tolerance. This squaring operation should be done on a moulder which costs about $22,000. But we do not have a moulder so they go through the SZM88.
>
> The location of the transfer machine is not optimal resulting in a material flow problem.
>
> No parts are routed through the Zuckermann on the spec sheets. The set-up man must be able to convert the individual standard specs to "88" specs. Eventually we hope to have certain spec sheets reworked to show both standard and 88 specifications.
>
> The Zuckermann is a 23 station machine. On the parts we run through the Zuckermann now it replaces about five conventional machining steps. Thus the single man 88 station replaces five men.

THE FUTURE OF THE TRANSFER MACHINE

Because of the special problems of the SZM88 in scheduling, set-up, costing, and maintenance Mr. Griffin felt he would be connected with the existing SZM88 operation well into the foreseeable future.

Right now everything about the Zuckermann is special. Although operation of the machine requires little training, set-up, maintenance and scheduling require special attention because the machine does not fit into the normal system. Stroud and I will continue to be responsible for these areas while actual operation will come under the control of the foreman of department 16. Even when we have the set-up, maintenance, and scheduling on this machine standardized we'll probably be adding more of these and similar machines in department 16. Mr. Westhaver and I have talked about the possibility of a series of transfer machines with each one as a separate line. While I don't envision any particular start-up problems on additional machines I'm sure there will be added complexities of scheduling.

Sarepta Paper Company (A)

In March of 1962, Mr. Joseph Small, Staff Assistant of the Executive Vice President of Sarepta Paper Company, was reviewing the work he had accomplished during the past two years. Small's time was usually divided between coordination of staff operations and the institution of cost-cutting devices and procedures.

An industry-wide profit squeeze was just beginning to seriously affect Sarepta although the squeeze had been in existence for several years. Mr. John Upton, Sarepta's President, often reminded his management team of the increasing severity of the situation. Within the past three months the price of one of Sarepta's product lines (making up 30 percent of its total volume) had been cut on two separate occasions and was presently at a level which Mr. Upton considered to be the absolute minimum for Sarepta.

To date, Small's accomplishments consisted of a number of procedural changes around the mill which were clearly improvements but which for the most part were difficult to allocate specific dollar savings to. However, Small believed that his two major improvements, which were materials handling devices, were showing specific dollar savings through increased manpower efficiency. Small realized that Mr. Upton wanted a larger more tangible savings than anything accomplished to date. He also knew that Mr. Upton did not consider any device or procedure which would cause labor relations difficulties or hard feelings among the workers as a prudent way to cut cost unless the resulting savings were necessary to remain competitive.

Small had come to Sarepta in 1960 from Allegiance Chemical Company where he had worked since graduating in Industrial Engineering from the University of Maine in 1950. While at Allegiance, Small had specialized in process control and production flow. Although his college training was not in chemistry, his work experience at Allegiance had helped him to acquire a good working knowledge of chemistry. As a result he felt perfectly at home in a discussion of any phase of the papermaking process.

COMPANY BACKGROUND

The Sarepta Paper Company, located in Wascom, Maine, is a nonintegrated[1] fine paper company which produces primarily specialty papers[2] for converting customers.[3] The company was formed in 1880 and was incorporated in 1920. Since its beginning the top management has come from one family, the Uptons, who were also the principal owners. Mr. John Upton is the third generation of Upton management. The Sarepta organization was quite often referred to by other paper companies as proud and progressive. Sarepta had developed considerable pride in its line of specialty papers and it was proud of the reputation for quality that it had in the paper industry. Sarepta's "progressive" label stems from the fact that it has been a leader in changing product lines to suit the various needs of the customer. Also Sarepta has been a leader in selling techniques by using its present direct selling method.

The American Paper and Pulp Association (APPA) classifies Sarepta as a medium-sized paper company with a daily production of 175 tons and an employment of approximately 600 persons. According to APPA there are approximately 85 nonintegrated paper mills in the New England area and roughly 20 of them have a product mix comparable to Sarepta. Sarepta's organization chart is shown in Exhibit 1.

Exhibit 1
ORGANIZATION CHART

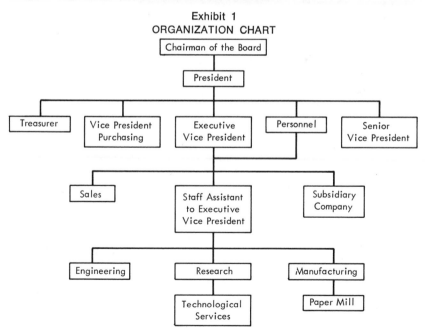

---

[1] Nonintegrated means that it does not have the facilities to make its own pulp—explained in section on Production (General).

[2] Specialty paper refers to high-quality grades of fine paper which usually have a specialized application (i.e., Thermofax paper).

[3] Converting customers buy paper and convert it to final form (i.e., wallpaper).

FINANCE

The balance sheets and income statements for 1960 and 1961 are presented in Exhibits 2 and 3. Sales have grown from approximately $12–$14 million just after World War II to the present level of $20 million. (Small had learned from the sales manager that the 1962 sales level had been forecasted to reach the $22–$24 million level. Because of the unstable profit situation, the expected profit as a percentage of sales were uncertain.) Until 1958, Sarepta was entirely owned by the Upton family. In 1958, 350,000 shares of common stock were sold publicly for $9.75 per share. Sarepta now has over 2,000 shareholders and its Class A common

Exhibit 2

SAREPTA PAPER COMPANY (A)

Balance Sheet

(all figures in thousands)

	1961	1960
Assets		
Current Assets:		
Cash	$ 506	$ 702
Accounts receivable	2,031	2,104
Inventory:		
Raw material and supplies	1,405	1,510
Work in process and finished goods	2,032	1,831
	$ 5,974	$ 6,147
Prepaid expenses	201	162
Total Current Assets	$ 6,175	$ 6,309
Fixed Assets:		
Land	$ 101	$ 85
Buildings	4,133	3,343
Machinery and equipment	7,205	6,305
	$11,439	$ 9,733
Less allowances for depreciation	4,481	3,934
	$ 6,958	$ 5,799
Total Assets	$13,133	$12,108
Liabilities		
Current Liabilities:		
Accounts payable	$ 1,743	$ 1,101
Payroll and other compensation	331	306
Profit sharing retirement plan	44	95
Taxes other than income taxes	110	108
Estimated federal income tax	330	331
Long-term debt due within one year	75	–
Total Current Liabilities	$ 2,633	$ 1,941
Long-term debt	2,025	2,100
Deferred federal income taxes	205	241
Stockholders' equity:		
Common stock—par value—$1.00 per share		
Class A	$ 441	$ 381
Class B	2,407	2,407
Retained Earnings	5,422	5,038
	$ 8,270	$ 7,826
Total Liabilities	$13,133	$12,108

stock is traded over the counter. Prior to this public issue all expansion and improvements had been financed from either retained earnings or debt.

Exhibit 3

SAREPTA PAPER COMPANY (A)

Statement of Earnings
(all figures in thousands)

	1961*	1960*
Net sales	$20,985	$19,413
Other income	38	70
	$21,023	$19,483
Costs and expenses:		
Cost of goods sold	$16,815	$15,833
Selling, general and administrative expenses†	2,823	2,521
Interest	126	97
	$19,764	$18,451
Earnings before federal tax	$ 1,259	$ 1,032
Allowance for federal income taxes (estimated)	654	538
Net income	$ 605	$ 494
Dividend—Class A Common Stock	$ 221	$ 191
Class B Common Stock	0	0

* Year ending December 31.
† Depreciation—1961—$567,000.
 1960—$472,000.

MARKETING

Until 1929, Sarepta's principal product was a magazine grade of paper made for a single national magazine. In addition there were a few specialty grades which were produced and sold to a small number of customers. At that time there was no formal sales force. In 1929, Sarepta lost its long-standing contract with the magazine due to a major policy change on the part of the magazine. Consequently, the first sales force was formed and Sarepta began to push direct selling. Direct selling may be generally defined as selling direct to converting customers who prepare the paper for final consumption (i.e., greeting cards and wallpaper). The alternatives to selling direct are the use of brokers, who carry no inventory, or merchants, who stock large quantities of paper and sell to customers of all sizes.

Direct selling has permitted Sarepta to establish a personal relationship with its customers and by doing so had kept Sarepta's management aware of the product needs of the customer. The fact that Sarepta has a total of only 125–150 customers means that it is possible for a 15-man sales force to serve them adequately. Also direct selling eliminates the need for an expensive advertising program to support brokers and merchants in their selling efforts.

The thrust of Sarepta's sales effort is based on quality, service, and price. Since the quality is usually specified according to the customers' particular needs, the only places for product differentiation are service and price. Direct selling lends itself to emphasis on service, therefore, Sarepta is in a good position to take advantage of the attributes of good customer service. Price is dependent on the published industry price level and the reasonable limits of variance around this level are determined by the cost picture of the company concerned.

Sarepta's product line[4] has undergone a general trend toward more specialty papers since its major change in 1929. In the last six years there has been a 40 percent change in the product line which is an indication of the growing importance of market sensitivity. Exhibit 4 gives the relative volumes of the eleven major types of paper produced in 1962 by Sarepta.

Exhibit 4
PRODUCT LINES AND RELATIVE SALES VOLUME

Product Line	*Volume (percent)*
1. Offset	14
2. Greeting card	12
3. Boardlining	3
4. Gumming	2
5. Envelope and stationery	2
6. Light weight business forms	7
7. Hanging paper	1
8. Direct process	35
9. Photocopy	7
10. Alpha and overlay	11
11. Surgical and X-ray	6
	100

RESEARCH AND DEVELOPMENT

Sarepta maintains a small R & D laboratory for the development of new pulps and the investigation of new chemical processes. The objectives are to develop the grade of paper desired by the customer and to assist manufacturing in making the pulp as cheaply as possible. The R & D laboratory employs 20 men on a full-time basis; eight of these are trained chemists and paper specialists.

---

[4] "Product line" refers to the different grades of paper.

PRODUCTION (GENERAL)

Sarepta is a nonintegrated paper company which means that it lacks the necessary facilities for the production of wood pulp. The overall difference between a nonintegrated and integrated process is shown in the following diagram:

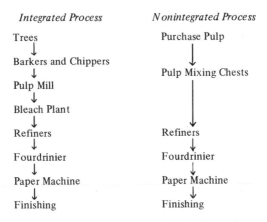

The obvious difference is what takes place before the pulp reaches the refiners. As a general rule only the larger paper companies have completely integrated processes. One of the main advantages of such an operation is that there is more control over the cost of the pulp which means there is more control over the basic cost structure of the final product. On the other hand, a considerably larger capital investment is required. Nonintegrated paper companies must operate under the major disadvantage of being dependent on a pulp supplier and having a product cost structure based on the price at which it can purchase pulp.

Sarepta's production facilities consist of five paper machines, each having different widths, lengths and operating characteristics. The variations in the designs of the different machines have resulted in some grades being more suitable to certain machines. It may be said, for purposes of production scheduling, that complete interchangeability of product lines with machines does not exist.

Sarepta's production operation is a three shift, 24 hours per day, six days per week process. Because of Maine "blue" laws Sunday can be used as a normal production day only six times a year. However, maintenance and other "nonproductive" activities may be performed every Sunday. Employees receive 1½ times normal pay for Saturday work and twice normal pay for Sunday work. Due to a special Sunday clean-up session performed by each shift every third week and because of the normally scheduled Sunday operation, the average pay for a production employee is considered to be 56 hours at the normal hourly rate.

Each paper machine is manned by a five-man crew which is made up of the following positions and wage rates:

Machine tender	$2.47–$2.63
Back tender	$2.26–$2.33
Third hand	$2.11–$2.17
Fourth hand	$2.07
Fifth hand	$2.33

In addition to base pay these five machine operators plus two additional beater operators (jobs explained in Production (Detail) section) receive a bonus based on a direct incentive system employing standards. The average bonus is equal to approximately 11 percent of the base wage rate. This is not to imply that there are only 35 men per shift associated with production, but rather these are the men directly responsible for the operation of the paper machines. Employees involved in pulp preparation and finishing are also considered production personnel but do not receive a direct bonus. These employees, along with all other hourly employees in the company, receive a plant-wide bonus which is determined by a formula based on the direct bonus given to the machine and beater operators.

The production employees are represented by the United Papermakers and Paperworkers Union and labor relations can be classified as good. Severe unemployment in and around Wascom has affected the attitude of workers toward job security. Sarepta employees are commonly known to be the highest paid employees in the surrounding area.

The crew-type operation of the paper machines tends to create a feeling of pride among the machine operators. They outwardly demonstrate pride in their competence in the "art" of papermaking and their ability to cope effectively with production problems. The production and over-all performance of each crew is thoroughly documented. This record is a necessary part of cost and production control but it also serves as a status incentive among the crews and consequently it reinforces the regular bonus incentive.

PRODUCTION (DETAIL)

A diagram of the process used by Sarepta is shown in Exhibit 5. Each of the paper machines and its associated equipment is similar to the layout in Exhibit 5 with only minor variations which are necessary to meet the individual machine requirements.

The purchased pulp, which is in sheets of approximately 30 inches × 50 inches having a thickness of $\frac{1}{8}$ inch is placed into the pulp mixer in bales to dissolve the solid pulp into the fibrous solution. From the pulp mixer the solution is pumped into the beater chest where beater-room additives are mixed. A beater engineer controls the beater as well as the amount and type of additives. Beater-room additives differ according to the grade

Exhibit 5
PULP AND PAPER PROCESS

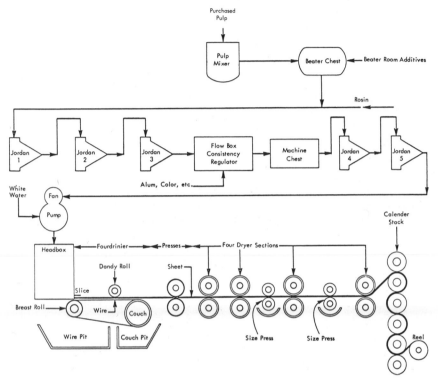

Courtesy IBM Corporation

of paper being produced. Typical additives are rosin, alum, caustic soda, calcium chloride, slime-control additives and brightness increasers such as titanium dioxide.

The stock, or washed pulp with additives, proceeds from the beater chest to a series of Jordans for refining. (Beaters and refiners are used to condition the fibers in the pulp.) A Jordan, which is a type of refiner is designed for cutting or brushing and is controlled by the machine tender. After the Jordans the stock passes to a consistency regulator where the percentage of dry pulp to total solution is controlled. A typical consistency would be 4 percent by weight. Also at that point other additives are added to the stock. The mixing chest, the next step in the process, is simply a holding point for the stock as it is fed into the final Jordans which allow the machine tender to make fine adjustments on the pulp fiber. After the last Jordan, the stock passes through cleaners for removal of undesirable nonfiber material, then it is diluted by recirculating water (known as white water) and is carried to the paper machine.

A paper machine, of the Fourdrinier type as used by Sarepta (see Exhibit 5), is made up of a headbox and wire for forming a sheet from the stock and presses and felts for smoothing, drying, sizing and finishing the sheet. The headbox is a reservoir from which all of the stock, both water and pulp, is delivered to the wire as a smooth sheet. The headbox slice opening is adjusted according to the speed of the wire, the consistency of the stock, the desired thickness and other variables. The wire which is an endless, moving bronze-wire cloth, allows the fibers to form a mat or web as the water drains away. At this point freeness, the ease with which water drains from the web, appears as a discernible line. The web appears shiny or wet on the headbox side of the line while the sheet appears dull on the other side. The freer the stock, the faster the water drains from the web and the closer the line is to the headbox.

Control of the sheet formation is of particular interest to Sarepta because of the stringent requirements of specialty papers. Formation, the way the fibers lie together and interlock, takes place on the wire as the sheet is formed by the slice. Only very slight changes can be made in formation after the stock has been deposited by the slice and a sheet formed. This fact points out the importance of the headbox to the success of the operation.

As a sheet moves with the wire, the dandy roll serves as a press while the couch roll, which is perforated and has a vacuum applied to it, sucks water from the sheet. From the couch to the first press the sheet is assisted by a felt which, like the wire, forms a continuous belt to assist the newly formed sheet into the dryers. The press, acting like the wringer on an old model washing machine, and the dryers, which are steam-heated rollers, serve to remove the moisture from the sheet as it progresses toward the dry end of the machine. A typical moisture content of a sheet entering the dryers is 65 percent and a typical moisture content of the finished product is 3 percent. Each section of the dryers is usually kept at a different temperature with the temperature progression being from low to high as the sheet moves toward the dry end.

Sizing, a material which increases the resistance of paper to penetration by liquids, is added to the sheet at the size presses. The final important point, as the sheet nears completion, is the calender stacks. The calender rolls are critical in determining the final thickness and finish of the paper. The calender stack adjustments are normally made by the back tender.

The reel after the calender stacks is the last point of the continuous process as shown in Exhibit 5. By means of a special reel arrangement, a full reel may be removed and a fresh reel begun without requiring that the paper machine be stopped. Once a full reel is removed it is usually rewound and cut into smaller reels. The rewinder is operated by the third hand and is considered a responsibility of the machine crew.

Completed paper is tested to insure that it meets the customers' specifications. Off-spec paper, paper which does not meet the required specifications, and waste paper resulting from trial runs and trimming is called broke and is returned to the pulp mixer to be re-entered into the process. Approximately 80 percent of all broke is placed back into the process.

There are numerous tests to which paper may be subjected in order to determine if the proper quality has been achieved. Some of the more common tests, which are universal to the industry, are basis weight, caliper, bursting strength, tensile strength, breaking strength, resistance to penetration by a liquid, finish and formation. Typical of specialized tests which are made on particular grades of paper according to their expected application are oil penetration, printability, and stiffness. Basis weight, caliper and bursting strength are defined as follows: basis weight—the weight in pounds of a ream of paper of standard size (a ream is usually 500 sheets each 24 inches $\times$ 36 inches); caliper—thickness measured in thousandths of an inch or points of caliper; bursting strength—strength in pounds per square, sometimes given in points—Mullen.

Historically at Sarepta, as in the entire paper industry, operator know-how has been relied upon exclusively for meeting the required specifications. Years of experience have taught the operators how different paper machine adjustments affect the quality of the paper. An experienced operator would know that basis weight is directly affected by stock flow rate, headbox level and stock consistency. Also he knows that caliper is affected by ironing at the calenders, by the presses and by the draw or differential, which is a result of the slightly higher speed of succeeding sections in stretching or drawing the sheet. Likewise finish is affected by ironing, by adding certain chemicals to the stock, by spraying starch or other sizing onto the sheet at the sizing press, by varying the drying rate and to a small extent by a change in the amount of refining.

An experienced operator also relies on such things as the feeling of slipperiness of the stock in the headbox, the location of the waterline on the wire, the sound of the machine, the crushing out at the calender or press rolls (undesirable accumulation of water resulting from excess moisture in the sheet), and a finger test of the relative velocities of the wire and the flow of stock at the slice. According to his best judgement an operator will relate these intuitive evaluations to the on-spec paper which has been produced in the past. These judgements must be made since there is no way to check characteristics such as bursting strength, porosity, or printability of paper continuously and simultaneously as the paper is being made. Consequently, the amount of off-spec paper produced is practically inversely proportioned to the accuracy of these judgements.

Operator judgement is particularly evident, and necessary, when a grade change occurs. He must preadjust the Jordans, headbox, consistency, wire and machine speed and slice opening as well as numerous other minor adjustments. Once the required operating changes have been made, variations in the stock will necessitate changes while the run is in progress.

PRODUCTION AND COST DATA

The elaborate records of production and cost, kept for every paper machine and every shift, are used to compile two cost figures used commonly by Sarepta to determine the effect of down time and off-specification paper on profits. Since time is such an important bench mark in a continuous process operation, both production and cost figures are commonly expressed in tons per hour and dollars per hour respectively.

The two cost figures of particular interest are the direct cost per hour and the marginal income per hour. The direct cost includes general overhead, direct labor and other costs which are not believed to change vis-à-vis normal variances in production. Marginal income is the average incremental income received per hour for a full hour of on-specification production. Marginal income is essentially the selling price minus the variable costs which are essentially raw material and power.

Production statistics which are continually reviewed for possible improvement are start-up time (time required in a grade change to obtain the required specifications) and off-specification time. As stated previously both of these times depend largely on operator know-how and intuition. Exhibit 6 presents average annual production and cost figures for all five paper machines.

Exhibit 6
SELECTED PRODUCTION AND COST DATA

Paper machine—number	1	2	3	4	5	Total
Average daily production (tons)	35	35	30	50	25	175
Start-up time (hours per year).	720	330	250	438	95	1,838
Off-spec time (hours per year)	110	210	140	275	150	885
Direct cost* (dollars per hour)	63	40	82	80	105	370
Marginal income* (dollars per hour)	131	83	163	185	211	773

* These terms are defined in the section on Production and Cost Data.

Raw material costs for Sarepta's nonintegrated process usually average between $150 to $165 per ton depending on the particular grade being processed. This cost includes an approximate broke reuse rate of 80 percent.

A NEW CONCEPT IN PAPERMAKING

As Mr. Small pondered his cost-cutting chore, he remembered having seen an advertisement for a computerized control system which was manufactured by International Business Machines. Although the advertisement was in a paper industry trade journal it was unclear as to just what benefits could be derived from such a system by a paper company. Since there were no actual systems in operation, there were no specific claims or statements which indicated the degree of success that could be achieved. Two other well-known computer manufacturers had also run similar advertisements. While Small was somewhat skeptical of the possible outcome, he decided to talk to a salesman from each company.

After discussing the proposed systems with the three companies, it appeared to Small that each of the systems followed the same principle—measurement of numerous variables at predetermined time intervals, comparison of measurements against standard data, and notification of intolerable variances between the actual and standard. The only significant differences between the different systems were price, experience in the field and service. Before any further detailed investigation was made Mr. Small decided that since IBM's system was the cheapest and since he thought IBM had a superior reputation for research, production, operating experience and service in all aspects of computer operation, it should be the system that he would investigate thoroughly for cost-cutting potential. Also because of the complexity of such an application and the unfamiliarity of Sarepta with computerized process control, Mr. Small and the IBM representatives felt that the system should be analyzed with respect to one paper machine. If proven successful, the system had the necessary computer capacity to be extended to the other four paper machines, and then even greater savings would be realized.

From what Mr. Small could see, a computer offered several potential cost advantages to Sarepta. If operated effectively, it would serve as an aid in reducing off-spec and start-up costs. Savings realized in these areas would be readily apparent and easily measured. However, Small hoped that the system might also be an aid toward making higher quality paper. Hopefully new lines could be introduced into the product mix which before could not be made to meet required specifications. For purposes of analysis Small knew that savings in this area could only be expressed as a hope or possible fringe benefit for having the system.

Small analyzed the cost and production data for the five machines (see Exhibit 6) and was convinced from that data that machine No. 4 would be the best to analyze with respect to the control system. However, there were two other cogent arguments for using No. 4. Historically the crews which operated it were thought to be the most competent and the most likely to cooperate in seeing that the system was used effectively. Also No. 4 already had more instrumentation than the other machines making the application cheaper and easier from the outset.

Exhibit 7 presents a diagram of the IBM 1710 system as it would be used by Sarepta. The paper machine would provide the system with actual readings, the card reader would give the standard values and the 1620 Central Processing Unit would perform the comparison of data. All readings, both standard and actual, would be printed out by typewriter with the variances being printed in red. A complete reading of all of the data

Exhibit 7
IBM 1710 CONTROL SYSTEM AS APPLIED TO A PAPER MACHINE

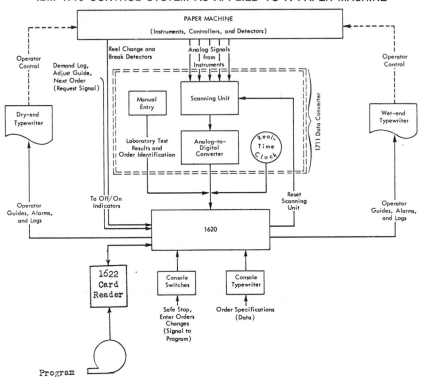

Courtesy IBM Corporation

would occur every 15 minutes while every 3 minutes variances from the standard would be printed. The operator could also receive a "demand log" (reading on all points whenever he wanted them) and a "break log" (a reading on all points at the time of a paper break).

Typical variables which could be easily measured and recorded are as follows:

a. Temperature.

b. Pressure.

c. Flow rate.

d. Position indicator.

e. pH.

f. Power.

g. Atmospheres of pressure—plus and minus.

h. Humidity as a function of dewpoint.

The paper machine sensors (see Exhibit 7) having analog outputs, would pass through transducers first to put their output in the form of milliampere (Ma) or millivolt (Mv) analog signals. Measurements of the pulse-type (i.e., on or off indicators) would be fed directly into the 1620 Central Processing Unit.

The IBM 1711 Data Converter would receive the analog signals and convert them into digital form. The digitized measurements (representing actual values) would then be fed into the 1620 Central Processing Unit which would also receive the standard data from the 1622 Card Reader and Punch. The comparison of actual and standard values would take place in the 1620 Central Processing Unit and the output would be a type-writer print out. Typewriters could be located at both the wet and dry ends of the machine, thereby, giving identical information to the machine tender and back tender.

The typewriter print out would take the form of the partial log sheet shown in Exhibit 8. Although it appears complex on first glance, a closer analysis shows that the sheet is simply a highly accurate logging device. It may be expanded or reduced to meet the needs of the particular paper machine which is being monitored. Also it should be noted that the values which are recorded are in units which are familiar to the machine opera-tors. All print out data is in paper machine language and not in computer language. For this reason, it was believed that only a minimum amount of training would be required for the machine operator to become familiar with the operation of the computer.

In determining the cost of the 1710 system to Sarepta, Mr. Small de-cided that all costs could be considered as related to the actual IBM equip-ment or related to the associated equipment such as sensors and computer room. The total purchase cost of the IBM equipment would be $175,000 with service contracts negotiated separately. However, the IBM salesman had not encouraged Small to purchase the equipment but rather he thought a monthly rental arrangement would be more suitable to Sarepta. The monthly rent for the entire system including normal service calls was $4,000. With the rental arrangement Sarepta would not be obligated for a period longer than 30 days. If Sarepta so desired, it could have the entire system removed with only 30 days notice to IBM.

After carefully reviewing the condition of all the instruments currently in use on the paper machine, Small decided that at least $25,000 would be required to purchase new sensors where necessary and to purchase the required transducers to give the system an "80 variable" capability. Small assumed that these expenditures would be capitalized and that a 10-year life was reasonable to expect. Another $25,000 was required to install the sensors and transducers and to make a room near the paper machines which could house the 1710. Since Sarepta maintenance personnel and carpenters were to perform this work, this second $25,000 was to be one-time expense as far as Small was concerned.

The operating expenses were more difficult for Small to estimate. Power and general overhead were tentatively set at $50 per month. In addition two men, schooled in the operation of the 1710, would be required on a full-time basis to operate the computer. Small knew of two men at Sarepta who were suitable for these two jobs, yet both would have to be

Exhibit 8

DAILY LOG SHEET
1710 SYSTEM

Rec	DATE	GRADE	TIME	Deckle Ash (1,2)	Refiner Consist Flow Rt. (3,4)	Refiner Temp Ph (5,6)	Refiner Power (7,8)	Refiner Power Hp/Ton (9,10)	(11,12)	Jordan Consist Flow Rt. (13,14)	Jordan Temp Ph (15,16)	Jordan Power Hp/Ton (17,18)	Jordan Freecon (19,20)	Temp/Ph Hd. Box (23,24)	Level Hd. Box / Bottle Pos. (25,26)	Apron Pos. / Slice Pos. (27,28)	Stock Fl. Hd. / Shower Wat. (29,30)	Make Up / O'flo (31,32)	(33,34)
1&2	4-25-62	6011000007622 0 F BRITE GRT DT	1203	865 / 140	300 / 300	80 / 43	230 / 100	75 / 749		250 / 400	85 / 42	240 / 400	350	85 / 44	130 / 250	200 / 65	1700 / 75	200 / 300	563 / 492
3&4	4-25-62	6011000007622 0 F BRITE GRT DT	1204	865 / 140	312 / 330	79 / 44	221 / 99	70 / 747		250 / 421	82 / 32	248 / 402	370	90 / 43	132 / 255	205 / 60	1700 / 75	201 / 302	560 / 490
5		1207 V9-69,75V19-369,350		V23-91,	85		1210	V27-	212,	200									
6&7	4-25-62	6011000007622 0 F BRITE GRT DT	1211	865 / 140	312 / 350	79 / 44	222 / 99	71 / 740		251 / 420	84 / 32	290 / 402	300	85 / 43	120 / 255	200 / 60	1700 / 75	200 / 302	563 / 490

Line 1 & 2 Represents standard print out

Line 3 & 4 Represents the timed routine print out of the log

Line 5   Represents exception routine

Line 6 & 7 Represents a sheet break print out caused by the sheet break interrupt.

NOTE: Small type will appear in red on computer typewriter.

sent to a three-week computer course. Also because of recent changes in work assignments Small believed that it was necessary to hire only one additional man to fill the two vacancies that would be created.

Small realized that although he had a large amount of information regarding the 1710 system and Sarepta's production operation he would be unable to make a cost analysis for Mr. Upton until he had made one critical assumption. The assumption which faced Small was just how much start-up and off-spec time could be eliminated by the computer application. Since there were no other 1710 applications in the paper industry, there was no past experience to draw from. After much deliberation Small decided that for the purposes of his analysis he would use a reduction in start-up time of 40 percent and a reduction in off-spec time of 60 percent. Small felt that such savings would not come initially but would result only from practice and diligent efforts on the part of the machine operators.

In thinking through these assumptions Small pondered the point of operator cooperation. He knew that job security would not be a source of discontent for it was obvious that the control system would not eliminate the need for crew members. A system with a closed loop designed to eliminate some of the routine tasks of the crew members (not eliminate jobs) was not even in the foreseeable future. However, Small was afraid there would be resistance to anything that might threaten to remove the art of the machine operators' work. It would be like making the skill required to be an artist no longer necessary so that anyone might be a successful painter. Clearly such a change would have a psychological impact on the employees. Small knew that his proposal to Upton would have to include a method of dealing effectively with any personnel objections that might arise. It was clear that regardless of the accuracy and thoroughness of the Control System, it would all be wasted unless the operators were willing to correlate their past paper machine experience with the printed warnings of the typewriter and take the required action.

Mirassou Vineyards (A)

IN 1966, there were serious questions being raised in the Mirassou family about what action should be taken regarding the vineyard's planting strategy, particularly in view of the recently proposed UpRight Harvester mechanical grape picker. The company was in the middle of establishing their own brand label wines in the market and shifting production from the rapidly developing and crowded San Jose area to more remote growing areas. Was the UpRight Harvester just another complication at this time in Mirassou's development, or was this the ideal moment to innovate new planting, growing, and harvesting methods?

BACKGROUND OF THE CALIFORNIA WINE INDUSTRY

In the mid-1960s, the California wine industry was experiencing an unprecedented boom. The popularity of wine in the United States was soaring. Per capita wine consumption per adult was approaching 2.5 gallons, and was expected to reach 3.4 gallons by 1980.[1] This growing demand, coupled with an expanding "drinking-age" population and growing disposable income among young Americans were all favorable trends.

The California wine industry accounted for approximately 74 percent of all wines consumed in the United States, compared to approximately 12 percent that were imported. The balance came from other states, including New York.

Wines were generally classified into three categories: table, dessert, and sparkling. Table and sparkling wines were legally classified as those containing not more than 14 percent alcohol, while dessert wines were those containing more than 14 percent alcohol.

Tables wines were further divided into *varietal* and *generic* wines.

---

[1] This description draws heavily from studies made by G. Michael Oberst and John W. Larsen, Wells Fargo Bank, N.A., San Francisco, California.

Varietal table wines were named for the principal grapes used in their production, i.e., Cabernet Sauvignon, Zinfandel, Barbera, Chenin Blanc and others. To bear a varietal name, by federal law, a wine must have derived at least 51 percent of its volume from the grape for which it was named and have the aroma and flavor of that grape. Generic wines were typically named for various wine producing districts in Europe because they possessed the general characteristic of wines from those areas, i.e., Burgundy, Chablis, Bordeaux (or claret) or others.

Table wines were characteristically lighter and drier (not sweet) tasting than dessert or sparkling wines, mostly due to the higher acidity and lower sugar content of the grapes from which they were made.

Dessert wines, and the subcategory called appetizer wines, had a stronger and sweeter taste because of higher sugar content, and in some cases, the addition of fruit flavoring. Sparkling wines could be either sweet or dry, but were characterized by the effervescent nature resulting from carbonation.

It had been estimated that shipments of table wine to United States markets, would rise from 78.6 million gallons in 1966 to approximately 374.0 million gallons in 1980.[2] Dessert wines would fall from 103.5 million gallons in 1966 to approximately 53.6 million gallons in 1980, while sparkling wines would jump from 9 million gallons to 63.7 million gallons in the same period.

GEOGRAPHIC CONSIDERATIONS

Certain grapes were closely identified with particular growing regions according to John W. Larsen of Wells Fargo Bank, N.A.

> The basic criterion for classification of the growing regions is a warm to temperate climate from April 1 through October 31. The Coastal region—and especially the North Coast—is the coolest area in which grapes are grown; its climate and soil conditions result in the longer maturing, low yield grapes which go into fine wines. The soil and hotter climate of the Central Valley and Southern California produce higher yield, faster maturing grapes for raisin, table and standard wine usage. Grapes for the sweet dessert wines are also generally found in Central and Southern California.
>
> Some grapes do best in particular regions. For example, the Cabernet Sauvignon, Pinot Noir, and Pinot Chardonnay grapes can be grown most successfully in parts of the North Coast. Likewise, Malvasia Bianca and Tinta Madeira, used for making dessert wines, do their best in the warmer areas. There are, of course, many exceptions to these generalities. Due to the limited acreage available and generally lower fertility in Coastal regions, an attempt has been made over the years to develop grapes which have all the wine making characteristics of a Coastal varietal but which will grow in the Valley and other hotter areas. An outstanding example

---

[2] G. Michael Oberst, Wells Fargo Bank, N.A.

of this is the Ruby Cabernet developed by the University of California at Davis. This grape is a cross between the Carignane and the Cabernet Sauvignon and it does well in hot regions.

In addition to the fact that growing region has a distinct bearing on the most suitable type of grape to plant, it affects price as well. Zinfandel is a grape which does relatively well in all California's growing regions. For example, Zinfandels grown in the [San Joaquin] Valley brought $135 per ton while those grown in the North Coast brought $325 per ton. The difference, of course, relates to sugar/acid balance and other measures of quality. Connoisseurs feel that a Zinfandel produced in the cooler area is notably superior in taste and aging characteristics. The market value notes this difference.

The really big and unique thing about the North Coast, which distinguishes it from any other wine producing area in the United States, is the fact that it can produce wines, properly aged, that have the same characteristics as the finer wines produced in Bordeaux and other areas in France. Even to the experienced palate, the taste difference between the two is barely noticeable. The climate and soil of a growing region clearly have quite a bearing on suitable varietals as well as on price. The grower should be knowledgeable as to the characteristics and limitations of the region under consideration.

SUMMARY OF THE WINE MAKING PROCESS

The annual grape harvest normally began in September and ended in late October. Following the harvest, the grapes were crushed in a stainless steel crush stemmer. The free running juice was drained off, and the remaining "pomace" (skins, etc.) was gently pressed for additional juice. The juice was then pumped into stainless steel fermentation tanks. The pomace was discarded in making white wines. For red wines, it was pumped into the fermentation tank with the juice to provide some of the "body" and "color" of the wines.

To control the heat generated by the natural fermentation process and to protect the delicacy and flavor of the wine, the juice was fermented under controlled temperature conditions. Red wines were allowed to ferment at a higher temperature than white wines in order to assist in the extraction of color from the skins which float to the top of the tank and form a "cap."

The fermented wine, either red or white, was then transferred between tanks several times so that the natural protein and other solid matter would settle. It was then rough filtered and stored in tanks.

White wines which benefit from wood aging were often stored in 60-gallon French or American oak barrels; others were left in stainless steel tanks. Red wines were typically aged and stored in wood barrels. Once the wine maker had tasted the wine and determined it had matured, it was bottled and corked for additional aging in glass, with wine breathing a very small amount of air through the cork. Following the initial aging, the wine was ready for sale.

From crush to shipment of bottled wine, white wines typically required one to´ two years, while red wines required an additional one to three years. Even at that point, many consumers bought these "young wines" to be laid down for additional bottle aging.

FIVE GENERATIONS OF WINE MAKING

The members of the Mirassou family were very proud of their long tradition of wine making in California. In 1848, Louis Pellier came to California from France in what proved to be an unfruitful search for gold. After a brief time, he turned to planting grape vines, and soon sent for fine cuttings from his native Bordeaux, France. The vines thrived, and in 1854, Louis' brother, Pierre, returned to France for more vines. On the long journey back to California, the ship was becalmed and the fresh water supply was exhausted. The resourceful Pierre Pellier made a deal with the ship's captain to buy his cargo of potatoes. Pierre inserted the cuttings in the moist potatoes he had slit open, thus saving the vines. Descendants of these vines still grew in the family vineyards. Henrietta Pellier, Pierre's daughter, married Pierre Mirassou, who was to become head of the family vineyards. Pierre Mirassou, Jr. eventually assumed control of the vineyard and was responsible for keeping the property and vines healthy during prohibition, when many California vineyards and wineries were closed.

Pierre Mirassou's grandsons, Norbert and Edmund, continued to operate the vineyard, even in the face of the "encroachment of civilization" in the rapidly growing San Jose and developing Santa Clara County areas. Their business had traditionally been involved in bulk production of high grade wines. The wine was produced at the winery in San Jose (at the lower end of the San Francisco Bay) and shipped in casks or barrels, or rail tank cars to other wineries, which processed it for distribution under their own labels.

The fifth generation (Edmund's sons: Daniel, Peter, and James—and Norbert's son, Steven, and son-in-law, Don Alexander) decided that the Mirassou family should take a higher profile. In 1966, the members of the fifth generation launched a "satellite business" of bottling and retailing fine wines[3] under the Mirassou family label.

Mirassou Sales, the name taken by the fifth generation's venture, was a major break with family tradition. Obviously, Mirassou Sales, if successful, was likely to be a competitor to the other wineries that bought most of the production of Mirassou Vineyards, the operation of the fourth generation. The Mirassous were warned by several executives in the wine industry that such a venture was almost certainly doomed to failure because

---

[3] Wines were generally grouped as to retail price: up to $1.50 per bottle were "standard"; $1.50 to $3.00 per bottle were "premium"; over $3.00 per bottle were "fine."

of the tremendous costs associated with promoting and establishing their market.

In 1966, the first bottles of wine under the Mirassou label were sold at locations other than the vineyard. In that year, only 3 percent of the Mirassou production was devoted to this venture.

SUB-DIVISIONITIS

The Mirassous began to suffer from what E. A. Mirassou called "sub-divisionitis." The expansion of housing developments and increased taxes in the increasingly populated areas in the San Francisco Bay area, made opportunity costs on land so high that several vineyards began the search for new growing areas. In the early 1960s, Mirassou began planting in the Monterey area of Central California, a distance of approximately 100 miles from their San Jose winery. (See Exhibits 1 and 2.)

In 1966, during this period of transition, the Mirassou family was ap-

Exhibit 1
LOCATION OF VINEYARDS

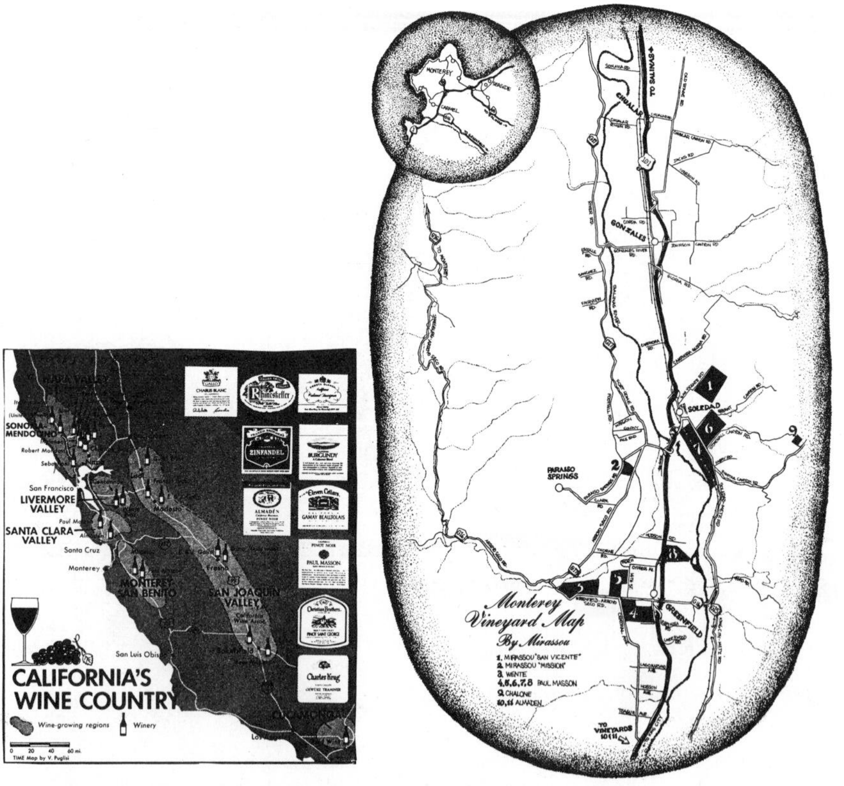

Reprinted by permission from TIME, the weekly newsmagazine; copyright Time Inc. Copyright 1972 by Mirassou Vineyards.

proached with a novel proposition—a proposal for a mechanized grape harvester that was being developed by the UpRight Harvester Company.

ECONOMICS OF GRAPE AND WINE PRODUCTION

One of the most important aspects of developing a vineyard was the long period from the time of planting vines until full production is reached. During the first three years, the production was zero. The yield of the vines slowly increased from the third through the sixth year. However, vines had a productive life of 35 to 40 years once they were established.

Exhibit 2
MIRASSOU ACREAGE UNDER CULTIVATION

	Santa Clara County			Monterey County		
Year	Uncul-tivated	Planted Developing*	Producing	Uncul-tivated	Planted Developing*	Producing
1960 0		0	300	0	0	0
1961 0		0	300	300	0	0
1962 0		0	300	640	300	0
1963 0		0	300	640	300	0
1964 0		0	300	640	300	0
1965 0		0	300	640	300	0
1966 0		0	300	640	0	300

* Approximately three years are required before grape production and six years are required to develop a fully producing vine after it is planted.

The costs of developing a vineyard in excess of costs of owning land (such as taxes, interest payments if financed, and opportunity losses) were largely associated with "culture" and "harvesting" costs. Cultural costs were those associated with establishing and tending the vineyard. The typical cultural costs for a large acreage vineyard development had been studied in some detail by the Wells Fargo Bank of California and are summarized in Exhibit 3.

The cost of land depended on the location, and often was not related to the suitability of the land for growing grapes. More typically, land prices were set by alternative land uses.

Approximately 180 gallons of wine are produced from a ton of grapes. Of this 180 gallons, approximately 150 gallons are free run juice of top quality, the remainder is pressed juice, which is sold or used for lesser quality wines or is further fermented for stock for distilled spirits (i.e., brandy).

The price buildup for a typical wine is shown in Exhibit 4. Mirassou Vineyards had traditionally sold wine in bulk to other wineries for blending purposes and to supplement limited production at prices lower than that

Exhibit 3
TYPICAL CULTURAL AND HARVEST COST AND YIELDS

	Year				
	1	2	3	4	5 (and thereafter)
Cultural Costs					
Management	50	50	50	50	50
String, wire, twine	0	30	2	2	2
Train vines.	0	55	12	12	12
Prune and tie	0	5	25	25	25
Control of small animals, deer, birds . . .	8	2	10	10	10
Water and labor.	18	20	12	12	12
Miscellaneous labor.	5	8	15	15	15
Repairs.	15	15	15	15	15
County taxes	20	21	21	21	21
Tillage	15	12	12	12	12
Fertilizer and labor.	0	12	14	14	14
Pest and disease control	7	8	17	17	17
Survey and planting	20	2	0	0	0
Rootings preparation.	20	2	0	0	0
Scatter and drive stakes	0	30	0	0	0
Stakes	0	200	0	0	0
Land preparation	200	0	0	0	0
Pipeline work	110	0	0	0	0
Total cost per acre	488	472	205	205	205
Harvesting Costs					
Labor (hand)	0	0	66	124	195
Total cost per acre	488	472	271	329	400
Typical Tonnage per Acre*					
Barber Grapes (approximately $95 per ton revenue)†.	0	0	4	7	10
Chenin Blanc Grapes (approximately $100 per ton revenue)†	0	0	5	10	12
Ruby Cabernet Grapes (approximately $110 per ton revenue)†	0	0	4	8	10

* Yield based on hand picking and normal cultural practices.
† Prices subject to considerable fluctuation depending on popularity of wines produced from the grape.
Source: Wells Fargo Bank, N.A.

typically received from primary distributors. Mirassou Sales (the Mirassou fifth generation's venture) served as the primary distributor.

THE "UPRIGHT" HARVESTER

The potential of mechanically picking wine grapes had intrigued producers for many years. The level of interest in mechanical picking had been closely correlated with the increased militancy of the farm laborers, particularly under the organizational efforts of Caesar Chavez. Many growers had become increasingly convinced that there would be a time when

Exhibit 4
TYPICAL TRADE MARKUP ON A CASE
OF WINE (CHENIN BLANC)

	Case of 12 Fifths
Juice	$ 0.72
Winery expenses	11.53
Profit to winery (target)	1.50
Cost to primary distributor	13.75
Markup of primary distributor	2.75
Cost to wholesaler	16.50
Markup of wholesaler	5.50
Cost to retailer	22.00
Markup of retailer	11.00
Retail price	$33.00

Profit

it would be impossible to depend on any substantial pool of unskilled itinerant unemployed laborers to work as harvesters during vintage season. It was described by one grower as "the type of work which most people don't want to do anyway, particularly in the hot, dry, and dustry California valleys where grapes grow best. It is not very romantic work, crawling on your knees under the vines." This situation was also reflected in the increased pay demanded by pickers. From 1956 to 1966, the pay per box of grapes increased from $0.15 to $0.38. This had resulted in a harvesting cost of approximately $18 per ton of grapes.

Additionally, some growers were experiencing lower yields of grapes picked per acre because of the unwillingness of workers to pick fruit that was difficult to reach.

The first effort to pick grapes mechanically was developed in the 1950s. It was a "sickle-bar cutter" that was a device that opened and closed like scissors. It was to cut off long stems of carefully trained grapevine branches. Unfortunately, it was found that it was difficult to train the branches in the necessary configuration, and the device was never commercially successful.

The next mechanical picking method that was attempted in the early 1960s involved suction. It was hoped that ripe grapes could be sucked off the vine with a vacuum hose. In theory, the ripe grapes would separate from the stems without the leaves. Several different attempts in the United States and Germany demonstrated that it was possible to pick substantially more grapes than were picked from the vines by workers. However, there was also the problem of sucking many of the leaves off the vines as well. Even the most successful of these devices, that could separate the grapes and leaves, tended to ingest some leaf particles. The chlorophyll from these particles tended to give the resulting wine a taste like alfalfa. The inability of the developers to correct this situation led to discarding the project by the mid-1960s and some very disgruntled growers who had lost valuable vines to the lusty experimental machines.

Viticulturists doing research at the University of California proposed a new growing method, using a wire trellis. (See Exhibit 5.) Their idea was that the fruitbearing canes should hang upon horizontally spaced wires separated three feet apart. Wallace Johnson, an inventor, engineer, and small grape grower, set out to develop a new approach to mechanical grape picking in conjunction with the trellis-growing method.

The device, which he named the UpRight Harvester straddled the rows of vines. (See Exhibit 6.) A series of finger-like "batons" mounted within the harvester would strike the wires. As the harvester progressed along the row, the vertical impact of the batons upward on the wires would gently dislodge the ripe grapes from the stems. These grapes would fall on "catching conveyors."

One man drove the harvester straddling the row of vines. The falling grapes were then caught and carried by the catching conveyors into conventional field boxes. As a field box was filled, it was dropped at the end of a row, and an additional field box would be attached. This entire operation could be handled by one man, but with two men it was a relatively easy task.

Mr. Johnson approached the members of the Mirassou family in 1966 with a proposal for the testing of the UpRight Harvester in their fields. He had been frustrated by earlier attempts at securing a meaningful test for several reasons. First, most growers were well aware of the failures of other mechanical harvesters. Second, mature, producing grape vines were valuable assets that were easily damaged. Growers were very concerned about stories of other devices that sucked all the leaves off the vines or made random hacks at the vines with large sickles. Third, even if the grapes could be picked, would the results be suitable for production of superior wine?

Perhaps the most difficult problem in getting any larger grower to go along with the scheme was the planting requirement. It was necessary for the grower to plant the vines in a unique pattern to allow enough room for the machine to drive down the rows astraddle the vines and room to produce the correct shaking motion of the branches. This essentially halved the number of vines per acre.

There was also some issue of whether the machine would actually be able to pick all varieties of grapes equally well. The structure of the vine and the actual mechanical connection of the grape to the stem were different for different varieties.

Based on Mr. Johnson's estimates, the $42,000 machine could pick an acre of grapes in approximately 60 minutes. However, because the UpRight Harvester would only remove the ripe grapes on each pass, it was necessary to make two passes over a field during the period that the grapes matured. However, in doing so, the pick would be considerably more

Exhibit 5
TRELLISED GRAPE VINES

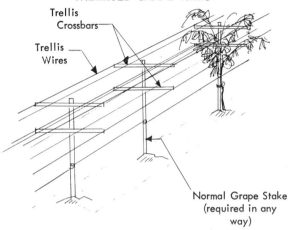

A. Schematic of trellised vines

B. View of conventional, untrellised vines

Exhibit 6
UPRIGHT MECHANICAL GRAPE HARVESTER

A. View of harvester straddling trellised vines in field

B. Close-up view showing harvester shaking
vines and collecting grapes. Conveyors and "V"
shaped grape catchers seen at the base of
the vines.

thorough. It was estimated by Johnson that the harvested fruit might increase 25 to 35 percent. Also, he pointed out that only ripe fruit would be harvested, while hand pickers tended to pick any fruit, mature or not, just to fill field boxes, since that was the basis of pay.

The penalty of the increased space between vines was perhaps not as great as it might first appear. Based on the work of the researchers at the University of California at Davis, there was some evidence that such spacing might increase the yield by as much as 50 percent per vine, when combined with a suggested pruning method.

ask about this

PROPOSED FIELD EXPERIMENTS

It was proposed to the Mirassou family that their new vineyards be planted and developed in accord with the planting requirements to accommodate the UpRight Harvester. However, if they were not prepared to take this step immediately, they might consider an alternative of preparing a limited test of the machine before such a major step. If a field were planted in one configuration, it could not be changed to the other without completely replanting because of the planting pattern.

Specifically, the plan being considered was to postpone any additional vineyard development until the demonstration could be made. The demonstration would require planting five rows of each of ten varieties of grapes to accommodate the harvester. This would represent the equivalent of a total of 20 acres.

This plan had the advantage of minimizing the risk to Mirassou of the cost of the destruction of the vines in these fields, and the opportunity loss associated with a two-year delay in developing the new fields. The possible gain was the opportunity to have the first newly planted vineyards that could be mechanically picked.

In attempting to make the decision, the Mirassou family was faced with the question of what the cost of the experiments would be to them, what the potential rewards would be if they proved successful. How would they measure success of the experiment, and given this measure, at what level of success would they go ahead to fully adopt the new growing technology?

The Kroger Company

IN LATE 1973 a number of Kroger executives were concentrating their efforts on the evaluation of SCAN, Sperry-Univac's automated super-market checkstand system.[1] SCAN utilized optical character recognition devices (scanners) in conjunction with a small computer to read and ring up the prices of items being passed over a specially designed checkstand counter. The optical character recognition devices electronically read symbols placed on grocery products and transmitted the message recorded in these symbols to computers which recorded prices. A prototype of the SCAN system had been installed in Kroger's Kenwood, Ohio supermarket in July 1972 so that the feasibility of the system could be tested under actual operating conditions. In reviewing the results of this test, Kroger hoped to determine the operating and marketing implications of the new technology, and to gain the insights required to make plans for the future.

COMPANY BACKGROUND

The Kroger Company, with sales of $3.8 billion, was the third largest grocery chain in the United States in 1973. The company had grown from a small midwestern chain of retail grocery outlets to a nationwide company employing 80,000 people in a variety of operations. These included 1,300 supermarkets under the Kroger, Market Basket, and Happy Foodstore names, numerous food processing and distribution activities, nearly 500 SuperRX Drugstores, and several smaller ventures including Top Value Enterprises which distributed trading stamps, manufactured toys, and had recently entered the amusement park business. Yet, in spite of the company's varied business activities, retail grocery operations remained the Kroger Company's principal endeavor, accounting for over 90 percent of annual sales in 1973.

---

[1] The system was originally developed by RCA. Ownership was transferred to Sperry-Univac in mid-1973.

Kroger was active in supermarket, superstore, and convenience store operations. The largest portion of their stores were supermarkets. The average size of the new stores in this category was 27,500 square feet, while the average for all of Kroger's present stores was 18,250 square feet. In 1972, the average sales volume for Kroger supermarkets was approximately $50,000 per week. The typical store stocked over 8,000 items, 1,300 of which bore Kroger's private label. Kroger superstores were large supermarkets featuring specialty shops and an extended line of groceries, meat, and produce. The sales volume of a superstore complex was typically more than triple that of the average supermarket. Convenience stores represented a new venture for Kroger in 1972, when the first was opened. These were essentially modern neighborhood grocery stores, and were franchised for operation by individual owners.

The company's after-tax earnings of $18.5 million in 1972 (Exhibits 1 and 2) had been the lowest in five years. Although profit margins were traditionally small for retail grocers, the extremely competitive nature of the retail grocery business, coupled with economic conditions, had further reduced margins and profits for the entire industry in the 1970s. Three factors in particular had contributed to this earnings decline, which averaged 32.5 percent for the 50 largest chains in 1972. First, labor costs had increased rapidly; the average wage for a grocery clerk had risen from $2.00 in 1960 to $3.98 in 1972. Second, the wholesale cost of merchandise had increased due to inflationary pressures, while governmental controls and consumer discontent kept retail prices from rising accordingly. Third, A & P, the nation's largest retail grocer, had cut prices substantially as a part of the WEO marketing campaign. This move served to further magnify the extremely competitive nature of the industry.

Kroger's threefold response to these competitive and environmental pressures was (1) to continue to upgrade their stores by closing 129, opening 59 new stores, and remodeling 57 others; (2) to maintain prices while seeking to provide increased customer services; and (3) to continue to emphasize operations improvements which would increase the productivity of the work force.

SUPERMARKET OPERATIONS

Kroger supermarketing activities were divided into 20 geographical divisions, each headed by a vice president. Each division, which was comprised of 45–120 stores, together with the warehouses, bakeries, and meat processing plants necessary to serve them, was a separate profit center. These divisions were further segmented into zones (10 stores per zone) and were headed by a zone manager who coordinated the merchandising and store management activities for his area with store managers. The principal duties of the store managers were to manage local merchandising activities, plan and control manpower and material requirements and costs, and to

Exhibit 1

THE KROGER COMPANY
Operating Results

CONSOLIDATED STATEMENT OF EARNINGS

Years Ended December 30, 1972 and January 1, 1972	1972 (52 Weeks)	1971 (52 Weeks)
Income:		
Sales	$3,790,532,448	$3,707,918,052
Equity in net earnings of unconsolidated companies	7,952,256	2,584,871
Total	$3,798,484,704	$3,710,502,923
Costs and Expenses:		
Merchandise costs including warehousing and transportation	$2,982,886,510	$2,920,964,393
Operating, general and administrative expenses	675,554,930	619,310,855
Rent	60,106,665	56,441,502
Depreciation and amortization	38,296,453	37,671,690
Interest on long-term debt	7,646,972	7,927,217
Other interest expense	779,990	1,900,321
Taxes based on income	10,033,915	30,017,865
Total	$3,775,305,435	$3,674,233,843
Earnings before extraordinary loss, and credit resulting from a change in the method of applying an accounting principle	$ 23,179,269	$ 36,269,080
Extraordinary loss, net of tax benefits	(5,340,920)	(4,056,000)
Credit resulting from a change in the method of applying an accounting principle	586,877	
Net Earnings	$ 18,425,226	$ 32,213,080
Average number of shares of common stock outstanding	13,448,068	13,392,141
Per share of common stock:		
Earnings before extraordinary loss, and credit resulting from a change in the method of applying an accounting principle	$ 1.73	$ 2.71
Extraordinary loss	(.40)	(.30)
Credit resulting from a change in the method of applying an accounting principle	.04	
Net earnings	$ 1.37	$ 2.41

CONSOLIDATED STATEMENT OF ACCUMULATED EARNINGS

Years Ended December 30, 1972 and January 1, 1972	1972	1971
Accumulated earnings — Beginning of the year	$ 273,635,341	$ 258,791,838
Net earnings for the year	18,425,226	32,213,080
	$ 292,060,567	$ 291,004,918
Dividends on common stock — $1.30 per share	17,406,554	17,369,577
Accumulated earnings — End of the year	$ 274,654,013	$ 273,635,341

oversee the order, receipt and display of merchandise. The store manager was typically assisted by an assistant store manager, and by various department heads such as the meat department manager, and the head cashier.

Merchandise accounted for the largest proportion of the costs of operating a store, averaging 80 percent of sales. Ordering was a critical part of managing the flow of this merchandise. It was important to see that stocks were neither too high, needlessly taking up valuable shelf and warehouse space, nor so low that stockouts were likely to occur. In addition, the

Exhibit 1 (*Continued*)

FIVE YEAR SUMMARY

EARNINGS STATISTICS	1972	1971	1970(c)	1969	1968
(thousands of dollars, except per share figures)					
Sales	$3,790,532	3,707,918	3,735,774	3,477,164	3,160,838
Earnings Before Extraordinary Items	$ 23,179(a)	36,269(b)	39,769	37,336(d)	33,857
Dividends	$ 17,407	17,370	17,192	17,034	17,091
Per Share					
Earnings Before Effect of LIFO	$ 1.87(a)	2.82(b)	3.29	3.12(d)	2.7
Earnings Before Extraordinary Items	$ 1.73(a)	2.71(b)	3.00	2.84(d)	2.63
Dividends	$ 1.30	1.30	1.30	1.30	1.30

BALANCE SHEET STATISTICS					
(thousands of dollars, except per share figures)					
Inventories	$ 300,549	271,918	262,598	271,889	233,177
Working Capital	$ 126,460	143,941	108,270	56,318	77,561
Property, Plant and Equipment, net	$ 325,212	317,798	336,574	305,254	260,962
Total Assets	$ 810,826	756,418	768,093	692,599	590,069
Long-Term Debt	$ 92,000	93,708	102,482	28,690	31,028
Shareowners' Equity	$ 353,360	351,891	332,767	309,579	282,064
Per Share of Common	$ 26.26	26.19	25.07	23.36	21.56

OTHER STATISTICS					
(dollars and shares in thousands)					
Depreciation and Amortization	$ 38,296	37,672	35,720	31,929	31,157
Capital Expenditures	$ 55,335	47,105	89,326	77,448	56,768
Common Shares Outstanding	13,455	13,436	13,274	13,252	13,082
Number of Shareowners	44,893	42,182	44,786	45,780	49,575
Number of Regular Employees	52,119	52,073	53,811	51,196	48,128

RETAIL FACILITIES					
(areas in thousands of square feet)					
Supermarkets					
Opened	59	67	99	58	58
Remodeled	57	74	85	112	107
Closed	126	157	94	41	46
Stores — End of Year	1,365	1,432	1,522	1,517	1,500
Total Area	24,896	25,688	26,457	25,917	25,194
Drug Stores					
Opened	46	47	53	37	41
Closed	28	20	3	3	3
Stores — End of Year	476	458	431	381	347
Total Area	4,525	4,253	3,946	3,482	3,172

(a) Represents earnings before extraordinary loss of $5,340,920 or $.40 per share arising from discontinuance of Family Center operations and credit of $586,877 or $.04 per share resulting from a change in the method of applying an accounting principle.
(b) Represents earnings before extraordinary loss of $4,056,000 or $.30 per share arising from discontinuance of Wisconsin operations.
(c) Fifty-three weeks.
(d) Represents earnings before extraordinary gain of $1,342,120 or $.10 per share arising from sale of investment.

TRANSFER AGENTS
The First National Bank of Cincinnati
111 E. Fourth Street
Cincinnati, Ohio 45202

Bankers Trust Company
485 Lexington Avenue
New York, New York 10017

REGISTRARS
The Central Trust Company
Fourth and Vine Streets
Cincinnati, Ohio 45202

Chemical Bank
20 Pine Street
New York, New York 10015

Source: Kroger Annual Report

control of pilferage, damaged goods, and pricing were important activities. Approximately 25–30 hours per week was spent by store personnel in reviewing stock and ordering goods.

Labor was the second largest cost element in supermarket operations averaging 9–10 percent of sales. Approximately 42 percent of the wages paid in a store were to the people manning the "front end," including checkers or cashiers, and baggers. Thirty-three percent of the labor cost accrued to the stockers, who unloaded, priced and stocked merchandise

Exhibit 2

THE KROGER COMPANY

Balance Sheet

CONSOLIDATED BALANCE SHEET

ASSETS	**DEC. 30, 1972**	JAN. 1, 1972
CURRENT ASSETS		
Cash	$ 35,125,543	$ 47,276,753
Short-term investments	20,006,111	11,982,495
Receivables	53,423,149	44,192,317
Inventories	300,548,848	271,918,122
Store and general supplies	3,745, 953	3,468,120
Prepaid and miscellaneous assets	18,634,426	15,714,058
Total current assets	$431,484,030	$394,551,865
PROPERTY, PLANT AND EQUIPMENT		
Land	$ 16,292,446	$ 17,951,202
Buildings	76,272,763	73,364,514
Equipment	360,870,394	349,487,893
Leaseholds and leasehold improvements	107,017,193	98,510,108
	$560,452,796	$539,313,717
Allowance for depreciation and amortization	235,240,764	221,516,182
Property, plant and equipment, net	$325,212,032	$317,797,535
INVESTMENTS AND OTHER ASSETS		
Investments in and advances to unconsolidated companies	$ 32,881,031	$ 22,200,091
Other investments, at cost, and other assets	7,198,047	7,817,826
Excess of cost of investments in consolidated subsidiaries over equities in net assets	14,050,755	14,050,648
Total investments and other assets	$ 54,129,833	$ 44,068,565
Total Assets	$810,825,895	$756,417,965

on the shelves. The balance of the labor costs in a supermarket were accounted for by the other organizational components, including the meat department, produce department, and supervision.

The Front End.   Since merchandise costs were largely determined by market forces, front end labor was a logical focus for cost control in the supermarket. The front end refers to that part of the operation where customers are checked out. The basic functions of front end personnel, including cashiers and baggers, were to (1) enter the cost of the merchan-

Exhibit 2 *(Continued)*

LIABILITIES	DEC. 30, 1972	JAN. 1, 1972
CURRENT LIABILITIES		
Current portion of long-term debt	$ 1,510,000	$ 1,708,000
Accounts payable	208,914,982	159,127,338
Accrued expenses	81,572,607	76,980,629
Accrued federal income and other taxes	13,026,643	12,794,711
Total current liabilities	$305,024,232	$250,610,678
OTHER LIABILITIES		
Long-term debt	$ 90,490,000	$ 92,000,000
Deferred federal income taxes	21,992,000	20,875,000
Employees' benefit fund	39,959,237	41,041,476
Total other liabilities	$152,441,237	$153,916,476
Total Liabilities	$457,465,469	$404,527,154

SHAREOWNERS' EQUITY		
Common capital stock, par $1, at stated value		
Authorized: 18,000,000 shares		
Issued: 1972 — 13,741,977; 1971 — 13,722,402	$ 88,555,289	$ 88,104,346
Accumulated earnings	274,654,013	273,635,341
	$363,209,302	$361,739,687
Common stock in treasury, at cost — 286,772 shares	9,848,876	9,848,876
Total Shareowners' Equity	$353,360,426	$351,890,811
Total Liabilities and Shareowners' Equity	$810,825,895	$756,417,965

Source: Kroger Annual Report

dise purchased by an individual customer into the cash register, (2) to enter the appropriate taxes which applied to customer purchases, (3) to total the cost of the purchases and taxes, (4) to receive payment and make change, including the handling of coupons, food stamps, etc., (5) to bag the items purchased by a customer, and (6) to assist the customer in removing his purchases from the checkout area and the store. In addition, front end personnel engaged in miscellaneous activities such as check cashing and looking up prices on unmarked items. Sometimes these people were assigned to other jobs, such as stocking shelves, when business was lighter than expected.

The checkstand is the focal point for front end activity. The typical Kroger store had 5–10 checkstands arranged in a row in the front of the store. One of these checkstands was usually designated as an "express" stand. There were for serving customers with 12 items, or less. The balance were "regular" checkstands and were for customers with any number of items. The number of checkstands at a store depended on the expected peak hourly demand.[2]

Most Kroger stores used double-belt checkstands. This type of checkstand (see Exhibit 3) was about 35″ high and 8′ long. It had two conveyor

Exhibit 3

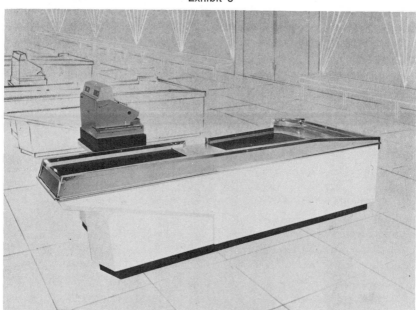

belts on it, separated by a metal plate. The customer unloaded his purchases from the shopping basket onto the first belt. The cashier, stationed at the side of the checkstand and in front of a cash register, used a foot pedal to move these goods to the metal plate. Here they were examined to determine the price, which was recorded on the register. The cashier then placed the item on the second belt which moved it to the bagging

[2] Peak demand depended on several factors, including the average sale per customer. Normally, however, a $30,000 per week store required three checkout units (including express); a $50,000 per week store required five checkouts; a $70,000 per week store needed seven checkouts; and a $100,000 per week store required nine checkout units.

station and began the process again with the next item.[3] The double-belt checkstand could be manned with one or more people. When one person operated the checkstand (a cashier), it was necessary for him to both check out the customer, make change, and to bag the groceries. A two-person manning mode utilized a cashier responsible for pricing out the items and making change, and a bagger, who helped the cashier to bag the groceries. A bagger could increase checkout speed by up to 50 percent. Sometimes, one bagger would assist two or more cashiers at one time.

In late 1972, Kroger began introducing the over-the-end (OTE) checkstand into some of its stores. This type of checkstand used a single belt which brought the goods to a cashier in the same way as the double belt stand. However, the OTE checkstand was designed so that the cashier stood directly behind this belt, received the goods in the left hand, priced at a register on the right and immediately bagged it at a bagging station on the cashier's left. Industrial engineering studies had shown this checkstand configuration would allow the cashier to check out a customer faster than the double-belt when the cashier was operating the stand alone. When a bagger was also assigned to the OTE, the checkstand was moved (on wheels) so that it was essentially the same as a double-belt stand. Initially, the OTE stands were 39″ high because methods studies had shown this to be the optimum height for reducing the work of the customer unloading the basket, and the cashier. However, customer resistance to this change was so high that ultimately the stand was lowered to the traditional 35½″. The OTE checkstand resulted in productivity increases of about 10 percent over the double-belt stand when a cashier alone was used with it. When baggers and cashiers both were used, the productivity associated with the OTE and double-belt checkstands was approximately the same. By 1973, the OTE checkstand had replaced the double-belt stand in 10 percent of Kroger's supermarkets.

Because sales by day and by hour fluctuated greatly, and because both labor costs and customer service are visibly affected by the number of people assigned to checkout operations at various times during a day, labor scheduling for front end operations was a critical activity. If, for instance, too many checkers were assigned to checkout counters during periods of light activity, sales dollars per manned checkstand hour (the standard industry productivity measure) would be low, but the customer service would be excellent. Conversely, if too few checkout counters were manned during periods of high activity, productivity would increase while customer service decreased. Customer service was generally measured by ascertaining the percentage of the time that more than a certain number of customers were either being served, or waiting in line to be checked out. Some division vice presidents used the rule of thumb that the percentage of time that more than two customers are in line (including the person being

---

[3] The average customer purchased 14 items, with an average price of about $0.56 per item.

checked out) should be held to 10 percent or less. Policy standards on customer service fluctuated with competitive pressures within a division at various times.

The Kroger Industrial Engineering Department had devised a front end labor scheduling procedure (see Exhibit 4) which had been adopted by approximately 90% of Kroger store managers. Mr. Bernie Brinkman,

Exhibit 4
LABOR SCHEDULING SHEET

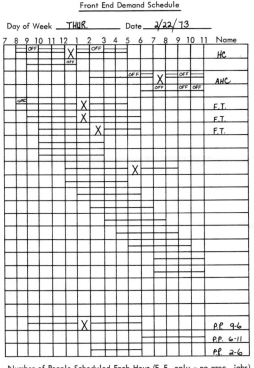

1. Est. Sales for Wk.
   (from budget) __102,000__

2. % of Wkly. Sales for day.
   (from IE 5571) __16__

3. Tot. Est. Sales for day.
   (mult. #2 x #1) __16,300__

4. Guide Hrs. allowable at
   ____O.R. for This Week
   _____.

5. F.E. Tot. Hrs. to be used This
   Day. (mult. #2 x #4).
   @200/mtr __81½__

6. Determine % of Daily Sale
   for each 1 hr. of this day
   (from IE 5571). Enter in
   Col. A Below

7. Complete Col. B Below
   (mult. #5 x hrly. % col. A)

Time	A 1 Hour Sales %	Sales $	B People Allowed Each Hour
9-10	4	650	3.5
10-11	6	980	5.0
11-12	7	1140	5.8
12-1	8	1300	6.5
1-2	7	1140	5.8
2-3	12	1950	9.5
3-4	10	1630	8.0
4-5	13	2120	10.6
5-6	9	1470	7.3
6-7	7	1140	5.8
7-8	7	1140	5.8
8-9	8	1300	6.5
9-10	3	490	2.9
10-11	1	160	1.5
			84.5

Total F.E. Hrs.
scheduled for day. __85½__

Total Office Hrs.
scheduled for day. __18½__

Total P.P. Hrs.
scheduled for day. __18__

__122 hrs.__

Number of People Scheduled Each Hour (F.E. only – no groc. jobs)

F.E. HANG.	7	8	9	10	11	12	1	2	3	4	5	6	7	8	9	10	11	Total
		3½	6	6	6½	6	9	8½	10	7	6	6	6	3	2			85½

Scheduling Instructions INCL BRKS 5¼ hrs.

A. Special Notes to denote schedule
 1. "Off" – Office Time.
 2. "C/O" or "B" – Carry Out or Bagging.
 3. List Grocery jobs – allow enough hours to complete specifically assigned task. Ex.–5 hrs. Cookies Crackers – Allow 5 hrs. for job and mark on schedule.
 4. All other time is considered register time.

B. Use bar line – ├─────┤ To denote work time.
 "X" out lunches – ├───── X ─────┤.

C. F.E. means front end.
Source: Company files.

Manager of Front End Operations at Kroger, estimated that this simple procedure, by helping the store manager to match checkout labor to demand during the day, saved the company over $300,000 in labor costs in each of the thirteen accounting periods in a year. It was also found that it resulted in improved customer service. The labor scheduling procedure involved obtaining estimates of the dollar sales volume of each store, by day, by hour. These sales estimates were then converted to checkstand requirements by using a standard productivity ratio, typically $200 per manned checkstand hour. Thus, if sales on Thursdays from 2–3 o'clock averaged $800.00, four checkstands would be scheduled for this time. Then, using a bar chart, the store manager could decide how he wanted to man these checkstands (cashier, cashier plus bagger, etc.) and indicate specific start and end times, lunch breaks, etc. for particular people.

TECHNOLOGICAL INNOVATION AT KROGER

During the 1950s, increases in labor productivity at Kroger had kept pace with increases in labor costs. Conditions in the 1960s, however, promised to yield net productivity losses as a result of increased labor costs. This realization led Kroger to search for ways to profitably substitute capital for labor with advances in technology. The high concentration of labor at the front end made this a particularly inviting area for investigation.

The recent history of Kroger technological innovation began in 1959 when Mr. Jack Strubbe[4] took charge of distribution and traffic, and a nascent industrial engineering group. Prior to this time, industrial engineers had not been widely used in the industry. Most of Kroger's management had developed from the store management and merchandising ranks, and were not technologically or engineering oriented. However, after a few years, the industrial engineering group began to have an impact on Kroger operations. The department developed and evaluated new equipment, labor standards for planning and controlling manpower allocations and costs, and had made numerous methods improvements. During this time, one industrial engineer had set up a mock front end in the second floor storage area of a Kroger store. He tested the effect on labor productivity of an optical scanning system for automatically reading and ringing up prices. While the notion of an automated front end was not new (Philco had briefly experimented with the idea in the 1950s), he showed that if the scanning concept could be developed technologically, significant labor savings could result.

In the mid-1960s, Jack Strubbe pursued this idea, and others, by initiating "Opportunity Days" at Kroger. Opportunity days were brainstorming sessions held with equipment suppliers. The intent of these sessions was to create and/or investigate opportunities for improving operations with

---

[4] Vice President, Distribution and Store Operations Services.

traditional suppliers, such as National Cash Register, and with those companies who normally did not trade with the grocery industry, but who might be able to bring their technological expertise to bear on Kroger's problems. The results of the opportunity day program were acceptable although not revolutionary. Traditional suppliers viewed them as a threat. Suppliers new to the industry felt that they did not know enough about grocery operations to take a chance at becoming deeply involved. Two companies did indicate an interest, however. The first was RCA, who became interested in automated front ends. The second was FMC, who became interested in developing an automated grocery warehouse. It was made clear at this time that Kroger did not wish to invest or share in the costs of these development programs, but that they would work with these companies.

The RCA interest continued and eventually culminated in a full test of the system at Kroger's Kenwood store in 1972. RCA divested itself of its interests in 1973, and Sperry-Univac bought out this system and continued the store test. The FMC interest resulted in Kroger's first automated warehouse in St. Louis in 1970. This was followed by several others at Nashville and Houston. In reviewing the results of the automated warehouse in 1973, Jack Strubbe said:

> We were looking for a 40 percent before-tax ROI[5] on our automated warehouse in St. Louis and got a loss. But there was enough promise there to try again at Houston and Nashville, and although we're not getting 40 percent there either, we have made improvements as we have gone along. . . . It's the experience of the industry that the first try doesn't make it. . . . I'd say with respect to automated warehousing that the problem is no longer in the technology or equipment, but in the tremendous problem of trying to change a group of support personnel that are not oriented mechanically or electronically, to the support of an extremely sophisticated mechanical and electronic system. General Motors installed an automated warehousing system similar to that of Houston's and had it on-stream in two months. Ours hasn't really come on yet.

INDUSTRY TRENDS IN FRONT END AUTOMATION

In 1969, most supermarket front ends relied upon various checkout processes which utilized mechanical cash registers as the basic component. In the years that followed, however, more and more stores began to convert to electronic checkout systems. In 1973, there were three basic types of electronic cash register systems being used or tested: the stand alone electronic cash register system (ECR), the manual point of sale systems

---

[5] Kroger normally looked for an 18–20 percent ROI on store properties, but sought higher returns on investments in areas where they were inexperienced, or the reliability of the project estimates were not proven.

(POS), and automated point of sale systems which utilized scanning devices (APOS).

Stand alone electronic registers functioned in much the same way as mechanical registers in that both relied upon manual keyboard input. However, an ECR may contain only 10 keys, while the mechanical versions typically had numerous rows of them. ECRs cost approximately the same as mechanical systems, averaging $2,950 per register,[6] but have several advantages over them. For instance, ECRs could automatically calculate and add in taxes, automatically handle multiple item sales, calculate trading stamps and coupons, record bottle refunds, and provide store management with the ability to easily track store or register sales for major categories of items.

Many chains had adopted or were testing ECR systems. Industry experience[7] had shown that ECRs could result in savings up to an equivalent of 10 percent of total sales taxes paid. It had been determined in two chains that taxes collected from the customer were only 68–75 percent of the taxes being paid to the state when mechanical registers were used, and the cashier was responsible for separating taxable and nontaxable items, as well as looking up the tax. In addition, some firms reported that increases in keying speed with full-touch electric keying averaged 15–25 percent. Since the time spent keying items represents 30–40 percent of total checkout time, this feature of the ECRs yielded increases in labor productivity and customer service.

A variety of POS systems were being offered by electronic equipment manufacturers in 1973. These systems, which included an in-store computer linked to a series of ECRs, cost an average of $58,000 for an eight register store. POS systems promised to couple the advantages of the ECR with those which could be obtained with the addition of a computer. These included monitoring individual registers during the time when personnel are trained, collecting department and store sales totals conveniently at any time, check and credit verification, electronic produce weighing and pricing, and a manual code-mode which enabled a store to track unit sales on selected items. It was possible to enter only a stock number for each purchase into the system. In this case, the computer could systematically supply the price while retaining sales data for reporting. Use of the code-mode in this way could slow down the checkout operation if the stock number was longer than the price, but in compensation, could provide the store manager with the ability to determine the effect of sales promotions, allowances, and new product introductions. Major sources of direct savings from POS systems, in addition to those which might accrue to stand alone ECRs, were the reduction in bad check losses, and additional labor savings resulting from rapid store closing procedures. Industry studies had shown

---

[6] The cost of a checkstand was between $900 and $1,500 so the total cost of a checkstand unit, including both the stand and the register, averaged $4,150.

[7] "1974: The Year of Electronics," *Progressive Grocer*, December 1973.

that median bad check losses were 0.05 percent of sales, 50 percent of which might be avoided with POS systems.

Closing out a register with POS systems was faster and more accurate than with manual or ECR registers. A register is closed out when the store is closed or when a checkstand is closed down for the day. It involves counting the cash in the register and reconciling the closing balance with the opening balance and the intervening sales totals. It takes approximately seven minutes to close out a manual register, and two hours for a head cashier to reconcile totals and account for all cash flow. With POS systems, a register can be closed out in 40 seconds, and the time to obtain totals and account for cash flow reduced substantially. In addition, the operator training period for both ECRs and POS systems had proven to be less than that for mechanical registers.

Several chains had adopted or were testing POS systems. The Jewel Tea Company, for instance, already had more than 600 POS checkout stands in operation in food stores by the end of 1973. Several manufacturers of POS systems held out the promise that their systems could be expanded to include optical scanning, although scanners were not yet being offered for sale by these companies.

The newest and most advanced checkout system (APOS) included electronic cash registers tied into mini-computers in conjunction with an optical character recognition device (scanner). These systems required that grocery items have a code placed on them which could be read by a scanner. In APOS systems, such as that of Sperry-Univac, the customer loaded his purchases onto a belt which fed them to the cashier at the other end. The cashier then positioned them so that the code was on the bottom, and pulled each item across the scanning eye which read and translated the code. The scanner then fed the information on the code to the computer which automatically rang up the price. The cashier had only to bag the item, unless it was uncoded. In this case, the price could be manually entered (Exhibit 5).

Both Kroger and the developers of APOS systems felt that they would be economical only if most of the manufacturers of the goods sold in grocery stores would place a universally accepted code on their products at the time of manufacture. This led to the creation of the universal product code (UPC). The UPC was a bar code denoting both the manufacturer's name and the item. Codes were assigned to manufacturers by the Distribution Number Bank, an administrative organization created by members of the retail food industry and various merchandise suppliers, who supported the concept. Their goal was to have 50 percent of supermarket products coded by the end of 1974, and 75 percent by the end of 1975. In 1973, the major grocery suppliers who had moved toward supplying their products with a UPC symbol, such as Quaker Oats, had incurred substantial costs in modifying their packaging equipment. These costs included capital expenditures for new packaging equipment or print-

Exhibit 5

Source: Company files.

ing devices, and increased operating costs due to the tight tolerances required in applying the code.

APOS systems promised to make all of the advantages of POS systems available to users, and in addition offered substantial additional advantages associated with the scanner. Assuming that an item had been coded by the manufacturer, it was not necessary to mark prices or make price changes on these items in the store. Prices would be maintained in the central computer, and the system would automatically ring up the price by referencing the code.[8] The savings associated with this system are indicated by the fact that twelve to sixteen hours were spent weekly changing prices in the average store and that approximately 10–15 percent of the

---

[8] Checkers could enter unpriced items by keying the item number and letting the system supply the price, or by keying in the price of the item directly.

time of those who stocked grocery shelves was spent in applying prices to goods. In addition APOS systems were expected to decrease checkout time significantly over POS systems, decrease pricing errors[9] substantially, and provide management with detailed sales information on all items. This information could be used to improve ordering and stocking decisions.

The SCAN system was the first integrated APOS system to be offered for sale. In late 1973, Sperry-Univac announced a lease arrangement costing about $3,500 per month for an average system, which included five scanning checkstands, an office console, a control center, and maintenance. Twenty to thirty percent of the lease cost would be fixed, regardless of the number of checkstands. This portion was for the central control units. The balance of the lease costs varied with the number of checkstands and the equipment options selected by the user.

The reaction of the industry to the three developments in front end automation, ECRs, POS, and APOS, is summed up in the following quote from *Groups and Chains:*[10]

> This is the year that is . . . the year the food retailing industry, or at least a large part of it, had been waiting for: 1973. The year of the big breakthrough toward the ultimate electronic front end system. With any number of manufacturers turning out prototypes and working models, and with supermarket chains announcing almost weekly commitments to this system or that system, all of this spurred by the adoption of the Universal Product Code (UPC), it would appear that the days of the long checkout lines in the supermarket are numbered.
>
> Yet, beneath all of the enthusiasm and pride reflected in the news releases emanating from manufacturers and retailers concerning new product developments and installations, the word for the bulk of the nation's retailers seems to be one of watching and waiting, a wanting to not necessarily be first, but definitely not to be last.

THE KENWOOD TEST

A test of the SCAN system was initiated by Kroger in July of 1972. The primary objectives of this test were to (1) determine the economics of operating an automated scanning system; (2) to determine the effects of the system on customer service, and to determine consumer acceptance; (3) to determine the reactions of grocery clerks and store management to the introduction of the new system. Kroger executives viewed this test as both a service to themselves and to the industry, to whom they would supply the results of the test.

The Kenwood store was selected as the site of the test because it was a typical suburban supermarket located in Cincinnati, Kroger's home city. Pretest sales at Kenwood averaged $70,400 per week. Both Sperry-Univac

---

[9] Industry average overrings minus underrings is a net underring of 0.6 percent of sales. Source: *Progressive Grocer,* December 1973.

[10] *Groups and Chains,* July 1973, page 8.

(RCA) and Kroger contributed to the operation of the Kenwood test. Sperry-Univac contributed the hardware and software, including checkstands, scanners and computer programs. Kroger's contribution included the test site, and about four man-years of effort from the Kroger Industrial Engineering group, which cooperated with Sperry-Univac (RCA) in arriving at hardware and software specifications, and measured the test results. In addition, Kroger bore the extra cost ($1,500 per wk) of applying coded labels to the 8,040,254 items[11] sold during the test with a "bullseye" scanning code, devised by Sperry-Univac. This code was to serve as a proxy for the UPC.

The test was designed upon classical lines in that control data was carefully collected from the Kenwood store before the automated checkstands were installed. In addition, three control stores were selected and monitored during the actual test period. Data was collected on pretest checkstand productivity, the time required to check out a customer, error rates, consumer and clerk attitudes, etc. Data on waiting line lengths was collected in both the test and pretest phases by installing motion picture cameras in the store which photographed the status of each line every fifteen minutes. The pretest checkstand configuration was a double-belt system with mechanical registers.

The scanning system was installed in July 1972 and was operated until November 1973 (fifteen months). Five scanning checkstands replaced the seven double-belt stands previously used in the store. Fewer scanning stands were used because of the increased checkout rate expected with them. The major results of the test were:

Sales. Sales at Kenwood were 9 percent higher during the test period than during the pretest period, while the average sales at the three control stores increased only 5.5 percent during the same periods.

Checker Productivity. Average sales per manned checkstand hour at Kenwood increased from $207 per hour in the pretest period to $300 per hour with scanning. The capacity of the system, measured by customers per peak hour per lane, also increased (Exhibit 6).

Customer Service. The average time each customer spent waiting in line decreased (Exhibit 6), while the average number of people per line increased with scanning (Exhibit 7). The consumer attitude survey indicated that an improvement in Kroger service had been perceived.

Customer Checkout Time. The average checkout time per order during the pretest period was 3.82 minutes per customer. This time was composed of 2.49 minutes per order for ringing and bagging, and 1.33 minutes per order during which the cashier was engaged in other activities or was idle. Comparable figures with scanning showed an average of 1.36 minutes to ring and bag per customer, and 1.24 minutes of miscellaneous time per customer, totaling 2.60 manned minutes per order.

---

[11] This repesented 95 percent of all of the items sold in this period.

Exhibit 6
KENWOOD TEST RESULTS

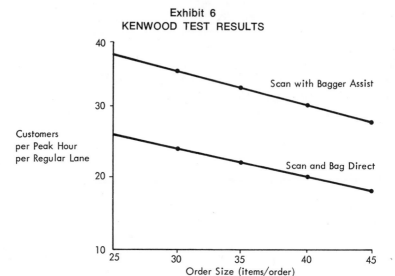

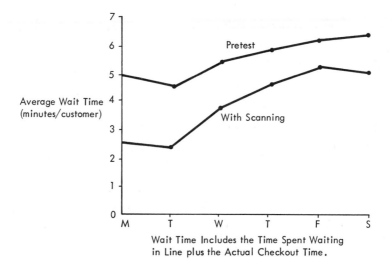

Wait Time Includes the Time Spent Waiting
in Line plus the Actual Checkout Time.

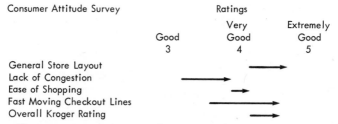

The arrows represent the change in consumer attitude between April 1972 (three months prior to scanning system installation) and January 1973 (six months after installation).

Source: *The Kroger Test*, Sperry-Univac Publication.

Exhibit 7
KENWOOD TEST RESULTS

Store: Kenwood   Double Belt Base—
Day: Saturday   Base Daily Sales: $14,000

                                         RCA (10/7 and 10/14)
                                           Test Daily Sales: $15,872

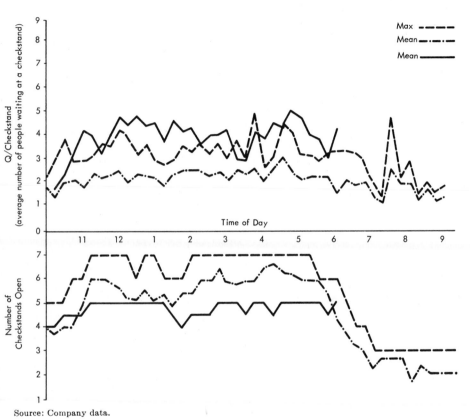

Source: Company data.

Checker Error. Checkout errors (overrings–underrings) were reduced by 75 percent with the scanning equipment.

Reliability. Total system downtime was reported as 1.5 hours in over 5,000 hours of operation.

Checker Acceptance. The Kenwood checkers were enthusiastic about the new system, and felt that the scanning system made their job easier. It was felt that it was easier to train a checker to operate this system than with the traditional manual cash registers.

DECEMBER 1973

By December 1973 the major results of the Kenwood test had been tabulated. While these results were promising, they raised many questions as well. For example, one Kroger executive compared the Kenwood store during the test period to a goldfish bowl, and wondered if the results had been contaminated by the attention paid to store personnel and customers during that period. Moreover, while the test results indicated some of the hard cash savings that could be made with a scanning system, the value of the "soft" savings accruing to customer attitudes, and the promise of better inventory and management control, were difficult to quantify. The ways in which the adoption of scanning technology would change the requirements for store and company management styles, techniques and personnel were also unclear.

Events concurrent and subsequent to the completion of the test also complicated the evaluation of the scanning system and the formulation of plans for the future. For example, while organized labor had shown little interest in the test while it was under way, an article appeared in the *Retail Clerks Advocate,* an organ of the retail clerks union, titled "RCIA Concerned Automation May Cut Jobs, Reduce Hours." The article stated, in reaction to a statement by Mr. Robert Cottrell, Director of Industrial Engineering, that scanning could increase productivity by 44 percent:

> That means, in effect, that unless collective bargaining cushions the impact of the scanner-computers, there will be a loss of jobs and reduced hours.

In November, IBM announced the 3660 Supermarket System. This system, which was similar to SCAN, was to have the capability of scanning UPC codes, could automatically ring up prices and was to include a sophisticated hardware, software and data-transmission package for store and warehouse sales reporting and inventory control. The latter feature of this system could be used in conjunction with IBM's System 370 computer. The basic IBM 3660 Supermarket System, including terminals, 8 scanners, and a controller-communications device for automatically transmitting orders to warehouses, was to cost $118,760 on a purchase basis.

When asked how fast Kroger and the grocery industry might move toward adopting automated checkout systems, Jack Strubbe said in late 1973:

> It depends on several things. For example, it depends on the degree of source symbol marking. It's a classic chicken-egg argument. I believe that while many manufacturers are working toward the application of the (UPC) symbol, before they get into a lot of big dough in applying it, they'll want to see what the retailers are going to do with it. On the other side, retailers aren't going to put it (scanning equipment) in until they get a high degree of the products they sell with source symbols on it.

SECTION THREE

Integration and Overview

7

Manufacturing—Missing Link in Corporate Strategy[1]

Wickham Skinner

A COMPANY'S manufacturing function typically is either a competitive weapon or a corporate millstone. It is seldom neutral. The connection between manufacturing and corporate success is rarely seen as more than the achievement of high efficiency and low costs In fact, the connection is much more critical and much more sensitive. Few top managers are aware that what appear to be routine manufacturing decisions frequently come to limit the corporation's strategic options, binding it with facilities, equipment, personnel, and basic controls and policies to a noncompetitive posture which may take years to turn around.

Research I have conducted during the past three years reveals that top management unknowingly delegates a surprisingly large portion of basic policy decisions to lower levels in the manufacturing area. Generally, this abdication of responsibility comes about more through a lack of concern than by intention. And it is partly the reason that many manufacturing policies and procedures developed at lower levels reflect assumptions about corporate strategy which are incorrect or misconstrued.

MILLSTONE EFFECT

When companies fail to recognize the relationship between manufacturing decisions and corporate strategy, they may become saddled with seriously noncompetitive production systems which are expensive and time-consuming to change. Here are several examples:

[1] Originally printed May–June 1969 in *Harvard Business Review*.

Company A entered the combination washer-dryer field after several competitors had failed to achieve successful entries into the field. Company A's executives believed their model would overcome the technical drawbacks which had hurt their competitors and held back the development of any substantial market. The manufacturing managers tooled the new unit on the usual conveyorized assembly line and giant stamping presses used for all company products.

When the washer-dryer failed in the market, the losses amounted to millions. The plant had been "efficient" in the sense that costs were low. But the tooling and production processes did not meet the demands of the marketplace.

Company B produced five kinds of electronic gear for five different groups of customers; the gear ranged from satellite controls to industrial controls and electronic components. In each market a different task was required of the production function. For instance, in the first market, extremely high reliability was demanded; in the second market, rapid introduction of a stream of new products was demanded; in the third market, low costs were of critical importance for competitive survival.

In spite of these highly diverse and contrasting tasks, production management elected to centralize manufacturing facilities in one plant in order to achieve "economies of scale." The result was a failure to achieve high reliability, economies of scale, or an ability to introduce new products quickly. What happened, in short, was that the demands placed on manufacturing by a competitive strategy were ignored by the production group in order to achieve economies of scale. This production group was obsessed with developing "a total system, fully computerized." The manufacturing program satisfied no single division and the serious marketing problems which resulted choked company progress.

Company C produced plastic molding resins. A new plant under construction was to come on-stream in eight months, doubling production. In the meantime, the company had a much higher volume of orders than it could meet.

In a strategic sense, manufacturing's task was to maximize output to satisfy large, key customers. Yet the plant's production control system was set up—as it had been for years—to minimize costs. As a result, long runs were emphasized. While costs were low, many customers had to wait, and many key buyers were lost. Consequently, when the new plant came on-stream, it was forced to operate at a low volume.

The mistake of considering low costs and high efficiencies as the key manufacturing objective in each of these examples is typical of the oversimplified concept of "a good manufacturing operation." Such criteria frequently get companies into trouble, or at least do not aid in the development of manufacturing into a competitive weapon. Manufacturing affects corporate strategy, and corporate strategy affects manufacturing. Even in an apparently routine operating area such as a production scheduling system, strategic considerations should outweigh technical and conventional industrial engineering factors invoked in the name of "productivity."

Shortsighted Views

The fact is that manufacturing is seen by most top managers as requiring involved technical skills and a morass of petty daily decisions and details. It is seen by many young managers as the gateway to grubby routine, where days are filled with high pressure, packed with details, and limited to low-level decision making—all of which is out of the sight and minds of top-level executives. It is generally taught in graduate schools of business administration as a combination of industrial engineering (time study, plant layout, inventory theory, and so on) and quantitative analysis (linear programming, simulation, queuing theory, and the rest). In total, a manufacturing career is generally perceived as an all-consuming, technically oriented, hectic life that minimizes one's chances of ever reaching the top and maximizes the chances of being buried in minutiae.

In fact, these perceptions are not wholly inaccurate. It is the thesis of this article that the technically oriented concept of manufacturing is all too prevalent; and that it is largely responsible for the typically limited contribution manufacturing makes to a corporation's arsenal of competitive weapons, for manufacturing's failure to attract the top talent it needs and *should* have, and for its failure to attract more young managers with general management interests and broad abilities. In my opinion, manufacturing is generally perceived in the wrong way at the top, managed in the wrong way at the plant level, and taught in the wrong way in the business schools.

These are strong words, but change is needed, and I believe that only a more relevant concept of manufacturing can bring change. I see no sign whatsoever that we have found the means of solving the problems mentioned. The new, mathematically based "total systems" approaches to production management offer the promise of new and valuable concepts and techniques, but I doubt that these approaches will overcome the tendency of top managemt to remove itself from manufacturing. Ten years of development of quantitative techniques have left us each year with the promise of a "great new age" in production management that lies "just ahead." The promise never seems to be realized. Stories of computer and "total systems" fiascoes are available by the dozen; these failures are always expensive, and in almost every case management has delegated the work to experts.

I do not want to demean the promise—and, indeed, some present contributions—of the systems/computer approach. Two years ago I felt more sanguine about it. But, since then, close observation of the problems in U.S. industry has convinced me that the "answer" promised is inadequate. The approach cannot overcome the problems described until it does a far better job of linking manufacturing and corporate strategy. What is needed is some kind of integrative mechanism.

PATTERN OF FAILURE

An examination of top management perceptions of manufacturing has led me to some notions about basic causes of many production problems. In each of six industries I have studied, I have found top executives delegating excessive amounts of manufacturing policy to subordinates, avoiding involvement in most production matters, and failing to ask the right questions until their companies are in obvious trouble. This pattern seems to be due to a combination of two factors:

1.   A sense of personal inadequacy, on the part of top executives, in managing production. (Often the feeling evolves from a tendency to regard the area as a technical or engineering specialty, or a mundane "nuts and bolts" segment of management.)

2.   A lack of awareness among top executives that a production system inevitably involves trade-offs and compromises and so must be designed to perform a limited task well, with that task defined by corporate strategic objectives.

The first factor is, of course, dependent in part on the second, for the sense of inadequacy would not be felt if the strategic role of production were clearer. The second factor is the one we shall concentrate on in the remainder of this article.

Like a building, a vehicle, or a boat, a production system can be designed to do some things well, but always at the expense of other abilities. It appears to be the lack of recognition of these trade-offs and their effects on a corporation's ability to compete that leads top management to delegate often-critical decisions to lower, technically oriented staff levels, and to allow policy to be made through apparently unimportant operating decisions.

In the balance of this article I would like to

1.   sketch out the relationships between production operations and corporate strategy;
2.   call attention to the existence of specific trade-offs in production system design;
3.   comment on the inadequacy of computer specialists to deal with these trade-offs;
4.   suggest a new way of looking at manufacturing which might enable the nontechnical manager to understand and manage the manufacturing area.

STRATEGIC IMPLICATIONS

Frequently the interrelationship between production operations and corporate strategy is not easily grasped. The notion is simple enough—

namely, that a company's competitive strategy at a given time places particular demands on its manufacturing function, and, conversely, that the company's manufacturing posture and operations should be specifically designed to fulfill the task demanded by strategic plans. What is more elusive is the set of cause-and-effect factors which determine the linkage between strategy and production operations.

Strategy is a set of plans and policies by which a company aims to gain advantages over its competitors. Generally a strategy includes plans for products and the marketing of these products to a particular set of customers. The marketing plans usually include specific approaches and steps to be followed in identifying potential customers, determining why, where, and when they buy, and learning how they can best be reached and convinced to purchase. The company must have an advantage, a particular appeal, a special push or pull created by its products, channels of distribution, advertising, price, packaging, availability, warranties, or other factors.

Contrasting Demands

What is not always realized is that different marketing strategies and approaches to gaining a competitive advantage place different demands on the manufacturing arm of the company. For example, a furniture manufacturer's strategy for broad distribution of a limited, low-price line with wide consumer advertising might generally require:

Decentralized finished-goods storage.

Readily available merchandise.

Rock-bottom costs.

The foregoing demands might in turn require:

1. Relatively large lot sizes.
2. Specialized facilities for woodworking and finishing.
3. A large proportion of low- and medium-skilled workers in the work force.
4. Concentration of manufacturing in a limited number of large-scale plants.

In contrast, a manufacturer of high-price, high-style furniture with more exclusive distribution would require an entirely different set of manufacturing policies. While higher prices and longer lead times would allow more leeway in the plant, this company would have to contend with the problems implicit in delivering high-quality furniture made of wood (which is a soft, dimensionally unstable material whose surface is expensive to finish and easy to damage), a high setup cost relative to running times in most wood-machining operations, and the need to make a large number of nonstandardized parts. While the first company must work with these problems too, they are more serious to the second company because its marketing strategy forces it to confront the problems head on. The latter's manufacturing policies will probably require:

Many model and style changes.
Production to order.
Extremely reliable high quality.

These demands may in turn require:

1. An organization that can get new models into production quickly.
2. A production control group that can coordinate all activities so as to reduce lead times.
3. Technically trained supervisors and technicians.

Consequently, the second company ought to have a strong manufacturing-methods engineering staff; simple, flexible tooling; and a well-trained, experienced work force.

In summary, the two manufacturers would need to develop very different policies, personnel, and operations if they were to be equally successful in carrying out their strategies.

Important Choices

In the example described, there are marked contrasts in the two companies. Actually, even small and subtle differences in corporate strategies should be reflected in manufacturing policies. However, my research shows that few companies do in fact carefully and explicitly tailor their production systems to perform the tasks which are vital to corporate success.

Instead of focusing first on strategy, then moving to define the manufacturing task, and next turning to systems design in manufacturing policy, managements tend to employ a concept of production which is much less effective. Most top executives and production managers look at their production systems with the notion of "total productivity" or the equivalent, "efficiency." They seek a kind of blending of low costs, high quality, and acceptable customer service. The view prevails that a plant with reasonably modern equipment, up-to-date methods and procedures, a cooperative work force, a computerized information system, and an enlightened management will be a good plant and will perform efficiently.

But what is "a good plant"? What is "efficient performance"? And what should the computer be programmed to do? Should it minimize lead times or minimize inventories? A company cannot do both. Should the computer minimize direct labor or indirect labor? Again, the company cannot do both. Should investment in equipment be minimized—or should outside purchasing be held to a minimum? One could go on with such choices.

The reader may reply: "What management wants is a combination of both ingredients that results in the lowest *total* cost." But the answer, too, is insufficient. The "lowest total cost" answer leaves out the dimensions of time and customer satisfaction, which must usually be considered too. Because cost *and* time *and* customers are all involved, we have to conclude that what is a "good" plant for Company A may be a poor or mediocre plant for its competitor, Company B, which is in the same industry but pursues a different strategy.

The purpose of manufacturing is to serve the company—to meet its needs for survival, profit, and growth. Manufacturing is part of the strategic concept that relates a company's strengths and resources to opportunities in the market. Each strategy creates a unique manufacturing task. Manufacturing management's ability to meet that task is the key measure of its success.

TRADE-OFFS IN DESIGN

It is curious that most top managements and production people do not state their yardsticks of success more precisely, and instead fall back on such measures as "efficiency," "low cost," and "productivity." My studies suggest that a key reason for this phenomenon is that very few executives realize the existence of trade-offs in designing and operating a production system.

Yet most managers will readily admit that there are compromises or trade-offs to be made in designing an airplane or a truck. In the case of an airplane, trade-offs would involve such matters as cruising speed, take-off and landing distances, initial cost, maintenance, fuel consumption, passenger comfort, and cargo or passenger capacity. A given stage of technology defines limits as to what can be accomplished in these respects. For instance, no one today can design a 500-passenger plane that can land on a carrier and also break the sonic barrier.

Much the same thing is true of manufacturing. The variables of cost, time, quality, technological constraints, and customer satisfaction place limits on what management can do, force compromises, and demand an explicit recognition of a multitude of trade-offs and choices. Yet everywhere I find plants which have inadvertently emphasized one yardstick at the expense of another, more important one. For example:

An electronics manufacturer with dissatisfied customers hired a computer expert and placed manufacturing under a successful engineering design chief to make it a "total system." A year later its computer was spewing out an inch-thick volume of daily information. "We know the location of every part in the plant on any given day," boasted the production manager and his computer systems chief.

Nevertheless, customers were more dissatisfied than ever. Product managers hotly complained that delivery promises were regularly missed—and in almost every case they first heard about failures from their customers. The problem centered on the fact that computer information runs were organized by part numbers and operations. They were designed to facilitate machine scheduling and to aid shop foremen; they were not organized around end products, which would have facilitated customer service.

How had this come about? Largely, it seemed clear, because the manufacturing managers had become absorbed in their own "systems approach"; the fascination of mechanized data handling had become an end in itself. As for top management, it had more or less abdicated responsibility. Because the company's growth and success had been based on engineering and because top management was R&D-oriented, policy-making executives saw production as a routine requiring a lower level of complexity and brainpower. Top management argued further that the company had production experts who were well paid and who should be able to do their jobs without bothering top-level people.

Recognizing Alternatives

To develop the notion of important trade-off decisions in manufacturing, let us consider Figure 7–1, which shows some examples.

In each decision area—plant and equipment, production planning and control, and so forth—top management needs to recognize the alternatives and become involved in the design of the production system. It needs to become involved to the extent that the alternative selected is appropriate to the manufacturing task determined by the corporate strategy.

Making such choices is, of course, an on-going rather than a once-a-year or once-a-decade task; decisions have to be made constantly in these trade-off areas. Indeed, the real crux of the problem seems to be how to ensure that the continuing process of decision making is not isolated from competitive and strategic facts, when many of the trade-off decisions do not at first appear to bear on company strategy. As long as a technical point of view dominates manufacturing decisions, a degree of isolation from the realities of competition is inevitable. Unfortunately, as we shall see, the technical viewpoint is all too likely to prevail.

TECHNICAL DOMINANCE

The similarity between today's emphasis on the technical experts—the computer specialist and the engineering-oriented production technician—and yesterday's emphasis on the efficiency expert—time-study man and industrial engineer—is impossible to escape. For 50 years, U.S. management relied on efficiency experts trained in the techniques of Frederick W. Taylor. Industrial engineers were kings of the factory. Their early approaches and attitudes were often conducive to industrial warfare, strikes, sabotage, and militant unions, but that was not realized then. Also not realized was that their technical emphasis often produced an inward orientation toward cost that ignored the customer, and an engineering point

Figure 7–1
SOME IMPORTANT TRADE-OFF DECISIONS IN MANUFACTURING—
OR "YOU CAN'T HAVE IT BOTH WAYS"

Decision Area	*Decision*	*Alternatives*
Plant and equipment	Span of process.	Make or buy.
	Plant size.	One big plant or several smaller ones.
	Plant location.	Locate near markets or locate near materials.
	Investment decisions.	Invest mainly in buildings or equipment or inventories or research.
	Choice of equipment.	General-purpose or special-purpose equipment.
	Kind of tooling.	Temporary, minimum tooling or "production tooling."
Production planning and control	Frequency of inventory taking.	Few or many breaks in production for buffer stocks.
	Inventory size.	High inventory or a lower inventory.
	Degree of inventory control.	Control in great detail or in lesser detail.
	What to control.	Controls designed to minimize machine downtime or labor cost or time in process, or to maximize output of particular products or material usage.
	Quality control.	High reliability and quality or low costs.
	Use of standards.	Formal or informal or none at all.
Labor and staffing	Job specialization.	Highly specialized or not highly specialized.
	Supervision.	Technically trained first-line supervisors or nontechnically trained supervisors.
	Wage system.	Many job grades or few job grades; incentive wages or hourly wages.
	Supervision.	Close supervision or loose supervision.
	Industrial engineers.	Many or few such men.
Product design engineering	Size of product line.	Many customer specials or few specials or none at all.
	Design stability.	Frozen design or many engineering change orders.
	Technological risk.	Use of new processes unproved by competitors or follow-the-leader policy.
	Engineering.	Complete packaged design or design-as-you-go approach.
	Use of manufacturing engineering.	Few or many manufacturing engineers.
Organization and management	Kind of organization.	Functional or product focus or geographical or other.
	Executive use of time.	High involvement in investment or production planning or cost control or quality control or other activities.
	Degree of risk assumed.	Decisions based on much or little information.
	Use of staff.	Large or small staff group.
	Executive style.	Much or little involvement in detail; authoritarian or nondirective style; much or little contact with organization.

of view that gloried in tools, equipment, and gadgets rather than in markets and service. Most important, the cult of industrial engineering tended to make top executives technically disqualified from involvement in manufacturing decisions.

Since the turn of the century, this efficiency-centered orientation has dogged U.S. manufacturing. It has created the image of "nuts and bolts," of greasy, dirty, detail jobs in manufacturing. It has dominated "production" courses in most graduate schools of business administration. It has alienated young men with broad management educations from manufacturing careers. It has "buffaloed" top managers.

Several months ago I was asked by a group of industrial engineers to offer an opinion as to why so few industrial engineers were moving up to the top of their companies. My answer was that perhaps a technical point of view cut them off from top management just as the jargon and hocus-pocus of manufacturing often kept top management from understanding the factory. In their isolation, they could gain only a severely limited sense of market needs and of corporate competitive strategy.

Enter the Computer Expert

Today the industrial engineer is declining in importance in many companies. But a new technical expert, the computer specialist, is taking his place. I use the term "computer specialist" to refer to individuals who specialize in computer systems design and programming.

I do not deny, of course, that computer specialists have a very important job to do. I do object, however, to any notion that computer specialists have more of a top management view than was held by their predecessors, the industrial engineers. In my experience, the typical computer expert has been forced to master a complex and all-consuming technology, a fact which frequently makes him parochial rather than catholic in his views. Because he is so preoccupied with the detail of a total system, it is necessary for someone in top management to give him objectives and policy guidance. In his choice of trade-offs and compromises for his computer system, he needs to be instructed and not left to his own devices. Or, stated differently, he needs to see the entire corporation as a system, not just one corner of it—i.e., the manufacturing plant.

Too often this is not happening. The computer is a nightmare to many top managers because they have let it and its devotees get out of hand. They have let technical experts continue to dominate; the failure of top management truly to manage production goes on.

How *can* top management begin to manage manufacturing instead of turning it over to technicians who, through no fault of their own, are absorbed in their own arts and crafts? How can U.S. production management be helped to cope with the rising pressures of new markets, more rapid product changes, new technologies, larger and riskier equipment decisions, and the swarm of problems we face in industry today? Let us look at some answers.

BETTER DECISION MAKING

The answers I would like to suggest are not panaceas, nor are they intended to be comprehensive. Indeed, no one can answer all the questions and problems described with one nice formula or point of view. But surely we can improve on the notion that production systems need only be "productive and efficient." Top management can manage manufacturing if it will engage in the making of manufacturing policy, rather than considering it a kind of fifth, independent estate beyond the pale of control.

The place to start, I believe, is with the acceptance of a theory of manufacturing which begins with the concept that in any system design there are significant trade-offs (as shown in Figure 7–1) which must be explicitly decided on.

Determining Policy

Executives will also find it helpful to think of manufacturing policy determination as an orderly process or sequence of steps. Figure 7–2 is a schematic portrayal of such a process. It shows that manufacturing policy must stem from corporate strategy, and that the process of determining this policy is the means by which top management can actually manage production. Use of this process can end manufacturing isolation and tie top management and manufacturing together. The sequence is simple but vital:

It begins with an analysis of the competitive situation, of how rival companies are competing in terms of product, markets, policies, and channels of distribution. Management examines the number and kind of competitors and the opportunities open to its company.

Next comes a critical appraisal of the company's skills and resources and of its present facilities and approaches.

The third step is the formulation of company strategy: How is the company to compete successfully, combine its strengths with market opportunities, and define niches in the markets where it can gain advantages?

The fourth step is the point where many top executives cut off their thinking. It is important for them to define the implications or "so-what" effects of company strategy in terms of specific manufacturing tasks. For example, they should ask: "If we are to compete with an X product of Y price for Z customers using certain distribution channels and forms of advertising, what will be demanded of manufacturing in terms of costs, deliveries, lead times, quality levels, and reliability?" These demands should be precisely defined.

The fifth and sixth steps are to study the constraints or limitations im-

Figure 7–2
THE PROCESS OF MANUFACTURING POLICY DETERMINATION

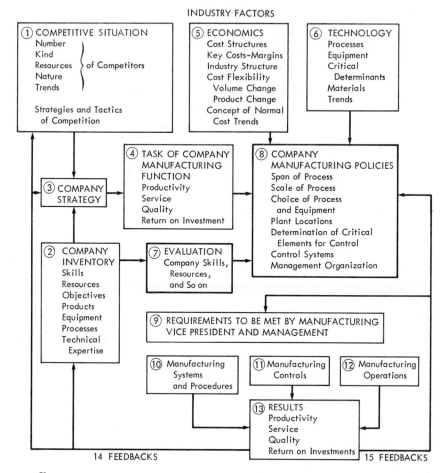

INDUSTRY FACTORS

① COMPETITIVE SITUATION
   Number
   Kind
   Resources } of Competitors
   Nature
   Trends

   Strategies and Tactics
     of Competition

⑤ ECONOMICS
   Cost Structures
   Key Costs–Margins
   Industry Structure
   Cost Flexibility
     Volume Change
     Product Change
   Concept of Normal
     Cost Trends

⑥ TECHNOLOGY
   Processes
   Equipment
   Critical
     Determinants
   Materials
   Trends

③ COMPANY
    STRATEGY

④ TASK OF COMPANY
    MANUFACTURING
    FUNCTION
   Productivity
   Service
   Quality
   Return on Investment

⑧ COMPANY
    MANUFACTURING POLICIES
   Span of Process
   Scale of Process
   Choice of Process
     and Equipment
   Plant Locations
   Determination of Critical
     Elements for Control
   Control Systems
   Management Organization

② COMPANY
    INVENTORY
   Skills
   Resources
   Objectives
   Products
   Equipment
   Processes
   Technical
     Expertise

⑦ EVALUATION
   Company Skills,
     Resources,
     and So on

⑨ REQUIREMENTS TO BE MET BY MANUFACTURING
    VICE PRESIDENT AND MANAGEMENT

⑩ Manufacturing
    Systems
    and Procedures

⑪ Manufacturing
    Controls

⑫ Manufacturing
    Operations

⑬ RESULTS
   Productivity
   Service
   Quality
   Return on Investments

14 FEEDBACKS   15 FEEDBACKS

Key
1. What the others are doing.
2. What we have got or can get to compete with.
3. How we can compete.
4. What we must accomplish in manufacturing in order to compete.
5. Economic constraints and opportunities common to the industry.
6. Constraints and opportunities common to the technology.
7. Our resources evaluated.
8. How we should set ourselves up to match resources, economics, and technology to meet the tasks required by our competitive strategy.
9. The implementation requirements of our manufacturing policies.
10. Basic systems in manufacturing (e.g., production planning, use of inventories, use of standards, and wage systems).
11. Controls of cost, quality, flows, inventory, and time.
12. Selection of operations or ingredients critical to success (e.g., labor skills, equipment utilization, and yields).
13. How we are performing?
14. Changes in what we have got, effects on competitive situation, and review of strategy.
15. Analysis and review of manufacturing operations and policies.

posed by the economics and the technology of the industry. These factors are generally common to all competitors. An explicit recognition of them is a prerequisite to a genuine understanding of the manufacturing problems and opportunities. These are facts that a nontechnical manager can develop, study, understand, and put to work. Figure 7–3 contains sample lists of topics for the manager to use in doing his homework.

Figure 7–3
ILLUSTRATIVE CONSTRAINTS OR LIMITATIONS
WHICH SHOULD BE STUDIED

A. Economics of the Industry
Labor, burden, material, depreciation costs.
Flexibility of production to meet changes in volume.
Return on investment, prices, margins.
Number and location of plants.
Critical control variables.
Critical functions (e.g., maintenance, production control, personnel).
Typical financial structures.
Typical costs and cost relationships.
Typical operating problems.
Barriers to entry.
Pricing practices.
"Maturity" of industry products, markets, production practices, and so on.
Importance of economies of scale.
Importance of integrated capacities of corporations.
Importance of having a certain balance of different types of equipment.
Ideal balances of equipment capacities.
Nature and type of production control.
Government influences.
B. Technology of the Industry
Rate of technological change.
Scale of processes.
Span of processes.
Degree of mechanization.
Technological sophistication.
Time requirements for making changes.

The seventh and eighth steps are the key ones for integrating and synthesizing all the prior ones into a broad manufacturing policy. The question for management is: "Given the facts of the economics and the technology of the industry, how do we set ourselves up to meet the specific manufacturing tasks posed by our particular competitive strategy?" Management must decide what it is going to make and what it will buy; how many plants to have, how big they should be, and where to place them; what processes and equipment to buy; what the key elements are which need to be controlled and how they can be controlled; and what kind of management organization would be most appropriate.

Next come the steps of working out programs of implementation, controls, performance measures, and review procedures (see Steps 9–15 in Figure 7–2).

CONCLUSION

The process just described is, in my observation, quite different from the usual process of manufacturing management. Conventionally, manufacturing has been managed from the bottom up. The classical process of the age of mass production is to select an operation, break it down into its elements, analyze and improve each element, and put it back together. This approach was contributed years ago by Frederick W. Taylor and other industrial engineers who followed in his footsteps.

What I am suggesting is an entirely different approach, one adapted far better to the current era of more products, shorter runs, vastly accelerated product changes, and increased marketing competition. I am suggesting a kind of "top-down" manufacturing. This approach starts with the company and its competitive strategy; its goal is to define manufacturing policy. Its presumption is that only when basic manufacturing policies are defined can the technical experts, industrial and manufacturing engineers, labor relations specialists, and computer experts have the necessary guidance to do their work.

With its focus on corporate strategy and the manufacturing task, the top-down approach can give top management both its entrée to manufacturing and the concepts it needs to take the initiative and truly manage this function. When this is done, executives previously unfamiliar with manufacturing are likely to find it an exciting activity. The company will have an important addition to its arsenal of competitive weapons.

Rochester Foods, Inc.

AS HE prepared for the arrival of the other members of his committee on the morning of February 5, 1973, Mr. Joseph Brady, Vice President—Merchandising and Director of Rochester Foods, Inc., reviewed the mandate of the committee and the job ahead of it. The "Task Force on Long-Term Meat Distribution Planning" had been set up by Mr. Paul Turner, RFI's president, to make recommendations regarding the company's meat distribution strategy over the following 5–10 years.

The need for such a group has been created both by RFI's projections for continued sales growth over the foreseeable future, and by the rapidly changing nature of the meat business—changes on the retail side, in the technology of meat preparation and distribution, in the supplier picture, and in RFI's competitors. These changes were expected to have important implications for the company's future growth and profitability.

The committee had begun by familiarizing itself with these trends, and the ways its suppliers and competitors were reacting to them. Several field trips had been made, and three alternative proposals for the direction in which the company should proceed had been generated. Paul Turner had originally suggested that a report be forthcoming by March 31, 1973, and with that date rapidly approaching Joseph Brady realized that the time was at hand for the task force to stop generating proposals and hammer out a recommendation.

COMPANY BACKGROUND

Rochester Foods' sales in 1972 were $202 million, almost double their value six years previously. They generated earnings of about $2.8 million (operating summaries for the years 1970–72 and the balance sheet for January 1973 are contained in Exhibit 1). Incorporated in New York in 1919, RFI still derived most of its business from that state in 1972, although its marketing area extended into Massachusetts and Vermont. Food products accounted for about 97 percent of total revenues.

Exhibit 1

ROCHESTER FOODS, INC.
Consolidated Income Statements: 1970–1972
(in millions)

	1970	1971	1972
Net sales	$162.8	$183.7	$202.0
Cost and expenses			
Cost of sales.	131.4	147.5	163.4
SG&A	26.2	30.0	32.0
Interest.	0.8	1.0	1.0
	$158.4	$178.5	$196.4
Earnings before tax.	4.4	5.2	5.6
Net earnings	2.2	2.6	2.8

Balance Sheet: January 1, 1973

Assets		Liabilities	
Cash	$ 2.5	Accounts payable.	$ 4.5
Accounts receivable.	2.0	Accrued expenses and taxes	1.0
Inventories.	7.5	Current maturities of long-term	
Total current assets.	$12.0	debt	1.5
Property, plant and equipment . . .	19.0	Total current liabilities.	$ 7.0
Less accumulated depreciation . . .	6.0	Long-term debt excluding current	
Total fixed assets	$13.0	maturities	6.0
Other assets		Stockholders' Equity	$12.0
Total Assets.	$25.0	Total Liabilities.	$25.0

The company served 130 supermarkets and retail outlets out of its central warehouse in West Rochester, New York. It owned and operated only 20 of these stores, but had a major equity interest in 70 others. The remaining 40 stores were served on a wholesale basis, with the company having leasehold relationships with 19 of them (wherein the lessees agreed to purchase a majority of their merchandise from RFI). Five of these 40 stores accounted for over 10 percent of the company's total sales in 1972.

In 1968 the Utica Tea chain of 25 stores had joined RFI on a wholesale basis, but since then there had been little change in the total number of stores, about 20 being added and dropped in that period. The stores were becoming bigger, however; the new stores were averaging about 12,000 square feet of selling space, and the average for all stores was now over 9,000 square feet. About 200,000 square feet of store space had been added since 1966, bringing the total to over 1.2 million square feet. The average weekly sales volume per store was about $30,000 in 1972, up from $23,000 four years previously.

BEEF MARKETING

Meat products accounted for about a quarter of RFI's sales volume in 1972, with almost 60 million pounds being sold. Of this total, beef accounted for 27 million pounds, or about 45 percent. This beef cost the company $16.5 million. The typical store bought about 4,000 pounds of fresh beef a week from the company. After removing the waste, roughly 20 percent, this resulted in sales of about 3,200 pounds of beef, of which over 600 pounds were ground. A typical meat department accounted for total sales of about $9,000 per week (about half of which were beef sales) and would employ 4 to 5 people. These people earned over $5 per hour, including fringe benefits.

U.S. consumption of meat and poultry was nearly 235 pounds per person in 1970, up 20 percent since 1960. Beef per capita consumption rose 33 percent to 113 pounds over the same period (it had doubled since 1951). Poultry consumption had increased 50 percent (to 50 pounds), but there had been almost no increase in the consumption of other kinds of meat. Despite the large and growing importance of beef to a grocery store ("it's what brings the customers in" was a typical comment), most stores claimed they barely broke even on fresh beef sales—one study claimed 70 percent actually lost money. This was due partly to industry pricing practices, which typically forced beef to carry lower gross margins than other meats, and partly to the higher labor costs associated with beef preparation. RFI estimated that the average markup on beef sales at its stores was only about 17 percent. They achieved a higher gross margin on luncheon meats, which required no preparation at all.

Beef sales were expected to increase in importance to retailers during the 1970s for several reasons. First, annual U.S. per capita consumption of beef was expected to reach 130 pounds by 1980. Moreover, if past trends were a reliable predictor, the American consumer would demand ever-improving quality in his beef (in 1951 only one-third of U.S. beef production was "choice" grade, while in 1971 over 60 percent was "choice," although about half of this apparent increase was attributable to a redefinition of government standards). Finally, beef prices were expected to continue inching upward. Beef production in the U.S. had increased by 2½ times since 1951, and would have to increase again by 25 percent by 1980 if the annual consumption rate of 130 pounds per person were to be attained. Achieving this increase would necessitate that beef producers "push at the margins" by: (1) moving into those fringe areas of the corn belt (and elsewhere) where beef production could be made economically more attractive than alternative uses of the land; (2) shifting from dairy operations; (3) increasing utilization of feedlots; or (4) increasing imports from beef exporting nations (who generally did not produce much of the kind of high quality beef demanded by American consumers). All of these avenues would probably lead to higher beef prices under the pressure of increasing demand.

In merchandising beef the store had to balance the purchasing and processing costs of various cuts against the sales drawing power of "the mix." As one meat man commented:

It's not something that lends itself to a simple formula, nor does it mean pushing the products with the highest current profitability. It's the fine art of balancing the profitable with the traffic builders. Too much advertised special in the case reduces profits; too little disappoints the customer.

The challenge to RFI was to maintain its beef sales as a profitable, and flexible, competitive weapon in the face of fluctuating prices and a changing environment.

BEEF ECONOMICS

A fuller understanding of the price-cost squeeze that beef processors face requires a short digression on the nature of beef and how it is processed. We begin with the observation that beef comes from cattle, and (despite intensive research and breeding) all cows have four legs and a front and a rear. This obvious fact has profound implications for the beef processor and the consumer. It means, for example, that the amount of sirloin that is available to the public is in relatively fixed ratio to the amount of ribs, and that eventually all of each must be sold to somebody. If beef is not in a form that makes someone want to buy it, it must be converted into a form that is salable. This can be costly, time-consuming, and wasteful.

Most cattle are saulghtered when they attain a weight of 1,000–1,100 pounds (feeding cattle of this size are worth $0.30–$0.40 per pound). The cleaned carcass, which weights 600–700 pounds, is first divided into sides and then into quarters, each weighing about 160 pounds. The quarters, in turn, are divided into the so-called "primal" wholesale cuts: chucks and ribs in the case of the forequarter, and loin, round, and flank in the case of the hindquarter (see Exhibits 2 and 3). About 15 minutes are required for a skilled man to "break" a quarter into its primal cuts. These cuts are bulky items; a round, for example, weighs about 70 pounds, and different chucks range from 70 to 100 pounds. The primal cuts are then divided into the retail cuts: the loin into sirloin steaks and T-bone steaks, for example, and the chuck into pot roast, blade roast, etc.

The basic problem faced by the beef processor, then, was how to sell a fixed amount of beef given different consumer preferences. This was complicated by the fact that a beef cut has no intrinsic cost or value. Whereas in an assembly process the cost of the finished item is determined from the cost of the component parts and the labor required to put them together, beef processing starts with a total cost and must somehow subdivide it into appropriate subcomponents, given the processing costs. Value is determined only by what the public (at the store level) is willing to pay for it and, therefore, changes with location. Hence, prices varied by processor and from day to day. Excerpts from a typical "yellow sheet,"

Exhibit 2
BEEF CHART—WHOLESALE AND RETAIL CUTS

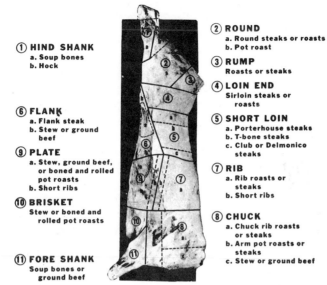

① **HIND SHANK**
   a. Soup bones
   b. Hock

⑥ **FLANK**
   a. Flank steak
   b. Stew or ground
      beef

⑨ **PLATE**
   a. Stew, ground beef,
      or boned and rolled
      pot roasts
   b. Short ribs

⑩ **BRISKET**
   Stew or boned and
      rolled pot roasts

⑪ **FORE SHANK**
   Soup bones or
      ground beef

② **ROUND**
   a. Round steaks or roasts
   b. Pot roast

③ **RUMP**
   Roasts or steaks

④ **LOIN END**
   Sirloin steaks or
      roasts

⑤ **SHORT LOIN**
   a. Porterhouse steaks
   b. T-bone steaks
   c. Club or Delmonico
      steaks

⑦ **RIB**
   a. Rib roasts or
      steaks
   b. Short ribs

⑧ **CHUCK**
   a. Chuck rib roasts
      or steaks
   b. Arm pot roasts or
      steaks
   c. Stew or ground beef

YIELDS OF WHOLESALE CUTS AND SUBDIVISIONS
Percentage of Carcass Weight

① to ⑥ HINDQUARTER 48.0%	⑦ to ⑪ FOREQUARTER .. 52.0%	
① to ③ Round and Rump . 24.0%	⑦ Rib 9.5%	
① Hind shank . 4.0%	⑧ Chuck 24.5	
② Buttock ... 15.5	⑨ Plate..... 8.0	
③ Rump 4.5	⑩ Brisket ... 6.0	
④ and ⑤ Full loin inc. suet. 20.5	⑪ Fore shank. 4.0	
④ Loin end ... 9.0		
⑤ Short loin .. 8.0		
Kidney knob . 3.5		
⑥ Flank........ 3.5		

   Numerals in circles refer to wholesale cuts and major subdivisions of
such cuts. Letters refer to retail cuts.
   Source: United States Department of Agriculture, Consumer and Marketing Service, Livestock Division.

Exhibit 3
BEEF BREAKDOWN BY WEIGHT*
(assumes live weight of 1,100 pounds)

Primal Cuts		*Retail Cuts*	
Chuck	130	Steaks	140
Rib.....................	45	Roasts	170
Loin	105	Ground beef..............	75
Round	120	Stew beef	25
Miscellaneous	50	Miscellaneous cuts	70
Roughmeats†	100	Total salable retail cuts........	480
Subtotal	550	Waste (fat, bone and shrink)......	170
Waste fat and bone	100	Total...............	650
Total...............	650		

   * Rough composite developed from U.S. Dept. of Agriculture, Economic Research Service, and Rochester Foods data.
   † Fifty percent fat.

which summarizes the daily status of beef prices, are contained in Exhibit 4.

The supply-demand picture was complicated by the fact that hotels and restaurants purchased sirloins and ribs almost exclusively, and were willing

Exhibit 4

EXCERPTS FROM "THE NATIONAL PROVISIONER DAILY MARKET AND NEWS SERVICE ("THE YELLOW SHEET")

BUTCHER CATTLE (Carcass, Carlot)—GENERAL RANGE—Good interest for all general range cattle. Holstein type strs. sold 52½ @ 53½¢ river basis, and 56¢ East. Choice heifers moved into Chgo. at 57½¢ Choice strs. 5/700 moved East at 60 @ 60½ in a good trade.

BUTCHER CATTLE (Primal Cuts)—Market still very strong with cuts advancing sharply, in light trade. Choice fores sold several times 51½¢ Chgo. basis. Choice heifer hinds traded 63½¢ Chgo. basis. Choice steer hinds traded at 67¢ East, equivalent 65¢ Chgo. basis. Choice heifer rounds few times at 70¢ Chgo. basis with partload reported at 71¢ Chgo. Choice steer rounds reported trading couple times at 70¢ Chgo. basis. Choice arm chucks sold several times at 55¢ Chgo. basis and choice arm backs traded 60¢ Chgo. basis. Trmd. loins about steady in view of strength of market. Choice ribs 25/35 reported at 79¢ Chgo. basis. Others available freely within quoted range. Choice full plates reported trading at 31¢ Chgo. basis. Choice navels traded at 28½¢ caf Chgo. Fresh 50% lean trmgs. available at printed sheet, with no reported trades.

INEDIBLE FATS—This market still rather unsettled with fair interest in bleachable fancy tallow at 6¢ Chgo. or basis; offerings held at 6⅛¢ to 6½¢. Some prime tallow sold at 5¾¢ Chgo. basis. Also some No. 2 tallow sold at 5¢ Chgo. basis. Yellow grease still offered and unsold at 5¢ Chgo.

LIVE CATTLE MARKET—In Omaha, slaughter strs. and heifers 75¢ to $1.25 higher. Cows 25¢ to 50¢ higher. Bulls firm. Feeders fully 50¢ higher. Steer top, $37.35, the highest since March, 1952; heifer top, $36.25, the highest since Feb., 1952. Unofficial estimated receipts tomorrow, 6,000 head.

to pay premium prices for these. The retailer, in contrast, depended more on the less tender (and less expensive) cuts. Hence, although the chuck accounted for about 25 percent of the weight of a beef carcass, it represented over 45 percent of retail beef sales.

BEEF TECHNOLOGY

In balancing supply and demand by juggling price, processing time and cost, the processor's job is complicated by two other aspects of beef processing: tenderization and shrink.

Tenderization occurred naturally during the first two to three weeks after slaughter, under the influence of certain enzymes in the meat. Many hotels and restaurants, therefore, aged beef for up to two weeks after purchase before serving. For beef processors and retailers to follow suit would necessitate a massive increase in inventory size and cost, as well as increase the loss due to "shrinkage" (see below), and was felt by many to be economically infeasible. As an alternative to natural aging, major beef processors had developed a variety of artifical tenderizing processes. For example, Swift & Co. had found that injecting an enzyme extracted from the juice of the papaya plant into the bloodstream of the animal immediately prior to slaughter helped to break down the enzymes faster; beef treated this way was sold under the name "Pro-Ten Beef." With or without such tenderizing treatment, the beef in most supermarkets was 6 to 15 days old: one day to kill and clean, one to two days to chill to 40° internal temperature, one day to cut, one to three days in transit, one to two days in a warehouse, one day in transit to a store and anywhere from one to five days at the store level.

The most critical, and visible, problem faced by the processor or retailer, however, was that of shrinkage. As beef aged it lost surface moisture ("evaporation shrink"). Not only did this mean loss of weight (and value, since meat was sold by the pound), but after four or five days the surface areas began to blacken and had to be cut away. The amount of shrinkage was proportional to the uncovered surface area; carcass beef was least vulnerable since most of its surface was covered by a layer of fat called "the bark," and shrinkage became increasingly costly as the meat was cut into smaller pieces. RFI estimated that at the retail stores carcass beef lost about 3 percent of its value over a six-day period due to shrinkage, with the rate gradually decreasing as dehydration caused the beef to form its own protective covering. Because of shrinkage, meat processors and retailers were under constant pressure to "move the beef through"; this often led to the availability of bargains as temporary surpluses developed at a particular location.

In an effort to control shrinkage and remove this pressure, a number of alternative processes had been developed in the past 20 years. Most of these treatments were variations of the "Cryovac" process, in which the meat was enclosed in a plastic bag and the air expelled. This allowed the meat to age naturally without dehydrating (although the meat did lose its "bloom", or red color, while it was in the bag). Cryovaced meat had a shelf life of three–six weeks. Different meat processors utilized different kinds of plastic covering or substituted a gas, such as carbon dioxide, for the vacuum. The major problem with this process, other than its cost, was the possibility of the rather fragile bag developing a leak during transportation or handling; when this occurred the meat began incurring shrinkage and spoilage at normal rates.

There had been considerably experimentation with frozen beef, which had a longer storage life than cryovaced beef. Major resistance had been encountered at the consumer level, however, The U.S. housewife bought meat largely on the basis of its appearance and feel, and tended to be suspicious of any packaging method that altered these. She also seemed to feel that frozen beef was somehow "less fresh" than unfrozen beef—even though her first act upon arriving home with her newly purchased fresh beef was usually to put it into her freezer. Until this attitude was overcome there was general agreement in the industry that frozen meat would not have wide acceptance.

THE BEEF INDUSTRY IN 1973

Prior to 1960 most of the beef produced in the U.S. passed through one of the major meat-packing firms (such as Armour or Swift). These companies arranged for the purchase of the cattle and transported them to packing plants near large metropolitan areas, which were often a substantial distance from the source of supply. There they were slaughtered and "broken" down into sides or quarters, and then shipped on to other plants closer to the final markets (hanging from overhead hooks in the truck or train van—hence the term "hanging meat"). Additional processing usually took place at these plants before the partially processed beef was shipped on to the individual retailer, who undertook its final "fabrication" into retail cuts. Only the largest retail chains owned their own central carcass processing facilities. This arrangement was costly because of the necessity for handling and transporting live cattle, and the multiplicity of additional processing and redistribution functions for dressed carcasses and by-products.

Letting the stores do as much of their own breaking and fabricating as possible reduced shrinkage and, within limits, enabled a store to tailor its preparation of retail cuts to the specialized needs of its clientele. On the other hand, decentralized processing was less efficient than central processing, and it was more difficult to control the over-all balance between the requirements of different stores (i.e., if one store sold mostly ribs and another mostly chuck, it was inefficient to send them each a forequarter).

The decade following World War II saw the advent of modern means of refrigerated transporation (refrigerated railroad cars and "piggy-back" trailers), the availability in rural areas of surplus farm labor resulting from the consolidation of farms, and technological advances in private communication systems, production equipment, and processing procedures—particularly vacuum packing. These factors made possible the emergence of a new kind of packing plant in areas of high density feeding: plants which purchased cattle directly from farmers and feeders through mobile buyers equipped with radios to confirm current market prices and schedule deliveries, which processed the beef in assembly line fashion under controlled conditions utilizing automated equipment, and then shipped it on to retailers in "boxed" form according to their specifications. Each box, weighing 50 pounds or more, would contain a single vacuum-packed (cryovaced) primal cut or several retail cuts. Boxed beef simplified the retailer's operation considerably, both because it eliminated much of his "backroom cutting" and because carcass processing usually left him with a number of unsalable cuts which he was forced either to mark down or to convert into lower priced cuts or ground beef. Therefore, it was particularly appropriate for smaller chains, whose sales volume could not justify the cost of central processing and control.

The largest and best known of these new companies was Iowa Beef Processors, which grew from near obscurity in the early 1960s to a sales volume of over $1 billion in 1971. Other companies (such as Monfort of Colorado, which had previously confined itself largely to feedlot activities) also jumped into the beef processing business. The major meat companies, however, were unwilling or unable to successfully follow the lead of these new entrants. During the same period a number of supermarket chains consolidated to the point where they could afford their own processing plants. Under this combined assault, coming at a time when many of their plants were becoming obsolete, delivery costs were skyrocketing, and a government consent decree enjoined them from integrating forward into either wholesaling or retailing, the influence of the traditional meat packers began to erode. It was Joseph Brady's belief, in fact, that it was only a matter of a few years before the major meat packers would no longer be conducting any significant beef processing operations in the upstate New York area.

RFI'S MEAT WAREHOUSE OPERATIONS

The company's 15,000 square foot central meat warehouse in West Rochester operated primarily as a transfer point; little meat was stored there for more than a few days. The warehouse had historically operated on a three-day-per-week delivery schedule, but had recently changed to a five-day delivery schedule under the pressure of increasing volume. Hanging meats (beef and pork) were received and shipped to the retail outlets on Mondays, Wednesdays and Fridays, and boxed meats (prepackaged chicken and branded packaged meats) on Tuesdays and Thursdays. There was little flexibility in the timing of the outbound shipments, which had to be made during daytime shifts to coincide with the hours of the retail stores.

It was difficult to balance the supply and demand for beef on a daily basis both because of unpredictable day-to-day variations in the retail demand and the nonuniform demand pattern during the week; about 40 percent of weekly demand occurred on Friday and Saturday. This skewed demand pattern, together with the logistical difficulties involved in obtaining beef from the midwest, made it necessary to hold about one-quarter of the incoming beef in the warehouse over the weekend.

RFI preferred to utilize carcass beef as much as possible because of its cost, quality, and natural protection against shrinkage. The amount that could be purchased, however, was dictated by the sales level of the slowest moving cut. Otherwise the stores would be forced to dispose of the excess cuts, usually at a loss. In 1971 about 35 percent of the beef purchased by RFI arrived in carcass form (as sides or quarters); the remaining demand was met through the purchase of hanging primal cuts, mostly chucks.

Although RFI officials felt that its ability to affect consumer preferences for different cuts of beef over the long term was limited, sales and "specials" could provide dramatic short-term changes. For example, the total poundage of a particular cut sold during a sale was often 5 to 10 times its volume during a nonsale period. It was difficult to determine, of course, the extent to which such specials actually increased the consumption of a cut, or whether they simply redistributed sales during the year. During a special the effective price of the cut was generally reduced by about 20 percent. On the other hand, a beef special often caused *total* store sales to increase by 10–15 percent.

The current meat warehouse capacity of about 1.5 million pounds of meat a week (under the current mix of meat types) was felt to be sufficient to meet RFI's projected sales volume through 1975—assuming that the company continued to grow at a rate of 10–15 percent per year and that no major acquisitions were made. The role of the task force that Joseph Brady directed was to make a recommendation regarding Rochester's meat operations after 1975.

ALTERNATIVE A: CONTINUATION OF THE CURRENT SYSTEM

The easiest and most obvious course of action was simply to expand the current warehouse facilities and continue to act as a transfer point for naked carcass and primal hanging beef shipped in from the midwest. This alternative offered a number of advantages, including better control over incoming quality and purchase cost (the number of suppliers was greater and negotiations with them easier) than would be the case with a boxed beef program. New warehouse space would cost about $45 per square foot.

While this alternative kept costs at the transfer point at a minimum, it permitted cost inefficiencies at each end of the supply chain. Hanging carcass beef contained approximately 100 pounds of waste fat and bone, which was shipped all the way to the retailer before it was separated and scrapped. In addition, up to 100 pounds of "rough meats" were produced in the course of breaking a carcass into its primal cuts; these were meat scraps that could be converted into ground beef. Rough meats contained 50 percent fat, however, and in order to keep the fat content of its ground beef under 20 percent (the usual standard) a retailer either had to cut out part of this fat by hand, or mix the rough cuts with other lean beef. Brady estimated that it took about an hour for a retail meatcutter to reduce 100 pounds of rough meats containing 50 percent fat to about 65 pounds of meat containing only 20 percent fat. The preparation of ground beef was a surprisingly difficult task, because of the problems of maintaining its color and freshness during a process that could entail considerable time and temperature variation. Ground beef was also more perishable than unground beef.

The freight rate from the midwest to Rochester averaged about $0.03 per pound. The trip took about 45 hours, and it was estimated that 0.35 percent shrink occurred enroute. Another 0.5 percent shrink occurred in carcass beef that remained in the warehouse over the weekend. The cost of shipping the meat from the central warehouse on to the retail stores averaged about $0.01 per pound.

From the point of view of the retail outlet, this alternative promised the lowest initial cost per pound, but required that the store carry out all of its own cutting. This increased its labor and equipment costs and led to variations in perceived value from store to store (which was affected mainly by the amount of trim left on the meat, and the amount of fat in the ground beef). Moreover, the amount of shrink at the store level was high; although it was difficult to get good information about this, Joseph Brady estimated that the average store held beef two–three days and that during this period the cooler shrink alone came to over 1 percent, while the *total* shrink (which included cooler shrink, cutting loss, waste, poor grading, scale errors, reworking and downgrading cuts, pilferage and incorrect register codings) was in the neighborhood of 4 percent and possibly higher. There was virtually no return from the discarded fat and bone (retail stores seldom got more than $0.015 per pound for it from local buyers). Finally, above and beyond the cost of the skilled labor required at the store level under this proposal—a meatcutter earned about $5.50 per hour and could convert a carcass into its primal cuts in about one hour—there was a serious doubt in Brady's mind as to whether men with this kind of skill would continue to be available to stores in the future. Experienced meatcutters were becoming increasingly difficult to locate, and young men were not going into the profession. Women found the work difficult because of the stength required to work with pieces of meat that often weighed more than 100 pounds.

ALTERNATIVE B: PACKER BOXED BEEF

The second alternative was to join the trend to a boxed beef program. Under this approach the packer would break the carcass into its primal cuts and vacuum pack and ship only the salable meat to RFI's central warehouse for distribution. The cost of this service was somewhat over $30 per carcass (see Exhibit 5 for a sample price calculation by Iowa Beef Processors), while prices for individually purchased primals varied widely (see Exhibit 5-A). There were a number of offsetting cost savings from such a program, however.

First, central cutting avoided shipment of the bone and waste that con-

Exhibit 5-A
IBP CATTLE-PAK FORMULA PRICE LIST

Date   January 19, 1972

Product	Size (pounds)	F.O.B. Price per CWT*
1. Straight cattle	650	$ 85.63
2. Straight cattle	750	84.61
3. Good cattle	650	79.90
4. Cattle-pak chux		68.40
5. Cattle-pak ribs		104.66
6. Cattle-pak rounds		97.09
7. Cattle-pak loins		92.92
		100.92
8. Eastern straight cattle	650	84.22
9. Eastern cattle-pak chux		69.57
10. Eastern cattle-pak rib		94.30
11. 80/20 coarse ground beef		59.66
12. 73/27 coarse ground beef		53.49

* Note: The prices for items 1, 2, 3 and 8 represent the prices per hundred pounds for boxed carcasses (of different grades and sizes) at the IBP plant; an illustration of how the price for item 1 was derived is contained in Exhibit 5B. Other prices refer to individual boxed primals or ground beef ("80/20" means "80 percent lean, 20 percent fat").

stituted about 15 percent of the original carcass weight. Moreover, because of the volume of renderable material accumulated by the packer, he could afford to process the fat and bone more efficiently and sell it in bulk. As a result, most packers were able to offer rebates to their customers amounting to about $0.05 per pound of the waste removed before shipment. Almost no shrinkage would take place enroute unless a leak developed in the plastic enclosure, which only occurred about 5 percent of the time. Samples of the promotional material issued by IBP are contained in Exhibit 6.

At the warehouse a boxed beef program would require a somewhat more sophisticated refrigeration system but would allow more efficient use of the warehouse space as well as eliminate the need for some equipment. No inspection of the incoming beef would be required, but Brady viewed this as a mixed blessing: purchasing boxed beef meant that his company would effectively lose control over the quality of the incoming meat, and how it was broken down and trimmed.

Although the retailer would pay more for his beef initially, a boxed beef program would offer him a number of advantages. First, it would eliminate the need for some manpower, or allow him to use the available manpower in more productive ways. The store manager would tend to handle fewer rough cuts and more of the ones that sold profitably for him. Second, it would decrease the amount of waste he handled, and the losses he incurred from shrinkage, "reworking," and the necessity to discount

Exhibit 5–B
IBP CATTLE-PAK PRICING STRAIGHT CATTLE

Date   January 19, 1972

	Yield	Price per Pound	Value
	650.00	at 58.10 cents	$377.65
Credits:		F.O.B. Plant	
Briskets	16.58	at 75.00 cents = $12.44	
Shank meat	17.23	at 58.00 cents = 9.99	
Inside skirts	2.08	at 60.00 cents = 1.25	
Outside skirts	1.88	at 75.00 cents = 1.41	
Plank steak	2.66	at 125.00 cents = 3.33	
Kidneys	1.69	at 13.50 cents = .23	
Hanging tenders.	1.17	at 50.00 cents = .59	
Short ribs	2.80	at 58.00 cents = 1.62	
IBP trim	3.18	at 73.00 cents = 2.32	
Regular trim*	100.49	at 31.00 cents = 31.15	
Fat and bone	99.84	at 4.74 cents = 4.73	
Cutting shrink.	3.25	at XXX cents = XXX	
Total pounds	252.85		

Total Credits	($ 69.06)†
Sub-Total	$308.59
Processing and packaging fees + ...	$ 31.50‡
Total Product Cost	$340.09
(Divided by yield:	397.15 pounds)
Price hundredweight F.O.B. IBP Plant . . .	$ 85.63§

* This is called "rough meats" in the text.
† The items listed under "Credits" would be left at the IBP plant, and the purchase cost reduced by $69.06 unless the purchaser specified that he wanted certain of these items. Joseph Brady felt that RFI would probably purchase all but the 100 pounds of waste fat and bone, unless it was decided to make ground beef a purchased item.
‡ This is the fee charged by IBP for breaking the carcass into primals and vacuum-packing it.
§ "Price per hundred pounds at the IBP plant."

slow-moving items. Cryovaced beef experienced slightly less than 1 percent shrink over a six-day period, on the average (this was largely due to the loss of fluids, which collected at the bottom of the package). Finally, it would eliminate the need for certain equipment. On the minus side it would require more sophisticated refrigeration equipment and more complex receiving and handling procedures. The retailer would also lose some of his ability to control quality.

Currently about 16 percent of RFI's total incoming beef tonnage was converted into ground beef at the store level. The adoption of a boxed beef program would give them the option of either preparing ground beef at Rochester from purchased frozen lean beef and the rough meats provided by the packer, or purchasing the ground beef directly from the packer. In-house centralized processing would require an equipment investment of about $75,000 and an annual cost of $50,000 to process up to

Exhibit 6

How you BENEFIT with CATTLE-PAK

1. Carcass shrinkage is virtually eliminated by vacuum packing.

2. Contamination is held to a minimum with vacuum packing.

3. Your weekend inventory is actual and carryover stock is always fresh.

4. Cattle-Pak cuts are controlled to a uniform standard. Only #3 and #2 cutability cattle are selected for Cattle-Pak.

5. Less backroom storage space required. Rails, hooks and reinforcing ceilings can be eliminated, saving up to 1,000′ per store unit.

6. Vacuum packed meats provide at least 21 days of marketing life if held at recommended temperature of 29-32°.

7. There is never a need for distressed sales.

8. No special meat deliveries. Rail trucks are eliminated.

9. The task of breaking cattle at the store level is eliminated.

10. More productivity from present work force.

11. Sales increase because employees can concentrate on merchandising and stocking the front of the store continuously.

12. Substantially increased NET PROFIT.

This Remains at IBP

Bone   Fat

CREDITS:

IBP allows full credit for all "Rough Meat" at our selling price — including bones, fat and trimmings.

ROUGH MEAT CUTS:

All cuts from the "Rough Meat" are available to you boneless, trimmed to Cattle-Pak specifications and vacuum packed, in any quantities you may require.

THESE SAVINGS ARE ABSOLUTE WITH CATTLE-PAK

FREIGHT: 700 lb. Carcass .02 $14.00 Per head
         450 lb. Cattle-Pak
                 Carcass .02 $ 9.00 Per Head
                                      $ 5.00

PLUS:

CARCASS SHRINK:
         700# ½ of 1% @ .45 $1.57
         450# Cattle-Pak   .00
                                     $6.57 Absolute
                                           Per Head
                                           Saving

PRESENTLY YOUR

BACKROOM SHRINK IS?

WAREHOUSE SHRINK IS?

THESE QUESTION MARKS ARE ELIMINATED BY CATTLE-PAK

5 million pounds of ground beef a year. But at that sales level it would reduce costs at the retail level by an estimated $120,000 per year (roughly half of this came from labor savings and the remainder from waste reduction). Packer produced ground beef, on the other hand, cost about $0.60 per pound (f.o.b. the packer; see Exhibit 5-A), but it removed what Joseph Brady considered to be an important marketing weapon from the retailer's control. He felt that a store's reputation in its community was largely determined by its meat program, and this in turn was heavily dependent on the quality of its ground beef.

In fact, the loss of control that a boxed beef program implied for all phases of their meat operations gave Brady considerable uneasiness. Entry into such a program tended to "lock in" the purchaser with a single packer, causing him to relinquish flexibility in cost negotiations.

ALTERNATIVE C: BREAKING AND FABRICATING BEEF AT WAREHOUSE

Boxed beef programs had particular appeal to small- and medium-sized chains; larger chains appeared to be moving to their own in-house vacuum processing of carcass beef. This would necessitate an expansion of RFI's warehouse and a considerable investment in new facilities. The operation there would become much more complex as well. Essentially, RFI would undertake an IBP type of service for its stores. Relationships with suppliers would remain the same as at present, however, as would the method of shipment from the midwest. RFI would retain control over the incoming quality characteristics of the beef. The retail outlets, on the other hand, would experience the same advantages and disadvantages as with purchased box beef: higher equipment and initial product cost, some labor savings, less handling of waste, and improved sanitation control. Central ground beef processing would also be possible under this option.

Moreover, through its ability to store beef centrally for longer periods, the company would be better able to balance out the fluctuations in consumer demand for different cuts that occurred from week to week, and gain more control over its product mix by coordinating beef "specials." This might enable RFI to purchase more of its beef in carcass form. It would be possible, in fact, to increase the percentage of carcass beef to over 80 percent of total requirements if the company were willing to increase the amount of beef it purchased by about 20 percent. This would leave RFI with a considerable number of excess loins and ribs with which it could attempt to penetrate the institutional (hotel and restaurant) market. Since carcass beef cost less than hanging primals, Brady estimated that this shift to more carcass purchases could reduce RFI's total beef purchase cost by $0.01–$0.02 per pound.

Joseph Brady's task force estimated that the initial investment required for a central processing plant would come to about $1 million; equipment costs accounted for about $400,000 of this, with additional floor space and increased inventory dividing up the remainder in equal parts. His estimate of the plant investment required was based on the assumptions that about 1,000 square feet of floor space would be required to process 100,000 pounds of beef per week, and that additional floor space would cost about $45 per square foot. The direct processing and packaging cost, including materials, would work out to about $0.025 per pound (of which $0.012 represented the direct labor cost) he estimated, while supervisory and clerical costs would amount to about 15 percent of the direct payroll cost. Maintenance, laundry and utility costs would come to another $15,000–$20,000 per month. On the other hand, Brady believed that a central processing facility in the Rochester area might be able to sell the waste fat and bone for $0.055 or more per pound.

The experience of other meat processors also provided a rough idea of the profitability of such an operation. For example, Monfort of Colorado operated a cryovac processing plant in which 1,000 men slaughtered and processed 2,200 head of cattle daily. Fixed investment in this plant amounted to about $10 million, and working capital investment about $16 million. Packing operations were reported to be returning between 1 percent and 2 percent on sales, yielding a 15 percent pre-tax return on investment. Monfort's margins tended to be somewhat higher than its other competitors such as Iowa Beef and Spencer Foods, both of whose earnings fluctuated about 1 percent on sales. These operations were much larger than the one that RFI was considering, however, and included slaughtering. Hence they utilized a considerable amount of automated equipment that might not be feasible for RFI. Within the past several years several grocery chains, including Kroger (annual grocery sales about $3.5 billion) and Stop & Shop (annual sales about $1 billion), had started up central meat processing facilities.

POLICY CONSIDERATIONS

As Joseph Brady considered the alternatives facing RFI, and tried to think of others not yet considered, he found himself contemplating the implications that these alternatives might have for the company as a whole, given some of the changes he suspected would be occurring in the environment over the next decade. In order to sort out and clarify some of these ideas in his own mind, he began jotting them down as follows:

CONJECTURES ABOUT FUTURE

1. Growth in business—not necessarily smooth and steady. Possibility of major acquisitions.
2. Trend toward bigger retail outlets, but also towards smaller, more specialized "convenience" stores which carry a limited product line and

offer drive-in service. Will this be an important factor, and is frozen meat the answer here?

3. Frozen meat. When and how will it overcome consumer resistance? Is this, or another, revolution near?

4. Labor cost. Now represents almost 10 percent of retail price and still going up. Growing power of unions, and resistance to working non-daylight hours.

5. Where are our retail meatcutters going to come from? Where are future store personnel going to come from? Pool of women workers, but are they willing—and able? How can we make cutting meat less strenuous?

Finally, he wondered how a boxed beef program, either in-house or purchased outside, could best be sold to the retail stores. Cryovaced beef would cost the store manager more per pound, but eventually it should save him money. How much he would save, of course, depended primarily on his ability to take full advantage of all the possible cost savings available from such a program—particularly labor costs. It might even be difficult for him to measure these cost savings, since Brady felt he would probably not lay off any meatcutters, but would utilize their freed-up time to perform other tasks. And, over a longer time frame, he would be able to increase his meat sales without having to hire additional workers. Such savings, however, were less visible than the direct cost figures that were generally available to him.

Zenith Radio Corporation (AR)

THE Zenith Radio Corporation was one of the leading manufacturers of consumer electronic products in the United States in 1965. Sales had grown from $142 million in 1956 to $625 million in 1965 while profits after taxes increased from $6.2 million to $33.6 million during this same period. (See Exhibit 1.) Television receivers accounted for approximately 75 to 85 percent of sales, the proportion rising with the surge in color television demand; other products included radios, phonographs, a limited amount of military gear and certain specialty products such as hearing aids. In the summer of 1966, the company was faced with the problem of deciding where and how to expand manufacturing capacity for consumer products.

HISTORY (1918–1961)

Zenith was founded as a partnership, the Chicago Radio Laboratory, by R. H. G. Matthews and Karl Hassel in 1919. One of their ventures was the construction of a long-wave radio receiver for the *Chicago Tribune,* which was used to pick up news dispatches from the Versailles Peace Conference from a long-wave station in France. This short circuiting of the congested trans-Atlantic cable enabled the *Tribune* to beat competition by 12 to 24 hours on conference stories.

In 1921 Eugene F. McDonald, a former Lieutenant Commander in the Navy, joined the partnership as general manager and provided funds badly needed for expansion. McDonald, in 1923, founded the Zenith Radio Corporation which he was to guide until his death in 1958. Originally the company was only a sales agent for the Chicago Radio Laboratory, but soon Zenith absorbed the partnership and entered the manufacturing end of the business. The company prospered in the late 1920s, establishing the reputation as a high-quality, innovation-oriented manufacturer of radio receivers.

The early depression years brought severe retrenchment for Zenith; sales dropped as low as $2 million in the year ended April 30, 1933, and losses were incurred from 1930 through 1933. The company survived relatively unscathed, however, in part because of an extremely conservative financial posture; expansion in the 1920s had not required an infusion of long-term debt and investment in inventories had been kept to a minimum. Furthermore, new low priced table and portable radio receivers, the latter selling for as little as $19.95, were introduced to fit the tenor of the times. Black ink appeared again in 1934 and, aside from a slight loss in 1946, the company has not experienced another deficit.

As the 1930s wore on, the notion of television began to generate excitement in the industry. Although Zenith indulged in a certain amount of R&D in this area and even originated Chicago's first television station in 1939, no attempt was made to market a commercial television set. The company's attitude is typified by a comment from the 1938 Annual Report:

> The management continues to believe that television is not yet ready for the public and refuses to be stampeded into the premature production of television receivers for sale to the public. We are manufacturing television receivers, which are being loaned to experienced observers, not sold. Any television receivers sold at this time may become obsolete shortly. Your company is ready but television is not.
>
> The management's definite stand on the matter of television has greatly increased the company's good will with radio dealers and the trade in general. The sales, even in the New York area, of television have been negligible. Television one day will be a great industry, but that day is not this year.
>
> The economic problems of television are far greater than the technical problems. One of the most important economic problems resolved itself into a vicious triangle. First, no radio manufacturer or broadcasting organization can afford the expense of supplying adequate television programs for a sufficient length of time to obtain circulation. Second, the advertisers will not contribute to and pay for the programs until circulation is acquired. Third, the public, which is the circulation, will not buy television receivers until they are assured of satisfactory and continued programs.

Immediately following World War II, the supply of component parts for consumer products became a grave problem for all manufacturers in the industry. To relieve this situation, the company in 1945 formulated a large-scale expansion program to provide manufacturing facilities for such components as coils, loud speakers and record changers.

Then, in 1948, the company put its first line of television receivers on the market. During that same year, in order to assure a source of picture tubes, the Rauland Corporation, a noted Chicago supplier, was acquired. Continued expansion of facilities, including a $4 million enlargement of

Exhibit 1

ZENITH RADIO CORPORATION and subsidiaries

FOR THE YEAR	1965
Net Sales (a)...	$470,503
Income Before Federal Income Taxes.................................	64,453
Federal Income Taxes..	30,900
Net Income...	33,553
Per Share (b)...	3.59
As a Percentage of Sales......................................	7.1%
As a Percentage of Beginning Stockholders' Equity..............	25.5%
Dividends Paid..	18,679
Per Share (b)...	2.00
Expenditures for Facilities..	10,852
Provision for Depreciation...	5,087
Number of Employees (Average).....................................	15,500

AS OF YEAR END	
Current Assets..	$ 172,368
Current Liabilities..	61,882
Working Capital..	110,486
Working Capital Ratio...	2.8
Property, Plants and Equipment, at Cost............................	65,121
Reserves for Depreciation and Amortization.........................	30,031
Net Property, Plants and Equipment................................	35,090
Stockholders' Equity..	147,972
Shares Outstanding (b)..	9,354,497

(a) Restated to exclude excise taxes; refer to Note 3 on page 9.
(b) Adjusted to give effect to three-for-one stock split on November 3, 1961, three-for-one stock split on May 6, 1959 and two-for-one stock split on March 31, 1958.

Table 1
ZENITH SALES AND PROFITS,
1949–1955
(millions of dollars)

Year	Sales	Profits
1949	77.0	2.7
1950	134.0	5.6
1951	110.0	5.3
1952	137.6	5.8
1953	166.7	5.6
1954	138.6	5.6
1955	152.9	8.0

TEN YEAR FINANCIAL REVIEW *(Dollars in Thousands Except for Per Share Data)*

1964	1963	1962	1961	1960	1959	1958	1957	1956
$362,314	$323,597	$289,804	$254,553	$235,772	$239,819	$180,634	$148,459	$131,570
48,383	43,228	40,937	38,355	32,476	35,430	25,741	17,341	13,299
24,100	22,375	21,300	20,340	17,250	18,800	13,625	9,175	7,120
24,283	20,853	19,637	18,015	15,226	16,630	12,116	8,166	6,179
2.61	2.27	2.16	1.99	1.70	1.88	1.37	.92	.70
6.7%	6.4%	6.8%	7.1%	6.5%	6.9%	6.7%	5.5%	4.7%
20.2%	19.2%	19.9%	20.4%	19.1%	23.5%	18.8%	16.6%	13.5%
14,378	12,381	10,896	10,499	8,160	7,732	4,925	2,462	2,462
1.55	1.35	1.20	1.167	.917	.872	.556	.278	.278
4,177	12,289	9,662	2,116	4,242	2,590	747	1,218	1,134
5,045	3,804	2,232	1,804	1,651	1,344	1,269	1,284	1,495
12,700	11,300	10,300	9,100	8,900	8,900	7,400	7,100	6,600
$142,445	$122,470	$108,300	$103,941	$ 97,365	$ 96,946	$ 80,844	$ 65,077	$ 57,986
42,178	35,196	35,087	34,700	29,080	35,542	27,850	19,889	19,875
100,267	87,274	73,213	69,241	68,285	61,404	52,994	45,188	38,111
3.4	3.5	3.1	3.0	3.3	2.7	2.9	3.3	2.9
54,706	50,146	39,203	31,006	28,807	24,592	22,154	21,615	20,480
25,360	20,421	17,141	16,378	14,721	13,252	12,003	10,893	9,644
29,346	29,725	22,062	14,628	14,086	11,340	10,151	10,722	10,836
131,768	120,122	108,524	98,641	88,179	79,604	70,656	64,450	49,318
9,307,537	9;199,129	9,104,029	9,031,542	8,935,842	8,864,352	8,864,352	8,864,352	8,864,352

assembly capacity in 1952, enabled Zenith to participate in the initial surge of demand for black and white television.

Relying on high-quality black and white television sets and a capable distribution network, Zenith gradually increased its share of the monochrome television market to over 20 percent, becoming the leader in that segment of the industry. While extensive research effort was expended on color devices, no attempt was made to introduce such a line until late 1961, over seven years after the first color sets became commercially available. The brief comments in the 1958 Annual Report are indicative of the position taken during this time, "The company had produced in its laboratories transistorized television receivers and in conjunction with the Rauland Corporation, is continuing research and development on color television receivers and tubes so that the company will be prepared to enter

Exhibit 1 *(Continued)*

ZENITH RADIO

CONSOLIDATED BALANCE

ASSETS	1965	1964
CURRENT ASSETS:		
Cash.	$ 36,284,991	$ 31,812,647
U.S. Government securities, at cost., ...	44,929,530	37,046,384
Receivables, less reserves of $2,800,000 in 1965 and $2,675,500 in 1964.	36,809,402	35,009,503
Inventories, priced at lower of cost (first-in, first-out) or market, including finished goods of $7,685,890 in 1965 and $9,424,615 in 1964. . .	54,344,303	38,576,480
Total current assets.	172,368,226	142,445,014
OTHER ASSETS:		
Receivable from settlement of litigation, less $1,000,000 in current receivables.	—	1,000,000
Prepaid expenses and other assets.	2,395,044	1,154,942
Total other assets.	2,395,044	2,154,942
PROPERTY, PLANTS AND EQUIPMENT, at cost.	65,121,293	54,706,313
Less — Reserves for depreciation and amortization. .	30,030,987	25,359,998
Net property, plants and equipment. . .	35,090,306	29,346,315
BROADCASTING STATIONS, PATENTS AND TRADEMARKS,		
at nominal value.	1	1
	$209,853,577	$173,946,272

Refer to page 9 for Notes To Financial Statements.

CORPORATION and subsidiaries

SHEETS December 31, 1965 and 1964

LIABILITIES	1965	1964
CURRENT LIABILITIES:		
Accounts payable and accrued liabilities..........	$ 39,149,346	$ 22,759,458
Salaries, wages and taxes........................	10,570,811	11,077,858
Contribution to Zenith Profit-Sharing Retirement Plan........................	12,107,345	8,324,130
Provision for Federal income taxes, less U.S. Government securities of $24,700,000 in 1965 and $19,300,000 in 1964...........	54,432	16,743
Total current liabilities..............	61,881,934	42,178,189
CAPITAL AND RETAINED EARNINGS:		
Capital stock, $1 par value per share; authorized, 12,000,000 shares; outstanding, 1965, 9,354,497 shares, 1964, 9,307,537 shares (Notes 1 and 2)........	9,354,497	9,307,537
Additional paid-in capital (increase in 1965 represents excess of proceeds over par value of stock sold under employee stock purchase plans)....................	5,617,197	4,334,780
Retained earnings per accompanying statement....	132,999,949	118,125,766
Total capital and retained earnings....	147,971,643	131,768,083
	$209,853,577	$173,946,272

Exhibit 1 *(Concluded)*

ZENITH RADIO

STATEMENTS OF CONSOLIDATED INCOME AND RETAINED EARNINGS AND SOURCE AND USE OF FUNDS for the years ended December 31, 1965 and 196

INCOME AND RETAINED EARNINGS

	1965	1964
NET SALES (Note 3)	$470,503,343	$362,313,884
COSTS AND EXPENSES:		
Cost of sales (Note 3)	351,017,161	267,232,322
Selling, advertising and administrative expenses	37,838,828	33,329,845
Contribution to Zenith Profit-Sharing Retirement Plan	12,107,345	8,324,130
Provision for depreciation	5,086,940	5,044,776
Total	406,050,274	313,931,073
INCOME BEFORE FEDERAL INCOME TAXES	64,453,069	48,382,811
PROVISION FOR FEDERAL INCOME TAXES	30,900,000	24,100,000
NET INCOME FOR THE YEAR	33,553,069	24,282,811
RETAINED EARNINGS:		
Cash dividends paid (1965—$2.00 per share; 1964—$1.55 per share)	(18,678,886)	(14,377,873)
Balance, beginning of year	118,125,766	108,220,828
Balance, end of year	$132,999,949	$118,125,766

SOURCE AND USE OF FUNDS

	1965	1964
SOURCE OF FUNDS:		
Net income for the year	$ 33,553,069	$ 24,282,811
Provision for depreciation	5,086,940	5,044,776
Sale of stock under employee stock purchase plans	1,329,377	1,740,997
	39,969,386	31,068,584
USE OF FUNDS:		
Cash dividends paid	18,678,886	14,377,873
Expenditures for facilities	10,851,795	4,177,128
All other, net	219,238	(478,850)
	29,749,919	18,076,151
INCREASE IN WORKING CAPITAL	$ 10,219,467	$ 12,992,433
WORKING CAPITAL, END OF PERIOD	$110,486,292	$100,266,825

into the manufacture of these receivers and tubes when the time is appropriate."

Company president, Joseph S. Wright, looking back on these events, commented in 1967, "We have learned a great deal from the problems others have had with new products. On the other hand, we have pioneered numerous innovations ourselves, many of which have been highly success-ful in building Zenith's markets." Examples of Zenith "firsts" were the superior picture contrast provided by the 1949 "black tube" television sets, turrent tuning for channel selection and fully transistorized hearing aids.

EXPANSION 1962–1965

In 1961 the company reported sales of $254 million and profits of $18 million. Capital expenditures in the period 1957–1961 had amounted to $10.9 million with net property, plant and equipment on the books of $14.6 million in 1961. Manufacturing facilities at that time consisted of over 2 million square feet of research, engineering and manufacturing facil-ities in the following locations:

Plant 1:	6001 West Dickens St., Chicago: Approximately 850,000 square feet devoted to black and white television assembly and phonograph production.
Plant 2:	1500 North Kostner St., Chicago: 600,000 square feet. Components manufacture for radio, televi-sion, and phonograph sets; also radio assembly; 1960 addition of 115,000 square feet for components.
Plant 3:	5801 West Dickens St., Chicago: Parts and Ser-vice Division.
Plant 4:	3501 West Potomac St., Chicago: Warehouse.
Plant 5:	6501 West Brand St., Chicago: Financial offices, hearing aids, engineering, special products and military products.
Rauland Corp.:	(Wholly owned subsidiary), 4245 North Knox St. Chicago: 380,000 square feet devoted to black and white picture tube research and production and special-purpose electronic tube research and production.
Wincharger Corp.:	(Wholly owned subsidiary), Sioux City, Iowa: Power generators.
Central Electronics, Inc.:	(Wholly owned subsidiary), Paris, Ill., 100,000 square feet constructed in 1961; manufacture of components for radio and television.
Zenith Radio Distributing Corporation:	(Wholly owned subsidiary), 912 West Washing-ton, Chicago.
Zenith Radio Research Corporation:	(Wholly owned subsidiary), Menlo Park, Calif., 30,000 square feet constructed in 1960; research.

Sales forecasts in 1961 were optimistic for all consumer electronic prod-ucts and it became apparent that the day of color television had finally arrived. Accordingly, Zenith announced a major plant expansion totalling $20.5 million that was to add over a million square feet of engineering and production space during the next two years. Several facilities were in-volved in this program, the major one being a 730,000 square foot Plant

6, across the Milwaukee Railroad tracks from Plant 1. It contained 325,000 square feet of color television and stereo assembly space, 250,000 square feet for receiving, shipping and storage and 155,000 square feet for new administrative quarters. Facilities at the Rauland Corporation were also expanded, and the first color television tube production was started on a pilot basis in late 1962. Annual capacity was to reach a rate of approximately one and a half million black and white tubes and one million color tubes a year by late 1965.

A long standing Zenith policy called for balanced picture tube and television set assembly capacity; however, substantial outside sales of tubes were encouraged countered by a comparable quantity of purchased tubes. According to Mr. Robert Alexander, Vice President of Manufacturing, this practice has given the company an excellent way of keeping a finger on industry quality standards. He felt that certain economies were also gained from larger production order quantities and concentration on a smaller number of sizes and styles. In 1965, the company announced a second major expansion of color picture tube capacity, a 700,000[1] square foot plant in Melrose Park, Illinois, designed to produce a million color tubes a year commencing at the end of 1966.

Hand wired chassis are a feature almost unique with Zenith television. Most of the other color set manufacturers employ printed circuit cards which permit automatic component insertion and soldering. Zenith has maintained and extensively advertised that their handcrafted sets are of superior quality, a claim which has been credited with providing at least some of the current market acceptance for Zenith television. In addition, Zenith executives believe that the company has gained the favor of many television supply and repair people because hand wired circuits are more accessible and easier to service than printed circuits and many repair men have not been trained on printed circuit units.

Model changes are introduced in May and December each year. The amount of operator retraining necessary is generally not extensive, however, because circuit modifications tend to evolve gradually; entire new lines are added less frequently. Historically retail television sales have had a pronounced seasonal pattern, peaking in the fourth quarter and lagging in the second quarter. The average factory price for Zenith color sets has been about $350 to $400 while black and white sets average $80 to $100.

"We have been very successful in matching production with sales," commented Mr. MacPherson. "The accurate analysis of the field situation has been one of Zenith's secret weapons. As a result we are able to operate with a minimum of finished goods inventory and still meet our distributor's requirements.[2] Other manufacturers produce for inventory in an attempt

---

[1] Including additions since purchase.

[2] Mr. Samuel Kaplan, Zenith Executive Vice President commented in the November 21, 1966, issue of *The Wall Street Journal*, "Our factory inventory is less than two days' supply."

to smooth production but it doesn't seem to work for them. Styles change or something else happens and they find themselves with as great a peak load as ever. We haven't experienced much of a seasonal pattern so far with color though."

MARKET CONDITIONS IN APRIL 1966

Market conditions for color television in the spring of 1966 were reflected in the following abstracts from an article in the April 12, 1966, issue of the *Wall Street Journal:*

Color TV Set Makers May Double '65 Sales in '66
But Won't Catch Demand Until '67
by Scott R. Schmedel

Although manufacturers of color television sets are whipping up production in an effort to double last year's sales, they still don't expect to catch up with consumer demand until well into 1967, and perhaps not even then.

Last year, 2,746,618 color sets were sold—compared with 8,027,981 black-and-white sets—a sharp jump from the 1,366,301 color sets sold in 1964 and the 743,000 of 1963.

This year, the industry expects to sell more than 5 million sets, aggravating inventory shortages that cropped up last year. "Inventories are still very low," says Joseph S. Wright, President of Zenith Radio Corp. "We've had less than a week's supply in the hands of our dealers for many months. We usually try to have five or six weeks' supply, and we prefer seven to eight," he adds.

Mr. Wright says he doesn't expect any change in the market "for the balance of this year and into next year sometime." And he notes, "we have persistently underestimated the strength of the demand."

Snowballing Color

By the end of 1965, 5.5 million color sets were installed in U.S. homes, equal to 10% of the black-and-white receivers in use. In 1966 alone, Radio Corp. of America, the industry leader, estimates another 5.5 million sets will be sold. Other manufacturers are a bit more cautious, but most agree the total will top 5 million.

The industry expects sales of color sets to snowball. Asserts S. R. Herkes, Vice President and General Manager of Motorola, Inc.: "If we have a 20% saturation of the market by the end of this year, the word-of-mouth will spark even more demand for color sets. I think 1967 will be a 10-million-set year, but regardless of what we can build in 1967 and 1968, the customers will be lined up to buy them."

The industry, however, isn't certain just how many sets it can sell this year and next because it doesn't know how many it can make. The key uncertainty is how many color picture tubes will be available.

There are 21 major assemblers of color sets, but only nine of them make picture tubes; the others buy their tubes from producers. The industry's ability to boost sales depends directly on the tens of millions of dollars the tube makers invest to increase their output—and on the makers' ability to overcome the quirks of making tubes on new production lines. Engineers claim the color picture tube is the most complicated consumer product ever built.

Output Data Vague

Industry statistics on tube production and capacity aren't available, but Mr. Herkes of Motorola says weekly output by all makers recently has been running "between the high 70,000s and the high 80,000s." The Electronic Industries Association's prelminary report on factory sales of color sets to distributors showed a total of 945,073 units through April 1, close to double the 481,097 of the like year earlier period.

Adding the formal and informal estimates of each company's prospects, however, indicates that tube production this year could accelerate to a surprisingly high 7 million tubes or more. In recently increasing its forecast of 1966 set sales to 5.5 million from 4.5 million, an upward revision of 22%, RCA was prompted primarily by the industry's plans to expand tube production.

There also are shortage of other set parts, although none is regarded as equaling the tube shortage. Parts containing copper, heavily used in electrical products, are such items, and wood cabinetry is another.

Rising copper and cabinet costs, in fact, along with the high consumer demand, are among the reasons why the price of color sets aren't declining as production increases. An average color set costs about $525 to $535, little changed overall in the past year.

Based on [publicly announced] plans, tube production in 1967 could range from 7 million to 10 million units. To most executives, a forecast of 10 million sets sold next year seems extremely high—but not impossible, depending on tube production. RCA believes consumer demand in 1967 will fall somewhere between 7 million and 9 million sets.

The mushrooming popularity of color TV is expected to cut into the market for black-and-white TV; sales will drop to about 7.6 million from the record 8 million of last year. So far this year, however, black-and-white sales are running ahead of last year. Even if they should fall off, total 1966 TV set sales, including color, almost certainty will surpass last year's record 10,774,599.

PLANS FOR EXPANSION

It became apparent to the Production Division that with the forecasted demands and management's agressive marketing policies, additional capacity would be needed in the very near future. In fact, Zenith could not make all the color television and stereo sets that could be sold in 1966. The relief anticipated by some industry observers in black-and-white television sales had not occurred for Zenith: sales of these units in the first half of 1966 continued to exceed those of the previous year. (See Exhibit 2.)

Exhibit 2
PRODUCTION DATA, 1963–1966
(in thousands of units)

INDUSTRY

(in thousands of units)

	Color	Black and White	Total
I. Television			
1963	700	7,203	7,903
1964	1,366	7,685	9,051
1965	2,747	8,028	10,795
1966*	4,700	7,800	12,500
II. Radio			
1963		9,975	
1964		10,771	
1965		13,282	
1966		15,600	

	Portable	Console	Total
III. Phonograph			
1963	3,405	1,624	5,029
1964	3,418	1,739	5,157
1965	4,046	1,709	5,755
1966*	4,000	2,000	6,000

* Estimated.

ZENITH PRODUCTION

1. 1963 annual report stated: Black and white television receiver production exceeded 1 million units for the fifth consecutive year.
2. 1964 annual report stated: Black and white and color receiver production exceeded 1,750,000 units and black and white exceeded 1 million units.
3. 1965 annual report stated: Black and white and color receiver production was in excess of 2 million units and black and white exceeded 1,500,000.

Mr. Alexander described the situation in these terms: "The sales forecasts made it clear to us in the spring of 1966 that more space would be needed almost immediately: a little bit here and there was simply not good enough. We have also found that a components plant is not always adaptable to the manufacture of larger assembled units. As a result we decided that an integrated plan should be put together that would lay out our requirements through 1970 taking into account that latest estimates of demand."

In May 1966, Mr. Donald MacGregor, the retired vice president of manufacturing, was engaged as a consultant to perform a thorough survey of Zenith manufacturing and engineering requirements and present a report of his findings to top management. The study took place in June and July

1966 and was completed August 1. A number of the manufacturing and engineering groups had developed proposals that had already been placed before management. Mr. MacGregor collected these and formulated others. His report indicated that the proposal for a 151,000 square foot addition to Plant 6 for color television manufacture, costing an estimated $2,730,000, would be needed almost immediately. A new 400,000 square foot, $6,330,000 plant for either color or black-and-white television, would be necessary within the next six months.

Those portions of the MacGregor report dealing with proposals for the Production Division are presented in Exhibit 3.

Exhibit 3

PRODUCTION DIVISION*

PROPOSALS FOR NEW FACILITIES

COLOR TELEVISION

Zenith produced 500,000 color TV sets last year—1965. Sales demand increased during the last half of the year, particularly in the last quarter, when the production capacity could not be increased to keep pace with the accelerating sales demand.

Early this year 1,000,000 color TV sets were scheduled for 1966—a 100 percent increase over 1965 actual production. The schedule was more a reflection of estimated possible production than of sales potential. It was predicated on the anticipated availability of color tubes, night shifts, reduced assembly of black-and-white sets, and fewer hi-fi stereo consoles than needed for expected sales demand.

The daily rate of color TV production must be upped from the present 3,500 to about 4,500 sets. Using all facilities available, this will require more night shifts, overtime, higher efficiencies, fewer rejects, and availability of parts—especially color tubes. Another of the major requirements for increased output is additional experienced, well-trained supervisory and technical personnel. The 1,000,000 figure is still a goal to be fought for, but to reach it will require some "good breaks" as well as superior and continuous production skills.

Next year's color TV sales forecast calls for a 50 percent increase over this year—a total of 1,500,000 sets. Obviously, with present facilities taxed to the limit, including night shifts and overtime, the 1967 schedule could only be accomplished with an increase of plant facilities, for which there is but slight prospect because of the considerable time required to plan, build, and equip new plants. Likewise, the hiring and training of new supervisors and technical personnel, under present conditions, may prove to be as time consuming, and even more difficult, that the planning, building, and setting up of new plants.

Possibly one or more plants, suitably located for adequate labor supply, technical and managerial personnel, transportation, and other important operational factors, can be purchased ready for occupancy. If so, time could be saved, but even though such a plant or plants were purchased soon, several months would be required to adapt the facility to Zenith's production require-

Exhibit 3 *(Continued)*

ments, and then several additional months to train the production and technical workers. In total, ten or twelve months, at best, would elapse from the time a plant is acquired to the beginning of production in significant volume.

If, on the other hand, a plant must be built, then the time span would necessarily be longer before the start of volume production. However, some time could be saved by starting a pilot operation while the plant is under construction, as was done at Paris, Illinois, about seven years ago.

* Reprinted from the MacGregor Report submitted August 1, 1966. Certain passages of proprietary nature have been eliminated.

The location of new facilities was not a direct issue at this time. However, it was a vital concern to the Manufacturing Group for a number of reasons, one of them being freight costs. Since purchased materials may represent 70 percent of the cost of goods sold, and the end products are fragile, have a high value and are often bulky, plants located at the center of the market and/or supplier area have an advantage in this regard.

Mr. MacGregor touched on another facet of the location problem: "Several proposals are for plants distant from the Chicago area. This is because of the labor scarcity here and the deteriorating quality of such job applicants when available. However, facility planning should be made with close attention to the advantages of centralization. For instance, Zenith and its subsidiaries have costly toolrooms and model shop equipment manned by highly paid and scarce tool and model makers located at Plants 1, 2, and 5, the Rauland Niles Plant and the Melrose Plant."

With the MacGregor report in hand on August 1, Zenith management then faced the task of deciding how to provide for the anticipated growth in demand for the company's products.

PROPOSAL I

151,000 Square Foot Addition
Adjoining Plant #6 on the East

The purpose of this Plant No. 6 addition is to increase production of Plant No. 6 color TV sets, to minimize night shifts and overtime, to obtain better material handling, and to lower color TV assembly costs. This new facility, together with other changes named below, will increase color TV output of Plant No. 6 from a present estimated 3,000 sets per day with maximum use of night shifts to 3,700 sets per day with nominal use of night shifts. This figure assumes the use for color sets of Plant No. 6 space presently employed for assembly of console stereo. It is also predicated on the purchase of the railroad vacant east of the Austin Avenue underpass.

Until recently, Production Division Management had favored the building of a production and warehouse facility of 340,000 square feet adjoining Plant

No. 6 to the east. This would have yielded about 5,250 color sets per day at Plant No. 6. However, this plan was abandoned for the following reasons:

A. Heavy manpower requirements.
B. Transportation difficulties inherent in adding 1,000 to 1,500 employees to the Plants No. 1 and No. 6 total.
C. Uncertainty as to whether air rights could be secured for the Austin Avenue underpass, or the possibility of many months or years of delay in getting such rights.

Summary

1.1	Construction Costs	
	Building–150,750 at $10.50 per sq. ft.	$1,582,875
	Other.	300,135
	Total.	$1,883,010
1.2	Purchase Cost of Land	$ 404,560
	Total.	$2,287,570
2.1	Occupancy Costs	
	Facilities, equipment and installation.	$ 442,500
2.2	Product: Color TV only	
	10 F.A. lines will produce 3,500 per day.	
	Total Cost.	$2,730,070

PROPOSAL II

Stereo Plant–Record Player–350,000 sq. ft.
1,500 Stereo–2,400 per day record players–1,800 people

1.1	Construction Costs	
	Building–350,000 sq.ft. × $8.00	$2,800,000
	Parking lot–Drives–Sidewalks	350,000
	Total.	$3,150,000
1.2	Purchase Cost of Land	
	40 acres × 43,560 × $53	$ 871,200
	Total.	$4,021,200
2.1	Occupancy Costs	
	Facilities, equipment & installation.	$ 911,500
	Total.	$4,932,700

PROPOSAL III

IV.	Components Plant–211,000 sq.ft.–1,500 people	
	1.1 Construction Costs	
	Building–211,000 × $8.00	$1,688,000
	Parking lot–Driveways–Sidewalks	193,000
	Total.	$1,881,000
	1.2 Purchase Cost of land	
	20 acres × 43,560 = 0	
	871,200 sq.ft. × $0.50 per sq.ft.	435,600
	Total.	$2,316,600
	2.1 Occupancy Costs	
	Facilities and equipment and installation	$ 874,700
	Total Cost.	$3,191,300

PROPOSAL IV

400,000 Square Foot Plant
for the Manufacture and
Assembly of Color (or B/W) TV

All present color TV facilities with maximum use of night shifts and overtime yield about 4,500 sets per day. Proposal I, for an addition to Plant No. 6, increases the daily yield of Plant No. 6 to about 3,700 sets, assuming nominal use of night shifts and minimum overtime. This also assumes the removal of console stereo from Plant No. 6 to a new plant (see Proposal II). With Plant No. 1 producing some 1,500 color TV sets daily (with night shifts and overtime), the total daily output of present color facilities plus the 151,000 square foot Plant No. 6 addition (Proposal I) will be approximately 151,000 square foot Plant No. 6 addition (Proposal I) will be approximately 5,200 sets. This falls considerably short of the average daily estimated sales requirements of 6,500 color TV sets for 1967 and 8,500 for 1968.

A new 400,000 square foot facility will produce about 2,100 color TV sets daily, bringing the total to 7,300.

	Color Sets Daily
Plant No. 1	1,500
Plant No. 6*	3,700
Proposal IV	2,100
Total	7,300

* Assuming approval of Proposal I (addition to Plant No. 6) and Proposal II (new 350,000 square foot console-stereo plant).

A daily output of 7,300 color sets meets the forecast sales requirements for 1967, but falls 1,200 short of the estimated 1968 demand. This shortage could possibly be met by maximum use of night shifts and overtime—a dangerous course to follow, especially in a tight labor market.

An additional 200,000 square feet would be required to build the indicated shortage of 1,200 color TV sets—thus, for a daily total of 8,500 sets, Proposal IV should provide for a 600,000 square foot plant instead of a 400,000 square foot plant. However, knowing that 1968 output per square foot of plant can only be an estimate subject to variations according to labor efficiencies, model mix, and design factors—also, that the 8,500 sets per day figure is likewise an estimate subject to future unknowns, then the conservative plan would seem to favor a 400,000 square foot plant, so designed as to permit easy and economical expansion to 600,000 square feet. This, as a matter of fact, might be started before completion of the 400,000 square foot plant—assuming that during the intervening months conditions had developed to make obvious the need for the larger facility. Of course, the location of the plant should be such as to provide labor availability for 3,000 to 3,500 color TV sets daily, and acreage should be sufficient for the larger plant, plus ample parking facilities.

Consideration has been given to retaining all color TV set production at Plants Nos. 1 and 6. At present, all black and white sets are made at Plant No. 1. If these black and white sets were to be transferred to a new plant and were replaced with color sets, the total output of Plants Nos. 1 and 6 would be 7,900 color sets daily. This figure might be increased, with maximum use of night shifts and overtime, to the indicated requirement of 8,500 daily for 1968, but this volume is doubtful and, of course, involves considerable extra costs and difficulties in maintaining quality standards because of crowding and other factors—all of which are present in current operations.

Another factor to be reckoned with is that Plant No. 1 is not too well adapted to color set manufacture. This is especially true with reference to Building No. 8. Moreover, converting Plant No. 1 to an all color plant would be a very costly operation. Weighting all factors, it seems preferable to set up a new 400,000 square foot plant for color, even though initially greater problems will be encountered in training supervisory and technical personnel.

For close liaison with Engineering headquarters this plant should be located as near as possible to Chicago. In any event, it will require a small staff of engineers as part of its organizational structure. From a transportation standpoint, the plant would best be situated south, southeast, or east of Chicago. In the unlikely event that an adequate labor supply could be found in an otherwise satisfactory location, there would be several advantages in combining this plant with the console-stereo plant (see Proposal II).

> Color TV Plant—400,000 sq.ft.
> 2,100 sets—1,850 employees
> III. Color TV Plant to Produce 2,100 Color Sets
>   1.1 Construction Costs
>   Building—400,000 sq.ft. × $8.00 . . . . $3,200,000
>   Parking lot—Drives—Sidewalks   350,000
>
>   Total. $3,550,000
>   1.2 Purchase Cost of Land
>   40 acres × 43,560 sq.ft. =
>   1,742,400 sq.ft. × $0.50 per sq.ft. . . . . $ 871,200
>
>   Total. $4,421,200
>   2.1 Occupancy costs
>   Facilities, equipment and installation $1,909,600
>   2.2 Product: Color TV
>   6 F.A. lines will produce 2,100 per day
>   Personnel approximately 1,850
>   Total Cost. $6,330,800

SUMMARY CHART

A Comparison of 1966 Production Capacities and Plant Areas—by Product Classes
with
1968 Forecast Sales Requirements and Estimated Plant Space Needs

Line	Subject	Television Black-White	Television Color	Console Stereo	Portable Phono.	Multi-Band Radio	Components	Warehouse	Military	TOTALS
1	1966 Maximum Unit Daily Output (A)	6,000	4,500	900	(D) 1,300	600				
2	1968 Unit Daily Sales Requirement (B)	5,700	8,500	1,200	2,300	690				
3	Percent Increase, 1968	Decrease 5%	90%	33%	77%	15%				
4	1966 Plant Area (Sq.Ft.) (A) (C)	790,000	930,000	130,000	33,000	60,000			(E) 70,000	2,013,000
5	1968 Plant Area Required (B) (C)	759,000	1,957,000		290,000				(E) 200,000	3,206,000
6	Percent Increase, 1968	Decrease 4%	90%		30%				185%	60%
	Estimated Costs for Additional Plant Areas to Meet 1968 Requirements	Addition to Plant No. 6 (See Proposal I)	New Plant (See Proposal IV)		New Plant (See Proposal II)		New Plant (See Proposal III)	New Warehouse (See Proposal V)		
7	Land	$ 405,000.	$ 870,000.		$ 871,000.		$ 435,000.	$ 545,000.		
8	Building (Cost)	1,885,000.	3,550,000.		3,150,000.		1,880,000.	2,050,000.		
9	Machinery, Moving, Set-Up	440,000.	1,910,000.		911,000.		875,000.	95,000.		
10	TOTAL	$2,730,000.	$6,330,000.		$4,932,000.		$3,190,000.	$2,690,000.		$19,872,000.
11	Building Area (Sq.Ft.)	151,000	(F) 400,000		350,000		211,000	300,000		1,412,000

Notes:
(A) Maximum Possible Use of Night Shifts and Overtime
(B) Moderate Use of Night Shifts; Minimum Overtime
(C) Including Rented Warehouse Space
(D) Zenith Only
(E) Includes Administrative, Sales, Engineering and Production
(F) See comments, preceding pages, on Lines 2 and 11

Roblin-Seaway Industries, Inc. (R)

INTRODUCTION

MR. DANIEL ROBLIN, JR., was considering the decision Roblin-Seaway Industries, Inc., should make regarding a vertical integration move. Mr. Roblin had on his desk a detailed report from A. J. Boynton & Co. evaluating a proposal to build continuous billet casting facilities. This proposal was designed to allow Roblin-Seaway Industries, Inc. to cast billets to supply its rod and bar mill rather than to continue the existing policy of purchasing billets. This proposal would also allow the company to consume steel scrap collected by its scrap division rather than to sell all the scrap to other steel companies.

BACKGROUND

Roblin-Seaway Industries, Inc., had been incorporated in 1960 in order to consolidate Roblin Incorporated and Seaway Steel Corporation. The purchase, processing, and sale of metal scrap by the Roblin Division and the manufacture and sale of steel rod and bar by the Seaway Steel Division remained the primary activities of Roblin-Seaway Industries, Inc., at the beginning of 1963. (See Exhibits 1 and 2 for recent financial statements.)

Daniel Roblin, Jr., had formed Roblin Incorporated in 1957 by merging the demolition and scrap operations of a family-owned business with another western New York scrap concern, Morrison & Risman Company. The Roblin Division purchased steel scrap from retail scrap dealers and industrial plants and received scrap from the division's building demolition activities.[1] The scrap was sorted, graded, sized, and baled in Roblin plants in Buffalo and Albany, New York. The metal was sold throughout the northeastern United States to steel mills, iron and steel foundries, and

---

[1] The Roblin Division purchased the scrap from the Seaway Steel rolling operation. This scrap amounted to 3 percent of the good production off the rolling mill.

Exhibit 1

ROBLIN-SEAWAY INDUSTRIES, INC., AND SUBSIDIARIES
Consolidated Balance Sheet
December 31, 1962 and December 31, 1961

Assets	*1962*	*1961*
Current Assets		
Cash	$ 143,178	$ 209,845
Accounts receivable	1,065,873	1,218,716
Inventories at lower of cost or market		
Raw materials	1,021,141	783,778
Finished goods	609,184	762,937
Scrap inventories	1,428,227	741,902
	$3,058,552	$2,288,617
Refundable taxes on income—estimated	80,212	-0-
Prepaid expenses	54,201	47,041
Total Current Assets	$4,402,016	$3,764,219
Plant and Equipment—based on cost		
Machinery and equipment	$1,136,622	$ 633,589
Furniture and fixtures	39,385	36,425
	$1,176,007	$ 670,014
Less allowances for depreciation	292,889	194,967
	$ 883,118	$ 475,047
	70,506	39,933
Leasehold improvements—net	$ 953,624	$ 514,980
Other Assets		
Advances to landlord ($25,000) and prepaid rentals	55,000	84,000
Cash surrender value of officers' life insurance	22,094	15,552
Sundry receivables and investments	21,047	36,864
Contracts to lease rolling mill assets, etc.	-0-	96,181
Deferred production development costs	58,276	-0-
Unamortized debt discount and expense	84,858	-0-
Unamortized organization expense	5,914	7,863
	$ 247,189	$ 240,460
	$5,602,829	$4,519,659

Liabilities		
Current Liabilities		
Notes payable—banks, partly secured	$1,772,155	$1,594,859
Accounts payable and accrued expenses	1,208,210	1,253,279
Salaries and wages and taxes thereon	69,431	66,936
Federal and state taxes on income-estimated	-0-	102,443
Current maturities of long-term debt	47,454	19,333
Dividend declared on preferred stock	4,980	4,980
Total Current Liabilities	$3,102,230	$3,041,830
Long-Term Debt (less current maturities)		
5½% debentures, due January 1, 1971	481,323	481,323
6% subordinated debentures, due January 1, 1978	710,000	-0-
6% convertible subordinated debentures, due July 1, 1982	467,000	-0-
Equipment purchase obligation	83,241	-0-
	$1,741,564	$ 481,323
Stockholders' Equity		
Preferred stock, 5½% cumulative, convertible:		
Authorized 3,700 shares; issued 3,622 shares	362,200	362,200
Class A stock, par value $0.10 a share:		
Authorized 1,750,000 shares; issued 305,341 shares	30,534	9,450
Common stock, par value $0.10 a share:		
Authorized 400,000 shares; issued 329,067 shares	32,907	15,928
Paid-in surplus	243,330	281,328
Retained earnings	90,064	327,600
	$ 759,035	$ 996,506
	$5,602,829	$4,519,659

Exhibit 2

ROBLIN-SEAWAY INDUSTRIES, INC., AND SUBSIDIARIES
Statement of Consolidated Income and Retained Earnings

	1962	1961
Net Sales	$13,898,306	$14,173,488
Cost of products and services sold	13,147,108	12,981,899
	$ 751,198	$ 1,191,589
Selling, administrative and general expense	690,429	763,028
Interest and other finance expense	256,556	155,929
	$ 946,985	$ 918,957
	($ 195,787)	$ 272,632
Sundry other income	25,055	9,106
Income–(Loss) before depreciation, amortization and taxes on income	($ 170,732)	$ 281,738
Provision for depreciation and amortization	107,802	77,653
Income–(Loss) before taxes thereon	($ 278,534)	$ 204,085
Taxes on income-estimated; (denotes refund)		
Federal	(75,688)	62,148
New York State Franchise	(4,487)	13,340
	$ (80,175)	$ 75,488
Net Income–(loss)	($ 198,359)	$ 128,597
Retained earnings at beginning of period	327,600	232,594
	$ 129,241	$ 361,191
Less cash dividends:		
On preferred stock	14,941	14,941
On Class A stock ($0.08 a share)	24,236	18,650
	$ 39,177	$ 33,591
Retained Earnings at End of Period	$ 90,064	$ 327,600

Statement of Consolidated Paid-up Surplus

Balance at January 1, 1962	$ 281,328
Less par value of 380,670 shares of Class A stock and common stock issued in connection with five-for-two stock split, plus fractions purchased	38,273
	$ 243,055
Add proceeds from sale of warrants	275
Balance at December 31, 1962	$ 243,330

brass, copper and aluminum foundries and ingot makers. As the demand for scrap had decreased in this country in the late 1950s, Roblin Incorporated had pioneered in the use of the Saint Lawrence Seaway to export scrap, first to Europe and then to Japan. In its last full year of independent operations, 1959, Roblin, Inc., reported a profit before taxes of $170,000 on sales of $6,500,000. These profits were achieved on a net worth of about $100,000 and long-term debts totalling about $400,000.

Seaway Steel Corporation had been formed in 1959 to take over the rolling operations of the Buffalo Bolt Company. When Houdaille Industries decided to suspend operations at its Buffalo Bolt Division after 104 years of production at the North Tonawanda (about 10 miles north of Buffalo, New York) plant, a group of five Buffalo businessmen (including Mr. Daniel A. Roblin, Jr.) purchased the real estate, the rolling mill machinery, and the steel billet inventory. The men set up a real estate corporation, Niagara Industrial Park, Inc., to own and manage the 30 acres of land and the 10 buildings (with a total of 500,000 square feet of factory floor space). The real estate corporation then leased a part of the land and facilities to the Seaway Steel Corporation.

The Seaway Steel Corporation was established to own and operate the rolling mill. The company was to manufacture and sell hot rolled steel rod and bar of "cold-heading" quality used to make nuts and bolts. Buffalo Bolt had sold rod and bar of this quality as well as consumed this rod and bar in its own operations. Manufacture of nuts and bolts at this location ended with the demise of Buffalo Bolt.

In addition to the steel rolling, Seaway Steel cast and rolled rods and bars of nickel. Some of the nickel was sold for use in electroplating and some was subsequently drawn into nickel wire and sold for the manufacture of welding rod, corrosion resistant filters and resistance wire. The nickel was sold for about $2,000 per ton and made up about 10 percent of the dollar volume of the sales of the Seaway Steel Division.

Roblin-Seaway, Inc., also had wholly or partly owned subsidiaries operating in the railway equipment industry, the demolition industry, and the Buffalo stevedore industry. Exhibit 3 shows financial data for each of the two major divisions in Roblin-Seaway.

SEAWAY STEEL PRODUCTS

The primary product of the Roblin-Seaway rolling mill was steel rod and bars of cold-heading quality ranging in diameter from approximately $5/16$ inch to $1\frac{1}{2}$. "Rod" and "bar" were the same products except that rod was sold in coil form and bar was sold in straight lengths. Although most of the mill products were round in cross-section, about 10 percent of the production was "flats," rectangular shapes from 1 inch $\times$ $5/8$ inch down to $7/16 \times 7/32$ inch.

The process used in mass production of manufacturing bolts from circular rod or wire required considerable plastic deformation to shape the head of the bolt. The upsetting (impact forming) of the head accentuated any surface defects on the metal such as seams or slivers. Because of these processing requirements, the metal had to be of a very high quality with great uniformity of structure and composition. The quality requirements demanded close control of the metal at all stages of the production: melting, rolling, heat treating, and drawing. Cold-heading quality rod and bar was produced in many different carbon steel and alloy steel compositions.

Because the Seaway rolling mill had been used exclusively for rolling metal of this quality and because the common ownership of the rolling

Exhibit 3
ROBLIN-SEAWAY INDUSTRIES, INC., AND SUBSIDIARIES†

	Roblin-Seaway, Incorporated			Roblin Division			Seaway Steel Division		
	1961 12 months	1962 12 months	1963 1st quarter	1961 12 months	1962 12 months	1963 1st quarter	1961 12 months	1962 12 months	1963 1st quarter
Net sales	$14,672,032	14,278,496	3,371,575	8,263,512	5,767,111	941,058	5,773,720	8,074,961	2,174,844
Tons	244,008	210,785	39,416	208,568	161,486	25,583	35,440	49,299	13,833
Purchases	$12,900,192	12,144,342	2,315,984	7,402,847	5,948,554	687,846	5,497,345	6,030,328	1,604,525
Tons	257,179	241,859	34,704	212,203	192,408	20,861	44,976	49,451	13,843
Beginning inventory	$ 780,969	2,288,617	3,041,897	462,790	670,183	1,344,683	318,179	1,618,434	1,537,214
Tons	14,540	27,711	58,949	13,103	16,738	47,806	1,437	10,973	11,143
Ending inventory	$ 2,288,617	3,058,552	2,880,441	670,183	1,344,682	1,204,810	1,618,434	1,543,870	1,541,747
Tons	27,711	58,785	54,237	16,738	47,660	43,084	10,973	11,125	11,153
Profit on material	$ 3,279,488	2,904,089	894,135	1,068,058	493,056	113,339	1,576,630	1,970,069	574,852
Variable manufacturing expenses	$ 1,765,998	1,687,422	538,931	394,311	235,606	58,269	882,175	1,079,446	317,396
Profit after variable manufacturing expenses	$ 1,513,490	1,216,667	355,204	673,747	257,450	55,070	694,455	890,623	257,456
Fixed manufacturing expenses	$ 515,308	515,769	152,384	207,139	190,578	48,424	265,681	272,842	81,336
Profit after fixed manufacturing expenses	$ 998,182	700,898	202,820	466,608	66,872	6,646	428,774	617,781	176,120
Division G.S. & A.	$ 511,819	553,842	130,989	222,997	237,841	41,760	225,222	225,441	63,965
Division profit (loss)	$ 486,363	147,056	71,831	243,611	(170,969)	(35,114)	203,552	392,340	112,155
Main office G.S. & A.	$ 102,401	140,117	34,510						
Other income	$ 9,106	25,055	3,915						
Other expense	$ 33,054	53,973	13,843						
Finance charges	$ 155,929	256,556	65,415						
Net profit (loss) before taxes	$ 204,085	(278,535)	(38,022)						
Taxes	$ 75,488	80,175*	—						
Net profit (loss) after taxes	$ 128,597	(198,360)	(38,022)						

* Tax credit.
† All tonnage figures refer to steel tonnage. The dollar sales figures include nonferrous scrap for the Roblin Division and nickel sales for the Seaway Steel Division.

mill and the bolt-making facilities had forced the Buffalo Bolt rolling mill management and crews to be particularly aware of the cost of poor quality, the Roblin-Seaway management was convinced that the Seaway quality was at least the equal of other manufacturers' and was probably better.

SEAWAY STEEL FACILITIES

Seaway Steel's equipment was located in two large and several smaller buildings leased from the real estate corporation described earlier. The primary production machinery was a 16-stand hot rolling mill designed to produce rounds and flats from 4 inch $\times$ 4 inch $\times$ 15 foot and $2\frac{1}{2}$ inch $\times$ $2\frac{1}{2}$ inch $\times$ 15 foot billets. The mill had the capability of coiling the metal coming out of the last stand or shearing it in straight lengths.

Although the rolling mill was over 30 years old, an analysis by a consulting firm at the time of the incorporation of Seaway Steel showed that the mill could be operated in competition with more modern mills. The only significant feature of more recent mills which the Seaway Steel mill lacked was repeater tables which guided the beginning of the bar out of one stand into the next.

Before entering the Seaway Steel mill, billets were heated to a red-hot condition in a billet heating furnace. The billets traveled through 10 stands in a straight line. The greatly lengthened bars then snaked back and forth through six stands located with common axes of rotation. As a bar came through a roll, a catcher grabbed the metal with a pair of tongs and looped the metal around and into the next pass.

The mill was prevented from rolling heavier coils from longer billets by the size of the coiling mechanisms and the width of the billet heating furnaces. Mr. Roblin estimated that it would cost $400,000 to enlarge these facilities. The alternative of providing thicker billets, for instance 6 inches $\times$ 6 inches, would require adding a stand or stands and the relocation of the billet heating furnaces as well as enlarging the coiling facilities. This would involve an investment of more than $500,000.

The large size of the mill crew (27 direct workers and 21 indirect workers) and the time required to change rolls, made size changes expensive. Although some small size changes could be accomplished by changing only the final rolls, other size or shape changes required changing all 16 roll stands. The 45 to 60-day delivery promises common in the industry were designed to provide mills with time to order and receive billets, (two to three weeks) and to fit the order into a monthly schedule which rolled each size only once. A firm emphasizing fast delivery would have to be prepared to make some adjustments in its delivery promises and rolling schedules on those occasions when a customer needed the metal faster.

The rate of production depended on the sizes rolled: $\frac{3}{4}$ inch diameter rod could be rolled at a rate of 26 tons per hour while $\frac{3}{16}$ inch diameter bar was rolled at a rate of 9 tons per hour. In a typical month of two-shift operations, about 60 different combinations of size, shape, and straightness might be produced. About one-eighth of the time might be spent changing roll sizes. On such a basis, 130 tons per 8-hour shift was considered the average productive capacity of the mill.

In order to facilitate the further manufacture of the rod or bar into nuts and bolts, a variety of different finishing operations were performed on the metal. Some customers performed these operations themselves, others purchased metal in treated form. Annealing and spheroidizing were the two principal forms of applying heat to develop desired properties. Seaway Steel had four annealing furnaces which had a combined capacity to anneal or spheroidize about 40 tons of steel in a 24-hour day. Standard charges for these processes were $19 per ton for annealing and $35 per ton for spheroidizing.

Most of the rod and bar produced by this mill was eventually drawn into wire by Seaway Steel or its customers. In addition to reducing the diameter of the metal, this process improved the surface quality and strength of the metal. Seaway Steel owned wire drawing machines, wire pointers, wire straighteners, and pickling and liming tanks. About 810 tons per month could be drawn to smaller dimensions and sold in wire form, but the current production volume of wire products was about 250 tons per month.

SEAWAY STEEL MARKET

The largest porton (70 percent) of Seaway Steel's sales of steel were to nut and bolt manufacturers, the fastener industry; the balance went to manufacturers of other forged and cold drawn products. Seaway Steel sold rod and bar in direct competition with most of the major steel companies and a number of smaller independent concerns. Prices tended to be the same from different suppliers in this market. One of the primary desires of rod and bar purchasers was the establishment of a relationship with a supplier which would enable the purchaser to receive steel in a time of steel shortage. From its establishment, Seaway Steel faced the very difficult task of convincing potential customers that Seaway Steel would provide a more reliable relationship than the relationship the customer enjoyed with his existing suppliers.

Seaway Steel had been fortunate in starting operations during the 1959 steel strike. The stock of billets purchased with the rolling mill and the opportunity to put the experienced Buffalo Bolt rolling mill crews to work allowed Seaway Steel to sell rod and bar while almost all the other mills in the country were strike bound.

The Seaway Steel management was also attempting to capitalize on the small size of the firm and the firm's ability to provide service to its customers. It was possible for a Seaway Steel customer to call up the president of Seaway Steel to ask him to change the rolling schedule to meet an urgent customer need. The company had advertised in trade journals its willingness to respond to such requests. In order to increase its flexibility, the company had started a policy of stocking billets of four of the common compositions.

Most manufacturers of nuts and bolts, like other steel consumers, purchased from several suppliers in an effort to increase their ability to obtain steel in times of steel shortages. The contractual relationship between Seaway Steel and the International Association of Machinists rather than the United Steelworkers of America provided a good argument for including Seaway Steel as one of a group of suppliers.

Against these advantages in the market, the Roblin-Seaway management was aware of the disadvantages faced by the company. Shortly after the Seaway Steel Corporation was formed, a well-known consulting firm was retained to examine the sales possibilities and to develop a suitable sales program. The consulting firm pointed out a number of difficulties.

1. The fastener industry was a declining industry. Although purchases of hot rolled bar and wire by the 300 firms in the fastener industry fluctuated greatly, the trend was downward. The consulting firm's figures of steel purchases in the size range supplied by Seaway Steel showed that annual purchases fell from 785,000 tons in 1954 through 1956 to 618,000 tons in 1957 through 1959.

2. The nut and bolt industry was dominated by a few firms. Seven firms were believed to consume over 50 percent of the steel in the fastener industry. Three of these firms were divisions of large integrated steel producers. It would probably be very difficult to persuade any one of the other four major concerns to replace an existing source with a small supplier like Seaway.

3. Transportation costs limited Seaway sales to the Detroit, Cleveland, Pittsburgh, Middle Atlantic, and New England areas, about 40 percent of the fastener industry was thus outside the geographic limitations of Seaway's sales.

4. Many customers were unable to see quality differences between suppliers of cold-heading rod and bar.

5. There was a tendency toward heavier coils which Seaway was unable to supply.

6. Some customers thought the dependence of Seaway on billets produced by integrated steel companies might mean that Seaway would be unable to supply its customers during periods of steel shortages.

The growth of Seaway Steel's sales from $4,400,000 in the first 12 months of its operation (September 1959 to September 1960) to $8,000,000 in 1962, indicated to the Roblin-Seaway management that these disadvantages were not as serious as they were originally thought to be.

STATEMENT OF THE PROBLEM

The Roblin Division sold about 160,000 tons of scrap in 1962 to integrated steel manufacturers. In the same year, the Seaway Steel Division purchased just under 50,000 tons of billets from the same or similar integrated steel manufacturers. The management of Roblin-Seaway had long been interested in filling the gap, that is, to use scrap in the manufacture of its own billets. Exhibit 4 gives some price data in these two markets.

Exhibit 4

SUMMARY STEEL STATISTICS

Quoted Mill Prices

	Billets Blooms Slabs Carbon Rerolling Bethlehem Mill, Lackawanna, N.Y.	*Hot Rolled Carbon Bars Bethlehem Mill, Lackawanna, N.Y.*	*Scrap No. 1 Bundles Buffalo*	*Annual Scrap Purchases by Steel Companies in Year Completed or Being Completed*
1/2/63	$80.00 per ton	$113.50 per ton	$21–$22 per ton	16,801,165 tons
12/27/61. . .	80.00	113.50	27– 28	17,890,128
12/28/60. . .	80.00	113.50	23– 24	18,172,856
12/30/59. . .	80.00	113.50	37– 38	19,924,920
12/31/58. . .	80.00	113.50	33– 34	16,359,790
1/8/58	77.50	108.50	29– 30	22,632,337
1/2/57	74.00	101.50	62– 63	27,499,845
12/27/55. . .	68.50	93.00	45– 46	26,366,539
12/29/54. . .	64.00	86.00	30– 31	18,711,322
12/31/53. . .	62.00	83.00	28– 29	24,703,474
12/31/52. . .	59.00	79.00	43– OPS Ceiling	25,784,695

Note: Although the quoted prices from the Bethlehem Steel Co., Lackawanna Mill (near Buffalo) given in *Steel* were for grades of lesser quality than the billets purchased by Seaway and the bar sold by Seaway Steel, they provide an indication of the movement of prices experienced by Seaway Steel. At the beginning of 1963 the average Seaway Steel purchase price for billets was $115.00 per ton and the average sale price for rod and bar was $153.00 per ton. Annealing added $19.00 to this price and spheroidizing added $33.00. The scrap price is a more accurate guide to the price of scrap sold by Roblin.

Source: The price columns were taken from weekly price quotations provided by *Steel* Magazine. Scrap volumes were provided by the American Iron & Steel Institute Annual Reports.

Until recent times, the traditional method of casting steel into large ingots and then rolling the ingots to blooms and then to billets had offered a number of very significant advantages over the intuitively more logical approach of casting steel to the desired billet dimensions. First, the large ingots allowed rapid casting and did not permit the steel to solidify before the open-hearth furnace load was poured into the molds. Second, for those products where surface condition was important it was cheaper to scarf (remove the surface imperfections) on a large ingot. Third, the working of the steel as it was rolled down in size improved the smoothness of the surface, filled in any cavities in the metal and increased the strength of the metal.

Installation of open-hearth furnaces, soaking pits, a blooming mill, and a billet mill to make steel in this fashion was prohibitively expensive for a firm of the size of Roblin-Seaway, Inc. (Either one of the mills by itself would cost $10 million to $15 million.)

Several technological advances raised the possibility of producing billets of acceptable quality with a much smaller capital investment. The first was the development of oxygen converters and electric furnaces which produced steel economically in much smaller quantities than open-hearth furnaces. The next was the development of a new continuous casting process. This process could be designed to cast quickly enough to keep up with the output of economically attractive oxygen converters or electric furnaces. In addition continuous casting provided a surface greatly superior to that of a cast ingot. Since experience had shown that the size reduction on Roblin-Seaway's rod and bar mill was sufficient to provide the necessary improvement in properties which was required for its products, the new casting process might be attractive.

Continuous casting involved pouring the molten metal into a mold with no bottom. As the metal solidified it was removed from the bottom of the mold thus providing space for a continuous stream of incoming molten metal. The concept of continuous casting was over 100 years old but it had only developed to the point of economic attractiveness after the Second World War. In 1962 there were more than 50 continuous casting machines in operation or in construction throughout the world. Although the machines produced a wide variety of shapes, volumes, and compositions, none of the installations were in the United States. Exhibit 5 is a schematic drawing of a continuous casting machine.

Mr. Roblin had hired A. J. Boynton & Co., an engineering consulting firm with experience in steelmaking processes, to evaluate the feasibility and economics of continuous casting.

Mr. Roblin had specified that the evaluation should be based on the use of two top charged direct arc electric furnaces equipped with oxygen lances. The modified 11-foot shell diameter furnaces would each have a cubic capacity of 18 tons and a melting capacity of 9 tons per hour. Mr. Roblin estimated that modified 12-foot-diameter furnaces with a cubic capacity of 20 tons and a melting capacity of 10 tons per hour could be installed for an additional $25,000 apiece.

Mr. Roblin had further specified that the process should be evaluated on the basis of a capacity of 60,000 tons of billets per year with a possible expansion to 120,000 tons. The facilities were to be located on the old Buffalo Bolt property.

Excerpts from the report are shown in the Appendix. The full report contained detailed descriptions of the equipment and facilities and complete staffing patterns. Only small portions of the report are reproduced here.

Exhibit 5
DIAGRAM OF CONTINUOUS CASTING PROCESS

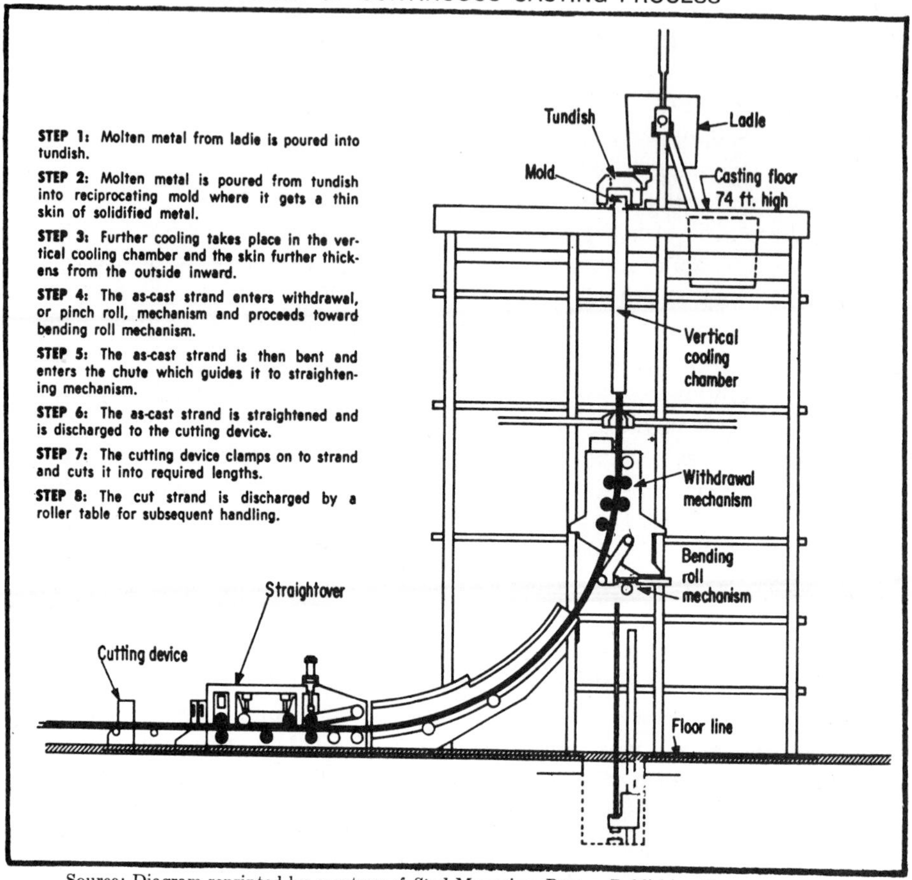
STEP 1: Molten metal from ladie is poured into tundish.
STEP 2: Molten metal is poured from tundish into reciprocating mold where it gets a thin skin of solidified metal.
STEP 3: Further cooling takes place in the vertical cooling chamber and the skin further thickens from the outside inward.
STEP 4: The as-cast strand enters withdrawal, or pinch roll, mechanism and proceeds toward bending roll mechanism.
STEP 5: The as-cast strand is then bent and enters the chute which guides it to straightening mechanism.
STEP 6: The as-cast strand is straightened and is discharged to the cutting device.
STEP 7: The cutting device clamps on to strand and cuts it into required lengths.
STEP 8: The cut strand is discharged by a roller table for subsequent handling.
Tundish
Ladle
Mold
Casting floor
74 ft. high
Vertical
cooling
chamber
Withdrawal
mechanism
Bending
roll
mechanism
Straightover
Cutting device
Floor line

Source: Diagram reprinted by courtesy of *Steel* Magazine, Penton Publishing Company.

In the report, the consulting firm suggested that Roblin-Seaway should purchase billets produced by the new process to see if they could be rolled into satisfactory rod and bar. Roblin-Seaway had followed this suggestion with billets of several different killed and semikilled compositions. Rod and bar produced from the continuous cast billets was very satisfactory and did not require extensive scarfing or conditioning before rolling.

In considering this proposal, Mr. Roblin believed that he would be able to secure the necessary financing. He thought that a program such as this might qualify for loans from the Small Business Administration, the Area Redevelopment Administration, and the New York State Job Development Agency. These organizations might be willing to loan $3 million on a 20-year loan at 4 percent. Additional financing at a higher rate of interest (he thought 6 percent might be an average figure) up to $1,500,000 could be raised from a bank, the equipment manufacturer, and further capitalization sold to the backers of Roblin-Seaway, Inc.

APPENDIX

CONSULTANTS' REPORT ON CONTINUOUS CASTING

A. *Process Description*

In the nonferrous metal field, the continuous casting machines in use are based on several widely different concepts of design and operation. This same condition does not hold for the steel casting applications, where most all of the production units are about identical in their basic operating principles.

Currently, a machine for continuously casting steel features the use of an open-ended, water-cooled, short copper mold arranged in a vertical position. The top end of the mold receives the stream of molten steel from an overhead ladle that contains part or all of a heat made in the steelmaking furnace(s). Control of the stream and maintenance of a clean separation of steel and slag are enhanced with the use of a small refractory lined vessel (referred to as a tundish) placed intermediate between the ladle and mold. The steel travels downward with the section exterior being solidified by indirect water cooling during passage through the mold. The steel section issues from the bottom end of the mold and receives additional uniform and controlled cooling by direct water sprays. When the interior of the section is completely solidified, the strand is cut to the desired lengths, and these individual lengths are routed for final cooling, stocking, and subsequent processing. The downward movement of the steel is achieved through the use of withdrawal rolls contacting the cast section ahead of the level of the cut-off unit. At the start of the cast, the travel of the strand is effected by utilizing a dummy billet threaded up through the withdrawal rolls and into the bottom of the mold.

Most all machines employ oxygen torches synchronized with the travel of the strand to cut the steel while in the vertical. More recently, several machines have been provided with rolls for bending the strand into a horizontal position prior to the cutting or shearing operation. This innovation serves to reduce the over-all height of the machine, and makes feasible a future possibility of continuously heating and rolling extremely long lengths of the cast steel section.

Though some machines in the past have employed a fixed mold, the units now being offered are based generally on furnishing a reciprocating mold. Such mold movement is effected either by cams, eccentrics, or spring mounting. It is in this matter of mold movement and such other features as rated casting speed and mold design, where there are discernible differences between the various machine builders.

Individual machines now in operation and/or under construction are designed to cast from one to eight strands out of a single ladle of steel. The multistrand machines are equipped with separate molds and often individual tundishes, drives, and withdrawal rolls to permit independent operation of each strand. Selection of the number of strands for a specific application is generally dictated by such considerations as:

1. Design casting speed, as influenced by the machine design, the section size, and the steel grades.
2. Time limit for holding steel in the supply ladle.
3. Type of supply ladle used, i.e., bottom pour, lip pour, or syphon.
4. Desired or required amount of steel to cast in the unit.
5. Advisability of providing reserve strands to accommodate necessary strand maintenance and possible breakdown.

B. *Productive Capacity*

Development of the annual production tonnage from the casting machine and the operating turn requirements is given by the succeeding figures. These figures are based on employing something less than the normal permissible time for casting, in order to secure sufficient time following a heat to clean

Annual desired production of good billets—tons	60,000
Estimated yield—cut billets on cooling beds to good finished billets—percent	98.0*
Annual production of cut billets on cooling bed—tons. . . .	61,224
Estimated yield—molten steel in molds to cut billets on cooling beds—percent	97.5
Annual molten steel in casting machine molds—tons	62,794 Total 18,838 (30%–2½-inch squares) 43,956 (70%–4-inch squares)
Estimated average casting speeds per strand—inches per minute.	–100 for 4-inch squares 180 for 2½-inch squares
Expected unit weight of cast sections (based on bulk density of 450 pounds per cubic feet)—pounds per lineal foot.	50 for 4-inch squares 19.5 for 2½-inch squares
Average casting rate per strand—pounds per minute	416.7 for 4-inch squares 292.5 for 2½-inch squares
Normal permissible time limit for casting ordinary carbon steel in 13- to 18-ton covered (and fired) lip-pour ladles previously preheated—minutes.	60 to 75
Selected average casting time per heat—minutes.	42½†
Average steel tonnage in molds during selected casting time—two strands—tons	17.7 for 4-inch squares 12.4 for 2½-inch squares
Selected average time of heat delivery—hours	1½ (16 heats per 24 hours)
Steel tonnage in molds per day (assuming all of one size cast in any one day)—tons	283.2 for 4-inch squares 198.4 for 2½-inch squares
Steel tonnage in molds per year—(based on 250 days per year—with 95 days on 2½-inch billets and 155 days on 4-inch billets)	43,896 for 4-inch squares 18,848 for 2½-inch squares 62,744 for both sizes (Checks within 0.1 percent of requirement figures)

* This yield figure is intended to reflect losses from off-analysis and low-temperature heats and poorly cooled billets. The figure is conservative and actually is largely a function of the care and experience of the labor force. After an adequate period of plant operation, some improvement in this yield figure should be realized.

† With heats provided every 1½ hours, this allows an average 47½ minutes between successive heats to remove the empty ladle, run out the end of the cast strand, clean up, ready casting unit for the next heat, receive a full ladle, allow steel to cool to casting temperature, and begin the casting operation. Time is available to change molds of the same size, but we question whether there will be sufficient time in these 47½ minutes to change mold size and make the machine adjustments necessary for casting a different billet size. Accordingly we have considered that the size of billets run will be changed a maximum of once a week, and that this changeover will be done on Saturday. Production cost estimate outlined later in this report includes the overtime expense for a crew to change molds and adjust the machine presumably each Saturday A.M.

up and make ready for the next successive heat. Operating figures are based on three eight-hour turns per day and five days per week.

In the matter of supplying steel to the casting machine, it has been noted earlier that the electric furnaces must deliver steel at the rate of one heat per 1½ operating hours. The weight of steel in the heat will include metal for ladle skulls and scrap, tundish and runner skulls and scrap, and occasionally, steel that is cast as scrap ingots during machine emergencies. The development of the demands on the furnaces is noted as follows:

Average steel tonnage in molds (two strands) from one heat—tons	17.7 for 4-inch squares 12.4 for 2½-inch squares
Estimated yield—molten steel in ladle to molten steel in molds—percent	98
Average steel tonnage in ladle—one heat—tons	18.1 for 4-inch squares 12.7 for 2½-inch squares
Required average heat time *per* considered furnace—tap-to-tap-hours.	3

As stated previously, the demands on the melt shop to supply steel for the continuous casting machine should pose no problems for the considered modified 11-foot electric furnaces. However, the difficulty that might be experienced will possibly be the inability of the casting machine to process the required 16 heats per day, every day, for five days per week and 50 weeks per year. If this situation is encountered and billet demand is at the full level of 60,000 tons per year, it will be necessary to operate the plant at more than 15 turns per week, maintaining perhaps a schedule of as much as 18 turns weekly.

Eventual Future Expansion

As demand may grow in the future beyond the initial 60,000 tons of billets per year, this growth, if not excessive, can be met by operating the facilities additional turns. If a 15 turns per week operation can produce the annual 60,000 tons, then in direct proportion, a 20-turn (per week) schedule would permit an increase in billet production to 80,000 tons per year. More realistically, we would expect the 20-turn operation would yield something less than the 80,000 tons of annual billet production, owing to the difficulty experienced in attempting to process 16 heats each day on the considered casting machine.

The procedure of securing an increase in plant output through the media of operating more turns has the advantage that no marked addition is required in investment. Production costs per ton of billet product, exclusive of fixed charges and overhead items, would remain almost unchanged.

If future demands envision a growth to as high a level as 120,000 tons of billets per year, then expansion of the physical plant facilities becomes necessary. Such expansion would include principally the following items of work as shown generally on Drawing No. 1191A-1:

a. Addition of a second casting machine (presumably also a two-strand unit).
b. An extension westward of the casting building.
c. Additional structure and facilities for billet cut-off, cooling, collection, and conditioning.
d. Extensions to the melt shop for additional scrap storage and relining areas.

The plant would operate on a 20-turns-per-week schedule, with each of the melt shop furnaces producing heats with a tap-to-tap time of about two hours. The 24 heats tapped daily from the two furnaces would be divided between the two casting machines, each machine receiving and processing 12 heats per day. Heat size, ranging from about 13 to 18 tons, would remain unchanged.

Such a plan for expansion offers a minimum of investment needs for a plant fulfilling the ultimate demands for billets. Further, the expanded operation would show some improvement in labor costs per billet ton (compared to the initial operation), due largely to an increase in the number of heats produced in the melt shop.

Alternate plans of some merit involve the use of larger electric furnaces, provision of additional strands for the initial casting machine, and operation at say an 18-turns-per-week schedule. For these cases, the investment in the initial construction is generally higher than the presently considered plan, though there possibly will be little difference in the total investment of the combined initial and eventual future construction. Advantages secured would appear to include a decrease in the production cost and a potential for the plant to ultimately produce annual billet tonnages even higher than the prescribed 120,000 tons. Since Seaway management has prescribed the furnaces to be considered for this analysis, detailed investigation of the desirability of providing larger furnaces for the project is considered to be beyond the scope of this report.

C. *Quality Considerations*

The continuous casting process has been applied commercially and successfully in a full range of billet sizes starting from about 2-inch squares and proceeding upwards to 10-inch squares and larger. Thus, the 2½-inch and 4-inch squares contemplated by Seaway should provide no difficulty insofar as section size is concerned. The 15-foot billet length is also no problem, and requires only a design and arrangement of the facilities to accommodate the desired lengths.

As to steel grades, all of the plain carbon steels ranging from the very low carbon contents up to nearly 1 percent carbon; most all of the low alloy steels, and many of the stainless steels and special high alloy steels have been continuously cast with good results. These have been primarily killed and semikilled steels.[1] Similar success has also been achieved in casting rimming steels but only in medium and large slab and bloom sections. The two major machine builders have both stated that it is not possible to continuously cast rimming steels in as small sizes as the 2½-inch and 4-inch squares.[2] Thus, the continuous casting process can satisfactorily produce all of Seaway's grade requirements except those specified as rimmed steels. These particular steels could, of course, be continuously cast successfully as semikilled or killed. However, it is advisable to determine whether customers will accept these substitutions.

A proper continuous casting operation that incorporates an optimum withdrawal roll pressure and uniform and adequate spray cooling will yield billets that are regular in shape and have a good smooth surface. Ripple marks that appear on the surface correspond generally to the mold reciprocations, and these marks will disappear in the initial stages of a succeeding rolling operation. To ensure full customer acceptance of rolled products made from continuously-cast billets, it will be necessary for Seaway to test roll sample billets that have been produced by this method.

In the matter of the internal structure, continuous-cast steel cross-sections show the expected cast columnar crystal structure with little or no segregation. Some central porosity is in evidence, particularly after etching, with the low-carbon steels showing more of this porosity than the higher-carbon grades. With a suitable intensity of the spray cooling below the mold, this porosity can be kept to a minimum. To develop the required physicals in the end product, the cast steel sections require hot working by forging or rolling, and this hot working operation[3] both modifies the cast structure and completely welds up the center porosity. Products rolled or forged from continuously-cast billets and slabs have been found to be at least equal in quality to rolled products derived from conventional ingots.

D. *Capital Costs of New Facilities*

The estimated capital requirements for the melting and continuous casting facilities described earlier in this report total $4,832,000. A summary of the

---

[1] The terms, "killed," "semikilled," and "rimmed" refer to the suppression of gas evolution in the casting of the steel. Killed steel requires the addition of deoxidizers to the molten steel to eliminate the formation of oxygen and carbon monoxide in the casting process. Semikilled steel allows a small amount of gases to evolve. These gases form small blowholes in the steel. Rimmed steel is produced where large amounts of gas are allowed to evolve in the ingot. This causes the formation of honeycomb blowholes near the bottom sides and scattered blowholes in the upper middle portion of a traditionally cast ingot.

[2] Apparently, the rapid cooling in the mold as a result of the high ratio of exposed surface area to billet weight (for the small billets) seriously affects the rimming action and gives rise to serious surface defects.

[3] Required area reduction ratios to be effected by hot working may range from as low as three to one to as high as ten to one, depending upon metal grade and quality and condition of the metal at pouring. One casting machine builder cites a ratio of six to one for carbon steels, and a range of eight to one to ten to one for alloy steel depending on its complexity. On the basis of advice received from Seaway, the smallest area reduction ratio being effected by the present mills is about nine to one. All other ratios are greater.

principal item groups making up this total is given in the following tabulation, supported by Estimate No. C-1191A-1 detail sheets[4] which are submitted with this report as an exhibit.

Account and/or Item Group		Estimated Capital Cost
A. Site Preparation		$ 110,500
B. Melting Department		
Building and structures	$ 610,500	
Cranes	220,000	
Equipment	775,200	
Equipment foundations	23,100	
Piping and wiring	54,000	
Total Melting Department		1,682,800
C. Casting Department		
Buildings and structures	$ 273,000	
Cranes	165,300	
Equipment	1,027,700	
Equipment foundations	20,200	
Piping and wiring	49,000	
Total Casting Department		$1,535,200
D. Auxiliary Departments and Operations		
Laboratory	−	
Mold and service machining	−	
Billet conditioning	6,000	
Melting and casting departments supply materials warehouse	−	
Lubricant storage facilities	−	
Total Auxiliary Departments and Operations		6,000
E. Utilities and Services		
Power supply and distribution	$ 145,500	
Compressed air supply and distribution	79,000	
Oxygen supply and distribution	3,000	
Drinking water supply and distribution	5,000	
Service water supply and distribution	101,500	
Sanitary, storm and return process water disposal systems	29,000	
Gas supply and distribution	5,000	
Communication facilities	10,000	
Fire protection facilities	5,000	
Change house	50,000	
Outside lighting	12,000	
Total Utilities and Services		445,000
F. Roadways, Trackwork, Parking Lot, Clock House		94,200
G. Operating Spares		*Not Included*
Subtotal		$3,873,700
H. General Expense		193,700
I. Contingencies		406,700
J. Engineering		357,900
Grand Total		$4,832,000

---

[4] Detail sheets are not included in this case.

E. *Estimated Production Cost*

The basis of the following production cost estimate is 60,000 and 45,000 net tons of acceptable billets produced per year, 70 percent 4-inch squares and 30 percent 2½-inch all 15-foot lengths carbon steel.

	Pounds per Ton of Billet	Unit Price	Costs per Ton at 60,000 Net Tons Produced*	Costs per Ton at 45,000 Net Tons Produced*
Cost of Metallics				
Steel scrap	2,214.3	$0.0134	$29.67	$29.67
Ferromanganese (7% O + 75% Mn)	12.8	0.127	1.63	1.63
Ferrosilicon (50% Si)	8.5	0.080	0.68	0.68
Aluminum shot	0.9	0.243	0.21	0.21
Total Metallics—Gross			$32.19	$32.19
Credit for scrap	108.6	0.0134	$ 1.46	$ 1.46
Total Metallics—Net			30.73	30.73
Melt Shop—Cost above Metallics				
Direct and indirect labor and assigned maintenance			3.84	3.84
Supervision, technical and clerical			1.22	1.63
Electric power (for melting)			5.34	5.66
Electrodes			3.65	3.65
Fluxes			0.79	0.79
Repairs and maintenance (labor and materials)			1.97	2.24
Furnace and ladle refractories			1.92	2.03
Oxygen			0.45	0.50
Water, gas and other utilities			0.43	0.46
Miscellaneous tools, supplies and lubricants			0.32	0.35
Yard switching and slag disposal			0.43	0.43
Employee benefits			0.76	0.82
Other expense			1.10	1.21
Total Melt Shop Cost above Metallics			22.22	23.61
Total Cost of Molten Steel			$52.95	$54.34

Casting—Cost above Metallics

Direct and indirect labor and assigned maintenance			$ 5.01
Supervision and clerical			1.23
Employee benefits			0.94
Molds	$0.71		
Tundish and runner refractories and nozzles	0.85		
Cutting gases	0.23		
Other miscellaneous supplies and materials	0.28		
Subtotal production supplies and materials		2.07	
Electric power, gas and other utilities		0.66	
Equipment maintenance		0.83	
Other miscellaneous costs		0.55	
Total Casting—Cost above Metallics			$11.29
Subtotal cost of finished billets stocked for			
heating and rolling			65.63
Depreciation†			10.74
Total cost of finished billets stocked for			
heating and rolling‡			$76.37

* Production at 60,000 tons per year is accomplished by working 15 turns per week. Production at 45,000 tons per year assumes 12 turns per week and a 7 percent smaller work crew.

† Based on a 10-year life, as per instructions from Seaway Steel management.

‡ Derived cost excluding interest, taxes, and insurance on investment; administrative and sales expense, general works overhead (plant superintendent, personnel and purchasing department, accounting and cost departments, plant protection, main office expense); product and raw materials inventory expense; locomotive crane expense; income taxes.

Dobbs House (A)

As JERRY MCKENZIE returned to New York in January 1971, he was still struggling with the decision he had been asked to make one month earlier by the president of the Squibb Corporation, the parent of Dobbs House. Consistent with Jerry's personal philosophy that every problem can be reduced to three alternatives, he saw his options as: (1) take a position with Dobbs House as Director of Corporate Planning with the first task of helping the General Manager of the Fast Foods Division; (2) become the General Manager of Fast Foods himself; or (3) continue in his present job on the corporate staff of Squibb in New York. Besides the personal problems involved in a move to Memphis (his wife did not relish the thought of moving south from her home in New York), Jerry, who had never been in a restaurant except to eat before this month, was unsure if he even understood the business well enough to make a well-reasoned decision or present a viable plan of action to Squibb management.

SQUIBB CORPORATION

Squibb Beech-Nut was formed on January 15, 1968 when E. R. Squibb & Sons, Inc. was spun off from the Olin Corporation and simultaneously merged with Beech-Nut, Inc. The merger brought together a leading pharmaceutical company and a well-known manufacturer and marketer of specialty foods, beverages, and confections. Previously, in 1966, Beech-Nut had acquired Dobbs Houses, Inc., a Memphis-based company engaged in airline catering, airport restaurants, coffee shops, and related services. Each of these activities was organized as a separate operating division of the parent corporation.

HISTORY OF DOBBS HOUSE

Dobbs House was variously described by the trade press as the "second largest airline caterer in the world" and as the "sleepy giant of the food industry out in Tennessee." The company was founded during the Depression by James K. Dobbs, Sr., who was described as "running it with an iron fist." Dobbs began his business career as an ambitious car salesman and became, among other things, the largest Ford dealer in the world.

He first became involved in the food business as an investor in the Toddle House chain that began as a 12-unit chain of 11-seat mobile food houses that could be relocated by truck. On moving, they were said to "toddle" from side to side, from which they received their name. At one point Toddle Houses were considered by many as the leader in the fast-food and hamburger business. Dobbs became dissatisfied with his partners and set out to build his own restaurant chain, called Dobbs Houses. He often located his Dobbs Houses across the street from Toddle Houses just as a challenge. In 1961, after years of competition, Dobbs bought out the Toddle House chain.

The "Dobbs concept" of the 1930s was to build small "mom and pop" snack bar units. His overall philosophy was "if you have *good food,* people will find you." A large sign and attractive site were considered by Dobbs as secondary. (See Exhibit 1.) Toddle and Dobbs Houses, open 24 hours

Exhibit 1
DOBBS HOUSE (A)

a day, featured real cream in their coffee, home-made pies, vegetable soup, and their own daily-ground hamburger meat. (See Exhibit 2.)

When James Dobbs Sr. died in 1961, his two sons alternated as president, but because of other interests, they elected to sell the company to Beech-Nut Life Savers in 1966. At the time of the sale, Dobbs Houses, Inc. was traded on the NYSE.

BACKGROUND OF JERRY MCKENZIE

Jerry McKenzie, born in 1941, attended an eastern prep school. After a spotty undergraduate career of two years at an Ivy-League school, he

Exhibit 2
DOBBS HOUSE (A)

Breakfast Varieties

served at any hour

Golden Brown Cream Waffle
with delicious syrup.........60
Golden Brown Pecan Waffle
with delicious syrup.........70
Humpty-Dumpty Eggs
with toast and jelly.........60
Two Eggs any style
with toast and jelly.........60
One Egg any style
with toast and jelly.........40

Delicious Pecan Roll 30
Genuine Country Sausage 55
One patty only 30
Crisp Bacon, 3 strips.........50
Smoked Ham................55
Crispy Hashed Brown Potatoes .30
Dry Cereal, served with milk ...30
Toast and Jelly 20
Orange or Tomato Juice 20-.35

Steakburger Combinations

Steakburger on Bun...........55
Steakburger with Cheese.......65
Doubleburger (two patties).....95
Masterburger
(two patties with cheese)....1.05
Steakburger Plate (one patty
on a bun with potatoes)......85
Steakburger and Vegetable Soup..90
*Above combinations served with
lettuce and tomato 5c extra*

*Steakburger meat from select
cuts of beef – grilled or
broiled to your taste*

Beverages

Hot Coffee (always fresh).......15
Sanka 20
Hot or Iced Tea.............15
Hot Chocolate..............20
Milk 20
Coca Cola 15

Tasty Sandwiches

Ham and Cheese,
with lettuce and tomato......75
Cheese, Bacon, Lettuce and
Tomato 75
Bacon and Egg,
with lettuce and mayonnaise ..75
Bacon, Lettuce and Tomato,
with mayonnaise 65
Ham, with lettuce,
tomato and mayonnaise......70
Grilled Cheese..............40
Fried Egg,
with lettuce and mayonnaise ..45
Lettuce and Tomato, mayonnaise .40

Soups/Salads

Vegetable Soup
prepared daily – piping hot ...40
Lettuce and Tomato Salad 35
Head Lettuce Salad 35
Tossed Vegetable Salad........35

*All salads chilled and served with
your choice of Mayonnaise, Honey
French or 1000 Isle Dressing*

From our Grill and Broiler

TENDERLOIN STEAK
PLATE 2.15
Tender and juicy, grilled to your
taste. Served with individual
Hashed Brown Potatoes,
Chilled Salad,
Choice of our famous Dressings

CHOPPED STEAK..........1.95
Choice cuts blended together by
experienced cooks. Served with
Individual Hashed Brown Potatoes,
Chilled Salad, Choice of our
famous Dressings

Desserts

Black Bottom Pie,
our specialty................35
Apple Pie, rich and tasty.......35
Chocolate Ice Box Cream Pie....35
Southern Karo Pecan Pie.......35

*We have special containers
for carrying out any of the
food on this menu*

the snack bar

Dobbs House
RESTAURANT

terminated his education and worked for a period as a lumberjack in Maine and then joined the Coast Guard. After a two-year stint with the Coast Guard, he moved to New York and obtained a job as a salesman with a chemical company. During this period he married and acquired a new degree of motivation. While holding a full-time job during the day, he finished four years of college in three years at night. After this, he received a Masters of Business Administration with honors from a well-known eastern business school.

Upon graduation, he joined Beech-Nut in 1967 on the recommendation of one of his professors, who was a director of the company. Up until his assignment to investigate Dobbs House, he had worked in various staff functions in New York establishing profit centers, information systems, accounting systems, strategic planning, and acquisition analysis.

He described his personal career strategy up to this point as an attempt at an end run to the top through energetic and high-profile activities in a corporate staff position.

DOBBS HOUSE AS OF 1970

Although Dobbs Houses was sold in 1966, the Dobbs brothers continued to be involved in management until they left active management in August 1970. It was at that time that Squibb management decided to

change Dobbs into what they described as a professionally-run company
(bottom up management and control).

Dobbs House consisted of three separately-managed divisions:

	Sales
Airline Catering and Restaurants (2 divisions)	$ 77 million
Fast Foods	29 million
Total	$106 million

The Airline Catering Division was traditionally profitable, but the 1969
and 1970 slump in airline traffic had seriously eroded the company's profit
margins.

The Airline Restaurant Division was also severely affected by the airline
traffic slump. To further aggrevate the situation, the Fast Foods Division
was showing declining sales and profits, since a record year in 1968. (See
Exhibit 3.) As a result, it appeared that the Dobbs House as a whole

Exhibit 3

FAST FOODS DIVISION INCOME STATEMENTS
January 1970, 1971

Item	January 1970		January 1971	
	Dollars	Percent	Dollars	Percent
Net Sales	$2,109,731	100.0	$2,094,114	100.0
Cost of Sales	1,878,974	89.1	1,963,053	93.8
Materials cost	$ 642,771	30.5	$ 628,460	30.0
Direct labor	668,644	31.7	754,942	36.1
Controllable operating expenses	284,105	13.5	272,955	13.0
Semi-fixed operation expenses	192,338	9.1	196,354	9.4
Managers' compensation	91,116	4.3	110,342	5.3
Gross margin	$ 230,757	10.9	$ 131,061	6.2
Division management	71,925	3.4	119,230	5.7
Earnings from operations	$ 158,832	7.5	$ 11,831	0.5
General and administrative	59,108	2.8	65,353	3.1
Operating income	$ 99,724	4.7	$ (53,522)	(2.6)
Other income, net of other deductions	47,730	2.3	55,000	2.6
Earnings before taxes	$ 147,454	7.0	$ 1,478	nil
Federal income taxes	70,776	3.4	741	nil
Net earnings after taxes	$ 76,678	3.6	$ 737	nil

would show flat earnings and the Fast Foods Division would show a loss
for the first time in over 35 years.

While the problems experienced in the airline-oriented divisions were
expected to be short-term, and probably outside the control of management, Squibb did not feel that the same was true of the traditionally stable
and profitable Fast Foods Division. The anxiety in Squibb's New York
offices was further increased by reports of failures of several fast-food

chains. The nervousness of the investment community was reflected by a tumble in the food service-lodging stock price index in 1970, shown in Exhibit 4. The fast-foods industry was described as "shark-infested waters," from which there would be few survivors.

Exhibit 4
FOOD SERVICE-LODGING AND DOW-JONES STOCK PRICE INDEXES 1970

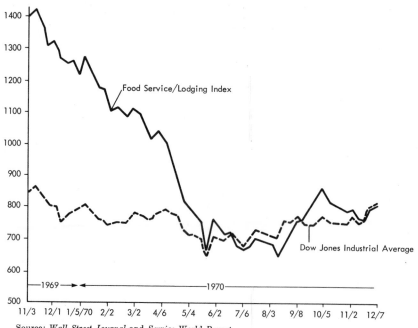

Source: *Wall Street Journal* and *Service World Report.*

REAL ESTATE COMMITMENTS

One of the reasons for several notable failures being experienced by other companies in the fast-food industry was associated with long-term real estate commitments. The success of a restaurant was often very dependent on site location. To secure attractive sites, it was generally necessary (and desirable) to make relatively long-term commitments in leases or purchases of real estate. Such leases represented substantial contingent liabilities, not represented on the balance sheets, if it became necessary to discontinue a location. While Squibb had only approximately $14 million invested in the Fast Foods Division, the possible loss due to unexpired lease write offs could potentially have been several times book investment.

COMPANY OPERATING STATISTICS

As of September 1970, there were 369 Snack Bars in operation in the Fast Foods Division. Exhibit 5 shows the approximate opening dates of

Exhibit 5
UNITS IN OPERATION BY YEAR OF OPENING

Opening Year	Number of Units	Percent of Total
1935–1939	11	3.0
1940–1944	1	0.3
1945–1949	4	1.1
1950–1954	9	2.4
1955–1959	90	24.4
1960–1964 134		36.2
1965–1969	94	25.5
1970 (9 months)	26	7.1
Total.	369	100.0

* Source: Consultant's report.

Exhibit 6
OPERATING UNITS AND REVENUES, 1963–1969

Year	Annual Snack Bar Revenues (in thousands)	Number of Units	Average Daily Sales
1963	$22,417	360	$184
1964	23,281	357	184
1965	23,856	343	187
1966	25,305	347	202
1967	24,106	340	197
1968	25,443	351	204
1969	27,092	354	215

Average Daily Sales of Competitors, 1969

Competitor	Average Daily Sales
Howard Johnson's	$ 950
International House of Pancakes	734
Denny's	967
Original House of Pancakes	819
Dutch Pantry	1,341
Waffle House	349

Source: Consultant's Report, various annual reports, and *Institutions Magazine*.

these units. Exhibit 6 shows the Annual Snack Bar revenue, the number of units in operation at the end of the year, and the average daily sales. Original plans to build over 50 new units in 1970 were abandoned when the Division's operating results softened. Interestingly, not until 1970 was the total number of units as large as it was in 1963. Monthly figures are shown in Exhibit 7, and the sales revenue rankings by opening year are shown in Exhibit 8. Aside from the expected general pattern of newer (and frequently larger) units doing better than older units, the units opened in

Exhibit 7
OPERATING UNITS AND REVENUES
(monthly, 1968–1970)

	1968		1969		1970	
	Number of Units	Daily Average	Number of Units	Daily Average	Number of Units	Daily Average
Jan.	340	$187	349	$222	354	$208
Feb.	345	197	351	205	353	208
Mar.	345	200	353	204	356	209
Apr.	345	199	353	203	359	209
May	343	201	355	208	361	216
June	343	209	353	216	362	217
July	344	210	352	220	367	222
Aug.	349	218	355	227	370	223
Sept.	348	206	353	212	369	210
Oct.	349	202	356	214	*	*
Nov.	351	206	357	216	*	*
Dec.	351	214	354	228	*	*

Source: Consultant's Report.
* Not available.

Exhibit 8
1969 SALES REVENUE, RANKED BY YEAR OF OPENING

	1969 Sales Revenues									
	Over $100M		$75M–100M		$50M–75M		Under $50M		Total	
Year of Unit Opening	Number	Percent	Number	Percent	Number	Percent	Number	Percent	Number	Percent
1968–69	11	25	11	25	13	30	9	20	44	100
1966–67	7	19	16	44	11	31	2	6	36	100
1964–65	14	46	6	20	8	27	2	7	30	100
1962–63	12	27	14	31	14	31	5	11	45	100
1960–61	10	14	16	23	29	42	15	21	70	100
1958–59	6	11	16	30	26	48	6	11	54	100
1956–57	4	14	7	24	10	34	8	28	29	100
1954–55	3	18	1	6	7	41	6	35	17	100
Before 1954	8	27	4	13	13	43	5	17	30	100
Total	75	21%	91	26%	131	37%	58	16%	355	100

Source: Consultant's Report.

1965–66 stand out as being unusually successful, though design of the units has not varied appreciably over the years. The only conclusion that management could draw was that in 1964–65 site selection was especially good. As seen in Exhibit 9, Dobbs House units were appreciably smaller than those of other fast-food operators.

The revenue of the Fast Foods Division was generated almost entirely from food sales (95.4 percent in 1968 and 97.7 percent in 1969). Liquor

Exhibit 9
AVERAGE UNIT SIZE AND SEATING CAPACITY

	Dobbs House Average			Fast Food Industry Average		
Year	Revenue per Year per Unit	Seats per Unit	Area per Unit, square feet	Revenue per Year per Unit	Seats per Unit	Area per Unit, square feet
1968*	72,500	25	1,145	140,000	36	1,700
1969†	76,500	28	1,004	165,000	49	1,850

* Units stated in 1968 and before.
† Units stated in 1969.
Source: Consultant's Report and *Nation's Restaurant News.*

and sundry sales amounted to only 0.1 percent in 1968 and 1969. Vending and other revenues amounted to 1.5 percent in 1968 and 2.2 percent in 1969.

CONSULTANT'S CONCLUSIONS

In preparation for the management transition from the Dobbs brothers to Squibb management, a consulting study of the situation at Dobbs House was completed by the end of 1970.

The consultant's report presented three major conclusions, together with several recommendations.

I. Over the coming decade success in the fast-food business will be increasingly hard to come by. The traditional requirements of cleanliness, high-quality food, good value, and good service will continue to be the prime prerequisites, but no longer will success in these basic operating areas be entirely sufficient. Three additional elements which will come increasingly into play:

Marketing. The first element will be marketing clout and expertise. The advertising and sales promotion abilities of the market leaders will continue to put strong competitive pressure on less capable smaller operators as the big chains attract greater numbers of their former customers. Long-term viability in the retail food business will require continuing and increasing advertising and sales-promotion inputs.

Research and Development. A second requirement for long-term success will be for food operators to invest a portion of their earnings in a formal research and development effort aimed at introducing new food items into existing types of restaurants and at creating and testing new restaurant concepts. The rate of change in the retail food business has increased and those operators who hope to share importantly in the growth of the market will have to be among the leaders in developing innovations in menus and restaurant styles that the merchandisable to consumers.

Format. Lastly, the retail food business will gradually evolve into one whereby the late 1970s, "style" (decor, pizazz on food selection and service, etc.) will be as important as "content" (cleanliness, food quality, etc.). The successful operators of the late 1970s will be the ones which "romance" the consumer, making a meal in their restaurants more than just a meal and, instead, somewhat of an experience.

II. Continued long-term success of the Snack Bar Division is by no means assured.

The current Snack Bars will become increasingly outdated over the coming decade as competition continues its expansion with bigger, more appealing units. While refurbishment of the old Dobbs units will help hold off the decline of consumer acceptance, it is nonetheless inevitable.

The long-term ability of the current Snack Bars to compete effectively against other major fast-food operations is in doubt, simply because the Snack Bars do not have the potential of generating the funds required to spend competitively on advertising and sales promotion. The upside sales potential of the current group of Snack Bars is probably limited to an average of $300 per day.

III. Signage is probably the weakest link in the entire Snack Bar Division's operation. There are at least four different signs currently in use in the Snack Bar Division, two for Toddle Houses (the old neon sign and the newer back-lighted one) and two for Dobbs Houses (the older oval one and the newer blue and white rectangular one).

All of the current signs are typically smaller, placed lower to the ground, and carry less noticeable graphics than the signs of major competitors such as Waffle House, Pickwick House or Denny's. Furthermore, Dobbs Houses is the only chain using two different names and such divergent styles of signs on shops in the same market. Furthermore, only a few Dobbs units have signs in front of the building.

CONSULTANT'S RECOMMENDATIONS

Emphasis should be placed on the development of novel restaurant concepts which will afford consumer positions which are strongly differentiated from those of current competitors. Most of the new restaurant chains of the 1970s will depend importantly on "style for their success. For many of them, decor, new and different food items, and unusual service will all be key elements in attracting customers.

The Division should proceed with a longer-term project of developing and testing the self-service/disposable ware coffee shop concept, which Division Management has begun. The Company will have to initiate a long-term development program (in addition to the short-term one discussed in the previous section) if it is going to have competitive operation in 10 or 15 years. Increasing numbers of major food manufacturers and retailers are looking for a way into the retail restaurant business and are investing money in the development and testing of new restaurants. General Mills is currently testing three restaurant concepts: Betty Crocker's Pie Shop and Ice Cream Parlor (pies, ice cream specialties, and sandwiches), Red Lobster Inns of America and Betty Crocker Restaurants and Bake Shops. The American consumer has been trained in the self-service ethic by the franchised-type of fast-food outlets. As labor and food costs continue to rise, there is no reason to believe that a large body of consumers will not prefer self-service to higher prices in a coffee shop.

The Snack Bar operations should undertake a limited program of newspaper advertising and sales promotion in its large markets. The objectives of the program would be to increase consumer awareness of Dobbs Houses, to build overall customer traffic and to promote added sales volume in current slack periods. Dobbs Houses could run two newspaper advertisements per week, on Monday and Wednesday. Both weekly insertions would advertise a "special" where Dobbs Houses would offer a food item at a reduced price or a free food item on a combination purchase (e.g., a free Coke with a steakburger). Total costs for this program in 30 of Dobbs biggest markets would cost about $600,000 per year. Since the advertising effort would cover 230 units accounting for about 60 percent of sales, an increase in sales of about 5.7 percent would payout the cost of the program on an on-going basis.

The Division should convert all units to the Dobbs name and adopt new signage. The recommended sign package would cost about $4,000 per unit converted. It includes a large oval road sign (9 feet $\times$ 12 feet) and a large rectangular sign (4 feet $\times$ 20 feet) for the roofs of existing units. Properly developed new signs would have the potential to materially increase sales volume in many units by increasing "impulse" traffic. The old oval Dobbs House signs are unattractive, small and typically so low to the ground as to be all but unnoticeable to passersby. The old neon Toddle House sign is an anachronism. The cost of the new signage will easily pay for itself. If one assumes that incremental sales volume generates a 65 percent contribution to profit and overhead (by taking out only the variable cost of food and minor supporting expenses), the signage costs would pay out with a $6,150 per year increase in sales per unit. On this basis an increase of only about 4 percent in average annual sales per unit would pay out the signage cost in two years.

The Division should retain its policy of having all units open 24 hours a day. Twenty-four hour operation is an important element in the success of a Snack Bar. Many customers first become acquainted with a Snack Bar during those hours when it is the only open restaurant in town. If they like it, they become good potential customers for other hours as well. A customer check survey disclosed a strong sales volume in the "typical" unit through 2 A.M. with a strong resurgence at 6 A.M. If all Snack Bars were to close between 2 A.M. and 6 A.M., the lost sales would cut $27 off the daily average (lowering it from $215 to $188). Assuming that about 40 percent of the sales dollars in that period are contributed to fixed overheads and profits, the profit loss is $11 per day or about 55 percent of the current daily profit of an average unit. To close between 2 A.M. and 5 A.M. would cut $18 off the daily average and about $7 (or 35 percent) off of daily contribution to profit and overheads.

Exhibit 10

OPERATING DATA OF SAMPLE UNITS, 1969

Operating statistics for 36 units in 1969 were randomly selected from the total 360 odd units in the Dobbs House chain. The sample was stratified to include four units of each ownership type [wholly-owned (1), owned building on leased land (2), and wholly-leased (3)] in combination with each location type [city (c), suburban (s), and rural (r)]. The size of each unit as measured by the number of seats was also noted [1 = 15 and under, 2 = 16 – 25, and 3 = 26 and over].

Unit	Owner-ship	Location	Size	Annual Revenue ($000)	Annual Expenses ($000)	Food	Labor	Other† Variable Cost	Unit‡ Overhead	Total Unit Cost	Total Expenses§ (Including Corporation Overhead)
						*Expenses, Percent Revenue**					
1	1	r	2	75	65	29	28	8	14	79	87
2	1	r	2	46	47	27	29	10	28	94	102
3	1	r	3	87	73	29	28	12	7	76	84
4	1	r	3	109	89	28	27	9	10	74	82
5	1	s	3	160	123	29	29	5	5	68	76
6	1	s	2	50	55	28	28	14	32	102	110
7	1	s	3	113	103	30	29	11	13	83	91
8	1	s	3	97	90	29	28	14	14	85	93
9	1	c	2	45	50	29	29	17	27	102	110
10	1	c	3	170	150	33	30	13	4	80	88
11	1	c	3	50	60	31	29	14	38	112	120
12	1	c	3	83	88	30	29	16	23	98	106
13	2	r	2	82	63	27	28	10	2	67	76
14	2	r	3	92	72	29	29	8	4	70	78
15	2	r	3	102	78	28	28	9	3	68	76
16	2	r	2	61	52	31	29	12	5	77	85

17	2	s	3	139	109	30	28	10	2	70	78
18	2	s	2	89	79	27	32	11	11	81	89
19	2	s	3	112	94	30	30	14	2	76	84
20	2	s	3	122	100	29	30	12	3	74	82
21	2	c	3	90	87	31	31	16	11	89	97
22	2	c	3	100	94	32	30	15	9	86	94
23	2	c	2	67	67	33	30	12	17	92	100
24	2	c	2	142	135	29	32	17	9	87	95
25	3	r	2	56	51	29	30	10	14	83	91
26	3	r	2	77	67	28	29	9	13	79	87
27	3	r	2	90	78	29	30	9	10	78	86
28	3	r	3	110	83	29	27	8	3	67	75
29	3	s	1	60	59	30	30	11	19	90	98
30	3	s	3	160	130	27	32	12	2	73	81
31	3	s	3	102	93	30	32	11	10	83	91
32	3	s	3	140	105	29	28	8	2	67	75
33	3	c	2	70	78	30	29	14	34	107	115
34	3	c	2	90	90	34	28	12	18	92	100
35	3	c	3	115	110	31	30	17	10	88	96
36	3	c	3	125	115	30	30	16	8	84	92

* These figures were obtained from similar data as shown in Exhibit 3 for individual units.
† Controllable Operating Expenses.
‡ Semi-Fixed Operating Expense and Managers' Compensation.
§ Division Management and General and Administrative.

JERRY MCKENZIE'S 30 DAYS AT DOBBS HOUSE

During his month at Dobbs House in Memphis, Jerry McKenzie took a relatively "low profile." He stated that he had been sent from New York to act as a consultant to "help" the organization in any way possible. To attempt to gauge the operations, he spent the majority of his time reading reports, attending meetings, and asking questions. He found that obtaining data was no problem. In fact, if anything, there was too much of it. The controller's report which he carried with him was humorously referred to as the "hernia book." It even had its own over-sized, custom-made carrying case. Selected material from the hernia book is summarized in Exhibit 10. Food and Labor percentages for competing chains are included in Exhibit 11.

Exhibit 11
FOOD AND LABOR COSTS AS PERCENT OF REVENUE
FOR SELECTED FAST-FOOD CHAINS, 1969

Operator	Food Cost Percent of Revenue	Labor Cost Percent of Revenue
Taco Bell	30	18
Arby's Roast Beef	40	16
Kentucky Fried Chicken	42	18
Hardee's Food Systems	40	22
A & W Root Beer	33	30
Dobbs House	31	32

By attending meetings and performance reviews of area managers, he felt he was able to gain a sense of the situation. He found, however, that most meetings were simply presentations of the things that were wrong; rarely was a plan of action for solving the problems discussed. (See Appendix.)

By taking the results from the consultants report plus the data available in Memphis, he constructed breakeven cost-revenue charts. He was unable, however, to determine in his mind which variables were most relevant and critical to the success of the business.

His initial reactions in examining the data was a sense of frustration. Clearly there were a number of units that were below breakeven volume. He was unsure, however, whether to stop operating the loss units or try to convert them to profitable operations.

Upon examining individual units he found they were profitable only because of unique situations. The high volume in one inner-city snack bar in Detroit was directly related to the number of prostitutes that used it as a base of operations. In another case, he found that a unit appeared to be successful because it was considered as the "clubhouse" of a motorcycle gang.

Complaints about the difficulties in hiring people to work in snack bars had been filed with the Memphis headquarters. It was almost impossible to find employees who were willing to work by themselves on late shifts.

During his third week at Memphis, Jerry had an interesting experience. Howard Berkowitz, a regional operations manager, had guessed Jerry McKenzie's purposes for being in Memphis. Howard, who had come from a restaurant family, held a bachelor's degree in hotel and restaurant management, and had approximately seven years of chain-restaurant experience, had been slightly dismayed by Jerry's graphs and numbers. Finally he said, "Jerry, I think I know why you are here. I like you, and I'd like to work with you. But you really don't know anything about this business. Maybe those charts will help, but if you sincerely want to learn, I'll show you what I know about how this business has to be run."

They drove to a local Dobbs House, and Howard showed Jerry around the unit. After a brief tour, Howard went into the kitchen and dumped the garbage pail on the floor. He rolled up his sleeves and began to rummage through the unappetizing and noxious heap of garbage. From this he pulled out unused containers of cream, dishes, dishrags, silverware, a salt shaker, and partially eaten food. He noted that the discarded dishes and silver were the result of carelessness by waitresses and busboys. Part of the food wastage was carelessness of the cook and waitresses. When a partially eaten steak was dissected, it was found to contain gristle. An inspection of other steaks in the refrigerator showed similar problems, though Dobbs House had paid for top quality meat.

Howard estimated the value of the contents of this garbage, annualized for this unit, was approximately $10,000.

RETURN TO NEW YORK

Now as Jerry returned to New York to make his report, he was trying to reconcile the findings of the consultants, the cost data, the interviews and meetings, and the vivid experience with the garbage pails.

His experiences with Howard Berkowitz left him with the gnawing feelings that there might be many key facets to running the business that he still did not know about or understand. He was also unsure that even if he had identified the true problems of the business that he would be able to effect any change. He had seen Dobbs management try to introduce several new ideas during the month, but most had been abandoned. For example, Dobbs headquarters staff had determined that reducing the size of the free matches with Dobbs advertising at the check-out counter could save over $100,000 per year in the 369 units. Trying to get each unit manager to make the switch had proven an almost impossible task; therefore the idea was discarded.

While the situation at Dobbs House could represent a personal opportunity, it held some risks. He now felt that the strategy of an "end run to the top" through brilliant staff work was not as likely to succeed as he once thought. Here was a chance to be an operating executive in a line position. However, if the situation proved to be hopeless, and he was unable to turn the Fast Foods Division around, his reputation would be tarnished for several years, with the possible loss of his job, and setback. The thought of being responsible for 3,500 Dobbs House cooks, waitresses, and other employees was rather chilling.

APPENDIX: MINUTES OF PROGRESS REVIEW MEETING OF JANUARY 29, 1971

Those attending were:

Phil Barksdale, General Manager.
Lamar Bell, Controller.
Howard Berkowitz, Regional Operations.
John Emerson, Training.
Sam Jones, Regional Operations.
Jack Larson, Regional Operations.
Bill Lynch, Personnel.

In the morning, we discussed money and inventory losses. Mr. Barksdale asked Steve Crain, our legal counsel, to discuss this matter. Mr. Barksdale stated that our policy concerning and regarding theft has been too lenient. In the couple of instances where we have tried to prosecute in the courts, we really haven't accomplished anything. Mr. Barksdale stated that we now are going to take a "hard nose" approach and will prosecute all offenders in the future.

Steve Crain was quick to point out that we have to be extremely careful in accusing anyone of stealing money or inventory. We must be sure we have all facts, figures, information, and witnesses. Our count must be right, and our procedure in conducting a cash audit must be exactly correct before we accuse anyone of any type of money theft or inventory shortage. Steve Crain pointed out that inventory losses are most difficult to prove and we have to be extremely careful in this matter. Mr. Barksdale asked Steve to develop written guidelines for our handling money and inventory losses. Steve Crain said he would do so as rapidly as possible. Upon completion of these written guidelines, he is to submit them to Mr. Barksdale, and Mr. Barksdale will submit them to corporate headquarters for approval.

During the discussion of inventory losses there was a general discussion of inventory being inflated over the past to make us look good for one particular month, and perhaps a lot of our people are carrying these inflated inventories forward. Each regional manager was advised to inform their area managers to conduct inventories as soon as possible in each of their commissary locations to determine whether or not the inventories are inflated or are accurate.

There then was a discussion of the money losses at the unit employee level. Mr. Barksdale said that we are more interested in the losses of large sums of money. However, he did explain that they are looking at a computer-type cash register, which would give us control that we do not now have. It would also determine sale mix for us. Mr. Barksdale assigned John Emerson, Lamar Bell, and Pat Maher to develop procedures for handling money at different levels in the operation.

In the afternoon we returned to our original agenda of talking about what we have accomplished in the last quarter, and what we hope to accomplish in the forthcoming quarter.

The first subject discussed was personnel. Bill Lynch gave us a summation of our Train the Trainor program.

One of the important things that Mr. Barksdale was concerned about what we had discussed back in October was that we had hoped to develop a "back-up procedure," so that all the city managers and unit managers would get a day off. Apparently, this is being done in a few areas. Mr. Barksdale set a deadline of March 1 to review progress on this procedure. He asked Bill Lynch to develop a flow chart similar to the one that Bob Ryan has submitted for his schedule of what is coming up in regards to personnel and what we can look forward to in the Fast Food Division.

We had a lengthy discussion as to what progress we have made with our training program in Houston, Miami, and Atlanta. Mr. Barksdale suggested that since personnel and training are so closely related, John Emerson and Bill Lynch should get together and get organized and establish objectives to get the program committed to writing. Mr. Barksdale also asked John Emerson to establish a flow chart similar to the one that Bill Lynch will establish, and perhaps they can get together and establish one to show how the program is going to be implemented and show what John Emerson has implemented up to now. In essence, Mr. Barksdale wants a plan of action—What are we going to do for the next year?

There was also a lengthy discussion between Mr. Barksdale and Bill Lynch. Mr. Barksdale feels that each area should have a person designated for training of personnel. For example, when we have information to go into the field in regards to personnel or training, the information would go to one particular individual rather than the way it is now being disseminated. Our communications must be improved. It was again brought up that not all of our people are aware of our fringe benefits, and we must get the information to the people. Bill Lynch and John Emerson are going to work on this.

The next area that was covered was that of the weekly and end-of-the-month reports. Lamar Bell explained that beginning in February the new weekly form will show the true gross margin; that is, it will include the semi-fixed and manager's compensation. Also, Lamar is developing a new form, which should make the area secretary's job much easier. John Simank and Peter Gonzales are to go over the form with each area secretary. The new form will be mailed out to the area office, and the area secretary will be told not to open the package until John and Peter arrive to go over it with them thoroughly.

The third area that Mr. Barksdale discussed was that of end-of-month inventory. Two people are required to sign the inventory form. The three regional managers agreed that it was being done. Not all were certain that it was being done in each and every instance. They are to follow up on this to be sure that it does get done, especially in the light of the inflated inventories that have been discovered recently. The regional managers thought that cost control in general has been greatly improved during the last quarter, especially in the payroll area.

There was a lengthy discussion in regards to part-time help receiving 50 cents an hour more than regular employees are receiving. It was pointed out that Norman Sidner is trying this in the Tampa Area. Mr. Barksdale asked Jack Larson to give him complete follow-up information on its effect on the payroll; its effect on the employees; and their reaction to part time help receiving this additional pay over regular full-time employees.

The next area that was discussed on the agenda was that of purchasing. Mr. Barksdale informed us that he has a master purchasing manual, and we will be working on distributing the parts that relate to the Fast Food Division as soon as possible. We know that the people in the field are asking for the Approved Products List and the new purchasing procedures that we told them about earlier.

The physical appearance of the units was discussed next. It was the general opinion of the regional managers that the unit physical appearance has improved in general. There seems to be some problems with air conditioners, especially in the southern part of the country and in Texas. However, it was felt that their units are in acceptable condition, and the general consensus was that we hold the line wherever possible as far as maintenance, painting, and roofing.

Mr. Barksdale asked the question, "What will make it difficult to make budget in future months?" The answers were: we would not be able to make the sales that we thought we would make; the budget is not realistic. Mr. Barksdale reviewed rather quickly that our goals are: (1) to meet the budget; (2) to upgrade people; (3) that proper training was to produce profit and sales.

Sam Jones was concerned about the ability of the people in the area to manage labor, food costs, and other controllable expenses because we have so many new people. Jack Larson feels that we are on top of the situation, and in general was in agreement with Sam and Howard that people are improving in their proficiency. Because of the introduction of performance reviews, people are becoming more knowledgeable about their business. It is expected that the morale of the employees will be much better during the second quarter.

Mr. Barksdale asked, "Should we expand the present Fast Foods business concept?" There was a unanimous answer of "No." Mr. Barksdale explained that we are definitely looking for new concepts in the future. It is important now to get the people, the controls, and the training procedures right before entering into any new concepts or ventures. Most important, we must build creditibility within our division and New York.

Mr. Barksdale said that in any cases where we have losing units to let Lamar know. Lamar and John Simank will investigate all possibilities to see whether or not it would be practical to keep the unit open or close it. Lamar also said that price increases are still being studied. Lamar reviewed the projects and responsibilities of several different people in the room, and everyone was of the general opinion that we were all slightly behind what we had hoped to accomplish. He felt that we had all done what we could in the last quarter, and would maintain the same pace in the second quarter.

Mr. Barksdale asked each individual what he thought had been accomplished during the last quarter. It was the general consensus that we had made tremendous progress, though it was not easy to see the evidence. We are making an investment in the future. We all felt it was frustrating. We were trying to accomplish so many things so rapidly.

All in the room gave Mr. Barksdale a unanimous vote of confidence.

Indexes

Case Index

Subject Index

W–X

This book has been set in 10 and 9 point Times Roman, leaded 2 points. Section numbers are in 18 point Scotch Roman italic and chapter numbers are 72 point Caslon Italic. Section and chapter titles are 18 point Scotch Roman. The size of the type page is 27 × 46½ picas.